Contents at a glance

SQL Server 2017
Administration Inside Out

William Assaf
Randolph West
Sven Aelterman
Mindy Curnutt

Published with the authorization of Microsoft Corporation by:
Pearson Education, Inc.

ISBN-13: 978-1-5093-0521-6
ISBN-10: 1-5093-0521-1

Library of Congress Control Number: 2017961300

Printed and bound in the United States of America.

1 18

Trademarks
Microsoft and the trademarks listed at *https://www.microsoft.com* on the "Trademarks" webpage are trademarks of the Microsoft group of companies. All other marks are property of their respective owners.

Warning and Disclaimer
Every effort has been made to make this book as complete and as accurate as possible, but no warranty or fitness is implied. The information provided is on an "as is" basis. The authors, the publisher, and Microsoft Corporation shall have neither liability nor responsibility to any person or entity with respect to any loss or damages arising from the information contained in this book or programs accompanying it.

Special Sales
For information about buying this title in bulk quantities, or for special sales opportunities (which may include electronic versions; custom cover designs; and content particular to your business, training goals, marketing focus, or branding interests), please contact our corporate sales department at corpsales@pearsoned.com or (800) 382-3419.

For government sales inquiries, please contact governmentsales@pearsoned.com.

For questions about sales outside the U.S., please contact intlcs@pearson.com.

Editor-in-Chief: Greg Wiegand
Acquisitions Editor: Trina MacDonald
Development Editor: Mark Renfrow
Technical Editor: Louis Davidson
Managing Editor: Sandra Schroeder
Senior Project Editor: Tracey Croom
Editorial Production: Octal Publishing, Inc.
Copy Editor: Octal Publishing, Inc.
Indexer: Octal Publishing, Inc.
Proofreader: Octal Publishing, Inc.
Cover Designer: Twist Creative, Seattle

for insp ...own.

...lliam Assaf

for putting up ... *MacBook.*

...olph West

in

...Aelterman

...dy Curnutt

Table of contents

Foreword

The world as we know it is being inundated with data. We live in a culture in which almost every individual has at least two devices, a smart phone, and a laptop or computer of some sort. Everything we do on these devices is constantly collecting, sharing, or producing data. This data is being used not only to help organizations make smarter decisions, but also to shape and transform how we as a society live, work, make decisions, and sometimes think.

This massive explosion can be attributed to the technological transformation that every business and nearly every industry is undergoing. Every click or purchase by an individual is now triggering some event that triggers another event that likely amounts to hundreds or possibly thousands of rows of data. Multiply this by every person in the world and now you have an unprecedented amount of stored data that no one could have ever imagined. Now, not only must organizations store this data, but also ensure that this data—this massive amount of data—is readily available for consumption at the click of a button or the swipe of a screen.

This is where the database comes into play. Databases are the backbone or back end to possibly every aspect of business today. Back when Ted Codd, the father of the relational database, came up with this seminal idea, he probably had no idea how widespread their use would be today. Initially, database usage was intended to store data and retrieve data. The primary purpose was to simply ensure the security, availability, and reliability of any information written by on-premises applications at varying scales.

Today, all of that has changed. Data must be available 24 hours per day, 7 days each week, primarily via the internet instead of just by way of on-premises applications. Microsoft SQL Server 2017 was designed with all of this in mind. It can support high-volume Online Transactional Processing (OLTP) databases and very large Online Analytical Processing (OLAP) systems out of the box. And, by taking advantage of Microsoft Azure, developers can grow and scale databases dynamically and transparently behind the scenes to accommodate planned and unplanned spikes in demand and resource utilization. In other words, the latest version of SQL Server was built to not only accommodate this new world of data, but to push the limits of what organizations are doing today and what they will be doing tomorrow and deeper into the future.

Close your eyes and imagine a world in which a DBA can configure a database system to automatically increase or decrease resource utilization based on end-user application usage. But that's not all. What if the relational database management system (RDBMS) could automatically tune performance based on usage patterns? All of this is now possible with SQL Server and Azure SQL Database. By using features such as the Query Store and Elastic Database Pools, DBAs can proactively design solutions that will scale and perform to meet any application Service-Level Agreement.

In addition to world-class performance, these databases also include security and high-availability features that are unparalleled to any other RDBMS. Organizations can build mission-critical secure applications by taking advantage of SQL Server out-of-the-box built-in features without purchasing additional software. These features are available both in the cloud and on-premises and can be managed using SQL Server Management Studio, SQL Server Data Tools, and SQL Operations Studio. All three tools are available to download for free, and will be familiar to DBAs and database developers.

Throughout this book, the authors highlight many of the capabilities that make it possible for organizations to successfully deploy and manage database solutions using a single platform. If you are a DBA or database developer looking to take advantage of the latest version of SQL Server, this book encompasses everything needed to understand how and when to take advantage of the robust set of features available within the product.

This book is based on the skills of a group of seasoned database professionals with several decades experience in designing, optimizing, and developing robust database solutions, all based on SQL Server technology. It is written for experienced DBAs and developers, aimed at teaching the advanced techniques of SQL Server.

SQL Server, Microsoft's core database platform, continues its maturity from supporting some of the smallest departmental tasks to supporting some the largest RDBMS deployments in the world. Each release not only includes capabilities that enhance its predecessor, but also boasts features that rival and exceed those of many competitors.

This trend continues with SQL Server 2017. This release, just like all past releases, continues to add capabilities to an already sophisticated and reliable toolkit. Features include a secure, elastic, and scalable cloud system; advanced in-memory technologies; faster and consolidated management and development experiences; and continued growth and enhancements in the area of high availability and disaster recovery. In addition, concerted efforts have been focused on making the number one secure RDBMS in the world even more secure, by adding capabilities such as row-level security, Always Encrypted, and dynamic data masking. Finally, and as always, performance is at the center of this release. With enhancements to the Query Store, DBAs can take a more proactive approach to monitoring and tuning performance.

All in all, this book is sort of like an "Inside Out" look of each of the core components of SQL Server 2017, with a few excursions into the depths of some very specific topics. Each chapter first provides and overview of the topic and then delves deeper into that topic and any corresponding related topics. Although it's impossible to cover every detail of every Transact-SQL statement, command, feature or capability, this book provides you with a comprehensive look into SQL Server 2017. After reading each page of this book, you will be able implement a cloud-based or on-premises scalable, performant, secure, and reliable database solution using SQL Server 2017.

Patrick LeBlanc, Microsoft

Introduction

The velocity of change for the Microsoft SQL Server DBA has increased this decade. The span between the releases of SQL Server 2016 and 2017 was only 16 months, the fastest new release ever. Gone are the days when DBAs had between three to five years to soak in and adjust to new features in the engine and surrounding technologies.

This book is written and edited by SQL Server experts with two goals in mind: to deliver a solid foundational skillset for all of the topics covered in SQL Server configuration and administration, and also to deliver awareness and functional, practical knowledge for the dramatic number of new features introduced in SQL Server 2016 and 2017. We haven't avoided new content—even content that stretched the boundaries of writing deadlines with late-breaking new releases. You will be presented with not only the "how" of new features, but also the "why" and the "when" for their use.

Who this book is for

SQL Server administration was never the narrow niche skillset that our employers might have suspected it was. Even now it continues to broaden, with new structures aside from the traditional rowstore, such as Columnstore and memory-optimized indexes, or new platforms such as Microsoft Azure SQL Database platform as a service (PaaS) and Azure infrastructure as a service (IaaS). This book is for the DBAs who are unafraid to add these new skillsets and features to their utility belt, and to give courage and confidence to those who are hesitant. SQL Server administrators should read this book to become more prepared and aware of features when talking to their colleagues in application development, business intelligence, and system administration.

Assumptions about you

We assume that you have some experience and basic vocabulary with administering a recent version of SQL Server. You might be curious, preparing, or accomplished with Microsoft Certifications for SQL Server. DBAs, architects, and developers can all benefit from the content provided in this book, especially those looking to take their databases to the cloud, to reach heights of performance, or to ensure the security of their data in an antagonistic, networked world.

This book mentions some of the advanced topics that you'll find covered in more detail elsewhere (such as custom development, business intelligence design, data integration, or data warehousing).

How this book is organized

This book gives you a comprehensive look at the various features you will use. It is structured in a logical approach to all aspects of SQL Server 2017 Administration.

Chapter 1, "Getting started with SQL Server tools" gives you a tour of the tooling you need, from the installation media to the free downloads, not the least of which is the modern, rapidly evolving SQL Server Management Studio. We also cover SQL Server Data Tools, Configuration Manager, performance and reliability monitoring tools, provide an introduction to PowerShell, and more.

Chapter 2, "Introducing database server components," introduces the working vocabulary and concepts of database administration, starting with hardware-level topics such as memory, processors, storage, and networking. We then move into high availability basics (much more on those later), security, and hardware virtualization.

Chapter 3, "Designing and implementing a database infrastructure" introduces the architecture and configuration of SQL Server, including deep dives into transaction log virtual log files (VLFs), data files, in-memory Online Transaction Processing (OLTP), partitioning, and compression. We spend time with TempDB and its optimal configuration, and server-level configuration options. Here, we also cover running SQL Server in Azure virtual machines or Azure SQL databases as well as hybrid cloud architectures.

Chapter 4, "Provisioning databases" is a grand tour of SQL Server Setup, including all the included features and their initial installation and configuration. We review initial configurations, a post-installation checklist, and then the basics of creating SQL Server databases, including database-level configuration options for system and user databases.

Chapter 5, "Provisioning Azure SQL Database," introduces Microsoft's SQL Server database-as-a-service (DBaaS) offering. This Azure cloud service provides a database service with a very high degree of compatibility with SQL Server 2017. You will read about the concepts behind Azure SQL Database, learn how to create databases, and perform common management tasks for your databases.

Chapter 6, "Administering security and permissions" begins with the basics of authentication, the configuration, management, and troubleshooting of logins and users. Then, we dive into permissions, including how to grant and revoke server and database-level permissions and role membership, with a focus on moving security from server to server.

Chapter 7, "Securing the server and its data" takes the security responsibilities of the SQL Server DBA past the basics of authentication and permissions and discusses advanced topics including the various features and techniques for encryption, Always Encrypted, and row-level security. We discuss security measures to be taken for SQL Server instances and Azure SQL databases as well as the Enterprise-level SQL Server Audit feature.

Chapter 8, "Understanding and designing tables," is all about creating SQL Server tables, the object that holds data. In addition to covering the basics of table design, we cover special table types and data types in-depth. In this chapter, we also demonstrate techniques for discovering and tracking changes to data.

Chapter 9, "Performance tuning SQL Server" dives deep into isolation and concurrency options, including READ COMMITTED SNAPSHOT ISOLATION (RCSI), and why your developers shouldn't be using NOLOCK. We review execution plans, including what to look for, and the Query Store feature that was introduced in SQL Server 2016 and improved in SQL Server 2017.

Chapter 10, "Understanding and designing indexes" tackles performance from the angle of indexes, from their creation, monitoring, and tuning, and all the various forms of indexes at our disposal, past clustered and nonclustered indexes and into Columnstore, memory-optimized hash indexes, and more. We review indexes and index statistics in detail, though we cover their maintenance later on in Chapter 13.

Chapter 11, "Developing, deploying, and managing data recovery" covers the fundamentals of database backups in preparation for disaster recovery scenarios, including a backup and recovery strategy appropriate for your environment. Backups and restores in a hybrid environment, Azure SQL Database recovery, and geo-replication are important assets for the modern DBA, and we cover those, as well.

Chapter 12, "Implementing high availability and disaster recovery" goes beyond backups and into strategies for disaster recovery from the old (log shipping and replication) to the new (availability groups), including welcome new enhancements in SQL Server 2017 to support cross-platform and clusterless availability groups. We go deep into configuring clusters and availability groups on both Windows and Linux.

Chapter 13, "Managing and monitoring SQL Server" covers the care and feeding of SQL Server instances, including monitoring for database corruption, monitoring database activity, and index fragmentation. We dive into extended events, the superior alternative to traces, and also cover Resource Governor, used for insulating your critical workloads.

Chapter 14, "Automating SQL Server administration" includes an introduction to PowerShell, including features available in PowerShell 5.0. We also review the tools and features needed to automate tasks to your SQL Server, including database mail, SQL Server Agent jobs, Master/Target Agent jobs, proxies, and alerts. Finally, we review the vastly improved Maintenance Plans feature, including what to schedule and how.

About the companion content

We have included this companion content to enrich your learning experience. You can download this book's companion content from the following page:

https://aka.ms/SQLServ2017Admin/downloads

The companion content includes helpful Transact-SQL and PowerShell scripting, as mentioned in the book, for easy reference and adoption into your own toolbox of scripts.

Acknowledgments

From William Assaf:

I'd like to thank the influencers and mentors in my professional career who affected my trajectory, and to whom I remain grateful for technical and nontechnical lessons learned. In no particular order, I'd like to thank Connie Murla, David Alexander, Darren Schumaker, Ashagre Bishaw, Charles Sanders, Todd Howard, Chris Kimmel, Richard Caronna, and Mike Huguet. There's definitely a special love/hate relationship developed between an author and a tech editor, but I couldn't have asked for a better one than Louis Davidson. Finally, from user groups to SQLSaturdays to roadshow presentations to books, I am indebted to my friend Patrick Leblanc, who climbed the ladder and unfailingly turned to offer a hand and a hug.

From Randolph West:

In June 2017, I told my good friend Melody Zacharias that I'd like to finish at least one of the many books I've started before I die. She suggested that I might be interested in contributing to this one. Piece of cake, I thought.

I have seven more gray hairs now. Seven!

I would like to thank Melody for recommending me in her stead, my husband for giving me space at the kitchen counter to write, and my dog Trixie for much needed distraction.

Trina, William, Louis, Sven and Mindy have been a great support as well, especially during the Dark Times.

This book would not be possible without the contributions of everyone else behind the scenes, too. Writing a book of this magnitude is a huge endeavour. (So help me if "endeavour" is the one word I get to spell the Canadian way!)

From Sven Aelterman:

I met William Assaf several years ago when I spoke at the Baton Rouge SQLSaturday. I have been back to this event many times since then and enjoyed preceding the Troy University Trojans' victory over Louisiana State University. (This just added in case the actual college football game doesn't make it in the history books. At least it will be recorded here.)

I am grateful for William's invitation to contribute two chapters to this book. William made a valiant attempt to prepare me for the amount of work "just" two chapters would be. Yet, I underestimated the effort. If it weren't for his support and that of Randolph West, technical editor Louis Davidson, editor Trina Macdonald, and even more people behind the scenes, the space for this acknowledgment might have been saved. They were truly a great team and valued collaborators. Without hesitation, I would go on the journey of book writing again with each of them.

My children, Edward and Sofia, and my wife, Ebony, have experienced firsthand that SQL Server can slow down time. "About two months" must have felt to them like months with 60 days each. I thank them for their patience while they had to share me with Azure and various table types. I hope that maybe my children will be inspired one day to become authors in their career fields.

Finally, I'd like to thank my coworkers at Troy University for inspiring me to do my best work. Working in a public higher education institution has some challenges, but the environment is so conducive to intellectual growth that it makes up for each challenge and then some.

From Mindy Curnutt:

I would like to thank Patrick LeBlanc for inviting me to participate in the creation of this book. Thanks also to Tracy Boggiano, for an amazing amount of help pulling together much of the chapter about automating administration. She's an MVP in my eyes! To everyone in the 2016-2017 TMW DBA Services "Team Unicorn": Eric Blinn, Lisa Bohm, Dan Andrews, Vedran Ikonic, and Dan Clemens, thank you for your proof reading and feedback. Thanks to my mom Barbara Corry for always swooping in to help with just about anything I needed. Of course, I couldn't have done any of this without the support of my husband, Chris Curnutt. He is always supportive despite long work hours, phone conversations with strange acronyms, and travel, he's also the love of my life. Last but not least, thanks to our two children, Riley and Kimball, who have supported and encouraged me in more ways than I can count.

Support and feedback

The following sections provide information on errata, book support, feedback, and contact information.

Errata & support

We've made every effort to ensure the accuracy of this book and its companion content. You can access updates to this book—in the form of a list of submitted errata and their related corrections—at:

https://aka.ms/SQLServ2017Admin/errata

If you discover an error that is not already listed, please submit it to us at the same page. If you need additional support, email Microsoft Press Book Support at *mspinput@microsoft.com*.

Please note that product support for Microsoft software and hardware is not offered through the previous addresses. For help with Microsoft software or hardware, go to *https://support.microsoft.com*.

Stay in touch

Let's keep the conversation going! We're on Twitter at *http://twitter.com/MicrosoftPress*.

Getting started with SQL Server tools

This chapter provides information about where to find many of the Microsoft tools used to manage and work with the Microsoft SQL Server platform. It also walks you through the installation, configuration, and basic utility of each tool.

The chapter is divided into five distinct sections:

- Installation Center
    - The Planning Tab
    - The Installation Tab

- Tools installed with the Database Engine

- SQL Server Management Tools

- SQL Server Data Tools

NOTE

Although SQL Server 2017 runs on Linux, many of the administration tools that work with the Windows Server version will work with the Linux version, too. We note the specific cases for which platform-specific tools are available.

SQL Server setup

You can install SQL Server 2017 natively on Windows and Linux. For development and testing environments, you can install SQL Server with Docker container images on Windows, Linux, and macOS.

The following section covers installing SQL Server natively on Microsoft Windows.

➤ **For more details on how to set up and configure SQL Server, read Chapter 4.**

Installing SQL Server by using the Installation Center

SQL Server Installation Center is the application that you use to install and add features to an instance of SQL Server. As illustrated in Figure 1-1, it can also serve as a launch point for downloading the installation packages for SQL Server Upgrade Advisor, SQL Server Management Tools, SQL Server Reporting Services, and SQL Server Data Tools.

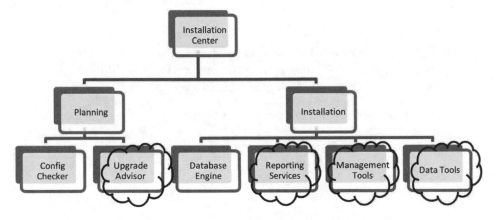

Figure 1-1 Installation Center components. Downloadable tools have a cloud outline.

It might seem a bit confusing, but on the Installation tab, the installers for SQL Server Reporting Services, SQL Server Management Tools, and SQL Server Data Tools, are merely links that redirect to a download location on the Microsoft website for each of these components' installation files. You also can download and install the tools independently without using Installation Center.

> NOTE
>
> **As a best practice, you should install SQL Server Management Studio and Data Tools only on client machines, not the production instance. This ensures a smaller installation and administration footprint on the server. It is therefore uncommon to use the Installation Center on client machines.**

The same is true for the Planning tab, on which the Upgrade Advisor (also known as the Data Migration Assistant) is simply a launch point for a continually updated .MSI file that you can download.

Inside OUT

How do I install SQL Server 2017 on Linux?

SQL Server is fully supported on Red Hat Enterprise Linux (RHEL), SUSE Linux Enterprise Server (SLES), and Ubuntu, using the built-in package manager for each distribution.

The main SQL Server package is the Database Engine. You can install the command-line tools, SQL Server Agent, Full-Text Search, and SQL Server Integration Services as optional packages.

For more information about installing SQL Server on Linux, visit Microsoft Docs at *https://docs.microsoft.com/sql/linux/sql-server-linux-setup*.

Planning before an upgrade or installation

When you first start the SQL Server Installation Center, it opens with the Planning tab preselected. This tab has two tools that you might find useful before installing or upgrading a SQL Server instance to SQL Server 2017: Configuration Checker and Upgrade Advisor.

Configuration Checker

The Configuration Checker tool checks for conditions that might prevent a successful SQL Server 2017 installation. When you click the Configuration Checker, a wizard runs against the local computer. There is no option to choose an alternate computer location. The wizard returns an HTML report listing all 13 installation requirement rules (facets) and the results of each test. Nine of these rules are universal to all Windows Configurations, and you can easily remedy most of them.

1. **FacetDomainControllerCheck.** We recommend that you do not install SQL Server 2017 on a Domain Controller. There are two reasons for this. First, it can compromise the security of both Active Directory and the SQL Server instance. Second, it can cause resource contention between the two services.

2. **FacetWOW64PlatformCheck.** Windows operating systems must be 64-bit to support a SQL Server 2017 installation.

3. **MediaPathLength.** The path for the location from which SQL Server 2017 is being installed must be fewer than 260 characters in length.

4. **NoRebootPackage.** The correct .NET Frameworks must already be installed.

5. **RebootRequiredCheck.**   No installation reboots can be pending.

6. **SetupCompatibilityCheck.**   No subsequent incompatible versions of SQL Server can be installed on the computer.

7. **SSMS_IsInternetConnected.**   Verifies that the computer is connected to the internet. This is required for validating a certificate when a .NET application starts.

8. **ThreadHasAdminPrivilegeCheck.**   The account running the setup file must have Local Administrator rights on the computer.

9. **WmiServiceStateCheck.**   Checks whether the Windows Management Instrumentation (WMI) service is started and running on the computer.

> ➤ You can find the most up-to-date Rules Documentation at *http://go.microsoft.com/ fwlink/?LinkID=398124*.

Upgrade Advisor

The Upgrade Advisor link on the Planning tab of Installation Center downloads the Data Migration Assistant installation package.

NOTE

The Data Migration Assistant is now continually updated by Microsoft. You can download the most recent version from *https://www.microsoft.com/download/details. aspx?id=53595*.

This application is really two tools in one, which you can use to create two project types:

● An assessment of upgrade or migration readiness

● A migration of data between versions of SQL Server and/or Microsoft Azure SQL Database

In both cases, the Source Server must be a SQL Server instance. The target server choices for all three Target Server Types accommodate both Assessment and Migration, as shown in Table 1-1.

Table 1-1 Data Migration Assistant assessment matrix

Target server type	Assessment	Migration
Azure SQL Database	X	X
SQL Server	X	X
SQL Server on Azure Virtual Machines	X	X

Assessment   The Assessment project type of the Data Migration Assistant detects database-specific compatibility issues between origin and destination SQL Server versions in the course of pre-upgrade discovery. It is common between versions for there to be deprecation and feature differences, and this is especially true if the Target Server Type is an Azure SQL database. If not addressed, some of these items might affect database functionality during or post upgrade. The tool neatly outlines all findings and makes recommendations.

The Assessment project type examines the following aspects of upgrading SQL Server:

- **Database compatibility.**   Looks at deprecated features and functionality issues that could be "show stoppers."

- **Feature parity.**   Identifies unsupported or partially supported features and functions that applications using the database might rely on. For example, if you plan to move to Azure SQL Database, these include Cross Database Queries, Server-Scoped Logon Triggers, and Trace Flags.

- **Benefits from new features.**   This feature is expected sometime soon and is not currently available.

- ➤ You can find more information online by searching for "Discontinued Database Engine Functionality in SQL Server *XXXX*," where *XXXX* is your Source SQL Server platform.

NOTE
You can find a list of SQL Server database features that are not supported in Azure SQL Database at *https://docs.microsoft.com/azure/sql-database/sql-database-transact-sql-information*.

Migration   Using the Migration project type of the Data Migration Assistant, an administrator can move a database's schema, data, and noncontained objects from a source server to a destination server. The wizard works by providing a user with the option to select a Source and Destination Server and to choose one or more databases for migration.

Moving to SQL Server   For SQL Server migrations, there must be a backup location that is accessible by both the source and destination servers, generally a UNC path. If this is a network location, the service running the source SQL Server instance must have write permissions for the directory. In addition, the service account running the destination SQL Server instance must have read permissions to the same network location.

If this poses a challenge, there is a check box labeled Copy The Database Backups To A Different Location That The Target Server Can Read And Restore From that you can select to break up the process into steps and utilize the (hopefully) elevated permissions of the administrator running the wizard.

When you select this option, the security privileges of the account of the individual running the Data Migration Assistant are used to perform the copy of the file from the backup location to the restore location. The user must have access to each of these locations with the needed read and write permissions for this step to succeed.

The wizard gives the user the option to specify the location to restore the data files and log files on the destination server.

As a final step, the wizard presents the user with a list of logins for migration consideration, with conflicting login names or logins that already exist identified. Where possible, the wizard attempts to map orphaned logins and align login security IDs (SIDs).

Moving to Azure SQL Database   The Data Migration Assistant tool performs an Azure SQL Database migration in two phases:

- **Schema.**   First, it generates a script of the database schema (you can save this script before deployment, for archival and testing purposes), which you deploy to the destination database.

- **Data.**   If you choose to move the data, another step is added after the creation of the tables on the destination database. This gives you the opportunity to verify that all of the tables exist in the destination database after the initial schema migration. Data migration makes use of Bulk Copy Program (BCP) under the hood.

The schema migration is required; the data migration is optional.

Installing or upgrading SQL Server

When it comes to administration and development tools used to work with SQL Server, the other important tab in Installation Center is the Installation tab. This tab contains a link to install the SQL Server Database Engine/Service. A few of the utilities discussed in this chapter are installed as options only during a full SQL Server Database Engine installation and cannot be downloaded and installed independently.

During an in-place upgrade of an existing SQL Server instance, you can neither add nor remove components. The process will simply upgrade existing components.

CAUTION
An in-place upgrade to SQL Server 2017 will uninstall SQL Server Reporting Services if it is installed.

If you have multiple versions installed on the same server (instance stacking), a number of shared components will be upgraded automatically, including SQL Server Browser and SQL Server VSS Writer.

➤ You can read more about multiple instances and versions of SQL Server on Microsoft Docs at *https://docs.microsoft.com/sql/sql-server/install/work-with-multiple-versions-and-instances-of-sql-server*.

Tools and services installed with the SQL Server Database Engine

SQL Server 2017 provides a number of optional tools and services that you can select during the installation process. We'll take a look at some of them in the sections that follow. (Note that this list is not an exhaustive listing and that some of these components might not be available in SQL Server 2017 on Linux.)

➤ For more information about configuring different features, see Chapter 4.

Machine Learning Services

SQL Server 2017 builds on the introduction in SQL Server 2016 of R, a statistics language used by data scientists, by introducing Python as a second machine learning (ML) language. As a result, these two languages are now classified as Machine Learning Services.

You can install R and Python independently or together, depending on your requirements. What's more, you can install these ML services directly in the Database Engine (in-database) or as standalone components.

The in-database option creates a secure integration between the Database Engine and the external runtimes containing the ML libraries. You can run queries using Transact-SQL (T-SQL) and make use of the Database Engine as the compute context.

If you decide to use of R or Python without installing SQL Server, you must choose the stand-alone option. Each service will then run in its own independent compute context.

NOTE

Installing any of the Machine Language Services requires agreeing to an additional license for each language option.

➤ You can read more about Machine Learning Services on Microsoft Docs at *https://docs.microsoft.com/sql/advanced-analytics/r/sql-server-r-services*.

Data Quality Services

The standardization, cleaning, and enhancement of data is critical to validity when performing analytical research. SQL Server Data Quality Services allows for both homegrown knowledge-base datasets and cloud-based reference data services by third-party providers.

Data Quality Services is a product that makes possible important data quality tasks, including the following:

- Knowledgebase-driven correction

- De-duplication

- Additional metadata enrichment

Data Quality Services has two parts: the Data Quality Server and the Data Quality Client. Data Quality Server has a dependency on the SQL Server Database Engine. Apart from that, you can install these two components on the same computer or on different computers. The tools are completely independent, and you can install one without having to install the other previously (i.e., the order doesn't matter).

To be functional, the Data Quality Client tool needs only to be able to connect to a Data Quality Server. There are certain operations the Data Quality Client can perform that require an installation of Microsoft Excel local to the client installation. It is commonplace to have the Data Quality Client on one or more workstations, not the SQL Server instance itself.

Data Quality Server

To install Data Quality Server, you must select its check box during SQL Server 2017 setup, which copies an installer file to your drive. After you have installed SQL Server 2017, to use Data Quality Server you must install it. In your Windows Start Menu, expand Microsoft SQL Server 2017, and then click SQL Server 2017 Data Quality Server Installer. This runs the DQSInstaller.exe file. The installation asks you to type and confirm a database master key password and creates three new databases into the SQL Server instance chosen to be host Server: DQS_Main, DQS_Projects, and DQS_Staging_Data.

Data Quality Client

The Data Quality Client is an application most commonly used in conjunction with master data management, data warehousing, or just plain data cleaning. It is typically used by a data steward who has a deep understanding of the business, and has domain knowledge about the data itself. You can use this tool to create knowledgebases surrounding data element rules, conversions, and mappings to help manage and align data elements. You also can use it to create and rune data quality projects and to perform administrative tasks.

To sign in to a Data Quality Server using the Data Quality Client tool, you must be either a member of the sysadmin server role or one of these three roles in the DQS_Main database:

- dqs_administrator

- dqs_kb_editor

- dqs_kb_operator

Command-line interface

You can use and administer SQL Server from a command line, which is especially relevant with Linux as a supported operating system (OS) for SQL Server. Both the SQLCMD and BCP utilities run on Windows, Linux, and macOS, with some minor differences.

SQLCMD

The SQLCMD is a tool that you can use to run T-SQL statements, stored procedures, or script files, using an ODBC connection to a SQL Server instance.

> ### WHAT DOES ODBC MEAN?
>
> **ODBC stands for Open Database Connectivity, which is an open-standard application programming interface (API) for communicating from any supported OS to any supported database engine.**

Although some people might consider the tool "old school" because it has been around since SQL Server 2005, it is still very popular because of its versatility. You can invoke SQLCMD from any of the following:

- Windows, Linux, or macOS command line

- Windows script files

- SQL Server Agent job step

- Using Windows PowerShell with the command line

NOTE

SQL Server Management Studio can invoke SQLCMD mode, which makes a lot of very useful functionality possible. Although it's technically part of SQLCMD, it is not strictly a command-line tool. You can read more about it at *https://docs.microsoft.com/sql/ relational-databases/scripting/edit-sqlcmd-scripts-with-query-editor*.

BCP

If you were thinking that SQLCMD is "old school," hold on to your hat. BCP makes SQLCMD look like the new kid on the block. BCP was first introduced in 1992 with the release of the very first edition of SQL Server. It's quite a testament that to this day BCP is still a practical way to work with SQL Server as a means to insert or export large quantities of data. It uses minimal logging techniques and bulk data flows to its advantage.

If you are thinking about SQL Server Integration Services right now, that's fine, but BCP is not nearly as powerful. You use BCP to move data between data files (text, comma-delimited, or other formats) and a SQL Server table.

You can use it to import files into SQL Server tables or to export data from SQL Server tables into data files. BCP requires the use of a format file to designate the structure of the receiving table and the data types allowed in each column. Fortunately, BCP helps you to create this format file quite easily.

There are a few things about BCP that you must understand and do for the tool to perform optimally (for more information go to *https://technet.microsoft.com/library/ms177445.aspx*):

- Use SELECT INTO syntax

- Put the database into the simple or bulk-logged recovery model

- Drop any nonclustered indexes on the destination table

- Insert sorted data and use the sorted_data option if a clustered index exists

- Run BCP on the same machine as the SQL Server

- Place source and destination files on separate physical drives

- Manually grow SQL data files in advance if growth is expected

- Take advantage of Instant File Initialization

- Use sp_tableoption to set table lock on bulk load (TABLOCK) to ON

Inside OUT

How do I download the most recent command-line tools?

The versions of SQLCMD and BCP installed with SQL Server 2017 on Windows are updated through a separate package that is available at *https://www.microsoft.com/download/details.aspx?id=53591*.

For features like Always Encrypted and Azure Active Directory authentication, a minimum of version 13.1 is required. It is entirely possible (and likely) to have more than one version of SQLCMD installed on a server, so be sure to check that you are using the correct version by running sqlcmd -?.

Separate installers are available for Linux and macOS versions of these command-line tools.

SQL Server PowerShell Provider

If you love to use a command line or if you have begun to use Windows PowerShell to help manage and maintain your SQL Servers, Microsoft offers the PowerShell Provider for SQL Server. Two features are required for you to use this:

- Windows PowerShell Extensions for Microsoft SQL Server

- SQL Server Management Objects (SMO)

Both are installed by default with the SQL Server Management Tools, but you also can download and install them separately through the Microsoft SQL Server Feature Pack.

The SQL Server PowerShell Provider uses SQL Server Management Objects. These objects were designed by Microsoft to provide management of SQL Server programmatically. There are many ways that developers and administrators can use Windows PowerShell to automate their work in SQL Server, especially when dealing with multiple server environments.

➤ To learn more, see Chapter 13.

SQL Server Configuration Manager

SQL Server Configuration Manager is a tool that uses the Microsoft Management Console as a shell. Because it is not a freestanding program, finding and opening the application can be a little tricky. To launch SQL Server Configuration Manager, on the Windows Start Menu, under Apps, search for SQLServerManager14.msc.

Administrators use SQL Server Configuration Manager to manage SQL Server Services. These services include the SQL Server Database Engine, the SQL Server Agent, SQL Server Integration Services, the PolyBase Engine, and others. SQL Server Configuration Manager provides a GUI to perform the following tasks associated with SQL Server–related services:

- Start or stop a service

- Alter the start mode (manual, automatic, disabled)

- Change startup parameters

- Create server aliases

- Change the Log On As accounts

- Manage client protocols, including TCP/IP default port, keep alive, and interval settings

- Manage FILESTREAM behavior

CHAPTER 1

Inside OUT

Can I manage SQL Server services from Windows Services Manager?

Although you can perform most of these same tasks using the Windows default services manager (Control Panel > Administrative Tools > Services), in this case we do not recommend using it.

The Windows Services Manager (services.msc) does not provide all of the various configuration options found in the SQL Server Configuration Manager. More important, it can omit adjusting important registry settings that needed to be changed, which will compromise the stability of your SQL Server environment.

You must always change SQL Server services using the SQL Server Configuration Manager. This is especially true for managing SQL Server Service Accounts.

Performance and reliability monitoring tools

The Database Engine Tuning Advisor, Extended Events, and Profiler tools are installed with the SQL Server Database Engine and do not require additional installation steps.

Database Engine Tuning Advisor

Among the many administrative tools Microsoft provides to work with SQL Server is the Database Engine Tuning Advisor. You can start it either from the Start menu or from within SQL Server Management Studio by clicking Tools and then Database Engine Tuning Advisor. Using this tool, you can analyze a server-side trace captured by SQL Server Profiler. It will analyze every statement that passes through the SQL Server and present various options for possible performance improvement.

NOTE

The Database Engine Tuning Advisor is not supported in Azure SQL Database.

The suggestions that Database Engine Tuning Advisor makes focus solely on indexing, statistics, and partitioning strategies. The Database Engine Tuning Advisor simplifies the implementation of any administrator-approved changes it suggests. You need to scrutinize these changes to ensure that they will not negatively affect the instance.

CAUTION

You should not run the Database Engine Tuning Advisor directly against a production server, because it can leave behind hypothetical indexes and statistics that can unknowingly persist. These will require additional resources to maintain. Use the is_hypothetical column in the sys.indexes system view to find hypothetical indexes for manual removal.

Extended events

Technically, the Extended Events GUI (client only) is installed with and is a built-in part of SQL Server Management Studio. An argument could easily be made that it belongs in the section later in the chapter that details tools within SQL Server Management Studio. However, we discuss it here with the other performance-specific tools for categorical reasons.

> You can read more about how extended events are supported in Azure SQL Database, with some differences, at *https://docs.microsoft.com/azure/sql-database/sql-database-xevent-db-diff-from-svr*.

SQL Server extended events is an event-handling system created with the intent to replace SQL Server Profiler. Think of it as the "new and improved" version of Profiler. It is more lightweight, full-featured, and flexible, all at once. Extended events offer a way of monitoring what's happening in SQL Server, with much less overhead than an equivalent trace run through the SQL Profiler. This is because extended events are asynchronous.

You access extended events through SQL Server Management Studio by connecting to a SQL Server instance and navigating to the Management folder. When you're there, expand the Extended Events node to display Sessions. Right-click this, and then, on the shortcut menu that opens, select the New Session Wizard. You can then use this wizard to schedule events to run at server startup or immediately after the event has been created.

NOTE

SQL Server Management Studio provides a simple extended events viewer called XEvent Profiler, which is meant to replace the standalone Profiler tool for monitoring activity in real time on a SQL Server instance.

Scripting extended events sessions via T-SQL can be a much quicker and consistent way to create a library of extended event sessions for reuse in multiple environments. This gives you the flexibility to start and stop them as needed, even as a job in SQL Server Agent.

Components

The following subsections describe the extended events components.

Events   Because Profiler has been deprecated, a number of new features in SQL Server have matching extended events, but not Profiler events. This means that using extended events to capture diagnostic and performance visibility (rather than Profiler) provides a much larger library of events to choose from than Profiler. Each event has its own set of default fields. In addition, there are global fields (known as actions) that you can add to the collection of any event, for example, `database_name`, `database_id`, `sql_text`, and `username`.

Targets (Data Storage Options)   Targets are basically the consumers, or recipients of events. Targets can log additional event context upon receipt of an event. The target options allow for different ways to view or even save event data. Although users can observe data during collection with extended events (watching the target in action), we do not recommend that you do so on a production machine. Targets come in two flavors:

- **File (`event_file` target).**   Best for large datasets, later analysis, remote analysis for retrieval by a consultant or tool, or historical record keeping/baselines. Options with this target setting are where to save the file and what to name it, what the maximum file size should be, should the file roll over and how many files total should be saved.

- **Memory (`ring_buffer` target).**   Best for smaller datasets or long sessions. With this option, the user can specify how many events to keep, how much memory to use (max), or how many events (per type) to keep.

Actions   These are instructions that specify what to do when an event fires. Actions are associated with events.

Predicates   These are filters that limit event firing and provide a more concise view of the issue being reviewed. Some examples are `LoginName`, `ApplicationName`, or SPID.

Scenarios for use

You can use extended events for a wide range of scenarios. As of SQL Server 2017, you can choose from more than 1,500 events. Here are some of the most common uses for extended events:

- Troubleshooting

- Diagnosing slowness

- Diagnosing deadlocks

- Diagnosing recompiles

- Debugging

- Login auditing

- Baselining

By scripting out an event session and using automation, you have a stock set of sessions that you can use to troubleshoot depending on the problem. You can deploy these solutions on any server that needs a closer examination into performance issues.

You can also use extended event trace to provide a baseline from which you can track code improvements or degradation over time.

Management data warehouse

The management data warehouse, introduced in SQL Server 2008, collects data about the performance of a SQL Server instance, and feeds the information back to an administrator in a Visual Analytic style format. Management data warehouse has its own relational database containing tables that are the recipient (target) of specific extended events collection activities.

Upon installation, the data warehouse provides three reports: Server Active History, Query Statistics History, and System Disk Usage. You can create additional reports and add them to the data warehouse collection.

Using the three-report configuration of management data warehouse makes it possible for a database administrator to do basic performance baselining and to plan for growth. It also allows for proactive tuning activities. It might be good practice to set this up when you install a new instance of SQL Server.

Installing a management data warehouse

Perform the following steps to install your management data warehouse:

1. In SQL Server Management Studio, in Object Explorer, expand the Management node, and then right-click Data Collection. On the shortcut menu that opens, point to Tasks, and then select Configure Management Data Warehouse, as shown in Figure 1-2.

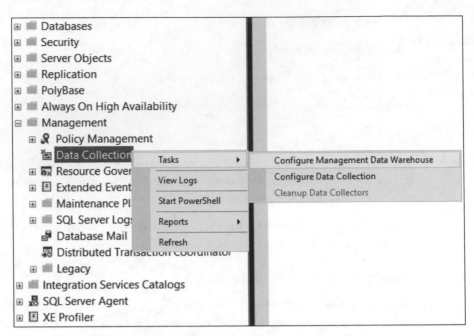

Figure 1-2 Navigating to the Management Data Warehouse menu item.

2.   In the Configure Management Data Warehouse Wizard, Select Create Or Upgrade A Management Data Warehouse, and then click Next.

3.   The server name is already populated, so either select the Management Data Warehouse database you are already using for collection by clicking it in the Database Name list box, or, to the right of the list box, click New. If you click New, in the New Database dialog box that opens, type the database name to which you want to store the information collected by the management data warehouse, as demonstrated in Figure 1-3.

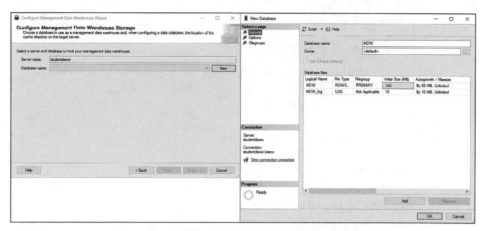

Figure 1-3 Creating a new database for collecting management data warehouse data.

4.   Select a user to map to the Management Data Warehouse role.

Setting up a data collection

After you install your management data warehouse, you need to set up a data collection to collect data from the server and databases of interest. Here's how to do that:

1.   In Object Explorer, expand the Management node, right-click Data Collection, point to Tasks, and then click Configure Data Collection.

2.   In the wizard that opens, select the Server Name and Database Name specified during the installation. Finish by choosing any other needed settings.

Go back and view Data Collection node. Things look different now: The Data Collection Sets in Object Explorer as well as the Data Collection node itself no longer displays a red down-arrow icon, as depicted in Figure 1-4.

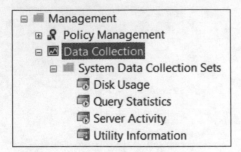

Figure 1-4 Active data collection sets.

Accessing reports

To access the management data warehouse reports, right-click Data Collection, point to Reports, and then move through the menus to the report that you would like to view, as shown in Figure 1-5.

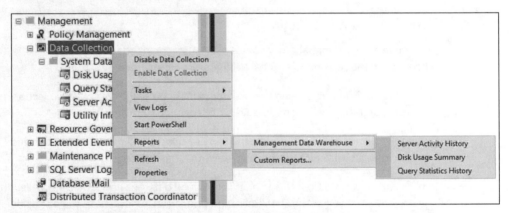

Figure 1-5 Accessing the management data warehouse reports.

SQL Server Reporting Services

Starting with SQL Server 2017, SQL Server Reporting Services is a separate download outside of the SQL Server installer. You can use SQL Server Reporting Services to create reports against a variety of data sources. It includes a complete set of tools for creating, managing, scheduling, and delivering reports. The reports can include charts, maps, data matrixes, and, with the addition of Microsoft Power BI, R, and Python, almost unlimited data visualizations that are rich and limited only by creativity.

You install SQL Server Reporting Services in Native mode, which provides a web portal interface to manage and organize reports and other items. Internet Information Services (IIS) is not required to use SQL Server Reporting Services, as it was in versions prior to SQL Server 2016.

Installation

You must download SQL Server Reporting Services separately, either by following the stub on the Installation Center screen or by going to *https://www.microsoft.com/download/details. aspx?id=55252.*

Completing the installation of SQL Server Reporting Services sets up and configures the following services and features:

- Installs the Report Server Service, which consists of the following:
    - Report Server Web Service
    - Web Portal for viewing and managing reports and report security
    - Report Services Configuraton Manager
- Configures the Report Service and Web Portal URLs
- Establishes the Service accounts needed for SQL Server Reporting Services to operate

> ➤ **You can read more about configuring SQL Server Reporting Services in Chapter 4.**

After the installation is complete, using administrative rights, browse to the following directories to verify that the installation was in fact successful and that the service is running:

- *http://localhost/Reports*

- *http://localhost/ReportServer*

If you are running a nondefault instance of SQL Server, you might need to use the Web Portal URL tab in the Report Services Configuration Manager dialog box to determine the exact path of both the Web Service URL and the Web Portal URL, as illustrated in Figure 1-6.

CHAPTER 1

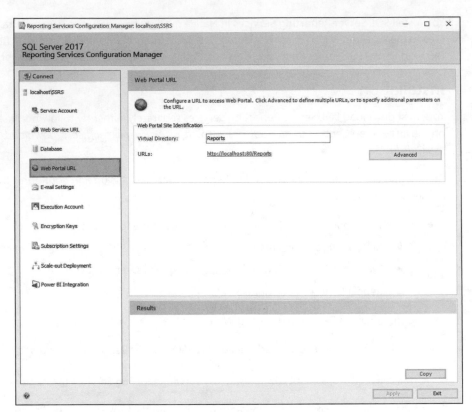

Figure 1-6 Web Portal URL setting in Reporting Services Configuration Manager.

Report Services Configuration Manager

The Report Services Configuration Manager simplifies customization of the behavior of features and capabilities offered by SQL Server Reporting Services. You can use it to perform the following tasks and more:

- Create or select existing Report Server databases

- Define the URLs used to access the Report Server and Report Manager

- Configure the Report Server Service Account

- Modify the connection string used by the Report Server

- Set up email distribution capability

- Integrate with a Power BI service

Inside OUT

Configuring SQL Server Reporting Services: the long and winding road...

The Configuration Manager in SQL Server Reporting Services comes with no shortage of customization options. Beyond the default, you can alter the configuration of almost any setting using the GUI, through SQL Server Management Studio, and also directly via web.config files, and even in some cases the Windows registry. Customizing accounts, IP addresses, ports, or behaviors can be quite an endeavor, the scope of which is far beyond what we can cover in this chapter.

You can find more information at *https://docs.microsoft.com/sql/reporting-services/install-windows/reporting-services-configuration-manager-native-mode*.

SQL Server Management Studio

SQL Server Management Studio is the de facto standard SQL Server database development and management tool. It provides a rich graphical interface and simplifies the configuration, administration, and development tasks associated with managing SQL Server and Azure SQL Database environments. SQL Server Management Studio also contains a robust script editor and comes stocked with many templates, samples, and script-generating features.

Inside OUT

Does SQL Server Management Studio support other operating systems?

SQL Server Management Studio is a Windows-only application; it does not work in Linux and macOS environments. Instead, you can use the free cross-platform Microsoft SQL Operations Studio to connect to SQL Server, Azure SQL Database and SQL Data Warehouse from Windows, Linux, and macOS.

SQL Operations Studio is an exciting addition to your toolkit.

Releases and versions

Since the release of SQL Server 2016, SQL Server Management Studio is a freestanding toolset that you can download and install independent of the Database Engine.

Initially, Microsoft went with monthly releases, but beginning in August of 2016, the company changed to a versioned release system that allows for more flexibility, and no longer uses a month/year naming convention.

Installing SQL Server Management Studio

To install SQL Server Management Studio, download the latest version of the product by either doing a web search or going to *https://docs.microsoft.com/sql/ssms/download-sql-server-management-studio-ssms*.

NOTE
You can install the standalone SQL Server Management Studio alongside versions of SQL Server Management Studio that were bundled with earlier versions of SQL Server.

CAUTION
Be forewarned! Although it is simply a "tool" and not the database engine itself, the download is almost 1 GB in size. If you already have a compatible version of SQL Server Management Studio installed, a smaller upgrade file is also available.

After you download the executable file, install and then watch the Package Progress and Overall Progress meter bars do their thing. There's not much more to it than that. The installation finishes with a Setup Completed message.

At this point, you can start the application by browsing through your Start Menu to Microsoft SQL Server Tools 17 > Microsoft SQL Server Management Studio 17. For ease of access, you might want to pin the program to your Start Menu or copy the icon to your desktop.

Upgrading SQL Server Management Studio

SQL Server Management Studio will notify you if an update is available. You can also manually check whether one is available. To do so, in SQL Server Management Studio, on the toolbar, select Tools, and then choose Check For Updates. The different versions of the SQL Server Management Studio components—the installed version and the latest available version—will display. If any updates are available, you can click the Update button to bring you to a webpage from which you can download and install the latest recommended version.

Now that the tools used to manage SQL Server are completely independent of the Database Engine, upgrading these components has become very easy. It has also become much safer to upgrade: there is no longer any concern about accidentally affecting your production environment (SQL Server Database Engine) because you upgraded your SQL Server Management Studio toolset.

Features of SQL Server Management Studio

The power of SQL Server Management Studio is in the many ways in which you can interact with one or more SQL Server instances. Listing each one would require its own book, so this section highlights only some useful features.

Object Explorer and Object Explorer Details

Object Explorer is the default SQL Server Management Studio view, providing both a hierarchical and tabular view of each instance of SQL Server and the child objects within those instances (including databases, tables, views, stored procedures, functions, and so on).

> NOTE
>
> **Object Explorer uses its own connection to the database server, and can block certain database-level activities, just like any other SQL Server Management Studio query.**

Object Explorer presents two panes (see Figure 1-7): the Object Explorer pane (left) and the Object Explorer Details pane (right). The Object Explorer pane is strictly hierarchical, whereas the Object Explorer Details pane is both hierarchical and tabular; as such, it provides additional functionality over its companion pane; for example, object search and multiple, and noncontiguous object selection and scripting. To display the Object Explorer Details pane, click View > Object Explorer Details, or press F7.

CHAPTER 1

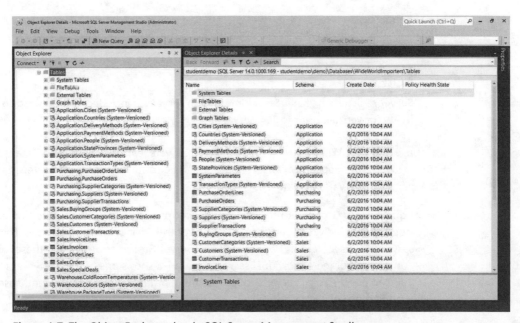

Figure 1-7 The Object Explorer view in SQL Server Management Studio.

Server Registration

The Server Registration feature within SQL Server Management Studio can save time and make it easier to manage a complex environment by saving a list of commonly accessed instances. Registering connections in advance for future reuse provides the following benefits:

- Preservation of connection information

- Creation of groups of servers

- Aliasing of servers with more meaningful names

- Ability to add detailed descriptions to both servers and server groups

- Import and export of registered server groups for sharing between machines or teammates

To access the Server Registration feature within SQL Server Management Studio, click View > Registered Servers, or press Ctrl+Alt+G. You can use SQL Server Management Studio to manage four different types of servers and services:

- Database Engine

- Analysis Services

- Reporting Services

- Integration Services

NOTE

Server registration of SQL Server Integration Services is included for backward compatibility for versions prior to SQL Server 2012.

Database Engine   When you use the Registered Servers feature to work with Database Engines, two nodes appear: Local Server Groups and Central Management Servers. Each of these has some very useful features:

- **Local Server Groups.**   The Local Server Groups node allows for the addition of either freestanding individual server registrations or the creation of server groups. Think of server groups as "folders" within the Local Server Groups node. Each of these folders can contain one or more individual servers. Figure 1-8 shows one of the many ways in which you can use the Local Server Groups feature to organize and save frequently used Database Engine connections.

Figure 1-8 The Local Server Group.

- **Exporting Registered Servers.**   To access the Export Registered Servers Wizard, right-click the Local Server Groups folder node or any folder or server nested within this node. On the shortcut menu, point to Tasks, and then click Export. From there, you have quite a bit of freedom; you can choose to export from any level within the tree structure and whether to include user names and passwords. In the preceding case, if you wanted to export only the Development Servers node and those servers within it, you could do so easily. Using the wizard, you can choose where to save the created file and then build out an XML document with the extension .regsrvr.

- **Importing Registered Servers.**   To access the Import Registered Servers Wizard, right-click the Local Server Groups folder node or any folder or server nested within this node. On the shortcut menu, point to Tasks, and then click Import. Browse to and select a previously created .regsrvr file, as demonstrated in Figure 1-9.

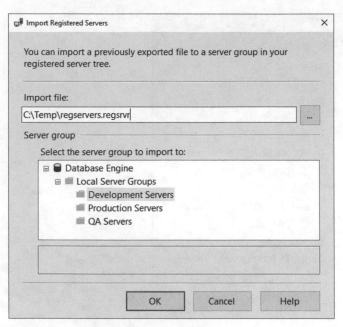

Figure 1-9 Importing registered servers.

From here you can choose in which folder you would like the imported object or object tree to reside. If you select a folder that already contains the same structures you are attempting to import, a message will appear asking you to approve or disapprove an update/overwrite to the existing object structure.

- **Central Management Servers.**   The second node available in the Database Engine feature is Central Management Servers. At first glance, this might appear to be almost the same thing as Local Server Groups: you're able to add servers and create folders with descriptive names to which you can add servers. And, yes, in this way, it is much the same. However, Centralized Management Servers includes some very significant differences.

    First, when using this feature, you must choose a SQL Server Database Engine to play the role of a Central Management Server (CMS). You can alias the server with a new name, but the server itself must exist. After you have chosen a server to play this role and have created a CMS, you can create new Server Groups or individual Server Registrations using the same methods explained in the Local Server Groups section.

Here is where things become interesting! If you right-click any level (a server, a group, or the CMS itself), you are presented with multiple options:

- New Query

- Object Explorer

- Evaluate Policies

- Import Policies

Anything that is run will be run against each of the servers in the chosen group's tree. Running a query against the CMS itself will result in the query being run against every server hierarchically present in all trees within the CMS. This is a very handy feature, but with great power comes great responsibility!

The default behavior of CMS is that multiple server results are merged into one result set. You can change and customize this behavior by going to Tools > Options > Query Results > SQL Server > Multiserver Results, and then turning on the Merge Results setting. Other behavior options available here include Add Login Name and Add Server Name to the result set from a CMS query.

When you create a CMS on an existing SQL Server, others can access and utilize the structure setup, so there is no need to Export or Import and keep folders and structures synchronized. This is great for team collaboration and efficiency.

Filtering objects

In the default Object Explorer view, SQL Server Management Studio lists objects within each category in alphabetical order. There are several main groups, or tree categories, that are common across all versions of SQL Server. These include the following:

- **Databases.** The full list of databases (including system databases) on the SQL Server instance. Database snapshots also appear here.

- **Security.** A diverse list of object types here, including Logins, Server Roles, Credentials, Cryptographic Providers, and Audits.

- **Server Objects.** These include Backup Devices, Endpoints, Linked Servers, and Triggers (server-level triggers).

- **Replication.** Information about Publishers and Subscriptions.

- **Always On High Availability.** Includes Failover Clustering and Availability Groups.

- **Management.**   Covers a number of diverse features and tools, including Policy Management, Data Collection, Resource Governor, Extended Events, Maintenance Plans, Database Mail, DTC (Distributed Transaction Coordinator), and SQL Server error logs.

- **SQL Server Agent.**   Covers jobs, alerts, operators, proxies, and error logs of its own.

- **Integration Services Catalogs.**   SQL Server Integration Services package catalog. Depends on SQL Server version.

By default, SQL Server Management Studio lists all objects alphabetically beneath each tree category. When working with databases that have a large quantity of objects, this can become quite aggravating as the user waits through potentially long list load times and expends energy scrolling and watching the screen very closely for the object in question.

Fortunately, SQL Server Management Studio has a filtering feature! You can apply filters to many object categories; for example, user databases, tables, views, stored procedures, table-valued functions, user-defined functions, and even database users.

You can configure filter settings in either the Object Explorer pane or the Objects Explorer Details pane independently. Table 1-2 lists the available filtering options.

Table 1-2 SQL Server Management Studio Filters and Options

Filter	Options
Name	Contains Equals Does Not Contain
Schema	Contains Equals Does Not Contain
Owner	Equals Does Not Equal
Is Natively Compiled	True False
Creation Date	Equals Less Than Less Than or Equal More Than More Than or Equal Between Not Between

After you have selected a filter, the suffix "(filtered)" appears in the Object Explorer or Object Explorer Details tree, above your filtered list.

To clear an applied filter and display all objects in a tree again, right-click a filtered category, select Filter, and then click Remove Filter.

Multi-Select   In the Object Explorer pane, you can select only one object at a time. The Object Explorer Details pane, however, provides a Multi-Select feature with which you can work on multiple objects at the same time (tables, views, jobs, and so on). Following the standard in the Windows environment, the Shift key allows for the selection of contiguous objects, whereas the Ctrl key allows for noncontiguous selecting. You can specify actions against multiple objects using the GUI or choose to script multiple objects at once. Scripting each object into its own file or merging all object scripting into one larger file are both available options.

Additional tools in SQL Server Management Studio

SQL Server Management Studio provides a number of time-saving tools and techniques for making you more productive. The following subsections provide just a few highlights.

IntelliSense tools

IntelliSense is a ubiquitous Microsoft technology found in many of its products that helps you with code completion. IntelliSense effectively reduces the amount of typing you do by offering shortcuts and autocompletion of keywords and object names, which also makes your code more accurate.

Additionally, SQL Server Management Studio comes with *snippets* to help you code more easily. Snippets are preconfigured code fragments that you can quickly drop into or around an existing block of code. The two options for using them are Insert Snippet and Surround With Snippets. You also can create your own snippets (you build them using XML), but that is beyond the scope of this discussion.

> NOTE
>
> **You can manage code snippets from the Tools menu, via the Code Snippets Manager option.**

Let's take a look at some use cases for snippets.

One of the options for SQL Server 2012 and later includes a snippet for an IF statement. After testing a block of code, you can quickly add the IF statement (including the BEGIN/END statements) by highlighting your code and choosing a snippet.

There are three ways to access snippets

- Use a keyboard shortcut

- Right-click and use the option from the context menu that opens

- On the Edit menu, point to IntelliSense, and then click the snippets option you want—Surround With, in the example shown in Figure 1-10.

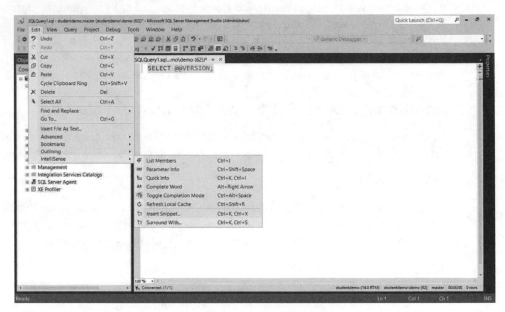

Figure 1-10 Accessing the Surround With snippet from the Edit menu.

You can double-click the Function folder to see the available snippets; clicking a snippet surrounds the highlighted code with the snippet template code. You also can insert "placeholder" text that you can replace later.

There are only a few stock Surround With snippets, but many Insert Snippets. You can find these by going to the Edit menu, pointing to IntelliSense, and then clicking Insert Snippet. You use them in the same manner you do for Surround With snippets, except that the code is placed at the current location of the cursor within a block of code. There are also keyboard shortcuts to use this feature. You can use Ctrl+K, Ctrl+S for Surround With snippets, and Ctrl+K, Ctrl+X for Insert Snippets.

Inside OUT

Did someone say keyboard shortcuts?

SQL Server Management Studio offers a large range of keyboard shortcuts for increasing productivity.

For example, you can show and hide the results pane of a query by using Ctrl+R. Accessing the Code Snippets Manager is as easy as using the combination Ctrl+K, Ctrl+B. Do you want to include the Actual Query Plan in a query? Use Ctrl+M. Ctrl+F5 parses a query before you run it to ensure that the syntax is correct. By far the most popular one is F5, which runs a query, but you can also use Ctrl+E to do that.

Customizing menus and shortcuts

SQL Server Management Studio is based on the Visual Studio integrated development environment (IDE), which means that it is customizable and extensible. Adding extensions is beyond the scope of this book, but the next few sections describe how to customize elements such as the toolbars and keyboard shortcuts.

Customize toolbars   SQL Server Management Studio installs with only the standard toolbar as the default. There are many other toolbars available for use. To access these options, on the toolbar, click Tools, and then click Customize. In the Customize dialog box, there are two tabs. on the first tab, Toolbars, you can select the toolbars that are useful in your work environment. Among the many choices are toolbars for working with Database Diagrams, extended events, XML, and even a web browser. On the second tab, the Commands tab, you can set up a custom toolbar or edit the drop-down menus and functionality of the existing toolbars.

Tool options   You also can customize the appearance of your SQL Server Management Studio interface. Click Tools and then Options to adjust color, font, keyboard hotkeys, length of strings in results, location of results, scripting preferences, international settings, theme, autorecovery timeframe, and more.

One very handy option is the Keyboard, Query Shortcuts feature. SQL Server Management Studio comes with several shortcuts already turned on (see Figure 1-11), but you can tailor these to your needs. Many long-time DBAs make heavy use of this feature to reduce the number of keystrokes to carry out common stored procedures.

Using shortcuts in SQL Server Management Studio, you can highlight text and then press the shortcut to run the associated stored procedure, supplying a parameter of the highlighted text. For instance, to see the text of a stored procedure or view, you can use the system procedure `sp_helptext`. By adding this stored procedure to the shortcut Ctrl+0 (which you can see in Figure 1-11), displaying the data definition language (DDL) of any scripted object within a database requires nothing more than a highlight of a name and simple key combination.

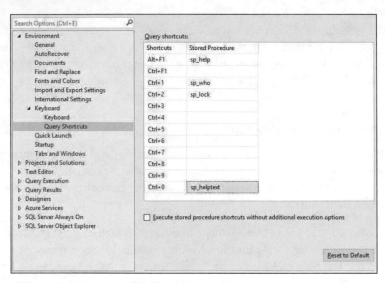

Figure 1-11 Managing query shortcuts.

Error logs

Each SQL Server instance maintains a distinct set of relevant error log messages that are accessible in two places: in the Management/Error Logs node, and in a context menu when you right-click an instance in the Registered Servers window. By default, these log files contain information about the SQL Server instance when coming online, what configuration settings were applied (or failed to apply), when backups occurred, when corruption is detected, when I/O is taking too long, partial stack dumps, and lots of other useful pieces of information. It's a great place to go to when troubleshooting stability or performance problems and to look for things that might cause trouble in the future.

To keep the log information to a reasonable and searchable size, the information is kept in a series of files rather than a single file. It is possible to close one file and start a new, blank file. Unfortunately, the default settings for cycling the log are not very useful.

By default, SQL Server keeps the six most-recent error log files. To configure the number of log files to maintain, in the SQL Server Management Studio Object Explorer, in the Management folder, right-click SQL Server Logs, and then select Configure. In the dialog box that opens, select the check box labeled Limit The Number Of Error Log Files Before They Are Recycled, and then, in the Maximum Number Of Error Log Files box, type a value. The value must be between 6 and 99.

> ➤ **For more about this and other post-installation checklist items, see Chapter 4.**

Every time the SQL Server service is restarted, it cycles the log file. This creates a brand new, empty log file and moves the previous log file down one spot in the list. Any log file older in sequence than the maximum specified number of files to keep is deleted.

You also can choose to manually cycle the log file by using the `sp_cycle_errorlog` command, or you can automate this process by using a SQL Server Agent job to perform this task. When working with SQL Server instances that are quite large and remain online for a long time-frame, this can prevent any single log file from becoming overly large and unwieldy.

No matter which method you use, the resulting action is the same: the current file is closed and a new, blank file is opened. If this causes the file count to exceed the maximum number of files, the oldest file is deleted.

Activity Monitor

Activity Monitor is a tool that provides information about what is currently running on the SQL Server and how that code might be affecting the instance. It provides the ability to easily view common hardware-specific performance metrics and a list of recently used queries (with metrics, code, and execution plans). You can sort all of the grids, and you can filter some of them. Out of the box, this is the place to begin if you need to do rudimentary troubleshooting and baselining.

To open the Activity Monitor window, In the Object Explorer pane, right-click the SQL Server instance, and then select Activity Monitor. The window opens in the Object Explorer Details pane.

Activity Monitor consists of six distinct parts:

- **Overview.**   Displays a basic version of what you might already be familiar with viewing in the Task Manager window but with a SQL Server flair, with four distinct graphs

- **Processes.**   Displays all nonsystem processes with open connections to the SQL Server instance

- **Resource Waits.**   Displays the Wait Events of active, open connections

- **Data File I/O.**   Displays a difference between two interval readings of the storage subsystem

- **Recent Expensive Queries.** Displays information about the most expensive queries from the past 30 seconds

- **Active Expensive Queries.** Displays a more detailed view of queries that are running at that moment

You can expand each of these six parts to show more information, with the Overview section expanded by default. If you want to sort or filter the results, click the column header of any of the columns in each section.

Activity Monitor overview

Four graphs cover the most basic overview of the instance. The % Processor Time is an average combined value for all logical processors assigned to the instance (see the section "Carving up CPU cores using an affinity mask" in Chapter 3). The other three graphs are Waiting Tasks (an instance-level value), Database I/O (all databases, measured in MB/sec) and Batch Requests/sec (all databases).

Each of the graphs display information in real time; however, you can configure the refresh interval by right-clicking any of the graphs. The default for each is 10 seconds; you can adjust this from as short as one second to as long as one hour. The graph settings are adjusted as a unified set, meaning that all four graphs use the same interval setting, so changing one interval changes them all. Likewise, selecting Pause on any of the graphs pauses the entire set.

Processes

The Processes section of Activity Monitor displays all nonsystem processes (also known as tasks) with open connections to the SQL Server instance, regardless of whether the process is actively running a query. Important metadata provided includes the following:

- **Session ID.** The session process identifier (SPID) of the current process

- **User Process.** Displays a 1 if this is a user process; 0 if it is a system process

- **Login.** The login name for the user running this process

- **Database.** The name of the database

- **Task State.** Populated from the list of possible tasks in the `task_state` column of the `sys.dm_os_tasks` dynamic management view

- **Command.** Populated from the list of command types in the `command` column of the `sys.dm_exec_requests` dynamic management view

- **Application.** The name of the application

- **Wait Time (ms).**   Amount of time that this task has been waiting, in milliseconds

- **Wait Type.**   The current wait type for this task

- **Wait Resource.**   The resource for which this task is waiting

- **Blocked By.**   If this task is being blocked by another process, this shows the SPID of the blocking process

- **Head Blocker.**   If there is a chain of blocking processes, this is the SPID of the process at the start of the blocking chain

- **Memory Use (KB).**   How much memory this process is using

- **Host Name.**   The host name of the machine that made this connection

- **Workload Group.**   The name of the Resource Governor workload group that this process belongs to (you can read more about the Resource Governor in Chapter 3)

To see the detailed T-SQL query being run (last T-SQL command batch), to trace the process in SQL Profiler, or to Kill the process, right-click any of the rows in the Processes pane.

Resource Waits

The Resource Waits section of the Activity Monitor tool displays the Wait Events of active, open connections, sorted by default by the Cumulative Wait Time in seconds. This can be very useful when you're trying to determine the root cause of a performance issue. Having a baseline for these counters when "things are good" is very useful later on when you're trying to gauge whether a problem being experienced is "new" or "normal." Understanding the meaning of certain wait times can help you to diagnose the root cause of slowness, be it drive, memory pressure, CPU, network latency, or a client struggling to receive and display a result set. Following are the wait statistics provided by this section:

- Wait Category

- Wait Time (ms/sec)

- Recent Wait Time (ms/sec)

- Average Waiter Count

- Cumulative Wait Time (sec)

➤ You can read more about Resource Waits at *https://technet.microsoft.com/library/cc879320.aspx*.

Data File I/O

The Data File I/O section of Activity Monitor displays the difference between two readings taken from the metadata stored in the `sys.dm_io_virtual_file_stats` dynamic management view. For this reason, when you first expand the section, you might not see results for a short while. The server needs to have at least two readings (so if your interval is 10 seconds, you'll wait 10 seconds before data appears). The information displayed shows each of the data files for all of the databases on the SQL Server, the file location and name, the megabytes per second read (MB/sec read), megabytes per second written (MB/sec written), and average response time in milliseconds (ms).

As a general rule, average response times of five milliseconds or less allow for acceptable performance, notwithstanding the occasional outlying peak.

Recent Expensive Queries

Activity Monitor's Recent Expensive Queries section displays information about the most expensive queries that have run on the SQL Server instance in the past 30 seconds. It includes both queries in flight and queries that finished. To see the full query text or to see the execution plan currently being used, right-click any of the queries listed. Here are the fields returned in this pane:

- Query
- Executions/Min
- CPU (ms/sec)
- Physical Reads/sec
- Logical Writes/sec
- Logical Reads/sec
- Average Duration (ms)
- Plan Count
- Database

Active Expensive Queries

If you're trying to determine what is running at this precise moment that might be causing performance issues, Active Expensive Queries is the place to look. This section of Activity Monitor is more granular than the aggregated "past 30 seconds" view provided in the Recent Expensive Queries section. In addition, the list of queries here shows some very interesting details that are available at only a granular level:

- Session ID

- Database

- Elapsed Time

- Row Count

- Memory Allocated

Again, you can see the full query text and the execution plan by right-clicking, but here you get an additional feature, Show Live Execution Plan, which might very well differ if a query is running long.

Inside OUT

Does Activity Monitor use resources?

In a nutshell, yes, it does. When you expand any of the detail areas in Activity Monitor, it must query the system metadata in real time to keep the columns and/or graphs populated on the screen. When you collapse the area, these queries stop.

Thus, after you have finished viewing a section, we recommend that you collapse that section, or close the Activity Monitor tab, to avoid any unnecessary "observer overhead."

SQL Server Agent

SQL Server Agent is a service on both Windows and Linux that you can use to schedule automated tasks, called Jobs, as illustrated in Figure 1-12. These Jobs are most commonly used to run routine maintenance (backups, index defragmentation, statistics updates, and integrity checks), but you can also use them to periodically run custom code.

NOTE

You can also filter SQL Server Agent nodes. This is described earlier in this chapter in the discussion on Object Explorer.

There is built-in functionality for Job Notifications that makes it possible for a person or group to receive communications about the status of a job, using the Database Mail feature. The setup provides a few straightforward configuration options as to when notifications are sent: Success, Failure, and Completion.

CHAPTER 1

➤ **For more information on configuring Database Mail and configuring SQL Agent to use Database Mail, see Chapter 13.**

SQL Server Agent's list of Jobs also includes any SQL Server Reporting Services subscriptions that have been created and scheduled on the server.

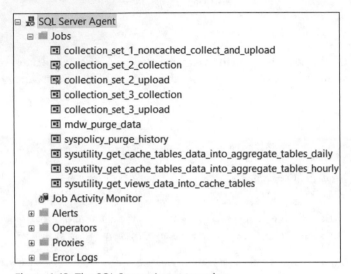

Figure 1-12 The SQL Server Agent tree view.

Job Activity Monitor

Job Activity Monitor gives a snapshot view of all jobs on a server. Using this feature, you can quickly see many attributes about the Jobs scheduled on a SQL Server instance. You can use many of these attributes to narrow the list of jobs being viewed. This can be especially handy if there are many hundreds of SQL Server Reporting Services reports scheduled, or the list of jobs is extensive. Table 1-3 lists the attributes.

Table 1-3 Job activity attributes

Job activity attribute	Values	Can use to filter?
Name		✓
Enabled	No Yes	✓

Status	Between Retries Executing Idle Not Idle Performing Completed Action Suspended Waiting for Step to Finish Waiting for Worker Thread	✓
Last Run Outcome	Canceled Failed In Progress Retry Succeeded Unknown	✓
Last Run Date Time		✓
Next Scheduled Run Date Time		✓
Job Category		✓
Is The Job Runnable?	Yes No	✓
Is The Job Scheduled?	Yes No	✓
Job Category ID		

Notifying operators with alerts

You can configure alerts to notify you when a specific event occurs. Unlike jobs that run on a schedule, alert notifications can be sent as a reaction to a scenario that has been set off. Examples include emailing the DBA team when a data or log file experiences auto growth, or when Target Server Memory drops below a certain threshold on a virtual machine. SQL Server Agent's alerting feature gives an administrator the ability to create alerts of three different types:

- **Event alerts.** Raised by SQL Server's Error and Severity mechanism. You can specify this for all databases or for a single database. You can use Error Number or Severity Level to set off an alert. Text within the System Message can be parsed to only alert in specific scenarios.

- **Performance condition alerts.** These utilize the entire library of SQL Server Performance Monitor counters. Any Counter Object can be chosen, the Sub Counter Object specified, the Counter Instance (if applicable), and a threshold (falls below, becomes equal to, rises above) at which an alert should fire. Figure 1-13 depicts setting up a Performance Condition Alert Definition to notify an administrator if Page Life Expectancy on an instance of SQL has dropped below five minutes.

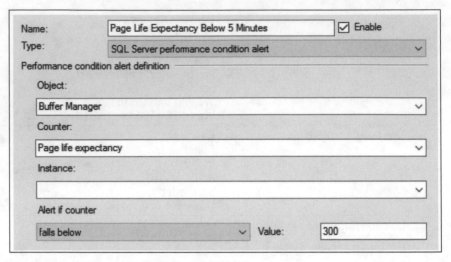

Figure 1-13 Creating a performance condition alert.

- **Windows Management Instrumentation (WMI) alerts.**   A WMI alert uses the Windows Management Instrumentation Event Provider to allow for more complicated actions upon event detection setting off an alert. One example is to use the alerting system to detect a deadlock and then save the XML deadlock graph information to a table for later analysis. Another use is to detect any DDL or system configuration changes that occur and to document them for review at a later time. Because the WMI Provider has access to many Server Event Classes and Properties, this feature is quite versatile. It does come with a couple of catches, however:

  - It requires that Service Broker is turned on in the msdb database of the instance.

  - If your code queries objects within a particular database on the server, Service Broker must be enabled on that database also.

  - It is not very GUI friendly and requires a bit more programming know-how than the other alert options.

  ➤ You can read more about creating WMI alerts in Chapter 13 as well as at *https://docs.microsoft.com/sql/ssms/agent/create-a-wmi-event-alert.*

A response to an alert can be to run a job, notify a list of operators, or both.

Operators

Operators are users or groups designated as points of contact to receive notifications from the SQL Server Agent. They are defined most commonly with email addresses, but there are additional delivery methods available.

Inside OUT

Azure SQL Database lacks SQL Server Agent

If you use SQL Server Management Studio to connect to an Azure SQL Database, you might notice the absence of SQL Server Agent.

Although at first this might seem puzzling, it makes perfect sense. SQL Server Agent is an OS service. Azure SQL Database is a database as a service (DBaaS), which is essentially a sole database (à la carte) minus the server and OS pieces of the platform.

The Azure environment comes with its own Azure Automation services, which you can use to schedule routines similar to what DBAs are used to with SQL Server Agent. But remember, with Azure SQL databases, point-in-time recovery is included automatically.

Another option is to use a Managed Instance, which is covered in Chapter 5.

SQL Server Data Tools

Similar to SQL Server Management Studio, SQL Server Data Tools is a free-standing installation of tools meant to be used with SQL Server. The SQL Server Data Tools installation provides a developer with tools for working with SQL Server Integration, Reporting, and Data Warehousing. The tools provided in SQL Server Data Tools run within a Visual Studio shell, without requiring the Visual Studio product outright. This shell is installed by using SQL Server Data Tools.

SQL Server Integration Services

SQL Server Integration Services is a versatile platform for importing, transforming, and exporting data. Frequently used for Extract, Transform, and Load (ETL) processes, SQL Server Integration Services can integrate with many external systems using standard tasks, interfaces and protocols.

SQL Server Integration Services manages these solutions using packages, which you create and modify via a graphical user interface.

SSISDB Upgrade Wizard

The SQL Server Integration Services Package Upgrade Wizard is a tool that you can use to upgrade SQL Server Integration Services packages that were created in versions earlier than SQL Server 2017. Although you most commonly access this tool from SQL Server Data Tools, you can also find and launch it from SQL Server Management Studio and also from the Windows command prompt. Part of the upgrade wizard in all of these scenarios involves the automated backup of the original packages.

From SQL Server Data Tools:

1. Open an Integration Services Project

2. Right-click SSIS Packages

3. Select Upgrade

From SQL Server Management Studio:

1. Connect to Integration Services

2. Expand Stored Packages

3. Right-click MSDB (File System)

4. Select Upgrade

From the Windows command prompt:

1. Navigate to the Microsoft SQL Server\140\DTS\Binn Folder

2. Locate and run the SSISUpgrade.exe file

The Import And Export Data Wizard

The SQL Server Import And Export Wizard is a tool that simplifies the copying of data from a source to a destination. It uses SQL Server Integration Services to copy data by creating a package in memory. You can choose to save the package the wizard creates for future reuse. The quantity of various sources and destination platforms that you can use can use with the wizard is generous. In some cases, you might need to download and install additional drivers and providers from a vendor or from a Microsoft Feature Pack. Table 1-4 lists examples of compatible data sources.

Table 1-4 Data sources in the Import And Export Wizard

Type	Details
Enterprise databases	SQL Server, Oracle, DB2
Text files	
Excel/Access	May require Access Runtime
Azure	Azure Blob Storage
Open source	PostgreSQL, MySQL
Others	ODBC, .Net Framework, OLEDB

Data Profiling Task and Viewer

You can use the Data Profiling Task within SQL Server Integration Services to clarify data patterns (normal versus abnormal) and identify data quality issues before they make their way to a destination (usually a data warehouse). The tool provides visibility around the data quality by calculating and documenting the metadata and statistical metrics shown in Table 1-5.

Table 1-5 Data profiling categories and details

Category	Details
Candidate keys	Key columns Key strength
Column length distribution	Minimum column length Maximum column length Detailed count by length Percentage distribution by length
Column null ratio	Null count by column Null percentage by column
Column statistics (numeric and date based column data types only)	Minimum value by column Maximum value by column Mean value by column Standard deviation by column
Column value distribution	Number of distinct values by column Most frequent values by column

The Data Profiling Task creates an XML output file. You can view this file by using the Data Profile Viewer, which is a standalone application and does not require Visual Studio or SQL Server Integration Services to run.

Figure 1-14 presents an example of the Data Profile Viewer displaying the XML created by a Data Profile Tasks, pointed at Microsoft's WideWorldImporters sample database and analyzing the `Sales.Customers` table.

CHAPTER 1

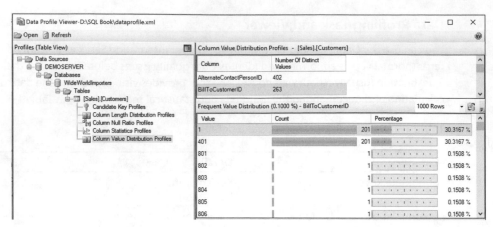

Figure 1-14 The Data Profile Viewer showing column distribution.

A note on deprecation

SQL Server 2017 introduces some exciting new features, but some features from earlier versions of SQL Server are deprecated and even discontinued. Deprecated features will be removed from a future version of the product, and you should not use them for new development. Discontinued features have already been removed, and might block upgrades to the latest database compatibility level, or migrations to Azure SQL Database.

Reference is made in several chapters of this book about features that have been deprecated, but the easiest way to stay up to date is to check the Microsoft documentation at *https:/docs. microsoft.com/sql/database-engine/deprecated-database-engine-features-in-sql-server-2017*.

You can also access the list of deprecated features by using the T-SQL query that follows, which provides a list of more than 250 features that are deprecated, along with a count of the number of occurrences on your SQL Server instance. We leave as an exercise for you to identify and resolve specific occurrences.

```
SELECT object_name, counter_name, instance_name, cntr_value, cntr_type
FROM sys.dm_os_performance_counters
WHERE object_name = 'SQLServer:Deprecated Features';
```

Introducing database server components

In this chapter, we cover the components that make up a typical database infrastructure. This chapter is introductory, the chapters that follow provide more detail about designing, implementing, and provisioning databases.

Although Microsoft SQL Server is new to Linux, Microsoft has, as much as possible, crafted it to work the same way that it does on Windows. We highlight places where there are differences.

No matter which configurations you end up using, there are four basic parts to a database infrastructure:

- Memory

- Processor

- Permanent storage

- Network

We also touch on a couple of high availability offerings, including improvements to availability groups in SQL Server 2017. We then look at an introduction to security concepts, including ways to access instances of SQL Server on-premises with Windows and Linux, and Microsoft Azure SQL Database. Finally, we take a brief look at virtualization.

Memory

SQL Server is designed to use as much memory as it needs, and as much as you give it. By default, the upper limit of memory that SQL Server can access, is limited only by the physical Random Access Memory (RAM) available to the server, or the edition of SQL Server you're running, whichever is lower.

CHAPTER 2

Understanding the working set

The physical memory made available to SQL Server by the operating system (OS), is called the *working set*. This working set is broken up into several sections by the SQL Server memory manager, the two largest and most important ones being the *buffer pool* and the *procedure cache* (also known as the *plan cache*).

In the strictest sense, "working set" applies only to physical memory. However, as we will see shortly, the buffer pool extension blurs the lines.

We look deeper into default memory settings in Chapter 3, in the section, "Configuration settings."

Caching data in the buffer pool

For best performance, you cache data in memory because it's much faster to access data directly from memory than storage.

The buffer pool is an in-memory cache of 8-KB data pages that are copies of pages in the database file. Initially the copy in the buffer pool is identical, but changes to data are applied to this buffer pool copy (and the transaction log) and then asynchronously applied to the data file.

When you run a query, the Database Engine requests the data page it needs from the Buffer Manager, as depicted in Figure 2-1. If the data is not already in the buffer pool, a page fault occurs (an OS feature that informs the application that the page isn't in memory). The Buffer Manager fetches the data from the storage subsystem and writes it to the buffer pool. When the data is in the buffer pool, the query continues.

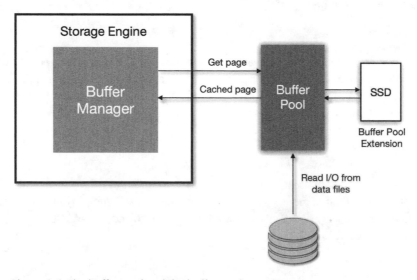

Figure 2-1 The buffer pool and the buffer pool extension.

The buffer pool is usually the largest consumer of the working set because that's where your data is. If the amount of data requested for a query exceeds the capacity of the buffer pool, the data pages will spill to a drive, either using the buffer pool extension or a portion of TempDB.

The buffer pool extension makes use of nonvolatile storage to extend the size of the buffer pool. It effectively increases the database working set, forming a bridge between the storage layer where the data files are located and the buffer pool in physical memory.

For performance reasons, this should be solid-state storage, directly attached to the server.

➤ To see how to turn on the buffer pool extension, read the section "Configuration settings" in Chapter 3. To learn more about TempDB, read the section "Physical database architecture," also in Chapter 3.

Caching plans in the procedure cache

Generally speaking, the procedure cache is smaller than the buffer pool. When you run a query, the Query Optimizer compiles a query plan to explain to the Database Engine exactly how to run the query. To save time, it keeps a copy of that query plan so that it doesn't need to compile the plan each time the query runs. It is not quite as simple as this, of course (plans can be removed, and trivial plans are not cached, for instance), but it's enough to give you a basic understanding.

The procedure cache is split into various cache stores by the memory manager, and it's also here where you can see if there are single-use query plans that are polluting memory.

➤ For more information about cached execution plans, read Chapter 9 or visit *https://blogs.msdn.microsoft.com/blogdoezequiel/2014/07/30/too-many-single-use-plans-now-what/*.

Lock pages in memory

Turning on the *Lock pages in memory* (LPIM) policy means that Windows will not be able to trim (reduce) SQL Server's working set.

Locking pages in memory ensures that Windows memory pressure cannot rob SQL Server of resources or shunt SQL Server memory into the Windows Server system page file, dramatically reducing performance. Windows doesn't "steal" memory from SQL Server flippantly; it is done in response to memory pressure on the Windows Server. Indeed, all applications can have their memory affected by pressure from Windows.

On the other hand, without the ability to relieve pressure from other applications' memory demands or a virtual host's memory demands, LPIM means that Windows cannot deploy enough memory to remain stable. Because of this concern, LPIM cannot be the only method to use to protect SQL Server's memory allocation.

The controversy of the topic is stability versus performance, in which the latter was especially apparent on systems with limited memory resources and older operating systems. On larger servers with operating systems since Windows Server 2008, and especially virtualized systems, there is a smaller but nonzero need for this policy to insulate SQL Server from memory pressure.

The prevailing wisdom is that the LPIM policy should be turned on by default for SQL Server 2017, provided the following:

- The server is physical, not virtual. See the section "Sharing more memory than we have (overcommit)" later in this chapter.

- Physical RAM exceeds 16 GB (the OS needs a working set of its own).

- Max Server Memory has been set appropriately (SQL Server can't use everything it sees).

- The Memory\Available Mbytes performance counter is monitored regularly (to keep some memory free).

If you would like to read more, Jonathan Kehayias explains this thinking in a Simple Talk article (*https://www.simple-talk.com/sql/database-administration/ great-sql-server-debates-lock-pages-in-memory/*).

Editions and memory limits

Since SQL Server 2016 Service Pack 1, many Enterprise edition features have found their way into the lower editions. Ostensibly, this was done to allow software developers to have far more code that works across all editions of the product.

Although some features are still limited by edition (high availability, for instance), features such as Columnstore and In-Memory OLTP are turned on in every edition, including Express. However, only Enterprise edition can use all available physical RAM for these features. Other editions are limited.

Inside OUT

In-Memory OLTP considerations

In-Memory OLTP requires an overhead of at least double the amount of data for a memory-optimized object. For example, if a memory-optimized table is 5 GB in size, you will need at least 10 GB of RAM available for the exclusive use of that table. Keep this in mind before turning on this feature in the Standard edition.

With Standard edition, as well, take care when using memory-optimized table-valued functions because each new object will require resources. Too many of them could starve the working set and cause SQL Server to crash.

You can read more at Microsoft Docs at *https://docs.microsoft.com/sql/relational-databases/in-memory-oltp/requirements-for-using-memory-optimized-tables.*

Central Processing Unit

The Central Processing Unit, or CPU, and often called the "brain" of a computer, is the most important part of a system. CPU speed is measured in hertz (Hz), or cycles per second. Current processor speed is measured in GHz, or billions of cycles per second.

Modern systems can have more than one CPU, and each CPU in turn can have more than one CPU core (which, in turn, might be split up into virtual cores).

For a typical SQL Server workload, single-core speed matters. It is better to have fewer cores with higher clock speeds than more cores with lower speeds, especially for non-Enterprise editions.

With systems that have more than one CPU, each CPU might be allocated its own set of memory, depending on the physical motherboard architecture.

Simultaneous multithreading

Some CPU manufacturers have split their physical cores into virtual cores to try to eke out even more performance. They do this via a feature called *simultaneous multithreading* (SMT). Intel calls this Hyper-Threading, so when you buy a single Intel® Xeon® CPU with 20 physical cores, the OS will see 40 virtual cores, because of SMT.

SMT becomes especially murky with virtual machines (VMs) because the guest OS might not have any insight into the physical versus logical core configuration.

SMT should be turned on for physical database servers. For virtual environments, you need to take care to ensure that the virtual CPUs are allocated correctly. See the section "Abstracting hardware away with virtualization" later in this chapter.

Non-Uniform Memory Access

CPUs are the fastest component of a system, and they spend a lot of time waiting for data to come to them. In the past, all CPUs would share one bank of RAM on a motherboard, using a shared bus. This caused performance problems as more CPUs were added because only one CPU could access the RAM at a time.

Multi-Channel Memory Architecture tries to resolve this by increasing the number of channels between CPUs and RAM, to reduce contention during concurrent access.

A more practical solution is for each CPU to have its own local physical RAM, situated close to each CPU socket. This configuration is called Non-Uniform Memory Access (NUMA). The advantages are that each CPU can access its own RAM, making processing much faster. However, if a CPU needs more RAM than it has in its local set, it must request memory from one of the other CPUs in the system (called *foreign memory access*), which carries a performance penalty.

SQL Server is NUMA-aware. In other words, if the OS recognizes a NUMA configuration at the hardware layer, where more than one CPU is plugged in, and each CPU has its own set of physical RAM (see Figure 2-2), SQL Server will split its internal structures and service threads across each NUMA node.

Since SQL Server 2014 Service Pack 2, the Database Engine automatically configures NUMA nodes at an instance level, using what it calls *soft-NUMA*. If more than eight CPU cores are detected (including SMT cores), soft-NUMA nodes are created automatically in memory.

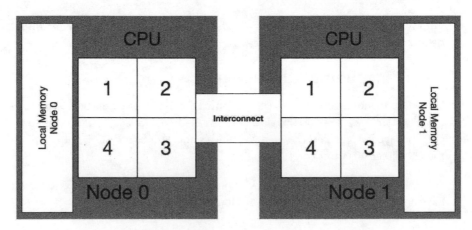

Figure 2-2 Two-socket NUMA configuration.

Inside OUT

Core counts and editions

SQL Server Standard edition has an artificial limit of 24 CPU physical cores that it can use. For instance, if a system contains two 16-core CPUs, for a total of 32 cores, Standard edition will need to be licensed for all 32 cores, even though it won't use eight of them.

Additionally, the NUMA distribution will be unbalanced because SQL Server will use the first 16 cores on the first CPU, and eight from the second CPU, unless you configure the SQL Server CPU usage using the affinity settings (for more information on how to do this, see the section "Configuration settings" in Chapter 3).

Be careful when choosing the hardware and edition for your SQL Server installation. If you're planning to install several VMs on one system, a better option would be Enterprise edition, licensed for all cores on the hardware. This would automatically cover all SQL Server VMs that you install on that hardware.

Disable power saving everywhere

Modern systems can use power saving settings to reduce the amount of electricity used by a server. Although this is good for the environment, it is bad for query performance because the CPU core speed might be reduced to save energy.

For all operating systems running SQL Server, turn on High Performance at the OS level, and double-check that High Performance is set at the BIOS level, as well. For dedicated VM hosts, this will require downtime to make the change.

Storing your data

When data is not in memory, it is *at rest*, and must be saved somewhere. Storage technology has evolved rapidly over the past few years, so we no longer think of storage as a mechanical hard drive containing one or more spinning metal disks with a magnetic surface. But, old habits die hard, and colloquially we still refer to a nonvolatile storage subsystem as "the disk," even if it might take another form. In this book, however, we refer to it as a "drive."

In the context of SQL Server, the storage subsystem should have low latency, so that when the database engine accesses the drive to perform reads and writes, those reads and writes should complete as quickly as possible. In the following list, we present some commonly used terms with respect to storage devices.

- **Drive.**   The physical storage device. This might be a mechanical drive, a solid-state drive with the same form-factor as a mechanical drive, or a card that plugs directly into the motherboard.

- **Volume.**   A logical representation of storage, as viewed by the OS. This might be one drive, part of a drive, or a logical section of a storage array. On Microsoft Windows, a volume usually gets its own drive letter or mount point.

- **Latency.**   Measured in milliseconds, latency is how long it takes for data to be read from a drive (seconds per read), and written to a drive (seconds per write).

- **IOPS.**   Input/output operations per second, or IOPS, is the number of reads and writes per second. A storage device might have differing performance depending on whether the IOPS are sequential or random. IOPS are directly related to latency by means of the queue depth.

- **Queue depth.**   The number of outstanding read and write requests in a storage device's request queue. The deeper the queue depth, the faster the drive.

SQL Server performance is directly related to storage performance. The move toward virtualization and shared storage arrays has placed more emphasis on random data access patterns. Low latency and high random IOPS will thus benefit the average SQL Server workload.

In the next two chapters, we go into more detail about the preferred storage configuration for SQL Server.

Types of storage

Nonvolatile storage can be split up into two main areas: *mechanical and solid-state*.

Mechanical hard drives

Traditional spinning disks have a built-in latency, called *seek time*, due to their shape and physical nature. The read/write head is mounted on an arm that must scan the surface of the disk as it spins, seeking a particular area to perform the I/O operation. If the data on the spinning disk is fragmented, it can take longer to access because the head must skip around, finding data or free space.

The standard interface for mechanical drives is Serial ATA (SATA) or Serial Attached SCSI (SAS).

As spinning disks increase in capacity, the tracks between data become narrower, which causes performance to decrease, and increases the likelihood of mechanical failure or data corruption. The limits are pushed because of the rotational energy in the disk itself, so there is a physical speed limit to the motor.

In other words, mechanical disks grow bigger but slower and more prone to failure.

Solid-state drives

Solid-state technology, which makes use of flash memory, eliminates seek time entirely because the path to each cell where the data is stored is almost instantaneous. This is what makes solid-state storage so much faster than mechanical storage.

Solid-state storage devices can take many different forms. The most common in consumer devices is a 2.5-inch enclosure with a SATA interface, which was common with mechanical laptop drives. This accommodates a drop-in replacement of mechanical storage.

In server architecture, however, flash memory can take several forms. For local storage, they make use of the Peripheral Component Interconnect Express (PCIe) interface and plug directly into the motherboard. An example of this is Non-Volatile Memory Express (NVMe).

As the technology evolves, the performance will only improve as capacity grows. Solid state is not perfect though; data can be written to a particular cell only a certain number of times before it fails. You might have experienced this yourself with thumb drives, which tend to fail after heavy usage. Algorithms to balance writes across cells, called *wear-leveling*, help to extend the lifespan of a solid-state device.

Another problem with flash memory is *write-amplification*. On a mechanical drive, if a file is overwritten, the previous file is marked for deletion, but is not actually deleted from the disk surface. When the drive needs to write to that area again, it overwrites the location without removing what was there before.

Solid-state drives must erase the location in question before writing the new data, which has a performance impact. The size of the cells might also require a larger area to be erased than the file itself (if it is a small file), which compounds the performance impact. Various techniques exist to mitigate write amplification, but this does reduce the lifespan of flash memory.

The performance problems with mechanical disks, and the lifespan problems with both mechanical and solid-state drives, can be mitigated by combining them into drive arrays, to reduce the risk of failure by balancing the load and increase performance.

Configuring the storage layer

Nonvolatile storage can stand alone, in the form of Direct-Attached Storage, or be combined in many ways to provide redundancy or consolidation, perhaps even offering different levels of performance in order to manage costs better. For example, archive data might not need to be stored on the fastest available drive if it is accessed infrequently.

CHAPTER 2

Direct-Attached Storage

Direct-Attached Storage (DAS) is plugged directly into the system accessing it. Also called local storage, it can comprise independent mechanical hard drives, solid-state drives, tape drives for backups, CD and DVD-ROM drives, or even enclosures containing storage arrays.

DAS has a lower latency than a Storage-Area Network or Network-Attached Storage (more on these later in the chapter) because there is no network to traverse between the system and the storage. However, it cannot be shared with other systems, unless the local file system is shared across the network using a protocol such as Server Message Block (SMB) 3.0.

For SQL Server, DAS comprising flash storage (solid-state) is preferred for TempDB, which is also supported (and recommended) in a Failover Cluster Instance. You can also use DAS for the buffer pool extension.

> ➤ **To see how you should best configure TempDB, see the section "Configuration settings" in Chapter 3.**

Storage arrays and RAID

Combining drives in an enclosure with a controller to access each drive, without any thought to redundancy or performance, is called *JBOD* (colloquially, "just a bunch of disks"). These drives might be accessed individually or combined into a single volume.

When done correctly, combining drives into an array can increase overall performance and/or lower the risk of data loss should one or more of the drives in the array fail. This is called Redundant Array of Independent Disks (RAID).

RAID offers several levels of configuration, which trade redundancy for performance. More redundancy means less raw capacity for the array, but this can reduce data loss. Faster performance can bring with it data loss.

Striping without parity (RAID 0) uses multiple drives to improve raw read/write performance, but with zero redundancy. If one drive fails, there is significant chance of catastrophic data loss across the entire array. JBOD configurations that span across drives fall under this RAID level.

Mirroring (RAID 1) uses two drives that are written to simultaneously. Although there is a slight write penalty because both drives must save their data at the same time, and one might take longer than the other, the read performance is nearly double that of a single drive because both drives can be read in parallel (with a small overhead caused by the RAID controller selecting the drive and fetching the data). Usable space is 50 percent of raw capacity, and only one drive in the array can be lost and still have all data recoverable.

Striping with parity (RAID 5) requires an odd number of three or more drives, and for every single write, one of the drives is randomly used for parity (a checksum validation). There is a larger write penalty because all drives must save their data and parity must be calculated and persisted. If a single drive is lost from the array, the other drives can rebuild the contents of the lost drive, based on the parity, but it can take some time to rebuild the array. Usable space is calculated as the number of drives minus one. If there are three drives in the array, the usable space is the sum of two of those drives, with the space from the third used for parity (which is evenly distributed over the array). Only one drive in the array can be lost and still have full data recovery.

Combinations of the base RAID configurations are used to provide more redundancy and performance, including RAID 1+0 (also known as RAID 10), RAID 0+1, and RAID 5+0 (also known as RAID 50).

In RAID 1+0, two drives are configured in a mirror (RAID 1) for redundancy, and then each mirror is striped together (RAID 0) for performance reasons.

In RAID 0+1, the drives are striped first (RAID 0), and then mirrored across the entire RAID 0 set (RAID 1). Usable space for RAID 0+1 and 1+0 is 50 percent of the raw capacity.

To ensure full recovery from failure in a RAID 1+0 or 0+1 configuration, an entire side of the mirror can be lost, or only one drive from each side of the mirror can be lost.

In RAID 5+0, a number of drives (three or more) is configured in a RAID 5 set, which is then striped (with no parity) with at least one other RAID 5 set of the same configuration. Usable space is $(x - 1) / y$, where x is the number of drives in each nested RAID 5 set, and y is the number of RAID 5 sets in this array. If there are nine drives, six of them are usable. Only one drive from each RAID 5 set can be lost with full recovery possible. If more than one drive in any of the RAID 5 sets is lost, the entire 5+0 array is lost.

SQL Server requires the best performance from a storage layer as possible. When looking at RAID configurations, RAID 1+0 offers the best performance and redundancy.

> ## NOTE
> Some database administrators tend to believe that RAID is an alternative to backups, but it does not protect 100 percent against data loss. A common backup medium is digital tape, due to its low cost and high capacity, but more organizations are making use of cloud storage options, such as Microsoft Azure Archive Storage and Amazon Glacier, for long-term, cost-effective backup storage solutions. Always make sure that you perform regular SQL Server backups that are copied securely off-premises.

CHAPTER 2

Centralized storage with a Storage-Area Network

A Storage-Area Network (SAN) is a network of storage arrays that can comprise tens, hundreds, or even thousands of drives (mechanical or solid-state) in a central location, with one or more RAID configurations, providing block-level access to storage. This reduces wasted space, and allows easier management across multiple systems, especially for virtualized environments.

Block-level means that the OS can read or write blocks of any size and any alignment. This offers the OS a lot of flexibility in making use of the storage.

You can carve the total storage capacity of the SAN into logical unit numbers (LUNs), and each LUN can be assigned to a physical or virtual server. You can move these LUNs around and resize them as required, which makes management much easier than attaching physical storage to a server.

The disadvantage of a SAN is that you might be at the mercy of misconfiguration or a slow network. For instance, the RAID might be set to a level that has poor write performance, or the blocks of the storage are not aligned appropriately.

Storage administrators might not understand specialized workloads like SQL Server, and choose a performance model that satisfies the rest of the organization to reduce administration overhead but which penalizes you.

Inside OUT

Fibre Channel versus iSCSI

Storage arrays might use Fibre Channel (FC) or Internet Small Computer Systems Interface (iSCSI) to connect systems to their storage.

FC can support data transfer at a higher rate than iSCSI, which makes it better for systems that require lower latency, but it comes at a higher cost for specialized equipment.

iSCSI uses standard TCP/IP, which makes it potentially cheaper because it can run on existing network equipment. You can further improve iSCSI throughput by isolating the storage to its own dedicated network.

Network-Attached Storage

Network-Attached Storage (NAS), is usually a specialized hardware appliance connected to the network, typically containing an array of several drives, providing file-level access to storage.

Unlike the SAN's block-level support, NAS storage is configured on the appliance itself, and file sharing protocols (such as SMB, Common Internet File System [CIFS] and Network File System [NFS]) are used to share the storage over the network.

NAS appliances are fairly common because they provide access to shared storage at a much lower monetary cost than a SAN. You should keep in mind security considerations regarding file-sharing protocols.

Storage Spaces

Windows Server 2012 and later support Storage Spaces, which is a way to manage local storage in a more scalable and flexible way than RAID.

Instead of creating a RAID set at the storage layer, Windows Server can create a virtual drive at the OS level. It might use a combination of RAID levels, and you can decide to combine different physical drives to create performance tiers.

For example, a server might contain 16 drives. Eight of them are spinning disks, and eight are solid state. You can use Storage Spaces to create a single volume with all 16 drives, and keep the active files on the solid-state portion, increasing performance dramatically.

SMB 3.0 file share

SQL Server supports storage located on a network file share that uses the SMB 3.0 protocol or higher because it is now fast and stable enough to support the storage requirements of the Database Engine (performance and resilience). This means that you can build a Failover Cluster Instance (see the section on this later in the chapter) without shared storage such as a SAN.

Network performance is critically important, though, so we recommend a dedicated and isolated network for the SMB file share, using network interface cards that support Remote Direct Memory Access (RDMA). This allows the SMB Direct feature in Windows Server to create a low-latency, high-throughput connection using the SMB protocol.

SMB 3.0 might be a feasible option for smaller networks with limited storage capacity and a NAS, or in the case of a Failover Cluster Instance without shared storage. For more information, read Chapter 12.

Connecting to SQL Server over the network

We have covered a fair amount about networking just discussing the storage layer, but there is far more to it. In this section, we look at what is involved when accessing the Database Engine over a network, and briefly discuss Virtual Local-Area Networks.

Unless a SQL Server instance and the application accessing it is entirely self-contained, database access is performed over one or more network interfaces. This adds complexity with authentication, given that malicious actors might be scanning and modifying network packets in flight.

CAUTION

Ensure that all TCP/IP traffic to and from the SQL Server is encrypted. For applications that are located on the same server as the SQL Server instance, this is not required if you're using the Shared Memory Protocol.

SQL Server 2017 requires strict rules with respect to network security, which means that older versions of the connectors or protocols used by software developers might not work as expected.

Transport Security Layer and its forerunner, Secure Sockets Layer, (together known as TLS/SSL, or just SSL), are methods that allow network traffic between two points to be encrypted. (For more information, see Chapter 7.) Where possible, you should use newer libraries that support TLS encryption. If you cannot use TLS to encrypt application traffic, you should use IPSec, which is configured at the OS level.

Protocols and ports

Connections to SQL Server are made over the Transport Control Protocol (TCP), with port 1433 as the default port for a default instance. Some of this is covered in Chapter 1, and again in Chapter 7. Any named instances are assigned random ports by the SQL Server Configuration Manager, and the SQL Browser service coordinates any connections to named instances. It is possible to assign static TCP ports to named instances by using the Configuration Manager.

There are ways to change the default port after SQL Server is installed, through the SQL Server Configuration Manager. We do not recommend changing the port, however, because it provides no security advantage to a port scanner, but some network administration policies require it.

Networking is also the foundation of cloud computing. Aside from the fact that the Azure cloud is accessed over the internet (itself a network of networks), the entire Azure infrastructure, which underlies both infrastructure-as-a-service (virtual machines with Windows or Linux running SQL Server) and platform-as-a-service (Azure SQL Database) offerings, is a virtual fabric of innumerable components tied together with networking.

Added complexity with Virtual Local-Area Networks

A Virtual Local-Area Network (VLAN) gives network administrators the ability to logically group machines together even if they are not physically connected through the same network switch.

It makes it possible for servers to share their resources with one another over the same physical LAN, without interacting with other devices on the same network.

VLANs work at a very low level (the data link layer, or OSI Layer 2), and are configured on a network switch. A port on the switch might be dedicated to a particular VLAN, and all traffic to and from that port is mapped to a particular VLAN by the switch.

High availability concepts

With each new version of Windows Server, terminology and definitions tend to change or adapt according to the new features available. With SQL Server now supported on Linux, it is even more important to get our heads around what it means when we discuss high availability.

At its most basic, high availability (HA) means that a service offering of some kind (for example, SQL Server, a web server, an application, or a file share) will survive an outage of some kind, or at least fail predictably to a standby state, with minimal loss of data and minimal downtime.

Everything can fail. An outage might be caused by a failed hard drive, which could in turn be a result of excessive heat, excessive cold, excessive moisture, or a datacenter alarm that is so loud that its vibrational frequency damages the internal components and causes a head crash.

You should be aware of other things that can go wrong, as noted in the list that follows; this list is certainly not exhaustive, but it's incredibly important to understand that assumptions about hardware, software, and network stability are a fool's errand:

- A failed network interface card

- A failed RAID controller

- A power surge or brownout causing a failed power supply

- A broken or damaged network cable

- A broken or damaged power cable

- Moisture on the motherboard

- Dust on the motherboard

- Overheating caused by a failed fan

- A faulty keyboard that misinterprets keystrokes

- Failure due to bit rot

- Failure due to a bug in SQL Server

CHAPTER 2

- Failure due to poorly written code in a file system driver that causes drive corruption

- Capacitors failing on the motherboard

- Insects or rodents electrocuting themselves on components (this smells really bad)

- Failure caused by a fire suppression system that uses water instead of gas

- Misconfiguration of a network router causing an entire geographical region to be inaccessible

- Failure due to an expired SSL or TLS certificate

- Running a DELETE or UPDATE statement without a WHERE clause (human error)

Why redundancy matters

Armed with the knowledge that everything can fail, you should build in redundancy where possible. The sad reality is that these decisions are governed by budget constraints. The amount of money available is inversely proportional to the amount of acceptable data loss and length of downtime. For business-critical systems, however, uptime is paramount, and a highly available solution will be more cost effective than being down, considering the cost-per-minute to the organization.

It is nearly impossible to guarantee zero downtime with zero data loss. There is always a trade-off. The business decides on that trade-off, based on resources (equipment, people, money), and the technical solution is in turn developed around that trade-off. The business drives this strategy using two values called the Recovery Point Objective and Recovery Time Objective, which are defined in a Service-Level Agreement (SLA).

Recovery Point Objective

A good way to think of Recovery Point Objective (RPO) is "How much data are you prepared to lose?" When a failure occurs, how much data will be lost between the last transaction log backup and the failure? This value is usually measured in seconds or minutes.

Recovery Time Objective

The Recovery Time Objective (RTO) is defined as how much time is available to bring the environment up to a known and usable state after a failure. There might be different values for HA and disaster recovery scenarios. This value is usually measured in hours.

Disaster recovery

HA is not disaster recovery (DR). They are often grouped under the same heading (HA/DR), mainly because there are shared technology solutions for both concepts, but HA is about keeping the service running, whereas DR is what happens when the infrastructure fails entirely. DR is like insurance: you don't think you need it until it's too late. HA costs more money, the shorter the RPO.

NOTE

A disaster is any failure or event that causes an unplanned outage.

Clustering

Clustering is the connecting of computers (nodes) in a set of two or more nodes, that work together and present themselves to the network as one computer.

In most cluster configurations, only one node can be active in a cluster. To ensure that this happens, a quorum instructs the cluster as to which node should be active. It also steps in if there is a communication failure between the nodes.

Each node has a vote in a quorum. However, if there is an even number of nodes, to ensure a simple majority an additional witness must be included in a quorum to allow for a majority vote to take place.

Inside OUT

What is Always On?

Always On is the name of a group of features, which is akin to a marketing term. It is not the name of a specific technology. There are two separate technologies that happen to fall under the Always On label, and these are addressed a little later in this chapter. The important thing to remember is that "Always On" does not mean "availability groups," and there is a space between "Always" and "On."

Windows Server Failover Clustering

As Microsoft describes it:

"Failover clusters provide high availability and scalability to many server workloads. These include server applications such as Microsoft Exchange Server, Hyper-V, Microsoft SQL Server, and file servers. The server applications can run on physical servers or virtual machines. [Windows Server Failover Clustering] can scale to 64 physical nodes and to 8,000 virtual machines." (https:// technet.microsoft.com/library/hh831579(v=ws.11).aspx).

The terminology here matters. Windows Server Failover Clustering is the name of the technology that underpins a Failover Cluster Instance (FCI), where two or more Windows Server Failover

Clustering nodes (computers) are connected together in a Windows Server Failover Clustering resource group and masquerade as a single machine behind a network endpoint called a Virtual Network Name (VNN). A SQL Server service that is installed on an FCI is cluster-aware.

Linux failover clustering with Pacemaker

Instead of relying on Windows Server Failover Clustering, SQL Server on a Linux cluster can make use of any cluster resource manager. Microsoft recommends using Pacemaker because it ships with a number of Linux distributions, including Red Hat and Ubuntu.

Inside OUT

Node fencing and STONITH on Linux

If something goes wrong in a cluster, and a node is in an unknown state after a set time-out period, that node must be isolated from the cluster and restarted or reset. On Linux clusters, this is called *node fencing*, following the STONITH principle ("Shoot the Other Node in the Head"). If a node fails, STONITH will provide an effective, if drastic manner of resetting or powering-off a failed Linux node.

Resolving cluster partitioning with quorum

Most clustering technologies make use of the quorum model, to prevent a phenomenon called *partitioning*, or "split brain." If there is an even number of nodes, and half of these nodes go offline from the view of the other half of the cluster, and vice versa, you end up with two halves thinking that the cluster is still up and running, and each with a primary node (split brain).

Depending on connectivity to each half of the cluster, an application continues writing to one half of the cluster while another application writes to the other half. A best-case resolution to this scenario would require rolling back to a point in time before the event occurred, which would cause loss of any data written after the event.

To prevent this, each node in a cluster shares its health with the other nodes using a periodic heartbeat. If more than half do not respond in a timely fashion, the cluster is considered to have failed. Quorum works by having a simple majority vote on what constitutes "enough nodes."

In Windows Server Failover Clustering, there are four types of majority vote: Node, Node and File Share, Node and Disk, and Disk Only. In the latter three types, a separate witness is used, which does not participate in the cluster directly. This witness is given voting rights when there is an even number of nodes in a cluster, and therefore a simple majority (more than half) would not be possible.

Always On FCIs

You can think of a SQL Server FCI as two or more nodes with shared storage (usually a SAN because it is most likely to be accessed over the network).

On Windows Server, SQL Server can take advantage of Windows Server Failover Clustering to provide HA (the idea being minimal downtime) at the server-instance level, by creating an FCI of two or more nodes. From the network's perspective (application, end users, and so on), the FCI is presented as a single instance of SQL Server running on a single computer, and all connections point at the VNN.

When the FCI starts, one of the nodes assumes ownership and brings its SQL Server instance online. If a failure occurs on the first node (or there is a planned failover due to maintenance), there are at least a few seconds of downtime, during which the first node cleans up as best it can, and then the second node brings its SQL Server instance online. Client connections are redirected to the new node after the services are up and running.

> ### Inside OUT
>
> *How long does the FCI failover take?*
>
> **During a planned failover, any dirty pages in the buffer pool must be written to the drive; thus, the downtime could be longer than expected on a server with a large buffer pool. You can read more about checkpoints in Chapter 3 and Chapter 4.**

On Linux, the principle is very similar. A cluster resource manager such as Pacemaker manages the cluster, and when a failover occurs, the same process is followed from SQL Server's perspective, in which the first node is brought down and the second node is brought up to take its place as the owner. The cluster has a virtual IP address, just as on Windows. You must add the virtual network name manually to the DNS server.

➤ You can read more about setting up a Linux cluster in Chapter 11.

FCIs are supported on SQL Server Standard edition, but are limited to two nodes.

The versatility of Log Shipping

SQL Server Transaction Log Shipping is an extremely flexible technology to provide a relatively inexpensive and easily managed HA and DR solution.

The principle is as follows: a primary database is in either the Full or Bulk Logged recovery model, with transaction log backups being taken regularly every few minutes. These transaction log backup files are transferred to a shared network location, where one or more secondary servers restore the transaction log backups to a standby database.

If you use the built-in Log Shipping Wizard in SQL Server Management Studio, on the Restore tab, click Database State When Restoring Backups, and then choose the No Recovery Mode or Standby Mode option (*https://docs.microsoft.com/sql/database-engine/log-shipping/configure-log-shipping-sql-server*).

If you are building your own log shipping solution, remember to use the RESTORE feature with NORECOVERY, or RESTORE with STANDBY.

If a failover occurs, the tail of the log on the primary server is backed up the same way (if available—this guarantees zero data loss of committed transactions), transferred to the shared location, and restored after the latest regular transaction logs. The database is then put into RECOVERY mode (which is where crash recovery takes place, rolling back incomplete transactions and rolling forward complete transactions).

As soon as the application is pointed to the new server, the environment is back up again with zero data loss (tail of the log was copied across) or minimal data loss (only the latest shipped transaction log was restored).

Log Shipping is a feature that works on all editions of SQL Server, on Windows and Linux. However, because Express edition does not include the SQL Server Agent, Express can be only a witness, and you would need to manage the process through a separate scheduling mechanism. You can even create your own solution for any edition of SQL Server, using Azure Blob Storage and AzCopy.exe, for instance.

Always On availability groups

As alluded to previously, this is generally what people mean when they incorrectly say "Always On." However, it's official name is Always On availability groups. In shorthand, you can refer simply to these as availability groups (or AGs).

What is an availability group, anyway? In the past, SQL Server offered database mirroring and failover clustering as two distinct HA offerings. However, with database mirroring officially deprecated since SQL Server 2012, coinciding with the introduction of availability groups, it is easier to think of availability groups as a consolidation of these two offerings as well as Log Shipping thrown in for good measure.

Inside OUT

What was database mirroring?

Database mirroring worked at the database level by maintaining two copies of a single database across two separate SQL Server instances, keeping them synchronized with a steady stream of active transaction log records.

Availability groups provide us with the ability to keep a discrete set of databases highly available across one or more nodes in a cluster. They work at the database level, as opposed to an entire server-instance level, like FCIs do.

Unlike the cluster-aware version of SQL Server, when it installed as part of an FCI, SQL Server on an availability group is installed as a standalone instance.

An availability group (on Windows Server through Windows Server Failover Clustering, and on Linux through a cluster resource manager like Pacemaker) operates at the *database level only*. As depicted in Figure 2-3, it is a set of one or more databases in a group (an *availability replica*) that are *replicated* (using Log Shipping) from a *primary replica* (there can be only one primary replica), to a maximum of eight *secondary replicas*, using synchronous or asynchronous *data synchronization*. Let's take a closer look at each of these:

- **Synchronous data synchronization.**   The log is hardened (the transactions are committed to the transaction log) on every secondary replica *before* the transaction is committed on the primary replica. This guarantees zero data loss, but with a potentially significant performance impact. It can be costly to reduce network latency to a point at which this is practical for highly transactional workloads.

- **Asynchronous data synchronization.**   The transaction is considered committed as soon as it is hardened in the transaction log on the primary replica. If something were to happen before the logs are hardened on all of the secondary replicas, there is a chance of data loss, and the recovery point would be the most recently committed transaction that made it successfully to all of the secondary replicas. With delayed durability turned on, this can result in faster performance, but higher risk of data loss.

CHAPTER 2

Inside OUT

What is delayed durability?

Starting in SQL Server 2014, delayed durability (also known as lazy commit) is a storage optimization feature that returns a successful commit before transaction logs are actually saved to a drive. Although this can improve performance, the risk of data loss is higher because the transaction logs are saved only when the logs are flushed to a drive asynchronously. To learn more, go to *https://docs.microsoft.com/sql/relational-databases/logs/control-transaction-durability*.

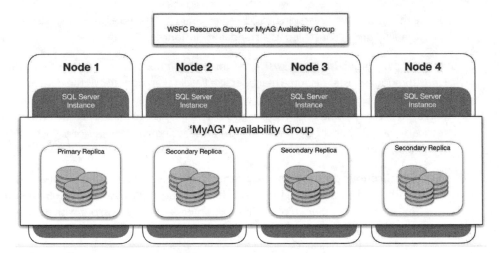

Figure 2-3 A Windows Server Failover Clustering cluster with four nodes.

You can use read-only secondary replicas for running reports and other operations that reduce the load on the primary replica. This also includes backups and database consistency checks, but you must also perform these on the primary replica when there is a low-usage period or planned maintenance window.

If the primary replica fails, one of the secondary replicas is promoted to the primary, with a few seconds of downtime while the databases run through crash recovery, and minimal data loss.

Read-scale availability groups

SQL Server 2017 introduces a new architecture that allows for multiple read-only secondary replicas, but does not offer HA. The major difference is that a read-scale availability group does not have a cluster resource manager.

What this allows is reduced contention on a business-critical workload by using read-only routing or connecting directly to a readable secondary replica, without relying on a clustering infrastructure on Windows or Linux.

> ➤ **For more information, go to Microsoft Docs at** *https://docs.microsoft.com/sql/ database-engine/availability-groups/windows/read-scale-availability-groups.*

Distributed availability groups

Instead of having an availability group on one cluster, a distributed availability group can span two separate availability groups, on two separate clusters (Windows Server Failover Clustering or Linux, each cluster can run on a different OS) that are geographically separated. Provided that these two availability groups can communicate with each other, you can configure them in a distributed availability group. This allows a more flexible DR scenario, plus it makes possible multisite replicas in geographically diverse areas.

The main difference from a normal availability group, is that the configuration is stored in SQL Server, not the underlying cluster. With a distributed availability group, only one availability group can perform data modification at any time, even though both availability groups have a primary replica. To allow another availability group to write to its primary replica database requires a manual failover, using FORCE_FAILOVER_ALLOW_DATA_LOSS.

Basic availability groups

SQL Server Standard edition supports a single-database HA solution, with a limit of two replicas. The secondary replica does not allow backups or read access. Although these limits can be frustrating, they do make it possible to offer another kind of HA offering with Standard edition.

> ➤ **For more information, go to Microsoft Docs at** *https://docs.microsoft.com/ sql/database-engine/availability-groups/windows/basic-availability-groups- always-on-availability-groups.*

Improve redundancy and performance with NIC teaming

NIC teaming, also known as *link aggregation*, uses two or more network interfaces to improve redundancy (failover), or increase the available bandwidth (bandwidth aggregation). In the Microsoft space, this is also called *load balancing and failover support* (LBFO). NIC teaming can work at the network-card level, where two or more NICs are combined into a virtual NIC on a server, or on a network switch level, where two or more network ports are aggregated.

When traffic encounters the aggregated network ports, the switch will know which port is the least busy at that time, and direct the packet to one of the other ports. This is how network load balancing works. There might be one or more servers behind each port, where the load balancing is distributed to multiple servers. Otherwise they might just be connected to a single server with multiple NICs, used just for redundancy, so that if one network interface card on the server fails, the server remains available.

Securing SQL Server

Security is covered in more depth in Chapter 6, and Chapter 7, so what follows is a basic over-view of server access security, not a discussion about permissions within SQL Server.

When connecting to SQL Server on Windows or Linux, or SQL Database in Azure, security is required to keep everyone out except the people who need access to the database.

Active Directory, using Integrated Authentication, is the primary method for connecting to SQL Server on a Windows domain. When you sign in to an Active Directory domain, you are provided a token that contains your privileges and permissions.

This is different from SQL Server Authentication, however, which is managed directly on the SQL Server instance and requires a user name and password to travel over the network.

Integrated authentication and Active Directory

Active Directory covers a number of different identity services, but the most important is Active Directory Domain Services, which manages your network credentials (your user account) and what you can do on the network (access rights). Having a network-wide directory of users and permissions facilitates easier management of accounts, computers, servers, services, devices, file sharing, and so on.

In this type of environment, SQL Server would be managed as just another service on the net-work, and the Active Directory Domain Service would control who has access to that SQL Server instance. This is much easier than having to manage per-server security, which is time consum-ing, difficult to troubleshoot, and prone to human error.

Inside OUT

Linux and Active Directory

SQL Server 2017 on Linux supports integrated authentication using Active Direc-tory. For more information, read the Microsoft Docs article titled "Active Directory Authentication with SQL Server on Linux," which is available at *https://docs.microsoft. com/sql/linux/sql-server-linux-active-directory-authentication*.

Authenticating with Kerberos

Kerberos is the default authentication protocol used in a Windows Active Directory domain; it is the replacement of NT LAN Manager (NTLM).

Kerberos ensures that the authentication takes place in a secure manner, even if the network itself might not be secure, because passwords and weak hashes are not being transferred over the wire. Kerberos works by exchanging encrypted tickets verified by a Ticket Granting Server (TGS; usually the domain controller).

A service account that runs SQL Server on a particular server, under an Active Directory service account, must register its name with the TGS, so that client computers are able to make a connection to that service over the network. This is called a *Service Principal Name*.

CAUTION

NTLM is the authentication protocol on standalone Windows systems and is used on older operating systems and older domains. You can also use NTLM as a fallback on Active Directory domains for backward compatibility.

The NTLM token created during the sign-in process consists of the domain name, the user name, and a one-way hash of the user's password. Unfortunately, this hash is considered cryptographically weak and can be cracked (decrypted) in a few seconds by modern cracking tools. It is incumbent on you to use Kerberos where at all possible.

Understanding the Service Principal Name

As shown in Figure 2-4, when a client logs into a Windows domain, it is issued a ticket by the TGS. This ticket is called a ticket-granting ticket (TGT), but it's easier to think of it as the client's credentials. When the client wants to communicate with another node on the network (for example, SQL Server), this node (or "principal") must have a Service Principal Name (SPN) registered with the TGS.

CHAPTER 2

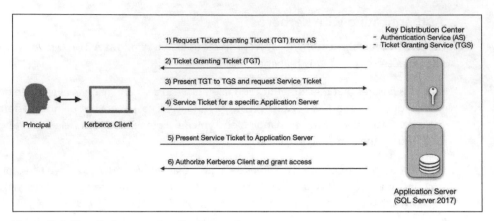

Figure 2-4 How Kerberos authentication works.

It is this SPN that the client uses to request access. After a verification step, a ticket and session key is sent from the TGS, to both the SQL Server and the client, respectively. When the client uses the ticket and session key on the SQL Server, the connection is authenticated by the SQL Server using its own copy of the session key.

For SQL Server to use Kerberos authentication instead of the older and less-secure NTLM, the Windows domain account that runs the SQL Server service, must register the SPN with the domain controller. Otherwise, the authentication will fall back to NTLM, which is far less secure. The easiest way to achieve this is to give the service account *Write ServicePrincipalName* permission in Active Directory Domain Service. To configure an SPN manually, you must use the Setspn.exe tool (built in to Windows).

Accessing other servers and services with delegation

Kerberos delegation allows an application (such as SQL Server, or Internet Information Services) to reuse end-user credentials to access a different server. This is intended to solve the so-called "double-hop issue," in which the TGS verifies only the first hop, namely the connection between the client and the registered server. In normal circumstances, any additional connections (the second hop) would require reauthentication.

Delegation impersonates the client by sending the client's TGT on the client's behalf. This in turn causes the TGS to send tickets and session keys to the original server and the new server, allowing authentication. Because the original connection is still authenticated using the same TGT, the client now has access to the second server.

For delegation to work, the service account for the first server must be trusted for delegation, and the second server must be in the same Active Directory forest or between forests with the appropriate trust relationship.

Azure Active Directory

Azure Active Directory (Azure AD) is concerned with identity management for internet-based (and on-premises) services, which use HTTP and HTTPS to access websites and web services, without the hierarchy associated with on-premises Active Directory.

You can use Azure AD for user and application authentication; for example, to connect to Azure SQL Database or Microsoft Office 365. There are no Organizational Units or Group Policy Objects. You cannot join a machine to an Azure AD domain, and there is no NTLM or Kerberos authentication. Instead, protocols like OAuth, OpenID Connect (based on OAuth 2.0), SAML, and WS-Federation are used.

You can authenticate (prove who you are), which then provides authorization (permission, or claims) to access certain services, and these services might not even be controlled by the service that authenticated you. Think back to network credentials. On an on-premises Active Directory, your user credentials know who you are (authentication), and what you can do (authorization).

Protocols like OpenID Connect blur these lines, by extending an authorization protocol (what you can do) into an authentication protocol, as well (who you are). Although this works in a similar manner to Kerberos, whereby an authorization server allows access to certain internet services and applications, permissions are granted with *claims*.

Asserting your identity by using claims

Claims are a set of "assertions of information about the subject that has been authenticated" (*https://docs.microsoft.com/azure/active-directory/develop/active-directory-authentication-scenarios#claims-in-azure-ad-security-tokens*).

Think of your user credentials as a security token that indicates who you are based on how you were authenticated. This depends on the service you originally connected to (i.e., Facebook, LinkedIn, Google, Office 365, or Twitter).

Inside that user object is a series of properties, or attributes, usually in the form of key–value pairs. Each set of attributes, or claims, is dependent on the authentication service used.

Authentication services like Azure AD might restrict the amount of information permissible in a user object, to provide the service or application just enough information about you to prove who you are, and give you access to the service you're requesting, without sharing too much about you or the originating authentication service.

CHAPTER 2

Federation and single sign-on

Federation is a fancy word that means an independent collection of websites or services that can share information between them using claims. An authentication service allows you to sign in on one place (LinkedIn, Facebook, or Microsoft) and then use that identity for other services controlled by other entities.

This is what makes claims extremely useful. If you use a third-party authentication service, that third party will make certain information available in the form of claims (key–value pairs in your security token) that another service to which you're connecting can access, without needing to sign in again, and without that service having access into the third-party service.

For example, suppose that you use LinkedIn to sign in to a blogging service so that you can leave a comment on a post. The blogging service does not have any access to your LinkedIn profile, but the claims it provides might include a URL to your profile image, a string containing your full name, and a second URL back to your profile.

This way, the blogging service does not know anything about your LinkedIn account, including your employment history, because that information is not in the claims necessary to leave a blog post comment.

Logging in to Azure SQL Database

Azure SQL Database uses three levels of security to allow access to a database. First is the firewall, which is a set of rules based on origin IP address or ranges and allows connections to only TCP port 1433.

The second level is authentication (proving who you are). You can either connect by using SQL Authentication, with a username and password (like connecting to a contained database on an on-premises SQL Server instance), or you can use Azure AD Authentication.

Microsoft recommends using Azure AD whenever possible, because it does the following (according to *https://docs.microsoft.com/azure/sql-database/sql-database-aad-authentication*):

- Centralizes user identities and offers password rotation in a single place

- Eliminates storing passwords by enabling integrated Windows authentication and other forms of authentication supported by Azure AD

- Offers token (claims-based) authentication for applications connecting to Azure SQL Database

The third level is authorization (what you can do). This is managed inside the Azure SQL database, using role memberships and object-level permissions, and works exactly the same way as it would with an on-premises SQL Server instance.

➤ You can read more about SQL Server security in Chapters 6 and 7.

Abstracting hardware with virtualization

Hardware abstraction has been around for many years, and, in fact, Windows NT was designed to be hardware independent. Taking this concept even further, virtualization abstracts the entire physical layer behind what's called a *hypervisor*, or *Virtual Machine Manager* (VMM) so that physical hardware on a host system can be logically shared between different VMs, or guests, running their own operating systems.

To a guest OS, the VM looks like normal hardware and is accessed in the same way.

As of this writing, there are two main players in the virtualization market: Microsoft Hyper-V and VMware.

Inside OUT

What is the cloud?

Cloud technology is just another virtualized environment, but on a much larger scale. Millions of servers are sitting in datacenters all over the world, running tens or hundreds of VMs on each server. The hypervisor and service fabric (the software that controls and manages the environment) is what differentiates each cloud vendor.

The move to virtualization has come about because physical hardware in many organizations is not being used to its full potential, and systems might spend hundreds of hours per year sitting idle. By consolidating an infrastructure, namely putting more than one guest VM on the same physical host, you can share resources between these guests, reducing the amount of waste and increasing the usefulness of hardware.

Certain workloads and applications are not designed to share resources, and misconfiguration of the shared resources by system administrators might not take these specialized workloads into account. SQL Server is an excellent example of this, given that it is designed to make use of all the physical RAM in a server by default.

If the resources are allocated incorrectly from the host level, contention between the guests takes place. This phenomenon is known as the *noisy neighbor*, in which one guest monopolizes resources on the host, and the other guests are negatively affected. With some effort on the part of the network administrators, this problem can be alleviated.

The benefits far outweigh the downsides, of course. You can move VMs from one host to another in the case of resource contention or hardware failure, and some hypervisors can orchestrate this without even shutting down the VM.

It is also much easier to take snapshots of virtualized file systems, which you can use to clone VMs. This can reduce deployment costs and time when deploying new servers, by "spinning up" a VM template, and configuring the OS and the application software that was already installed on that virtual hard drive.

Over time, the cost benefits become more apparent. New processors with low core counts are becoming more difficult to find. Virtualization makes it possible for you to move physical workloads to VMs (now or later) that have the appropriate virtual core count, and gives you the freedom to use existing licenses, thereby reducing cost.

> David Klee writes more on this in his article "Point Counterpoint: Why Virtualize a SQL Server?" available at *http://www.davidklee.net/2017/07/12/point-counterpoint-why-virtualize-a-sql-server*.

Resource provisioning for VMs

Setting up VMs requires understanding their anticipated workloads. Fortunately, as long as resources are allocated appropriately, a VM can run almost as fast as a physical server on the same hardware, but with all of the benefits that virtualization offers.

It makes sense, then, to overprovision resources for many general workloads.

Sharing more memory than you have (overcommit)

You might have 10 VMs running various tasks such as Active Directory Domain Controllers, DNS servers, file servers, and print servers (the plumbing of a Windows-based network, with a low RAM footprint), all running on a single host with 16 GB of physical RAM.

Each VM might require 4 GB of RAM to perform properly, but in practice, you have determined that 90 percent of the time, each VM can function with 1 to 2 GB RAM each, leaving 2 to 3 GB of RAM unused per VM. You could thus *overcommit* each VM with 4 GB of RAM (for a total of 40 GB), but still see acceptable performance, without having a particular guest swapping memory to the drive as a result of low RAM, 90 percent of the time.

For the remaining 10 percent of the time, for which paging unavoidably takes place, you might decide that the performance impact is not sufficient to warrant increasing the physical RAM on the host. You are therefore able to run 10 virtualized servers on far less hardware than they would have required as physical servers.

CAUTION

Because SQL Server makes use of all the memory it is configured to use (limited by edition), it is not good practice to overcommit memory for VMs that are running SQL Server. It is critical that the amount of RAM assigned to a SQL Server VM is available for exclusive use by the VM, and that the Max Server Memory setting is configured correctly (see Chapter 3).

Provisioning virtual storage

In the same way that you can overcommit memory, so too can you overcommit storage. This is called *thin provisioning*, in which the VM and guest OS are configured to assume that there is a lot more space available than is physically on the host. When a VM begins writing to a drive, the actual space used is increased on the host, until it reaches the provisioned limit.

This practice is common with general workloads, for which the space requirements grow predictably. An OS like Windows Server might be installed on a guest with 127 GB of visible space, but there might be only 250 GB of actual space on the drive, shared across 10 VMs.

For specialized workloads like SQL Server and Microsoft SharePoint (which is underpinned by SQL Server anyway), thin provisioning is not a good idea. Depending on the performance of the storage layer and the data access patterns of the workload, it is possible that the guest will be slow due to drive fragmentation or even run out of storage space (for any number of reasons, including long-running transactions, infrequent transaction log backups, or a growing TempDB).

It is therefore a better idea to use thick provisioning of storage for specialized workloads. That way the guest is guaranteed the storage it is promised by the hypervisor, and is one less thing to worry about when SQL Server runs out of space at 3 AM on a Sunday morning.

When processors are no longer processors

Virtualizing CPUs is challenging because the CPU works by having a certain number of clock cycles per second (which we looked at earlier in this chapter). For logical processors (this refers to the physical CPU core, plus any logical cores if SMT is turned on), every core shares time slices, or *time slots*, with each VM. Every time the CPU clock ticks over, that time slot might be used by the hypervisor or any one of the guests.

Just as it is not recommended to overprovision RAM and storage for SQL Server, you should not overprovision CPU cores either. If there are four quad-core CPUs in the host (four CPU sockets populated with a quad-core CPU in each socket), this means that there are 16 cores available for use by the VMs (32 when accounting for SMT).

Inside OUT

Virtual CPUs and SMT (Hyper-Threading)

Even though it is possible to assign as many virtual CPUs as there are logical cores, we recommend that you limit the number of vCPUs to the number of physical cores available (in other words, excluding SMT) because the number of execution resources on the CPU itself is limited to the number of physical cores.

Virtual CPU

A virtual CPU (vCPU) maps to a logical core, but in practice, the time slots are shared evenly over each core in the physical CPU. A vCPU will be more powerful than a single core because the load is parallelized across each core.

One of the risks of mixing different types of workloads on a single host is that a business-critical workload like SQL Server might require all the vCPUs to run a large parallelized query. If there are other guests that are using those vCPUs during that specific time slot and the CPU is over-committed, SQL Server's guest will need to wait.

There are certain algorithms in hypervisors that allow vCPUs to cut in line and take over a time slot, which results in a lag for the other guests, causing performance issues. Assume that a file server has two logical processors assigned to it. Further assume that on the same host, a SQL Server has eight logical processors assigned to it. It is possible for the VM with fewer logical processors to "steal" time slots because it has a lower number of logical processors allocated to it.

There are several ways to deal with this, but the easiest solution is to keep like with like. Any guests on the same host should have the same number of virtual processors assigned to them, running similar workloads. That way, the time slots are more evenly distributed, and it becomes easier to troubleshoot processor performance. It might also be practical to reduce the number of vCPUs allocated to a SQL Server instance so that the time slots are better distributed.

CAUTION

A VM running SQL Server might benefit from fewer vCPUs. If too many cores are allocated to the VM, it could cause performance issues due to foreign memory access because SQL Server might be unaware of the underlying NUMA configuration. Remember to size your VM as a multiple of a NUMA node size.

You can find more information on VMware's blog at *https://blogs.vmware.com/vsphere/2012/02/vspherenuma-loadbalancing.html.*

The network is virtual, too

Whereas before, certain hardware devices might be used to perform discrete tasks, such as network interface cards, routers, firewalls, and switches, these tasks can be accomplished exclusively through a software layer, using virtual network devices.

Several VMs might share one or more physical NICs on a physical host, but because it's all virtualized, a VM might have several virtual NICs mapped to that one physical NIC.

This allows a number of things that previously might have been cumbersome and costly to set up. Software developers can now test against myriad configurations for their applications without having to build a physical lab environment using all the different combinations.

With the general trend of consolidating VMs, virtual networking facilitates combining and consolidating network devices and services into the same environment as the guest VMs, lowering the cost of administration and reducing the need to purchase separate hardware. You can replace a virtualized network device almost immediately if something goes wrong, and downtime is vastly reduced.

Summary

SQL Server now runs on Linux, but for all intents and purposes, it's the same as the Windows version, and many of the same rules apply.

Whether running on physical or virtual hardware, databases perform better when they can be cached in memory as much as possible and are backed by persistent storage that is redundant, and has low latency and high random IOPS.

As data theft becomes more prevalent, consider the security of the database itself, the underlying OS and hardware (physical or virtual), the network, and the database backups, too.

When considering strategies for SQL Server HA and DR, design according to the organization's business requirements, in terms of the RPO and RTO. Chapter 11 and Chapter 12 cover this in depth.

CHAPTER 2

Designing and implementing a database infrastructure

This chapter covers the architecture of a database infrastructure, including the different types of database files as well as how certain features work under the hood to ensure durability and consistency, even during unexpected events. We cover what certain configuration settings mean, and why they are important.

Next, we look at some of these same concepts in the context of Microsoft Azure, including Microsoft SQL Server on Virtual Machines (infrastructure as a service), and Azure SQL Database (database as a service, a component of the larger platform as a service).

Finally, we investigate the hybrid cloud, taking the best features and components from on-premises and Azure, and examining how to make them interact.

Physical database architecture

The easiest way to observe the physical implementation of a SQL Server database is by its files. Every SQL Server database comprises at least two main kinds of file:

- **Data.** The data itself is stored in one or more filegroups. Each filegroup in turn comprises one or more physical data files.

- **Transaction Log.** This is where all data modifications are saved until committed or rolled back. There is usually only one transaction log file per database.

NOTE

There are several other file types used by SQL Server, including logs, trace files, and memory-optimized filegroups, which we discuss later in this chapter.

Data files and filegroups

When a user database is initially created, SQL Server uses the model database as a template, which provides your new database with its default configuration, including ownership, compatibility level, file growth settings, recovery model (full, bulk-logged, simple), and physical file settings.

By default, each new database has one transaction log file (this is best practice and you should not change this unless necessary), plus one data *filegroup*. This data filegroup is known as the *primary filegroup*, comprising a single data file by default. It is known as the primary data file, which has the file extension .mdf (see Figure 3-1).

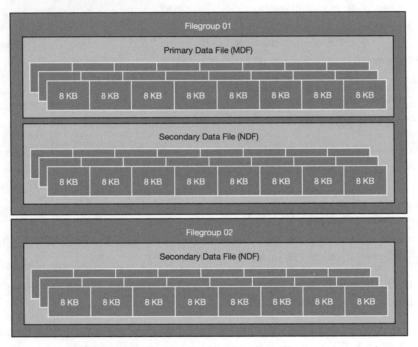

Figure 3-1 The data files as they make up one or more filegroups in a database.

You can have more than one file in a filegroup, which provides better performance through parallel reads and writes. Secondary data files generally have the file extension .ndf.

However, the real benefit comes with adding new filegroups and splitting your logical data storage across those filegroups. This makes it possible for you to do things like piecemeal backups and restore at a filegroup level in Enterprise edition.

Inside OUT

Filegroups and partial recovery

If you have a large database (more than 100 GB), we recommend that you separate your data into multiple filegroups based on a business rule (one per year, for instance), and avoid using the primary filegroup for user data entirely.

Should a disaster occur, you can restore your primary filegroup and most current data immediately (using partial restore), which brings the database online much quicker than having to restore everything from a single filegroup.

You can also age-out data into a filegroup that is set to read-only, and store it on slower storage than the current data, to manage storage costs better.

If you use table partitioning (see the section "Table partitioning" later in the chapter), splitting partitions across filegroups makes even more sense.

Mixed extents and uniform extents

SQL Server data pages are 8 KB in size. Eight of these contiguous pages is called an *extent*, which is 64 KB in size.

There are two types of extents in a SQL Server data file:

- **Mixed Extent.**   *(Optional)* The first eight pages of a data file. Each 8-KB page is assigned to its own separate object (one 8-KB page per object).

- **Uniform Extent.**   Every subsequent 64-KB extent, after the first eight pages of a data file. Each uniform extent is assigned to a single object.

Mixed extents were originally created to reduce storage requirements for database objects, back when mechanical hard drives were much smaller and more expensive. As storage has become faster and cheaper, and SQL Server more complex, this causes contention (a hotspot) at the beginning of a data file, especially if a lot of small objects are being created and deleted.

Since SQL Server 2016, mixed extents are turned off by default for TempDB and user databases, and turned on by default for system databases. If you want, you can configure mixed extents on a user database by using the following command:

```
ALTER DATABASE <dbname> SET MIXED_PAGE_ALLOCATION ON;
```

CHAPTER 3

Contents and types of data pages

At certain points in the data file, there are system-specific data pages (also 8 KB in size). These help SQL Server recognize the different data within each file.

Each data page begins with a header of 96 bytes, followed by a body containing the data itself. At the end of the page is a slot array, which fills up in reverse order, beginning with the first row, as illustrated in Figure 3-2. It instructs the Database Engine where a particular row begins on that particular page. Note that the slot array does not need to be in any particular order after the first row.

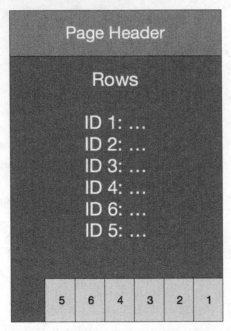

Figure 3-2 A typical 8-KB data page, showing the header, the data, and slot array.

There are several types of pages in a data file:

- **Data.**   Regular data from a heap, or clustered index at the leaf level (the data itself; what you would see when querying a table).

- **Index.**   Nonclustered index data at the leaf and nonleaf level as well as clustered indexes at the nonleaf level.

- **Large object data types.** These include `text`, `ntext`, `image`, `nvarchar(max)`, `varchar(max)`, `varbinary(max)`, Common Language Runtime (CLR) data types, `xml`, and `sql_variant` where it exceeds 8 KB. Overflow data can also be stored here (data that has been moved "off-page" by the Database Engine), with a pointer from the original page.

- **Global Allocation Map** (GAM).   Keeps track of all free extents in a data file. There is one GAM page for every GAM interval (64,000 extents, or roughly 4 GB).

- **Shared Global Allocation Map** (SGAM).   Keeps track of all extents that can be mixed extents. It has the same interval as the GAM.

- **Page Free Space** (PFS).   Keeps track of free space inside heap and large object pages. There is one PFS page for every PFS interval (8,088 pages, or roughly 64 MB).

- **Index Allocation Map** (IAM).   Keeps track of which extents in a GAM interval belong to a particular allocation unit (an allocation unit is a bucket of pages that belong to a partition, which in turn belongs to a table). It has the same interval as the GAM. There is at least one IAM for every allocation unit. If more than one IAM belongs to an allocation unit, it forms an *IAM chain*.

- **Bulk Changed Map** (BCM).   Keeps track of extents that were modified by bulk-logged operations since the last full backup. Used by transaction log backups in the bulk-logged recovery model.

- **Differential Changed Map** (DCM).   Keeps track of extents that were modified since the last full or differential backup. Used for differential backups.

- **Boot Page.**   Only one per database. This contains information about the database.

- **File Header Page.**   One per data file. This contains information about the file.

➤ To read more about the internals of a data page, read Paul Randal's post, "Anatomy of a page," at *https://www.sqlskills.com/blogs/paul/inside-the-storage-engine-anatomy-of-a-page*.

CHAPTER 3

Inside OUT

What about memory-optimized objects?

Even memory-optimized objects rely on the storage subsystem (the transaction log must still be written to, though in a highly-efficient manner) and require significant IOPS (refer to Chapter 2, "Introducing database server components," to read more about storage).

Memory-optimized features use their own filegroup, called the *memory-optimized filegroup*. It is implemented in a similar fashion as the FILESTREAM filegroup, in that all objects are stored in folders on the underlying file system.

All data files and delta file pairs for memory-optimized objects are stored here. Microsoft recommends a minimum of four storage containers for this filegroup, spread across physical drives.

These file pairs record changes to the tables and are used during recovery (including when the SQL Server is restarted) to repopulate the objects in memory (if using the default SCHEMA_AND_DATA durability). You can remove the memory-optimized filegroup only by dropping a database.

According to Microsoft, you must provide four times the drive space that your memory-optimized tables require. To see more, go to *https://docs.microsoft.com/sql/relational-databases/in-memory-oltp/the-memory-optimized-filegroup*.

Verifying data pages by using a checksum

By default, when a data page is read into the buffer pool, a checksum is automatically calculated over the entire 8-KB page and compared to the checksum stored in the page header on the drive. This is how SQL Server keeps track of page-level corruption. If the checksum stored on the drive does not match the checksum in memory, corruption has occurred. A record of this suspect page is stored in the msdb database.

The same checksum is performed when writing to a drive. If the checksum on the drive does not match the checksum in the data page in the buffer pool, page-level corruption has occurred.

Although the PAGE_VERIFY property on new databases is set to CHECKSUM by default, it might be necessary to check databases that have been upgraded from previous versions of SQL Server, especially those created prior to SQL Server 2005.

You can monitor checksum verification on all databases by using the following query:

```
SELECT name, databases.page_verify_option_desc
FROM sys.databases;
```

You can mitigate data page corruption by using Error-Correcting Code Random Access Memory (ECC RAM). Data page corruption on the drive is detected by using DBCC CHECKDB and other operations.

➤ For information on how to proactively detect corruption, read the section "Database corruption" in Chapter 13, "Managing and monitoring SQL Server."

Recording changes in the transaction log

The transaction log is the most important component of a SQL Server database because it is where all units of work (*transactions*) performed on a database are recorded, before the data can be written (*flushed*) to the drive. The transaction log file usually has the file extension .ldf.

Inside OUT

How many transaction log files should I have per database?

Although it is possible to use more than one file to store the transaction logs for a database, we do not recommend this, because there is no performance or maintenance benefit to using multiple files. To understand why and where it might be appropriate to have more than one, see the section "Inside the transaction log file with virtual log files" later in the chapter.

A successful transaction is said to be *committed*. An unsuccessful transaction is said to be *rolled back*.

In Chapter 2, we saw that when SQL Server needs an 8-KB data page from the data file, it copies it from the drive and stores a copy of this page in memory in an area called the *buffer pool*, while that page is required. When a transaction needs to modify that page, it works directly on the copy of the page in the buffer pool. If the page is subsequently modified, a log record of the modification is created in the *log buffer* (also in memory), and that log record is then written to the drive.

By default, SQL Server uses a technique called Write-Ahead Logging (WAL), which ensures that no changes are written to the data file before the necessary log record is written to the drive in a permanent form (in this case, persistent storage).

However, SQL Server 2014 introduced a new feature called *delayed durability*. This does not save every change to the transaction log as it happens; rather, it waits until the log cache grows to a certain size (or `sp_flushlog` runs) before flushing it to the drive.

CAUTION

If you turn on delayed durability on your database, keep in mind that the performance benefit has a downside of potential data loss if the underlying storage layer experiences a failure before the log can be saved.

> ➤ You can read more about log persistence and how it affects durability of transactions at *https://docs.microsoft.com/sql/relational-databases/logs/control-transaction-durability*.

Until a commit or rollback occurs, a transaction's outcome is unknown. An error might occur during a transaction, or the operator might decide to roll back the transaction manually because the results were not as expected. In the case of a rollback, changes to the modified data pages must be undone. SQL Server will make use of the saved log records to undo the changes for an incomplete transaction.

Only when the transaction log file is written to can the modified 8-KB page be saved in the data file, though the page might be modified several times in the buffer pool before it is flushed to the drive.

> ➤ See later in this section about how checkpoints flush these modified (dirty) pages to the drive.

Our guidance, therefore, is to use the fastest storage possible for the transaction log file(s), because of the low-latency requirements.

Inside the transaction log file with virtual log files

A transaction log file is split into logical segments, called *virtual log files* (VLFs). These segments are dynamically allocated when the transaction log file is created and whenever the file grows. The size of each VLF is not fixed and is based on an internal algorithm, which depends on the version of SQL Server, the current file size, and file growth settings. Each VLF has a header containing a Minimum Log Sequence Number and whether it is active.

Inside OUT

What is a Log Sequence Number?

Every transaction is uniquely identified by a Log Sequence Number (LSN). Each LSN is ordered, so a later LSN will be greater than an earlier LSN. The LSN is also used by database backups and restores. For more information, see the Chapter 11, "Developing, deploying, and managing data recovery," and Chapter 13.

Figure 3-3 illustrates how the transaction log is circular. When a VLF is first allocated by creation or file growth, it is marked inactive in the VLF header. Transactions can be recorded only in active portions of the log file, so the SQL Server engine looks for inactive VLFs sequentially, and as it needs them, marks them as active to allow transactions to be recorded.

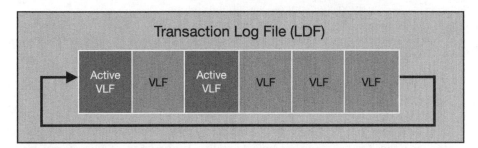

Figure 3-3 The transaction log file, showing active and inactive VLFs.

Marking a VLF inactive is called *log truncation*, but this operation does not affect the size of the physical transaction log file. It just means that an active VLF has been marked inactive and can be reused.

Several processes make use of the transaction log, which could delay log truncation. After the transactions that make use of an active VLF are committed or rolled back, what happens next depends on a number of factors:

- The recovery model:
    - **Simple.**   A checkpoint is issued implicitly after a transaction is committed.
    - **Full/bulk-logged.**   A transaction log backup must take place after a transaction is committed. A checkpoint is issued implicitly if the log backup is successful.

- Other processes that can delay log truncation:
    - **Active backup or restore.**   The transaction log cannot be truncated if it is being used by a backup or restore operation.
    - **Active transaction.**   If another transaction is using an active VLF, it cannot be truncated.
    - **Database mirroring.**   Mirrored changes must be synchronized before the log can be truncated. This occurs in high-performance mode or if the mirror is behind the principal database.
    - **Replication.**   Transactions that have not yet been delivered to the distribution database can delay log truncation.

- **Database snapshot creation.**   This is usually brief, but creating snapshots (manu-ally or through database consistency checks, for instance) can delay truncation.

- **Log scan.**   Usually brief, but this, too, can delay a log truncation.

- **Checkpoint operation.**   See the section "Flushing data to the storage subsystem by using checkpoints" later in the chapter.

➤ To learn more, read "Factors That Can Delay Log Truncation" at *https://technet.microsoft.com/library/ms345414.aspx.*

After the checkpoint is issued and the dependencies on the transaction log (as just listed) are removed, the log is truncated by marking those VLFs as inactive.

The log is accessed sequentially in this manner until it gets to the end of the file. At this point, the log wraps around to the beginning, and the Database Engine looks for an inactive VLF from the start of the file to mark active. If there are no inactive VLFs available, the log file must create new VLFs by growing in size according to the auto growth settings.

If the log file cannot grow, it will stop all operations on the database until VLFs can be reclaimed or created.

Inside OUT

What do I do if I run out of space in the transaction log file?

If a transaction log runs out of space because no inactive VLFs are available, you first must take a transaction log backup (if the database is in the Full or Bulk-Logged recovery model). Failing that, you can grow the transaction log file. If there is insuf-ficient space on the drive to grow the transaction log file, you can assign a second log file to the database on a different drive.

In most cases, a transaction log file runs out of space because the database is in the full or bulk-logged recovery model, and transaction log backups are not being taken regularly. We recommend that you to allow transaction log files to grow automati-cally, with a fixed auto growth size, and to take regular transaction log backups.

Flushing data to the storage subsystem by using checkpoints

Recall from Chapter 2 that any changes to the data are written to the database file asynchro-nously, for performance reasons. This process is controlled by a *database checkpoint*. As its name implies, this is a database-level setting that can be changed under certain conditions by modifying the Recovery Interval or by running the CHECKPOINT command in the database context.

The checkpoint process takes all the modified pages in the buffer pool as well as transaction log information that is in memory and writes that to the storage subsystem. This reduces the time it takes to recover a database because only the changes made after the latest checkpoint need to be rolled forward in the Redo phase (see the section "Restarting with recovery" later in the chapter).

The Minimum Recovery LSN

When a checkpoint occurs, a log record is written to the transaction log stating that a checkpoint has commenced. After this, the Minimum Recovery LSN (MinLSN) must be recorded. This LSN is the minimum of either the LSN at the start of the checkpoint, the LSN of the oldest active transaction, or the LSN of the oldest replication transaction that hasn't been delivered to the transactional replication distribution database.

In other words, the MinLSN "...is the log sequence number of the oldest log record that is required for a successful database-wide rollback." (*https://docs.microsoft.com/sql/relational-databases/sql-server-transaction-log-architecture-and-management-guide*)

> ➤ To learn more about the distribution database, read the section "Replication" in Chapter 12, "Implementing high availability and disaster recovery."

This way, crash recovery knows to start recovery only at the MinLSN and can skip over any older LSNs in the transaction log if they exist.

The checkpoint also records the list of active transactions that have made changes to the database. If the database is in the simple recovery model, the unused portion of the transaction log before the MinLSN is marked for reuse. All dirty data pages and information about the transaction log are written to the storage subsystem, the end of the checkpoint is recorded in the log, and (importantly) the LSN from the start of the checkpoint is written to the boot page of the database.

NOTE

In the full and bulk-logged recovery models, a successful transaction log backup issues a checkpoint implicitly.

Types of database checkpoints

Checkpoints can be activated in a number of different scenarios. The most common is the automatic checkpoint, which is governed by the recovery interval setting (see the Inside OUT sidebar that follows to see how to modify this setting) and typically takes place approximately once every minute for active databases (those databases in which a change has occurred at all).

NOTE

Inactive databases with no transactions would not require a frequent checkpoint, because nothing has changed in the buffer pool.

CHAPTER 3

Other checkpoint events include the following:

- Database backups (including transaction log backups)

- Database shutdowns

- Adding or removing files on a database

- SQL Server instance shutdown

- Minimally logged operations (for example, in a database in the simple or bulk-logged recovery model)

- Explicit use of the CHECKPOINT command

Inside OUT

How do I set the recovery interval?

According to Microsoft Docs, the recovery interval "...defines an upper limit on the time recovering a database should take. The SQL Server Database Engine uses the value specified for this option to determine approximately how often to issue automatic checkpoints on a given database." (*https://docs.microsoft.com/sql/database-engine/configure-windows/configure-the-recovery-interval-server-configuration-option*). You can also visit that page to learn how to configure this setting.

We recommend that you not increase this value unless you have a very specific need. A longer recovery interval can increase database recovery time, which can affect your Recovery Time Objective (RTO).

Try to keep your transactions as short as possible, which will also improve recovery time. You can read more about coding efficient transactions at *https://technet.microsoft.com/library/ms187484.aspx*.

There are four types of checkpoints that can occur:

- **Automatic.** Issued internally by the Database Engine to meet the value of the recovery interval setting. On SQL Server 2016 and higher, the default is one minute.

- **Indirect.** Issued to meet a user-specified target recovery time, if the TARGET_RECOVERY_TIME has been set.

- **Manual.** Issued when the CHECKPOINT command is run.

- **Internal.** Issued internally by various features, such as backup and snapshot creation, to ensure consistency between the log and the drive image.

➤ For more information about checkpoints, visit Microsoft Docs at *https://docs.microsoft. com/sql/relational-databases/logs/database-checkpoints-sql-server*.

Restarting with recovery

Whenever SQL Server starts, recovery (also referred to as crash recovery or restart recovery) takes place on every single database (on one thread per database, to ensure that it completes as quickly as possible) because SQL Server does not know for certain whether each database was shut down cleanly.

The transaction log is read from the latest checkpoint in the active portion of the log, namely the LSN it gets from the boot page of the database (see the section "The Minimum Recovery LSN" earlier in the chapter) and scans all active VLFs looking for work to do.

All committed transactions are rolled forward (*Redo portion*) and then all uncommitted transactions are rolled back (*Undo portion*). The total number of rolled forward and rolled back transactions are recorded with a respective entry in the ERRORLOG file.

SQL Server Enterprise edition brings the database online immediately after the Redo portion is complete. Other editions must wait for the Undo portion to complete before the database is brought online.

➤ **For more information about database corruption and recovery, see Chapter 13.**

The reason why we cover this in such depth in this introductory chapter is to help you to understand why drive performance is paramount when creating and allocating database files.

When a transaction log is first created or file growth occurs, the portion of the drive must be zeroed-out (the file system literally writes zeroes in every byte in that file segment).

Instant file initalization does not apply to transaction log files for this reason, so keep this in mind when growing or shrinking transaction log files. All activity in a database will stop until the file operation is complete.

As you can imagine, this can be time consuming for larger files, so you need to take care when setting file growth options, especially with transaction log files. You should measure the performance of the underlying storage layer and choose a fixed growth size that balances performance with reduced VLF count. Consider setting file growth for transaction log files in multiples of 8 GB. At a sequential write speed of 200 MBps, this would take under a minute to grow the transaction log file.

MinLSN and the active log

As mentioned earlier, each VLF contains a header that includes an LSN and an indicator as to whether the VLF is active. The portion of the transaction log, from the VLF containing the MinLSN to the VLF containing the latest log record, is considered the active portion of the transaction log.

All records in the active log are required in order to perform a full recovery if something goes wrong. The active log must therefore include all log records for uncommitted transactions, too, which is why long-running transactions can be problematic. Replicated transactions that have not yet been delivered to the distribution database can also affect the MinLSN.

Any type of transaction that does not allow the MinLSN to increase during the normal course of events, affects overall health and performance of the database environment because the transaction log file might grow uncontrollably.

When VLFs cannot be made inactive until a long-running transaction is committed or rolled back or if a VLF is in use by other processes (including database mirroring, availability groups, and transactional replication, for example), the log file is forced to grow. Any log backups that include these long-running transaction records will also be large. The recovery phase can also take longer because there is a much larger volume of active transactions to process.

> ➤ You can read more about transaction log file architecture at *https://docs.microsoft.com/sql/ relational-databases/sql-server-transaction-log-architecture-and-management-guide*.

Table partitioning

All tables in SQL Server are already partitioned, if you look deep enough into the internals. It just so happens that there is one partition per table by default. Until SQL Server 2016 Service Pack 1, only Enterprise edition could add more partitions per table.

This is called *horizontal partitioning*. Suppose that a database table is growing extremely large, and adding new rows is time consuming. You might decide to split the table into groups of rows, based on a *partitioning key* (typically a date column), with each group in its own partition. In turn, you can store these in different filegroups to improve read and write performance.

Breaking up a table this way can also result in a query optimization called *partition elimination*, by which only the partition that contains the data you need is queried.

However, table partitioning was not designed primarily as a performance feature. Partitioning tables will not automatically result in better query performance, and, in fact, performance might be worse due to other factors, specifically around statistics (please see Chapter 8 for more about designing partitioned tables).

Even so, there are some major advantages to table partitioning, which benefit large datasets, specifically around rolling windows and moving data in and out of the table. This process is called *partition switching*, by which you can switch data into and out of a table almost instantly.

Assume that you need to load data into a table every month and then make it available for querying. With table partitioning, you put the data that you want to insert into a completely separate table in the same database, which has the same structure and clustered index as the main table. Then, a switch operation moves that data into the partitioned table almost instantly (it requires a shared lock to update the tables' metadata), because no data movement is needed.

This makes it very easy to manage large groups of data or data that ages-out at regular intervals (sliding windows) because partitions can be switched out nearly immediately.

Inside OUT

Should I use partitioned tables or partitioned views?

Because table partitioning is available in all editions of SQL Server as of 2016 Service Pack 1, you might find it an attractive option for smaller databases. However, it might be more prudent to use partitioned views, instead.

Partitioned views make use of a database view that is a union query against a group of underlying tables. Instead of querying a partitioned table directly, you would query the view.

Using key constraints on the primary key for each base table still allows the query optimizer to use "partition" elimination (base table elimination). Performance-wise, moving data in and out of the partitioned view would be almost instantaneous because you need to update only the view itself to add or remove a particular base table.

Data compression

SQL Server supports several types of data compression to reduce the amount of drive space required for data and backups, as a trade-off against higher CPU utilization.

➤ You can read more about data compression in Microsoft Docs at *https://docs.microsoft.com/ sql/relational-databases/data-compression/data-compression*.

In general, the amount of CPU overhead required to perform compression and decompression depends on the type of data involved, and in the case of data compression, the type of queries running against the database, as well. Even though the higher CPU load might be offset by the savings in I/O, we always recommend testing before implementing this feature.

Row compression

You turn on row compression at the table level. Each column in a row is evaluated according to the type of data and contents of that column, as follows:

- Numeric data types and their derived types (i.e., `integer`, `decimal`, `float`, `datetime`, and `money`) are stored as variable length at the physical layer.

- Fixed-length character data types are stored as variable length strings, where the blank trailing characters are not stored.

- Variable length data types, including large objects, are not affected by row compression.

- Bit columns actually take up more space due to associated metadata.

Row compression can be useful for tables with fixed-length character data types and where numeric types are overprovisioned (e.g., a `bigint` column that contains only integers).

➤ **You can read more about row compression in Microsoft Docs at** *https://docs.microsoft.com/ sql/relational-databases/data-compression/row-compression-implementation.*

Page compression

You turn on page compression at the table level, as well, but it operates on all data pages associated with that table, including indexes, table partitions, and index partitions. Leaf-level pages (see Figure 3-4) are compressed using three steps:

1. Row compression

2. Prefix compression

3. Dictionary compression

Non-leaf-level pages are compressed using row compression only. This is for performance reasons.

Inside OUT

What is the difference between leaf-level and non-leaf-level pages?

Clustered and nonclustered indexes in SQL Server are stored in a structure known as a B+ tree. The tree has a root node, which fans out to child nodes, with the data itself at the leaf level.

Any nodes that appear between the root and leaf levels are called intermediate, or non-leaf-level nodes. Data in the leaf level is accessed (through a seek or a scan operation) by using page identifiers in the root and intermediate levels, which contain pointers to the respective starting key values in the leaf level. When the leaf level is reached, the slot array at the end of each page contains a pointer to the exact row.

Figure 3-4 presents an example of a clustered index.

➤ You can read more about indexes in Chapter 10, "Understanding and designing indexes," and Chapter 13. To learn more about the B+ tree structure, visit *https://technet.microsoft.com/library/ms177443.aspx*.

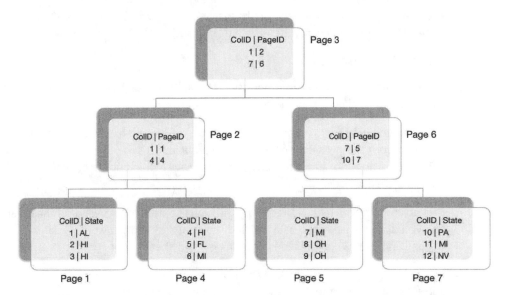

Figure 3-4 A typical clustered index with leaf and non-leaf levels, clustered on CollD.

Prefix compression works per column, by searching for a common prefix in each column. A row is created just below the page header, called the *compression information* (CI) structure, containing a single row of each column with its own prefix.

If any of a column's rows on the page match the prefix, its value is replaced by a reference to that column's prefix.

Dictionary compression then searches across the entire page, looking for repeating values, irrespective of the column, and stores these in the CI structure. When a match is found, the column value in that row is replaced with a reference to the compressed value.

If a data page is not full, it will be compressed using only row compression. If the size of the compressed page along with the size of the CI structure is not significantly smaller than the uncompressed page, no page compression will be performed on that page.

Unicode compression

You can achieve between 15 and 50 savings percentage by using Unicode compression, which is implemented automatically on Unicode data types, when using row or page compression. The savings percentage depends on the locale, so the saving is as high as 50 percent with Latin alphabets. This is particularly useful with `nchar` and `nvarchar` data types.

Backup compression

Whereas page- and row-level compression operate at the table level, backup compression applies to the backup file for the entire database.

Compressed backups are usually smaller than uncompressed backups, which means fewer drive I/O operations are involved, which in turn means a reduction in the time it takes to perform a backup or restore. For larger databases, this can have a dramatic effect on the time it takes to recover from a disaster.

Backup compression ratio is affected by the type of data involved, whether the database is encrypted, and whether the data is already compressed. In other words, a database making use of page and/or row compression might not gain any benefit from backup compression.

The CPU can be limited for backup compression in Resource Governor (you can read more about Resource Governor in the section "Configuration settings" later in the chapter).

In most cases, we recommend turning on backup compression, keeping in mind that you might need to monitor CPU utilization.

Managing the temporary database

SQL Server uses the temporary database (TempDB) for a number of things that are mostly invisible to us, including temporary tables, table variables, triggers, cursors, table sorting, snapshot isolation, read-committed snapshot isolation, index creation, user-defined functions, and many more.

Additionally, when performing queries with operations that don't fit in memory (the buffer pool and the buffer pool extension), these operations spill to the drive, requiring the use of TempDB. In other words, TempDB is the working area of every database on the instance, and there is only one TempDB per instance.

Storage options for TempDB

Every time SQL Server restarts, TempDB is cleared out. If the files don't exist, they are re-created. If the files are configured at a size smaller than their last active size, they will automatically be shrunk or truncated. Like the database file structure described earlier, there is usually one TempDB transaction log file, and one or more data files in a single filegroup.

For this reason, performance is critical, even more than with other databases, to the point that the current recommendation is to use your fastest storage for TempDB, before using it for user database transaction log files.

Where possible, use solid-state storage for TempDB. If you have a Failover Cluster Instance, have TempDB on local storage on each node.

Recommended number of files

Only one transaction log file should exist for TempDB.

The best number of TempDB data files for your instance is almost certainly greater than one, and less than or equal to the number of logical processor cores. This guidance goes for physical and virtual servers.

> ➤ You can read more about processors in Chapter 2. Affinity masks are discussed later in this chapter.

The default number of TempDB data files recommended by SQL Server Setup should match the number of logical processor cores, up to a maximum of eight, keeping in mind that your logical core count includes symmetrical multithreading (e.g., Hyper-Threading). Adding more TempDB data files than the number of logical processor cores would rarely result in positive performance. Adding too many TempDB data files could in fact severely harm SQL Server performance.

Increasing the number of files to eight (and other factors) reduces TempDB contention when allocating temporary objects. If the instance has more than eight logical processors allocated, you can test to see whether adding more files helps performance, and is very much dependent on the workload.

You can allocate the TempDB data files together on the same volume (see the section "Types of storage" in Chapter 2), provided that the underlying storage layer is able to meet the low-latency demands of TempDB on your instance. If you plan to share the storage with other database files, keep latency and IOPS in mind.

CHAPTER 3

Inside OUT

Do I need Trace Flags 1118 and 1117 for TempDB?

On versions prior to SQL Server 2016, Trace Flag 1118 turned off mixed extents at the instance level, which reduced contention when creating and deleting many temporary objects.

Trace Flag 1117 ensured that all files allocated to any database grew at the same rate.

Because trace flags are instance-wide, it meant that all databases were affected by these trace flags, even though they mainly benefited TempDB.

Since SQL Server 2016, these trace flags have no effect. Instead, uniform extents are turned on by default for TempDB (MIXED_PAGE_ALLOCATION was mentioned previously in this chapter), as is the setting to autogrow all files at the same time.

Configuration settings

SQL Server has scores of settings that you can tune to your particular workload. There are also best practices regarding the appropriate settings (e.g., file growth, memory settings, and parallelism). We cover some of these in this section.

➤ Chapter 4, "Provisioning databases," contains additional configuration settings for provisioning databases.

Many of these configurations can be affected by Resource Governor, which is a workload management feature of the Database Engine, restricting certain workload types to a set of system resources (CPU, RAM, and I/O).

Managing system usage by using Resource Governor

Using Resource Governor, you can specify limits on resource consumption at the application-session level. You can configure these in real time, which allows for flexibility in managing workloads without affecting other workloads on the system.

A resource pool represent the *physical resources* of an instance, which means that you can think of a resource pool itself as a mini SQL Server instance. To make the best use of Resource Governor, it is helpful to logically group similar workloads together into a *workload group* so that you can manage them under a specific resource pool.

This is done via *classification*, which looks at the incoming application session's characteristics. That incoming session will be categorized into a workload group based on your criteria. This facilitates fine-grained resource usage that reduces the impact of certain workloads on other, more critical workloads.

CAUTION

There is a lot of flexibility and control in classification because Resource Governor supports user-defined functions (UDFs) to classify sessions. This also means that a poorly written UDF can render the system unusable. Always test classifier functions and optimize them for performance. If you need to troubleshoot a classifier function, use the Dedicated Administrator Connection (DAC) because it is not subject to classification.

For example, a reporting application might have a negative impact on database performance due to resource contention at certain times of the day, so by classifying it into a specific workload group, you can limit the amount of memory or disk I/O that reporting application can use, reducing its effect on, say, a month-end process that needs to run at the same time.

Configuring the page file (Windows)

Windows uses the page file (also known as the swap file) for virtual memory for all applications, including SQL Server, when available memory is not sufficient for the current working set. It does this by offloading (paging out) segments of RAM to the drive. Because storage is slower than memory (see Chapter 2), data that has been paged out is also slower when working from the system page file.

The page file also serves the role of capturing a system memory dump for crash forensic analysis, a factor that dictates its size on modern operating systems with large amounts of memory. This is why the general recommendation for the system page file is that it should be at least the same size as the server's amount of physical memory.

Another general recommendation is that the page file should be set to System Managed, and, since Windows Server 2012, that guideline has functioned well. However, in servers with large amounts of memory, this can result in a very large page file, so be aware of that if the page file is located on your operating system (OS) volume. This is also why the page file is often moved to its own volume, away from the OS volume.

On a dedicated SQL Server instance, you can set the page file to a fixed size, relative to the amount of Max Server Memory assigned to SQL Server. In principle, the database instance will use up as much RAM as you allow it, to that Max Server Memory limit, so Windows will preferably not need to page SQL Server out of RAM.

> **NOTE**
>
> If the *Lock pages in memory* policy is on (recommended on a physical server only), SQL Server will not be forced to page out of memory, and you can set the page file to a smaller size. This can free up valuable space on the OS drive, which can be beneficial to the OS.

➤ For more about Lock pages in memory, see Chapter 2 as well as the section by the same name later in this chapter.

Taking advantage of logical processors by using parallelism

SQL Server is designed to run on multiple logical processors (for more information, refer to the section "Central Processing Unit" in Chapter 2).

In SQL Server, parallelism makes it possible for portions of a query (or the entire query) to run on more than one logical processor at the same time. This has certain performance advantages for larger queries, because the workload can be split more evenly across resources. There is an implicit overhead with running queries in parallel, however, because a controller thread must manage the results from each logical processor and then combine them when each thread is completed.

The SQL Server query optimizer uses a cost-based optimizer when coming up with query plans. This means that it makes certain assumptions about the performance of the storage, CPU and memory, and how they relate to different query plan operators. Each operation has a cost associated with it.

SQL Server will consider creating parallel plan operations, based on two parallelism settings: *Cost threshold for parallelism* and *Max degree of parallelism*. These two settings can make a world of difference to the performance of a SQL Server instance if it is using default settings.

Query plan costs are recorded in a *unitless* measure. In other words, the cost bears *no relation* to resources such as drive latency, IOPS, number of seconds, memory usage, or CPU power, which can make query tuning difficult without keeping this in mind.

Cost threshold for parallelism

This is the minimum cost a query plan can be before the optimizer will even consider parallel query plans. If the cost of a query plan exceeds this value, the query optimizer will take parallelism into account when coming up with a query plan. This does not necessarily mean that every plan with a higher cost is run across parallel processor cores, but the chances are increased.

The default setting for cost threshold for parallelism is 5. Any query plan with a cost of 5 or higher will be considered for parallelism. Given how much faster and more powerful modern server processors are, many queries will run just fine on a single core, again because of the overhead associated with parallel plans.

Inside OUT

Why doesn't Microsoft change the defaults?

Microsoft is reticent to change default values, because of its strong support of backward compatibility. There are many applications in use today that are no longer supported by their original creators that might depend on default settings in Microsoft products. Besides, if it is a best practice to change the default settings when setting up a new instance of SQL Server, it does not make much of a difference either way.

NOTE

Certain query operations can force some or all of a query plan to run serially, even if the plan cost exceeds the cost threshold for parallelism. Paul White's article "Forcing a Parallel Query Execution Plan" describes a few of these. You can read Paul's article at *http://sqlblog.com/blogs/paul_white/archive/2011/12/23/forcing-a-parallel-query-execution-plan.aspx*.

It might be possible to write a custom process to tune the cost threshold for parallelism setting automatically, using information from the Query Store. Because the Query Store works at the database level, it helps identify the average cost of queries per database and would be able to find an appropriate setting for the cost threshold relative to your specific workload.

➤ You can read more about the Query Store in the section "Execution plans" in Chapter 9.

Until we get to an autotuning option, you can set the cost threshold for parallelism to 50 as a starting point for new instances, and then monitor the average execution plan costs, to adjust this value up or down (and you should adjust this value based on your own workload).

Cost threshold for parallelism is an advanced server setting; you can change it by using the command `sp_configure 'cost threshold for parallelism'`. You can also change it in SQL Server Management Studio by using the Cost Threshold For Parallelism setting, in the Server Properties section of the Advanced node.

Max degree of parallelism

SQL Server uses this value, also known as MAXDOP, to select the maximum number of logical processors to run a parallel query plan when the cost threshold for parallelism is reached.

The default setting for MAXDOP is 0, which instructs SQL Server to make use of all available logical processors to run a parallel query (taking processor affinity into account—see later in this chapter).

The problem with this default setting for most workloads is twofold:

- Parallel queries could consume all resources, preventing smaller queries from running or forcing them to run slowly while they find time in the CPU scheduler.

- If all logical processors are allocated to a plan, it can result in foreign memory access, which, as we explain in Chapter 2 in the section on Non-Uniform Memory Access (NUMA), carries a performance penalty.

Specialized workloads can have different requirements for the MAXDOP. For standard or Online Transaction Processing (OLTP) workloads, to make better use of modern server resources, the MAXDOP setting must take NUMA nodes into account.

If there is more than one NUMA node on a server, the recommended value for this setting is the number of logical processors on a single node, up to a maximum value of 8.

For SQL Server instances with a single CPU, with eight or fewer cores, the recommended value is 0. Otherwise, you should set it to a maximum of 8 if there are more than eight logical processors.

MAXDOP is an advanced server setting; you can change it by using the command `sp_configure 'max degree of parallelism'`. You can also change it in SQL Server Management Studio by using the Max Degree Of Parallelism setting, in the Server Properties section of the Advanced node.

SQL Server memory settings

Since SQL Server 2012, the artificial memory limits imposed by the license for lower editions (Standard, Web, and Express) apply to the buffer pool only (see *https://docs.microsoft.com/sql/sql-server/editions-and-components-of-sql-server-2017*).

This is not the same thing as the Max Server Memory, though. According to Microsoft Docs, the Max Server Memory setting controls all of SQL Server's memory allocation, which includes, but is not limited to the buffer pool, compile memory, caches, memory grants, and CLR (Common Language Runtime, or .NET) memory (*https://docs.microsoft.com/sql/database-engine/configure-windows/server-memory-server-configuration-options*).

Additionally, limits to Columnstore and memory-optimized object memory are over and above the buffer pool limit on non-Enterprise editions, which gives you a greater opportunity to make use of available physical memory.

This makes memory management for non-Enterprise editions more complicated, but certainly more flexible, especially taking Columnstore and memory-optimized objects into account.

Max Server Memory

As noted in Chapter 2, SQL Server uses as much memory as you allow it. Therefore, you want to limit the amount of memory that each SQL Server instance can control on the server, ensuring that you leave enough system memory for the following:

- The OS itself (see the algorithm below)

- Other SQL Server instances installed on the server

- Other SQL Server features installed on the server; for example, SQL Server Reporting Services, SQL Server Analysis Services, or SQL Server Integration Services

- Remote desktop sessions and locally run administrative applications like SQL Server Management Studio

- Antimalware programs

- System monitoring or remote management applications

- Any additional applications that might be installed and running on the server (including web browsers)

The appropriate Max Server Memory setting will vary from server to server. A good starting place for the reduction from the total server memory is 10 percent less, or 4 GB less than the server's total memory capacity, whichever is the greater reduction. For a dedicated SQL Server instance and 16 GB of total memory, an initial value of 12 GB (or a value of 12288 in MB) for Max Server Memory is appropriate.

> ### NOTE
> **SQL Server is supported on servers with as little as 4 GB of RAM, in which case a Max Server Memory value of 2,048 MB is recommended.**

OS reservation   Jonathan Kehayias has published the following algorithm that can help with reserving the appropriate amount of RAM for the OS itself. Whatever remains can then be used for other processes, including SQL Server by means of Max Server Memory:

- 1 GB of RAM for the OS

- Add 1 GB for each 4 GB of RAM installed, from 4 to 16 GB

- Add 1 GB for every 8 GB RAM installed, above 16 GB RAM

> ➤ To learn more, read Kehayias, J and Kruger, T, *Troubleshooting SQL Server: A Guide for the Accidental DBA* (Redgate Books, 2011).

Assuming that a server has 256 GB of available RAM, this requires a reservation of 35 GB for the OS. The remaining 221 GB can then be split between SQL Server and anything else that is running on the server.

Performance Monitor to the rescue   Ultimately, the best way to see if the correct value is assigned to Max Server Memory is to monitor the Memory\Available MBytes value in Performance Monitor. This way, you can ensure that Windows Server has enough working set of its own, and adjust Max Server Memory downward if this value drops below 300 MB.

Max Server Memory is an advanced server setting; you can change it by using the command `sp_configure 'max server memory'`. You can also change it in SQL Server Management Studio by using the Max Server Memory setting, in the Server Properties section of the Memory node.

Max Worker Threads

Every process on SQL Server requires a thread, or time on a logical processor, including network access, database checkpoints, and user threads. Threads are managed internally by the SQL Server scheduler, one for each logical processor, and only one thread is processed at a time by each scheduler on its respective logical processor.

These threads consume memory, which is why it's generally a good idea to let SQL Server manage the maximum number of threads allowed automatically.

However, in certain special cases, changing this value from the default of 0 might help performance tuning. The default of 0 means that SQL Server will dynamically assign a value when starting, depending on the number of logical processors and other resources.

To check whether your server is under CPU pressure, run the following query:

```
SELECT AVG(runnable_tasks_count)
FROM sys.dm_os_schedulers
WHERE status = 'VISIBLE ONLINE';
```

If the number of tasks is consistently high (in the double digits), your server is under CPU pressure. You can mitigate this in a number of other ways that you should consider before increasing the number of Max Worker Threads.

In some scenarios, lowering the number of Max Worker Threads can improve performance.

> ➤ You can read more about setting Max Worker Threads on Microsoft Docs at *https://docs.microsoft.com/sql/database-engine/configure-windows/configure-the-max-worker-threads-server-configuration-option*.

Lock pages in memory

The Lock pages in memory policy can cause instability if you use it incorrectly. But, you can mitigate the danger of OS instability by carefully aligning Max Server Memory capacity for any installed SQL Server features (discussed earlier) and reducing the competition for memory resource from other applications.

When reducing memory pressure in virtualized systems, it is also important to avoid over-allocating memory to guests on the virtual host. Meanwhile, locking pages in memory can still prevent the paging of SQL Server memory to the drive due to memory pressure, a significant performance hit.

> ➤ For a more in-depth explanation of the Lock pages in memory policy, see Chapter 2.

Optimize for ad hoc workloads

Ad hoc queries are defined, in this context, as queries that are run only once. Applications and reports should be running queries many times, and SQL Server recognizes them and caches them over time.

By default, SQL Server caches the runtime plan for a query after the first time it runs, with the expectation of using it again and saving the compilation cost for future runs. For ad hoc queries, these cached plans will never be reused yet will remain in cache.

When Optimize For Ad Hoc Workloads is set to True, a plan will not be cached until it is recognized to have been called twice. The third and all ensuing times it is run would then benefit from the cached runtime plan. Therefore, it is recommended that you set this option to True.

For most workloads, the scenario in which plans might only ever run exactly twice is unrealistic, as is the scenario in which there is a high reuse of plans.

This is an advanced server setting; you can change it by using the command `sp_configure 'optimize for ad hoc workloads'`. You can also change it in SQL Server Management Studio by using the Optimize For Ad Hoc Workloads setting, in the Server Properties section of the Advanced node.

Carving up CPU cores using an affinity mask

It is possible to assign certain logical processors to SQL Server. This might be necessary on systems that are used for instance stacking (more than one SQL Server instance installed on the same OS) or when workloads are shared between SQL Server and other software. Virtual machines (VMs) are probably a better way of allocating these resources, but there might be legitimate or legacy reasons.

CHAPTER 3

Suppose that you have a dual-socket NUMA server, with both CPUs populated by 16-core processors. Excluding simultaneous multithreading (SMT), this is a total of 32 cores, and SQL Server Standard edition is limited to 24 cores, or four sockets, whichever is lower.

When it starts, SQL Server will allocate all 16 cores from the first NUMA node, and eight from the second NUMA node. It will write an entry to the ERRORLOG stating this case, and that's where it ends. Unless you know about the core limit, you will be stuck with unbalanced CPU core and memory access, resulting in unpredictable performance.

One way to solve this without using a VM, is to limit 12 cores from each CPU to SQL Server, using an *affinity mask* (see Figure 3-5). This way, the cores are allocated evenly and combined with a reasonable MAXDOP setting of 8, foreign memory access is not a concern.

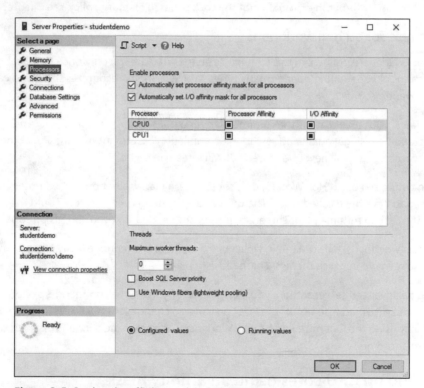

Figure 3-5 Setting the affinity mask in SQL Server Management Studio.

By setting an affinity mask, you are instructing SQL Server to use only specific cores. The remaining unused cores are marked as offline. When SQL Server starts, it will assign a scheduler to each online core.

Inside OUT
How do I balance schedulers across processors if I limit affinity?

It is possible that an external process (i.e., outside of SQL Server) is also bound to a particular core. This can result in queries being blocked by that external process.

To avoid this unexpected behavior, you can use Trace Flag 8002, which lets SQL Server decide which core the scheduler will use to run your query.

For more information about this potential issue, you can read Klaus Aschen-brenner's article "Setting a Processor Affinity in SQL Server – the (unwanted) Side-Effects," which is available at *http://www.sqlpassion.at/archive/2017/10/02/ setting-a-processor-affinity-in-sql-server-the-unwanted-side-effects*.

CAUTION
Affinity masking is not a legitimate way to circumvent licensing limitations with SQL Server Standard edition. If you have more cores than the maximum usable by a certain edition, all logical cores on that machine must be licensed regardless.

Configuring affinity on Linux

For SQL Server on Linux, even when an instance is going to be using all of the logical processors, you should use the ALTER SERVER CONFIGURATION option to set the PROCESS AFFINITY value, which maintains efficient behavior between the Linux OS and the SQL Server Scheduler.

You can set the affinity by CPU or NUMA node, but the NUMA method is simpler.

Suppose that you have four NUMA nodes. You can use the configuration option to set the affinity to use all the NUMA nodes as follows:

```
ALTER SERVER CONFIGURATION SET PROCESS AFFINITY NUMANODE = 0 TO 3;
```

> ➤ You can read more about best practices for configuring SQL Server on Linux at *https://docs. microsoft.com/sql/linux/sql-server-linux-performance-best-practices*.

File system configuration

This section deals with the default file system on Windows Server. Any references to other file systems, including Linux file systems are noted separately.

The NT File System (NTFS) was originally created for the first version of Windows NT, bringing with it more granular security than the older File Allocation Table (FAT)–based file system as well as a journaling file system. You can configure a number of settings that deal with NTFS in some way to improve your SQL Server implementation and performance.

CHAPTER 3

Instant file initialization

As stated previously in this chapter, transaction log files need to be zeroed-out at the file-system in order for recovery to work properly. However, data files are different, and with their 8-KB page size and allocation rules, the underlying file might contain sections of unused space.

With instant file initialization, which is an Active Directory policy (Perform volume maintenance tasks), data files can be instantly resized, without zeroing-out the underlying file. This adds a major performance boost.

The trade-off is a tiny, perhaps insignificant security risk: data that was previously used in drive allocation currently dedicated to a database's data file now might not have been fully erased before use. Because you can examine the underlying bytes in data pages using built-in tools in SQL Server, individual pages of data that have not yet been overwritten inside the new alloca-tion could be visible to a malicious administrator.

> ## NOTE
> It is important to control access to SQL Server's data files and backups. When a database is in use by SQL Server, only the SQL Server service account and the local administrator have access. However, if the database is detached or backed up, there is an opportu-nity to view that deleted data on the detached file or backup file that was created with instant file initialization turned on.

Because this is a possible security risk, the Perform Volume Maintenance Tasks policy is not granted to the SQL Server service by default, and a summary of this warning is displayed during SQL Server setup.

Even so, turning on instant file initialization was a common post-installation step taken for many SQL Servers by DBAs, so this administrator-friendly option in SQL Server Setup is a welcome and recommended time-saving addition.

Without instant file initialization, you might find that the SQL Server wait type PREEMPTIVE_OS_WRITEFILEGATHER is prevalent during times of data-file growth. This wait type occurs when a file is being zero initialized; thus, it can be a sign that your SQL Server is wasting time that could skipped with the benefit of instant file initialization. Keep in mind that PREEMPTIVE_OS_WRITEFILEGATHER will also be generated by transaction log files, which cannot benefit from instant file initialization.

Note that SQL Server Setup takes a slightly different approach to granting this privilege than SQL Server administrators might take. SQL Server assigns Access Control Lists (ACLs) to auto-matically created security groups, not to the service accounts that you select on the Server Configuration Setup page. Instead of granting the privilege to the named SQL Server service account directly, SQL Server grants the privilege to the per-service security identifier (SID) for the SQL Server database service; for example, the NT SERVICE\MSSQLSERVER principal. This means that the SQL Server service will maintain the ability to use instant file initialization even if its service account changes.

If you choose not to select the Perform Volume Maintenance Tasks privilege during SQL Server setup but want to do so later, go to the Windows Start menu, and then, in the Search box, type **Local Security Policy**. Next, in the pane on the left expand Local Policies (see Figure 3-6), and then click User Rights Assignment. Find the Perform Volume Maintenance Tasks policy, and then add the SQL Server service account to the list of objects with that privilege.

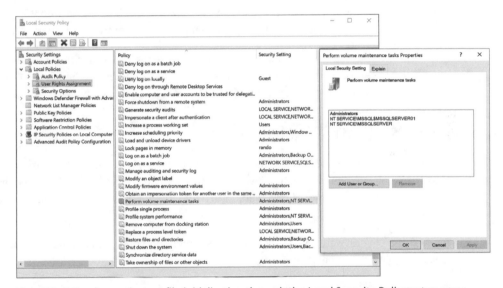

Figure 3-6 Turning on instant file initialization through the Local Security Policy setup page.

You can easily check to determine whether the SQL Server Database Engine service has been granted access to instant file initialization by using the `sys.dm_server_services` dynamic management view via the following query:

```
SELECT servicename, instant_file_initialization_enabled
FROM sys.dm_server_services
WHERE filename LIKE '%sqlservr.exe%';
```

NTFS allocation unit size

SQL Server performs best with an allocation unit size of 64 KB.

Depending on the type of storage, the default allocation unit on NTFS might be 512 bytes, 4,096 bytes (also known as Advanced Format 4K sector size), or some other multiple of 512.

Because SQL Server deals with 64-KB extents (see the section "Mixed extents and uniform extents" earlier in the chapter), it makes sense to format a data volume with an allocation unit size of 64 KB, to align the extents with the allocation units.

NOTE
We cover aligned storage in more detail in Chapter 4.

Other file systems

The 64-KB recommendation holds for SQL Server utilizing other file systems, as well:

- **Windows Server.**   The Resilient File System (ReFS) was introduced with Windows Server 2012. It has seen significant updates since then, most recently in Windows Server 2016.

- **Linux.**   SQL Server on Linux is supported on both the XFS and ext4 file systems. For ext4, the typical block size is 4 KB, though blocks can be created up to 64 KB. For XFS, the block size can range from 512 bytes to 64 KB.

Azure and the Data Platform

No book about SQL Server is complete without an overview of the Data Platform in Microsoft's cloud offering, despite the risk that it will be outdated by the time you read it. Notwithstanding the regular release cadence of new features in Azure, the fundamental concepts do not change as often.

Azure offers several ways to consider the management and querying of data in a SQL Server or SQL Server-like environment.

This section is divided into three main areas:

- **Infrastructure as a service.**   SQL Server running on an Azure Virtual Machine.

- **Platform as a service.**   Azure SQL Database and Azure SQL Data Warehouse (database as a service).

- **Hybrid cloud.**   Combines the best features of on-premises SQL Server with Azure.

Infrastructure as a service

Take what you've learned in the previous two chapters about VMs, and that's infrastructure as a service (IaaS) in a nutshell, optimized for a SQL Server environment.

As we detail in Chapter 2, a VM shares physical resources with other VMs. In the case of Azure Virtual Machines, there are some configurations and optimizations that can make your SQL Server implementation perform well, without requiring insight into the other guest VMs.

When creating a SQL Server VM in Azure, you can choose from different templates, which provide a wide range of options for different virtual hardware configurations, OS, and, of course, version and edition of SQL Server.

Azure VMs are priced according to a time-based usage model, which makes it easier to get started. You pay per minute or per hour, depending on the resources you need, so you can start small and scale upward. In many cases, if performance is not acceptable, moving to better virtual hardware is very easy and requires only a few minutes of downtime.

Azure VM performance optimization

Many of the same rules that we outlined for physical hardware and VMs apply also to those Azure VMs used for SQL Server. These include setting Power Saving settings to High Performance, configuring Max Server Memory usage correctly, spreading TempDB over several files, and so on.

Fortunately, some of these tasks have been done for you. For instance, power-saving settings are set to High Performance already, and TempDB files are configured properly when you configure a new Azure VM running SQL Server 2016 or higher.

However, Azure VMs have a limited selection for storage. You don't have the luxury of custom Direct-Attached Storage or Storage-Area Networks dedicated to your environment. Instead, you can choose from the following options:

- Standard or Premium Storage

- Unmanaged or Managed Disks

- SQL Server data files in Microsoft Azure

Inside OUT

What is Azure Blob Storage?

Coming from a database background, you think of a "blob" as a large object in binary format, which is stored using the data types `nvarchar(max)` or `varbinary(max)`.

In a similar vein, Azure Blob Storage is a service for storing unstructured text or binary data as objects (or *blobs*), accessible using HTTP or HTTPS. You can think of these blobs as files.

Virtual hard drives

Virtual hard drives (VHDs) in Azure are provided through Standard and Premium Storage offerings:

- **Standard Storage.**   Designed for low-cost, latency-insensitive workloads (*https://docs. microsoft.com/azure/storage/common/storage-standard-storage*).

- **Premium Storage.**   Backed by solid-state drives. This is designed for use by low-latency workloads such as SQL Server.

Given our previously stated guidance to use the fastest drive possible, SQL Server is going to make better use of Premium Storage, because SQL Server's main performance bottleneck is TempDB, followed closely by transaction log files, all of which are drive-bound.

Inside OUT

Can I use Standard Storage for SQL Server?

Yes, you can choose Standard Storage instead of Premium Storage drives for your SQL Server VM, but we do not recommend it unless you have a large number of Standard drives in a striped configuration.

With Premium Storage, you will pay for the entire drive, even if you use only a portion of it. With Standard Storage, you pay only for what you are using. Although this is an attractive cost-saving opportunity, the storage is not dedicated and is much slower.

Standard Storage has a maximum of 500 IOPS (60 MBps throughput), and is shared with other users, which will negatively affect SQL Server's performance.

It is possible to choose between unmanaged and managed disks:

- **Unmanaged disks.**   VHDs are managed by you, from creating the storage account and the container, to attaching these VHDs to a VM and configuring any redundancy and scalability.

- **Managed disks.**   You specify the size and type of drive you need (Premium or Standard), and Azure handles creation, management, and scalability for you.

Unmanaged disks give you more control over the drive, whereas managed disks are handled automatically, including resiliency and redundancy. Naturally, managed disks have a higher cost associated with them, but this comes with peace of mind.

As of this writing, there are several sizes to choose for Premium Storage, with more offerings being added all the time. Table 3-1 lists these offerings.

Table 3-1 Premium Storage offerings in Azure Storage

Disk type	P4	P6	P10	P20	P30	P40	P50
Size (GB)	32	64	128	512	1,024	2,048	4,095
IOPS	120	240	500	2,300	5,000	7,500	7,500
Throughput (MBps)	25	50	100	150	200	250	250

Maximum throughput can be limited by Azure VM bandwidth.

Microsoft recommends a minimum of two P30 drives for SQL Server data files. The first drive is for transaction logs, and the second is for data files and TempDB.

Disk striping options

To achieve better performance (and larger drive volumes) out of your SQL Server VM, you can combine multiple drives into various RAID configurations by using Storage Spaces on Windows-based VMs, or MDADM on Linux-based VMs. Depending on the Azure VM size, you can stripe up to 64 Premium Storage drives together in an array.

NOTE
Even though some testing is required, there is a chance that you could achieve acceptable performance by striping a large number of Standard Storage drives together.

An important consideration with RAID is the stripe (or block) size. A 64-KB block size is most appropriate for an OLTP SQL Server environment, as noted previously. However, large data warehousing systems can benefit from a 256-KB stripe size, due to the larger sequential reads from that type of workload.

➤ **To read more about the different types of RAID, see Chapter 2.**

Storage account bandwidth considerations

Azure Storage costs are dictated by three factors: bandwidth, transactions, and capacity. Bandwidth is defined as the amount of data transferred to and from the storage account.

For Azure VMs running SQL Server, if the storage account is located in the same location as the VM, there is no additional bandwidth cost.

➤ **To read more about using Azure Blob Storage with SQL Server, go to *https://docs.microsoft. com/sql/relational-databases/tutorial-use-azure-blob-storage-service-with-sql-server-2016*.**

CHAPTER 3

However, if there is any external access on the data, such as log shipping to a different location or using the AzCopy tool to synchronize data to another location (for example), there is a cost associated with that.

> ➤ **For more information about AzCopy, go to Microsoft Docs at *https://docs.microsoft.com/ azure/storage/common/storage-use-azcopy*.**

Drive caching

For SQL Server workloads on Azure VMs, it is recommended that you turn on ReadOnly caching on the Premium Storage drive when attaching it to the VM, for data files, and TempDB. This increases the IOPS and reduces latency for your environment, and it avoids the risk of data loss that might occur due to ReadWrite caching.

For drives hosting transaction logs, do not turn on caching.

> ➤ **You can read more about drive caching at *https://docs.microsoft.com/azure/ virtual-machines/windows/sql/virtual-machines-windows-sql-performance*.**

SQL Server data files in Azure

Instead of attaching a data drive to your machine running SQL Server, you can use Azure Storage to store your user database files directly, as blobs. This provides migration benefits (data movement is unnecessary), high availability (HA), snapshot backups, and cost savings with storage. Note that this feature is neither recommended nor supported for system databases.

To get this to work, you need a storage account and container on Azure Storage, a Shared Access Signature, and a SQL Server Credential for each container.

Because performance is critical, especially when accessing storage over a network, you will need to test this offering, especially for heavy workloads.

There are some limitations that might affect your decision:

- FILESTREAM data is not supported, which affects memory-optimized objects, as well. If you want to make use of FILESTREAM or memory-optimized objects, you will need to use locally attached storage.

- Only .mdf, .ndf, and .ldf extensions are supported.

- Geo-replication is not supported.

> ➤ **You can read more (including additional limitations) at *https://docs.microsoft.com/sql/ relational-databases/databases/sql-server-data-files-in-microsoft-azure*.**

Virtual machine sizing

Microsoft recommends certain types, or series, of Azure VMs for SQL Server workloads, and each of these series of VMs comes with different size options.

➤ **You can read more about performance best practices for SQL Server in Azure Virtual Machines at** *https://docs.microsoft.com/azure/virtual-machines/windows/sql/ virtual-machines-windows-sql-performance.*

It is possible to resize your VM within the same series (going larger is as simple as choosing a bigger size in the Azure portal), and in many cases, you can even move across series, as the need arises.

You can also downgrade your VM to a smaller size, to scale down after running a resource-intensive process, or if you accidentally overprovisioned your server. Provided that the smaller VM can handle any additional options you might have selected (data drives and network interfaces tend to be the deciding factor here), it is equally simple to downgrade a VM to a smaller size by choosing the VM in the Azure portal.

NOTE

Some administrators might prefer managing Azure resources using a scripting environment as opposed to the Azure portal, especially when there are tens, hundreds, or even thousands of resources. All features available in the portal are also available in PowerShell modules for Azure. Additionally, the Azure command-line interface (Azure CLI) is a cross-platform toolset that works on macOS, Linux, and Windows.

Both growing and shrinking the VM size does require downtime, but it usually takes just a few minutes at most.

To quote directly from Microsoft Docs:

"Dv2-series, D-series, G-series, are ideal for applications that demand faster CPUs, better local disk performance, or have higher memory demands. They offer a powerful combination for many enterprise-grade applications." (https://docs.microsoft.com/azure/cloud-services/ cloud-services-sizes-specs)

This makes the D-series (including Dv2 and Dv3) and G-series well suited for a SQL Server VM.

However, choosing the right series can be confusing, especially with new sizes and series coming out all the time. The ability to resize VMs makes this decision less stressful.

CHAPTER 3

NOTE

You pay separately for Premium Storage drives attached to Azure VMs. Keep this in mind when identifying the right VM for your workload.

Locating TempDB files on the VM

Many Azure VMs come with a temporary drive, which is provisioned automatically for the Windows page file and scratch storage space. The drive is not guaranteed to survive VM restarts and does not survive a VM deallocation.

A fairly common practice with Azure VMs is to place the SQL Server TempDB on this temporary drive because it uses solid-state storage and is theoretically faster than a Standard Storage drive.

However, this temporary drive is thinly provisioned. Remember in Chapter 2 how thin provisioned storage for VMs is shared among all the VMs on that host.

Placing the TempDB on this drive is risky, because it can result in high latency, especially if other guests using that underlying physical storage have done the same thing. This is also affected by the series of VM.

To keep things simple, place TempDB on its own dedicated Premium Storage drive (if the VM supports it) or at least sharing a larger Premium Storage drive with other databases. For example, a P30 drive is 1,024 MB in size, and provides 5,000 IOPS.

Platform as a service

With platform as a service (PaaS), you can focus on a particular task without having to worry about the administration and maintenance surrounding that task, which makes it a lot easier to get up and running.

You can use database as a service (DBaaS), which includes Azure SQL Database and Azure SQL Data Warehouse, to complement or replace your organization's data platform requirements. This section focuses on Azure SQL Database.

Azure SQL Database provides you with a single database (or set of databases logically grouped in an elastic pool) and the freedom not to concern yourself with resource allocation (CPU, RAM, storage, licensing, OS), installation, and configuration of that database.

You also don't need to worry about patching and upgrades at the OS or instance level, nor do you need to think about index and statistics maintenance, TempDB, backups, corruption, or redundancy. In fact, the built-in support for database recovery is excellent (including point-in-time restores), so you can even add on long-term backup retention to keep your backups for up to 10 years.

Microsoft's Data Platform is about choosing the right component to solve a particular problem, as opposed to being all things to all people.

Azure SQL Database and Azure SQL Data Warehouse are part of a larger vision, taking the strengths of the database engine and combining them with other Azure components, breaking the mold of a self-contained or standalone system. The change in mindset is necessary to appreciate it for what it offers, instead of criticizing it for its perceived shortcomings.

Differences from SQL Server

SQL Server is a complete, standalone relational database management system designed to create and manage multiple databases and the associated processes around them. It includes a great many tools and features, including a comprehensive job scheduler.

Think of Azure SQL Database, then, as an offering at the database level. Because of this, only database-specific features are available. You can create objects such as tables, views, user-defined functions, and stored procedures, as well as memory-optimized objects. You can write queries. And, you can connect an application to it.

What you can't do with Azure SQL Database is run scheduled tasks directly. Querying other databases is extremely limited. You can't restore databases from a SQL Server backup. You don't have access to a file system, so importing data is more complicated. You can't manage system databases, and in particular, you can't manage TempDB.

There is currently no support for user-defined SQL Server CLR procedures. However, the native SQL CLR functions, such as those necessary to support the `hierarchyid` and geospatial data types, are available.

On-premises environments usually use only Integrated Authentication to provide single sign-on and simplified login administration. In such environments, SQL authentication is often turned off. Turning off SQL authentication is not supported in Azure SQL Database. Instead of Integrated Authentication, there are several Azure Active Directory authentication scenarios supported. Those are discussed in more detail in Chapter 5, "Provisioning Azure SQL Database."

Azure SQL Database does not support multiple filegroups or files. By extension, several other Database Engine features that use filegroups are unavailable, including FILESTREAM and FileTable.

> ➤ You can read more about FILESTREAM and FileTable in Chapter 8.

Most important, Azure SQL databases are limited by physical size, and resource usage.

The resource limits, known as Database Transaction Units (DTUs), force us to rethink how we make the best use of the service. It is easy to spend a lot of wasted money on Azure SQL Database because it requires a certain DTU service level at certain periods during the day or week, but at other times is idle.

CHAPTER 3

It is possible to scale an Azure SQL database up and down as needed, but if this happens regularly, it makes the usage, and therefore the cost, unpredictable. Elastic pools (see the upcoming section on this) are a great way to get around this problem by averaging out DTU usage over multiple databases with elastic DTUs (eDTUs). That said, Azure SQL Database is not going to completely replace SQL Server. Some systems are not designed to be moved into this type of environment, and there's nothing wrong with that. Microsoft will continue to release a standalone SQL Server product.

On the other hand, Azure SQL Database is perfect for supporting web applications that can scale up as the user base grows. For new development, you can enjoy all the benefits of not having to maintain a database server, at a predictable cost.

Azure SQL Database service tiers

Azure SQL Database is available in four service tiers: Basic, Standard, Premium, and Premium RS. Premium RS offers the same performance profile as the Premium tier, but without HA. This is useful for replaying high-performance workloads or for development and testing using the Premium tier feature set in a preproduction environment.

Just as with choosing between SQL Server 2017 editions, selecting the right service tier is important. The Basic and Standard service tiers do not support Columnstore or memory-optimized objects. The Basic tier provides only seven days of backups versus 35 days on the higher tiers. Premium and Premium RS have a much lower I/O latency than Standard tier.

However, it is fairly easy to switch between service tiers on Azure SQL Database, especially between the different levels in each tier, and when combined with elastic pools, this gives you great flexibility and predictable usage costs.

Finally, Microsoft operates under a cloud-first strategy, meaning that features will appear in Azure SQL Database before they make it to the latest on-premises products. Given the length of time it takes for many organizations to upgrade, the benefits are even more immediate and clear.

Elastic database pools

As noted earlier, Azure SQL Database has limits on its size and resources. Like Azure VMs, Azure SQL Database is pay-per-usage. Depending on what you need, you can spend a lot or a little on your databases.

Elastic pools increase the scalability and efficiency of your Azure SQL Database deployment by providing the ability for several databases in a pool to share DTUs. In that case, the combined DTUs are referred to as elastic DTUs (eDTUs).

Without using elastic pools, each database might be provisioned with enough DTUs to handle its peak load. This can be inefficient. By grouping databases with different peak load times in an elastic pool, the Azure fabric will automatically balance the DTUs assigned to each database depending on their load, as depicted in Figure 3-7. You can set limits to ensure that a single database does not starve the other databases in the pool of resources.

Figure 3-7 An elastic database pool showing databases sharing their DTUs.

The best use case for elastic pools is one in which databases in the pool have low average DTU utilization, with spikes that occur from time to time. This might be due to a reporting-type query that runs once a day, or a help desk system that can experience a lot of traffic at certain times of the day, for instance.

The elastic pool evens out these spikes over the full billing period, giving you a more predictable cost for an unpredictable workload across multiple databases.

Multitenant architecture   Azure SQL databases in an elastic database pool gives you the ability to provision new databases for your customer base with predictable growth and associated costs. Management of these databases is much easier in this environment because the administrative burden is removed. Performance is also predictable because the pool is based on the combined eDTUs.

However, not all scenarios will benefit from the use of elastic pools. The most beneficial are those in which databases experience their peak load at separate times. You would need to monitor the usage patterns of each customer and plan which elastic database pool they work best in, accordingly.

Database consolidation   In an on-premises environment, database consolidation means finding a powerful enough server to handle the workload of many databases, each with its own workload pattern. Similarly, with elastic database pools, the number of databases is limited by the pool's eDTU size. For example, the current maximum pool size is 4,000 eDTUs in a Premium pool. This means that you can operate up to 160 databases (at 25 DTUs each) in that single pool, sharing their resources.

CHAPTER 3

Combined with autoscale settings, depending on DTU boundaries, consolidation makes a lot of sense for an organization with many small databases, just as it does with an on-premises SQL Server instance.

Elastic database query

Perhaps the most surprising limitation in Azure SQL Database is that support for cross-database queries is very limited. This means that it is not possible to write a query that uses a three-part or four-part object name to reference a database object in another database or on another server. Consequently, semantic search is not available.

As a workaround, you can place the databases that you want to combine in a logical group inside an elastic database pool. This makes it possible for you to perform cross-database queries on them as well as to connect to external data in the form of Microsoft Excel, Microsoft Power BI, and so on.

There are some limitations. As of this writing, elastic database query is still in preview. On the Standard tier, the first query can take several minutes to run because the functionality to run the query needs to be loaded first. Additionally, access is currently read-only for external data.

Performance does improve on the higher tiers as costs increase, but this is not meant to replicate home-grown systems that have many databases tightly bound together.

Elastic database jobs

SQL Server has the ability to run the same query against multiple databases from a list of registered servers, or Central Management Server. In a similar manner, the elastic database jobs feature gives you the ability to run a script written in Transact-SQL (T-SQL) against databases in an elastic database pool.

Because this makes use of other Azure services, including Azure Cloud Service and Azure Service Bus, there is an additional cost associated with elastic database jobs because of the way the platform is designed.

For example, in a software as a service (SaaS) scenario in which each customer receives its own database instance, the schemas of all databases must be kept synchronized. An elastic pool job can target the databases that are part of a custom group of databases. A job is inserted into a control database (a standalone Azure SQL database). The *controller* (one of two worker roles created with the Cloud Service) then reads the job, and a second worker role runs that job task against each database in the pool using an *activator* (making use of the Azure Service Bus component). Finally, the results are stored in the control database, and diagnostics are saved to an Azure Storage container.

➤ You can read about Elastic Scale in Chapter 5, and find out more about elastic database jobs, such as their architecture and setup, at *https://docs.microsoft.com/azure/sql-database/ sql-database-elastic-jobs-overview*.

Sharding databases with Split-Merge

Azure SQL Database is designed for SaaS scenarios because you can start off small and grow your system as your customer base grows. This introduces a number of interesting challenges, including what happens when a database reaches its maximum DTU limit and size, for example.

Sharding is a technique by which data is partitioned horizontally across multiple nodes, either to improve performance or the resiliency of an application. In the context of Azure SQL Database, sharding refers to distributing data across more than one database when it grows too large. (If this sounds like table partitioning, you're mostly right.)

It is all very well to add more databases (shards) to support your application, but how do you distribute your data evenly across those new databases?

The Split-Merge tool can move data from constrained databases to new ones while maintaining data integrity. It runs as an Azure web service, which means there is an associated cost. The tool uses *shard map management* to decide what data segments (*shardlets*) go into which database (*shard*) using a metadata store (an additional standalone Azure SQL Database) and is completely customizable.

➤ To read about how this process works in detail, go to *https://docs.microsoft.com/azure/ sql-database/sql-database-elastic-scale-overview-split-and-merge*.

Hybrid cloud with Azure

Azure SQL Database is not designed to completely replace SQL Server. Many thousands of organizations all over the world are quite happy with the security, performance, and low latency offered by hosting their environment on-premises but would like to make use of certain components in the cloud.

The most common implementation of a hybrid cloud is with Azure Active Directory (Azure AD). Instead of having to manage user accounts in two places (on-premises and in Azure, for Microsoft Office 365, for example), you can synchronize your Active Directory Domain Service with Azure AD, and manage it all in one place.

Mixing your on-premises and Azure environments, in whichever way you do it, falls under the definition of a hybrid cloud, and Microsoft has some interesting ways of helping you achieve this, especially around the data platform and SQL Server.

CHAPTER 3

Keeping cold data online and queryable by using Stretch Database

In larger organizations, it can be expensive to maintain historic (cold) data in a SQL Server database, when you consider not only the storage, but also the associated maintenance and administration costs. Additionally, data retention laws require organizations to store data for several years, which can be cumbersome.

Stretch Database is designed to balance the needs of keeping cold data online, by reducing the cost of storing and managing that data locally and reducing RTO and RPO mandated in a Service-Level Agreement (SLA).

Because historic data can account for a large percentage of an existing database, removing cold data from an on-premises database can significantly reduce the storage, time, and other resources for necessary tasks like backups, index and statistics maintenance, data consistency checks, and so on, while still making it available to be queried.

Stretch Database is activated at the instance level, but you move rows at a database and table level. If your cold data is already stored in a separate archive table, you can move the entire table. If your cold data is in a large table that also contains active, or hot data, you can set up a filter to move only the older rows.

No application changes are needed, but there are some considerable limitations to using Stretch Database:

- Constraints in the migrated data are not enforced for uniqueness (including primary key and unique constraints), and you cannot move tables containing foreign keys and check constraints.

- You cannot perform any data modification on migrated data (updates and deletes), and you cannot insert rows directly (they must be moved in by the Stretch Database functionality).

- You cannot perform data modification on the data that is eligible for migration.

- You cannot create indexes on views that refer to Stretch-configured tables, and you cannot move tables that are used in existing indexed views.

- Filters on indexes are not propagated on migrated data, which can cause issues with unique filtered indexes.

There are also limits to the type of data and indexes that can participate in a Stretch Database:

- `text`, `ntext`, and `image` data types are not permitted.

- `timestamp` (`rowversion`), `xml`, and `sql_variant` types are not permitted.

- CLR (Common Language Runtime, or .NET) data types are not permitted (including `geography`, `geometry`, and `hierarchyid`).

- Computed columns are not permitted.

- Full-text, XML, and spatial indexes are not permitted.

Finally, the costs for Stretch Database are based on both storage and compute models. This means that you will pay for storage even if you never query the data. If you query the data, you will also pay for the compute costs (priced according to a Database Stretch Unit, or DSU) as well as any data transfer.

These limitations might exist for good reasons, but those reasons could be enough cause to consider alternatives. However, for ease of use, Stretch Database works as advertised.

Automated backups with SQL Server Managed Backups

With SQL Server on Azure VMs, you can automate SQL Server native backups that write directly to Azure Blob Storage. (This works with an on-premises version of SQL Server, as well, but latency can be an issue.)

By default, the schedule depends on the transaction workload, so a server that is idle will have fewer transaction log backups than a busy server. This reduces the total number of backup files required to restore a SQL Server database in a disaster recovery (DR) scenario.

You can also use advanced options to define a schedule. However, you must set this up before turning on Managed Backups to avoid unwanted backup operations. Additionally, the retention period is customizable, with the maximum being 30 days.

You can configure these backups at the instance or database level, providing much needed flexibility for smaller database environments that would not ordinarily have a full-time database administrator on hand.

You can fully encrypt backups through SQL Server backup encryption, and Azure Blob Storage is encrypted by default (for data at rest).

> ➤ **You can read more about encryption in Chapter 7.**

There is an associated cost with the Azure Storage container required to store these database backups, but when the retention period is reached, older files will be cleared out, keeping the costs consistent. If you were building your own custom backup solution, you would incur similar costs anyway, and there is a good chance the managed backup storage costs will be lower.

> ➤ To read more about SQL Server Managed Backup to Microsoft Azure, go to *https://docs.microsoft.com/sql/relational-databases/backup-restore/ sql-server-managed-backup-to-microsoft-azure*.

Azure Stack

Microsoft recently announced its version of a private cloud, in which you can install certain Azure services on-premises, on Microsoft-approved hardware. This brings the power of Azure to your own datacenter, for faster development.

After you have developed the solutions that best suit your organization, you can deploy your applications and solutions to the Azure region that makes the most sense, or just keep them on-premises, hosted on Azure Stack.

You can expose Azure SQL databases as a service by using the SQL Server resource provider. This gives your users the ability to create databases without having to provision a VM every time. Think of it as an on-premises version of Azure SQL Database.

Keep in mind that certain features like elastic pools, and scaling databases, are not available at this time.

> ➤ You can read more about Azure SQL databases on Azure Stack at *https://docs.microsoft.com/ azure/azure-stack/azure-stack-sql-resource-provider-deploy*.

Private networking between on-premises and Azure

When creating an environment in the Azure cloud, you begin with an Azure Virtual Network (VNet). This logically groups your services (including Azure VMs) together into a virtual network or networks, depending on your requirements. This is free to set up, and you can connect to it over the public internet.

Many organizations want to ensure a secure channel between their environments, be it between Azure VNets, or between their on-premises network and Azure. You can achieve this by way of a Virtual Private Network (VPN).

A VPN encrypts traffic over any network (including the internet), through a tunnel it creates. All traffic that travels through that tunnel is secure, which means that no bad actors will be able to monitor the traffic. However, there is a performance overhead with encrypting that traffic, which makes the connection slightly slower.

There are two main ways that Azure implements connections between your on-premises environment and Azure itself. One of these is through a traditional VPN service over the internet (site-to-site), and the other is through a dedicated connection that does not use the public internet (Azure ExpressRoute).

Site-to-site VPN   There are two different types of problems that you need to deal with when connecting systems to an Azure VNet: connecting two Azure VNets together, and connecting an external network to an Azure VNet.

To connect two Azure VNets together in the same region, you can create a peering network—in other words, no part of the VNet goes out to the internet, which is priced (very reasonably) per gigabyte transferred.

If you want a VPN gateway, instead, which creates a connection between your on-premises network and an Azure VNet, those are priced according to the maximum bandwidth you would require (100 Mbps, 500 Mbps, 1 Gbps, and 1.25 Gbps), and charged at an hourly rate (which, depending on what you need, is also reasonably priced).

Azure ExpressRoute   If those speeds are not satisfactory, and you want to connect your on-premises network to your Azure VNet, you can use ExpressRoute.

With its low latency, ExpressRoute expands your existing network to the virtually limitless services available in Azure, depending on your budget, of course.

According to Microsoft Docs:

ExpressRoute is "...*excellent for scenarios like periodic data migration, replication for business continuity, disaster recovery, and other high-availability strategies.*" (*https://azure.microsoft.com/services/expressroute*)

This type of bandwidth gives you the flexibility of moving entire VMs from on-premises to Azure, for test environments and migrations. Your customers can use Azure web services that take data from your on-premises environment without ever going over the public internet.

You can also use it for creating a DR site, using SQL Server Log Shipping. Perhaps you want to extend your availability group to the cloud, which you can do by using a distributed availability group (see Chapter 2). Using ExpressRoute, you can treat Azure as an extension of your own network, as illustrated in Figure 3-8.

CHAPTER 3

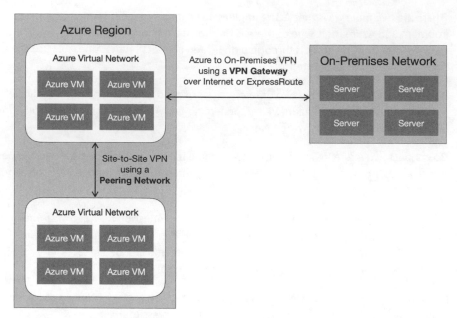

Figure 3-8 Azure virtual networks can connect to an on-premises network in various ways.

Inside OUT

How fast can data be transferred over a VPN connection?

Network speed is measured in bits per second (bps). Because there are eight bits in a byte, a single byte would take eight seconds to be transmitted at 1 bps, at the theoretical maximum throughput (perfect network conditions).

For speeds in the gigabit-per-second (Gbps) range, it will take at least eight seconds to transfer 1 GB at a speed of 1 Gbps. It will take slightly longer due to latency and other overheads, like encryption.

Additionally, transferring data over large distances incurs latency. A network packet will take approximately 65 milliseconds to move across the continental United States and back again. You must consider both network speed *and* latency when planning migrations, as well as DR and HA scenarios.

Provisioning databases

In this chapter, we review the process of installing and configuring a Microsoft SQL Server instance as well as the creation or migration of databases. We pay special attention to new features introduced in SQL Server 2017 and even some added since SQL Server 2016 Service Pack 1, including those features that have been expanded for the first time from the Enterprise edition to the Standard edition of SQL Server. We review some basic checklists for you to verify every time and, when necessary, direct you to where you can find more details on critical steps elsewhere in this book as well as other sources of information.

What to do before installing SQL Server

Before you run the SQL Server installer, there are a number of factors and settings that you should consider, some of which you cannot easily change after installation. Pay special attention to sections in this chapter regarding server volume alignment (whether this is a physical or virtual server, or whether the volumes are physical drives or Storage-Area Network–based), version and edition choices, and new features of the SQL Server 2017 installer.

CAUTION

We recommended that you do not install SQL Server on the same server as a domain controller. In some scenarios, it is not supported and can even cause Setup to fail.

Deciding on volume usage

When you're configuring a Microsoft Windows Server, before starting the SQL Server installer, consider the volumes. Although you can move user and system database data and log files to other locations after installation, it's best to plan your volumes prior to installation.

NOTE

The examples in this chapter assume that your Windows operating system installation is on the C volume of your server.

One of the basic guiding principles for a SQL Server installation is that anywhere you see "C:\", change it to another volume. This helps minimize SQL Server's footprint on the operating system (OS) volume, especially if you install multiple SQL Server instances, which can have potential disaster recovery implications in terms of volume-level backup and restores.

NOTE

For Microsoft Azure SQL Database virtual machines (VMs), do not set the installation directories for any settings on the D:\ "Temporary Storage" volume. This folder is wiped upon server restart! The only exception is that the TempDB data files can exist on the D drive if certain other considerations are taken. For more about this, see Chapter 3.

If this is the first SQL Server instance you are installing on a server, you will have the opportunity to change the location of shared features files, the data root directory for the instance (which contains the system databases), default database locations for user database files, and their backups. If this is not the first SQL Server 2017 instance installation on this server, the shared features directory locations (for Program Files and Program Files x86) will already be set for you, and you cannot change it.

Inside OUT

What if I am tight on space on the C drive when installing SQL Server?

There are some easy ways and some tricky ways to minimize the footprint of a SQL Server installation on the OS volume of your server (typically the C drive, as it is for this example). In general, SQL Server Setup and cumulative updates will delete temporary files involved in their installation, but not log files or configuration files, which should have minimal footprint. Outside of log files, we recommend that you do not delete any files installed by SQL Server Setup or cumulative updates. Instead, let's take a look at some proactive steps to move these files off of the C volume.

Some parts of SQL Setup will install on the OS volume (typically, and in this and future examples, the Windows C volume). These files, which are staging areas for SQL Server Setup, are created on the OS volume in a C:\Program Files\Microsoft SQL Server\140\ Setup Bootstrap\ subfolder structure, where 140 is specific to the internal version number (14.0) of SQL 2017. This folder is used for future cumulative updates or feature changes.

If you're extremely tight on space before installing SQL Server, you will also find that the root binaries installation directory will be, by default, C:\Program Files\ Microsoft SQL Server\. When you're using the SQL Server Setup user interface, there is no option to change this. You will, however, find this installation directory folder path listed as the INSTANCEDIR parameter in the config file that is generated by SQL Server Setup. We talk more about how to use the config file to install SQL Server in the section "Automating SQL Server Setup by using configuration files" later in the chapter.

You should place as much of the installation as possible on other volumes. Keep in mind that a full-featured installation of SQL Server 2017 can consume more than 7 GB. You will want to move some of those binaries for feature installations to other folders.

The following sample scenario is a good starting point (the volume letters don't matter):

- **Volume C.**   OS only

- **Volume E.**   SQL Server installation files, SQL Server data files

- **Volume F.**   SQL Server log files

- **Volume G.**   SQL Server TempDB data and log files (we look at TempDB data files in more detail later in the chapter)

- **Volume H.**   SQL Server backups

Where do you go from here? Here are some avenues that you might take with respect to volumes:

- Use additional volumes for your largest data files (larger than 2 TB) for storage manageability

- Use an additional volume for your most active databases and their log files

- Use an additional volume for large amounts of FILESTREAM data

- Use an additional volume for large replicated database snapshot files

> ## Inside OUT
>
> ### *Why separate files onto different volumes?*
>
> There are reasons to separate your SQL Server files onto various volumes, and not all of them are related to performance. You should separate your files onto different volumes even if you exclusively use a Storage-Area Network (SAN).
>
> We know that more discrete Input/Output (I/O) on a physical server with dedicated drives means better performance. But even in a SAN, separating files onto different volumes is also done for stability. If a volume fills and has no available space, files cannot be allocated additional space. On volume C, 0 bytes free could mean Windows Server stability issues at worst, user profile and remote desktop problems at least, and possible impact to other applications.
>
> In the aforementioned scenario, if the E or F volumes fill up because of unmonitored SQL Server file growth over time, the problems presented would be limited to SQL Server and, likely, only to the database(s) whose data or log files that have filled.

Important SQL Server volume settings

There are some settings that you need to consider for volumes that will host SQL Server data and log files, and this guidance applies specifically to these volumes (for other volumes—for example, those that contain the OS, application files, or backup files—the default Windows settings are acceptable unless otherwise specified):

- When adding these volumes to Windows, there are three important volume configuration settings that you should check for yourself or discuss with your storage administrator. When creating new drives, opt for GUID Partition Table (GPT) over Master Boot Record (MBR) drive types for new SQL Server installations. GPT is a newer drive partitioning scheme than MBR, and GPT drives support files larger than 2 TB, whereas the older MBR drive type is capped at 2 TB.

- The appropriate file unit allocation size for SQL Server volumes is 64 KB, with few exceptions. Setting this to 64 KB for each volume can have a significant impact on storage efficiency and performance. The Windows default is 4 KB, which is not optimal.

  To check the file unit allocation size for an NT File System (NTFS) volume, run the following from the Administrator: Command Prompt, repeating for each volume:

  ```
  Fsutil fsinfo ntfsinfo d:
  Fsutil fsinfo ntfsinfo e:
  ...
  ```

The file unit allocation size is returned with the Bytes Per Cluster; thus 64 KB would be displayed as 65,536 (bytes).

Correcting the file unit allocation size requires formatting the drive, so it is important to check this setting prior to installation.

If you notice this on an existing SQL Server instance, your likely resolution steps are to create a new volume with the proper file unit allocation size and then move files to the new volume during an outage. Do *not* format or re-create the partition on volumes with existing data: you will lose the data.

Note that new Azure VM drives follow the Windows default of 4 KB; thus, you must reformat them to 64 KB.

- There is a hardware-level concept related to file unit allocation size called "disk starting offset" that deals with how Windows, storage, disk controllers, and cache segments align their boundaries. Aligning disk starting offset was far more important prior to Windows Server 2008. Since then, the default partition offset of 1,024 KB has been sufficient to align with the underlying disk's stripe unit size, which is a vendor-determined value. This should be verified in consultation with the drive vendor's information.

  To access the disk starting offset information, run the following from the Administrator: Command Prompt:

  ```
  wmic partition get BlockSize, StartingOffset, Name, Index
  ```

  A 1024 KB starting offset is a Windows default; this would be displayed as 1048576 (bytes) for Disk #0 Partition #0.

  Similar to the file unit allocation size, the only way to change a disk partition's starting offset is destructive—you must re-create the partition and reformat the volume.

SQL Server editions

NOTE

This book is not intended to be a reference for licensing or sales-related documentation; rather, editions are a key piece of knowledge for SQL administrators to know.

Following are brief descriptions for all of the editions in the SQL Server family, including past editions that you might recognize. It's important to use the appropriate licenses for SQL Server even in preproduction systems.

- **Enterprise edition.**   Appropriate for production environments. Not appropriate for preproduction environments such as User Acceptance Testing (UAT), Quality Assurance (QA), testing, development, and sandbox. For these environments, instead use the free Developer edition.

- **Developer edition.**   Appropriate for all preproduction environments. Not allowed for production environments. This edition supports the same features and capacity as Enterprise edition and is free.

- **Standard edition.**   Appropriate for production environments. Lacks the scale and compliance features of Enterprise edition that might be required in some regulatory environments. Limited to the lesser of 4 sockets or 24 cores and also 128 GB of buffer pool memory, whereas Enterprise edition is limited only by the OS for compute and memory.

NOTE

In case you missed it, in Service Pack 1 of SQL Server 2016, a large number of features in Enterprise edition features were moved "down" into Standard, Web, and Express editions, including database snapshots, Columnstore indexes (limited), table partitioning, data compression, memory-optimized OLTP, PolyBase, SQL Audit, and the new Always Encrypted feature. Standard and Web edition also gained the ability to use the Change Data Capture (CDC) feature.

- **Web edition.**   Appropriate for production environments, but limited to low-cost server environments for web applications.

- **Express edition.**   Not appropriate for most production environments or preproduction environments. Appropriate only for environments in which data size is small, is not expected to grow, and can be backed up with external tools or scripts (because Express edition has no SQL Server Agent to back up its own databases). The free Express edition is ideal for proof-of-concepts, lightweight, or student applications. It lacks some critical features and is severely limited on compute (lesser of 1 socket or 4 cores), available buffer pool memory (1,410 MB), and individual database size (10 GB cap).

- **Express with Advanced Services.**   Similar to Express edition in all caveats and limitations. This edition includes some features related to data tools, R integration, full-text search, and distributed replay that are not in Express edition.

- **Business Intelligence edition.**   This edition was a part of the SQL Server 2012 and SQL Server 2014 products but was removed in SQL Server 2016.

- **Datacenter edition.**   This edition was part of SQL Server until SQL 2008 R2 and has not been a part of the SQL Server product since SQL Server 2012.

NOTE

When you run the SQL Server 2017 installer, you are prompted to install a number of features outside of the core database features. Installing SQL Server features on multiple Windows servers requires multiple licenses, even if you intend to install each SQL Server instance's features only once.

There is an exception to this rule, and that is if you have licensed all physical cores a virtual host server with SQL Server Enterprise and purchased Software Assurance. Then, you can install any number or combination of SQL Server instances and their standalone features on virtual guests.

Changing SQL Server editions and versions

Upgrading editions in-place is supported by a feature of the SQL Server 2017 installer. You can upgrade in the following order: Express, Web, Standard, Enterprise. You also can upgrade Developer edition to Enterprise, Standard, or Web edition in SQL Server 2017.

It is important to note that you cannot downgrade a SQL Server version or licensed edition. This type of change requires a fresh installation and migration. For example, you cannot downgrade in-place from SQL Server 2017 Enterprise edition to Standard edition.

Upgrading versions in-place is supported but not recommended, if at all possible. Instead, we strongly recommend that you perform a fresh installation of the newer version and then move from old to new instances. This method offers major advantages in terms of duration of outage, rollback capability, and robust testing prior to migration. And, by using DNS aliases or SQL aliases, you can ease the transition for dependent application and connections.

Although in-place upgrades to SQL Server 2017 are not recommended, they are supported from as early as SQL Server 2008 on Windows Server 2012, assuming that the earlier versions are not 32-bit installations. Beginning with SQL Server 2016, SQL Server is available only for 64-bit platforms. SQL Server 2017 requires Windows Server 2012 or later.

You cannot perform an in-place upgrade from SQL Server 2005 to SQL Server 2017; however, you can attach or restore its databases to SQL Server 2017, though they will be upgraded to compatibility level 100, which is the version level for SQL 2008.

CHAPTER 4

Installing a new instance

In this section, we discuss how to begin a new SQL Server 2017 instance installation, upgrade an existing installation, or add features to an existing instance.

It's important to note that even though you can change *almost* all of the decisions you make in SQL Server Setup after installation, those changes potentially require an outage or a server restart. Making the proper decisions at installation time is the best way to ensure the least administrative effort. Some security and service account decisions should be changed only via the SQL Server Configuration Manager application, not through the Services console (services. msc). This guidance will be repeated elsewhere for emphasis.

We begin by going through the typical interactive installation. Later in this chapter, we go over some of the command-line installation methods that you can use to automate the installation of a SQL Server instance.

Planning for multiple SQL Server instances

You can install as many as 50 SQL Server instances on a Windows Server; however, we do not recommend this. In a Windows failover cluster, the number of SQL Server instances is reduced by half if you're using shared cluster drives.

Only one of the SQL Server instances on a server can be the default instance. All, or all but one, of the SQL Server instances on a SQL Server will be named instances. The default instance is addressable by the name of the server alone, whereas named instances require an instance name. The SQL Browser service then is required to handle traffic between multiple instances on the SQL Server.

➤ **For more information about the SQL Server browser, go to Chapter 7.**

For example, you can reach the default instance of a SQL Server by connecting to *servername*. All named instances would have a unique instance name, such as *servername/ instancename*.

In application connection strings, *servername/instancename* should be provided as the Server or Data Source parameter.

Installing a SQL Server instance

The instructions in this chapter are the same for the first installation or any subsequent installations, whether for the default or any named instances of SQL Server 2017. As opposed to an exhaustive step-by-step instruction list for installations, we've opted to cover the important decision points and the information you need, plus new features introduced in SQL Server 2016 and 2017.

Inside OUT

What if I have a new Azure VM?

You do not need to install SQL Server on new Azure VMs, because provisioning new Windows Servers with SQL Server are easily available in the Azure Marketplace.

There are two types of SQL Server licensing agreements for Azure VMs:

- SQL Server VM images in the Azure Marketplace contain the SQL Server licensing costs as an all-in-one package. The SQL Server license is included in the per-minute pricing of the VM, is billed regularly along with other Azure assets, and does not need to be purchased separately.

- If you'd like to bring your existing Enterprise licensing agreement, there are three options:

    - Bring-your-own-license (BYOL) VM images available for you to provision using the same process and then later associate your existing Enterprise license agreements. The image names you're looking for here are pre-fixed with BYOL.

    - Manually upload an .iso to the VM and install SQL Server 2017 as you would on any other Windows Server.

    - Upload an image of an on-premises VM to provision the new Azure VM.

It is important for you to keep in mind that you cannot change from the built-in licensing model to the BYOL licensing model after the VM has been provisioned. You need to make this decision prior to creating your Azure VM.

Inside the SQL Server Installation Center

While logged in as a local Windows administrator, begin by mounting the installation .iso to the Windows server. These days, this rarely involves inserting a physical disc or USB flash drive; although you can use them if necessary. Unpacking the contents of the .iso file to a physical file folder over the network would also provide for a faster SQL Setup experience.

You should not run Setup with the installation media mounted over a remote network connection, via a shared remote desktop drive, or any other high-latency connection. It would be faster to copy the files locally before running Setup.

Start Setup.exe on the SQL Server Setup media, running the program as an administrator. If AutoPlay is not turned off (it usually is), Setup.exe will start when you first mount the media or double-click to open the .iso. Instead, as a best practice, right-click Setup.exe and then, on the shortcut menu that appears, click Run As Administrator.

We'll review here a few items (not all) in the SQL Server Installation Center worth noting before you begin an installation.

In the tab pane on the left, click Planning to open a long list of links to Microsoft documentation websites. Most helpful here might be a standalone version of the System Configuration Checker, which you run during SQL Server Setup later, but it could save you a few steps if you review it now. A link to download the Upgrade Advisor (now renamed to the Data Migration Assistant) is also present, a helpful Microsoft-provided tool when upgrading from prior versions of SQL Server.

On the Maintenance page, you will find the following:

- A link to launch the relatively painless Edition Upgrade Wizard. This is for changing your existing installation's edition, not its version (SQL 2012, 2014, 2016, 2017) or platform (x86 versus 64-bit). You can upgrade from "lower" editions to higher editions, but keep in mind that downgrading editions is not possible and would require that you install a new SQL Server. For example, you cannot downgrade from Enterprise to Standard edition without a new installation. For complete details on Edition upgrade paths, visit *https://docs.microsoft.com/sql/database-engine/install-windows/ supported-version-and-edition-upgrades#includesscurrentincludessscurrent-m dmd-edition-upgrade*

- The Repair feature is not a commonly used feature. It's use is necessitated by a SQL Server with a corrupted Windows installation. You might also need to repair an instance of SQL Server when the executables, .dll files, or registry entries have become corrupted before repair. A failed SQL Server in-place upgrade or cumulative update installation might also require a Repair, which could be better than starting from scratch.

- Whereas adding a node to an existing SQL Server failover cluster is an option in the Installation menu, removing a node from an existing SQL Server failover cluster is an option in the Maintenance menu.

- A link to the Update Center for SQL Server (Technet Article ff803383) provides information on the latest cumulative updates for each version of SQL Server.

- On the Tools menu, there is a link to the Microsoft Assessment and Planning (MAP) Toolkit for SQL Server, which is a free download that can be invaluable when you're performing an inventory of your SQL Server presence in a network. It's also capable of searching for SQL Server instances by a variety of methods and generating CIO-level reports.

- On the Advanced menu, there is a link to perform an installation based on a configuration file, which we discuss later in this chapter in the section "Automating SQL Server Setup by using configuration files."

There are also links to wizards for advanced failover cluster installations.

➤ We discuss Failover Cluster Instances (FCIs) in Chapter 12.

Installing SQL Server

In the SQL Server Installation Center, in the pane on the left side, click Installation. Although what follows in this chapter is not a step-by-step walk-through, we'll cover key new features and decision points.

> ## Inside OUT
>
> *Where are SQL Server Management Studio, SQL Server Data Tools, and SQL Server Reporting Services?*
>
> SQL Server Management Studio, SQL Server Data Tools (for Visual Studio 2015 and higher), and SQL Server Reporting Services are no longer installed with SQL Server's traditional setup media. These products are now updated regularly (monthly usually) and available for download.
>
> As of SQL Server 2016, Management Tools is no longer an option on the Feature Selection page. Although both tools are listed in the SQL Server Installation Center, they are simply links to free downloads.
>
> Remember to keep up-to-date versions of SQL Server Management Studio and SQL Server Data Tools on administrator workstations and laptops. Communicate with your team so that everyone is using the same releases of these free tools for on-premises SQL Server as well as Azure SQL Database administration.
>
> The standalone version of SQL Server Reporting Services is now a 90-MB download that launches its own installer, but it still needs a SQL Server Database Engine instance as part of the license and to host the two Report Server databases. Note that this isn't a licensing change and that SQL Server Reporting Services isn't free, you will need to provide a license key or choose a nonproduction edition to install (Evaluation, Developer, or Express).

Installing options and features

In this section, we discuss the installation details of other features of SQL Server, including new options in Setup that were not available in previous versions.

Data analytics and artificial intelligence features

The Feature Selection page has a pair of new options in SQL Server 2017, both greatly expanding SQL Server's footprint into the big data field. Let's take a look at each option.

PolyBase Query Service For External Data   The PolyBase Query Engine makes it possible to query Hadoop nonrelational data or Azure Blob Storage files by using the same Transact-SQL (T-SQL) language with which SQL Server developers are already familiar. You may have only one SQL Server Instance with the PolyBase feature installed on a Windows Server.

As strange as this sounds, this functionality of SQL Server requires that you install the Oracle SE Java Runtime Environment (JRE). If while on the Feature Rules page you encounter the error "Oracle JRE 7 Update 51 (64-bit) or higher is required," you can ignore the message and, in the background, proceed with the installation of Oracle JRE 7. You do not need to restart Windows or SQL Server Setup after a successful installation of the Oracle JRE, and on the Feature Rules page, the Re-Run button should clear that error so that you can proceed with SQL Server Setup.

This is a manual installation that is not contained in the Setup components or automatically downloaded by the Smart Setup (more on that later). To download the latest version, visit the Oracle JRE site at *http://www.oracle.com/technetwork/java/javase/downloads/index.html*.

Choose the JRE download because the Server JRE does not include an installer for Windows Platforms. Choose the Windows x64 Offline installer, which is a self-installing .exe file, and then complete the installation.

You must configure at least six individual ports in a range (with TCP 16450 through 16460 the default) for the PolyBase Engine. You can move forward with the defaults if these ranges are unclaimed in your network.

Later, on the Server Configuration page, you will choose a service account for the SQL Server PolyBase Engine service and the SQL Server PolyBase Data Movement service. We recommend a dedicated Windows Authenticated service account, with a special note that if it is a part of a scale-out of PolyBase instances, all of the instances should use the same service account.

Finally, after SQL Server Setup is complete, if you installed both the Database Engine and PolyBase at the same time, the two PolyBase services will be in the "Change Pending" state. They are unable to connect because, by default, TCP is not an activated protocol for the SQL Server instance. This is a common post-installation to-do item for other reasons, so turning on the TCP protocol for the new SQL Server instance, followed by restarting the SQL Server service, is required.

After the new SQL Server installation is complete, review the "Hadoop Connectivity" setting by using `sp_configure`. The setting ranges from 0 to 7, with options 1 through 6 dealing mostly with older versions of Hortonworks Data Platform. Setting 7 allows for the connectivity with recent Hortonworks HDP versions as well as Azure Blob storage. To change this `sp_configure` setting, you must run the RECONFIGURE step and also restart the SQL Server service, and then manually start the two SQL Server PolyBase services.

> **NOTE**
>
> **Complete information on the settings for Hadoop connectivity are available in the documentation at** *https://docs.microsoft.com/sql/database-engine/configure-windows/polybase-connectivity-configuration-transact-sql*.

Additional steps, including a firewall change, are needed to install this feature as part of a Poly-Base Scale-Out Group of multiple SQL Server instances, with one PolyBase Engine service per Windows Server.

Machine learning features   The newly named Machine Learning Services (In-Database or the standalone Machine Learning Server) feature makes it possible for developers to integrate with R language and/or Python language extensions using standard T-SQL statements. Data scientists can take advantage of this feature to build advanced analytics, data forecasting, and algorithms for machine learning. Formerly called the Revolution R engine, SQL Server 2017 installs version 9 of the Microsoft R Open Server, supported for both Windows and Linux.

This feature adds the SQL Server Launchpad service. You cannot configure the service account for the Launchpad service; it will run as a dedicated NT Service\MSSQLLaunchpad virtual account. The standalone installation of Machine Learning Services does not create the SQL Server Launchpad service and is intended for models that do not need a SQL Server.

After the new SQL Server installation is complete, you must turn on a security option to allow external scripts. This makes it possible for you to run non-T-SQL language scripts, and in the SQL Server 2017 release of this feature, R and Python are the only languages supported. (In SQL Server 2016, only R was supported, thus the name change from R Services to Machine Learning Services.) Use `sp_configure` to select the External Scripts Enabled option, reconfigure, and restart the SQL Server service.

Grant Perform Volume Maintenance Tasks feature of SQL Server Setup

On the same Server Configuration Setup page on which service accounts are set, you will see a check box labeled Grant Perform Volume Maintenance Task Privilege To The SQL Server Database Engine Service. This option was added in SQL Server 2016.

This automates what used to be a standard post-installation checklist step for SQL DBAs since Windows Server 2003. The reason to grant this permission to use instant file initialization is to speed the allocation of large database data files, which could dramatically reduce the Recovery Time Objective (RTO) capacity for disaster recovery.

This can mean the difference between hours and minutes when restoring a very large database. It also can have a positive impact when creating databases with large initial sizes, or in large autogrowth events; for example, with multiple data files in the TempDB (more on this next). It is recommended that you allow SQL Setup to turn on this setting.

➤ **For more information on instant file initialization, see Chapter 3.**

Default settings for the TempDB database

Starting with SQL Server 2016, SQL Server Setup provides a more realistic default configuration for the number and size of TempDB data files. This was a common to-do list for all post-installation checklists for DBAs since the early days of SQL Server.

The TempDB database page in SQL Server Setup provides not only the ability to specify the number and location of the TempDB's data and log files, but also their initial size and autogrowth rates. The best number of TempDB data files is almost certainly greater than one, and less than or equal to the number of logical processor cores. Adding too many TempDB data files could in fact severely degrade SQL Server performance.

➤ **For more information on the best number of TempDB data files, see Chapter 3.**

Specifying TempDB's initial size to a larger, normal operating size is important and can improve performance after a SQL Server restart when the TempDB data files are reset to their initial size. Setup accommodates an individual TempDB data file initial size up to 256 GB. For data file initial sizes larger than 1 GB, you will be warned that Setup could take a long time to complete if instant file initialization is turned on by granting the Perform Volume Maintenance Task for the SQL Server Service Account. (This should be accomplished automatically by Setup; see the previous section.)

All TempDB files autogrow at the same time, keeping file sizes the same over time. Previously only available as a server-level setting via trace flag 1117, TempDB data files have behaved in this way by default since SQL Server 2016.

Note also the new naming convention for the second TempDB data file and beyond: tempdb_mssql_*n*.ndf. A SQL Server uninstallation will automatically clean up TempDB data files with this naming convention—for this reason, we recommend that you follow this naming convention for TempDB data files.

➤ **TempDB is discussed in greater detail in Chapter 3.**

Figure 4-1 depicts a VM with four logical processors. Note that the number of files is by default set to the number of logical processors. The sizes, autogrowth settings, and data directories have been changed from their defaults, you should consider doing the same.

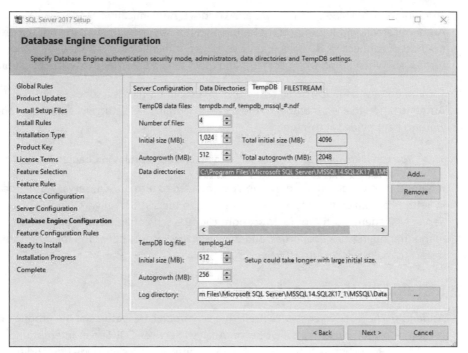

Figure 4-1 The Database Engine Configuration page in SQL Server 2017 Setup, including the TempDB tab.

Mixed Mode authentication

SQL Server supports two modes of authentication: Windows and SQL Server.

> ➤ You can read more on this topic in Chapter 7, but it is important to note this decision point here.

Ideally, all authentication is made via Windows Authentication, through types of server principals called *logins*, that reference Domain accounts in your Enterprise edition. These domain accounts are created by your existing enterprise security team, which manages password policy, password resets, password expiration, and so on.

A redundant security model for connecting to SQL Server also exists within each instance: SQL Server Authenticated logins. Logins are maintained at the SQL Server level, are subject to local policy password complexity requirements, are reset/unlocked by SQL DBAs, have their own password change policy, and so forth.

Turning on Mixed Mode (SQL Server and Windows Authentication Mode) activates SQL Server Authenticated login. It is important to note that it is not on by default and not the preferred method of connection. By default, only Windows Authentication is turned on and cannot be turned off. When possible, applications and users should use Windows Authentication.

Turning on Mixed Mode also activates the "sa" account, which is a special built-in SQL Server Authentication that is a member of the server sysadmin role. Setup will ask for a strong password to be provided at this time.

➤ **You can learn more about the "sa" account and server roles in Chapter 7.**

It is important to keep in mind that you do not need to turn on SQL Server Authentication in Setup; you can do this later on by connecting to the SQL Server via Object Explorer in SQL Server Management Studio. To do so, right-click the server name and then, on the shortcut menu that opens, click Properties, and then click the Security page. You must perform a service restart to make this change effective.

Installing other core features

Aside from the SQL Server service itself, three common core features of the product might be common to your installations. SQL Server Analysis Services, SQL Server Integration Services, and SQL Server Reporting Services are part of the license and are provided at no additional cost. If you need them, this section covers installing these features using Setup. Later in this chapter, we review the post-installation steps necessary to use them.

Installing SQL Server Analysis Services

Installing SQL Server Analysis Services requires you to make a decision at installation time regarding the mode in which it can be installed. Each instance of SQL Server Analysis Services can be in only one mode, which means that with a single license, you can run only the classic Multidimensional mode, the newer Tabular mode (introduced in SQL 2012), or the Power Pivot mode. Ask your business intelligence decision makers which platform you should use. Following are brief descriptions of each mode:

- **Multidimensional mode.**   This is the familiar SQL Server Analysis Services setup that was first introduced in SQL 2000. This is also the mode to support data mining.

- **Tabular mode.**   This is the newer SQL Server Analysis Services setup that was first introduced in SQL 2012, using the in-memory VertiPaq processing engine. For the first time in SQL Server 2017, this is the default installation mode selected on the Analysis Services Configuration page of Setup.

- **Power Pivot mode.**   This mode installs SQL Server Analysis Services in the Power Pivot for SharePoint mode.

Inside OUT

What if you choose the wrong SQL Server Analysis Services mode?

If you choose one SQL Server Analysis Services mode at installation but your business intelligence developers want another mode, the supported option is to uninstall and reinstall the SQL Server Analysis Services feature. Changing the SQL Server Analysis Services mode from Multidimensional to Tabular, or vice versa, after installation is not supported and administrators are specifically warned not to do this.

Packages developed for each mode are not supported for the other. If no databases have been deployed to the SQL Server Analysis Services server instance, changing the DeploymentMode property in the MSMDSRV.ini file should make it possible to change an existing instance, but, again, this is not a supported change. The file is located in *%Programfiles%\Microsoft SQL Server\MSAS13.TABULAR\OLAP\Config*.

Installing SQL Server Integration Services

The SQL Server Integration Services instance for SQL Server 2017 is installed once per server per version, not once per instance, like other features. However, starting in SQL Server 2017, a new Integration Services Scale Out Configuration is available. We discuss this new feature further in the next section.

Also unlike other features, you can install SQL Server Integration Services on a 32-bit OS; however, we do not recommend this. A 64-bit version of SQL Server Integration Services is installed on 64-bit operating systems. If you worry about connecting to 32-bit servers, data sources, or applications installations (such as Microsoft Office), don't—those connections are not dependent on the 32-bit/64-bit installation and are handled at the package or connection-string level.

A standalone installation of SQL Server Integration Services without a matching SQL Server Database Engine is possible but not recommended. For the modern Project Deployment model of SQL Server Integration Services, the storage and logging of packages will still be dependent on a SQL Server Database Engine, and the execution of packages on a schedule would still require a SQL Agent service. Isolation of the SQL Server Integration Services workload is not best isolated in this way. A dedicated installation including the SQL Server Database Engine and SQL Server Agent is a better configuration to isolate SQL Server Integration Services package runtime workloads from other database workloads.

Installations of different versions of SQL Server Integration Services are installed side by side on a server; specifically, the service SQL Server Integration Services 14.0 is compatible with prior versions.

Outside of configuring the service account, you do not need any additional configuration when installing SQL Server Integration Services during SQL Server Setup. The default virtual service account is NT Service\MsDtsServer140. Note that this account is different from the Scale Out Master and Scale Out Worker service accounts, and is used differently. Let's talk about the Scale Out feature now.

Installing SQL Server Integration Services Scale Out configuration

A new feature in SQL Server 2017, Integration Services now supports a Scale Out configuration by which you can run a package on multiple SQL Server instances. This also allows for high availability of SQL Server Integration Services, with the secondary.

The master node talks to worker nodes in a SQL Server Integration Services Scale Out, with the communication over a port (8391 by default) and secured via a new Secure Sockets Layer (SSL) certificate. The SQL Server installer can automatically create a 10-year self-signed certificate and endpoint for communication at the time the master node is set up.

When adding another SQL Server Integration Services installation as a Scale Out Worker, start the new SQL Server Integration Services Manage Scale Out window via SQL Server Management Studio. Right-click the Catalog you have created, and then click Manage Scale Out. At the bottom of the page, click the + button to add a new Scale Out Worker node. Provide the server name to which to connect. If using a named instance, still provide only the server name of the node; do not include the instance name. A dialog box confirms the steps taken to add the Worker node, including copying and installing certificates between the Worker node and Master node, updating the endpoint and HttpsCertThumbprint of the worker, and restarting the Worker's Scale Out service. After the worker node is added, refresh the Worker Manager page, and then click the new Worker node entry, which will be red. You must turn on the Worker Node by clicking Enable Worker.

You also can copy and install the certificates manually between servers. You will find them in %program files%\Microsoft SQL Server\140\DTS\Binn\.

The Worker and Master nodes do not appear in SQL Server Configuration Manager (as of SQL 2017 RC2) but do appear in Services.msc.

One major security difference with Scale Out is that even though the SQL Server Integration Services Service Account doesn't run packages or need permission to do very much, the Scale Out Master and Worker service accounts actually do run packages. By default, these services run under virtual accounts NT Service\SSISScaleOutMaster140 and NT Service\SSISScaleOutWorker140, but you might want to change these to a Windows-authenticated Domain service account that will be used to run packages across the Scale Out.

Installing SQL Server Reporting Services

Starting with SQL Server 2017, SQL Server Reporting Services is no longer found in the SQL Server Setup media; it is instead available as a simplified, unified installer and a small download. SQL Server Reporting Services is now a 90-MB download that launches its own installer but still needs a SQL Server Database Engine instance as part of the license and to host the two Report Server databases. Note that SQL Server Reporting Services isn't free, and that the separate installer isn't a licensing change. You will need to provide a license key upon installation or choose a nonproduction edition to install (Evaluation, Developer, or Express).

The "native" mode of SQL Server Reporting Services is now the only mode in SQL Server 2017. If you are familiar with Reporting Services Report Manager in the past, accessible via the URL http://servername/Reports, that is the "native mode" installation of Reporting Services.

You'll notice the Report Server Configuration Manager in a new location, in its own Program Files menu, Microsoft SQL Server Reporting Services. After installation, start the Report Server Configuration Manager (typically installed in a path like *Program Files (x86)\Microsoft SQL Server\140\Tools\Binn\RSConfigTool.exe*). The Report Server Configuration Manager application itself is largely unchanged since SQL 2008.

The virtual service account "NT SERVICE\SQLServerReportingServices" is the default SQL Server Reporting Services service account. It is a second-best option, however: we recommend that you create a new domain service account to be used only for this service; for example, "*Domain*\svc_*ServerName*_SSRS" or a similar naming convention. You will need to use a domain account if you choose to configure report server email with "Report server service account (NTLM)" authentication.

If you choose to change the SQL Server Reporting Services service account later, use only the Reporting Services Configuration Manager tool to make this change. Like other SQL Server services, never use the Services console (services.msc) to change service accounts.

After installation, you will need to follow-up on other changes and necessary administrative actions; for example, configuring the SQL Server Reporting Services Execution Account, email settings, or backing up the encryption key using Reporting Services Configuration Manager.

SQL Server 2017 Reporting Services also can integrate with Microsoft Power BI dashboards. A page in the Report Server Configuration Manager supports registering this installation of SQL Server Reporting Services with a Power BI account. You will be prompted to sign into Azure Active Directory. The account you provide must be a member of the Azure tenant where you intend to integrate with Power BI. The account should also be a member of the system administrator in SQL Server Reporting Services, via Report Manager, and a member of the sysadmin role in the SQL Server that hosts the Report Server database.

CHAPTER 4

Inside OUT

Where is SQL Server Reporting Services SharePoint Integrated mode?

There is no more SharePoint Integrated mode, the simplified "native" mode download is the only installation available. This matches the moves that Microsoft has made in other areas that step away from the SharePoint on-premises product in favor of SharePoint Online features and development.

Instead, you can integrate SQL Server Reporting Services native mode with on-premises SharePoint sites via embedded SQL Server Reporting Services reports, including SQL Server Reporting Services reports stored in the Power BI Report Server.

Similarly, there is no future support for SQL Server Reporting Services integration with SharePoint Online.

"Smart Setup"

Since SQL Server 2012, the SQL Server installer has had the ability to patch itself while within the Setup wizard. The Product Updates page is presented after the License Terms page, and, after you accept it, it is downloaded from Windows Update (or Windows Server Update Services) and installed along with other SQL Server Setup files.

This is recommended, and so a SQL Server 2017 Setup with internet connectivity is the easiest way to carry out installation. This also could be described as a way to "slip-stream" updates, including hotfixes and cumulative updates, into the SQL Server installation process, eliminating these efforts post-installation.

For servers without internet access, there are two Setup.exe parameters that support downloading these files to an accessible location and making them available to Setup. When starting the SQL Server 2017 .iso's Setup.exe from Windows PowerShell or the command line (you can read more about this in the next section), you can set the /UpdateEnabled parameter to FALSE to turn off the download from Windows Update. The /UpdateSource parameter can then be provided as an installation location of unpacked .exe files. Note that the /UpdateSource parameter is a folder location, not a file.

Setting up logging

SQL Server Setup generates a large number of logging files for diagnostic and troubleshooting purposes. These logs should be the first place you go when you have an issue with Setup.

After you proceed past the Ready To Install page, and regardless of whether Setup was a complete success, it generates a number of log files in the following folder:

%programfiles%\Microsoft SQL Server\140\Setup Bootstrap\Log*YYYYMMDD_HHMMSS*\

Here's an example:

C:\Program Files\Microsoft SQL Server\140\Setup Bootstrap\Log\20170209_071118\

However, when you run Setup using the /Q or /QS parameters for unattended installation, the log file is written to the Windows %temp% folder.

A log summary file of the installation is created that uses the following naming convention:

Summary_*instancename_YYYYMMDD_HHMMSS*.txt

Setup generates similar files for the Component and Global Rules portions of Setup as well as a file called Detail.txt. These files might contain the detailed error messages you are looking for when troubleshooting a failed installation. The Windows Application Event log might also contain helpful information in that situation.

Finally, a System Configuration Check report .htm file is generated each time you run Setup, as well.

You'll also find the new SQL Server instance's first error log encoded at UTC time in this folder, showing the log from startup, similar to the normal SQL Server Error Log.

Automating SQL Server Setup by using configuration files

Let's dig more into what we can do with Setup.exe outside of the user interface. You can use configuration files to automate the selection process when installing SQL Server, which helps to create a consistent configuration.

Values provided in configuration files can prepopulate or override Setup settings. They also can configure Setup to run with the normal user interface or silently without any interface.

Starting Setup from prompt

You can start setup.exe from either Windows PowerShell or the command prompt, providing repeatability and standardization of parameter options. You also can use it to prefill sections of the Setup wizard or to change the default behavior of Setup.

For the purposes of the installer, ensure that you always use the Administrator level for these two prompts. The title on each page should be preceded by "Administrator: "; for example, Administrator: Windows PowerShell.

To start Windows PowerShell or command prompt as Administrator, in the Start menu, search for the desired application, right-click it, and then, on the shortcut menu that opens, select Run As Administrator.

Figure 4-2 shows an example of starting Setup.exe from the Windows PowerShell prompt, and Figure 4-3 shows starting it from the command prompt.

```
PS E:\> .\setup.exe /ACTION=install /UPDATEENABLED=false /UPDATESOURCE="d:\downloaded install files"
Microsoft (R) SQL Server 2017 RC2 14.00.900.75
Copyright (c) 2017 Microsoft.  All rights reserved.
```

Figure 4-2 Starting Setup.exe from the Windows PowerShell prompt.

```
E:\>setup.exe /ACTION=install /UPDATEENABLED=false /UPDATESOURCE="D:\downloaded install files"
Microsoft (R) SQL Server 2017 RC2 14.00.900.75
Copyright (c) 2017 Microsoft.  All rights reserved.
```

Figure 4-3 Starting Setup.exe from the command prompt.

Sometimes, you also might find it necessary to start Setup from the command line or Windows PowerShell because of a workaround for a specific problem.

Generating a configuration file

Writing a configuration file by hand is not necessary and can be tedious. Instead of going through that effort, you can let SQL Server Setup create a configuration file for you. Here's how to do that. Work your way through the normal SQL Server Setup user interface, completing everything as you normally would, but pause when you get to the Ready To Install page. Near the bottom of this page is a path (see Figure 4-4). At that location, you'll find a generated configuration file, ready for future use.

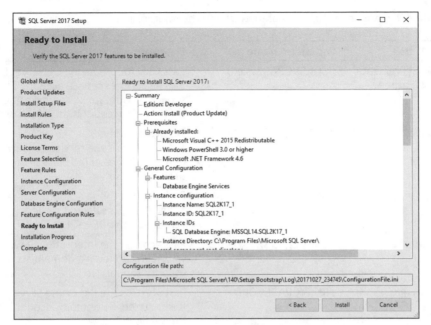

Figure 4-4 The Ready To Install page displays a summary of the installation steps that are about to begin as well as the Configuration File Path that has been prepared based on the selections.

Installing by using a configuration file

Now that you have a configuration file that you either prepared yourself or generated by using a previous walk-through of Setup, you can take the next step to automating or standardizing your installation.

You can start Setup.exe with a configuration file by using the /CONFIGURATIONFILE parameter of Setup.exe, or by navigating to the Advanced page of the SQL Server Installation Center that starts with Setup.exe in Windows. Then, start Setup.exe with a configuration file by selecting the Install Based On A Configuration File check box. A message appears, asking you to browse to the .ini file. After you select the appropriate file, Setup.exe will start with those options.

One thing to keep mind, however, is that configuration files generated by Setup.exe do not store the passwords you provided for any service accounts. If you do want to configure service account credentials in your configuration file, for security reasons, do not store the service account passwords in plain text in a configuration file. You should instead store them securely and provide them when you run Setup.exe. Each service's account information is available in a Setup.exe runtime parameter, which are listed in Table 4-1.

CHAPTER 4

Table 4-1 Common Setup.exe parameters and their purposes

Service	Parameter name	Description
SQL Server Database Engine	/SQLSVCPASSWORD	Password for the main SQL Server Database Engine Services service account. This is the service account for sqlservr.exe. It is required if a domain account is used for the service.
SQL Server Agent	/AGTSVCPASSWORD	Password for the SQL Server Agent service account. This is the service account for sqlagent.exe. It is required if a domain account is used for the service.
sa password	/SAPWD	Password for the sa account. It is required if Mixed Mode is selected, or when /SECURITYMODE=SQL is used.
Integration Services	/ISSVCPASSWORD	Password for the Integration Services service. It is required if a domain account is used for the service.
Reporting Services (Native)	/RSSVCPASSWORD	Password for the Reporting Services service. It is required if a domain account is used for the service.
Analysis Services	/ASSVCPASSWORD	Password for the Analysis Services service account. It is required if a domain account is used for the service.
PolyBase	/PBDMSSVCPASSWORD	Password for the PolyBase engine service account.
Full-Text filter launcher service	/FTSVCPASSWORD	Password for the Full-Text filter launcher service.

For example, in the snippet that follows, the PROD_ConfigurationFile_Install.INI has provided the account name of the of the SQL Server Database Engine service account, but the password is provided when Setup.exe runs:

```
Setup.exe /SQLSVCPASSWORD="securepasswordhere"
/ConfigurationFile="d:\SQLInstaller\Configuration
Files\PROD_ConfigurationFile_Install.INI"
```

You can provide further parameters like passwords when you run Setup. Parameter settings provided will override any settings in the configuration file, just as the configuration file's settings will override any defaults in the Setup operation. Table 4-2 lists and describes the parameters.

Table 4-2 Common Setup.exe parameters of which you should be aware

Parameter usage	Parameter	Description
Unattended installations	/Q	Specifies Quiet Mode with no user interface and user interactivity allowed.
Unattended installations	/QS	Specifies Quiet Mode with user interface but no user interactivity allowed.
Accept license terms	/IACCEPTSQLSERVERLICENSETERMS	Must be provided in any Configuration File looking to avoid prompts for installation.
R open license accept terms	/IACCEPTROPENLICENSEAGREEMENT	Similarly, must provide this parameter for any unattended installation involving either of the two R Server options.
Configuration file	/CONFIGURATIONFILE	A path to the configuration .ini file to use.
Instant file initialization	/SQLSVCINSTANTFILEINIT	Set to true to Grant Perform Volume Maintenance Task privilege to the SQL Server Database Engine Service (recommended)
TempDB data file count	/SQLTEMPDBFILECOUNT	Set to the number of desired TempDB data files to be installed initially.

Post-installation server configuration

After you install SQL Server, there are a number of changes to make or confirm on the Windows Server and in settings for SQL Server.

Post-installation checklist

You should run through the following checklist on your new SQL Server instance. The order of these items isn't necessarily specific, and many deal with SQL server and/or Windows configuration settings. Evaluate whether these are appropriate for your environment, but you should consider and apply them to most SQL Server installations.

1. Check your SQL Server version.

2. Configure the Maximum Server Memory setting.

CHAPTER 4

3. Surface Area Configuration.

4. Set up SQL Agent.

5. Turn on TCP/IP.

6. Verify power options.

7. Configure antivirus exclusions.

8. Optimize for ad hoc workloads.

9. Lock pages in memory.

10. System page file.

11. Backups, index maintenance, and integrity checks.

12. Backup service master and database master keys.

13. Default log retention.

14. Suppress successful backup messages.

Let's take a look at each of these in more detail in the subsections that follow.

Check your SQL Server version

After you install SQL Server, check the version number against the latest cumulative updates list, especially if you did not opt to or could not use Windows Update during SQL Server Setup. You can view the version number in SQL Server Management Studio's Object Explorer or via a T-SQL query on either the following two built-in functions:

```
SELECT @@VERSION;
select SERVERPROPERTY('ProductVersion');
```

NOTE

Take the opportunity before your SQL Server enters production to patch it. For informa-tion about the latest cumulative updates for SQL Server, search for KB321185 or visit *https://support.microsoft.com/help/321185/how-to-determine-the-version,-edition-and-update-level-of-sql-server-and-its-components.*

Configure the Maximum Server Memory setting

We discussed the Maximum Server Memory setting in Chapter 3, in the section "Configuration settings," but it is definitely on the list to set post-installation for any new SQL Server instance.

This setting is accessible via SQL Server Management Studio, in Object Explorer, on the Server Properties page. On the Memory page, look for the Maximum Server Memory (In MB) box. This value defaults to 2147483647, which does not limit the amount of memory SQL Server can access in the Windows server. This value is also available in `sp_configure`, when Show Advanced Options is turned on, under the configuration setting Max Server Memory (MB).

> ➤ **You can read more about why you should limit the Max Server Memory setting in Chapter 3.**

An example of configuring a Windows Server with one SQL Server instance and 64 GB of memory, to use a Max Server Memory setting of 58982 MB, as illustrated in Figure 4-5.

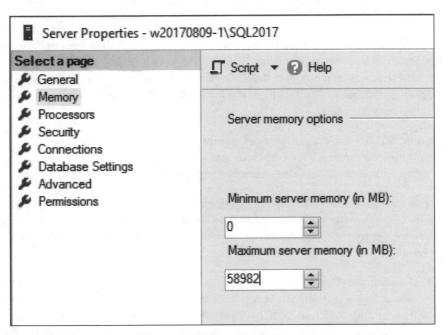

Figure 4-5 The Server Properties dialog box with the Memory page selected.

Keep lowering this number if you have other applications on the server that will be consuming memory, including other SQL Server instances. We discuss this more in the next section. If you observe over time that during normal operations your server's total memory capacity is nearly exhausted (less than 2 GB free), lower the Maximum Server Memory setting further. If there is sufficient padding available (more than 8 GB free), you can consider raising this setting.

Lowering this setting after installation and during operation does not return SQL Server memory back to the OS immediately; rather, it does so over time during SQL Server activity. Similarly, increasing this setting will not take effect immediately.

Just above the Maximum Server Memory setting is the Minimum Server Memory setting, which establishes a floor for memory allocation. It is not generally needed. You might find this setting useful for situations in which the total system memory is insufficient and many applications, including SQL Server instances, are present. The minimum server memory is not immediately allocated to the SQL Server instance upon startup; instead, it does not allow memory below this level to be freed for other applications.

Maximum server memory settings for other features

Other features of SQL Server have their own maximum server memory settings. As you will notice by their default settings, for servers on which both the SQL Server Database Engine and SQL Server Analysis Services and/or SQL Server Reporting Services are installed, competition for and exhaustion of memory is likely in environments with a significant amount of activity. It is recommended that you protect the Database Engine by lowering the potential memory impact of other applications.

Limiting SQL Server Analysis Services memory   SQL Server Analysis Services has not just one maximum server memory limit, but four, and you can enforce limits by hard values in bytes or by a percentage of total physical memory of the server.

You can change these via SQL Server Management Studio by connecting to the SQL Server Analysis Services instance in Object Explorer. Right-click the server, and then, on the shortcut menu, click Properties. The memory settings described here are available and nearly identical for Multidimensional and Tabular installations:

- **LowMemoryLimit.**   A value that serves as a floor for memory, but also the level at which SQL Server Analysis Services begins to release memory for infrequently used or low-priority objects in its cache. The default value is 65, or 65 percent of total server physical memory (or the Virtual Address Space technically, but Analysis Services, among other features, is not supported on 32-bit systems, and so this is not a concern).

- **TotalMemoryLimit.**   A value that serves as a threshold for SQL Server Analysis Services to begin to release memory for higher priority requests. It's important to note that this is not a hard limit. The default is 80 percent of total server memory.

- **HardMemoryLimit.**   This is a hard memory limit that will lead to more aggressive pruning of memory from cache and potentially to the rejection of new requests. By default, this is displayed as 0 and is effectively the midway point between the `TotalMemoryLimit` and the server physical memory. The `TotalMemoryLimit` must always be less than the `HardMemoryLimit`.

- **VertiPaqMemoryLimit.**   For SQL Server Analysis Services installations in Tabular mode only, the Low Memory setting is similarly enforced by the `VertiPaqMemoryLimit`, which has a default of 60, or 60 percent of server physical memory. After this threshold is reached, and only if `VertiPaqPagingPolicy` is turned on (it is by default), SQL Server Analysis Services begins to page data to the hard drive using the OS page file. Paging to a drive can help prevent out-of-memory errors when the `HardMemoryLimit` is met.

Figure 4-6 shows the General page of the Analysis Server Properties dialog box, as started in Object Explorer, and the locations of the preceding memory configuration properties.

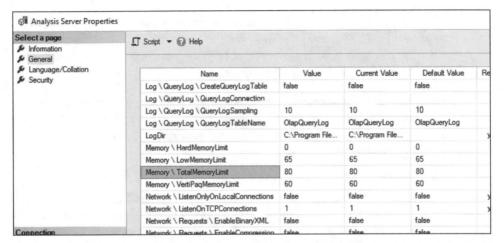

Figure 4-6 The General page in the Analysis Server Properties dialog box showing the default settings.

Limiting SQL Server Reporting Services memory   You can configure memory settings only in the rsreportserver.config file, which is a text file that is stored at %ProgramFiles%\Microsoft SQL Server Reporting Services\SSRS\ReportServer.

NOTE

This location has changed from previous versions, but the config file name has not.

Four options are available for limiting SQL Server Reporting Services memory utilization, and all are based on numbers contained in tags within this .config file, so be sure to make a backup of it before editing.

Two of the settings are in the .config file by default; two more are available to administrators to use in advanced scenarios.

CHAPTER 4

Let's take a look at each one:

- **MemorySafetyMargin.**   The percentage of `WorkingSetMaximum` that SQL Server Reporting Services will use before taking steps to reduce background task memory utilization and prioritize requests coming from the web service, attempting to protect user requests. User requests could still be denied.

- **MemoryThreshold.**   The percentage of `WorkSetMaximum` at which SQL Server Reporting Services will deny new requests, slow down existing requests, and page memory to a hard drive until memory conditions improve.

Two more settings are instead given values automatically upon service startup, but you can override them in the .config file. Two older memory settings from SQL Server 2005 with which SQL DBAs might be familiar are `MemoryLimit` and `MaximumMemoryLimit`, but those two values have been ignored since SQL Server 2008.

- **WorkingSetMaximum.**   By default, this is the total server physical memory. This setting does not appear by default in the .config file, but you can override it to reduce the amount of memory of which SQL Server Reporting Services will be aware. This value is expressed in kilobytes of memory.

- **WorkingSetMinimum.**   By default, this value is 60 percent of the `WorkingSetMaximum`. If SQL Server Reporting Services needs memory below this value, it will use memory and not release it due to memory pressure. This setting does not appear by default in the .config file, but you can override it to increase the variability of SQL Server Reporting Services' memory utilization.

These four settings can appear in the rsreportserver.config file. As demonstrated here, you should override the default settings to 4 GB maximum and 2 GB minimum (each expressed in KB):

```
<MemorySafetyMargin>80</MemorySafetyMargin>
<MemoryThreshold>90</MemoryThreshold>
<WorkingSetMaximum>4194304</WorkingSetMaximum>
<WorkingSetMinimum>2097152</WorkingSetMinimum>
```

Limiting Machine Learning Server memory   Similar to SQL Server Analysis Services and SQL Server Reporting Services, the Machine Learning Server has a .config file at %ProgramFiles%\ Microsoft SQL Server\MSSQL14.MSSQLSERVER\MSSQL\Binn\rlauncher.config.

By default, Machine Learning Server is similar to 20 percent of total server memory. You can override this by adding a tag to the .config file to provide a value for `MEMORY_LIMIT_ PERCENT`. This value is not in the .config file by default.

Remember to make a backup of this config file before editing. Following is an example of the contents of the rlauncher.config file, with the default memory limit changed to 25 percent:

```
RHOME=C:\PROGRA~2\MICROS~1\MSSQL1~4.SQL\R_SERV~2
MPI_HOME=C:\Program Files\Microsoft MPI
INSTANCE_NAME=SQL2K17
TRACE_LEVEL=1
JOB_CLEANUP_ON_EXIT=1
USER_POOL_SIZE=0
WORKING_DIRECTORY=C:\Program Files\Microsoft SQL
Server\MSSQL14.SQL2K17\MSSQL\ExtensibilityData
PKG_MGMT_MODE=0
MEMORY_LIMIT_PERCENT=25
```

Surface Area Configuration

If you are a veteran SQL Server DBA, you will remember when SQL Server Surface Area Configuration was a separate application. Surface Area Configuration was moved to the Facets menu starting with SQL Server 2008.

To view Surface Area Configuration in SQL Server Management Studio, in Object Explorer, connect to the SQL Server, right-click the server, and then, on the shortcut menu, click Facets. (Note that this window sometimes takes a moment to load.) In the dialog box that opens, change the value in the list box to Surface Area Configuration.

Keep in mind that all of these options should remain off unless needed and properly configured because they present a specific potential for misuse by an administrator or unauthorized user. In typical installations of SQL Server 2017, however, you will need three of these options:

- Database Mail (more about this in Chapter 14. You also can turn this setting on or off via the Database Mail XPs option in `sp_configure`.

  ### NOTE
  Keep in mind that enterprise Simple Mail Transfer Protocol (SMTP) servers have an "allow list" of IP addresses; you will need to add this server's IP to this list to send email.

- Remote Dedicated Admin Connection (more on this in Chapter 7). You also can turn this setting on or off via the remote admin connections option in `sp_configure`.

- CLR Integration, which you will need to turn on to use SQL Server Integration Services. You also can turn this setting on or off via the `clr enabled` option in `sp_configure`.

You should turn on other options in Surface Area Configuration only if they are specifically required by a third-party application and you are aware of the potential security concerns.

Setting up SQL Agent

There are a number of post-installation tasks to set up in SQL Agent before SQL Server can begin to help you automate, monitor, and back up your new instance.

➤ **Chapter 7 and Chapter 14 cover these topics in greater detail.**

You need to do the following:

1. Change the SQL Agent service from Manual to Automatic startup.

2. To send email notifications for alerts or job status notifications, you must set up a Database Mail account and profile (see Chapter 14).

3. Set up an Operator for a distribution group of IT professionals in your organization who would respond to a SQL Server issue.

4. Configure SQL Server Agent to use Database Mail.

5. Set up SQL Server Alerts for desired errors and high severity (Severity 21+) errors.

At the very least, these steps are put in place so that SQL Server can send out a call for help. Even if you have centralized monitoring solutions in place, the most severe of errors should be important enough to warrant an email.

You can choose to configure a large number of Windows Management Instrumentation (WMI) conditions, Perfmon counter conditions, SQL Server Error messages by number or severity in SQL Server Alerts. However, do not overcommit your inboxes, and do not set an inbox rule to Mark As Read and file away emails from SQL Server. By careful selection of emails, you can assure yourself and your team that emails from SQL Server will be actionable concerns that rarely arrive.

Turning on TCP/IP

The common network protocol TCP/IP is off by default, and the only protocol that is on is Shared Memory, which allows only local connections. You will likely not end up using Shared Memory to connect to the SQL Server for common business applications; rather, you'll use it only for local connections in the server.

When you connect to SQL Server using SQL Server Management Studio while signed in to the server, you connect to the Shared_Memory endpoint whenever you provide the name of the server, the server\instance, localhost, the dot character ("."), or (local).

TCP/IP, however, is ubiquitous in many SQL Server features and functionality. Many applications will need to use TCP/IP to connect to the SQL Server remotely. Many SQL Server features require it to be turned on, including the Dedicated Admin Connection (DAC), the AlwaysOn availability groups listener, and Kerberos authentication.

In the SQL Server Configuration Manager application, in the left pane, click SQL Server Network Configuration. Browse to the protocols for your newly installed instance of SQL Server. The default instance of SQL Server, here and in many places, will appear as MSSQLSERVER.

After turning on the TCP/IP protocol, you need to do a manual restart of the SQL Server service.

Turning on Named Pipes is not required or used unless an application specifically needs it.

Verifying power options

The Windows Server Power Options setting should be set to High Performance for any server hosting a SQL Server instance.

Windows might not operate the processor at maximum frequency during normal or even busy periods of SQL Server activity. This applies to physical or virtual Windows servers.

Review the policy and ensure that the group policy will not change this setting back to Balanced or another setting.

Configuring antivirus exclusions

Configure any antivirus software installed on the SQL Server to ignore scanning extensions used by your SQL Server data and log files. Typically, these will be .mdf, .ldf, and .ndf.

Also, configure any antivirus programs to ignore folders containing full-text catalog files, backup files, replication snapshot files, SQL Server trace (.trc) files, SQL Audit files, Analysis Services database, log and backup files, FILESTREAM and FileTable folders, SQL Server Reporting Services temp files and log files.

Processes might also be affected, so set antivirus programs to ignore the programs for all instances of the SQL Server Database Engine service, Reporting Services service, Analysis Services service, and R Server (RTerm.exe and BxlServer.exe).

In SQL Server FCIs (and also for availability groups), also configure antivirus software to exclude the MSCS folder on the quorum drive, the MSDTC directory on the MSDTC share, and the Windows\Cluster folder on each cluster node, if they exist.

Optimizing for ad hoc workloads

The server-level setting to Optimize For Ad Hoc Workloads doesn't have the most intuitive name.

We are not optimizing ad hoc queries; we are optimizing SQL Server memory usage to prevent ad hoc queries from consuming unnecessary cache.

➤ For more about the Optimize For Ad Hoc Workloads setting, see Chapter 2.

For the unlikely scenario in which a large number of queries are called only two times, setting this option to True would be a net negative for performance.

However, like other design concepts in databases, we find that there are either one or many. There is no two.

➤ To read more about cached execution plans, see Chapter 9.

Lock pages in memory

You should consider using this setting for environments in which instances of SQL Server are expected to experience memory pressure due to other applications, server limitations, or over-allocated virtualized systems; however, this is an in-depth topic to be considered carefully.

➤ For more about the Lock pages in memory setting, see Chapter 2.

➤ For more about the Windows page file, see Chapter 3.

Inside OUT

How do I know if the permission to Lock pages in memory is in effect?

Starting with SQL Server 2016 SP1, you can check whether the Lock pages in memory permission has been granted to the SQL Server Database Engine service. Here's how to do that:

```
select sql_memory_model_desc
--Conventional = Lock pages in memory privilege is not granted
--LOCK_PAGES = Lock pages in memory privilege is granted
--LARGE_PAGES = Lock pages in memory privilege is granted in Enterprise mode
--with Trace Flag 834 ON
from sys.dm_os_sys_info;
```

Backups, index maintenance, and integrity checks

Backups are a critical part of your disaster recovery, and they should begin right away.

Begin taking database backups, at least of the master and msdb databases immediately. You should also back up other Setup-created databases, including ReportServer, ReportServer-TempDB, and SSISDB right away.

> ➤ **For more information on backups, index maintenance, and monitoring, see Chapter 12.**

As soon as your new SQL Server instance has databases in use, you should be performing selective index maintenance and integrity checks, regularly.

> ➤ **For more information on automating maintenance, see Chapter 13.**

Backing up service master and database master keys

You also should back up service master keys and any database master keys as they are created, storing their information securely.

> ➤ **For more information on service master and database master keys, see Chapter 6.**

To back up the instance service master key, use the following:

```
BACKUP SERVICE MASTER KEY TO FILE = 'localfilepath or_UNC' ENCRYPTION BY PASSWORD =
'complexpassword'
```

And as soon as they come into existence as needed, in each user database, back up individual database master keys, as follows:

```
BACKUP MASTER KEY TO FILE = 'localfilepath_or_UNC' ENCRYPTION BY PASSWORD =
'complexpassword'
```

Increasing default error and agent history retention

By default, SQL Server maintains the current SQL Server error log plus six more error logs of history. Logs are cycled each time the SQL Server service is started, which should be rare, but you also can manually cycle them via the `sp_cycle_errorlog`.

However, one eventful, fun weekend of server troubleshooting or maintenance could wipe out a significant amount of your error history. This could make the task of troubleshooting periodic or business-cycle related errors difficult or impossible. You need visibility into errors that occur only during a monthly processing, monthly patch day, or periodic reporting.

In SQL Server Management Studio, in Object Explorer, connect to the SQL Server instance. Expand the Management folder, right-click SQL Server Logs, and then, on the shortcut menu, click Configure. Select the Limit The Number Of Error Logs Before They Are Recycled check box and type a value larger than 6. You might find that a value between 25 and 50 will result in more useful log history contained for multiple business cycles.

Similarly, you might find that the SQL Server Agent history is not sufficient to cover an adequate amount of job history, especially if you have frequent job runs.

In SQL Server Management Studio, in Object Explorer, connect to the SQL Server instance. Right-click SQL Server Agent, and then click Properties. Click the History page. This page is not intuitive and can be confusing. The first option, Limit Size Of The Job History Log, is a rolling job history retention setting. You might find it a good start to simply add a 0 to each value, increasing the maximum log history size in rows from the default of 1,000 to 10,000, and also increase the maximum job history per job in rows from the default of 100 to 1,000.

The second option, Remove Agent History, along with its companion Older Than text box is not a rolling job history retention setting; rather, it is an immediate and manual job history pruning. Select this second check box, and then click OK and return to this page; you will find the second check box is cleared. Behind the scenes, SQL Server Management Studio ran the msdb.dbo. sp_purge_jobhistory stored procedure to remove job history manually.

➤ For more information about SQL Server Agent job history, see Chapter 13.

Suppress successful backup messages

By default, SQL Server writes an event to the error log upon a successful database backup, whether it be FULL, DIFFERENTIAL, or TRANSACTION LOG.

On instances with many databases and with many databases in FULL recovery mode with regular transaction log backups, the amount of log activity generated by just their successful frequent log backups could flood the log with clutter, lowering log history retention.

> ### NOTE
> It is important to note that you can review successful backup history by querying the msdb system database, which has a series of tables dedicated to storing the backup history for all databases, including msdb.dbo.backupset and msdb.dbo.backupmediafamily. The built-in "Backup and Restore Events" report in SQL Server Management Studio provides access to this data, as well.

➤ **For more on backups, see Chapter 11.**

SQL Server Trace Flag 3226 is an option that you can turn on at the instance level to suppress successful backup notifications.

There are many trace flags available to administrators to alter default behavior—many more options than there are user interfaces to accommodate them in SQL Server Management Studio. Take care when turning them on and understand that many trace flags are intended only for temporary use when aiding troubleshooting.

Because Trace Flag 3226 should be a permanent setting, simply starting the trace by using DBCC TRACEON is not sufficient, given that the trace flag will no longer be active following a SQL Server service restart. Instead, add the trace flag as a startup parameter to the SQL Server Database Engine service by using SQL Server Configuration Manager.

Use the syntax –T*flagnumber*, as illustrated in Figure 4-7.

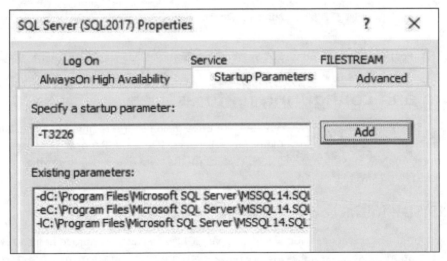

Figure 4-7 Specifying a startup parameter in the SQL Server Properties dialog box.

After you specify the trace flag, click Add. The change will not take effect until the SQL Server Database Engine service is restarted. Figure 4-8 shows that Trace Flag 3226 is now a part of the startup.

CHAPTER 4

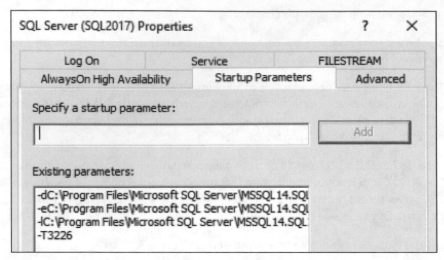

Figure 4-8 The Startup Parameters tab in the SQL Server Properties dialog box, with Trace Flag 3226 now appearing in the Existing Parameters box.

➤ **For more information on SQL Server Configuration Manager, see Chapter 1.**

Installing and configuring features

SQL Server installation is now complete, but three main features require post-installation configuration, including SQL Server Integration Services, SQL Server Reporting Services, and SQL Server Analysis Services. You will need to perform the steps detailed in this section before use if these features were installed.

SSISDB initial configuration and setup

Among the best features added by SQL Server 2012 were massive improvements to SQL Server Integration Services, specifically with a new server-integrated deployment, built-in performance data collector, environment variables, and more developer quality-of-life improvements.

When the Integration Services Catalog is created, a new user database called SSISDB is also created. You should back it up and treat it as an important production database.

You should create the SSISDB catalog database soon after installation and before a SQL Server Integration Services development can take place. You will need to do this only once. Because this will involve potential Surface Area Configuration changes and the creation of a new strong password, a SQL DBA, not a SQL Server Integration Services developer, should perform this and store the password securely alongside others generated at the time of installation.

In Object Explorer, connect to your instance, right-click Integration Services Catalog, and then, on the shortcut menu, click Create Catalog. In this single-page setup, you must select the Enable CLR Integration check box, decide whether SQL Server Integration Services packages should be allowed to be run at SQL Server Startup (we recommend this due to maintenance and cleanup performed then), and provide an encryption password for the SSISDB database.

The encryption password is for the SSISDB database master key. After you create it, you should then back up the SSISDB database master key.

> **For more information on database master keys, see Chapter 7.**

The SSISDB database will contain SQL Server Integration Services packages, their connection strings, and more data about the packages. The encryption would not allow these sensitive contents to be decrypted by a malicious user who gains access to the database files or backups. This password would be required if the database were moved to another server, so you should store it in a secure location within your enterprise.

NOTE
If you receive an error when creating the SSSIDB catalog that reads "The catalog backup file 'C:\Program Files\Microsoft SQL Server\140\DTS\Binn\SSISDBBackup.bak' could not be accessed" or similar, it is likely because SQL Server Integration Services was not actually installed, so the template database backup was not copied from the SQL Server media. You can run SQL Server Setup again or copy the SSISDBBackup.bak file from another SQL Server installation of the same version.

SQL Server Reporting Services initial configuration and setup

If you did not select the Install And Configure check box in SQL Server Setup, you will have more tasks to complete here, but there are still tasks to perform upon first installation of a SQL Server Reporting Services native-mode installation.

Open the Reporting Services Configuration Manager application, connect to the newly installed SQL Server Reporting Services instance, and then review the following options, from top to bottom:

- **Service Account.** You can change the SQL Server Reporting Services service account here. Remember that you should use only the Reporting Services Configuration Manager tool to make this change.

- **Web Service URL.** The web service URL is not for user interaction; rather, it is for the Report Manager and custom applications to programmatically connect to the SQL Server Reporting Services instance.

By default, a web service on TCP Port 80 is created called ReportServer. For named instances, the web service will be called ReportServer_*instancename*. The URL for the webservice would then be

http://*servername*/ReportServer

or:

http://*servername*/ReportServer_*instancename*

To accept defaults, at the bottom of the application window, click Apply.

You can optionally configure an SSL certificate to a specific URL here, and the Reporting Services Configuration Manager will make the changes necessary.

- **Database.**   Each reporting service requires a pair of databases running on a SQL Server instance. If you selected the Install And Configure check box in SQL Server Setup, the databases will have been created for you with the names ReportServer and ReportServerTempDB, or, for a named instance, ReportServer$*InstanceName* and ReportServer$*InstanceName*TempDB. Both of these databases are important and you should create backups. The ReportServerTempDB is not a completely transient database like the SQL Server instance's TempDB system database.

  To set the databases for a new instance, click Change Database, and then follow the Create A New Report Server Database Wizard. This will add both databases to the instance.

- **Web Portal URL.**   The web portal URL is the user-friendly website that hosts links to reports and provides for administrative features to the SQL Server Reporting Services instance. This is the link to share with users if you will be using the SQL Server Reporting Services portal.

  By default, the URL for the web portal is /Reports

  Http://*servername*/Reports for the default instance

  or:

  Http://*servername*/Reports_*InstanceName* for named instances

  You can change the name from the default here if desired. To proceed, at the bottom of the application window, click Apply.

- **Email Settings.**   You use these email settings are used for sending reports to user subscribers via email. SQL Server Reporting Services uses its own Email Settings and does not inherit from the SQL Server instance's Database Mail settings. This setting is optional if you do not intend to send reports to subscribers via email.

  First introduced in SQL Server 2016 was the ability for SQL Server Reporting Services to authenticate to an external SMTP server using anonymous (No Authentication), Basic, or NT LAN Manager (NTLM) authentication, which will use the SQL Server Reporting Services service account to authenticate to the SMTP server.

Prior to SQL Server 2016, authentication to external SMTP servers required the installation of a local SMTP server to provide a relay to the external, Azure-based (such as SendGrid) or cloud-based SMTP server. With SQL Server 2016 and 2017, SMTP connections can be made directly to these external SMTP servers.

NOTE

Keep in mind that enterprise SMTP servers have an allow list of IP addresses, and you will need to add this server's IP to this list to send email.

- **Execution Account.** You can provide this domain account optionally to be used when reports are configured to run on a schedule, to run without credentials (select the Credentials Are Not Required Option) or to connect to remote servers for external images.

  The execution account should not be the same as the SQL Server Reporting Services service account.

  This account should have minimal read-only access to any data sources or remote connections that will require it. You also can give it EXECUTE permissions for data sources that use stored procedures, but you should never give it any additional SQL Server permissions or let it be a member of any SQL Server server roles, including sysadmin.

- **Encryption Keys.** Immediately after installation and after the two SQL Server Reporting Services databases have been created, back up this instance's encryption keys. This key is used to encrypt sensitive information such as connection strings in the two databases. If the databases are restored to another server and this key is not available from the source server, credentials in connection strings will not be usable and you will need to provide them again for the reports to run successfully on a new server.

  If you can no longer locate the backup of a key, use the Change operation on this page to replace the key, and then back it up.

  To restore the original key to a new server to which the databases have been moved, use the Restore operation on this page.

- **Subscription Settings.** Use this page to specify a credential to reach file shares to which report subscriptions can be written. Reports can be dropped in this file share location in PDF, Microsoft Excel, or other formats for consumption.

  Multiple subscriptions can use this file share credential, which can be used on this page in a central location.

  This account should be different from the SQL Server Reporting Services execution account to serve its purpose appropriately.

CHAPTER 4

- **Scale-Out Deployment.**   Visit this page on multiple SQL Server Reporting Services instances to join them together. By using the same SQL Server Reporting Services databases for multiple SQL Server Reporting Services instances, multiple front ends can provide processing for heavy reporting workloads, including heavy subscription workloads. The server names can be used in a network load balancer such as a Network Load Balancing Cluster.

  Upon first installation, the Scale-Out Deployment page will show that the instance is "Joined" to a single server scale-out.

  Each scale-out instance of SQL Server Reporting Services must use the same settings on the Database page of the Reporting Services Configuration Manager. Connect to each instance in the scale-out and visit this page by opening it on each SQL Server Reporting Services instance to view the status, add servers to the scale-out, or remove servers.

- **PowerBI Integration.**   Visit this page to associate the SQL Server Reporting Services instance to a Microsoft Power BI account, specifically to an account in Azure Active Directory. The administrator joining the Power BI instance to the SQL Server Reporting Services instance must be a member of the Azure Active Directory, a system administrator of the SQL Server Reporting Services instance, and a sysadmin on the SQL Server instance that hosts the SQL Server Reporting Services databases.

➤ **For the latest information on Power BI/SQL Server Reporting Services integration and the latest Azure authentication features, search for MT598750 or visit *https://docs.microsoft.com/sql/reporting-services/install-windows/power-bi-report-server-integration-configuration-manager*.**

SQL Server Analysis Services initial configuration and setup

No additional steps are required after setup to begin using a new SQL Server Analysis Services instance.

Because of the nature of SQL Server Analysis Services databases, their size, and how they are populated, typically they are not updated on a schedule, but you can do so by passing an XMLA command via a SQL Server Agent job step: type **SQL Server Analysis Services Command**. You also can initiate manual backups of SQL Server Analysis Services databases in Object Explorer in SQL Server Management Studio as well as restore SQL Server Analysis Services databases.

When installing SQL Server Analysis Services, a security group should have been chosen to grant permissions to SQL Server Analysis Services server administrators, granting a team full access to the server.

If you need to add a different group to the administrator role of the SQL Server Analysis Services instance, open SQL Server Management Studio, and then, in Object Explorer, connect to the Analysis Services instance. Right-click the server, and then, on the shortcut menu, click Properties. On the Security page, you can add additional windows-authenticated accounts or groups to the administrator role.

Adding databases to a SQL Server instance

Now that your SQL Server is installed and SQL Server features are configured, it is time to put your SQL Server instance to use. In SQL Server Management Studio, you'll see four system databases there already, plus additional databases for SQL Server Reporting Services and SQL Server Integration Services perhaps if you have installed these features. Now it is time to create user databases.

We have discussed a number of database configurations in Chapter 3, including the physical configuration of files and storage.

For information on Azure SQL Databases, refer to Chapter 5. The remainder of this chapter refers to SQL Server instance databases.

Considerations for migrating existing databases

As an administrator, you'll be faced with the need to move a database from one instance to another, perhaps for the purposes of refreshing a preproduction environment, moving to a new SQL Server instance, or promoting a database into production for the first time.

When copying a database into a new environment, keep in mind the following:

- Edition

- Version and compatibility mode

- SQL logins

- Database-scoped configurations

- Database settings

- Encryption

Let's look at each of these in more detail.

Edition

Generally speaking, databases progress upward in terms of cost and feature set, beginning with Express edition, Web, Standard, and finally Enterprise edition. (Developer edition is the same as Enterprise edition, except for the ability to use it in a production environment.) Moving a database up from Express, Web, or Standard edition expands the features available for use in the database.

The concern for DBAs is when databases need to move down from Enterprise, Standard, or Web edition. A large number of features that had historically been exclusive to Enterprise edition were included in Standard edition for the first time with SQL Server 2016 SP1, expanding what we can do with Standard edition as developers and administrators.

You will encounter errors related to higher-edition features when restoring or attaching to an instance that does not support those editions. For example, when attempting to restore a data-compressed database to tables to an instance that does not support data compression, you will receive an error message similar to "cannot be started in this edition of SQL Server because part or all of object '*somecompressedindex*' is enabled with data compression." In this case, you will need to manually remove data compression from the database in the source instance and then create a new backup or detach the database again before migrating to the lower-edition instance. You cannot turn off the use of higher-edition features on the lower-edition instance.

You can foresee this problem by using a dynamic management view that lists all edition-specific features in use. Keep in mind that some features are supported in all editions but are limited. For example, memory-optimized databases are supported even in Express edition but with only a small amount of memory that can be allocated.

For example,

```
USE [WIDEWORLDIMPORTERS];
SELECT FEATURE_NAME
FROM SYS.DM_DB_PERSISTED_SKU_FEATURES;
```

returns the following rows:

```
feature name
Compression
Partitioning
ColumnStoreIndex
InMemoryOLTP
```

Version and compatibility mode

SQL Server databases upgraded from an older version to a new version will retain a prior compatibility mode. Compatibility mode is a database-level setting.

For example, restoring or attaching a database from SQL 2012 to SQL 2017 will result in the database assuming the SQL 2012 (11.0) compatibility mode inside the SQL 2017 environment. This is not necessarily a problem, but it does have consequences with respect to how you can use features and improvements and potentially how it performs.

You can view the compatibility level of a database in SQL Server Management Studio. To do so, in Object Explorer, right-click a database, and then, on the shortcut menu, click Properties. In the pane on the left, click Options. On the Options page, the Compatibility Level list box displays the current setting. You can change that setting or use the ALTER DATABASE command to change the COMPATIBILITY_LEVEL setting. You can also view this setting for all databases in the system catalog via sys.databases; look for the compatibility_level column.

SQL Server provides database compatibility modes for backward compatibility to database-level features, including improvements to the query optimizer, additional fields in dynamic management objects, syntax improvements, and other database-level objects.

For the scenario in which a SQL Server 2017 (internal version 140) instance is hosting a database in SQL Server 2012 (internal version 110) compatibility mode, it is important to note that applications are still connecting to a SQL Server 2017 instance. Only database-level features and options are honored in the prior compatibility modes.

For example, some recent syntax additions such as the new STRING_SPLIT() or OPENJSON functions, added in SQL Server 2016, will not work when run in the context of a database in a prior compatibility mode. Some syntax improvements, such as DATEFROMPARTS() and AT TIME ZONE, will work in any database in any compatibility mode in SQL Server 2017.

SQL Server 2017 supports compatibility levels down to SQL Server 2008 (internal version 100).

Changing the database compatibility level does not require a service restart to take place, but we strongly recommend that you do *not* perform this during normal operating hours. Promoting the database compatibility mode should be thoroughly tested in preproduction environments. Even though syntax errors are extremely unlikely, other changes to the query optimizer engine from version to version could result in performance changes to the application that must be evaluated prior to rollout to a production system. When you do upgrade production from a prior compatibility level, you should do so during a maintenance period, not during user activity.

> ➤ **For more information on the differences between compatibility modes since SQL 2005, reference MSDN article bb510680 or visit *https://docs.microsoft.com/sql/t-sql/statements/ alter-database-transact-sql-compatibility-level*.**

CHAPTER 4

Inside OUT

When should I keep a database in a prior compatibility mode?

It is a common oversight to forget to promote the database compatibility level to the new SQL Server version level after a database upgrade. You are missing out on new database features, but there can be good reasons to keep a database in a prior compatibility mode, though you should consider all of them temporary.

The most common reason to run a database in prior compatibility mode is not technical at all; rather, the administrator might be handcuffed by vendor support or software certification. Many changes from version to version in SQL Server are additive and rarely regressive.

One notable exception is one of the new features introduced in SQL Server 2014: improvements to the Cardinality Estimator resulted in poor query performance in rare situations. In the case of complex, fine-tuned and/or large chunks of poor-performing code, reverting to the previous Cardinality Estimator is the most realistic near-term solution. Changing the database's compatibility mode down to SQL 2012 might have resolved the issue, but two less-drastic options are available.

Trace flag 9481 will force a database in SQL 2014 compatibility mode to use the legacy Cardinality Estimation model from SQL 2012 and earlier. The LEGACY_CARDINALITY_ESTIMATION database option is also available starting with SQL Server 2016, to force the old Cardinality Estimation model into use for that database only. It has the same effect in the database at Trace Flag 9481.

NOTE

You can upgrade the SSISDB database, which contains the SQL Server Integration Services Catalog, independently of other databases by using the SSISDB Database Upgrade Wizard. This makes it easier to move your SQL Server Integration Services packages and environments from server to server by restoring or attaching a database from a previous version to a SQL Server 2017 Server.

SQL logins

SQL-authenticated logins and their associated database users are connected via security identifier (SID), not by name. When moving a database from one instance to another, the SIDs in the SQL logins on the old instance might be different from the SIDs in the SQL logins on the new instance, even if their names match. After migration to the new instance, SQL-authenticated logins will be unable to access databases where their database users have become "orphaned," and you must repair this. This does not affect Windows Authenticated logins for domain accounts.

This condition must be repaired before applications and end users will be able to access the database in its new location. Refer to the section "Solving orphaned SIDs" in Chapter 6.

The database owner should be included in the security objects that should be accounted for on the new server. Ensure that the owner of the database, listed either in the Database Properties dialog box or the `sys.databases owner_sid` field, is still a valid principal on the new instance.

For databases with Partial Containment, contained logins for each type will be restored or attached along with the database, and this should not be a concern.

Database-scoped configurations

Database-scoped configurations were introduced in SQL Server 2016 (and also in Azure SQL Database v12) and represent a container for a set of options available to be configured at the database level. in earlier versions, these settings were available only at the server or individual query, such as Max Degree of Parallelism (MaxDOP).

> ➤ **For more information on Parallelism and MaxDOP, go to Chapter 9.**

You should evaluate these options for each database after it is copied to a new instance to determine whether the settings are appropriate. The desired MaxDOP, for example, could change if the number of logical processors differs from the system default.

You can view each of these database-scoped configurations in SQL Server Management Studio. In Object Explorer, right-click a database, and then, on the shortcut menu, click Properties. In the pane on the left, click Options. A heading just for database-scoped configurations appears at the top of the Other Options list. You can also view database-scoped configurations in the dynamic management view sys.database_scoped_configurations.

Database configuration settings

You should review database-specific settings at the time of migration, as well. You can review them with a quick glance of the sys.databases catalog view, or from the database properties window in SQL Server Management Studio.

The following is not a list of all database settings, but we will cover these and many more later in the chapter. You should pay attention to these when restoring, deploying, or attaching a database to a new instance.

- **Read Only.**   If the database was put in READ_ONLY mode before the migration to prevent data movement, be sure to change this setting back to READ_WRITE.

- **Recovery Model.**   Different servers might have different backup and recovery methods. In a typical environment, the FULL recovery model is appropriate for production environments when the data loss tolerance of the database is smaller than the frequency of full backups, or when point-in-time recovery is appropriate. If you are copying a database from a production environment to a development environment, it is likely you will want to change the recovery model from FULL to SIMPLE. If you are copying a database from a testing environment to a production environment for the first time, it is likely you will want to change the recovery model from SIMPLE to FULL.

> ➤ For more information about database backups and the appropriate recovery model, see Chapter 11.

- **Page Verify Option.**   For all databases, this setting should be CHECKSUM. The legacy TORN_PAGE option is a sign that this database has been moved over the years up from a pre-SQL 2005 version, but this setting has never changed. Since SQL 2005, CHECKSUM has the superior and default setting, but it requires an administrator to manually change.

- **Trustworthy.**   This setting is not moved along with the database. If it was turned on for the previous system and was a requirement because of external assemblies, cross-database queries, and/or Service Broker, you will need to turn it on again. It is not recommended to ever turn on this setting unless it is made necessary because of an inflexible architecture requirement. It could allow for malicious activity on one database to affect other databases, even if specific permissions have not been granted. It is crucial to limit this setting and understand cross-database permission chains in a multitenant or web-hosted shared SQL Server environment.

> ➤ For more on object ownership, see Chapter 6.

Transparent data encryption

Transparent data encryption (TDE) settings will follow the database as it is moved from one instance to another, but the certificate and the certificate's security method will not. For example, the server certificate created to encrypt the database key and the private key and its password are not backed up along with the database. These objects must be moved to the new instance along with the database *prior to* any attempt to restore or attach the database.

CAUTION

Restoring an unencrypted database over an encrypted database is allowed. When would you inadvertently do this? If you restore a backup from the database before it was encrypted, you will end up with an unencrypted database. You must then reapply transparent data encryption.

➤ **For more information on transparent data encryption, see Chapter 7.**

Moving existing databases

There are a number of strategies for moving or copying a SQL Server database from one instance to another. You should consider each as it relates to necessary changes to application connection strings, DNS, storage, and security environments. We'll review a number of options for migration in this section.

Restoring a database backup

Restoring a backup is an easily understandable way to copy data from one instance to another. You can also carry out this method in such a way as to minimize the outage impact.

Let's compare two different simplified migration processes. Following is a sample migration checklist using a FULL backup/restore:

➤ **For more information on the types of database backups and database restores, see Chapter 11.**

1. Begin application outage.

2. Perform a FULL backup of the database.

3. Copy the database backup file.

4. Restore the FULL backup.

5. Resolve any SQL-authenticated login security issues or any other changes necessary before use.

6. In applications and/or DNS and/or aliases, change connection strings.

7. End application outage.

In the preceding scenario, the application outage must last the entire span of the backup, copy, and restore, which for large databases could be quite lengthy, even with native SQL Server backup compression reducing the file size.

Instead, consider the following strategy:

1.   Perform a FULL compressed backup of the database.

2.   Copy the database backup file.

3.   Restore the FULL backup WITH NORECOVERY.

4.   Begin application outage.

5.   Take a differential backup and then a log backup of the database.

6.   Copy the differential backup file and the log backup file to the new server.

7.   Restore the differential backup file WITH NORECOVERY.

8.   Restore the transaction log backup WITH RECOVERY.

9.   Resolve any SQL-authenticated login security issues or any other changes necessary before use.

10.   In applications and/or DNS and/or aliases, change the connection strings.

11.   End application outage.

In this scenario, the application outage spans only the duration of the differential and transaction log's backup/copy/restore operation, which for large databases should be a tiny fraction of the overall size of the database. This scenario does require more preparation and scripting in advance, and it requires coordination with the usual backup system responsible for transaction log backups. By taking a manual transaction log backup, you can create a split transaction log backup chain for another system, for which you should take account.

Attaching detached database files

Detaching, copying, and attaching database files will also get the job of getting the database in place on a new instance. It is relatively straightforward to disassociate (detach) the files from the old SQL Server, copy the files to the new instance, and then attach the files to the new SQL Server. This is largely limited by the data transfer speed of copying the files. You might also consider moving the SAN drives to the new server to decrease the time spent waiting for files to copy.

Attaching copied database files can be faster than restoring a full database backup; however, it lacks the ability to minimize the outage by taking advantage of transaction log backups (see earlier).

Copying the full set of database files (remember that the database might contain many more files than just the .mdf and .ldf files, including secondary data files and FILESTREAM containers) is not faster than restoring a transaction log backup during the application outage, and it is not a true recovery method. Because database backup files can also be compressed natively by SQL Server, the data transfer duration between the Windows servers will be reduced by using the backup/restore strategy.

Moving data with BACPAC files

A BACPAC file is an open JSON-format file that contains the database schema and row data, allowing for the migration of databases, ideally, at the start of a development/migration phase and not for large databases. SQL Server Management Studio can both generate and import BACPAC files, and the Azure portal can import them when moving an on-premises SQL Server to an Azure SQL database.

Creating a database

In this section, we review the basics of database settings and configuration. As a DBA, you might not create databases from scratch regularly, but you should be familiar with all the settings and design decisions that go into their creation, including, adding database files and the tools involved.

Managing default settings

It is important to understand the role of the model database when creating new databases, regardless of the method of creation. The model database and its entire contents and configuration options are copied to any new database, even TempDB upon service restart. For this reason, never store any data (even for testing) in the model database. Similarly, do not grow the model database from its default size, because this will require all future databases to be that size or larger.

However, the location of the model database's files is not used as a default for new databases. Instead, the default location for database files is stored at the server level. You can view these default storage locations, which should be changed and must be valid, in the Server Properties dialog box in SQL Server Management Studio, on the Database Settings page. There you will find the default locations for Data, Log, and Backup files. These locations are stored in the registry.

On this page, you'll also see the default recovery interval setting, which is by default 0, meaning that SQL Server can manage the frequency of internal automatic CHECKPOINTs. This typically results in an internal checkpoint frequency of one minute. This is an advanced setting that can be (though rarely is) changed at each database level, though it should not be changed at the server level or database level except by experienced administrators.

Also on the Database Settings page of Server Properties you will find the default index fill factor and default backup compression setting. These are server-level defaults applied to each database, but you cannot configure them separately for each database. You can configure them independently at each index level and with each backup statement, respectively.

> ## Inside OUT
>
> *Watch out for the default data and log file locations: they can cause future cumulative updates to fail!*
>
> Portions of cumulative updates reference the default file locations. You might see errors such as "operating system error 3 (The system cannot find the path specified.)" in the detailed log of the cumulative update.
>
> The patches will fail if these default database locations change to an invalid path, if the complete subfolder path does not exist, or if SQL Server loses permissions to access the locations. You will need to restart the cumulative update after correcting the problem with the default locations.

Among the settings inherited by new databases from the model database unless overridden at the time of creation are the following:

- Initial data and log file size

- Data and log file Autogrowth setting

- Data and log file Maximum size

- Recovery model

- Target Recovery Time (which would override the system default recovery interval)

- All Database-Scoped Configurations including the database-level settings for Legacy Cardinality Estimation, Max DOP, Parameter Sniffing, and Query Optimizer Fixes.

- All the Automatic settings, including auto close, auto shrink, auto create/update statistics. (We discuss each of these later in the chapter.)

Inside OUT

Your SQL Server Management Studio connections to the model database will block CREATE DATABASE statements.

Close or disconnect SQL Server Management Studio query windows that use the model database context. If you are configuring the model database by using T-SQL commands, you can leave SQL Server Management Studio query windows open. Create database statements need to reference the model database. User connections, including query windows in SQL Server Management Studio with the model database context, can block the creation of user databases.

You might see the error "Could not obtain exclusive lock on database 'model'. Retry the operation later. CREATE DATABASE failed. Some file names listed could not be created. Check related errors. (Microsoft SQL Server, Error: 1807)".

For applications like SharePoint that create databases, this could lead to application errors.

Owning the databases you create

The login that runs the CREATE DATABASE statement will become the owner of any database you create, even if the account you are using is not a member of the sysadmin group. Any principal that can create a database becomes the owner of that database, even if, for example, they have only membership to the dbcreator built-in server role.

Ideally, databases are not owned by named individual accounts. You might decide to change each database to a service account specific to that database's dependent applications. You must do this after the database is created. You cannot change the database owner via SQL Server Management Studio; instead, you must use the ALTER AUTHORIZATION T-SQL statement.

➤ For more information on the best practices with respect to database ownership and how to change the database owner, see Chapter 6.

Creating additional database files

Every SQL Server database needs at least one data file and one log file. You can use additional data files to maximize storage performance. (We discuss physical database architecture in detail in Chapter 3.)

CHAPTER 4

However, adding additional log files long term is not a wise decision. There is no performance advantage to be gained with more than one transaction log file for a database. SQL Server will not write to them randomly, but sequentially.

The only scenario in which a second transaction log file would be needed is if the first had filled up its volume. If no space can be created on the volume to allow for additional transaction log file data to be written, the database cannot accept new transactions and will refuse new application requests. In this scenario, one possible troubleshooting method is to temporarily add a second transaction log file on another volume to create the space to allow the database transactions to resume accepting transactions. The end resolution involves clearing the primary transaction log file, performing a one-time-only shrink to return it to its original size, and removing the second transaction log file.

Using SQL Server Management Studio to create a new database

You can create and configure database files, specifically their initial sizes, in SQL Server Management Studio. In Object Explorer, right-click Databases, and then, on the shortcut menu, click New Database to open the New Database dialog box.

After you have configured the new database's settings but before you click OK, you can script the T-SQL for the CREATE DATABASE statement.

Here are a few suggestions when creating a new database:

- Pregrow your database and log file sizes to an expected size. This avoids autogrowth events as you initially populate your database. You can speed up this process greatly by using the Perform Volume Maintenance Task permission for the SQL Server service account so that instant file initialization is possible.

    ➤ **We covered instant file initialization earlier in this chapter.**

- Consider the SIMPLE recovery model for your database until it enters production use. Then, the FULL or BULK_LOGGED recovery models might be more appropriate.

    ➤ **For more information database backups and the appropriate recovery model, see Chapter 11.**

- Review the logical and physical files names of your database and the locations. The default locations for the data and log files are a server-level setting but you can override them here. You also can move the files later on (we cover this later in this chapter).

- As soon as the database is created, follow-up with your backup strategy to ensure that it is covered as appropriate with its role.

Deploying a database via SQL Server Data Tools

You can also deploy developed databases to a SQL Server instance using a Database Project in SQL Server Data Tools. For databases for which objects will be developed by your team or another team within your enterprise, SQL Server Data Tools provides a professional and mature environment for teams to develop databases, check them into source control, generate change scripts for incremental deployments, and reduce object scripting errors.

SQL Server Data Tools can generate incremental change scripts or deploy databases directly. It also has the option to drop or re-create databases for each deployment, though this is turned off by default.

You might find it easiest to create the new database by using SQL Server Management Studio and then deploy incremental changes to it with SQL Server Data Tools.

Database properties and options

In this section, we review some commonly changed and managed database settings. There are quite a few settings on the Options page in Database Properties, many involving rarely changed defaults or ANSI-standard deviations for legacy support.

You can view each of these settings in SQL Server Management Studio via Object Explorer. To do so, right-click a database, and then, on the shortcut menu, click Properties. In the Database Properties dialog box, in the pane on the left, click Options. You also can review database settings for all databases in the sys.databases catalog view.

The subsections that follow discuss the settings that you need to consider when creating and managing SQL Server databases.

Collation

Collations exist at three levels in a SQL Server instance: the database, the instance, and TempDB. The collation of the TempDB database by default matches the collation for the instance and should differ only in otherwise unavoidable circumstances. Ideally, the collations in all user databases match the collation at the instance level and for the TempDB, but there are scenarios in which and individual database might need to operate in a different collation.

Oftentimes databases differ from the server-level collation to enforce case sensitivity, but you can also enforce language usage differences (such as kana or accent sensitivity) and sort order differences at the database level.

The default collation for the server is decided at installation and is preselected for you based on the regionalization settings of the Windows Server. You can override this during installation. Some applications, such as Microsoft Dynamics GP, require a case-sensitive collation.

CHAPTER 4

Whereas the server-level collation is virtually unchangeable, databases can change collation. You should change a database's collation only before code is developed for the database or only after extensive testing of existing code.

Be aware that unmatched collations in databases could cause issues when querying across those databases, so you should try to avoid collation differences between databases that will be shared by common applications.

For example, if you write a query that includes a table in a database that's set to the collation SQL_Latin1_General_CP1_CI_AS (which is **c**ase **i**nsensitive and **a**ccent **s**ensitive) and a join to a table in a database that's also set to SQL_Latin1_General_CP1_CS_AS, you will receive the following error:

```
Cannot resolve the collation conflict between "SQL_Latin1_General_CP1_CI_AS" and
"SQL_Latin1_General_CP1_CS_AS" in the equal to operation.
```

Short of changing either database to match the other, you will need to modify your code to use the COLLATE statement when referencing columns in each query, as demonstrated in the following example:

```
… FROM
CS_AS.sales.sales s1
INNER JOIN CI_AS.sales.sales s2
ON s1.[salestext] COLLATE SQL_Latin1_General_CP1_CI_AS = s2.[salestext]
```

In contained databases, collation is defined at two different levels: the database and the catalog. You cannot change the catalog collation cannot from Latin1_General_100_CI_AS_WS_KS_SC. Database metadata and variables are always in the catalog's collation. The COLLATE DATABASE_DEFAULT syntax can also be a very useful tool if you know the collation before execution.

Recovery model

The FULL recovery model is appropriate for production environments when the data loss tolerance of the database is smaller than the frequency of full backups or when point-in-time recovery is appropriate. If you are copying a database from a production environment to a development environment, it is likely you will want to change the recovery model from FULL to SIMPLE. If you are copying a database from a testing environment to a production environment for the first time, it is likely that you will want to change the recovery model from SIMPLE to FULL.

> ➤ **For more information on database backups and the appropriate recovery model, see Chapter 11.**

Compatibility level

SQL Server provides database compatibility modes for backward compatibility to database-level features, including improvements to the query optimizer, additional fields in dynamic management objects, syntax improvements, and other database-level objects.

Compatibility mode is a database-level setting, and databases upgraded from an older version to a new version will retain a prior compatibility mode. For example, some new syntax additions in SQL Server 2016 such as the new `STRING_SPLIT()` or `OPENJSON` functions will not work when run in the context of a database in a prior compatibility mode. Other syntax improvements, such as `DATEFROMPARTS()` and `AT TIME ZONE`, will work in any database in any compatibility mode in SQL Server 2017.

SQL Server 2017 supports compatibility levels down to SQL Server 2008 (internal version 100), the same as SQL Server 2016.

Database compatibility does not require a service restart to take place, but we strongly recommend that you do *not* perform this during normal operating hours. Promoting the database compatibility mode should be thoroughly tested in preproduction environments. Even though syntax errors are extremely unlikely, other changes to the query optimizer engine from version to version could result in performance changes to the application that must be evaluated prior to rollout to a production system. When you do upgrade production from a prior compatibility level, you should do so during a maintenance period, not during user activity.

You should review database-specific settings at the time of migration, as well. You can review them from a quick scroll of the sys.databases catalog view or from the database properties window in SQL Server Management Studio.

The following is not a list of all database settings, but you should pay attention to these when restoring, deploying, or attaching a database to a new instance.

Containment type

Partially contained databases represent a fundamental change in the relationship between server and database. They are an architectural decision that you make when applications are intended to be portable between multiple SQL Server instances or when security should be entirely limited to the database context, not in the traditional server login/database user sense.

> ➤ **For more information about the security implications of contained databases, see Chapter 6.**

Azure SQL databases are themselves a type of contained database, able to move from host to host in the Azure platform as a service (PaaS) environment, transparent to administrators and users. You can design databases that can be moved between SQL Server instances in a similar fashion, should the application architecture call for such capability.

Changing the Containment Type from None to Partial converts the database to a partially contained database, and should not be taken lightly. We do not advise changing a database that has already been developed without the partial containment setting, because there are differences with how temporary objects behave and how collations are enforced. Some database features, including Change Data Capture, Change Tracking, replication, and some parts of Service Broker are not supported in partially contained databases. You should carefully review, while logged in as a member of the sysadmin server role or the db_owner database role, the system dynamic management view sys.dm_db_uncontained_entities for an inventory of objects that are not contained.

Autoclose

You should turn on this setting only in very specific and resource-exhausted environments. It activates the periodic closure of connections and the clearing of buffer allocations, when user requests are done. When active, it unravels the very purpose of application connection pooling; for example, rendering certain application architectures useless and increasing the number of login events. You should never turn on this settings as part of performance tuning or trouble-shooting exercise of a busy environment.

Auto Create statistics

When you turn on this setting, the query optimizer automatically create statistics needed for runtime plans, even for read-only databases (statistics are stored in the tempdb for read-only databases). Some applications, such as SharePoint, handle the creation of statistics automatically: due to the dynamic nature of its tables and queries, SharePoint handles statistics creation and updates by itself. Unless an application like SharePoint insists otherwise, you should turn on this setting. You can identify autocreated statistics in the database as they will use a naming convention similar to _WA_Sys_<column_number>_<hexadecimal>.

Inside OUT

What are statistics?

SQL Server uses statistics to describe the distribution and nature of the data in tables. The query optimizer needs the Auto Create setting turned on so that it can create single-column statistics when compiling queries. These statistics help the query optimizer create optimal runtime plans. Without relevant and up-to-date statistics, the query optimizer may not choose the best way to execute queries. Unless an application has been specifically designed to replace the functionality of Auto Create and Auto Update statistics, such as SharePoint, these two settings should be turned on.

Autocreate incremental statistics

Introduced in SQL 2014, this setting allows for the creation of statistics that take advantage of table partitioning, reducing the overhead of statistics creation. This setting has no impact on nonpartitioned tables. Because it can reduce the cost of creating and updating statistics, you should turn it on.

This will have an effect only on new statistics created after this setting is turned on. When you turn it on, you should update the statistics on tables with partitions, including the INCREMENTAL = ON parameter, as shown here:

```
UPDATE STATISTICS [dbo].[HoriztonalPartitionTable] [PK_HorizontalPartitionTable] WITH
RESAMPLE, INCREMENTAL = ON;
```

You also should update any manual scripts you have implemented to update statistics to use the ON PARTITIONS parameter when applicable. In the catalog view sys.stats, the is_incremental column will equal 1 if the statistics were created incrementally, as demonstrated here:

```
UPDATE STATISTICS [dbo].[HoriztonalPartitionTable] [PK_HorizontalPartitionTable] WITH
RESAMPLE ON PARTITIONS (1);
```

Autoshrink

You should never turn on this setting. It will automatically return any free space of more than 25 percent of the data file or transaction log. You should shrink a database only as a one-time operation to reduce file size after unplanned or unusual file growth. This setting could result in unnecessary fragmentation, overhead, and frequent rapid log autogrowth events.

Auto Update Statistics

When turned on, statistics will be updated periodically. Statistics are considered out of date by the query optimizer when a ratio of data modifications to rows in the table has been reached. The query optimizer checks for and updates the out-of-date statistic before running a query plan and therefore has some overhead, though the performance benefit of updated statistics usually outweighs this cost. This is especially true when the updated statistics resulted in a better optimization plan. Because the query optimizer updates the statistics first and then runs the plan, the update is described as synchronous.

Auto Update Statistics Asynchronously

This changes the behavior of the Auto Update Statistics by one important detail. Query runs will continue even if the query optimizer has identified an out-of-date statistics object. The statistics will be updated afterward.

> ### NOTE
> It is important to note that you must turn on Auto Update Statistics for Auto Update Statistics Asynchronously to have any effect. There is no warning or enforcement in SQL Server Management Studio for this, and though a Connect Item with this concern was raised in 2011, it was marked Closed as "Won't Fix."

Inside OUT

Should I turn on Auto Update Statistics and Auto Update Statistics Asynchronously in SQL Server 2017?

Yes! (Unless the application specifically recommends not to, such as SharePoint.)

Starting in SQL Server 2016 (and with database compatibility mode 130), the ratio of data modifications to rows in the table that helps identify out-of-date statistics has been aggressively lowered, causing statistics to be automatically updated more frequently. This is especially evident in large tables in which many rows were regularly updated. In SQL Server 2014 and earlier, this more aggressive behavior was not on by default, but could be turned on via Trace Flag 2371 starting with SQL 2008 R2 SP1.

It is more important starting with SQL Server 2016 than in previous versions to turn on Auto Update Statistics Asynchronously, which can dramatically reduce the overhead involved in automatic statistics maintenance.

Allow Snapshot Isolation

This setting allows for the use of Snapshot Isolation mode at the query level. When you turn this on, the row versioning process begins in TempDB, though this setting does little more than allow for this mechanism to be used in this database. To begin to use Snapshot Isolation mode in the database, you would need to change code; for example, to include SET TRANSACTION ISOLATION LEVEL SNAPSHOT.

➤ For much more on Snapshot Isolation and other isolation levels, see Chapter 9.

Is Read Committed Snapshot On

Turning on this setting changes the default isolation mode of the database from READ COMMITTED to READ COMMITTED SNAPSHOT. You should not turn this on during regular business hours; instead, do it during a maintenance window. Ideally, however, this setting is on and accounted for during development.

There will be an impact to the utilization of the TempDB as well as a rise in the IO_COMPLETION and WAIT_XTP_RECOVERY wait types, so you need to perform proper load testing. This setting, however, is potentially a major performance improvement and the core of enterprise-quality concurrency.

Page Verify Option

For all databases, this setting should be CHECKSUM. The legacy TORN_PAGE option is a sign that this database has been moved over the years up from a pre-SQL 2005 version, but this setting has never changed. Since SQL 2005, CHECKSUM has the superior and default setting, but it requires an administrator to manually change.

Trustworthy

It is not recommended to ever turn on this setting unless it is made necessary because of an inflexible architecture requirement. Doing so could allow for malicious activity on one database to affect other databases, even if specific permissions have not been granted. Before turning on this setting, you should understand the implications of cross-database ownership chains in a multitenant or web-hosted shared SQL Server environment.

> ➤ **For more on object ownership, see Chapter 6.**

Database Read-Only

You can set an older database, or a database intended for nonchanging archival, to READ_ONLY mode to prevent changes. Any member of the server sysadmin role or the database db_owner role can revert this to READ_WRITE, so you should not consider this setting a security measure.

Database-Scoped Configurations

First introduced in SQL Server 2016 (and also in Azure SQL Database v12), Database-Scoped Configurations are a set of options previously available only at the server or individual query, such as Max Degree of Parallelism (MaxDOP). You can now change settings easily via database options that previously were available only via trace flags at the server level.

You can view each of these Database-Scoped Configurations in SQL Server Management Studio. In Object Explorer, right-click a database, and then, on the shortcut menu, click Properties. In the Database Properties dialog box, in the pane on the left, click Options. On the Options page, a heading just for Database-Scoped Configurations appears at the top of the Other Options list.

The current database context is important for determining which database's properties will be applied to a query that references objects in multiple databases. This means that the same query, run in two different database contents, will have different execution plans, potentially because of differences in each database's Max DOP setting, for example.

Query Store

Introduced in SQL Server 2016, the Query Store is a built-in reporting mechanism and data warehouse for measuring and tracking cached runtime plans. Though useful, it is not on by default, and you should turn it on as soon as possible if you intend to use it to aid performance tuning and troubleshooting cached runtime plans.

➤ **For more information on the Query Store, see Chapter 9.**

Indirect checkpoints

If your database was created in SQL Server 2016 or 2017, your database is already configured to use indirect checkpoint, which became the default for all databases in SQL Server 2016. However, databases created on prior versions of SQL Server will continue to use the classic automatic checkpoint, which has been in place since SQL Server 7.0 and tweaked only since.

This is an advanced topic, and one that we won't dive into too deeply, save for one configuration option that you should change on databases that have been upgraded from versions prior to SQL Server 2016.

What is a checkpoint? This is the process by which SQL Server writes to the drive both data and transaction log pages modified in memory, also known as "dirty" pages. Checkpoints can be issued manually by using the CHECKPOINT command but are issued in the background for you, so issuing CHECKPOINT is rarely necessary and is usually limited to troubleshooting.

What is automatic checkpoint? Prior to SQL Server 2016 and since SQL Server 7.0, by default all databases used automatic checkpoint. The rate with which dirty pages were committed to memory has increased with versions, as disk I/O and memory capacities of servers have increased. The goal of automatic checkpoint was to ensure that all dirty pages were managed within a goal defined in the server configuration option Recovery Interval. By default, this was 0, which meant it was automatically configured. This tended to be around 60 seconds, but was more or less unconcerned with the number of pages dirtied by transactions between checkpoints.

What is indirect checkpoint? This is a new strategy of taking care of "dirty pages" that is far more scalable and can deliver a performance difference especially on modern systems with a large amount of memory. Indirect checkpoints manage dirty pages in memory differently; instead of scanning memory, indirect checkpoints proactively gather lists of dirty pages. Indirect checkpoints then manage the list of dirty pages and continuously commit them from memory to the drive, on a pace to not exceed an upper bound of recovery time. This upper bound is defined in the database configuration option TARGET_RECOVERY_TIME. By default, in databases created in SQL Server 2016 or higher, this is 60 seconds. In databases created in SQL Server 2012 or 2014, this option was available but set to 0, which indicates that legacy automatic checkpoints are in use.

So, even though the recovery time goal hasn't really changed, the method by which it is achieved has. Indirect checkpoints are significantly faster than automatic checkpoints, especially as servers are configured with more and more memory. You might notice an improvement in the performance of backups specifically.

You can configure a database that was created on an older version of SQL Server to use indirect checkpoints instead of automatic checkpoints with a single command. The TARGET_RECOVERY_TIME will be 0 for older databases still using automatic checkpoint. The master database will also have a TARGET_RECOVERY_TIME of 0 by default, though msdb and model will be set to 60 starting with SQL Server 2016.

Consider setting the TARGET_RECOVERY_TIME database configuration to 60 seconds to match the default for new databases created in SQL Server 2016 or higher, as shown here:

```
ALTER DATABASE [olddb] SET TARGET_RECOVERY_TIME = 60 SECONDS WITH NO_WAIT;
```

You can check this setting for each database in the TARGET_RECOVERY_TIME_IN_SECONDS column of the system view sys.databases.

NOTE

There is a specific performance degradation involving nonyielding schedulers or excessive spinlocks that can arise because of this setting being applied to the TempDB by default, as of SQL Server 2016. It is not common. It is identifiable and resolvable with analysis and custom solution to disable indirect checkpoints on the TempDB, detailed in this blog post from the SQL Server Tiger Team: *https://blogs.msdn.microsoft.com/sql_server_team/indirect-checkpoint-and-tempdb-the-good-the-bad-and-the-non-yielding-scheduler/.*

Moving and removing databases

In this section, we review the steps and options to moving databases and the various methods and stages of removing databases from use.

Moving user and system databases

In this section, we discuss moving database files, which becomes necessary from time to time, either because of improper initial locations or the addition of new storage volumes to a server. Relocating system and user databases is similar to each other, with the master database being an exception. Let's look at each scenario.

CHAPTER 4

Locating SQL Server files

As we discussed in our earlier checklist, you can review the location of all database files by querying the catalog view sys.master_files. If you did not specify the intended location for the data files while you were on the Data Directories page of the Database Engine Configuration step of SQL Server Setup, you will find your system database files on the OS volume at %programfiles%\Microsoft SQL Server*instance*\MSSQL\Data.

> #### NOTE
>
> In sys.master_files, the physical_name of each database file, the logical name of each database file (in the Name field of this view), and the name of the database do not need to match. It is possible, through restore operations, to accidentally create multiple databases with the same logical file names.

Ideally, there should be no data or log files on the OS volume, even system database files. You can move these after SQL Server Setup is complete, however.

When you're planning to move your database data or log files, prepare their new file path location by granting FULL CONTROL permissions to the per-SID name for the SQL Server instance. (Note that this is not necessarily the SQL Server service account.) For the default instance, this will be NT SERVICE\MSSQLSERVER; for default instances, it will be NT SERVICE\MSSQL$*instancename*.

Inside OUT

Where does SQL Server keep track of the locations of database files?

When the SQL Server process is started, only three pieces of location information are provided to the service:

- The location of the master database data file
- The location of the master database log file
- The location of the SQL Server error log

You can find this information in the startup parameters of the SQL Server service in the SQL Server Configuration Manager application. All other database file locations are stored in the master database.

Database actions: offline versus detach versus drop

Earlier in this chapter, we discussed strategies to move user database files by using the OFFLINE status. Let's discuss the differences between various ways to remove a database from a SQL Server instance.

The OFFLINE option is one way to quickly remove a database from usability. It is also the most easily reversed, as demonstrated here:

```
SET ONLINE;
```

You should set maintenance activities to ignore databases that are offline because they cannot be accessed, maintained, or backed up. The data and log files remain in place in their location on the drive and can be moved. The database is still listed with its files in sys.master_files.

Taking a database offline is an excellent intermediate administrative step before you DETACH or DROP a database; for example, a database that is not believed to be used any more. Should a user report that she can no longer access the database, the administrator can simply bring the database back online—an immediate action.

You can separate a database's files from the SQL Server by using a DETACH. The data and log files remain in place in their location on the drive and can be moved. But detaching a database removes it from sys.master_files.

To reattach the database, in SQL Server Management Studio, in Object Explorer, follow the Attach steps. It is not as immediate an action and requires more administrative intervention than taking the database offline.

When reattaching the database, you must locate at least the primary data file for the database. The Attach process will then attempt to reassociate all the database files to SQL Server control, in their same locations. If their locations have changed, you must provide a list of all database files and their new locations.

> NOTE
> If you are detaching or restoring a database to attach or copy it to another server, do not forget to follow-up by moving SQL Server logins and then potentially reassociating orphaned database users with their logins. For more information, review Chapter 7.

CHAPTER 4

Inside OUT

When moving user database files, why should I use offline/online instead of detach/attach?

There are a number of reasons you need to take a user database offline instead of the strategy of detaching, moving, and reattaching the files.

While the database is offline, database information remains queryable in sys.master_files and other system catalog views. You can still reference the locations of database files after taking the database offline to ensure that everything is moved. Also, it is not possible to detach a database when the database is the source of a database snapshot or part of a replication publication. Taking a database offline is the only method possible in these scenarios.

Note that you cannot detach or take system databases offline. A service restart is necessary to move system databases, including the master database.

Finally, a DROP DATABASE command, issued when you use the Delete feature of Object Explorer, removes the database from the SQL Server and deletes the database files on the drive. An exception to the delete files on drive behavior is if the destination database is offline. Deleting an offline database and detaching a database are therefore similar actions.

Dropping a database does not by default remove its backup and restore history from the msdb database, though there is a check box at the bottom of the Drop Database dialog box in SQL Server Management Studio that you can select for this action. The stored procedure msdb.dbo.sp_delete_database_backuphistory is run to remove this history. For databases with a long backup history that has not been maintained by a log history retention policy, the step to delete this history can take a long time and could cause SQL Server Management Studio to stop responding. Instead, delete old backup and restore history incrementally by using msdb.dbo.sp_delete_backuphistory and/or run the msdb.dbo.sp_delete_database_backuphistory procedure in a new SQL Server Management Studio query window.

➤ For more information on backup and restore history, see Chapter 13.

Moving user database files

You can move user databases without a SQL Server instance restart and without disrupting other databases by taking the database offline, updating the files, moving them, and then bringing the database online again.

Use the following steps to move user database files:

1. Perform a manual full backup of the soon-to-be affected databases.

2. During a maintenance outage for the database and any applications that are dependent, begin by taking the user database offline and then running a T-SQL script to alter the location of each database file.

3. Here's an example of the T-SQL statements required:

```
ALTER DATABASE database_name SET OFFLINE WITH ROLLBACK IMMEDIATE
ALTER DATABASE database_name MODIFY FILE ( NAME = logical_data_file_name,
FILENAME = 'location\physical_data_file_name.mdf' );
ALTER DATABASE database_name MODIFY FILE ( NAME = logical_log_file_name,
FILENAME = 'location\physical_log_file_name.ldf' );
ALTER DATABASE database_name SET ONLINE
```

4. While the database is offline, physically copy the database files to their new location. (You will delete the old copies when you've confirmed the new configuration.) When the file operation is complete, bring the database back online.

5. Verify that the data files have been moved by querying sys.master_files, which is a catalog view that returns all files for all databases. Look for the physical_name volume to reflect the new location correctly.

6. After you have verified that SQL Server is recognizing the database files in their new locations, delete the files in the original location to reclaim the drive space.

7. After you have successfully moved the database files, you should perform a manual backup of the master database.

Moving system database files, except for master

You cannot move system database files while the SQL Server instance is online; thus, you must stop the SQL Server service.

NOTE

If you plan to move all of the system databases to a different volume, you also will need to move the SQL Server Agent Error Log, or SQL Server Agent will not be able to start.

You can do this in SQL Server Management Studio. In Object Explorer, connect to the SQL Server instance, and then expand the SQL Server Agent folder. Right-click Error Logs, and then, on the shortcut menu that opens, click Configure. Provide a new Error Log File location for the SQLAGENT.OUT file.

CHAPTER 4

Verify that the SQL Server Agent per-SID name for the SQL Server Agent service has FULL CONTROL permissions to the new folder. The per-service SID account will be NT Service\SQLSERVERAGENT for default instances or NT Service\SQLAgent$*instancename* for named instances.

When you later restart the SQL Server service and the SQL Server Agent service, the Agent error log will be written to the new location.

1. Begin by performing a manual full backup of the soon-to-be affected databases.

2. For model, msdb, and TempDB, begin by running a T-SQL script (similar to the script for moving user databases). SQL Server will not use the new locations of the system databases until the next time the service is restarted. You cannot set the system databases to offline.

3. During a maintenance outage for the SQL Server instance, stop the SQL Server instance, and then copy the database files to their new location. (You will delete the old copies when you've confirmed the new configuration.) The only exception here is that the TempDB data and log files do not need to be moved—they will be re-created automatically by SQL Server upon service start.

4. When the file operation is complete, start the SQL Server service again.

5. Verify that the data files have been moved by querying sys.master_files. Look for the physical_name volume to reflect the new location correctly.

6. After you have verified that SQL Server is recognizing the database files in their new locations, delete the files in the original location to reclaim the drive space.

7. After you have successfully moved the database files, perform a manual backup of the master database.

If you encounter problems starting SQL Server after moving system databases to another volume—for example if the SQL Server service account starts and then stops—check for the following:

1. Verify that the SQL Server service account and SQL Server Agent service account have permissions to the new folders location. Review the following link for a list of File System Permissions Granted to SQL Server service accounts: *https://docs.microsoft.com/sql/database-engine/configure-windows/configure-windows-service-accounts-and-permissions#Reviewing_ACLs*

2. Check the Windows Application Event Log and System Event Log for errors.

3. If you cannot resolve the issue, if necessary, start SQL Server with Trace Flag T3608, which does not start the SQL Server fully, only the master database. You then can move all other database files, including the other system databases, back to their original location by using T-SQL commands issued through SQL Server Management Studio.

Moving master database files

Moving the master database files is not difficult, but it is a more complicated process than that for the other system databases. Instead of issuing an ALTER DATABASE ... ALTER FILE statement, you must edit the parameters passed to the SQL Server service in SQL Server Configuration Manager.

1. On the Startup Parameters page, notice that there are three entries containing three files in their current paths. (If you have other startup parameters in this box, do not modify them now.)

    Edit the two parameters beginning with –d and –1 (lowercase "L"). The –e parameter is the location of the SQL Server Error Log; you might want to move that, as well.

    After editing the master database data file (-d) and the master database log file (-l) locations, click OK. Keep in mind that the SQL Server service will not look for the files in their new location until the service is restarted.

2. Stop the SQL Server service, and then copy the master database data and log files to their new location. (You will delete the old copies when you've confirmed the new configuration.)

3. When the file operation is complete, start the SQL Server service again.

4. Verify that the data files have been moved by querying sys.master_files, a dynamic management view that returns all files for all databases. Look for the physical_name volume to reflect the new location correctly.

5. After you have verified that SQL Server is recognizing the database files in their new locations, delete the files in the original location to reclaim the drive space.

Single-user mode

By default, all databases are in MULTI_USER mode. Sometimes, it is necessary to gain exclusive access to a database with a single connection, typically in SQLCMD or in a SQL Server Management Studio query window.

For example, when performing a restore, the connection must have exclusive access to the database. By default, the restore will wait until it gains exclusive access. You could attempt to discontinue all connections, but there is a much easier way: setting a database to SINGLE_USER mode removes all other connections but your own.

CHAPTER 4

Setting a database to SINGLE_USER mode also requires exclusive access. If other users are connected to the database, running the following statement will be unsuccessful:

```
ALTER DATABASE database_name SET SINGLE_USER;
```

It is then necessary to provide further syntax to decide how to treat other connections to the database.

- **WITH NO_WAIT.** The ALTER DATABASE command will fail if it cannot gain exclusive access to the database It is important to note that without this statement or any other WITH commands, the ALTER DATABASE command will wait indefinitely.

- **WITH ROLLBACK IMMEDIATE.** Rollback all conflicting requests, ending other SQL Server Management Studio Query window connections, for example.

- **WITH ROLLBACK AFTER n SECONDS.** Delays the effect of WITH ROLLBACK IMMEDIATE by *n* SECONDS, which is not particularly more graceful to competing user connections, just delayed.

For example:

```
ALTER DATABASE databasename
SET SINGLE_USER WITH ROLLBACK IMMEDIATE;
```

Instead of issuing a WITH ROLLBACK, you might choose to identify other sessions connected to the destination database; for example, by using the following:

```
SELECT *
FROM sys.dm_exec_sessions
WHERE
db_name(database_id) = 'database_name';
```

And then evaluate the appropriate strategy for dealing with any requests coming from that session, including communication with that user and closing of unused connections to that database in dialog boxes, SQL Server Management Studio query windows, or user applications.

After you have completed the activities that required exclusive access, set the database back to MULTI_USER mode:

```
ALTER DATABASE database_name SET MULTI_USER;
```

You need to gain exclusive access to databases prior to a restore. This script to change the database to SINGLE_USER and back to MULTI_USER is a common step wrapped around a database restore.

➤ **For more information on database restores, see Chapter 11.**

### CHAPTER 5

Provisioning Azure SQL Database

This chapter delves into Microsoft Azure SQL Database, the Microsoft SQL Server–compatible relational database offering in the Microsoft Azure cloud. Azure SQL Database is designed so that cloud applications can take advantage of relational database services without the overhead of managing the actual database engine. Azure SQL Database is also designed to meet requirements from hosting a single database associated with an organization's line-of-business application to hosting thousands of databases for a global software-as-a-service offering. In this chapter, we look at basic Azure SQL Database concepts and how to provision databases and manage them.

We first introduce fundamental concepts of Azure and database-as-a-service. Next, you'll learn how to create your first server and database. These sections include thorough coverage of the available options and why each one matters. Also covered are the current limitations of Azure SQL Database compared to SQL Server 2017. You will find there aren't many left, but, still, a successful deployment requires planning for missing features.

Security must be on your checklist when deploying any database, and perhaps even more so in the cloud. This chapter includes coverage of all the security features specific only to Azure SQL Database. For security features common to SQL Server, refer to Chapter 6 and Chapter 7. This chapter then reviews features designed to prepare your cloud-hosted database for disaster recovery. Finally, we present an overview of different methods that you can use to move on-premises SQL Server databases to Azure SQL Database.

Throughout the chapter, you will also find many PowerShell samples to complete tasks. This is important because the flexibility of cloud computing offers quick setup and teardown of resources. Automation through scripting becomes a must-have skill—unless you prefer to work overtime clicking around in the web GUI. If you need an introduction to PowerShell, a solid place to start is *https://docs.microsoft.com/powershell/scripting/getting-started/getting-started-with-windows-powershell*.

One area that is beyond the scope for this book is creating an Azure subscription. There are many options for creating an Azure subscription and there are ways to obtain free monthly Azure credits for developers or IT professionals. You can consult the resources at *https://azure. microsoft.com/get-started/* to begin your journey to the cloud.

Azure and database-as-a-service concepts

You have likely already heard or read many different definitions of cloud computing. Rather than add yet one more, we will briefly discuss some key features of cloud computing and how they apply to Azure SQL Database. The first concept relates to accounting: expenses. With traditional on-premises environments, there is usually a significant initial outlay of capital. This is called capital expenditure, or "CapEx." Expenses in Azure, on the other hand, fall under the category of operational expenditure, or "OpEx." With OpEx, there is no initial monetary outlay and mostly no longterm financial commitment. The fees you pay are pay-per-use charges and are all inclusive: hardware, licensing, electricity, monitoring, and so on.

Under some Azure subscription models, you are incentivized for committing to a minimum annual spend in return for a reduced service cost. It is important to note that OpEx might not be cheaper than CapEx overall—that depends on how efficiently services are provisioned and used. Those considerations are beyond the scope of this text, but we strongly encourage you to plan for optimizing your resource allocation early.

The second concept in cloud computing is *elasticity*. Elasticity means that the resources you provision are not fixed in terms of capacity. In on-premises environments, you would provision hardware and software (licensing) sufficient to accommodate peak demand. In Azure, elasticity gives you the ability to scale up and down or out and in as needed to accommodate demand at any given moment.

Finally, *control* also becomes a discussion topic. With on-premises deployments of SQL Server, the DBA team decides which hardware to select, when to apply patches, and when to upgrade to a major new release. With Azure SQL Database, it's the team at Microsoft that makes these decisions. The team announces major changes and updates using a variety of channels, and, as a cloud DBA, one of your tasks will include regularly reviewing these announcements. You will need to thoroughly understand your Azure environment to determine which changes or updates will affect your application(s).

Database-as-a-service

Azure provides many types of services, including virtual machines (VMs), web applications, and, of course, Azure SQL Database. Cloud services are often categorized in one of three types: infrastructure-as-a-service (IaaS), platform-as-a-service (PaaS), and software-as-a-service (SaaS). In this book, we refer to Azure SQL Database as database-as-a-service (DBaaS), which is a specialized type of PaaS.

There is an alternative way to host SQL Server databases in the cloud, which is using Azure VM images, which can come with a SQL Server version preinstalled. In that case, you are using IaaS. With IaaS, you gain increased control and complete feature parity with on-premises deployments. IaaS also introduces more responsibility for sizing the VM specifications appropriately and managing software updates for both the operating system (OS) and SQL Server.

We encourage you to consider the implications of choosing between IaaS and PaaS for hosting your databases in the cloud. A discussion of these implications is available in Chapter 3.

Managing Azure: The Azure portal and PowerShell

When you are ready to begin using Azure, you will need to deploy, manage, and eventually tear down resources when applications are retired or upgraded. To manage on-premises Microsoft environments, you might use various GUI tools (often based on the Microsoft Management Console) or PowerShell. In Azure, the primary GUI is the Azure portal. As mentioned at the beginning of the chapter, you should also become comfortable using PowerShell. A third option for managing Azure is the Azure Command-Line Interface (CLI). You can use the Azure CLI across platforms (Windows, macOS, and Linux) and within the portal using Azure Cloud Shell (in preview as of writing). In this chapter, the focus is on the GUI and the portal, with only a few key operations illustrated using Azure CLI.

For managing Azure and Azure SQL Database using PowerShell, you should always use the latest Azure PowerShell module. The module is updated frequently, so be sure to check for updates regularly. You can install the PowerShell module using the following PowerShell command, run with Administrator privileges:

```
Install-Module AzureRM
```

If you need to update the module, use the following:

```
Update-Module AzureRM
```

TROUBLESHOOTING

Installing modules using the `Install-Module` cmdlet requires PowerShell version 3 or higher. You might need to install the NuGet Package Provider first, but you will be prompted to do so.

If you prefer a GUI to install or update the Azure PowerShell module, use the Web Platform Installer (WebPI) from *http://www.microsoft.com/web/downloads/platform.aspx*. If you use the WebPI to install the module, you also need to use WebPI to update it. The PowerShell `Update-Module` cmdlet will not be able to update the module if it was installed using the WebPI.

CHAPTER 5

After installing or updating the module, you might want to test whether you can successfully connect to your Azure subscription. Use the following command to sign in to Azure using a Microsoft account or an Azure Active Directory account:

```
Login-AzureRmAccount
```

TROUBLESHOOTING

To run the Azure cmdlets, you might need to change the PowerShell runtime policy to "RemoteSigned." Use `Set-ExecutionPolicy RemoteSigned` **from an elevated PowerShell command window.**

The `Login-AzureRmAccount` cmdlet will output the active subscription. If you need to switch the subscription, you can use the `Get-AzureRmSubscription` cmdlet to see a list of all subscriptions your account can manage. You can then use the `Select-AzureRmSubscription` cmdlet to change the active subscription to another one. This is illustrated using the commands that follow and assumes that you have a subscription with the name "Pay-As-You-Go."

```
Get-AzureRmSubscription
Select-AzureRmSubscription -SubscriptionName 'Pay-As-You-Go'
```

NOTE

This section intentionally does not cover managing the database itself. This is discussed in later sections.

Azure governance

Even relatively modest on-premises environments require governance—the organizational processes and procedures by which the environment is managed and responsibilities are delineated. Governance is also a necessity in cloud environments. In this chapter, we can't delve into all of the governance issues related to cloud operations. We do, however, discuss some features of Azure that allow governance to be formalized.

Azure resources are organized in a hierarchy of containers. The container at the top level is the subscription. The subscription is primarily a billing boundary—all resources in a single subscription appear on a single bill and have the same billing cycle. There are also life cycle consequences: should a subscription be discontinued, all resources within the subscription will stop. (Eventually, the subscription will be deleted.) Security configuration is also associated with the subscription: a subscription trusts a single Azure Active Directory (Azure AD) instance. This means that all user accounts used to manage resources within the subscription must exist within the trusted Azure AD instance. Microsoft accounts or user accounts from other Azure AD instances can be added as external users to the trusted instance. An organization can choose to have multiple Azure subscriptions that trust the same Azure AD instance.

A single subscription can have many resources of several types, of which Azure SQL Database is just one. To allow organizing these resources by life cycle and to provide a security boundary, *resource groups* exists. Resource groups are logical containers that have a name and a little metadata. The resources in a resource group are deleted if the resource group itself is deleted, hence the life cycle relationship between the resources and the resource group. Using Role-Based Access Control, permissions can be granted on a resource group and those permissions will apply to the resources within the group. Configuring permissions this way can be a huge timesaver and increase visibility into permission assignments. This is discussed in more detail in the section "Security in Azure SQL Database" later in the chapter.

NOTE

You can move resources between resource groups and between subscriptions. When moving resources, the Azure region in which they are located will not change, even if the target resource group's location is different. The location of a resource group determines only where that resource groups' metadata is stored, not where the actual resources are hosted.

Figure 5-1 illustrates the relationship between the subscription, resource group, and resource.

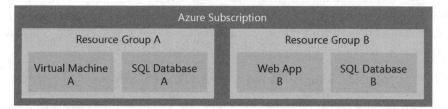

Figure 5-1 The container relationship between Azure subscription, resource groups, and resources.

Logical SQL Servers

The Azure SQL Database service introduces a concept called a *logical SQL Server*. This "server" is quite different from what you might be used to on-premises. An Azure SQL Server is best described as a connection endpoint and less as an instance or a server. For example, a logical SQL Server does not provide compute or storage resources. It does not provide much configuration. And although there is a virtual master database, there is no model, TempDB, or msdb—those are abstracted away.

In addition to missing several features of an on-premises SQL Server, there are also features that are unique to logical SQL servers: firewall configuration and elastic pools to name just two.

> ➤ **You can find more information about firewall configuration later in this chapter. We covered elastic pools in Chapter 3.**

For now, you should consider that your logical SQL server determines the geographic region where your data will be stored. When a single server hosts multiple databases, these databases are collocated in the same Azure region, but they might not be hosted on the same hardware. That is of no consequence to you when using the databases, but the point serves to illustrate the purely *logical* nature of the concept.

Cloud-first

If you've been working with SQL Server for a few years, you've likely noticed the increased release cadence. This is a direct result of the *cloud-first* approach in SQL Server product development that Microsoft adopted a few years ago. Cloud-first in this context means that new features are generally first made available in Azure SQL Database as a preview feature. Those preview features are usually opt-in and are closely monitored by the product team. The close monitoring allows the team to quickly identify usage patterns and issues. These features are then included in the next SQL Server release. Examples of features released this way are Always Encrypted, dynamic data masking, and graph tables.

Database Transaction Unit

Database Transaction Units (DTUs) are likely the Azure SQL Database concept that new adopters struggle with the most. DBAs must comprehend what it means and come to terms with the fact that this single measure is how you determine the level of performance to expect for your database.

A DTU is a blended measure of hardware resources that are provided for the database. This blend includes CPU, memory, and data and transaction log I/O. An increase in DTU results in a linear increase in each of the hardware resources. Thus, when doubling the DTUs for a database, you are effectively doubling how much CPU, memory, and I/O is assigned to your database. The relative mix of these hardware measures was determined by Microsoft using a benchmark developed for this purpose. This benchmark is called the Azure SQL Database Benchmark. It is designed to be representative of common Online Transaction Processing (OLTP) workloads.

> ➤ To read a detailed description of the benchmark, go to *https://docs.microsoft.com/azure/ sql-database/sql-database-benchmark-overview*.

As you'll learn in the section on provisioning Azure SQL Database, when creating a database, you specify the number of DTUs for that database by specifying the pricing tier and service objective. Additional differences between the pricing tiers are also discussed in that section.

Inside OUT

How do you know how many DTUs to provision?

Accurately provisioning DTUs for your database workload prevents slow response times or excessive charges. There are techniques that you can use to optimize your DTU estimations. When planning for migration from on-premises to Azure SQL Database, you can use the Azure SQL Database DTU Calculator.

The DTU Calculator is a tool available as an executable or a PowerShell script that will measure processor time, drive reads and writes, and log bytes per second for your on-premises database server using performance counters. The tool creates a CSV file with the values measured over 60 minutes. This CSV file is then uploaded to the DTU Calculator website, which returns an analysis and recommendation. The DTU Calculator is not affiliated with Microsoft. You can find the DTU Calculator at *https://dtucalculator.azurewebsites.net*.

After your database is in the cloud, you can review your DTU usage and identify the queries that use the most resources by using the Query Performance Insight (QPI) blade in the portal. QPI uses information from Query Store, so verify that it is turned on if you want to use QPI. For more information on QPI, go to *https://docs.microsoft.com/azure/sql-database/sql-database-query-performance*.

CHAPTER 5

Resource scalability

Scalability is a key feature of cloud computing. You can scale up or scale down an Azure SQL database with minimal impact to applications. This scaling activity is completed while the database is online. You can initiate the scaling operation from the portal or by using PowerShell. Depending on the size of the database and the nature of the scale operation, the operation can take several hours to complete.

NOTE

Scaling down is possible only if your database is not currently larger than the maximum size of the destination tier or service objective. Any backups that are older than the retention period for the destination tier are also immediately deleted.

When managing many databases, each with potentially many different scaling needs, you should also consider running these databases in an elastic pool. An elastic pool is a grouping of databases on a single logical server that share the DTUs available within the pool. We discuss elastic pools in depth in the section "Provisioning an elastic pool" later in the chapter.

Elastic scale in Azure SQL Database is also achieved using the elastic database tools client library which is available for .NET and Java applications. Applications developed using this library can save their data in different Azure SQL databases based on data-dependent routing rules while retaining the ability to run SELECT queries across all shards. This is a popular model for SaaS applications because you can assign each SaaS customer its own database.

➤ You can find more information on the elastic database tools at *https://docs.microsoft.com/ azure/sql-database/sql-database-elastic-scale-get-started*.

Provisioning a logical SQL server

Creating a logical SQL server (just called "server" from here on) is the first step in the process of deploying a database. The server determines the region that will host the database(s), provides fundamental access control and security configuration (more on that later), and the fully quali-fied domain name (FQDN) of the endpoint.

NOTE
Using the Azure portal, it is possible to provision a new server while creating a new data-base. All other methods require two separate steps or commands, so for consistency, we will discuss each separately in this chapter. This will allow the focus to remain on each distinct element (server and database) of your provisioning process.

You'll be interested to know that provisioning a server does not incur usage charges. Azure SQL Database is billed based on the DTUs assigned to each database or elastic pool. The server acts only as a container for databases and provides the connection endpoint. This is also why there are no performance or sizing specifications attached to a server.

Inside OUT

When should you create a new logical SQL server?

The logical SQL server determines the region where the databases are located. Your databases should be in the same region as the applications that access them, both to avoid cross-region traffic charges as well as to have the lowest possible latency when running queries.

Security considerations can also dictate how many logical SQL servers you operate. Because the server admin login and Azure AD principal assigned as server admins have complete control and access to all databases on a server, you might set up different servers for different applications or different environments, such as development, test, and production. On the other hand, the threat detection feature (discussed in detail in the section "Security in Azure SQL Database" later in the chapter) is charged per logical server. Therefore, it's likely that you'll want to strike a balance between manageability, cost, and security.

The final factors when considering creating a new server or reusing an existing one is the database life cycle and billing aggregation. The database life cycle is tied directly to the server, so if you operate databases with very different life cycles, you could benefit from improved manageability by hosting those on different servers. As it relates to billing, whereas your usage is charged per database, you might find benefits in aggregating charges for specific databases. You can aggregate charges easily by using a resource group. Recall that all databases are tied to the resource group of the server where they are hosted. Therefore, if you want to aggregate charges for specific databases, these databases should be deployed to separate servers, each in a different resource group.

Creating a server using the Azure portal

To provision a server using the Azure portal, you use the SQL Server (logical server only) blade. You need to provide the following information to create a server:

- **Server name.** The server name becomes the DNS name of the server. The domain name is fixed to database.windows.net. This means that your server name must be globally unique and lowercase. There are also restrictions as to which characters are allowed, though those restrictions are comparable to on-premises server names.

- **Server admin login.** This user name is best compared to the "sa" account in SQL Server. However, you cannot use "sa" or other common SQL Server identifiers for this user name; they are reserved for internal purposes. You should choose a generic name rather than a name derived from your name because you cannot change the server admin login later.

- **Password.**   Unlike on-premises SQL Server, it's not possible to turn off SQL Server Authentication. Therefore, the password associated with the server admin login should be very strong and carefully guarded. Unlike the login itself, Azure users with specific roles can change it.

  ➤ You can read more about Role-Based Access Control to your Azure SQL Database resources later in the chapter.

- **Subscription.**   The subscription in which you create the server determines which Azure account will be associated with databases on this server. Database usage charges are billed to the subscription.

- **Resource group.**   The resource group where this server will reside. Review the section on Azure governance earlier in the chapter to learn about the importance of resource groups.

- **Location.**   This is the Azure region where the database(s) are physically located. Azure SQL Database is available in most regions worldwide. You should carefully consider the placement of your servers and, by consequence, databases. Your data should be in the same region as the compute resources (Azure Web Apps, for example) that will read and write the data. When you locate the applications that connect to the server in the same region, you can expect latency in the order of single-digit milliseconds.

When creating a new server using the Azure portal, the new server's firewall allows connections from all Azure resources. In the current GUI, the check box indicating this setting is unavailable. You can read more about the firewall in the section "Server and database-level firewall" later in the chapter. We recommend that you configure the firewall to allow connections from known IP addresses only before deploying any databases.

Creating a server by using PowerShell

To provision a server using PowerShell, use the New-AzureRmSqlServer cmdlet, as demonstrated in the code example that follows. Of course, you'll need to modify the values of the variables in lines 1 through 3 to fit your needs. These commands assume that a resource group with the name SSIO2017 already exists and that the resource group name will also become the server name. The server will be created in the active Azure subscription.

```
$resourceGroupName = 'SSIO2017'
$serverName = $resourceGroupName.ToLower()
$Cred = Get-Credential -UserName dbadmin -Message "Pwd for server admin"
New-AzureRmSqlServer -ResourceGroupName $resourceGroupName `
    -ServerName $serverName `
    -Location $location -SqlAdministratorCredentials $Cred
```

In this script, the `Get-Credential` cmdlet is used to obtain the password for the dbadmin server administrator. This cmdlet opens a dialog box that asks for the password. All values needed to create a server are provided as parameters to the `New-AzureRmSqlServer` cmdlet.

NOTE

Throughout this chapter, the Azure PowerShell sample scripts all build upon the existence of a server named ssio2017 in a resource group named SSIO2017. You will need to choose your own server name because it must be globally unique. The sample scripts available for download are all cumulative and define the value just once, which makes it easy to make a single modification and run all the sample scripts.

Establishing a connection to your server

With a server created, you can establish a connection. Azure SQL Database supports only one protocol for connections: TCP. In addition, you have no control over the TCP port number; it is always 1433.

TROUBLESHOOTING

Connection troubleshooting

Some corporate networks might block connections to internet IP addresses with a destination port of 1433, so if you have trouble connecting, check with your network administrators.

Using SQL Server Management Studio 17 as an example to connect to the newly created server, Figure 5-2 shows the different values entered in the Connect To Server dialog box. When you first establish the connection, you will be prompted by SQL Server Management Studio to create a firewall rule to allow this connection (see Figure 5-3). You will need to sign in with your Azure account to create the firewall rule.

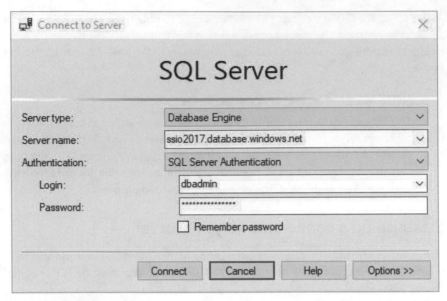

Figure 5-2 The Connect To Server dialog box, showing values to connect to the newly created logical SQL server.

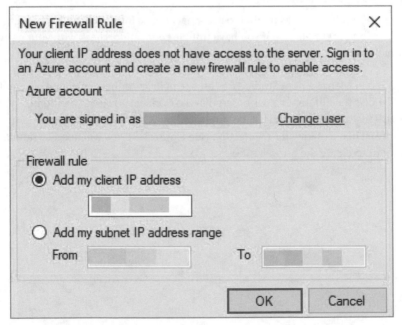

Figure 5-3 The New Firewall Rule dialog box that opens if the IP address attempting to connect is not included in any existing firewall rule.

Connections to Azure SQL Database are always encrypted, even if it is not specified in the connection string. For older client libraries, you might need to specify encryption explicitly in the connection string because these libraries might not support the automatic upgrade of the connection. If you neglect to specify it explicitly, you will receive an error message. Use `Encrypt=True` in the connection string if needed.

You might be tempted to look up the IP address of your server and use the IP address instead of the FQDN to connect. This is not recommended, because the IP address for the server is really the IP address of a connection gateway. This IP address is subject to change at any time as the Azure fabric conducts updates or failovers.

NOTE

During upgrade windows or Azure infrastructure failures, you might experience a brief period of connectivity loss while the DNS infrastructure and your client(s) retain the cached IP address. The configured time-to-live (TTL) of the DNS entries is purposefully short: five minutes.

Deleting a server

Deleting a server is a permanent, irreversible operation. You should delete a server only if you no longer need that server's name and are confident that you will not need to restore any databases that are or were hosted on it.

Because there is no cost associated with maintaining a server, likely the only reason to delete one is when you have reached the limit of servers permitted in a single subscription. As of this writing, that limit is six servers, but you can request an increase by contacting Azure Support.

Provisioning a database in Azure SQL Database

After provisioning a server, you are ready to provision your first database. Provisioning a database incurs charges associated with the pricing tier that you select. As a reminder, pricing for Azure SQL Database is per database or elastic pool, not per server.

You can create a database from one of three sources: Blank, Sample, or Backup. A Blank database is just that: there are no user database objects. If you choose Sample (AdventureWorksLT), the new database will have the lightweight Adventure Works schema and data. If you choose Backup, you can restore the most recent daily backup of another Azure SQL Database in the subscription. The sections that follow discuss the process of provisioning a database using the Azure portal, PowerShell, Azure CLI, and Transact-SQL (T-SQL).

CHAPTER 5

NOTE

You can provision a new logical SQL server while provisioning a new database only by using the Azure portal. All other methods require two separate steps or commands.

Creating a database using the Azure portal

There are several methods to begin creating a new database in Azure SQL Database using the Azure portal. One method is to start from the Overview blade of an existing server. You can also start from the Create New Service blade. The method you choose determines which values you will need to provide; for example:

- **Database name.**   The database name must be unique within the server and meet all requirements for a database name in SQL Server.

- **Subscription.**   Select the subscription that will be used to bill the charges for this database. The subscription you select here will narrow down the list of server choices later. This parameter is not shown when the process is started from a server.

- **Resource group.**   Here, you will choose to create a new resource group or use an existing one. If you choose to create a new resource group, you will also need to create a new server. But note that choosing an existing resource group will not narrow the list of server choices later.

- **Collation.**   The collation selected here becomes the database's default collation. Unlike on-premises, there is no GUI to set the new database's collation name. You will need to correctly type the collation name from memory or refer to a list of valid SQL Server collation names.

- **Source.**   You select one of three values that match the aforementioned options: Blank database, Sample (AdventureWorksLT), or Backup.

- **Backup.**   You will be prompted to provide this only when you've selected Backup as the source of the new database. The database you select will be restored to its most recent daily backup, which means it might be up to 24 hours old.

➤ You can read more about options for restoring database backups in the section "Understanding default disaster recovery features" later in the chapter.

- **Server.**   You can select an existing server in the selected subscription or create a new server. The existing servers that are listed are filtered to the subscription you selected earlier, but not to the resource group. If you select a server in a different resource group than the group you selected earlier, the resource group value will be updated automatically to reflect the correct selection. That is because the life cycle of a database is tied to the life cycle of the server, and the life cycle of the server is tied to the resource group. Therefore, a database cannot exist in a different resource group than its server. This server value is locked when the process is started from a logical SQL server.

- **Pricing tier.**   When creating a standalone database, you need to select a pricing tier. The pricing tier determines the hourly usage charges and several architectural aspects of your database. We discuss pricing tiers in a later section. It is possible to mix pricing tiers within a server, underscoring the notion that the server is a mere logical container for databases and has no relationship to any performance aspects. While selecting the pricing tier, you also can set a maximum database size. Your database will not be able to run INSERT or UPDATE T-SQL statements when the maximum size is reached.

- **Elastic database pool.**   You can make this selection only when adding this database to an existing or new elastic database pool. We discuss elastic pools in detail in the section "Provisioning an elastic pool" later in the chapter.

Creating a database by using PowerShell

The script that follows illustrates how to create a new Standard-tier standalone database with the S0 service objective on an existing server named ssio2017. The database collation is set to `Latin1_General_CI_AS`. The `-Collation`, `-Edition`, and `-RequestedService ObjectiveName` parameters are optional; we show them here because they would be commonly specified. Their respective defaults are `SQL_Latin1_General_CP1_CI_AS` (generally not desired), `Standard`, and S0. Pay attention to the server name: it is lowercase because the parameter value must match exactly. Logical SQL server names cannot contain uppercase characters.

```
$resourceGroupName = 'SSIO2017'
$serverName = $resourceGroupName.ToLower()
$databaseName = 'Contoso'
New-AzureRmSqlDatabase -ResourceGroupName $resourceGroupName `
    -ServerName $serverName -DatabaseName $databaseName -Edition Standard `
    -RequestedServiceObjectiveName "S0" -CollationName Latin1_General_CI_AS
```

Other optional parameters include the following:

- **CatalogCollation.**   This collation parameter determines the collation of character data in the database's metadata catalog. Note that you cannot set this database property in the GUI. This value defaults to `SQL_Latin1_General_CP1_CI_AS`, which is different from SQL Server, where it defaults to DATABASE_DEFAULT.

- **ElasticPoolName.**   When specified, this database will be added to the existing elastic pool on the server. The next section covers elastic pools.

- **MaxSizeBytes.** Sets the maximum database size in bytes. You cannot set just any value here; there is a list of supported maximum sizes. The available maximum sizes depend on the selected pricing tier.

- **SampleName.** Specify AdventureWorksLT if you want the database to have the available sample schema and data.

- **Tags.** This parameter is common to many Azure cmdlets. You can use it to specify an arbitrary number of name–value pairs. Tags are used to add custom metadata to Azure resources. You can use both the Azure portal and PowerShell to filter resources based on tag values. You can also obtain a consolidated billing view for resources with the same tag values.

  A usage example is -Tags @{"Tag1"="Value 1";"Tag 2"="Value 2"}, which would associate two name–value pairs to the database. The name of the first tag is Tag1 with Value 1, and the name of the second tag is Tag 2 with Value 2.

After creating the database, you can retrieve information about it by using the Get-AzureRmSqlDatabase cmdlet, as shown here:

```
Get-AzureRmSqlDatabase -ResourceGroupName SSIO2017 -ServerName ssio2017 `
    -DatabaseName Contoso
```

Creating a database by using Azure CLI

The Azure CLI makes it possible for you to use the same set of commands to manage Azure resources regardless of the platform of your workstation: Windows, macOS, Linux, and even using the portal's Cloud Shell.

NOTE

Installing the Azure CLI on different operating systems is not covered in this text. Guidance for each OS is available at *https://docs.microsoft.com/cli/azure/install-azure-cli*.

The Azure CLI command that follows creates a database with the same parameters as those found in the preceding PowerShell script. After creating the database, the new database's properties are retrieved.

> ➤ You can find the full list of supported CLI commands for Azure SQL Database at *https://docs.microsoft.com/cli/azure/sql/db*.

```
az sql db create --resource-group SSIO2017 --server ssio2017
    --name Contoso --collation Latin1_General_CI_AS
    --edition Standard --service-objective S0
az sql db list --resource-group SSIO2017 --server ssio2017
    --name Contoso
```

NOTE

For clarity, the long parameter names have been used in the preceding example. Many parameters for the `az` command also have a shorthand version. For example, instead of using `--resource-group`, you can use `-g`. The `--help` (shorthand: `-h`) parameter shows both the long and shorthand parameter names, if a shorthand version is available.

Creating a database by using T-SQL

The T-SQL script that follows creates a new Azure SQL database with the same properties as used in both of the previous examples. To create a new database, connect to the server on which the new database will reside; for example, using SQL Server Management Studio 17:

```
CREATE DATABASE Contoso COLLATE Latin1_General_CI_AS
    (EDITION = 'standard', SERVICE_OBJECTIVE = 'S0');
```

Because the T-SQL command is run in the context of a server, you do not need to, nor can you, provide a server name or resource group name. You cannot use T-SQL to create a database based on the AdventureWorksLT sample, but you can use it to restore a database from a backup using the `AS COPY OF` clause, as shown here:

```
CREATE DATABASE Contoso_copy AS COPY OF Contoso;
```

Selecting a pricing tier and service objective

Azure SQL Database is billed by the hour. The selection of a pricing tier and service objective determines how much you will be charged for your database. However, there are additional considerations. Specific pricing and other details might change by the time the ink on this page has dried; thus, we will discuss some general concepts that you should be aware of and how they would influence your selection of a tier.

NOTE

You can find current pricing for Azure SQL Database at *https://azure.microsoft.com/ pricing/details/sql-database/*.

The Basic tier provides the lowest available DTUs. For giving up some availability guarantees and performance, you also pay significantly less. This tier is suitable for development purposes and perhaps very small-scale applications.

The Standard and Premium tiers are the two main choices for production databases. At first glance, you will notice that the Premium tier provides considerably more DTUs and does so at a higher cost per DTU compared to Standard. This is because of architectural differences between these tiers. The database files in Standard tier databases are stored in Azure blob storage. This means that the files are not local to the database engine. In the Premium tier, they are stored on local solid-state drives (SSDs). This difference in locality of the database files has performance implications, as you might expect. Further, there is also a difference in how intraregion high availability (HA) is handled. HA for Standard tier databases is ensured by using replication of the Azure blobs. In the Premium tier, HA is achieved by using Always On features.

Finally, the Premium RS tier provides the same performance objectives as the Premium tier but at a lower cost. This is due to a less-stringent Service-Level Agreement (SLA) for the Premium RS tier. You should consider using this tier for scenarios in which performance trumps availability, such as development and test or during migration activities.

Scaling up or down

Azure SQL Database scale operations are conducted with minimal disruption to the availability of the database. A scale operation is performed by the service using a replica of the original database at the new service level. When the replica is ready, connections are switched over to the replica. Although this will not cause data loss and is completed in a time frame measured in seconds, active transactions might be rolled back. The application should be designed to handle such events and retry the operation.

Scaling down might not be possible if the database size exceeds the maximum allowed size for the lower service objective or pricing tier. If you know that you will likely scale down your database, you should set the maximum database size to a value equal to or less than the maximum database size for the service objective to which you might scale down.

Scaling is always initiated by an administrator. Unlike some Azure services, there is no auto-scale functionality in Azure SQL Database. You could, however, consider deploying databases to an elastic pool (discussed in the next section) to achieve automatic balancing of resource demands for a group of databases. Another option to scale without administrator intervention would be to use Azure Automation to monitor DTU usage and within defined limits initiate scaling. You can use the PowerShell `Set-AzureRmSqlDatabase` cmdlet to set a new pricing tier by using the `-Edition` parameter, and a new service objective by using the `-RequestedServiceObjectiveName` parameter.

Provisioning an elastic pool

For an introduction to elastic pools, refer to Chapter 3. Elastic pools are created per server, and a single server can have more than one elastic pool. The number of eDTUs available depends on the pricing tier, as is the case with standalone databases. Beyond the differences between tiers described in the preceding section, which also apply to elastic pools, the relationship between the maximum pool size and the selected eDTU, and the maximum number of databases per pool are also different per tier.

You can create elastic pools in the Azure portal, by using PowerShell, the Azure CLI, or the REST API. After an elastic pool is created, you can create new databases directly in the pool. You also can add existing databases to the pool or move them out of it.

In most of the next sections, no distinction is made between standalone databases or elastic pool databases. Management of standalone databases is not different from management of databases in elastic pools. Also, whether a database is in an elastic pool or standalone makes no difference for establishing a connection.

To create a new elastic pool on the ssio2017 server and move the existing Contoso database to the pool, use the following PowerShell script:

```
$resourceGroupName = 'SSIO2017'
$serverName = $resourceGroupName.ToLower()
$databaseName = 'Contoso'
$poolName = 'Contoso-Pool'
# Create a new elastic pool
New-AzureRmSqlElasticPool -ResourceGroupName $resourceGroupName `
    -ServerName $serverName -ElasticPoolName $poolName `
    -Edition 'Standard' -Dtu 50 `
    -DatabaseDtuMin 10 -DatabaseDtuMax 20
# Now move the Contoso database to the pool
Set-AzureRmSqlDatabase -ResourceGroupName $resourceGroupName `
    -ServerName $serverName -DatabaseName $databaseName `
    -ElasticPoolName $poolName
```

This script creates a new pool named Contoso-Pool in the Standard tier and provides 50 total eDTUs. A single database will be assigned no less than 10 DTU and no more than 20 DTU. The parameters –Dtu, –DatabaseDtuMin and –DatabaseDtuMax have a list of valid values depending on the selected tier and one another.

Limitations of Azure SQL Database

Although Azure SQL Database provides a very high level of compatibility with SQL Server 2017, there are differences in the available feature set, a lower maximum database size, and missing related services. The limitations of the Database Engine are covered in Chapter 3. This section covers limitations specific to Azure SQL Database sizing and other SQL services. The last sub-section in this section covers managed instances, which provide additional compatibility and remove many of the limitations we'll look at here.

Database limitations

Azure SQL Database is subject to certain size limitations. Primary among these is the maximum database size. The maximum size of a database varies based on the pricing tier. The size of a database includes only the size of the data; the size of transaction logs is not counted. If you are designing an application for the cloud, the size limitations are less of a restriction when deciding to adopt Azure SQL Database. This is because an application designed for the cloud should shard its data across several database instances. In addition to overcoming database size limitations, the benefits of sharding also include faster disaster recovery and the ability to locate the data closer to the application if the application runs in different Azure regions.

To provide predictable performance for Azure SQL Database, there are limits to the number of concurrent requests, concurrent logins, and concurrent sessions. These limits differ by service tier and service objective. If any limit is reached, the next connection or query attempt will fail with error code 10928.

> ➤ You can find an exhaustive list of these operational limits online at *https://docs.microsoft.com/azure/sql-database/sql-database-resource-limits*.

One final limitation to be aware of is that a single server has an upper limit on the total DTUs it can host as well as on the total number of databases. For a large deployment, this might require distributing databases across servers. We recommend against operating at or near this limit because overall performance can become suboptimal. As of this writing, you should limit the number of databases per server to around 1,000.

NOTE
These limitations are subject to change frequently, so be sure to review current limitations before deciding whether Azure SQL Database is right for you.

Other SQL Server services

In addition to the database engine, an on-premises deployment of SQL Server can include SQL Server Agent to schedule maintenance tasks or other activities, SQL Server Integration Services to load or extract data, SQL Server Analysis Services to support analytical workloads, and SQL Server Reporting Services to provide report functionality. These services are not included in Azure SQL Database. Instead, comparable functionality is often available through separate Azure services. A complete discussion of the available alternatives in Azure is beyond the scope of this book. The descriptions that follow are intended to merely name some of the alternatives and their high-level uses and direct you to an online starting point to learn more:

- **SQL Server Agent.**   To schedule recurring tasks for Azure SQL Database instances, DBAs should consider using Azure Automation. Azure Automation is a service that makes it possible for you to reliably run potentially long-running PowerShell scripts. You can use Azure Automation to automate management of any Azure or third-party cloud service, including Azure SQL Database. In addition, there is a gallery of reusable scripts available.

➤ You can find more information about using Azure Automation with Azure SQL Database at *https://docs.microsoft.com/azure/sql-database/sql-database-manage-automation*. You can find an introduction to Azure Automation at *https://docs.microsoft.com/azure/automation/automation-intro*.

● **SQL Server Integration Services.**   Instead of SQL Server Integration Services, you would use Azure Data Factory to perform tasks such as extracting data from various sources, transforming it by using a range of services, and finally publish it to data stores for consumption by business intelligence tools or applications. We should note that you can use SQL Server Integration Services to extract data from and load data to Azure SQL Database, and that you can use Data Factory to extract data from and load data to on-premises data stores. The decision about which service to use depends largely on where most of your data resides, which services you plan on using for transforming the data, and whether you allow a cloud service to connect to your on-premises environment using a gateway service. Recently, Microsoft also announced the Azure-SSIS integration runtime in Data Factory, which you can use to deploy SQL Server Integration Services packages.

➤ You can learn more about Data Factory at *https://azure.microsoft.com/services/data-factory/*.

● **SQL Server Reporting Services.**   Several years ago, Microsoft offered a reporting service in Azure that was highly compatible with SQL Server Reporting Services: SQL Reporting Services. It was discontinued, however, and instead Microsoft Power BI is now recommended. Power BI is a powerful tool to create interactive visualizations using data from various sources. You can embed Power BI dashboards and reports in applications. You can also access them directly using a web browser or mobile app.

➤ You can learn more about Power BI at *https://powerbi.microsoft.com*.

● **SQL Server Analysis Services.**   To replace SQL Server Analysis Services, there are several alternative Azure services. Foremost, there is Azure Analysis Services. It is built on SQL Server Analysis Services and, as such, existing tabular models can be migrated from on-premises SQL Server Analysis Services deployments to the cloud.

➤ You can learn more about Azure Analysis Services at *https://docs.microsoft.com/azure/analysis-services/analysis-services-overview*.

Second, for data warehousing terabytes or petabytes of relational data, there is Azure SQL Data Warehouse. SQL Data Warehouse is based on SQL Server and provides a compatible interface. Compared with Azure SQL Database, however, SQL Data Warehouse can scale storage and compute independently. This makes SQL Data Warehouse suitable for storing enormous amounts of data that might only occasionally need to be processed.

➤ To learn more about Azure SQL Data Warehouse go to *https://azure.microsoft.com/services/sql-data-warehouse/*.

Another alternative to SQL Server Analysis Services is Azure Data Lake. Data Lake is much more extensive than SQL Server Analysis Services, but we mention it here because of its ability to capture data and prepare it for analytical workloads. Unlike SQL Server Analysis Services, though, Data Lake can store unstructured data in addition to relational data.

➤ **You can learn more about Data Lake at** *https://docs.microsoft.com/azure/data-lake-store/data-lake-store-overview*.

Overcoming limitations with managed instances

As of this writing in limited preview, managed instances in Azure SQL Database are one of the newest features. Managed instances have been designed to further reduce feature disparity between SQL Server and Azure SQL Database, provide additional integration with other Azure features, and maintain the benefits of DBaaS. The goal for managed instances is to make more lift-and-shift migrations possible from on-premises or Azure VM deployments to DBaaS.

In terms of achieving near 100 percent compatibility with SQL Server, a managed instance provides features not available in standard Azure SQL databases, including the following:

- SQL CLR

- SQL Server Agent

- Cross-database and cross-instance queries and transactions

- FILESTREAM and FileTable

Most notable in terms of added functionality, managed instances run in an Azure Virtual Network. This Virtual Network can act as a network boundary between the Azure resources within the Virtual Network and those outside (including other Azure customers' resources). You also can use a Virtual Network to create a LAN-like network environment between your on-premises environment and the Azure cloud.

Security in Azure SQL Database

As with many cloud services that fall in the PaaS category, there are certain security operations that are handled for you by the cloud provider. As it relates to security in Azure SQL Database, this includes patching the OS and the database service.

Other aspects of security must be managed by you, the cloud DBA. Some of these aspects, such as Transparent Data Encryption (TDE) are shared with on-premises SQL Server 2017. Others are specific to Azure SQL Database and include firewall configuration, access control, and auditing and threat detection. We discuss these features of Azure SQL Database in the upcoming sections. Microsoft's commitment regarding Azure SQL Database is to not differentiate the tiers with security features. All the features discussed in this section are available in all pricing tiers, though some require additional charges.

Security features shared with SQL Server 2017

An important security consideration is access control. Azure SQL Database implements the same permission infrastructure that's available in SQL Server 2017. This means that database and application roles are supported, and you can set very granular permissions on database objects and operations using the Data Control Language (DCL) statements GRANT and REVOKE. Refer to Chapter 6 for more information.

TDE is on by default for any new database. This hasn't always been the case, so if your database has been around for a long time, you should verify whether it is turned on. When TDE is on for a database, not only are the database files encrypted, but the geo-replicated backups are also encrypted. You will learn more about backups in the section "Preparing Azure SQL Database for disaster recovery" later in the chapter. TDE is covered in Chapter 7.

Other security features shared with SQL Server 2017 are dynamic data masking, row-level security, and Always Encrypted. Chapter 7 looks at these features in detail.

Server and database-level firewall

A server is accessed using an FQDN, which maps to a public IP address. To maintain a secure environment, managing firewall entries to control which IP addresses can connect to the logical server or database is a requirement.

> ### NOTE
> You can associate a server with a Virtual Network offering enhanced network security. Managed instances are currently always associated with a Virtual Network.

When creating a new server using the Azure portal, by default *any* Azure resource is permitted through the server-level firewall. This might appear convenient, but it leaves the server open to unauthorized connection attempts from an attacker who merely needs to create an Azure service such as a web app. Servers created using other methods—for example, PowerShell—do not have any default firewall rules, which means any connection attempt is refused until at least one firewall rule is created.

Database-level firewall rules take precedence over server firewall rules. After you have created database firewall rules, you can remove the server firewall rule(s) and still connect to the database. However, if you will be hosting several databases that need to accept connections from the same IPs on a single server, keeping the firewall rules at the server level might be more sensible. It is also convenient to keep server-level firewall rules in place for administrative access.

You can find server-level firewall rules in the virtual master database in the `sys.firewall_rules` catalog view. Database-level firewall rules are in the user database in the `sys.database_firewall_rules` catalog view. This makes the database more portable, which can be advantageous in combination with contained users. Especially when using geo-replication, which we discuss in the section "Preparing Azure SQL Database for disaster recovery" coming up later in the chapter, having portable databases avoids unexpected connection issues when failing-over databases to another server.

➤ **You can learn more about contained databases in Chapter 6.**

Setting the server-level firewall

You can create server-level firewall rules by using the Azure portal, PowerShell, Azure CLI, or T-SQL. As seen earlier, SQL Server Management Studio might prompt you to create a firewall rule when establishing a connection, though you would not use this method to create firewall rules for your application's infrastructure. To create a firewall rule, you need to provide the following:

- **Rule name.**   The rule name has no impact on the operation of the firewall; it exists only to create a human-friendly reminder about the rule. The rule name is limited to 128 characters. The name must be unique in the server.

- **Start IP address.**   The first IPv4 address of the range of allowed addresses.

- **End IP address.**   The end IPv4 address can be the same as the start IP address to create a rule that allows connections from exactly one address. The end IP address cannot be lower than the start IP address.

NOTE

When creating firewall rules using the Azure portal, you must create them one at a time. After you add a new rule, you must click the Save button even though the UI appears to allow adding additional new rules.

Inside OUT

Automate firewall rule management

Managing the firewall rules in a dynamic environment, such as one in which databases on a server are accessed from numerous Azure Web App instances, which often scale up and down and out and in, can quickly become error-prone and resource intensive. Rather than resorting to allowing any Azure resource to pass through the server-level firewall, you should consider automating the firewall rule management.

The first step in such an endeavor is to create a list of allowed IP addresses. This list could include static IP addresses, such as from your on-premises environment for management purposes, and dynamic IP addresses, such as from Azure Web Apps or Virtual Machines. In the case of dynamic IP addresses, you can use the AzureRM PowerShell module to obtain the current IP addresses of Azure resources.

After you build the list of allowed IP addresses, you can apply it by looping through each IP, attempting to locate it in the current firewall rule list, and adding it if necessary. In addition, you can remove any IP addresses in the rule list but not on the allowed list.

If you want to create a server-level firewall rule that allows access from any Azure resource, you would create a rule using `0.0.0.0` as both the start and end IP address of the rule. Using PowerShell, the `New-AzureRmSqlServerFirewallRule` cmdlet provides the `-AllowAllAzureIPs` parameter as a shortcut: you do not need to provide a rule name, start, or end IP address.

TROUBLESHOOTING

When SQL Server Management Studio offers to create a server-level firewall rule, you will need to sign in with an Azure AD user account whose default directory matches the directory that is associated with the subscription where the logical SQL server exists. If this is not the case, the creation of the firewall rule will fail with an HTTP status code 401 error.

Setting the database-level firewall

Configuring database-level firewall rules requires that you have already established a connection to the database. This means you will need to at least temporarily create a server-level firewall rule to create database-level firewall rules.

You can create and manage database-level firewall rules only by using T-SQL. Azure SQL Database provides the following stored procedures to manage the rules:

- **sp_set_database_firewall_rule.**   This stored procedure creates a new firewall rule or updates an existing firewall rule.

- **sp_delete_database_firewall_rule.**   This stored procedure deletes an existing databaselevel firewall rule using the name of the rule.

CHAPTER 5

The following T-SQL script creates a new database-level firewall rule allowing a single (fictitious) IP address and then updates the rule by expanding the single IP address to a range of addresses, and finally deletes the rule:

```
EXEC sp_set_database_firewall_rule N'Headquarters', '1.2.3.4', '1.2.3.4';
EXEC sp_set_database_firewall_rule N'Headquarters', '1.2.3.4', '1.2.3.6';
SELECT * FROM sys.database_firewall_rules;
EXEC sp_delete_database_firewall_rule N'Headquarters';
```

Access control using Azure AD

To set up single sign-on (SSO) scenarios, easier login administration, and secure authentication for application identities, you can turn on Azure AD authentication. When Azure AD authentication is turned on for a server, an Azure AD user or group is given the same permissions as the server admin login. In addition, you can create contained users referencing Azure AD principals. This means that user accounts and groups in an Azure AD domain can authenticate to the databases without needing a SQL login.

For cases in which the Azure AD domain is federated with an Active Directory Domain Services domain, you can achieve true SSO comparable to an on-premises experience. The latter case would exclude any external users or Microsoft accounts that have been added to the directory; only federated identities can take advantage of this. Furthermore, this also requires a client that supports it, which, as of this writing, is only SQL Server Management Studio.

> **NOTE**
>
> The principal you set as the Active Directory admin for the server must reside in the directory that is associated with the subscription where the server resides. The directory that is associated with a subscription can be changed, but this might have effects on other configuration aspects, such as Role-Based Access Control, which we describe in the next section.

To set an Active Directory admin for a server, you can use the Azure portal, PowerShell, or Azure CLI. You use the PowerShell `Set-AzureRmSqlServerActiveDirectoryAdministrator` cmdlet to provision the Azure AD admin. The `-DisplayName` parameter references the Azure AD principal. When you use this parameter to set a user account as the administrator, the value can be the user's display name or user principal name (UPN). When setting a group as the administrator, only the group's display name is supported.

> **TROUBLESHOOTING**
>
> **Setting the Active Directory admin if the group's display name is not unique**
>
> If the group you want to designate as administrator has a display name that is not unique in the directory, the optional `-ObjectID` parameter is required. You can retrieve the `ObjectID` from the group's properties in the Portal.

NOTE

If you decide to configure an Azure AD principal as server administrator, it's always preferable to designate a group instead of a single user account.

After you set an Azure AD principal as the Active Directory admin for the server, you can create contained users in the server's databases. Contained users for Azure AD principals must be created by other Azure AD principals. Users authenticated with SQL authentication cannot validate the Azure AD principal names, and, as such, even the server administrator login cannot create contained users for Azure AD principals. Contained users are created by using the T-SQL CREATE USER statement with the FROM EXTERNAL PROVIDER clause. The following example statements create an external user for an Azure AD user account with UPN l.penor@contoso.com and for an Azure AD group Sales Managers:

```
CREATE USER [l.penor@contoso.com] FROM EXTERNAL PROVIDER;
CREATE USER [Sales Managers] FROM EXTERNAL PROVIDER;
```

By default, these newly created contained users will be members of the PUBLIC database role and will be granted CONNECT permission. You can add these users to additional roles or grant them additional permissions directly like any other database user. Chapter 6 has further coverage on permissions and roles.

TROUBLESHOOTING

Users are unable to connect using Azure AD credentials

The workstation from which users will connect must have .NET Framework 4.6 or later and the Microsoft Active Directory Authentication Library for Microsoft SQL Server installed. These prerequisites are installed with certain developer and DBA tools but they might not be available on end-user workstations. If not, you can obtain them from the Microsoft Download Center.

You also can add Azure AD application identities as external users. For an application identity to access a database, a certificate must be installed on the system running the application.

> ➤ You can find more information and a sample on the SQL Server Security
> Blog at *https://blogs.msdn.microsoft.com/sqlsecurity/2016/02/09/*
> *token-based-authentication-support-for-azure-sql-db-using-azure-ad-auth/*.

Role-Based Access Control

All operations discussed thus far have all assumed that your user account has permission to create servers, databases, and pools and can then manage these resources. If your account is the service administrator or a co-administrator, no restrictions are placed on your ability to add, manage, and delete resources. Most enterprise deployments, however, will require more fine-grained control over permissions to create and manage resources. Using Azure Role-Based Access Control (RBAC), administrators can assign permissions to Azure AD users, groups, or service principals at the subscription, resource group, or resource level.

RBAC includes several built-in roles to which you can add Azure AD principals. The built-in roles have a fixed set of permissions. You also can create custom roles if the built-in roles do not meet your needs.

> ➤ You can find a comprehensive list of built-in roles and their permissions at *https://docs. microsoft.com/azure/active-directory/role-based-access-built-in-roles*.

Three of the built-in roles relate specifically to Azure SQL Database:

- **SQL DB Contributor.**   This role can primarily create and manage Azure SQL databases but not any security-related settings. For example, this role can create a new database on an existing server and create alert rules.

- **SQL Security Manager.**   This role can primarily manage security settings of databases and servers. For example, this role can create auditing policies on an existing database but cannot create a new database.

- **SQL Server Contributor.**   This role can primarily create and manage servers but not databases or any security-related settings.

Note that the permissions do not relate to server or database access; instead, they relate to managing the resources in Azure. Indeed, users assigned to these RBAC roles are not granted any permissions in the database, not even CONNECT permission.

NOTE

In concrete terms, this means that an Azure AD user in the SQL Server Contributor role can create a server and thus define the server administrator login's username and password. Yet, the user's Azure AD account does not get any permissions in the database at all. If you want the same Azure AD user to have permissions in the database, including creating new users and roles, you will need to use the steps in this section to set up the Azure AD integration and create an external database user for that Azure AD account.

Auditing and threat detection

Azure SQL Database provides auditing and threat detection to carry out monitoring of database activity using Azure tools. In on-premises deployments, *extended events* are often used for monitoring. SQL Server builds upon extended events for its SQL Server Audit feature (discussed in Chapter 7). This feature is not present in Azure SQL Database in the same form, but a large subset of extended events is supported in Azure SQL Database.

➤ You can find more details about support for extended events at *https://docs.microsoft.com/azure/sql-database/sql-database-xevent-db-diff-from-svr.*

Azure SQL Database auditing creates a record of activities that have taken place in the database. The types of activities that can be audited include permission changes, T-SQL batch execution, and auditing changes themselves. As of this writing, there is no official list of supported audit actions available.

➤ Audit actions are grouped in audit action groups, and a list of audit action groups is available in the PowerShell reference for the `Set-AzureRmSqlDatabaseAuditing` cmdlet at *https://docs.microsoft.com/powershell/module/azurerm.sql/set-azurermsqldatabaseauditing.*

Auditing and threat detection are separate but related features: threat detection is possible only if auditing is turned on. The features are configured on the same blade in the Azure portal. Auditing is available at no charge, but there is a monthly fee per server for activating threat detection.

You can turn on both features at the server and database level. When auditing is turned on at the server level, all databases hosted on that server are audited. After you turn on auditing on the server, you can still turn it on at the database level, as well. This will not override any server-level settings; rather, it creates two separate audits. This is not usually desired.

Auditing logs server and database events to an Azure storage account. The Azure storage account must be in the same region as the server. This is a sensible requirement; you would not want to incur data transfer charges for the audit data or deal with the latency of such a transfer.

Configuring auditing

To configure auditing, you need to create or select an Azure storage account. We recommend that you aggregate logging for all databases in a single storage account. When all auditing is done in a single storage account, you will benefit from having an integrated view of audit events.

You also need to decide on an audit log retention period. You can choose to keep the audit logs indefinitely or you can select a retention period. The retention period can be at most nine years with a daily granularity.

NOTE

As of this writing, two auditing types are available: Blob and Table. Table auditing has been deprecated for a while, and you should not use it for any new audit configuration. This section is completely written from the perspective of using Blob storage as the auditing type.

CHAPTER 5

The following PowerShell script sets up auditing for the Contoso database on the ssio2017 server:

```
$resourceGroupName = 'SSIO2017'
$location = "southcentralus"
$serverName = $resourceGroupName.ToLower()
$databaseName = 'Contoso'
$storageAccountName = "azuresqldbaudit"
# Create a new storage account
$storageAccount = New-AzureRmStorageAccount -ResourceGroupName $resourceGroupName `
    -Name $storageAccountName -Location $location -Kind Storage `
    -SkuName Standard_LRS -EnableHttpsTrafficOnly $true
# Use the new storage account to configure auditing
$auditSettings = Set-AzureRmSqlDatabaseAuditing `
    -ResourceGroupName $resourceGroupName `
    -ServerName $serverName -DatabaseName $databaseName `
    -StorageAccountName $storageAccountName -StorageKeyType Primary `
    -RetentionInDays 365 -State Enabled
```

The first cmdlet in the script creates a new storage account with the name `azuresqldbaudit`. Note that this name must be globally unique, so you will need to update the script with a name of your choosing before running the script. Storage account names can contain only lowercase letters and digits. (For more details on the `New-AzureRmStorageAccount` cmdlet, see *https://docs.microsoft.com/powershell/module/azurerm.storage/new-azurermstorageaccount*.) The second cmdlet, `Set-AzureRmSqlDatabaseAuditing`, configures and turns on auditing on the database using the newly created storage account. The audit log retention period is set to 365 days.

NOTE

To set auditing at the server level, use the `Set-AzureRmSqlServerAuditing` **cmdlet.**

By default, all actions are audited. You cannot use the Azure portal to customize which events are audited; instead, you use PowerShell (or the REST API) to indicate specific action groups that you want to audit. The `-AuditActionGroup` parameter takes an array of strings that identify the groups to audit.

➤ **You can find the list of group names at** *https://docs.microsoft.com/powershell/module/azurerm.sql/set-azurermsqldatabaseauditingpolicy#optional-parameters*.

Viewing audit logs

There are several methods that you can use to access the audit logs. The method you use largely depends on your preferences as well as the tools that you have available on your workstation. We discuss the methods in this section in no particular order.

> ➤ You can find a full list of methods to access the audit logs at *https://docs.microsoft.com/ azure/sql-database/sql-database-auditing#subheading-3.*

If your goal is to quickly review recent audit events, you can see the audit logs in the Azure portal. In the Auditing & Threat Detection blade for a database, click View Audit Logs to open the Audit Records blade. This blade shows the most recent audit logs, which you can filter to restrict the events shown by latest event time or show only suspect SQL injection audit records. This approach is rather limited because you cannot aggregate audit logs from different databases and the filtering capabilities are minimal.

A more advanced approach is to use SQL Server Management Studio. SQL Server Management Studio 17 and later support opening the audit logs directly from Azure storage. Alternatively, you can use the Azure Storage Explorer to download the audit logs and open them using older versions of SQL Server Management Studio or third-party tools. The audit logs are stored in the sqldbauditlogs blob container in the selected storage account. The container follows a hierarchical folder structure: logicalservername\DatabaseName\SqlDbAuditing_AuditName\ yyyymmdd. The blobs within the date folder are the audit logs for that date (in Coordinated Universal Time [UTC]). The blobs are binary extended event files (.xel).

NOTE

Azure Storage Explorer is a free and supported tool from Microsoft. You can download it from *https://azure.microsoft.com/features/storage-explorer/.*

After you have obtained the audit files, you can open them in SQL Server Management Studio. On the File menu, click Open, and then click Merge Audit Files to open the Merge Audit Files dialog box, as shown in Figure 5-4.

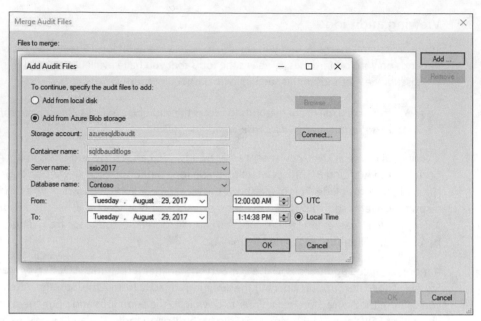

Figure 5-4 SQL Server Management Studio 17 and later support opening and merging multiple Azure SQL Database audit files directly from an Azure storage account.

A third way of examining audit logs is by using the `sys.fn_get_audit_file` T-SQL function. You can use this to perform programmatic evaluation of the audit logs. The function can work with locally downloaded files or you can obtain files directly from the Azure storage account. To obtain logs directly from the Azure storage account, you must run the query using a connection to the database whose logs are being accessed. The following T-SQL script example queries all audit events logged to the azuresqldbaudit storage account from August 29, 2017, for the Contoso database on the ssio2017 server:

```
SELECT * FROM sys.fn_get_audit_file ('https://azuresqldbaudit.blob.core.windows.net/
sqldbauditlogs/ssio2017/Contoso/SqlDbAuditing_Audit/2017-08-29/', default, default);
```

➤ You can find more information on the `sys.fn_get_audit_file` function at *https://docs. microsoft.com/sql/relational-databases/system-functions/sys-fn-get-audit-file-transact-sql*.

Configuring threat detection

With auditing turned on, you can optionally turn on threat detection. Threat detection examines the audit logs for anomalies and alerts the Azure service administrators and co-administrators or a list of configured email addresses. There are three types of threats that can be detected:

- **SQL injection.** This threat type detects the possible occurrence of a SQL injection attack.

- **SQL injection vulnerability.** This type detects the possible existence of a SQL injection vulnerability in the queries that are run.

- **Anomalous client login.** This type detects logins that are unusual, such as from a geographic location from which a user has not previously signed in.

You can turn off these threat types individually if you do not want to detect them.

Inside OUT

Which audit action groups should be turned on for threat detection to work?

Threat detection requires that auditing is turned on for the database or server, but it does not require that any specific audit action groups are turned on.

However, to effectively analyze threat detections, the following audit action groups are recommended: BATCH_COMPLETED_GROUP, SUCCESSFUL_DATABASE_AUTHENTICATION_GROUP, and FAILED_DATABASE_AUTHENTICATION_GROUP.

Turning on these groups will provide details about the events that caused the threat detection to alert.

Preparing Azure SQL Database for disaster recovery

Hosting your data on Microsoft's infrastructure does not mean that you can avoid preparing for disasters. Even though Azure has high levels of availability, both due to human error and significant adverse events, your data can still be at risk. Azure SQL Database provides default and optional features that will ensure HA for your databases when properly configured.

Understanding default disaster recovery features

Without taking any further action after provisioning a database, the Azure infrastructure takes care of several basic disaster recovery (DR) preparations. First among these is the replication of data files across fault and upgrade domains within the regional datacenters. This replication is not something you see or control, but it is there. This would be comparable to the on-premises use of Always On availability groups or storage tier replication. The exact method of replication of the database files within a datacenter depends on the chosen tier. (We discussed this earlier in the section "Selecting a pricing tier and service objective.") As Azure SQL Database evolves, the methods Microsoft employs to achieve local HA are of course subject to change.

Regularly scheduled backups are also configured by default. A full backup is scheduled weekly, differential backups take place every few hours, and transaction log backups every 5 to 10 minutes. The exact timing of backups is managed by the Azure fabric based on overall system workload and the database's activity levels. These backups are retained for a specified period, which depends on the pricing tier.

You can use these backups to restore the database to a point-in-time within the retention period. You also can restore a database that was accidentally deleted to the same server from which it was deleted. Remember: deleting a server irreversibly deletes all databases and backups. You should generally not delete a server until the backup retention period has expired, just in case. After all, there is no cost associated with a server without databases.

You also can restore databases to another Azure region. This is referred to as a geo-restore. This restores databases from backups that are geo-replicated to other regions using Azure Storage replication. If your database has TDE turned on, the backups are also encrypted.

Although these default features provide valuable DR options, they are likely not adequate for production workloads. For example, the Estimated Recovery Time (ERT) for a geo-restore is less than 12 hours with a Recovery Point Objective (RPO) of less than one hour. Further, the maximum backup retention period is 35 days for the Standard, Premium, and Premium RS tiers, and only seven days for the Basic tier. Some of these values are likely unsuitable for mission-critical databases, so you should review the optional DR features in the next sections and configure those as needed to achieve an acceptable level of risk for your environment.

Manually backing up a database

In addition to the automatic, built-in backup discussed in the preceding section, you might have a need to back up a database manually. This might be necessary if you need to restore a database in an on-premises or IaaS environment. You might also need to keep database backups for longer than the automatic backups' retention period, though we encourage you to read the section "Using Azure Backup for long-term backup retention" later in the chapter to understand all options for long-term archival.

The term "backup" is somewhat inappropriate insomuch as the method to create a manual backup is exporting the database to a BACPAC file. (You can read more about BACPAC files in Chapter 4. A significant difference between a database backup and an export is that the export is not transactionally consistent. During the data export, Data Manipulation Language (DML) statements in a single transaction might have completed before and after the data in different tables was extracted. This can have unintended consequences and can even prevent you from restoring the export without dropping foreign key constraints.

Azure SQL Database can, however, provide you with a transactionally consistent export using a three-step procedure: first, make a copy of the database. The copy is guaranteed to be transactionally consistent. Then, export the copy. Because no applications are accessing this copy, no data manipulation is taking place during the export. Finally, delete the copy to avoid incurring continued charges. You can perform this procedure by using the Azure portal, but because it involves multiple steps, and some steps can be long-running, it lends itself perfectly to using a PowerShell script.

A database export's destination is an Azure blob, so a storage account is required. The following script determines a name for the database copy based on the existing database and the current time:

```
# Set variables
$resourceGroupName = 'SSIO2017'
$location = "southcentralus"
$serverName = $resourceGroupName.ToLower()
$databaseName = 'Contoso'
# Create a name for the database copy
$d = (Get-Date).ToUniversalTime()
$databaseCopyName = "$databaseName-Copy-" + ($d.ToString("yyyyMMddHHmmss"))
$storageAccountName = 'azuresqldbexport'
# Ask interactively for the server admin login username and password
$cred = Get-Credential
# Create a new Azure storage account
$storAcct = New-AzureRmStorageAccount -ResourceGroupName $resourceGroupName `
    -Name $storageAccountName -Location $location `
    -SkuName Standard_LRS

# Get the access keys for the newly created storage account
$storageKey = Get-AzureRmStorageAccountKey -ResourceGroupName $resourceGroupName `
    -Name $storageAccountName
# Create a database copy - this copy will have the same tier as the original
$newDB = New-AzureRmSqlDatabaseCopy -ResourceGroupName $resourceGroupName `
    -ServerName $serverName -DatabaseName $databaseName `
    -CopyDatabaseName $databaseCopyName
# Prepare additional variables to use as the storage location for the BACPAC
$containerName = "mydbbak"
$container = New-AzureStorageContainer -Context $storAcct.Context -Name
$bacpacUri = $container.CloudBlobContainer.StorageUri.PrimaryUri.ToString() + "/" + `
    $databaseCopyName + ".bacpac"
# Initiate a database export of the database copy - see Firewall troubleshooting
$exportRequest = New-AzureRmSqlDatabaseExport -ResourceGroupName $resourceGroupName `
    -ServerName $NewDB.ServerName -DatabaseName $databaseCopyName `
    -StorageKeytype StorageAccessKey -StorageKey $storageKey[0].Value `
    -StorageUri $bacpacUri `
    -AdministratorLogin $cred.UserName -AdministratorLoginPassword $cred.Password
```

```
# Run a loop while the export is progressing
Do {
    $exportStatus = Get-AzureRmSqlDatabaseImportExportStatus `
        -OperationStatusLink $ExportRequest.OperationStatusLink
    Write-Host "Exporting... sleeping for 5 second..."
    Start-Sleep -Seconds 5
} While ($exportStatus.Status -eq "InProgress")
# Delete the copied database to avoid further charges
Remove-AzureRmSqlDatabase -ResourceGroupName $resourceGroupName `
    -ServerName $serverName -DatabaseName $databaseCopyName
```

First, a new storage account is created in the same Azure region as the database server to avoid cross-region traffic charges. The script then creates the database copy on the same database server. Next, the new storage account is used for the export of the database copy. The export operation is asynchronous, so a loop is used to wait for completion of the export. Finally, when the export is completed, the database copy is deleted. As in previous scripts, the storage account name you create must be globally unique, so change the value of the variable in the script before running it.

This script produces several lines of output. At the end of the script, if everything was successful, you can use the Azure Storage Explorer to access the new storage account and download the BACPAC file for further use. Alternatively, you can leave the BACPAC file in Azure Storage and use related commands to import the database file later, should a restore become necessary.

TROUBLESHOOTING

BACPAC exports require a firewall rule to allow all Azure services

The Azure SQL Database Export Service, which is used to export to a BACPAC file, can run anywhere in the Azure region of the source database server. Because the IP address of the host running the service is not known in advance, you will need to open the server firewall to allow all Azure IP addresses to access the server. For more information, review the section "Server and database-level firewall" earlier in the chapter.

Configuring geo-replication

If your disaster recovery needs are such that your data cannot be unavailable for a period of up to 12 hours, you will likely need to configure geo-replication. When you geo-replicate a database, there are one or more active secondary databases to which all transactions are replicated. Geo-replication takes advantage of the Always On feature also found in on-premises SQL Server.

You can configure geo-replication in any pricing tier and any region. To configure georeplication, you will need to provision a server in another region, though you can do this as part of the configuration process if you are using the Azure portal.

In the event of a disaster, you would be alerted via the Azure portal of reliability issues in the datacenter hosting your primary database. You would need to manually failover to a secondary database—using geo-replication only, there is no automatic failover (but keep reading to learn about failover groups, which do provide automatic failover capability). Failover is accomplished by selecting (one of) the secondary database(s) to be the primary.

Because the replication from primary to secondary is asynchronous, an unplanned failover can lead to data loss. The RPO for geo-replication, which is an indicator of the maximum amount of data loss expressed as a unit of time, is five seconds. Although no more than five seconds of data loss during an actual disaster is a sound objective, when conducting DR drills, no data loss is acceptable. A planned change to another region, such as during a DR drill or to migrate to another region permanently, can be initiated as a planned failover. A planned failover will not lead to data loss because the selected secondary will not become primary until replication is completed.

Unfortunately, a planned failover cannot be initiated from the Azure portal. The PowerShell cmdlet `Set-AzureRmSqlDatabaseSecondary` with the `-Failover` parameter and without the `-AllowDataLoss` parameter will initiate a planned failover. If the primary is not available due to an incident, you can use the portal (see Figure 5-5) or PowerShell to initiate a failover with the potential for some data loss, as just described. If you have multiple secondaries, after a failover, the new primary will begin replicating to the remaining available secondaries without a need for further manual configuration.

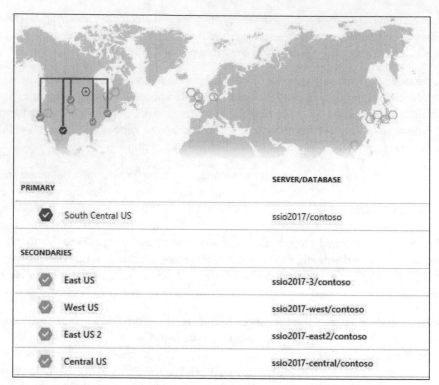

PRIMARY		SERVER/DATABASE
✅	South Central US	ssio2017/contoso

SECONDARIES		
✅	East US	ssio2017-3/contoso
✅	West US	ssio2017-west/contoso
✅	East US 2	ssio2017-east2/contoso
✅	Central US	ssio2017-central/contoso

Figure 5-5 The Azure portal showing geo-replication configured with the maximum of four secondaries. The recommended region for geo-replication, North Central US, is indicated using the purple hexagon. There is no replica hosted in that region.

NOTE

When you first configure geo-replication using the Azure portal, the UI will inform you of the recommended region for the geo-replicated database. You are not required to configure the secondary in the recommended region, but doing so will provide optimal performance for the replication between regions. The recommendation is based on Microsoft's knowledge of connectivity between its datacenters in different regions.

For each secondary database, you will be charged the same hourly charges as a primary database, with the same pricing tier and service objective. A secondary database must have the same pricing tier as its primary, but it does not need to have the same service objective or performance level. For example, a primary database in the Standard tier with service objective S2 can be geo-replicated to a secondary in the Standard tier with service objective S1 or S3, but it cannot be geo-replicated to a secondary in the Basic or Premium tier.

To decide whether your service objective for secondaries can be lower than that of the primary, you will need to consider the read-write activity ratio. If the primary is write-heavy—that is, most database operations are writes—the secondary will likely need the same service objective to be able to keep up with the primary. However, if the primary's utilization is mostly toward read operations, you could consider lowering the service objective for the secondary. You can monitor the replication status in the Azure portal or use the PowerShell `Get-AzureRmSql` `DatabaseReplicationLink` cmdlet to ensure that the secondary can keep up with the primary.

As of this writing, geo-replication introduces a limitation on the scalability of databases. When a primary database is in a geo-replication relationship, its pricing tier cannot be upgraded (for example, from Standard to Premium) without first upgrading all secondaries. To downgrade, you must downgrade the primary before any secondaries can be downgraded. As a best practice, when scaling up or down, you should make sure that the secondary database has the higher service objective longer than the primary. In other words, when scaling up, first scale up secondary databases; when scaling down, scale down secondary databases second.

Inside OUT

What are other uses for geo-replication?

The judicious configuration of geo-replication and application programming can make it possible for you to downgrade your primary Azure SQL database to a lower service objective. Because secondaries are readable, you can use them to run read-only queries. By directing some of the read queries, such as for reporting or Extract, Transform, and Load (ETL) purposes, to secondary databases, fewer DTUs may be used by the primary.

In addition to potentially lowering service objective requirements, you also can use active geo-replication during application upgrades and to move a database to another server or region with minimal downtime.

Setting up failover groups

As discussed in the previous section, geo-replication represents a very capable option for DR planning. Geographically distributing relational data with an RPO of five seconds or less is a goal that not many on-premises environments can achieve. However, the lack of automatic failover and the need to configure failover on each database individually creates overhead in any deployment, whether it has a single database in a shop with a single (overworked?) DBA or many hundreds or thousands of databases. Further, because a failover causes the writable database to be hosted on a different logical server with a different DNS name, connection strings must be updated or the application must be modified to try a different connection.

Failover groups, currently in public preview, build on top of geo-replication to address these shortcomings. Configured at the server level, a failover group can include one, multiple, or all databases hosted on that server. All databases in a group are recovered simultaneously. By default, failover groups are set to automatically recover the databases in case of an outage, though you can turn this off. With automatic recovery turned on, you need to configure a grace period. This grace period offers a way to direct the Azure infrastructure to emphasize either availability or data guarantees. By increasing the grace period, you are emphasizing data guarantees because the automatic failover will not occur if it would result in data loss until the outage has lasted as long as the grace period. By decreasing the grace period, you are emphasizing availability. As of this writing, the minimum grace period is at least one hour, although this is expected to change to allow much shorter grace periods. In practical terms, this means that if the secondary database in the failover group is not up to date one hour after the outage, the failover will occur, resulting in data loss.

When you configure a failover group, two new DNS CNAME records are created. The first CNAME record refers to the read-write listener and it points to the primary server URL. During a failover, this record is updated automatically so that it always points to the writable replica. The read-write listener's FQDN is the name of the failover group prepended to database.windows. net. This means that your failover group name must be globally unique. The second CNAME record points to the read-only listener, which is the secondary server's URL. The read-only listener's DNS name is the name of the failover group prepended to secondary.database.windows. net. If the failover group name is ssio2017, the FQDN of the read-write listener will be ssio2017. database.windows.net and the FQDN of the secondary will be ssio2017.secondary.database. windows.net.

NOTE

As of this writing, a failover group can have only one secondary. For high-value databases, you should still configure additional secondaries to ensure that in case of a failover, HA isn't lost.

You can create failover groups with existing geo-replication already in place. If the failover group's secondary server is in the same region as an existing geo-replication secondary, the existing secondary will be used for the failover group. If you select a region for the failover secondary server where no replica is yet configured, a new secondary server and database will be created during the deployment process. If a new secondary database is created, it will be created in the same tier and with the same service objective as the primary.

Unlike with geo-replication, the Azure portal supports initiating a planned failover for failover groups. You can also initiate a planned failover by using PowerShell. Planned failovers will not cause data loss. Both interfaces also support initiating a forced failover, which, as with geo-replication's unplanned failover, can lead to data loss within the five-second RPO window.

Inside OUT

Auditing, threat detection, and geo-replication

When configuring auditing for geo-replicated databases, you should configure auditing at the server level on both the primary and secondary server. You should not turn on auditing at the database level. By configuring auditing at the server level, the audit logs will be stored in the same region as the server, thereby avoiding cross-region traffic.

As a side effect of configuring auditing on the secondary databases' server, you can set a different retention period, though we do not recommend this configuration, because valuable correlations between events on the primary and secondary can be lost. As described in the security section, you can use SQL Server Management Studio to merge audit files from different servers and databases to analyze them together.

You should apply the same configuration for threat detection. The current Azure portal GUI indicates that threat detection is not supported on secondary databases. However, if threat detection is turned on for the secondary server, it will cover the secondary database.

NOTE

DR and business continuity planning should not just consider the Azure SQL Database resources, but also other Azure services your application uses. These other services might include Azure Web Apps, Virtual Machines, DNS, storage accounts, and more. You can find more information on designing highly available services that include Azure SQL Database at *https://docs.microsoft.com/azure/sql-database/ sql-database-designing-cloud-solutions-for-disaster-recovery*.

Using Azure Backup for long-term backup retention

To meet compliance and regulatory requirements, you might need to maintain a series of long-term database backups. Azure SQL Database can provide a solution using long-term backup retention. When you configure long-term backup retention, you are taking advantage of another Azure service: Azure Backup. With Backup, you can elect to have the weekly full backups retained for a maximum of 10 years. You can configure the retention period with a granularity of weeks.

Long-term backup retention is configured at the server level, but databases on the server can be selectively included or excluded. Before you can set up long-term backup retention, you must create a Recovery Services vault in the same resource group and region. When a vault is available, you must create or select a retention policy. As its name indicates, the retention policy determines how long the weekly backups are retained in the vault. After you configure long-term backup retention, the next scheduled full backup will be the first backup added. In other words, existing backups are not added to the vault.

> **NOTE**
>
> **For more information on creating a vault as well as step-by-step guidance, see** *https://docs.microsoft.com/azure/sql-database/ sql-database-long-term-backup-retention-configure.*

Each database in a single server can have a separate retention policy, but all backups from a single server are kept in the same vault, as illustrated in Figure 5-6. Pricing for Azure Backup is based on the number of protected "nodes" and the storage consumed. In the case of Azure SQL Database, a "node" is a single database, and the storage consumed is the size of the database backup file. When a database is deleted, you will continue to be charged for the vault's contents; however, the charges will decrease over time as backup files older than the retention period are deleted.

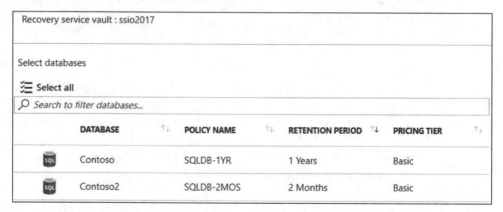

Figure 5-6 Long-term backup retention of two databases on the same server. The Contoso database's retention period is set to one year and Contoso2 database's retention period is set to two months. Both databases use the ssio2017 vault.

> **NOTE**
>
> **As of this writing, control of long-term backups is very limited. You are not able to access the backup files directly nor can you choose to delete specific files.**

You can configure long-term backup retention by using the Azure portal or PowerShell. Although only primary or standalone databases are backed up and will therefore be the only databases that have backups to be added to the vault, you should configure long-term backup retention on geo-replicated secondaries, as well. This ensures that in case of a failover, backups from the new primary database will be added to its vault, without further intervention. After a failover, a full backup is immediately taken and that backup is added to the vault. Until a failover takes place, no additional costs are incurred for configuring retention on the secondary server.

NOTE

As noted earlier, when the server hosting a database is deleted, the database backups are immediately and irrevocably lost. This applies to long-term backup retention, as well. For as long as the logical SQL server is around, you will be able to restore a database up to the retention period, even if the database itself was deleted. We should stress again that there is no cost to keeping a logical SQL server around, so exercise restraint and caution before deleting servers.

Moving to Azure SQL Database

Now that we have covered the critical aspects of provisioning and managing Azure SQL Database, we will briefly review options for moving data from SQL Server to Azure SQL Database. The source could be an on-premises SQL Server database or one hosted in an Azure or third-party cloud VM. The migration method you choose largely depends on the tolerance for downtime and the complexity of the preparation.

Among the options for migration, here are some of the most common ones:

- **BACPAC.** BACPAC files have been mentioned previously in this chapter for possible on-premises use. You also can use them in the reverse direction. When a BACPAC file has been generated for an on-premises database, it needs to be uploaded to a standard-tier Azure storage account. From there, you can import the BACPAC file to an existing server using the Azure portal or PowerShell. Although this migration method is simple and scalable to many databases, for large databases, the entire process might take longer than is acceptable. The Microsoft SQL Server CAT offers a lengthy article on using BACPAC for moving SQL Server to Azure SQL Database, which you can read at *https://blogs.msdn. microsoft.com/sqlcat/2016/10/20/migrating-from-sql-server-to-azure-sql-database-using-bacpac-files/*.

TROUBLESHOOTING

BACPAC imports require a firewall rule for all Azure Services

The Azure SQL Database Import Service, which is used for the import of BACPAC files, can run anywhere in the Azure region of the destination server. Because the IP address of the host running the service is not known, you will need to open the server firewall to allow all Azure IP addresses to access the server. We discuss this in the section "Server and database-level firewall" earlier in the chapter.

- **Transactional replication.**   Setting up replication makes it possible to move schema and data with minimal downtime. If using replication, it is also possible to migrate only a subset of the data from the source. The downside is that replication requires changing the schema of the database that is to be moved. Also, you will need to allow direct communication from your SQL Server to Azure. Chapter 12 has detailed coverage on replication with SQL Server.

- **Custom development.**   You can transfer schema and data by using custom scripts or SQL Server Integration Services. With increasing schema complexity, the complexity of the custom development also increases. SQL Server Data Tools or third-party schema and data migration tools can help in this effort.

- **Microsoft Data Migration Assistant (DMA).**   This option is the newest available. You can use the DMA tool to assess the schema of the source database and verify compatibility with Azure SQL Database. If issues are detected, detailed guidance on how to resolve them is provided. Finally, the tool can prepare and run a migration workflow. The tool should be at least version 3.2; earlier versions did not have the migration workflow. You can also find references to another tool: the SQL Azure Migration Wizard. This tool, however, was created for the previous iteration of Azure SQL Database (v11) and is no longer developed. It still works, but it will apply Azure SQL Database v11 compatibility rules, which are much more restrictive than the current v12.

- Azure Database Migration Service. As of this writing, this service is in preview. It is a comprehensive service that supports Azure SQL Database, managed instances, and SQL Server on Azure VMs. You can learn more about it at *https://azure.microsoft.com/services/database-migration/*.

NOTE

Migration operations can be resource intensive. To minimize the duration of the migration, you should consider using the Premium RS tier during the migration. Recall from earlier in the chapter that the Premium RS tier offers the same performance as the Premium tier but at a lower cost. The lower cost is due to lower availability guarantees. Lower availability should not be a concern during the migration process. After all, if something goes wrong during the migration, you have a recovery plan in place, right? If the maximum database size is configured appropriately, the database can be scaled down to the Standard tier upon completion of the migration. The trade-off, of course, is that during the migration you will be charged a significantly higher hourly rate.

When considering moving databases, you should review schema compatibility as early as possible. You can use the SQL Server Data Tools to find incompatible object definitions. By importing the database schema in SQL Server Data Tools and then changing the destination platform to Microsoft Azure SQL Database v12, SQL Server Data Tools will list the incompatible schema elements. Unlike DMA, SQL Server Data Tools does not provide guidance on resolution, though.

In this chapter, we look at the Microsoft SQL Server permissions, from authentication through to data access, starting from the ground floor on up. We discuss practical administrative tasks that DBAs need to do and why, including handling orphaned security identifiers (SIDs), security migration, SQL Server Agent runtime permissions, and more. Many of these principles apply equally to SQL Server and Microsoft Azure SQL Database; when they differ, we will point this out.

Logins and users

Given that we're starting on the ground floor of security, let's begin by establishing an important distinction in terminology:

- A *principal* is an entity that is given access.

- The *scope* of a principal depends on that to which it can be given access.

- Server Authentication is made via principals named *logins*.

- Database access is made via principals named *users*.

- Other types of principals include *roles* (server, database, and application)

In each database, a user can be associated with one server login.

Logins might not be associated with users in all databases, and it is possible for users to exist without any association to a login, though oftentimes this occurs accidentally. (We talk about this scenario more later on.) Table 6-1 presents a quick comparison.

Table 6-1 Comparison of users and logins

Database user	Server login
• Set a database context • Linked to a server login • Does not have a password • Assigned to database roles • Stored in the user database • Brought along with a User DB Restore • Given access to SELECT, UPDATE, EXECUTE, CREATE TABLE, and so on.	• Authenticates sessions to a SQL Server • Can be linked to Active Directory (Windows Authentication) • Or can have a password (SQL Authentication) • Assigned to server roles • Stored in the master database • Not affected by User DB Restore • Given access to RESTORE, CONNECT, CREATE DATABASE, and so on.

It is important to understand this terminology and the differences between these objects, not just for interacting with SQL Server, but for communicating with fellow SQL administrators and developers.

Different types of authentication

Figure 6-1 illustrates that there are five ways to connect to a SQL Server instance in SQL Server Management Studio. Let's begin with the authentication methods with which DBAs are most familiar.

Logins and users are not associated by their names that you see in SQL Server Management Studio; instead, they are associated by a SID binary value. How the SID is generated for each login is based on the type of authentication used by the login. You can view the SID for a login in the sys.server_principals view.

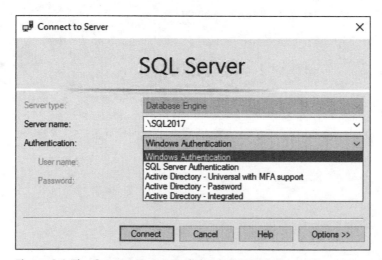

Figure 6-1 The Connect To Server dialog box in SQL Server Management Studio.

Windows Authentication

Windows-authenticated logins take advantage of authentication that's built in to Windows clients to seamlessly pass credentials in a Windows or domain environment. This is the only authentication method that is turned on by default, and we strongly recommend it for use in most applications.

For Windows-authenticated logins, the Windows SID for the account or group is used. For domain accounts, this SID will be the same from Windows server to Windows server.

In a typical business environment, using Windows Authentication means that account creation/termination, Active Directory security group membership, and password policy are handled by an existing corporate security administration infrastructure. In fact, using Active Directory security groups is a best practice for centrally managed role-based authentication (RBA).

SQL Server Authentication

SQL Server Authentication is a method that stores user names and passwords in the master database of the SQL Server instance. SQL DBAs must manage password complexity policy, password resets, locked-out passwords, password expiration, and changing passwords on each instance that uses SQL Server Authentication. In these and other ways, it is redundant to Windows Authentication—but creates more work for the SQL DBA.

The SID assigned to a newly created SQL Server–authenticated login is generated by the SQL Server. This is why two logins with the same names on two SQL Server instances will have different SIDs (more on this later).

You can use SQL Server Authentication to connect to on-premises SQL Server instances, Azure virtual machine–based SQL Server instances, and databases in Azure SQL Database, but other methods of authentication are preferred in all cases.

SQL Server Authentication also covers database-level authentication, which is used by contained database users.

The last three authentication types are exclusive to Azure-based resources, specifically Azure SQL Database or Azure SQL Data Warehouse, using Azure Active Directory (Azure AD) credentials.

Active Directory Universal Authentication

Universal Authentication uses Azure two-factor authentication, and you can use it for connecting to Azure SQL Database or SQL Data Warehouse resources. SQL Server Management Studio can use the Azure Authenticator application or other two-factor methods.

Currently, this feature is limited to authentication with Azure AD accounts for connecting to a database in Azure SQL Database or Data Warehouse, though further Microsoft development around two-factor authentication for server access is likely—and welcomed.

This method, like the next two Azure AD–based authentication methods, was first supported by SQL Server Management Studio as of SQL Server 2016.

Active Directory Password Authentication

Azure AD accounts can be used for authentication with a user name and password, using Azure Users that have been created in the Azure tenant and granted access to the Azure SQL Database or SQL Data Warehouse.

This authentication method makes it possible for you to use your Azure account to sign in to SQL Server from outside Azure AD via a user name and password. This is more secure than SQL Server–based authentication because it is linked to an Azure AD account that is, in theory, managed by an existing Enterprise Security group.

You can use this method, for example, to grant Microsoft Office 365 accounts direct access to a database in Azure SQL Database over the web.

As of SQL Server 2016 and SQL Server Data Tools for Visual Studio 2015, SQL Server Management Studio supports this authentication method.

Active Directory Integrated Authentication

You can use Azure AD accounts for authentication very similarly to Windows Authentication, for use when you can sign in to Windows with your Azure AD credentials. No user name or password is requested; instead, your profile's local connections are used.

For example, you can use this authentication method when connected via Remote Desktop to an Azure AD–authenticated session on a virtual machine (VM) in Azure.

Other types of logins

You can create another type of login aside from Windows or SQL Server authentication; however, this type of login has limited uses.

You can create a login that is mapped directly to a certificate or to an asymmetric key. Secure access to the SQL Server instance is then possible by any client with the public key of the certificate, using a nondefault endpoint that you create specifically for this type of access.

The Service Broker feature of SQL Server, used for asynchronous messaging and queueing, supports Certificate-Based Authentication, for example.

You also can use these logins to sign database objects, such as stored procedures. This encrypts the database objects and is common for when the code of a third-party application is proprietary and not intended to be accessible by customers.

For example, the ##MS_PolicyEventProcessingLogin## and ##MS_PolicyTsqlExecutionLogin## logins, created automatically with SQL Server, are certificate-based logins.

Authentication to SQL Server on Linux

You can make SQL Server connections to instances running on the Linux operating system by using Windows Authentication and SQL Authentication.

In the case of SQL Authentication, there are no differences when connecting to a SQL Server instance running on Linux with SQL Server Management Studio.

It is also possible to join the Linux server to the domain (by using the realm join command), using Kerberos, and then connect to the SQL Server instance on Linux just as you would connect to a SQL Server instance on Windows Server. The steps necessary are detailed in the SQL Server on Linux documentation at *https://docs.microsoft.com/sql/linux/sql-server-linux-active-directory-authentication*.

NOTE

There are otherwise very few significant differences between SQL Server on Linux and SQL Server on Windows Server for the purposes of the rest of this chapter, and indeed, for most of the chapters in this book.

Inside OUT

I've created a SQL Server 2017 on Linux VM in Azure. How do I connect to it?

If you are using a Linux VM running Azure, you need a Network Security Group inbound security rule to allow connections to the SQL instance. Without it, your authentication attempt will wait and eventually fail with Error 1225, "The remote computer refused the network connection."

After allowing network connections to your Azure VM, you must then do an initial configuration of the SQL Server. Connecting via Bash on Ubuntu on Windows or PuTTY, or similar tool, run the following command:

```
sudo /opt/mssql/bin/mssql-conf setup
```

You will be asked to accept the license terms and to provide the "sa" password. You then will be able to connect to the SQL Instance in Azure via SQL Server Management Studio with SQL Authentication using the "sa" account and the password you provided.

You can make connections to the Linux operating system itself via the Windows 10 built-in Bash shell (a feature introduced with the Creator's edition update). Windows Server 2016 built 1709 and later have been updated to include the Windows Subsystem for Linux feature. For more information, visit: *https://msdn.microsoft.com/commandline/wsl/install-on-server*.

Solving orphaned SIDs

An orphaned SID is a user who is no longer associated with its intended login. The user's SID no longer matches, even if the User Name and Login Name do.

Any time you restore a (noncontained) database from one SQL Server to another, the database users transfer, but the server logins in the master database do not. This will cause SQL Server–authenticated logins to break, but Windows-authenticated logins will still work.

Why?

The key to this common problem that many SQL DBAs face early in their careers is the SID and, particularly, how the SID is generated.

For Windows-authenticated logins based on local Windows accounts and SQL Server–authenticated logins, this SID will differ from server to server.

The SID for the login is associated with the user in each database based on the matching SID. The names of the login and user do not need to match, but they almost certainly will, unless you are a SQL DBA intent on confusing your successors. But know that it is the SID, assigned to the login and then applied to the user, that creates the association.

The most common problem scenario is as follows:

1. A database is restored from one SQL Server instance to another.

2. The SIDs for the Windows-authenticated logins and their associated users in the restored database will not be different, so Windows-authenticated logins will continue to authenticate successfully and grant data access to end users via the database users in each database.

The SIDs for any SQL Server–authenticated logins will be different on each server. So, therefore, will the associated database users' SIDs in each database. When restoring the database from one server to another, the SIDs for the server logins and database users no longer match. Their *names will still match*, but data access cannot be granted to end users.

3. The SID must now be rematched before SQL Server–authenticated logins will be allowed access to the restore database.

Problem scenario

A database exists on Server1 but does not exist on Server2.

Original state

Server1

SQL Login = Katherine

SID = 0x5931F5B9C157464EA244B9D381DC5CCC

Database User = Katherine

SID = 0x5931F5B9C157464EA244B9D381DC5CCC

Server2

SQL Login = Katherine

SID = 0x08BE0F16AFA7A24DA6473C99E1DAADDC

Then, the database is restored from Server1 to Server2. Now, we find ourselves in this problem scenario:

Orphaned SID

Server1

SQL Login = Katherine

SID = 0x5931F5B9C157464EA244B9D381DC5CCC

Database User = Katherine

SID = 0x5931F5B9C157464EA244B9D381DC5CCC

Server2

SQL Login = Katherine

SID = 0x08BE0F16AFA7A24DA6473C99E1DAADDC

Database User = Katherine

SID = 0x5931F5B9C157464EA244B9D381DC5CCC ← Orphaned SID

The resolution

The resolution for the preceding example issue is quite simple:

```
ALTER USER Katherine WITH LOGIN = Katherine;
```

The SID of the user is now changed to match the SID of the login on Server2; in this case, 0x08BE0F16AFA7A24DA6473C99E1DAADDC. Again, the relationship between the Server Login and the Database User has nothing to do with the name.

You can use the script that follows to look for orphaned SIDs. This should be a staple of your DBA toolbox. It's important to understand that this script only *guesses* that logins and user names should have the same name. If you are aware of logins and users that do not have the same name and should be matched on SID, you will need to check for them manually.

> ### NOTE
> Are you accustomed to using sp_change_users_login to fix orphaned SIDs? That stored procedure has been deprecated and replaced by the ALTER USER ... WITH LOGIN statement.

```
Select
        DBUser_Name       =       dp.name
,       DBUser_SID        =       dp.sid
,       Login_Name        =       sp.name
,       Login_SID         =       sp.sid
,       SQLtext           =       'ALTER USER [' + dp.name + ']
                                  WITH LOGIN = [' + ISNULL(sp.name, '???') + ']'
        from sys.database_principals dp
        left outer join sys.server_principals sp
        on dp.name = sp.name
        where
                dp.is_fixed_role = 0
        and sp.sid <> dp.sid
        and dp.principal_id > 1
        and dp.sid <> 0x0
        order by dp.name;
```

You should check for orphaned SIDs every time you finish a restore that brings a database from one server to another; for example, when refreshing a preproduction environment.

Preventing orphaned SIDs

Orphaned SIDs are preventable. You can re-create SQL Server–authenticated logins on multiple servers, each having the same SID. This is not possible using SQL Server Management Studio; instead, you must accomplish this by using the CREATE LOGIN command, as shown here:

```
CREATE LOGIN [Katherine] WITH PASSWORD=N'strongpassword', SID =
0x5931F5B9C157464EA244B9D381DC5CCC;
```

Using the SID option, you can manually create a SQL login with a known SID so that your SQL Server–authenticated logins on multiple servers will share the same SID. Obviously, the SID must be unique on each instance.

In the previous code example we used sys.server_principals to identify orphaned SIDs. You can also use sys.server_principals to identify the SID for any SQL Server–authenticated login.

Creating SQL Server–authenticated logins with a known SID is not only helpful to prevent orphaned SIDs, but it could be crucially timesaving for migrations involving large numbers of databases, each with many users linked to SQL Server–authenticated logins, without unnecessary outage or administrative effort.

We'll look more closely at this topic later in this chapter when we examine SQL Server security migrations.

Factors in securing logins

In this section, we cover some important topics for logins specifically, including login options, SQL Server configuration, and security governance.

Using mixed mode

Mixed mode is simply a description of a SQL Server that can accept both Windows Authentication and SQL Server Authentication.

If the content of this chapter refers to SQL Server Authentication as redundant, often unnecessary, and problematic for administrators, that's intentional: using SQL Server Authentication (aka configuring the SQL Server instance in mixed mode) creates additional administrative overhead of which DBAs need to be aware.

CHAPTER 6

As the DBA of a SQL instance, be sure to emphasize to developers and application administrators that Windows Authentication, via named domain accounts or service accounts, is always preferred to SQL Server Authentication.

Use SQL Server Authentication to connect to SQL Server instances only in special cases; for example, when Windows-authenticated accounts are impossible to use or for network scenarios involving double-hop authentication when Kerberos is not available.

Since SQL Server 2005, user names and passwords of SQL Server–authenticated logins are no longer transmitted as plain text during the login process. And, unlike early versions of SQL Server, passwords are not stored in plain text in the database. However, any SQL Server–authenticated login could potentially have its password reverse-engineered by a malicious actor who has access to or a copy of the master database .mdf file. For these reasons and more, Windows-authenticated accounts are far more secure.

This is not an option for Azure SQL databases.

Setting the default database

Each login includes a default database option, which you should set appropriately depending on how the login is to be used.

A login will fail if its default database is not accessible, including if the database is restoring, offline, or dropped from the instance. The login will fail even if it is a member of the sysadmin server role, so you should never change the default database of a known administrator login. (The sysadmin role has all permissions to the SQL Server instance. We will talk more about the sysadmin role and other server-level roles later in this chapter.)

Similarly, if you specify an inaccessible database as the Initial Catalog or Initial Database in various connections strings, your login attempt might fail.

Administrator logins should keep the master (the default setting) or TempDB as their default database because the SQL Server cannot start up without the presence of those databases.

This guidance follows even for logins that are not a member of the sysadmin server role. There might be some cases for which a default database set to a user database is appropriate; for example, for a login that will be used only for a single database. In this way, the default database setting might be helpful because login will be denied new connections if that single database is inaccessible, moved to another instance, or dropped from the instance.

Enforcing password policies

As stated earlier, one of the problems with SQL Server Authentication is that it is itself a redundant security system within each SQL Server. Included in each server, and in each user, is whether a SQL login must adhere to the machine's password policy. It is not required to be enforced.

The policies applied from the machine's local security policy, inherited from the domain if applicable, include minimum length and complexity requirements.

The Enforce Password Policy check box is selected by default when you open the Login – New dialog box (Figure 6-2) in SQL Server Management Studio, but you can clear the check box to turn off this option. So, with SQL Server Management Studio it is possible to create a login with a noncomplex (or even blank) password. When you create it in code, the CHECK_POLICY option is not required but defaults to ON.

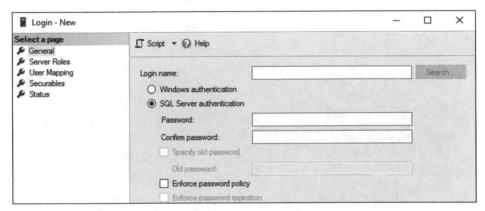

Figure 6-2 The blank Login – New dialog box in SQL Server Management Studio.

You should keep in mind that if you turn on the CHECK_POLICY option on an existing login that did not already have it on, the existing password is not affected. The policy will be enforced the next time the password is changed. Applications and end users can still sign in to the SQL instance by using the existing, potentially noncomplex password. Subsequent DBAs might assume that the password policy is enforced on the existing password. Therefore, do not turn on CHECK_POLICY on a login without then immediately changing the password, or at least setting the MUST_CHANGE option at the same time so that the user must change her password on the next login.

In addition to enforcing password policy, you can optionally enforce a maximum password age by selecting the Enforce Password Expiration check box. You also can force a user to change her password on her next login, but keep in mind that although SQL Server Management Studio has built-in behavior to allow for this password to be changed with a simple dialog box, other applications might not have the ability for users to change their passwords interactively, and they will instead see only a failed login.

Providing logins to the DBA team

In all but the most rudimentary IT departments, SQL DBAs need access to production SQL Server instances but need their access governed and contained to certain uses and privileges. In this section, we cover why and how you should do this.

Windows Authentication means that SQL DBAs will need to sign in to a Windows instance using their domain credentials. Then, they connect to the SQL Server instance with Windows Authentication and begin their work. DBAs use this same method whether they are connecting to a production environment SQL Server or a development environment SQL Server, though next we'll talk about using different credentials for each.

Inside OUT

What is a "production" environment, and how is it different?

In the upcoming section, we talk about "production" versus "preproduction." What does that mean? Let's take a look at what each environment actually is:

- **Production.**   This is the main system of record. It might, for example, connect to the actual instruments or machines, or control life-critical systems, or customer-facing applications, or contains the business' valuable data. It is subject to disaster recovery plans, needs high availability, and is "the server" to which the CEO of your company refers.

- **Preproduction.**   These systems resemble the production environment but aren't visible to the actual machinery (physically or metaphorically speaking) of the business. Preproduction servers shouldn't contain actual customer or patient information, and don't have the same tight disaster recovery (DR) requirements. They go by many names, including Development, Test, Quality Assurance (QA), User Acceptance Testing (UAT), Business Acceptance Testing (BAT), and many others.

Developers, report writers, and quality assurance testers should ideally have access only to preproduction systems. If they need to troubleshoot a production problem, only senior developers are given access, and even then, only temporarily.

DBAs need to have access to SQL Server instances in all environments, but, still, we need to discuss how best to arrange for access to production systems.

To illustrate, let's consider the following scenario: tasked with backing up and restoring a database from the production environment to the development environment, the DBA uses the connections already open in SQL Server Management Studio, copies the backup to a network share, and then begins the restore. The restore is 50 percent complete when a user calls to ask, "Is the SQL Server down?"

What do you think has happened?

If your DBA team isn't already using *two or more* Windows-authenticated accounts, you should consider segmenting each DBA's production database access from the account they use for the rest of their day-to-day activities, including preproduction systems, but also email, office applications, Office 365, and more.

Consider creating "admin-level" accounts for each DBA that have no preproduction access, office applications or Office 365 access, Virtual Private Network (VPN), or even internet access. The idea is to encourage your DBA team to use its admin accounts only for administrative activities.

For example, Katherine is a DBA and uses Domain\Katherine to access her "everyday" activities such as email, instant messaging, preproduction SQL instances, source control, Office 365, VPN, and more. But this domain account has limited access to production SQL Servers—for example, she can access server-level DMV's, activity levels, SQL Agent job history, and the SQL Server error log. But she cannot create logins, read or update live production data, alter databases, and so on.

To perform any of those tasks, Katherine opens a remote desktop session to another server using Domain\admin-Katherine. This activity is deliberate and requires heightened awareness— the production databases are important! Starting SQL Server Management Studio from within the remote desktop session, Domain\admin-Katherine is a member of the sysadmin server role and can accomplish anything she needs to in the production environment. When she's done, she logs out.

Domain\admin-Katherine also has no VPN access; thus, if it is compromised, it cannot be used to both gain access to the corporate network remotely and access SQL Servers.

In the end, you might have good regulatory, corporate policy, security, or private reasons to separate a DBA's "everyday" access from production SQL Server instance access. However, access to the production servers using their "admin-" account (many other naming conventions are common) requires deliberate steps and mental awareness of the task at hand, so the risk of accidentally running intended-for-development tasks in production is considerably reduced.

Later in this chapter, in the section "Creating custom server roles," we talk about fixed server roles that you can use to separate duties among a team of DBAs, and a custom server role that you can create to set up read-only access to an entire server.

CHAPTER 6

Login security

In this section, we discuss some important special logins to be aware of, including special administrative access, which you should control tightly.

The "sa" login

The "sa" login is a special SQL Server–authenticated login. It is a known member of the sysadmin server role with a unique SID value of 0x01, and you can use it for all administrative access. If your instance is in mixed mode (in which both Windows Authorization and SQL Server Authentication are turned on), DBAs can use the sa account.

The sa account also has utility as the authorization (aka owner) for database objects, schemas, availability groups, and the databases themselves. This known administrator account, however, has obvious potential consequences.

Applications, application developers, and end users should never use the sa account. This much should be obvious. If it is, consider changing the password and assigning any entities who were using it the permissions necessary and appropriate for their role. The sa account, like any SQL Server–authenticated account, could potentially have its password reverse-engineered by a malicious actor who has access to or a copy of the master database .mdf file.

The sa account is a common vector for brute-force attacks to compromise a SQL Server. For this reason, if your SQL Server is exposed to the internet, we recommend that you rename or disable the sa account.

Because its password is commonly known to multiple administrators, it also can serve as an anonymous backdoor for malicious or noncompliant activity by current or former employees.

Because your SQL Server instance's DBAs should be using Windows Authentication for all administrative access (more on that later), no DBA should actively use the sa account. Its password doesn't need to be known to DBAs. There are no use cases nor best practices that require accessing the SQL Server by using the sa account.

The BUILTIN\Administrators group

If you have experience administering SQL Server 2005 or older, you'll remember the BUILTIN\ Administrators group, which was created by default to grant access to the sysadmin server role to any account that is also a member of the local Windows Administrator group.

Beginning with SQL Server 2008, this group was no longer added to SQL Server instances by default, because it is an obvious and serious security back door. Although it was potentially convenient for administrators, it was also targeted by malicious actors.

Do not add the BUILTIN\Administrators group to your SQL Server instance—it is no longer there by default for a reason.

Service accounts

In Chapter 4 we discuss service accounts, but it is worth pointing out that service accounts are logins, as well.

Service accounts are usually given the minimal permissions needed to run the services to which they are assigned by SQL Server Configuration Manager. For this reason, do not use the Windows Services (services.msc) to change SQL Server feature service accounts. Changing the instance's service account with the Windows Services administrative page will likely result in the service's failure to start.

It is not necessary to grant any additional SQL Server permissions to SQL Server service accounts. (You might need to grant additional NT File System (NTFS)–level permissions to file locations, etc.) Although the SQL Server Agent service account likely needs to be a member of the sysadmin role, the SQL Server service account does not. For these reasons and more, different service accounts for different services is necessary.

You also should never grant the NT AUTHORITY\SYSTEM account, which is present by default in a SQL Server instance, any additional permissions. Many Windows applications run under this system account and should not have any nonstandard permissions.

CHAPTER 6

Inside OUT

What about service accounts for instances in my Always On availability group?

For SQL Servers in an Always On availability group, the SQL Server service on each replica instance does not need to have the same domain service account, though this is the simplest approach.

If each replica SQL Server service account is different, you must create a login for each other replica's domain service account on each replica.

Though not recommended, if you choose to use nondomain service accounts for each SQL Server instance, you must create the Database Mirroring EndPoint (not to be confused with the deprecated database mirroring feature) using an encrypted certificate for the instance.

We also recommend that you so not use local or built-in service accounts, including the machine account, though it is also possible to do by granting each machine's network service account a login on each other's replica. This is definitely not a secure approach.

For more on Always On availability groups, see Chapter 12.

Contained databases

Contained databases can be a confusing topic because they break many of the conventions we've covered thus far in this chapter. Contained databases shift many of server-level concepts to the database level in a move that allows databases to be more mobile between server environments. This has advantages specific to high availability and cloud-based designs.

Databases created or altered on a SQL Server instance by using CONTAINMENT = PARTIAL bypass the server's authentication, creating authentication directly at the database level, and creating the confusing concept of a "Contained SQL user with password."

NOTE

Currently, only partially contained databases are offered by SQL Server 2017 because some objects still cross the database boundary, such as management of the SQL instance's endpoints. A fully contained database has no external dependencies even for metadata, temporary objects, and configuration. This level of containment is not available in SQL Server 2017.

Table 6-2 compares contained database users to database users and server logins (previously shown in Table 6-1).

Table 6-2 Comparing users, logins, and contained users

Database user	Server login	Contained database user
• Set a database context • Linked to a server login • Does not have a password • Assigned to database roles • Stored in the user database • Brought along with a User DB Restore • Given access to SELECT, UPDATE, EXECUTE, CREATE TABLE, etc.	• Authenticates to a SQL Server • Can be linked to Active Directory (Windows Authentication) • Or can have a password (SQL Authentication) • Assigned to server roles • Stored in the master database • Not affected by User DB Restore • Given access to RESTORE, CONNECT, CREATE DATABASE, etc.	• Authenticates to a SQL Server • Has a password (SQL Authentication) • Assigned to database roles • Stored in the database • Brought along with a User DB Restore • Given access to database-level permissions typically granted to both logins and users

You can move contained databases from SQL Server instance to instance without the need to re-create server-level objects, such as server-level security (logins). Some features are only partially contained, however. Use the views `sys.dm_db_uncontained_entities` and `sys.sql_modules` to return information about uncontained objects or features. By determining the containment status of the elements of your database, you can discover what objects or features must be replaced or altered to promote containment.

A significant security factor to be aware of with contained databases is that any user with the ALTER ANY USER permission, and of course any user who is a member of the db_owner fixed database role, can grant access to the database and therefore the server's resources. Users with this permission could grant access to net new users and applications independently of the SQL Server instance's administrators.

Though the concept of creating databases with the specific `CONTAINMENT` option does not exist in Azure SQL Database (in v12), contained databases were developed specifically to assist with the concept of a cloud-based database as a service, to allow Azure SQL databases to be mobile between different cloud hosts, and to assure very high levels of availability.

Permissions in SQL Server

In this section, we cover the basics of SQL Server permissions, how you grant, revoke, and deny them, and how you should apply them.

Understanding Permissions for Data Definition Language and Data Manipulation Language

Statements in Transact-SQL (T-SQL), and the permissions that can be applied to them, can be sorted into two basic categories of actions: Data Manipulation Language (DML) and Data Definition Language (DDL).

DML

These six statements access and modify data in tables and are commonly used:

- BULK INSERT
- DELETE
- INSERT
- MERGE
- SELECT
- UPDATE

NOTE

Where are permissions for MERGE? There is no MERGE permission; instead, the syntax requires individual permissions to SELECT from the source tables and SELECT, INSERT, UPDATE, and/or DELETE on the target tables.

Where are permissions for IDENTITY_INSERT? Although it probably precedes your DML activity, IDENTITY_INSERT is actually a DDL operation and so, since SQL 2008 R2, IDENTITY_INSERT requires that the user have ALTER permissions on the table. In versions prior to SQL 2008 R2, the user must have owned the table, been a member of the sysadmin server role, or a member of the db_owner and db_ddladmin roles.

Three more DML statements are deprecated and are needed to modify permissions for the deprecated `text`, `ntext`, and `image` data types. Do not use them, except for legacy support.

- READTEXT

- UPDATETEXT

- WRITETEXT

DDL

A large number of statements are used to create, modify, and destroy objects in instances and databases. Their base categories include the following:

- ALTER

- CREATE

- DROP

- TRUNCATE TABLE

- ENABLE TRIGGER

- DISABLE TRIGGER

- UPDATE STATISTICS

Inside OUT

Why is TRUNCATE *a DDL command, when it* DELETEs *rows?*

For the job of removing all rows from a table, the TRUNCATE TABLE command accomplishes the task faster than a DELETE statement without a WHERE clause.

This is because individual rows are not logged as deleted, rather the data pages are deallocated. The TRUNCATE operation is written to the transaction log and can be rolled back within of an explicit transaction because the pages are not fully deallocated until the transaction commits. TRUNCATE is a deallocation of data pages, as opposed to a DELETE, which removes rows from a table.

If this sounds like something closer to a DROP than a DELETE, you're right!

Modifying permissions

A third category of action can be described as modifying permissions, or Data Control Language (DCL), and there are three statements to use when modifying a principal's permissions:

- GRANT

- DENY

- REVOKE

GRANT allows a permission to occur, DENY disallows it, and REVOKE removes the current GRANT or DENY on the object specified. Here is the basic syntax:

```
GRANT|DENY|REVOKE permission
ON objecttype::Securable
TO principal
```

However, the ON portion of the permission statement could be optional to apply to a current context. For example, you can omit the portion to GRANT a permission to a principal for the current database by doing this:

```
GRANT EXECUTE TO [domain\katie.sql]
```

Keep in mind that this statement would grant EXECUTE permissions for any stored procedure in the database, but not to each stored procedure individually. Any stored procedures created in the future could also be run by the principal.

CHAPTER 6

Overlapping permissions

GRANT and DENY oppose each other, though DENY wins. To demonstrate, consider the following opposing GRANT and DENY statements run from an administrative account on the WideWorldImporters sample database:

```
GRANT SELECT on SCHEMA::sales to [domain\katie.sql];
DENY SELECT on OBJECT::sales.InvoiceLines to [domain\katie.sql];
```

As a result, the database user [domain\katie.sql] would have permissions to SELECT every object in the sales schema, except for the sales.SalesInvoice table. Let's assume that no other permissions or role memberships have been granted to the database user [domain\katie.sql].

If this is run by [domain\katie.sql]

```
use WideWorldImporters;
go
SELECT TOP 100 * FROM sales.Invoices;
SELECT TOP 100 * FROM sales.InvoiceLines;
```

the result is this:

```
Msg 229, Level 14, State 5, Line 4
The SELECT permission was denied on the object 'InvoiceLines', database 'WideWorldIm-
porters', schema 'sales'.

(100 row(s) affected)
```

The sales.Invoices table was still accessible to [domain\katie.sql] because it was in the sales schema, even though the user was denied access to sales.InvoiceLines.

Let's continue to explore this scenario. First, from an administrative account, let's remove the GRANT and DENY we issued in the previous command. As a result, we are back to our original state. No permissions or role memberships have been granted to the database user [domain\katie.sql]:

```
REVOKE SELECT on SCHEMA::sales to [domain\katie.sql]
REVOKE SELECT on OBJECT::sales.Invoices to [domain\katie.sql]
```

> ### NOTE
>
> You can use the syntax REVOKE *permission* TO or REVOKE *permission* FROM syntax interchangeably. This is to make the syntax a little easier to understand.

This results in the following when [domain\katie.sql] runs the same pair of SELECT statements:

```
Msg 229, Level 14, State 5, Line 4
The SELECT permission was denied on the object 'Invoices', database
'WideWorldImporters', schema 'sales'.
Msg 229, Level 14, State 5, Line 5
The SELECT permission was denied on the object 'InvoiceLines', database
'WideWorldImporters', schema 'sales'.
```

Now, from an administrative account, let's GRANT overlapping GRANT and DENY statements, only this time the GRANT and DENY are reversed:

```
DENY SELECT on SCHEMA::sales to [domain\katie.sql]
GRANT SELECT on OBJECT::sales.InvoiceLines to [domain\katie.sql]
```

This also results in permission denied errors when [domain\katie.sql] runs the same pair of SELECT statements:

```
Msg 229, Level 14, State 5, Line 4
The SELECT permission was denied on the object 'Invoices', database
'WideWorldImporters', schema 'sales'.
Msg 229, Level 14, State 5, Line 5
The SELECT permission was denied on the object 'InvoiceLines', database
'WideWorldImporters', schema 'sales'.
```

The DENY on the entire sales schema overlapped and won.

Inside Out

What is wrong in the preceding demonstration?

In the previous sample code snippets, for simplicity, we're granting access to an individual named user, Domain\Katie.SQL. When possible, you should avoid this. Ideally, you should grant permissions to the users or logins of Active Directory security groups, or to custom database or server roles.

You should create domain security groups for access roles based around job function, levels of oversight, zones of control, and so on. Your Active Directory environment might already have groups for different job functions, including SQL DBAs (for both their "everyday" and administrative accounts). If not, request that a smart list of groups be created so that you can implement proper security in your SQL Server.

Granting commonly needed permissions

Granting a domain account membership to the sysadmin role is appropriate only for administrator accounts; it is inappropriate for developers, power users, and analysts. What permissions might they need, short of "all of them"?

As a DBA, you should be aware of permissions that your IT colleagues can be granted short of the server sysadmin role or database db_owner roles.

Many of these common securables are server-level and so are not supported in Azure SQL Database v12. They are not supported even when run in the master database of the Azure SQL Database server.

The following subsections present some examples of permissions that you can grant developers in a production database that do not grant them access to view table data or change database objects.

ALTER TRACE

```
GRANT ALTER TRACE TO [server_principal]
```

A developer might need this permission to trace the SQL Server as part of a troubleshooting expedition into the SQL Server. (Though you should remind him after granting this permission that traces are deprecated, and extended events are a much better diagnostic tool.

> ➤ **For more information, see Chapter 13.**

Because ALTER TRACE is a server-level securable, developers would be able to trace all events on the server, from all databases and processes. Certain sensitive events cannot be traced; for example, the T-SQL statement of CREATE LOGIN for a SQL authenticated login.

ALTER ANY EVENT SESSION

```
GRANT ALTER ANY EVENT SESSION TO [server_principal]
```

A developer might need this permission to trace the SQL Server as part of a troubleshooting expedition into the SQL Server, after you tell them about extended events. This will grant them access to create extended events sessions with T-SQL commands, but will not give them access to view server metadata in the New Extended Events Session Wizard in SQL Server Management Studio. For that, they will need one further commonly granted developer permission: VIEW SERVER STATE (discussed shortly).

Similar to traces, extended events sessions can capture events on the server from all databases and processes. You cannot trace certain sensitive events; for example, the T-SQL statement of CREATE LOGIN for a SQL authenticated login.

However, as of Azure SQL Database v12, for developers to view extended events sessions, you must grant them an ownership-level permission CONTROL DATABASE (discussed in just a moment). In production environments, this isn't recommended for developers or non-administrators.

VIEW SERVER STATE

```
GRANT VIEW SERVER STATE TO [server_principal]
```

This permission at the server level allows the principal to view a large number of server metadata objects, system views, and dynamic management views (DMVs), many of which could be invaluable to a developer who is looking to troubleshoot, analyze, or performance tune.

Many of the DMVs mentioned in Chapter 12 need only the VIEW SERVER STATE permission.

This is a relatively safe permission to grant. With VIEW SERVER STATE, the principal still has no access to data, database objects, logins, or passwords. This is a read-only permission at the server level and is a great alternative to granting administrative permissions.

VIEW DEFINTION

```
GRANT VIEW DEFINTION ON schema.objectname TO [database_principal]
```

This provides permission to the developer to view the T-SQL code of database objects, without the rights to read or change the objects. This is known as the metadata of the objects.

Developers might need access to verify that code changes have deployed to production; for example, to compare the code of a stored procedure in production to what is in source control. This is also a safe permission to grant developers because it does not confer any SELECT or any modification permissions.

Instead of going through each object in a database, you might instead want to GRANT VIEW ANY DEFINITION TO [principal]. This applies the permission to all objects in the current database context. You can revoke it easily.

SHOWPLAN

```
GRANT SHOWPLAN TO [server_principal]
```

As part of performance tuning, developers almost certainly need access to view a specific query's runtime plan, for queries against any database on the server. Seeing the execution plan is not possible even if the developer has the appropriate SELECT or EXECUTE permissions on the database objects in the query. This applies to both estimated and actual runtime plans.

The SHOWPLAN permission, however, is not enough: developers also must have the appropriate read or read/write permissions to run the query that generates the plan.

Non-administrators and developers can still view *aggregate* cached runtime plan statistics via the DMV sys.dm_exec_cached_plans without the SHOWPLAN permission, if they have the VIEW SERVER STATE permission.

CONNECT ALL DATABASES

```
GRANT CONNECT ALL DATABASES TO [server_principal]
```

Introduced in SQL Server 2014, this is a quick way to allow a login to set its context to any current or future database on the server. It grants no other permissions. Although it does not create a user in each database for the login, it behaves as if a user had been granted in each database for login, and has been given no other rights.

This permission alone doesn't seem very useful, but it could be handy for setting up a DBA's "everyday" account or, rather, granting this securable to a Windows-authenticated group to which all DBA "everyday" accounts belong. Consider granting this permission and the next, as well, SELECT ALL USER SECURABLES, to grant read-only access to a server, including each database on the server.

SELECT ALL USER SECURABLES

```
GRANT SELECT ALL USER SECURABLES TO [server_principal]
```

Introduced in SQL Server 2014, this permission grants the ability to SELECT from all readable database objects in all user databases. The object types include tables, views, table-valued functions. EXECUTE permissions are not implied. This is a fast way to give administrators access to read from all current and future databases and their objects, but is not appropriate for non-administrative end users or application logins.

Keep in mind that production data could contain sensitive, personally identified, or personal health information. In some regulatory environments, granting this permission would not be appropriate and might fail regulatory audit, unless SELECT permission on sensitive tables was denied, masked, or those tables were encrypted, perhaps with the Always Encrypted feature.

Similarly, you could also use this permission to DENY SELECT access to all data on a server. This could ensure that administrators can accomplish a variety of other server-level tasks in production systems with safe assurance that they cannot casually access data using their "everyday" accounts. Keep in mind that members of the sysadmin server role would not be affected by any DENY permission.

> ➤ For more information on encryption of sensitive data, including Always Encrypted, see Chapter 7.

IMPERSONATE

```
GRANT IMPERSONATE ON USER::[database_principal] TO [database_principal]
GRANT IMPERSONATE ON LOGIN::[server_principal] TO [server_principal]
```

The IMPERSONATE permission allows the user of the EXECUTE AS statement and also the EXECUTE AS clause to run a stored procedure. This permission can create a complicated administrative environment and should be granted only after you have an understanding of the implications and potential inappropriate or malicious use. With this permission, it is possible to impersonate a member of the sysadmin role and assume those permissions, so this permission should be granted in controlled scenarios, and perhaps only temporarily.

This permission is most commonly granted for applications that use EXECUTE AS to change their connection security context. You can grant the IMPERSONATE permission on logins or users.

Logins with the CONTROL SERVER permission already have IMPERSONATE ANY LOGIN permission, which should be limited to administrators only. It is unlikely that any application that uses EXECUTE AS would need its service account to have permission to IMPERSONATE any login that currently or ever will exist. Instead, service accounts should be granted IMPERSONATE permissions only for known, appropriate, and approved principals that have been created for the explicit purpose of being impersonated temporarily.

An EXECUTE AS statement should eventually be followed by a REVERT. We use EXECUTE AS and discuss more about this statement later in this chapter.

CONTROL SERVER|DATABASE

```
GRANT CONTROL SERVER TO [server_principal]
GRANT CONTROL ON DATABASE::[Database_Name] TO [database_principal]
```

This effectively grants all permissions on a server or database and is not appropriate for developers or non-administrators.

Granting the CONTROL permission is not exactly the same as granting membership to the sysadmin server role or a db_owner database role, but it has the same effect. Members of the sysadmin role are not affected by DENY permissions, but owners of the CONTROL permission might be.

Ownership versus authorization

Database ownership is an important topic and a common check-up finding for SQL Server administrators. The concept of an ownership chain is complicated to explain; in this section, we cover the topic of database ownership and its impact.

Beginning with SQL Server 2008, "ownership" was redefined as "authorization." Ownership is now a casual term, whereas AUTHORIZATION is the concept that establishes this relationship between an object and a principal.

CHAPTER 6

Changing the AUTHORIZATION for any object, including a database, is the preferred, unified terminology than describing and maintaining object ownership with a variety of syntax and management objects. In the case of a database, however, although AUTHORIZATION does not imply membership in the db_owner role, it does grant the equivalent highest level of permissions.

For this reason, and for reasons involving the database ownership chain, named individual accounts (for example, your own [domain*firstname.lastname*]) should not be the AUTHORIZATION of a database.

The problem—which many developers and administrators do not realize—is that when a user creates a database, that user is the "owner" of the database, and that user principal's SID is listed as the owner_sid in sys.databases.

If the database's "owner_sid" principal account was ever to be turned off or removed in Active Directory, and you move the database to another server without that principal, you will encounter problems with IMPERSONATION and AUTHORIZATION of child objects, which could surface as a wide variety of errors or application failures. This is because the owner_sid is the account used as the root for authorization for the database. It must exist and be a valid principal.

For this reason, DBAs should change the AUTHORIZATION of databases to either a known high-level, noninteractive service account or to the built-in sa principal (sid 0x01). It is a standard item on any good SQL Server health check.

If there are databases with sensitive data that should not allow any access from other databases, they should not have the same owner_sid as less-secure databases, and you should not turn on Cross Database Ownership Chaining at the server level (it is not by default).

Changing database ownership

When "ownership" was redefined as "authorization," the stored procedure sp_changedbowner was deprecated in favor of the ALTER AUTHORIZATION syntax; for example:

```
ALTER AUTHORIZATION ON DATABASE::[databasename]  TO [server_principal];
```

In SQL Server databases, the new owner can be a SQL Server–authenticated login or a Windows-authenticated login. To change the ownership of a database by running the ALTER AUTHORIZATION statement, the principal that's running needs the TAKE OWNERSHIP permission and the IMPERSONATE permission for the new owner.

The new owner of the database must not already exist as a user in the database. If it does, the ALTER will fail with the error message: "The proposed new database owner is already a user or aliased in the database." You will need to drop the user before you can run the ALTER AUTHORIZATION statement.

For Azure SQL Database, the new owner can be a SQL Server–authenticated login or a user object federated or managed in Azure AD, though groups are not supported.

To change the ownership of a database in Azure SQL Database, there is no sysadmin role of which to be a member. The principal that alters the owner must either be the current database owner, the administrator account specified upon creation, or the Azure AD account associated as the administrator of the database. As with any permission in Azure SQL Database, only Azure AD accounts can manage other Azure AD accounts. You can manage SQL Server–authenticated accounts by SQL Server–authenticated or Azure AD accounts.

Understanding views, stored procedures, and function permissions

In similar ways, views, stored procedures, and functions abstract the permissions necessary to read and write from tables and other views. In this section, we explore how views, stored procedures, and user-defined functions make it possible to access underlying database objects. Views, stored procedures, and functions can simplify the minimum permissions you need to assign.

Simply put, EXECUTE permissions on stored procedures and SELECT permissions on views allow a user to access data from the objects in the same database that are included in the procedure or view definition, without explicit permissions on the objects included in the procedure or view definition.

This is an important concept to understand, so that you as a DBA can follow a principle of least privilege and grant only the minimum rights necessary for an application or end user to access data. We could even go so far as to DENY SELECT access to application users and still provide them with data access via the stored procedures, view, and functions we have designed for appropriate data access.

How views, stored procedures, and functions allow access

Stored procedures require EXECUTE to run, but do not require the user to have all underlying object permissions (SELECT, INSERT, DELETE). Similarly, views and functions require SELECT to run, but do not require the user to have all underlying object permissions, either.

In the case of stored procedures there are three important caveats that would break this abstraction and require that whoever is running the procedure also have permissions to the underlying database objects:

- The procedure cannot perform any ALTER operations, which are not abstracted by the stored procedure. This includes IDENTITY_INSERT.

- The procedure does not perform any dynamic SQL Server command such as `sp_executesql` or EXEC (@SQL) to access data. This is a built-in safeguard against SQL Server injection attacks.

- The underlying database objects referenced by the stored procedure have an ownership chain; that is, they have the same ownership chain.

Not violating any of those conditions, thanks to the intact database permission chain, you can GRANT EXECUTE permission to a principal and *no other permissions,* and you can run the procedure successfully. Now, the database principal has no way to access the database objects outside of your stored procedure.

Views and functions work similarly, without the first two caveats (they obviously don't apply), and you can use them to provide a horizontal or vertical partition of a table to users who do not have explicit SELECT permissions to that table.

A demonstration of permissions with views, stored procedures, and functions

Let's demonstrate with a simple lab exercise, in which we will create a testing user and a testing table in the WideWorldImporters database. Run all of the code in this demonstration section while logged in as a member of the sysadmin role:

```
USE [master]
GO
CREATE LOGIN DenyPrincipal WITH PASSWORD=N'deny'
GO
GRANT CONNECT SQL TO DenyPrincipal
ALTER LOGIN DenyPrincipal ENABLE
GO
USE [WideWorldImporters]
GO
CREATE USER DenyPrincipal FOR LOGIN DenyPrincipal
GO
CREATE TABLE dbo.DenyPrincipalTable (
ID INT IDENTITY (1,1) NOT NULL CONSTRAINT PK_DenyPrincipalTable PRIMARY KEY,
Text1 VARCHAR(100) )
GO
INSERT INTO dbo.DenyPrincipalTable (Text1) VALUES ('test')
GO 3
```

We've inserted three rows into the dbo.DenyPrincipalTable.

Now let's test various ways to access this table, without granting any permissions to it.

Inside OUT

When testing with EXECUTE AS, how can I determine what my current security context is?

The section that follows uses the EXECUTE AS statement, which makes it possible for you to simulate the permissions of another principal. If you are using SQL Server Management Studio, this will affect only the current query window.

Be sure to always follow an EXECUTE AS with a REVERT, which stops the impersonation and restores your own permissions. Each execution of REVERT affects only one EXECUTE AS.

If you run into issues, you can always find out what principal you are running by using this statement:

```
SELECT ORIGTNAL LOGIN(), CURRENT_USER;
```

It will provide you with two values:

- **ORIGINAL_LOGIN().**   The name of the login with which you actually connected. This will not change even after you use EXECUTE AS USER or EXECUTE AS LOGIN. This is the not the name of the user you originally connected with, but could be helpful to remember how you originally connected.

- **CURRENT_USER.**   The name of the user whose security content you have assumed, and is the equivalent of USER_NAME(). The result similar to SUSER_ NAME() and SUSER_SNAME() on SQL Server instances, but on Azure SQL Database v12, SUSER_NAME() results an SID and SUSER_SNAME() is not supported in Azure SQL Database v12.

Test permissions using a view   Now, we will create a view on the table dbo.DenyPrincipal Table and try to access it. Note that we just created the [DenyPrincipal] database principal and have not granted it any other permissions. Outside of what is granted to the [public] role (more on that later), [DenyPrincipal] has no permissions. Execute this and all following code in this section while logged in as a member of the sysadmin role:

```
CREATE VIEW dbo.denyview WITH SCHEMABINDING AS

SELECT DenyView = text1 FROM dbo.DenyPrincipalTable

GO

GRANT SELECT ON dbo.denyview TO [DenyPrincipal]
GO
```

The [DenyPrincipal] principal now has access to the view dbo.DenyView, but not to the table dbo.DenyPrincipalTable.

Now, attempt to read data from the table:

```
EXECUTE AS USER = 'DenyPrincipal';
SELECT * FROM dbo.DenyPrincipalTable;
GO
REVERT;
```

This results in the following error:

```
Msg 229, Level 14, State 5, Line 41
The SELECT permission was denied on the object 'DenyPrincipalTable', database 'Wide-
WorldImporters', schema 'dbo'.
```

Why? Remember that we have granted no permissions to the DenyPrincipalTable. This is as intended.

But the user [DenyPrincipal] can still access the data in column text1 via the view:

```
EXECUTE AS USER = 'DenyPrincipal';
select * from dbo.DenyView;
GO
REVERT;
```

Here are the results:

```
DenyView
test
test
test
```

Note also that [DenyPrincipal] has access only to the columns (and if desired, the rows) that the view dbo.DenyView provides. Applications can use views and stored procedures to provide appropriate SELECT, INSERT, UPDATE and DELETE access to underlying table data by blocking access to rows and columns and no SELECT access directly to the table.

> ➤ For more information on techniques to grant appropriate data access, including Always Encrypted, see Chapter 7.

Test permissions using a stored procedure   Let's prove the same abstraction of permissions by using a stored procedure, and then also demonstrate when it fails:

```
CREATE PROC dbo.DenySproc AS
BEGIN
SELECT DenySproc = text1
FROM dbo.DenyPrincipalTable;
END
```

```
GO
GRANT EXECUTE ON dbo.DenySproc to [DenyPrincipal];
GO

EXECUTE AS USER = 'DenyPrincipal';
EXEC dbo.DenySproc;
GO
REVERT;
GO
```

Here are the results:

DenySproc
test
test
test

It works! Without any access to the dbo.DenyPrincipalTable table, the user DenyPrincipal was able to access the table data.

Now, let's break the stored procedure's ability to abstract the permissions:

```
CREATE PROC dbo.DenySproc_adhoc
AS
BEGIN
DECLARE @sql nvarchar(1000)
SELECT @sql = 'select ExecSproc_adhoc = text1 FROM dbo.DenyPrincipalTable';
EXEC sp_executesql @SQL;
END
GO
GRANT EXECUTE ON dbo.DenySproc_adhoc to [DenyPrincipal];
GO
EXECUTE AS USER = 'DenyPrincipal';
EXEC dbo.DenySproc_adhoc;
GO
REVERT;
```

Here are the results:

```
Msg 229, Level 14, State 5, Line 75
The SELECT permission was denied on the object 'DenyPrincipalTable', database 'Wide-
WorldImporters', schema 'dbo'.
```

Note that we used the dynamic SQL command sp_executesql, passing in a string of T-SQL, which as a security feature automatically breaks the permission abstraction. Note also that the failure message indicates that the user [DenyPrincipal] does not have permission to SELECT from the underlying table.

Test permissions using a table-valued function Finally, you'll find that table-valued functions work in the same way. Let's create an inline table-valued function to demonstrate:

```
CREATE FUNCTION dbo.DenyFunc ()
RETURNS TABLE
AS RETURN
    SELECT DenyFunc = Text1
    FROM dbo.DenyPrincipalTable;
GO
GRANT SELECT ON dbo.DenyFunc TO [DENYPRINCIPAL];
GO
EXECUTE AS USER = 'DenyPrincipal';
SELECT * FROM DenyFunc();
GO
REVERT;
GO
```

Here are the results:

```
DenyFun
test
test
test
```

Using a function also works! Without any access to the `dbo.DenyPrincipalTable` table, the user `DenyPrincipal` was able to access the table data via the table function `DenyFunc()`.

Access a table even when SELECT is denied Let's take it one step further and DENY SELECT permissions to [DenyPrincipal]. Will we still be able to access the underlying table data via a view and stored procedure?

```
DENY SELECT ON dbo.DenyPrincipalTable TO [DenyPrincipal];
GO
EXECUTE AS USER = 'DenyPrincipal';
SELECT * FROM dbo.denyview; --test the view
GO
EXEC dbo.DenySproc; --test the stored procedure
GO
SELECT * FROM DenyFunc();
GO
REVERT;
GO
```

Yes! And, again, here are the results:

```
DenyView
test
test
test
```

DenySproc
test
test
test

DenyFunc
test
test
test

Understanding server roles

In this section, we review the server roles built in to SQL Server, with a focus on when and why they should be granted. Several server roles are built in to SQL Server, including the one you are likely most familiar with, the sysadmin. You can create your own custom server roles, as well, which we discuss in the next section.

Logins are granted membership to other server roles most commonly for situations in which the DBA team will be separated in terms of responsibility or when service accounts need access to perform server-level operations.

Assigning server role membership appropriately

Too often, vendor specifications and developers request inappropriate permissions to be given to end users and service accounts via fixed server roles. In this section, we look at the server roles built in to SQL Server, with a focus on when and why you should grant them.

Note that server roles are not a feature of Azure SQL Database, though database roles (covered later in this chapter) are provided.

To manage user assignment server roles, SQL Server Management Studio provides the membership page in the Login Properties dialog box (Figure 6-3). By default, only the Public check box is selected (you cannot clear it). Initially, a new login is assigned to only the public built-in server role, from which that login cannot be removed.

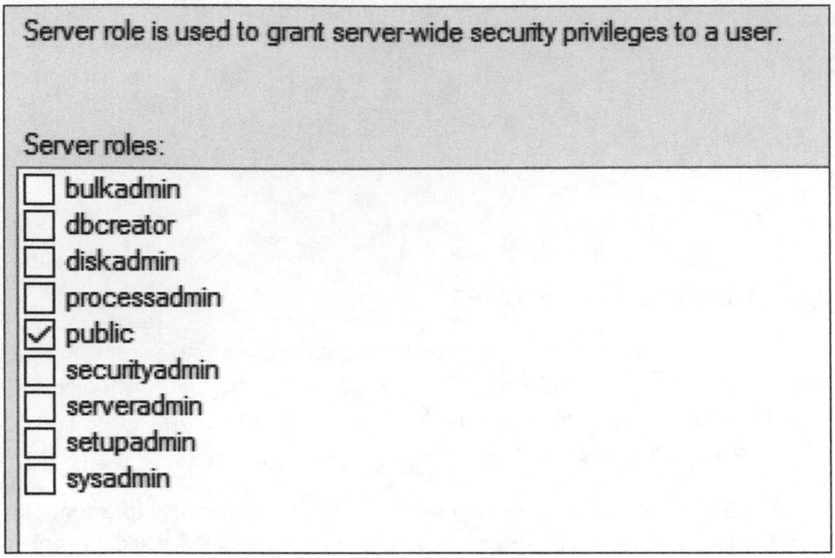

Figure 6-3 The server role membership page from the Login Properties dialog box in SQL Server Management StudioBy default, only the public role is selected (and cannot be cleared).

You also can use T-SQL to add and remove members from server roles, as shown in this example:

```
ALTER SERVER ROLE serveradmin ADD MEMBER [domain\katie.sql]
GO
ALTER SERVER ROLE processadmin DROP MEMBER [domain\katie.sql]
GO
```

Let's explore the list of built-in server roles, beginning with the unlimited sysadmin role.

- **sysadmin.** The sysadmin server role has unrestricted access to all operations. It is appropriate for DBA administrative accounts only. Although software vendors or other accounts can request membership to the sysadmin server role to simplify their installations, this is not appropriate, and a responsible DBA should push back on granting membership to this role.

  When granting the sysadmin role, it is unnecessary to grant membership to any other server role. Granting membership to every server role is comedically the equivalent of pushing all the buttons on an elevator.

  The sysadmin role is also granted certain other permissions, especially in SQL Server Management Studio. The sysadmin role is nearly the equivalent of the GRANT CONTROL SERVER permission, with some differences. The most notable is the fact that the sysadmin role is unaffected by any DENY permissions; for example:

```
USE Master;
GO
CREATE LOGIN [domain\katie.sql] FROM WINDOWS;
GO
GRANT CONTROL SERVER TO  [domain\katie.sql] ;
DENY VIEW SERVER STATE TO  [domain\katie.sql];
GO
EXECUTE AS LOGIN = 'domain\katie.sql';
SELECT * FROM sys.dm_exec_cached_plans;
GO
REVERT;
GO
```

Where the DENY would have no effect on a user that is a member of the sysadmin server role, here is the result:

```
Msg 300, Level 14, State 1, Line 7
VIEW SERVER STATE permission was denied on object 'server', database 'master'.
Msg 297, Level 16, State 1, Line 7
The user does not have permission to perform this action.
```

- **bulkadmin.**   The bulkadmin server role has been granted permissions to perform BULK INSERT operations from local files. It could be suitable for service accounts for unattended processes that perform automated mass data movement. Bulk operations from any local folders are allowed; this is the main difference between granting membership to this role and granting the ADMINISTER BULK OPERATIONS permission.

    Principals with this permission can use bcp, SQL Server Integration Services, or T-SQL to perform BULK INSERT statements. Note that for BULK INSERT operations, permissions to INSERT into the destination tables are additionally required, and permissions to ALTER TABLE for the destination table might also be required.

- **dbcreator.**   Service accounts for applications that generate databases automatically, such as Microsoft SharePoint On-Premises, can be granted membership to this server role instead of sysadmin, to allow databases to be created. You can create new databases directly or via the restore from a backup.

    The dbcreator server role has the CREATE ANY DATABASE permission. Keep in mind that this permission also gives the user the capability to ALTER and DROP any database for which that user has AUTHORIZATION.

- **diskadmin.**   A subset of the serveradmin fixed server role, the diskadmin server role has the rights to affect drive resources; for example, to create and drop backup devices.

    In addition to other permissions, diskadmin has been granted the ALTER RESOURCES permission, which is fairly limited, poorly documented, and is not recommended to grant individually. Instead, grant membership only to the diskadmin role.

CHAPTER 6

- **processadmin.**   This role grants admin-level visibility to sessions and requests, and to view and reset server performance information. These permissions can prove useful to non-administrators who monitor activity. You will likely find it useful for these types of users to combine processadmin with SQL Agent job-related permissions, discussed later in this chapter.

  The role is granted the ALTER ANY CONNECTION permissions, allowing members of this role to view and stop sessions. The role is also granted VIEW and ALTER SERVER STATE, making it possible for members to view a wide array of helpful DMVs.

  Any connection can view its own sessions in the sys.dm_exec_sessions, but with the ALTER ANY CONNECTION permission, a connection can view all sessions and requests active on the server, including system sessions below session_id 50.

  The ALTER SERVER STATE allows access to DBCC SQLPERF, a well-documented command that can view and reset wait and latch statistics as well as view space utilization data from transaction log files. In Azure SQL Database, resetting wait and latch statistics is not supported.

- **public.**   To be as plain as possible, no permissions should ever be granted to the public server role (or corresponding public roles in each database, discussed later.)

  Every login is a member of the public server role. Every user is a member of the public database role. Do not grant any additional permissions to the public roles, because they will be granted to all current and future logins and users.

  securityadmin.   The security admin permission should be considered as close to sysadmin as it gets. The ability to create logins at the server level and users in each database, to grant and revoke permissions at the server and database level, should not be granted lightly. Members of the securityadmin role can create and add logins to the sysadmin role, so membership should be given scrutiny equivalent to the sysadmin role.

  Membership in the securityadmin role is required by some service accounts to delegate the management of security to applications, especially those that create databases procedurally and thus need to provision security for them; for example, the setup and farm accounts for Microsoft SharePoint On-Premises installations.

  The securityadmin role possesses the ALTER ANY LOGIN permission and more, including security permissions inside each database, plus management of account status and passwords for SQL Server–authenticated logins.

- **Serveradmin.**   Membership in the serveradmin server role grants the ability to alter and create endpoints, sp_configure settings, and to SHUTDOWN the SQL Server instance. The role is also granted VIEW and ALTER SERVER STATE, allowing the permission to view a wide array of helpful DMVs.

The ALTER SERVER STATE allows access to DBCC SQLPERF, a well-documented command that can view and reset wait and latch statistics as well as view space utilization data from transaction log files. In Azure SQL Database, resetting wait and latch statistics is not supported.

The serveradmin has no access to data or database-level settings or security-related permissions, and so is often combined with other roles to provide a subset of administrative capability.

- **Setupadmin.**   The setupadmin role only grants permissions to deal with linked servers using T-SQL statements. To use SQL Server Management Studio to set up linked servers, the sysadmin role is required.

Creating custom server roles

Beginning with SQL Server 2012, you can create custom server roles to help you further define the roles that various administrators and non-administrators can serve. This can be especially helpful when crafting a package of less-than-sysadmin permissions for deployment managers, security administrators, auditors, developers, integration testers, or external access.

Inside a DBA team, we might seek to break down duties and grant permissions to suit, for example, junior administrators or high availability administrators, who should not need full sysadmin rights.

The key to creating custom server roles is to have a good understanding of the permissions involved to perform certain tasks and then divvying up permissions. You also can make custom server roles to be members of any built-in server role except for sysadmin.

Similarly, you have the ability to create custom database roles in each database. We discuss that later in this chapter.

Following is an example of a potentially useful custom server role. You could create it to allow read-only access to administrators to a server. In the section "Providing logins to the DBA team" earlier in the chapter, we discussed separating the Windows credentials used by DBAs into an "everyday" account and an administrative account. This custom server role could be useful to provide read-only access to a DBA's "everyday" account.

```
--Create a new custom server role

CREATE SERVER ROLE SupportViewServer;

GO
--Grant permissions to the custom server role
--Run DMVs, see server information
```

CHAPTER 6

```
GRANT
VIEW SERVER STATE
to SupportViewServer;
--See metadata of any database

GRANT
VIEW ANY DATABASE
to SupportViewServer;

--Set context to any database

GRANT
CONNECT ANY DATABASE
to SupportViewServer;

--Permission to SELECT from any data object in any databases

GRANT
SELECT ALL USER SECURABLES
to SupportViewServer;

GO

--Add the DBA team's accounts
ALTER SERVER ROLE SupportViewServer ADD MEMBER [domain\Katherine]
ALTER SERVER ROLE SupportViewServer ADD MEMBER [domain\Colby]
ALTER SERVER ROLE SupportViewServer ADD MEMBER [domain\David]
...
```

Understanding database roles

In this section, we review the database roles, both built-in and custom, with a focus on when and why they should be granted. The same list of roles applies to SQL Server and Azure SQL Database.

Similar to server roles, database roles (Figure 6-4) in each database provide for packages of permissions to ease the provisioning of database users. You also can create your own user-defined database roles to further customize the packages of permissions granted to users.

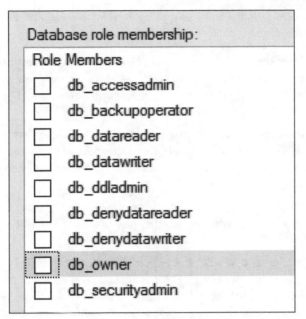

Database role membership:

Role Members
☐ db_accessadmin
☐ db_backupoperator
☐ db_datareader
☐ db_datawriter
☐ db_ddladmin
☐ db_denydatareader
☐ db_denydatawriter
☐ db_owner
☐ db_securityadmin

Figure 6-4 The Database Role Membership page from the User Properties dialog box in SQL Server Management Studio for a SQL Server instance.

Let's examine the list of built-in database roles, their permissions, and appropriate use.

- **db_owner.** The db_owner database role's name is a bit misleading because it can have many members. It provides unrestricted access to the database to make any/all changes to the database and contained objects. This is not the same as being identified as the owner_sid within the database. Changing the AUTHORIZATION for the database to a principal confers the same rights as db_owner because the server principal will be mapped to the dbo built-in user when accessing the database, which is a member of the db_owner role.

    The db_owner role does not grant the CONTROL DATABASE permission but is equivalent. Similar to how the sysadmin server role operates, the db_owner ignores any DENY permissions.

    The only users in the database who can add or remove members from built-in database roles are members of the db_owner role and the principal that holds AUTHORIZATION for the database.

➤ For more on AUTHORIZATION, the equivalent of "ownership" terminology, see the section "Ownership versus authorization" earlier in the chapter.

- **db_accessadmin.**   The db_accessadmin role not only has the right to create and manage database users and database roles, but to create schemas, grant permissions on all database objects. Among other permissions, the db_accessadmin has the ALTER ANY LOGIN and CREATE SCHEMA permissions.

   Members of the db_accessadmin role can create users with or without an association to existing logins. However, members of the db_accessadmin database role cannot fix orphaned users or change the login that a user is assigned to, because they do not have the CONTROL DATABASE permission.

   Even though members of the db_accessadmin role can create schemas, they cannot change the authorization for schemas, because they do not have the ALTER ANY SCHEMA permission.

   Keep in mind that in a contained database, members of the db_accessadmin role (and the db_owner role) can create users with passwords, allowing new access to the SQL Server. Because of the high level of control over permissions and membership in the database, this role should be considered as important as the db_owner role and not given out lightly.

   Because of the high level of control over permissions and membership in the database, this role should be considered as important as the db_owner role and not given out lightly.

- **db_backupoperator.**   The db_backupoperator role has permissions to BACKUP DATABASE (including full and differential backups), BACKUP LOG, and to CHECKPOINT the database. Note that this role has no rights to RESTORE the database, because that requires server-level permissions found in the sysadmin and dbcreator fixed server roles, or the owner of the database.

- **db_datareader.**   The db_datareader role given rights to SELECT from any object in the database, including tables and views. This is a heavy-handed and brute-force way to give access to application accounts, and it ignores the ability for views to abstract the permissions necessary to read from tables. It is preferable to add permissions to individual objects or schemas instead of granting SELECT access to all objects, your database might not always need to grant SELECT permissions to all tables and views.

- **db_datawriter.**   The db_datawriter permission can INSERT, UPDATE, or DELETE any table in the database. This is a heavy-handed and brute-force way to give access to application accounts, and it ignores the ability for stored procedures to provide approved or audited methods for data changes by abstracting the permissions necessary to write to tables. You should instead grant write permissions on specific objects to specific principals, or use stored procedures to accomplish writes.

- **db_ddladmin.**   The db_ddladmin role has the rights to perform DDL statements to alter any object in the database, but it has no permission to create or modify permissions, users, roles, or role membership. This role also does not have the permission to EXECUTE objects in the database, even objects that members of this role create. There is no built-in database role that provides EXECUTE permissions, which you should grant more granularly than at the database level.

- **db_denydatareader.**   The inverse of db_datareader, the db_denydatareader role denies SELECT on all objects.

- **db_denydatawriter.**   The inverse of db_datawriter, the db_denydatawriter role denies INSERT, UPDATE, and DELETE on all objects.

- **db_securityadmin.**   Members of the db_securityadmin role can manage fixed database roles (but not change their membership), create and manage custom roles, role membership, and GRANT, REVOKE, and DENY permissions on database objects in the database.

  Note that members of the db_accessadmin role can create and manage users, but members of the db_securityadmin cannot.

- **public.**   To be as clear as possible, no permissions should *ever* be granted to the public database role (or the public server role, discussed earlier in this chapter).

  Every database user is a member of the public database role. Do not grant any additional permissions to the public roles in any database, because they will be granted to all current and future users.

Inside OUT

Avoid these common security antipatterns in the databases you manage.

Here are two common worst practices in the wild from software vendors:

- Grant EXECUTE on stored procedures, or to the entire database context, to public to ensure that all users have the ability to call all current and future stored procedures.

- Grant SELECT on the entire database context to public to ensure that all users aren't blocked from the ability to read data from views and tables.

This public-permissioned strategy belies a fundamental arrogance about the relationship between the end user and the vendor application. Software developers should never assume that their application's security apparatus will be the only way to access the database.

CHAPTER 6

> In reality, an enterprise's power users, analysts, and developers will access the vendor's database with other applications, including but not limited to SQL Server Management Studio; Microsoft Office applications, including Excel and Access; or ad hoc business intelligence tools such as Microsoft Power BI. Users will have unrestricted access to all data and procedures in the database when connecting to the database with other tools.
>
> In this day and age of multiplatform devices and data access, it's wise to assume that users can connect to your data outside of the primary application. Database security should be enforced in the database, as well, not solely at the application layer. Instead of ever granting permissions to public roles, grant only appropriate EXECUTE | SELECT | INSERT | UPDATE | DELETE permissions to specific principals linked to domain security groups.

Creating custom database roles

You can create custom database roles to help further define the roles that various application users or service accounts need for proper data access. Instead of assigning distinct packages of administrative permissions, here you assign packages of data access and database object permissions. Custom database roles can own schemas and objects, just like database user principals.

As with server roles, the key to creating custom database roles is to have a good understanding of the permissions involved and the appropriateness of data access. It is unlikely that all users in a database will need the same data access, and not all read-only access will be the same.

```
--Create a new custom database role
USE [WideWorldImporters]
GO

-- Create the database role
CREATE ROLE SalesReadOnly AUTHORIZATION [dbo];
GO

-- Grant access rights to a specific schema in the database
GRANT EXECUTE
ON [Website].[SearchForSuppliers]
TO SalesReadOnly;
GO
```

NOTE

Like users, custom database roles can themselves can be made members of other database roles. However, it is not a recommended security practice to add a custom database role as a member of a fixed database role. You should assign permissions for custom roles directly, to prevent future accidental escalation of permissions.

Assigning database role membership appropriately

However, as of this writing, SQL Server Management Studio does not provide the same membership page for Azure SQL Database users. Instead, you must use T-SQL code to add and remove database users from built-in or custom groups; for example:

```
--Add User to built-in database role
ALTER ROLE db_owner ADD MEMBER [domain\katie.sql];
GO

-- Add User to custom database role
ALTER ROLE SalesReadOnly ADD MEMBER [domain\James]
ALTER ROLE SalesReadOnly ADD MEMBER [domain\Alex]
ALTER ROLE SalesReadOnly ADD MEMBER [domain\Naomi]
ALTER ROLE SalesReadOnly ADD MEMBER [domain\Amos]
ALTER ROLE SalesReadOnly ADD MEMBER [domain\Shed]
GO

--Remove User from database role
ALTER ROLE SalesReadOnly DROP MEMBER [domain\Shed];
GO
```

Using the Dedicated Administrator Connection

The Dedicated Administrator Connection (DAC) is an admin-only reserved connection into the SQL Server instance or Azure SQL Database for use as an emergency method to authenticate to the server when some problematic condition is otherwise preventing authentication.

Examples could be misconfiguration of security, misconfiguration of the Resource Governor, misconfiguration of prompts created FOR LOGON, or other interesting conditions that block even members of the sysadmin server role.

Only one member at a time of the server sysadmin role can connect using the DAC, so similar to a database in single-user mode, do not attempt to connect to the DAC via Object Explorer in SQL Server Management Studio. (Object Explorer cannot connect to the DAC, by design.)

In SQL Server Management Studio, you might see an error message that says Failed To Connect To Server, but in the background, the query window has in fact connected to the DAC, evidenced by the server name in the bottom of the window. This occurs only when reusing a previously connected query window in SQL Server Management Studio. You can avoid the error by opening a new Database Engine Query window in SQL Server Management Studio, but the result is the same.

The DAC also has resource limitations intended to limit the impact of DAC commands. You will not be able to perform all administrative tasks through the DAC; for example, you cannot issue BACKUP or RESTORE commands from the DAC. You should instead use the DAC only for diagnostic and remediation of the issues that prevent normal access, and then return to a normal connection. Do not use the DAC to carry out long-running queries against user data, DBCC CHECKDB, or to query the dm_db_index_physical_stats DMV.

When connecting to a database in Azure SQL Database with the DAC, you must specify the database name in your connection string or connection dialog box. Because you cannot change database contexts with the USE syntax in Azure SQL Database, you should always make connections directly to the desired database in Azure SQL Database, via the database or initial catalog parameters of the connection string.

There are several ways to sign in to a SQL Server instance or Azure SQL Database using the DAC via a login that is a member of the sysadmin role:

- In SQL Server Management Studio, open a new query or change the connection of a query, providing the servername as usual, but preceded by ADMIN:; for example:

  ADMIN:servername

  Or, for a named instance (ensure that the SQL browser is running):

  ADMIN:servername\instancename

- From a command prompt, you can connect to the DAC via sqlcmd with the parameter –A; for example:

  C:\Users\Katie>sqlcmd -S servername –A

  Or, for a named instance (ensure that the SQL browser is running):

  C:\Users\Katie>sqlcmd -S servername\instancename -A

- In SQL Server Management Studio, change a query window to SQLCMD mode, and then use the following query:

  :CONNECT ADMIN:servername

  Or, for a named instance (ensure that the SQL browser is running):

  :CONNECT ADMIN:servername\instancename

- In Windows PowerShell, the DedicatedAdministratorConnection parameter of the Invoke-SQLCMD cmdlet provides a connection to the DAC. For example:

  Invoke-SQLCmd -ServerInstance servername -Database master -Query "Select @@Server-name" -DedicatedAdministratorConnection

  Or, for a named instance (ensure that the SQL browser is running):

  Invoke-SQLCmd -ServerInstance servername\instnacename -Database master -Query "Select @@Servername" -DedicatedAdministratorConnection

Allowing remote DACs

By default, DACs are allowed only locally. You also can use the Surface Area Configuration dialog box in the Facets section of SQL Server Management Studio to allow remote DAC connections via the `RemoteDacEnabled` setting. You also can use `sp_configure` to turn on the Remote Admin Connections option.

We recommend that you do because it could prove invaluable to gain access to a SQL Server when remote desktop protocol or similar technologies are unable to connect to the Windows host of the SQL Server instance. Turning on the Remote DAC does not require a service restart.

The endpoint port that SQL Server uses to listen to DACs is announced in the SQL Server error log upon startup; for example, you will see this shortly after the SQL Server service starts: "Dedicated admin connection support was established for listening locally on port 1434." This is the default port for default instances, whereas named instances will use a randomly-assigned port, changed each time the service is started.

Connecting to the DAC remotely with SQL Server Management Studio is also possible by addressing the port number of the DAC instead of the `ADMIN:` syntax. For example, providing a connection string in SQL Server Management Studio to *servername\instancename*,49902 would connect to the DAC endpoint.

Moving SQL Server logins and permissions

Moving SQL Server logins from one SQL Server instance to another instance is an eventuality for any SQL Server DBA. It comprises several steps.

Moving Windows-authenticated logins, SQL Server–authenticated logins, and all server-level permissions are three discrete steps that are accomplished via different methods. The end goal of your maturity as a DBA is to use SQL Server Management Studio's dialog boxes as little as possible, because GUI-driven solutions to this scenario are the most time consuming and could result in an unagreeable amount of button-clicking. T-SQL scripts are superior in terms of manageability, repeatability, and to deepen your understanding of the underlying security objects.

In a server migration, keep in mind that all database-level permissions, database roles, and users will be moved with the backup/restore of each database.

In this section, we discuss various methods of migrating security, some of which apply to either SQL Server instances or Azure SQL Database.

Moving logins by using SQL Server Integration Services (SQL Server only)

Since SQL Server 2008 R2, and updated for SQL 2017, SQL Server Integration Services has shipped with a Transfer Logins task that you can use to move logins from one server to another, including between different versions of SQL Server.

You use SQL Server Data Tools to create a new SQL Server Integration Services project. As Figure 6-5 shows, this provides an in-the-box, do-it-yourself alternative to the steps that follow, which involve custom scripts to migrate permissions from one server to another. The task is highly configurable, allowing for both Windows- and SQL Server–authenticated logins to be created on the far side, with their original SIDs if desired. A Fail/Replace/Skip option is provided for login names that already exist on the destination.

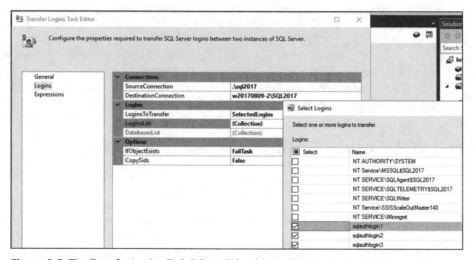

Figure 6-5 The Transfer Logins Task Editor dialog box in SQL Server Integration Services.

Logins created by the Transfer Logins task arrive at the destination server turned off; you must turn them on again before you can use them.

Unfortunately, until the SQL Server Integration Services SQL Management Object connection manager supports an Azure SQL Database connection, this solution does not work for Azure SQL Database.

Keep in mind that this SQL Server Integration Services task does not move any of the role memberships or server permissions that these logins might have been granted on the source instance.

➤ To read more, see the sections "Moving server roles by using T-SQL (SQL Server only)" and "Moving server permissions by using T-SQL (SQL Server only)" later in this chapter.

Moving Windows-authenticated logins by using T-SQL (SQL Server only)

This is the easiest of the steps, assuming that the source and target SQL Server instance are in the same domain. Moving Windows-authenticated logins is as easy as scripting out the CREATE LOGIN statements for each login.

You do not necessarily need to use Object Explorer in SQL Server Management Studio for this operation. The system catalog view sys.server_principals contains the list of Windows-authenticated logins (types 'U' for Windows user, and 'G' for Windows group). The default_database_name and default_language_name also are provided and you can script them with the login.

Here's a sample script:

```
--Create windows logins
SELECT
CreateTSQL_Source = 'CREATE LOGIN ['+ name +']

FROM WINDOWS WITH

DEFAULT_DATABASE=['+default_database_name+'],

DEFAULT_LANGUAGE=['+default_language_name+']'
FROM sys.server_principals
WHERE type in ('U','G')
AND name NOT LIKE 'NT %'
AND is_disabled = 0
ORDER BY name, type_desc;
```

Keep in mind that this script does not generate T-SQL for any of the role memberships or server permissions that these logins might have been granted on the source instance.

> ➤ To read more, see the sections "Moving server roles by using T-SQL (SQL Server only)" and "Moving server permissions by using T-SQL (SQL Server only)" later in this chapter.

Moving SQL Server–authenticated logins by using T-SQL (SQL Server only)

A time-honored reference for this task has been made available by Microsoft for years yet was never implemented with the SQL Server product itself. Since roughly 2000, many DBAs have referenced Microsoft support article 918992, "How to transfer logins and passwords between instances of SQL Server" (*https://support.microsoft.com/help/918992/*), which provides scripts to create a pair of stored procedures, sp_hexadecimal and sp_help_revlogin.

With the aid of these stored procedures, it is possible to generate a hash of a SQL Server–authenticated password with its login and then re-create the SQL Server–authenticated login on another server with the same password. It is not possible to reverse-engineer the SQL Server–authenticated login password, but you can re-create it without the need to change dependent application connection strings.

But don't stop there! Note that these provided stored procedures only re-create the SQL Server–authenticated logins; they do not re-create any of the role memberships or server permissions that those logins might have been granted on the source instance. In the next two sections, we discuss moving server roles and server permissions.

Moving server roles by using T-SQL (SQL Server only)

Instead of clicking through the dialog boxes for each role, you can script the transfer of server role membership via SQL Server internal catalog views. Here's a sample script, note that it includes options to add logins to server roles, using syntax for both before and after SQL Server 2012:

```
--SERVER LEVEL ROLES
SELECT DISTINCT
    SERVER_ROLE_NAME  =  QUOTENAME(R.NAME)
,   ROLE_TYPE  =  R.TYPE_DESC
,   PRINCIPAL_NAME  =  QUOTENAME(M.NAME)
,   PRINCIPAL_TYPE  =  M.TYPE_DESC
,   SQL2008R2_BELOW_CREATETSQL      = 'SP_ADDSRVROLEMEMBER  @LOGINAME=  '''+M.NAME+''',
                                         @ROLENAME = '''+R.NAME+''''
,   SQL2012_ABOVE_CREATETSQL      = 'ALTER SERVER ROLE [' + R.NAME + '] ADD MEMBER
                                         [' + M.NAME + ']'
FROM      SYS.SERVER_ROLE_MEMBERS AS RM
INNER JOIN SYS.SERVER_PRINCIPALS R ON RM.ROLE_PRINCIPAL_ID = R.PRINCIPAL_ID
INNER JOIN SYS.SERVER_PRINCIPALS M ON RM.MEMBER_PRINCIPAL_ID = M.PRINCIPAL_ID
WHERE R.IS_DISABLED = 0 AND M.IS_DISABLED = 0 -- IGNORE DISABLED ACCOUNTS
AND M.NAME NOT IN ('DBO', 'SA') -- IGNORE BUILT-IN ACCOUNTS
ORDER BY QUOTENAME(R.NAME);
```

Moving server permissions by using T-SQL (SQL Server only)

Moving server permissions can be extremely time consuming if you choose to do so by identifying them on the Securables page of each SQL Server Login Properties dialog box.

Instead, we advise that you script the permissions to re-create on the destination server by using internal catalog views. Following is a sample script:

```
--SERVER LEVEL SECURITY
    PERMISSION_STATE  =  RM.STATE_DESC
,   PERMISSION  =  RM.PERMISSION_NAME
,   PRINCIPAL_NAME  =  QUOTENAME(U.NAME)
,   PRINCIPAL_TYPE  =  U.TYPE_DESC
```

```
,   CREATETSQL_SOURCE = RM.STATE_DESC + N' ' + RM.PERMISSION_NAME +
    CASE WHEN E.NAME IS NOT NULL THEN 'ON ENDPOINT::[' + E.NAME + '] ' ELSE '' END +
    N' TO ' + CAST(QUOTENAME(U.NAME COLLATE DATABASE_DEFAULT) AS NVARCHAR(256)) + ';'
FROM SYS.SERVER_PERMISSIONS RM
INNER JOIN SYS.SERVER_PRINCIPALS U
ON RM.GRANTEE_PRINCIPAL_ID = U.PRINCIPAL_ID
LEFT OUTER JOIN SYS.ENDPOINTS E
ON E.ENDPOINT_ID = MAJOR_ID AND CLASS_DESC = 'ENDPOINT'
WHERE U.NAME NOT LIKE '##%' - IGNORE SYSTEM ACCOUNTS
AND U.NAME NOT IN ('DBO', 'SA'- IGNORE BUILT-IN ACCOUNTS
ORDER BY RM.PERMISSION_NAME, U.NAME;
```

Moving Azure SQL Database logins

It is not possible to use sp_hexadecimal and sp_help_revlogin against a Azure SQL Database server for SQL Server–authenticated logins. Scripting an Azure SQL Database login from SQL Server Management Studio obfuscates any password information, just as it does on a SQL Server instance.

And because you do not have access to sys.server_principals, sys.server_role_members, or sys.server_permissions, scripting these server-level permissions in Azure SQL Database isn't possible. (The system catalog view sys.server_principals is a dependent of sp_help_revlogin.)

Further, creating a login with a password HASH is not supported in Azure SQL Database (as of v12).

As of this writing, the solution for migrating Azure SQL Database logins from one server to another is to have the original script or to re-create the logins on the destination server with a new password.

The three types of Azure-authenticated principals are actually stored in the Azure SQL database, not at the Azure SQL server level, and are administered via the Azure portal. Like other database users and permissions, you can move those principals to a destination server along with the database itself.

Other security objects to move

Do not forget to move other server-level objects to the destination server, as appropriate.

Other security objects include Linked Server connections and SQL Server Audits, for which you can generate scripts, albeit without passwords in the case of Linked Servers. Given this hindsight, it is definitely advantageous to securely store your linked server creation scripts with their passwords.

CHAPTER 6

You also should re-create SQL Server Credentials (and any corresponding proxies in use by SQL Server Agent) on the destination server, although you cannot script credentials (you must re-create them manually). You can script proxies in SQL Server Agent by using SQL Server Management Studio, and you should re-create them, including their assigned subsystems.

Alternative migration approaches

Strangely, there is no easy way to accomplish this goal graphically within the SQL Server Management Studio dialog boxes or to "generate scripts" of all SQL Server server-level security.

There are some third-party products available to accomplish the task. There is also a free package of Windows PowerShell cmdlets available, including some designed to assist with security migrations. You can find these in the dbatools free open-source GPL-licensed Windows PowerShell project, which is available at *http://www.dbatools.io*.

If your SQL Server resides on a VM, performing a clone of the instance at the VM level might provide some transportability for the VM from one environment to another, to bypass the process of rebuilding a SQL Server instance altogether. For version upgrades, hardware changes, or partial migrations, a VM-level clone is obviously not a solution.

Moving the master database

There is also one more potential SQL Server–based method of server login information migration that is no less complex or troublesome. If you are moving from the exact same version of SQL Server to another, a backup and restore of the master database from one SQL Server instance to another is a potential, albeit not recommended, solution. (This obviously does not apply to Azure SQL Database.)

However, restoring a master database from one server to another involves myriad potential changes to server-specific encryption keys, service account, user permissions, and server identification information. These changes might or might not be supported configuration changes. The process is not outlined in any support documentation, and we do not recommend it.

Keep in mind that a migration of the master database is advisable only when the destination server of the restored database has the identical volume letters and NTFS permissions, access to the same service accounts, in addition to the same SQL Server version and edition.

### CHAPTER 7

Securing the server and its data

In recent years, security has become incredibly important to organizations of all sorts, in all industries and government entities, as well. All you need to do is to pay attention to the news to see that the number of leaks and hacks of sensitive information is increasing almost daily.

IT organizations around the world—not just in Europe—should consider the implementation of a European privacy law known as the *General Data Protection Regulation* (GDPR; effective May 25, 2018) as a wake-up call to review how they handle and manage customer information.

Continuing on from Chapter 6, which focused on authorization, this chapter covers features in SQL Server and the underlying operating system (OS) that help you to secure your server and the databases that reside on it.

We begin with what it means to encrypt data. We then move on to understanding how networks transmit and secure data. We conclude with the different features in SQL Server and Microsoft Azure SQL Database that can help you to achieve a secure environment.

Defense in depth means combining different features and strategies to protect your data as much as possible. We show how this strategy can protect your data during regular operations as well as minimize the fallout should your data be stolen.

At the OS level, the defensive strategies for Windows and Linux are similar. But because entire books already have been written on securing these platforms, this chapter will look at OS security only from a high level and focus mainly on securing your data with SQL Server 2017 and Azure SQL Database.

Introducing security principles and protocols

Security is about finding a balance between the value of your data and the cost of protecting it. Ultimately, the organization makes this call, but at least you have the technical tools available to undertake these measures to protect your data.

SQL Server implements a number of security principles through cryptography and other means, which you can use to build up layers of security to protect your environment.

Computer cryptography is implemented through some intense mathematics that use very large prime numbers. However, even if you're wary of math, you need not be afraid in this chapter: we don't delve that deeply into it, although we do cover some terminology that might sound scary.

This section explains various security principles and goes into some detail about encryption. It also covers network protocols and how cryptography works. This will aid your understanding of how SQL Server and network security protects your data.

Securing your environment with defense in depth

Securing a SQL Server environment (or for that matter, a cloud infrastructure, including Azure SQL Database) requires a number of protections that work together to make it difficult for an attacker to get in, snoop around, steal or modify data, and then get out.

Defense in depth is about building layers of protection around your data and environment.

Perimeter security should include logical and physical segmentation; for example, keeping sensitive servers and applications on a separate part of the network, perhaps off-premises in a separate datacenter or in the Azure cloud. You would then want to protect these connections; for example, by using a Virtual Private Network (VPN).

You should have a firewall and other network defenses to protect against *external network attacks*. From a physical aspect, don't let just anyone plug a laptop into an unattended network point, or allow them to connect to your corporate wireless network and have access to the production environment.

From within the network, you need to implement *authentication* (who you are) and *authorization* (what you can do), preferably through Active Directory.

> NOTE
> **Integrated authentication with Active Directory is supported on Linux.**

On the *servers* themselves, you should ensure that the file system is locked down, that SQL Server permissions are set correctly, and that file shares (if any) are secured, and using the latest sharing protocols.

On the *application* side, you can implement coding practices that protect against things like SQL injection attacks, and you can implement encryption in your database (and backup files).

Inside OUT

What is SQL injection?

One of the most prevalent attack vectors for a database is to manipulate the software application or website to attack the underlying database.

SQL injection is a technique that exploits applications that do not sanitize input data. A carefully crafted Uniform Resource Identifier (URI) in a web application, for example, can manipulate the database in ways that a naïve application developer is not expecting.

If a web application exposes database keys in the Uniform Resource Locator (URL), for example, an industrious person could carefully craft a URL to read protected information from a table by changing the key value. An attacker might be able to access sensitive data or modify the database itself by appending Transact-SQL (T-SQL) commands to the end of a string to perform malicious actions on a table or database.

In a worst-case scenario, a SQL injection attack would take a few seconds, the entire database could be exfiltrated (data removed without your knowledge), and you might hear about it only when your organization is blackmailed or sensitive data is leaked.

You can avoid SQL injection easily by ensuring that all data input is escaped, sanitized, and validated. To be very safe, all SQL Server queries should use parameterization.

You can read more about defending against SQL injection attacks on Microsoft Docs at *https://docs.microsoft.com/sql/relational-databases/security/sql-injection*.

The Open Web Application Security Project (OWASP) is also an excellent resource to identify and defend against potential vulnerabilities, including SQL injection. You can visit the OWASP website at *https://www.owasp.org*.

CHAPTER 7

The difference between hashing and encryption

In a security context, data that is converted in a repeatable manner to an unreadable, fixed-length format using a cryptographic algorithm and that *cannot* be converted back to its original form is said to be *hashed*.

Data that is converted to an unreadable form that *can* be converted back to its original form using a *cryptographic key* is said to be *encrypted*.

Cryptographic algorithms can be defeated in certain ways, the most common being *brute-force* and *dictionary* attacks. Let's take a quick look at each one:

- **Brute-force attack.**   In a brute-force attack, the attacking code checks every possible combination of a password, passphrase, or encryption key against the hashing or encryption service, until it finally arrives at the correct value. Depending on the type of algorithm and the length of the password, passphrase, or key, this can take a few milliseconds, to as long as millions of years (yes, you read that correctly).

- **Dictionary attack.**   A dictionary attack is a lot faster to perform, so a malicious actor would attempt this first. Dictionary attacks take a list of words from a dictionary (which can include common words, passwords, and phrases) and use these against the hashing or encryption service. Dictionary attacks take advantage of the fact that human beings are bad at remembering passwords and tend to use common words.

As computers become more powerful and parallelized, the length of time to run a brute-force attack continues to decrease. Countermeasures do exist to protect against some of these attacks, and some encryption systems cannot be defeated by a brute-force attack. These countermeasures are beyond the scope of this book, but it is safe to say that sufficiently complex algorithms and long encryption keys will take several years to compromise.

Hashing

A *cryptographic hash function* (an algorithm) takes *variable-length data* (usually a password) and applies a mathematical formula to convert it to a fixed size, or *hash value*.

This is the recommended method of securing passwords. When a password has been hashed correctly, it cannot be decrypted into its original form. Used with a random *salt* (a random string applied along with the hash function), this results in passwords that are impossible to reconstruct, even if the same password is used by different people.

To validate a password, it must be hashed using the same hash function again, with the same salt, and compared against the stored hash value.

Because hash values have a fixed size (the length depends on the algorithm used), there is a possibility that two sets of data (two different passwords) can result in the same hash value. This is called a *hash collision*, and it is more likely to occur with shorter hash value lengths. This is why longer hashes are better.

NOTE

Make sure that you use passwords that are at least 15 characters in length and, preferably, more than 20 characters. If you use a password manager, you don't need to memorize passwords, and brute-force attacks take exponentially longer for each additional character you choose. Don't be shy about using phrases or sentences either. The password length matters more than its complexity.

Inside OUT

Why should I use a salt, and what is a rainbow table?

If you don't use a random salt, the same hash value will be created each time the hash function is applied against a particular password. Additionally, if more than one person uses the same password, the same hash value will be repeated.

Imagine that a malicious actor has a list of the most commonly used passwords and knows which hash function you used to hash the passwords in your database. This person could build a catalog of possible hash values for each password in that list. This catalog is called a *rainbow table*.

It becomes very simple to just look up the hash values in your database against the rainbow table and deduce which password was used. Thus, you should always use a random salt when hashing passwords in your database. Rainbow tables become all but useless in this case.

Encryption

Data encryption is the process of converting human-readable data, or *plain text*, into an encrypted form by applying a cryptographic algorithm called a key (the *cipher*) to the data. This process makes the encrypted data (the *ciphertext*) unreadable without the appropriate key to unlock it. Encryption facilitates both the secure transmission and storage of data.

Over the years, many ciphers have been created and subsequently defeated (*cracked*) because those algorithms were considered weak. In many cases, this is because both CPUs and Graphics Processor Units (GPUs) have become faster and more powerful, reducing the length of time it takes to perform brute-force and other attacks. In other cases, the implementation of the cryptographic function was flawed, and attacks on the implementation itself have been successful.

Inside OUT

Why are GPUs used for cracking passwords?

A GPU is designed to process identical instructions (but not necessarily the same data) in parallel across hundreds or thousands of cores, ostensibly for rendering images on a display many times per second.

This coincides with the type of work required to crack passwords through brute force, because those thousands of cores can each perform a single arithmetic operation per clock cycle through a method called *pipelining*.

Because GPUs can operate at billions of cycles per second (GHz), this results in hundreds of millions of hashes per second. Without a salt, many password hashes can be cracked in a few milliseconds, regardless of the algorithm used.

A primer on protocols and transmitting data

Accessing data from an Azure SQL database or SQL Server database involves the transmission of data over a network interface, which you need to do in a secure manner. A *protocol* is a set of instructions for transmitting that information over a specific network port.

A *Transmission Control Protocol* (TCP) *port* is one of 65,535 possible connections to a networked device; in this case, the device is a server running Windows or Linux. It is always associated with an IP address and a protocol.

Official and unofficial standards over the years have resulted in a set of commonly used ports. For instance, TCP ports 1433 and 1434 are reserved for SQL Server, whereas TCP ports 80 and 443 are reserved for HTTP and HTTPS, respectively. TCP port 22 is reserved for Secure Shell (SSH), User Datagram Protocol (UDP) port 53 is used for Domain Name Services (DNS), and so on.

The internet protocol suite

To discuss security on a network, you need to understand cryptographic protocols. To discuss the network itself, you need to discuss the biggest network of them all: the internet.

The internet is a network of networks (it literally means "between networks") which transmits data using a suite of protocols, including TCP, which sits on top of *Internet Protocol* (IP). TCP/IP is the most common network protocol stack in use today. Most of the services on the internet, as well as local networks, rely on TCP/IP.

NOTE

The full internet protocol suite comprises TCP, IP, Address Resolution Protocol (ARP), Internet Control Message Protocol (ICMP), UDP, and Internet Group Management Protocol (IGMP). All of these are required to implement the full TCP/IP stack.

IP is a connectionless protocol, meaning that each individual unit of transfer, also known as a *network packet* or *datagram*, contains the data itself—the *payload*—and a *header* that indicates where it came from and where it needs to go (the routing information).

IP network packets are delivered using a "best effort" model, meaning that they might be delivered out of order, with no delivery guarantee at all. This low overhead makes the protocol fast and allows packets to be sent to several recipients at once (*multicast* or *broadcast*).

TCP provides the necessary instructions for reliability, sequencing (the order of packets), and data integrity. If a packet is not received by the recipient, or a packet is received out of order, TCP can resubmit the data again, using IP as its delivery mechanism.

Versions of IP in use today   Version 4 of the Internet Protocol (IPv4) has a 32-bit address space, which provides nearly 4.3 billion addresses (2^{32}, or approximately 4.3×10^9). Unfortunately, when this version was first proposed in September 1981, very few people predicted that the internet would be as large and important as it is today. With billions of humans online, and billions of devices connected, the available IPv4 address space is all but depleted.

> ➤ You can read the Internet Protocol, Version 4 Specification, known as Internet Engineering Task Force Request For Comments #791, at *https://tools.ietf.org/html/rfc791*.

Tricks like Network Address Translation (NAT), which uses private IP addresses behind a router with a single valid public IP address representing that entire network, have held off the depletion over the years, but time and address space has run out.

Version 6 of the Internet Protocol (IPv6), has an address space of 128 bits which provides more than 340 undecillion addresses (2^{128}, or approximately 3.4×10^{38}). This number is so staggeringly huge that, even with networks and devices being added every minute, including the upward trend of the Internet of Things, each of these devices can have its own unique address on the internet, without ever running out of addresses.

> ➤ You can read the Internet Protocol, Version 6 Specification, known as Internet Engineering Task Force Request For Comments #8200, at *https://tools.ietf.org/html/rfc8200*.

CHAPTER 7

Inside OUT

What is the Internet of Things?

Until recently, computing devices such as servers, desktop computers, laptops, and mobile devices have been the only devices connected to the internet.

Today, a huge variety of objects embedded with electronics are finding their way online, including coffee machines, security cameras, home automation systems, vehicle trackers, heart monitors, industrial measurement devices, and many, many more.

Ignoring the fact that many of these devices should not have publicly accessible internet addresses in the first place, the growth trend is exponential, and IPv6 is making this massive growth possible.

Cloud platforms such as Azure have services dedicated to managing the communication and data requirements of these devices, including an Azure SQL database.

Making sense of an IP address   An IP address is displayed in a human-readable notation but is binary under the hood:

- **IPv4.**   The address is broken up into four subclasses of decimal numbers, each subclass ranging from 0 to 255, and separated by a decimal point. For example, 52.178.167.109 is a valid IPv4 address.

- **IPv6.**   The address is broken up into eight subclasses of hexadecimal numerals, each subclass being four digits wide, and separated by a colon. If a subclass contains all zeroes, it can be omitted. For example, 2001:d74f:e211:9840:0000:0000:0000:0000 is a valid IPv6 address that can be simplified to 2001:d74f:e211:9840:: with the zeroes omitted (note the double-colon at the end to indicate the omission).

Adoption of IPv6 across the internet is taking decades, so a hybrid solution is currently in place by which IPv4 and IPv6 traffic is shared across IPv6 and IPv4 devices, respectively. If that doesn't sound like enough of a headache, let's add routing into the mix.

Finding your way around the internet

Routing between networks on the internet is performed by the Border Gateway Protocol (BGP), which sits on top of TCP/IP.

BGP is necessary because there is no map of the internet. Devices and entire networks appear and disappear all the time. BGP routes billions of network packets through millions of routers based on a best guess scenario. Packets are routed based on trust: routers provide information to one another about the networks they control, and BGP implicitly trusts that information.

BGP is thus not secure, because it was designed solely to fix the scalability of the internet, which was (and still is) growing exponentially. It was a "quick fix" that became part of the fabric of the infrastructure long before security was a concern.

Efforts to secure BGP have been slow. It is therefore critical to assume that your own internet traffic will be hijacked at some point. If this happens, proper cryptography can prevent third parties from reading your data.

A brief overview of the World Wide Web

A lot of people conflate the World Wide Web (the web) with the internet, but the web is a single component of the greater internet, along with email (and other services that have seemingly faded into obscurity but are still in use today, such as File Transfer Protocol and Voice over IP).

> ### NOTE
> Based on publicly available information, Microsoft processes around 500 billion emails per month through its various services, including Microsoft Office 365 and Outlook Mail (the web version).

The web uses the Hypertext Transport Protocol (HTTP), which sits on top of TCP/IP. A web server provides mixed media content (text, graphics, video, and other media) in Hypertext Markup Language (HTML) format, which is transmitted using HTTP and then interpreted and rendered by a web browser.

The web grew quickly for two reasons. First, the internet became commercialized after originally being an academic and military project for several decades. The web itself then became wildly popular because of the introduction of the first graphical web browser, NCSA Mosaic, in the 1990s. The spiritual successors to Mosaic were Netscape Navigator and Microsoft Internet Explorer, during a period of internet history known as the "browser wars."

> ➤ You can learn more about the commercial beginnings of the web and the so-called "Internet Era," by listening to the Internet History Podcast, available at *http://www.internethistorypodcast.com*.

Modern web browsers include Microsoft Edge, Google Chrome, Mozilla Firefox, and Apple Safari.

> ### NOTE
> The modern web browser is hugely complex, doing a lot more than rendering HTML, but for the purposes of this discussion and in the interest of brevity, we gloss over those extras.

CHAPTER 7

How does protocol encryption fit into this?

The explosive adoption of the web in the 1990s created the need for secure transactions as public-facing organizations began to transition their sales online into electronic commerce, or *e-commerce*, ventures. Consumers wanted to use their credit cards safely and securely so that they could shop and purchase goods without leaving the comfort of their homes.

Remember that the internet is built on the Internet Protocol, which is stateless and has routing information in the header of every single packet. This means that anyone can place a hardware device (or software) in the packet stream, do something with the packet, and then pass it on (modified or not) to the destination, without the sender or recipient having any knowledge of this interaction. Because this is a fundamental building block of a packet-switching network, it's very difficult to secure properly.

As we discussed earlier, encryption transforms data into an unreadable format. Now, if someone connected to the same network were to intercept encrypted packets, that person couldn't see what you're doing. The payload of each packet would appear garbled and unreadable, unless this person has the key to decrypt it.

A secure version of HTTP was created by Netscape Communications in 1994, which was dubbed HTTPS (HTTP Secure, or HTTP over Secure Sockets Layer [SSL]). Over the years, the moniker of HTTPS has remained, but it has come to be known as HTTP over Transport Layer Security (TLS) as standards improved.

When we talk about data moving over the network, that usually means TCP/IP is involved, and we need to transmit that data securely.

Symmetric and asymmetric encryption

You can encrypt data in two ways: symmetric and asymmetric. Each has its advantages and disadvantages.

Symmetric encryption (shared secret)

A secret key, which is usually a password, passphrase, or random string of characters, is used to encrypt data with a particular cryptographic algorithm. This secret key is shared between the sender and the recipient, and both parties can encrypt and decrypt all content by using this secret key.

If the key is accidentally leaked to a third party, the encrypted data could be intercepted, decrypted, modified, and reencrypted again, without either the sender or recipient being aware of this. This type of attack is known as a *man-in-the-middle* attack.

Asymmetric encryption (public key)

Also known as public key encryption (PKE). A key–pair is generated, comprising a private key and a public key, and the public key can be widely distributed. The *public key* is used to encrypt data, and the *private key* is used to decrypt that data.

The advantage is that the private key never needs to be shared, which makes this method far more secure because only you can use your private key to decrypt the data. Unfortunately, asymmetric encryption does require a lot more processing power, plus both parties need their own key–pairs.

> ## Inside OUT
>
> *What encryption method should I use for SQL Server?*
>
> For practical purposes, SQL Server manages the keys internally for both symmetric and asymmetric encryption.
>
> Owing to the much larger overhead of asymmetric encryption, however, you should encrypt any data in SQL Server that you want you protect by using symmetric key encryption.
>
> Using the encryption hierarchy, layers above the data can be protected using passwords or asymmetric keys (we discuss this in the next section).

Digital certificates

Public keys require discoverability, which means that they need to be made publicly available. If a sending party wants to sign a message for the receiving party, the burden is on the sender to locate the recipient's public key in order to sign a message.

For small-scale communications between two private entities, this might be done by sharing their public keys between each other.

For larger-scale communications with many senders and one recipient (such as a web or database server, for example), a certificate authority can provide the public key through a digital certificate, which the recipient (the website or database administrator) can install on the server directly.

This certificate serves as an electronic signature for the recipient, which includes its public key. The authority, known as a Certification Authority, is trusted by both the sender and the recipient, and the sender can verify that the recipient is indeed who it claims to be.

Digital certificates, also known as *Public Key Certificates*, are defined by the X.509 standard. Many protocols use this standard, including TLS and its predecessor, SSL.

> ➤ **You can read more about how digital certificates and TLS relate to SQL Server and Azure SQL Database later in this chapter.**

Certification Authority

A Certification Authority (CA) is an organization or entity that issues digital certificates, which include the name of the owner, the owner's public key, and start and expiration dates.

The certificate is automatically revoked after it expires, and the CA can revoke any certificate before then.

For the certificate to be trusted, the CA itself must be trustworthy. It is the responsibility of the CA to verify the owner's identity so that any certificates issued in that owner's name can be trusted.

In recent months, several CAs have lost their trustworthy status, either because their verification process was flawed or their signing algorithms were weak. Take care when choosing a CA for your digital certificates.

Encryption in SQL Server

Encryption is but one part of securing your environment. SQL Server provides a full encryption hierarchy, starting at the OS layer (including the network stack and file system), working all the way down the levels of the database, through to individual cells in a table.

Figure 7-1 shows this hierarchy.

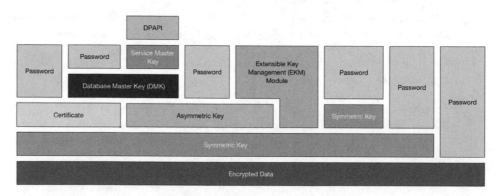

Figure 7-1 The SQL Server encryption hierarchy.

Data protection from the OS

At the top of the hierarchy, protecting everything below it, is the OS. Windows Server provides an Application Programming Interface (API) for system- and user-level processes to take advantage of data protection (encryption) on the file system.

In other words, SQL Server and other applications can make use of this data protection API to have Windows automatically encrypt data on the drive without having to encrypt data through other means.

SQL Server Enterprise edition uses the Data Protection API (DPAPI) for Transparent Data Encryption (TDE).

Inside OUT

How does data protection work for SQL Server on Linux?

The mechanism that Microsoft created for getting SQL Server to run on Linux and Docker containers, is called the Platform Abstraction Layer (PAL). It aligns all code specific to the OS in one place, forming a bridge with the underlying platform.

All APIs, including file system and DPAPIs, are included in the PAL. This makes SQL Server 2017 entirely platform agnostic.

To read more about the PAL, visit the official SQL Server Blog at *https://blogs.technet. microsoft.com/dataplatforminsider/2016/12/16/sql-server-on-linux-how-introduction/*.

The encryption hierarchy in detail

Each layer of the hierarchy protects the layer below it by using a combination of keys (asymmetric and symmetric) and certificates (refer to Figure 7-1).

Each layer in the hierarchy can be accessed by a password at the very least, unless an Extensible Key Management (EKM) module is being used. The EKM module is a standalone device that holds symmetric and asymmetric keys outside of SQL Server.

The Database Master Key (DMK) is protected by the Service Master Key (SMK), and both of these are symmetric keys. The SMK is created when you install SQL Server and is protected by the DPAPI.

If you want to use TDE on your database (see the section "Configuring TDE on a user database" later in this chapter), it requires a symmetric key called the Database Encryption Key (DEK), which is protected by an asymmetric key in the EKM module or by a certificate through the DMK.

This layered approach helps to protect the data from falling into the wrong hands.

There are two considerations when deciding how to secure a SQL Server environment, which you can implement independently.

- **Data at rest.**   In the case of TDE, this is decrypting the data on a drive as it is read into the buffer pool, and encrypting the data as it is flushed to a drive from the buffer pool. (You could also encrypt your storage layer independently from SQL Server, but this does not form part of the encryption hierarchy.)

- **Data in motion.**   Protecting the data during transmission over a network connection. Any network protocols and APIs involved must support encrypting and decrypting the data as it moves in and out of the buffer pool.

Data is in motion from the moment it is read from or written to the buffer pool in SQL Server or Azure SQL Database. Between the buffer pool and the underlying storage, data is considered to be at rest.

NOTE

TDE encrypts database backup files along with the data and transaction log files. However, the TDE feature is available only with the SQL Server Enterprise edition and Azure SQL Database.

Using EKM modules with SQL Server

Organizations might choose to take advantage of a separate security appliance called a Hardware Security Module (HSM) or EKM device to generate, manage, and store encryption keys for the network infrastructure outside of a SQL Server environment.

SQL Server can make use of these keys for internal use. The HSM/EKM device can be a hardware appliance, a USB device, a smart card, or even software, as long as it implements the Microsoft Cryptographic Application Programming Interface (MCAPI) provider.

EKM is an advanced SQL Server setting and is turned off by default. To use the key or keys from an HSM/EKM device, you need to turn on EKM by using the `sp_execute 'EKM provider enabled'` command with the appropriate parameter. Then, the device must be registered as an EKM module for use by SQL Server.

After the HSM/EKM device creates a key for use by SQL Server (for TDE, for instance), the device exports it securely into SQL Server via the MCAPI provider.

The module might support different types of authentication (Basic or Other), but only one of these types can be registered with SQL Server for that provider.

If the module supports Basic authentication (a user name and password combination), SQL Server uses a credential to provide transparent authentication to the module.

Inside OUT

What is a credential?

In SQL Server, a credential is a record of authentication information that the Database Engine uses to connect to external resources.

These credentials provide security details for processes to impersonate Windows users on a network, though they can also be used to connect to other services like Azure Blob Storage and, of course, an HSM/EKM device.

Credentials that will be used by all databases can be created in the master database by using the CREATE CREDENTIAL command, or per individual database using the CREATE DATABASE SCOPED CREDENTIAL command.

Chapter 6 contains more information on logins, and Chapter 13 goes into more detail about credentials.

➤ To read more about EKM in SQL Server, go to *https://docs.microsoft.com/sql/relational-databases/security/encryption/extensible-key-management-ekm*.

Cloud security with Azure Key Vault

You can use Azure Key Vault in addition to, or as a drop-in replacement of, a traditional HSM/EKM device. SQL Server can use Key Vault on-premises or running in a VM in the cloud.

Key Vault is implemented as an EKM provider inside SQL Server, using the SQL Server Connector (a standalone Windows application) as a bridge between Key Vault and the SQL Server instance.

To make use of Key Vault, you must create the vault, along with a valid Azure Active Directory (Azure AD) first.

Begin by registering the SQL Server service principal name in Azure AD. After the service principal name is registered, you can install the SQL Server Connector and turn on EKM in SQL Server.

➤ You can read more about service principal names and Kerberos in Chapter 2.

You must then create a login that SQL Server will use for accessing Key Vault, and then map that login to a new credential that contains the Key Vault authentication information.

➤ A step-by-step guide for this process is available on Microsoft Docs at *https://docs.microsoft.com/sql/relational-databases/security/encryption/setup-steps-for-extensible-key-management-using-the-azure-key-vault.*

Master keys in the encryption hierarchy

Since SQL Server 2012, both the SMK and DMK are symmetric keys encrypted using the Advanced Encryption Standard (AES) cryptographic algorithm. AES is faster and more secure than Triple Data Encryption Standard (3DES), which was used in SQL Server prior to 2012.

Note, however, that when you upgrade from an older version of SQL Server—those that were encrypted using 3DES—you must regenerate both the SMK and DMK to upgrade them to AES.

The SMK

The SMK is at the top of the encryption hierarchy in SQL Server. It is automatically generated the first time the SQL Server instance starts, and it is encrypted by the DPAPI in combination with the local machine key (which itself is created when Windows Server is installed). The key is based on the Windows credentials of the SQL Server service account and the computer credentials. (On Linux, the local machine key is likely embedded in the PAL when SQL Server is installed.)

Inside OUT

What is the difference between DES, 3DES, and AES?

Data Encryption Standard (DES) was a symmetric key algorithm developed in the 1970s, with a key length of 56 bits (2^{56} possible combinations). It has been considered cryptographically broken since 1998. In 2012 it was possible to recover a DES key in less than 24 hours if both a plain-text and cipher-text pair were known.

Its successor, 3DES, applies the DES algorithm three times (each time with a different DES key) to each block of data being encrypted. However, with current consumer hardware, the entire 3DES keyspace can be searched, making it cryptographically weak.

AES (Advanced Encryption Standard) uses keys that are 128, 192, or 256 bits in length. Longer keys are much more difficult to crack using brute-force methods, so AES is considered safe for the foreseeable future. It also happens to be much faster than 3DES.

If you need to restore or regenerate an SMK, you first must decrypt the entire SQL Server encryption hierarchy, which is a resource-intensive operation. You should perform this activity only in a scheduled maintenance window. If the key has been compromised, however, you shouldn't wait for that maintenance window.

CAUTION

It is essential that you back up the SMK to a file and then copy it securely to an off-premises location. Losing this key will result in total data loss if you need to recover a database or environment.

To back up the SMK, you can use the T-SQL script shown that follows, but be sure to choose a randomly generated password. The password will be required for restoring or regenerating the key at a later stage. Keep the password separate from the SMK backup file so that they cannot be used together if your secure backup location is compromised. Ensure that the folder on the drive is adequately secured. After you back up the key, transfer and store it securely in an off-premises location.

```
BACKUP SERVICE MASTER KEY TO FILE = 'c:\SecureLocation\service_master_key'
    ENCRYPTION BY PASSWORD = '<UseAReallyStrongPassword>';
GO
```

The DMK

(Refer back to Figure 7-1 to see how the DMK is protected by the SMK.)

The DMK is used to protect asymmetric keys and private keys for digital certificates stored in the database. A copy of the DMK is stored in the database for which it is used as well as in the master database. The copy is automatically updated by default if the DMK changes. This allows SQL Server to automatically decrypt information as required. A DMK is required for each user database that will make use of TDE.

CAUTION

Don't forget to back up the DMK to a file, as well, and copy it securely to an off-premises location.

It is considered a security best practice to regenerate the DMK periodically to protect the server from brute-force attacks. The idea is that it will take longer for a brute-force attack to break the key than the length of time for which the key is in use.

For example, suppose that you encrypt your database with a DMK in January of this year. In July, you regenerate the DMK, which will cause all keys for digital certificates to be reencrypted with the new key. If anyone had begun a brute-force attack on data encrypted with the previous DMK, all results from that attack will be rendered useless by the new DMK.

You can back up the DMK by using the T-SQL script that follows. The same rules apply as with backing up the SMK (choose a random password, store the file off-premises, and keep the password and backup file separately). This script assumes that the master key exists.

```
USE WideWorldImporters;
GO
BACKUP MASTER KEY TO FILE = 'c:\SecureLocation\wwi_database_master_key'
    ENCRYPTION BY PASSWORD = '<UseAReallyStrongPassword>';
GO
```

➤ You can read more about the SMK and DMK on Microsoft Docs at *https://docs.microsoft.com/sql/relational-databases/security/encryption/sql-server-and-database-encryption-keys-database-engine*.

Encrypting data by using TDE

Continuing with our defense-in-depth discussion, an additional way to protect your environment is to encrypt data at rest, namely the database files (and when TDE is turned on, all backups of that database).

There are third-party providers, including storage vendors, that provide excellent on-disk encryption for your Direct-Attached Storage (DAS) or Storage-Area Network (SAN), as a file system solution or at the physical storage layer. Provided that your data and backups are localized to this particular solution, and no files are copied to machines that are not encrypted at the file-system level, this might be an acceptable solution for you.

However, if you have the Enterprise edition of SQL Server, you can use TDE, which encrypts the data, transaction log, and backup files at the file-system level by using a DEK.

If someone manages to acquire these files via a backup server, Azure Blob Storage archive, or by gaining access to your production environment, that person will not be able to simply attach the files or restore the database without the DEK.

The DEK is a symmetric key (shared secret) that is secured by a certificate stored in the master database. If using HSM/EKM or Key Vault, the DEK is protected by an asymmetric key in the EKM module, instead. The DEK is stored in the boot record of the protected database (page 0 of file 1) so that it is easily available during the recovery process.

NOTE
TDE is invisible to any applications that use it. No changes are required in those applications to take advantage of TDE for the database.

In the data file, TDE operates at the page level, because all data files are stored as 8-KB pages. Before being flushed from the buffer pool, the contents of the page are encrypted, the checksum is calculated, and then the page is written to the drive. When reading data, the 8-KB page is read from the drive, decrypted, and then the contents are placed into the buffer pool.

> **NOTE**
>
> Even though encryption might to some degree increase the physical size of the data it is protecting, the size and structure of data pages is not affected. Instead, the number of pages in the data file might increase.

For log files, the contents of the log cache are also encrypted before writing to and reading from the drive.

> ➤ To read more about checkpoint operations and active virtual log files (VLFs) in the transaction log, refer to Chapter 3.

Backup files are simply the contents of the data file, plus enough transaction log records to ensure that the database restore is consistent (redo and undo records of active transactions when the backup is taken). In other words, the contents of new backup files are encrypted by default after TDE is turned on.

Configuring TDE on a user database

To use TDE on SQL Server Enterprise edition, you need to create a DMK if you don't already have one.

Verify that it is safely backed up and securely stored off-premises. If you have never backed up the DMK, you will be warned by the Database Engine after using it that it has not yet been backed up. If you don't know where that backup is, back it up again. This is a crucial detail to using TDE (or any encryption technology).

Next, you will create a digital certificate or use one that you have acquired from a CA. In the next example, the certificate is created on the server directly.

Then, you create the DEK, which is signed by the certificate and encrypted using a cryptographic algorithm of your choice.

Although you do have a choice of algorithm, we recommend AES over 3DES for performance and security reasons, and you have a choice of three AES key sizes: 128, 192, or 256 bits. Remember that larger keys are more secure but will add additional overhead when encrypting data. If you plan to rotate your keys every few months, you can safely use 128-bit AES encryption because no brute-force attack (using current computing power) should be able to attack a 128-bit key in the months between key rotations.

After you create the DEK, you turn on encryption on the database. The command completes immediately, but the process will take place in the background because each page in the database will need to be read into the buffer pool, encrypted, and flushed to the drive.

CHAPTER 7

CAUTION

Turning on TDE on a user database will automatically turn on TDE for TempDB, as well, if it is not already on. This can add overhead that adversely affects performance for unencrypted databases that make use of TempDB. If you want to turn off TDE on TempDB, all user databases must have it turned off first.

The script that follows provides a summary of the steps to turn on TDE:

```
USE master;
GO
-- Remember to back up this Database Master Key once it is created
CREATE MASTER KEY ENCRYPTION BY PASSWORD = '<UseAReallyStrongPassword>';
GO
CREATE CERTIFICATE WideWorldServerCert WITH SUBJECT = 'WWI DEK Certificate';
GO
USE WideWorldImporters;
GO
CREATE DATABASE ENCRYPTION KEY
    WITH ALGORITHM = AES_128
    ENCRYPTION BY SERVER CERTIFICATE WideWorldServerCert;
GO
ALTER DATABASE WideWorldImporters SET ENCRYPTION ON;
GO
```

Verifying whether TDE is turned on for a database

To determine which databases are encrypted with TDE, you can issue the following command:

```
SELECT name, is_encrypted FROM sys.databases;
```

If a user database is encrypted, the `is_encrypted` column value for that database will be set to 1. TempDB will also show a value of 1 in this column.

Protecting sensitive columns with Always Encrypted

Although TDE is really useful for encrypting the entire database at the file-system level, it doesn't prevent database administrators and other users from having access to sensitive information within the database.

The first rule of storing sensitive data is that you should avoid storing it altogether when possible. Credit card information makes sense in a banking system, but not in a sales database, for instance.

NOTE

Many third-party systems can encrypt your data securely, as well, but are beyond the scope of this chapter. It is good to keep in mind that there is a small but inherent risk in storing encryption keys with data, as SQL Server does. Your organization must balance that risk against the ease of managing and maintaining those keys.

If you must store sensitive data, Always Encrypted protects how data is *viewed* at the column level. It works with applications that use particular connection types (*client drivers*; see the next section) to interact with SQL Server. These client drivers are protected by a digital certificate so that only specific applications can view the protected data.

Always Encrypted was introduced in SQL Server 2016 and has been available on all editions since SQL Server 2016 Service Pack 1. To use this feature, the database makes use of two types of keys: *column encryption keys* and *column master keys* (dicussed shortly).

The encryption used by Always Encrypted is one of two types:

- **Deterministic encryption.**   This is the same as generating a hash value without a salt. The same encrypted value will always be generated for a given plain-text value. This is useful for joins, indexes, searching, and grouping, but it makes it possible for people to guess what the hash values represent.

- **Randomized encryption.**   This is the same as generating a hash value with a salt. No two of the same plain-text values will generate the same encrypted value. Although this does improve security of the data, it does not permit joins, indexes, searching, and grouping for those encrypted columns.

For values that are not expected to participate in joins or searches, you can safely use randomized encryption. Choose deterministic encryption for values like social security numbers and other government-issued values because it helps for searching and grouping.

Because the whole intention of Always Encrypted is to prevent unauthorized persons from viewing data (including database administrators), you should generate the keys elsewhere and store them in a trusted key store (in the the operating system's key store for the database server and the application server, or an EKM module such as Key Vault), away from the database server. The person who generates the keys should not be the same person who is administering the database.

Client application providers that support Always Encrypted

The following providers currently support Always Encrypted:

- .NET Framework 4.6 or higher

CHAPTER 7

- Microsoft JDBC Driver 6.0 or higher

- ODBC Driver 13.1 for SQL Server or higher

It is anticipated that .NET Standard will be supported in the near future.

The connection between the Database Engine and application is made by using a client-side encrypted connection. Each provider has its own appropriate method to control this setting:

- **.NET Framework.**   Set the Column Encryption Setting in the connection string to `enabled`, or configure the `SqlConnectionStringBuilder.ColumnEncryption Setting` property to `SqlConnectionColumnEncryptionSetting.Enabled`.

- **JDBC.**   Set the `columnEncryptionSetting` to `Enabled` in the connection string, or configure the `SQLServerDataSource()` object with the `setColumnEncryption Setting("Enabled")` property.

- **ODBC.**   Set the `ColumnEncryption` connection string keyword to `Enabled`, use the `SQL_COPT_SS_COLUMN_ENCRYPTION` preconnection attribute, or through the Data Source Name (DSN) using the `SQL_COLUMN_ENCRYPTION_ENABLE` setting.

Additionally, the application must have the `VIEW ANY COLUMN MASTER KEY DEFINITION` and `VIEW ANY COLUMN ENCRYPTION KEY DEFINITION` database permissions in order to view the Column Master Key and Column Encryption Key.

The Column Master Key and Column Encryption Key

The Column Master Key (CMK) protects one or more Column Encryption Keys (CEK).

The CEK is encrypted using AES encryption and is used to encrypt the actual column data. You can use the same CEK to encrypt multiple columns, or you can create a CEK for each column that needs to be encrypted.

Metadata about the keys (but not the keys themselves) is stored in the database's system catalog views:

- sys.column_master_keys

- sys.column_encryption_keys

This metadata includes the *type* of encryption and *location* of the keys, plus their *encrypted values*. Even if a database is compromised, the data in the protected columns cannot be read without access to the secure key store.

➤ To read more about considerations for key management, go to *https://docs.microsoft.com/sql/relational-databases/security/encryption/overview-of-key-management-for-always-encrypted*.

Using the Always Encrypted Wizard

The easiest way to configure Always Encrypted is by using the Always Encrypted Wizard in SQL Server Management Studio. As noted previously, you need to have the following permissions before you begin:

- VIEW ANY COLUMN MASTER KEY DEFINITION

- VIEW ANY COLUMN ENCRYPTION KEY

If you plan on creating new keys, you also need the following permissions:

- ALTER ANY COLUMN MASTER KEY

- ALTER ANY COLUMN ENCRYPTION KEY

In SQL Server Management Studio, in Object Explorer, right-click the name of the database that you want to configure. In the Always Encrypted Wizard, in the pane on the left, click Tasks, and then, on the Tasks page, click Encrypt Columns.

On the Column Selection page, choose the a column in a table that you want to encrypt, and then select the encryption type (deterministic or randomized). If you want to decrypt a previously encrypted column, you can choose Plaintext here.

On the Master Key Configuration page, you can create a new key by using the local OS certificate store or by using a centralized store like Key Vault or an HSM/EKM device. If you already have a CMK in your database, you can use it, instead.

NOTE

Memory-optimized and temporal tables are not supported by this wizard, but you can still encrypt them by using Always Encrypted.

➤ You can read more about Always Encrypted on Microsoft Docs at *https://docs.microsoft.com/sql/relational-databases/security/encryption/always-encrypted-database-engine*.

CHAPTER 7

Securing data in motion

Data in motion is data that SQL Server provides over a network interface. Protecting data in motion requires a number of considerations, from the perimeter security, to cryptographic protocols for the communication itself, and the authorization of the application or process accessing the data.

This section first goes into more detail about network encryption with TLS, which operates on the network itself, and then dives into row-level security and data masking. The latter features do not make use of encryption, but form part of your defense-in-depth strategy to protect data in motion from prying eyes.

Unlike Always Encrypted, which encrypts data at rest and only decrypts it when being read, row-level security and data masking hide or show data depending on who's asking for it and how it is queried.

Securing network traffic with TLS

We touched briefly on TLS earlier in this chapter in the discussion about TCP/IP, but we did not go into much detail. Now, it's time we look at it more closely.

So, what is TLS, and how does it affect SQL Server and Azure SQL Database? The name is revealing. TLS is a security layer on top of a transport layer, or in technical terms, a *cryptographic protocol*. As we pointed out at the beginning of this chapter, most networks use the TCP/IP protocol stack. In other words, TLS is designed to secure the traffic on TCP/IP-based networks.

How does TLS work?

With TLS protection, before two parties can exchange information, they need to mutually agree on the encryption key and the cryptographic algorithm to use, which is called a *key exchange* or *handshake*. TLS works with both symmetric and asymmetric encryption, which means that the encryption key could be a shared secret or a public key (usually with a certificate).

After the key exchange is done, the handshake is complete, and a secured communication channel allows traffic between the two parties to flow. This is how data in motion is protected from external attacks.

> **NOTE**
> Remember that longer keys mean better security. Public keys of 1,024 bits (128 bytes) are considered short these days, so some organizations now prefer 2,048-bit, or even 4,096-bit public key certificates for TLS.

A brief history of TLS

Just as earlier cryptographic protocols have been defeated or considered weak enough that they will eventually be defeated, so too have SSL and its successor, TLS, had their challenges:

- The prohibition of SSL 2.0 is covered at *https://tools.ietf.org/html/rfc6176*.

- Known attacks on TLS are available at *https://tools.ietf.org/html/rfc7457*.

TLS 1.2 was defined in 2008, and is the latest public version. It is vulnerable to certain attacks, like its predecessors, but as long as older encryption algorithms are not used (for instance 3DES, RC4, and IDEA), it is good enough for the moment.

Where possible, you should be using TLS 1.2 everywhere. SQL Server ships with TLS 1.0, 1.1, and 1.2 support out of the box, so you will need to turn off 1.0 and 1.1 at the OS level to ensure that you use TLS 1.2.

> ➤ You can see how to turn off older versions of TLS in the Microsoft Knowledge Base article at *https://support.microsoft.com/help/3135244*.

As of this writing, TLS 1.3 is a draft specification.

NOTE

Although we do not recommend 3DES for TLS, you can still use 3DES lower in the SQL Server security hierarchy for securing DEKs because these are protected by the SMK, the DMK, and a Certificate, or entirely by an HSM/EKM module like Key Vault.

Row-level security

Protecting the network itself is good and proper, but this does not protect assets within the network from, for example, curious people snooping on salaries in the HR database. Or, suppose that your database contains information for many customers, and you want only customers to view their own data, without having knowledge of other data in the same tables.

Row-level security performs at the database level to restrict access through a security policy, based on group membership or execution context. It is functionally equivalent to a WHERE clause.

Access to the rows in a table is protected by an inline table-valued function, which is invoked and enforced by the security policy.

The function checks whether the user is allowed to access a particular row, while the security policy attaches this function to the table. So, when you run a query against a table, the security policy applies the predicate function.

There are two types of security policies supported by row-level security, both of which you can apply simultaneously:

- Filter predicates, which limit the data that can be seen
- Block predicates, which limits the actions a user can take on data

Hence, a user might be able to see rows, but cannot insert, update, or delete rows that look like rows they can see. This concept is covered in more detail in the next section.

CAUTION

There is a risk of information leakage if an attacker writes a query with a specially crafted WHERE clause and, for example, a divide-by-zero error, to force an exception if the WHERE condition is true. This is known as a *side-channel attack*. It might be wise to limit the ability of users to run ad hoc queries when using row-level security.

Filtering predicates for read operations

You can silently filter rows that are available through read operations. The application has no knowledge of the other data that is filtered out.

Filter predicates affect all read operations (this list is taken directly from the official documentation at *https://docs.microsoft.com/sql/relational-databases/security/row-level-security*):

- **SELECT.**   Cannot view rows that are filtered.
- **DELETE.**   Cannot delete rows that are filtered.
- **UPDATE.**   Cannot update rows that are filtered. It is possible to update rows that will be subsequently filtered. (The next section covers ways to prevent this.)
- **INSERT.**   No effect (inserting is not a read operation). Note, however, that a trigger could cause unexpected side effects in this case.

Blocking predicates for write operations

These predicates block access to write (or *modification*) operations that violate the predicate. Block predicates affect all write operations:

- **AFTER INSERT.**   Prevents inserting rows with values that violate the predicate. Also applies to bulk insert operations.
- **AFTER UPDATE.**   Prevents updating rows to values that violate the predicate. Does not run if no columns in the predicate were changed.
- **BEFORE UPDATE.**   Prevents updating rows that currently violate the predicate.
- **BEFORE DELETE.**   Blocks delete operations if the row violates the predicate.

Dynamic data masking

Data masking works on the premise of limiting exposure to data by obfuscation. Without requiring too many changes to the application or database, it is possible to mask *portions* of columns to prevent lower-privilege users from seeing, for example, full credit card numbers and other sensitive information.

The mask is defined in the column definition of the table, using MASKED WITH (FUNCTION = [type]) syntax (and you can add masking after table creation by using ALTER COLUMN syntax).

There are four types of masks that are available:

- **Default.** The column is masked according to the data type (not its default value). Strings will use "XXXX" (fewer if the length is less than four characters); numerics will use a zero value; dates will use midnight on January 1st, 1900; and binary will use a single byte binary equivalent of zero.

- **Email.** Only the first letter and the trailing domain suffix is not masked; for example, "aXXX@XXXXXXX.com".

- **Random.** This replaces a numeric data type with a random value between a range you specify.

- **Custom String.** Only the first and last letters are not masked. There is a custom padding string in the middle, which you specify.

> ➤ You can read more about dynamic data masking, including samples of how to set it up, at *https://docs.microsoft.com/sql/relational-databases/security/dynamic-data-masking*.

Limitations with masking data

Dynamic data masking has some significant limitations. It does not work on Always Encrypted columns, nor FILESTREAM or COLUMN_SET column types. Additionally, GROUP BY and WHERE clauses are excluded, as are INSERT and UPDATE statements. Computed columns are also excluded, but if the computed column depends on a masked column, the computed column inherits that mask and returns masked data. Finally, a masked column cannot be a used as a FULLTEXT index key.

CAUTION

It is possible to expose masked data with carefully crafted queries. This can be performed by using a brute-force attack or using inference based on the results. If you are using data masking, you should also limit the ability of the user to run ad hoc queries and ensure that their permissions are sound.

Azure SQL Database

All of the security features discussed thus far work equally on SQL Server and Azure SQL Database, namely TDE, Always Encrypted, row-level security and dynamic data masking.

That's great if you're just comparing SQL Server to Azure SQL Database, but there are some features unique to Azure SQL Database that are worth looking at, which we'll do in the next section. But keep in mind that because Azure features and products are always changing, this is only a brief overview.

Azure SQL Database Threat Detection

The risks of having a publicly accessible database in the cloud are numerous. To help protect against attacks, you can activate Threat Detection, which runs 24 hours per day on each of your Azure SQL Database servers (called nodes) for a monthly fee. This service notifies you by email whenever atypical behavior is detected.

Some of the interesting threats include SQL injection attacks and potential vulnerabilities as well as unfamiliar database access patterns, including unfamiliar logins or access from unusual locations. Each notification includes possible causes and recommendations to deal with the event.

Threat Detection ties into the Azure SQL Audit log (discussed in the next section); thus, you can review events in a single place and decide whether each one was expected or malicious.

Although this does not prevent malicious attacks (over and above your existing protections), you are given the necessary tools to mitigate and defend against future events. Given how prevalent attacks like SQL injection are, this feature is very useful in letting you know if that type of event has been detected.

You can turn on Threat Detection through the Azure portal, or through PowerShell.

> ➤ **To read more on configuring Azure SQL Database Threat Detection with PowerShell, go to** *https://docs.microsoft.com/azure/sql-database/scripts/ sql-database-auditing-and-threat-detection-powershell*.

Built-in firewall protection

Azure SQL Database is secure by default. All connections to your database environment pass through a firewall. No connections to the database are possible until you add a rule to the firewall to allow access.

To provide access to all databases on an Azure SQL server, you must add a server-level firewall rule through the Azure portal or through PowerShell with your IP address as a range.

> ➤ **To read more about protecting your Azure SQL Database, see Chapter 5.**

Auditing with SQL Server and Azure SQL Database

Auditing is the act of tracking and recording events that occur in the Database Engine.

Since SQL Server 2016 Service Pack 1, the Audit feature is available in all editions, as well as in Azure SQL Database. Chapter 5 covers configuring auditing in Azure SQL Database in depth.

SQL Server Audit

There is a lot going on in the Database Engine. SQL Server Audit uses extended events to give you the ability to track and record those actions at both the instance and database level.

> ### NOTE
> **Although extended events carry minimal overhead, it is important that you carefully balance auditing against performance impact. Use targeted auditing by only capturing the events that are necessary to fulfil your audit requirements.**

➤ **You can read more about extended events in Chapter 13.**

Audits are logged to event logs or audit files. An event is initiated and logged every time the audit action is encountered, but for performance reasons, the audit target is written to asynchronously.

The permissions required for SQL Server auditing are complex and varied, owing to the different requirements for reading from and writing to the Windows Event Log, the file system, and SQL Server itself.

Requirements for creating an audit

To keep track of events (called actions), you need to define a collection, or *audit*. The actions you want to track are collected according to an *audit specification*. Recording those actions is done by the *target* (destination).

- **Audit.** The SQL Server audit object is a collection of server actions or database actions (these actions might also be grouped together). Defining an audit creates it in the off state. After it is turned on, the destination receives the data from the audit.

- **Server audit specification.** This audit object defines the actions to collect at the instance level or database level (for all databases on the instance). You can have multiple Server Audits per instance.

- **Database audit specification.** You can monitor audit events and audit action groups. Only one database audit can be created per database per audit. Server-scoped objects must not be monitored in a database audit specification.

- **Target.**   You can send audit results to the Windows Security event log, the Windows Application event log, or an audit file on the file system. You must ensure that there is always sufficient space for the target. Keep in mind that the permissions required to read the Windows Application event log are lower than the Windows Security event log, if using the Windows Application event log.

An audit specification can be created only if an audit already exists.

➤ To read more about audit action groups and audit actions, go to *https://docs.microsoft.com/ sql/relational-databases/security/auditing/sql-server-audit-action-groups-and-actions*.

Inside OUT

What if an audit shuts down the instance or prevents SQL Server from starting?

SQL Server can be shut down by a failure in the audit. You will find an entry in the log saying MSG_AUDIT_FORCED_SHUTDOWN. You can start SQL Server in single-user mode using the -m option at the command line, which will write an entry to the log saying MSG_AUDIT_SHUTDOWN_BYPASSED.

An audit initiation failure also can prevent SQL Server from starting. In this case, you can use the -f command-line option to start SQL Server with minimal configuration (which is also single-user mode).

In minimal configuration or single-user mode, you will be able to remove the offending audit that caused the failure.

Creating a server audit in SQL Server Management Studio

Verify that you are connected to the correct instance in SQL Server Management Studio. Then, in Object Explorer, expand the Security folder. Right-click the Audits folder, and then, on the shortcut menu that opens, select New Audit.

In the Create Audit dialog box that opens, configure the settings to your requirements, or you can leave the defaults as is. Just be sure to enter in a valid file path if you select File in the Audit Destination list box. We also recommend that you choose an appropriate name to enter into the Audit Name box (the default name is based on the current date and time).

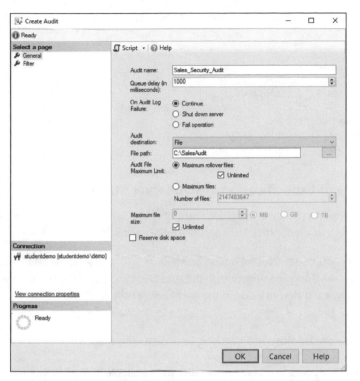

Figure 7-2 Creating an audit in SQL Server Management Studio.

Remember to turn on the audit after it is created. It will appear in the Audit folder, which is within the Security folder in Object Explorer. To do so, right-click the newly created audit, and then, on the shortcut menu, click Enable Audit.

Create a server audit by using T-SQL

The server audit creation process can be quite complex, depending on the destination, file options, audit options, and predicates. As just demonstrated, you can configure a new audit by using SQL Server Management Studio, and then create a script of the settings before clicking OK, which produces a T-SQL script, or you can do it manually.

> ➤ **To read more about creating a server audit in T-SQL visit** *https://docs.microsoft.com/ sql/t-sql/statements/create-server-audit-transact-sql.*

To create a server audit in T-SQL, verify that you are connected to the appropriate instance, and then run the code in Listing 7-4. (You'll need to change the audit name and file path accordingly.) Note that the next example also sets the audit state to ON. It is created in the OFF state by default.

This audit will not have any effect until an audit specification and target are also created.

```
USE master;
GO
-- Create the server audit.
CREATE SERVER AUDIT Sales_Security_Audit
    TO FILE (FILEPATH = 'C:\SalesAudit');
GO
-- Enable the server audit.
ALTER SERVER AUDIT Sales_Security_Audit
    WITH (STATE = ON);
GO
```

Create a server audit specification in SQL Server Management Studio

In Object Explorer, expand the Security folder. Right-click the Server Audit Specification folder, and then, on the shortcut menu, click New Server Audit Specification.

In the Create Server Audit Specification dialog box (Figure 7-3), in the Name box, type a name of your choosing for the audit specification. In the Audit list box, select the previously created server audit. If you type a different value in the Audit box, a new audit will be created by that name.

Now you can choose one or more audit actions, or audit action groups.

➤ A full list of audit actions and audit action groups is available at *https://docs.microsoft.com/sql/relational-databases/security/auditing/sql-server-audit-action-groups-and-actions*.

NOTE
If you have selected an audit group action, you cannot select Object Class, Object Schema, Object Name, and Principal Name, because the group represents multiple actions.

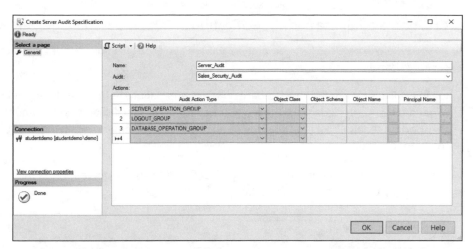

Figure 7-3 Creating a Server Audit Specification in SQL Server Management Studio.

Remember to turn on the server audit specification after you create it, by using the context menu.

Create a server audit specification by using T-SQL

In much the same way as you create the audit itself, you can create a script of the configuration from a dialog box in SQL Server Management Studio, or you can create the specification manually, as shown in the script that follows. Note that the server audit specification refers to a previously created audit.

```
USE [master];
GO
-- Create the server audit specification.
CREATE SERVER AUDIT SPECIFICATION Server_Audit
FOR SERVER AUDIT Sales_Security_Audit
    ADD (SERVER_OPERATION_GROUP),
    ADD (LOGOUT_GROUP),
    ADD (DATABASE_OPERATION_GROUP),
WITH (STATE = ON);
GO
```

CHAPTER 7

Creating a database audit specification in SQL Server Management Studio

As you would expect, the location of the database audit specification is under the database security context.

In Object Explorer, expand the database on which you want to perform auditing, and then expand the Security folder. Right-click the Database Audit Specifications folder, and then, on the shortcut menu, click New Database Audit Specification. Remember again to use the context menu to turn it on.

Figure 7-4 shows an example of capturing SELECT and INSERT operations on the Sales.CustomerTransactions table by the dbo user.

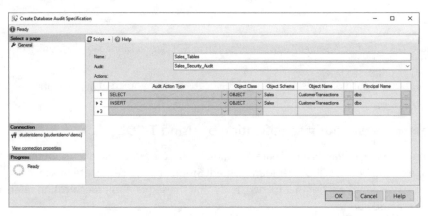

Figure 7-4 Creating a database audit specification in SQL Server Management Studio.

Creating a database audit specification by using T-SQL

Again, verify that you are in the correct database context. Create the database audit specification by referring to the server audit that was previously created, and then specify which database actions you want to monitor, as demonstrated in the next example.

The destination is already specified in the server audit, so as soon as this is turned on, the destination will begin logging the events as expected.

```
USE WideWorldImporters;
GO
-- Create the database audit specification.
CREATE DATABASE AUDIT SPECIFICATION Sales_Tables
    FOR SERVER AUDIT Sales_Security_Audit

    ADD (SELECT, INSERT ON Sales.CustomerTransactions BY dbo)
    WITH (STATE = ON);
GO
```

Viewing an audit log

You can view audit logs either in SQL Server Management Studio or in the Security Log in the Windows Event Viewer. This section describes how to do it by using SQL Server Management Studio.

NOTE

To view any audit logs, you must have CONTROL SERVER **permission.**

In Object Explorer, expand the Security folder, and then expand the Audits folder. Right-click the audit log that you want to view, and then, on the shortcut menu, select View Audit Logs.

Note that the Event Time is in UTC format. This is to avoid issues regarding time zones and daylight savings.

Figure 7-5 shows two audit events that have been logged. In the first, the audit itself has been changed (it was turned on). The second event is a SELECT statement that was run against the table specified in the database audit specification example presented earlier.

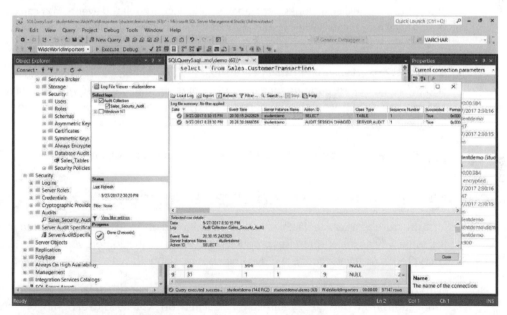

Figure 7-5 File Viewer dialog box for viewing a SQL Server audit.

There are many columns in the audit that you cannot see in Figure 7-5, notable among them are Server Principal ID (SPID), Session Server Principal Name (the logged-in user), and the Statement (the command that was run). The point here being that you can capture a wealth of information.

NOTE

You can also view the audit log in an automated manner by using the built-in T-SQL system function `sys.fn_get_audit_file`**, though the data is not formatted the same way as it is through the File Viewer in SQL Server Management Studio. See more at** *https://docs.microsoft.com/sql/relational-databases/system-functions/ sys-fn-get-audit-file-transact-sql.*

Auditing with Azure SQL Database

With Azure SQL Database auditing, you can track database activity and write it to an audit log in an Azure Blob storage container, in your Azure Storage account (you are charged for storage accordingly).

This helps you to remain compliant with auditing regulations as well as see anomalies (as discussed earlier in the section "Azure SQL Database Threat Detection") to give you greater insight into your Azure SQL Database environment.

Auditing gives you the ability to retain an audit trail, report on activity in each database, and analyze reports, which includes trend analysis and security-related events. You can define server-level and database-level policies. Server policies automatically cover new and existing databases.

If you turn on server auditing, that policy applies to any databases on the server. Thus, if you also turn on database auditing for a particular database, that database will be audited by both policies. You should avoid this unless retention periods are different or you want to audit for different event types.

➤ **You can read more about Azure SQL Database auditing in Chapter 5.**

Securing Azure infrastructure as a service

Infrastructure as a service (IaaS), or SQL Server running on an Azure VM, is secured in much the same way as the on-premises product. Depending on the edition, you can use TDE, Always Encrypted, row-level security, and dynamic data masking.

With Azure IaaS, setting up a VM in a resource group is secure by default. If you want to allow connections from outside of your Azure virtual network, you need to allow not only the connection through the OS firewall (which is on by default in Windows Server), but you also can control connections through a Network Security Group.

In addition to that, you can control access through a network appliance, such as a firewall or NAT device. This provides finer-grained control over the flow of network traffic in your virtual network, which is needed to set up Azure ExpressRoute, for example (Chapter 3 covers this in some detail).

Network Security Group

A Network Security Group (NSG) controls the flow of traffic in and out of the entirety (or part) of an Azure virtual network *subnet*.

Inside OUT

What is a subnet?

A subnet, short for subnetwork, is a logical separation of a larger network into smaller sections, making the network easier to manage and secure.

Subnetting can be vastly complex and is definitely beyond the scope of this book. There are subnet calculators online that you should refer to if you're doing this yourself. Because Azure Virtual Networks make use of subnets, here is a high-level overview.

Subnets are identified by a *network ID*, which is rendered in *network prefix notation* (also known as CIDR, or Classless Interdomain Routing). You will recognize this as a network address in IPv4 format followed by a prefix of /8, /16, or /24, and so on. The lower (*shorter*) the prefix, the more addresses are available.

This is a shorthand for the IP addresses that are available in that subnet, with the network address as the starting value. For example, 192.168.1.0/24 means that there are 256 possible addresses, starting at 192.168.1.1, up to and including 192.168.1.254. All subnets reserve the first address (in this case, 192.168.1.0) for the network identifier, and the last address (in this case, 192.168.1.255) for the broadcast address.

In the Azure classic deployment model, an NSG would provide security for an individual virtual machine. With the Azure Resource Manager deployment model, an NSG can provide security for an entire subnet, which affects all the resources in that subnet (see Figure 7-6). If you require more control, you can associate the NSG with an individual network interface card (NIC), thus restricting traffic further.

NOTE

When creating a VM using the Azure Resource Manager, it will come with at least one virtual NIC, which in turn, you manage through an NSG. This is an important distinction from the classic provider (in which the NSG worked at the VM level) because individual NICs can belong to different NSGs, which provides finer control over the flow of network traffic on individual VMs.

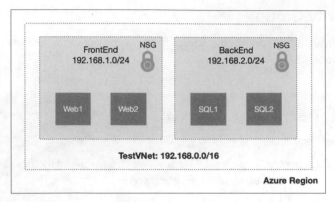

Figure 7-6 A typical virtual network, with each subnet secured by a security group.

As with typical firewalls, the NSG has rules for incoming and outgoing traffic. When a packet hits a port on the virtual network or subnet, the NSG intercepts the packet and checks whether it matches one of the rules. If the packet does not qualify for processing, it is discarded (dropped).

Rules are classified according to source address (or range) and destination address (or range). Depending on the direction of traffic, the source address could refer to inside the network or outside on the public internet.

This becomes cumbersome with more complex networks, so to simplify administration and provide flexibility, you can use service tags to define rules by service name instead of IP address. Storage, SQL and Traffic are currently supported, with more to come in the future.

You can also use default categories, namely VirtualNetwork (the IP range of all addresses in the network), AzureLoadBalancer (the Azure infrastructure load balancer), and Internet (IP addresses outside the range of the Azure Virtual Network).

> ➤ You can read more about Azure Virtual Network security and service tags at *https://docs. microsoft.com/azure/virtual-network/security-overview*.

User-defined routes and IP forwarding

As a convenience to Azure customers, all VMs in an Azure Virtual Network are able to communicate with one another by default, irrespective of the subnet in which they reside. This also holds true for virtual networks connected to your on-premises network by a VPN, and for Azure VMs communicating with the public internet (including those running SQL Server).

> ➤ You can read more about Virtual Private Networks in Chapters 2 and 3.

In a traditional network, communication across subnets like this requires a gateway to control (route) the traffic. Azure provides these *system routes* for you automatically.

You might decide that this free-for-all communication is against your network policy and that all traffic from your VMs should first be channeled through a network appliance (such as a firewall or NAT device). Virtual appliances are available in the Azure Marketplace at an additional cost, or you could configure a VM yourself to run as a firewall.

A user-defined route with IP forwarding makes this happen. With a user-defined route, you create a subnet for the virtual appliance and force traffic from your existing subnets or VMs through the virtual appliance.

In Microsoft's own words:

"[t]o allow a VM to receive traffic addressed to other destinations, you must enable IP Forwarding for the VM. This is an Azure setting, not a setting in the guest operating system." (https://docs.microsoft.com/azure/virtual-network/virtual-networks-udr-overview)

> ### CAUTION
> With user-defined routes, you cannot control how traffic *enters* the network from the public internet. They only control how traffic *leaves* a subnet, which means that your virtual appliance must be in its own subnet. If you want to control traffic flow from the public internet as it enters a subnet, use a Network Security Group, instead.

Until you create a routing table (by user-defined route), subnets in your Virtual Network rely on system routes. A user-defined route adds another entry in the routing table, so a technique called Longest Prefix Match (LPM) kicks in to decide which is the better route to take, by selecting the most specific route (the one with the longest prefix). As seen earlier in Figure 7-6, a /24 prefix is longer than a /16 prefix, and a route entry with a higher prefix takes precedence.

If two entries have the same LPM match, the order of precedence is as follows:

- User-defined route

- BGP route

- System route

Remember BGP? It's used for ExpressRoute. As we mentioned in Chapter 3, ExpressRoute is a VPN service by which you can connect your Azure Virtual Network to your on-premises network, without going over the public internet. You can specify BGP routes to direct traffic between your network and the Azure Virtual Network.

CHAPTER 7

Additional security features in Azure networking

There are additional features for improving the management and security of an Azure Virtual Network, as it relates to SQL Server or Azure SQL Database, which are worth discussing here. As of this writing, some of these features are still in preview.

Virtual network service endpoints

Service endpoints make it possible for you to restrict access to certain Azure services that were traditionally open to the public internet so that they are available only to your Azure Virtual Network, as illustrated in Figure 7-7.

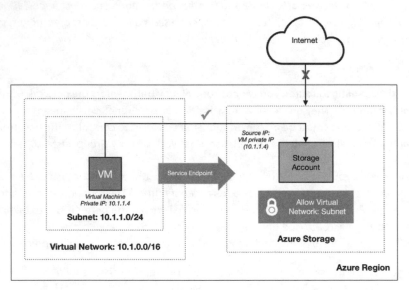

Figure 7-7 A service endpoint protecting an Azure Storage account.

Configurable through the Azure portal (or PowerShell), you can block public internet access to your Azure Storage and Azure SQL Database accounts. Additional service endpoints will be introduced in the future.

➤ To read more about Virtual Network service endpoints, go to *https://docs.microsoft.com/ azure/virtual-network/virtual-network-service-endpoints-overview*.

Distributed-denial-of-service protection

Azure's protection against distributed-denial-of-service (DDoS) attacks for Virtual Networks has been improved, which is timely, given that attacks against publicly accessible resources are increasing in number and complexity. The basic service included in your subscription provides real-time protection by using the scale and capacity of the Azure infrastructure to mitigate attacks (see Figure 7-8).

For an additional cost, you can take advantage of built-in machine learning algorithms to protect against targeted attacks, with added configuration, alerting, and telemetry.

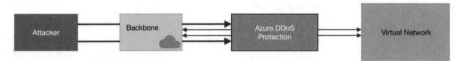

Figure 7-8 Azure DDoS protection defending a virtual network against attacks.

You also can use the Azure Application Gateway web application firewall to help protect against more sophisticated attacks.

Combined with Azure SQL Database auditing and NSGs, these features provide a comprehensive suite of protection against the latest threats.

> ➤ **To read more about Azure DDoS protection, go to** *https://azure.microsoft.com/services/ddos-protection*.

CHAPTER 7

Understanding and designing tables

This chapter discusses a fundamental concept in relational databases: tables. Tables are the database objects that actually store the data in the database. Thoroughly understanding the concepts in this chapter is a requirement for designing and maintaining an effective database. We first discuss table design fundamentals, including data types, keys, and constraints. Next, we cover several specialized table types, such as temporal tables and graph tables. Then, we examine the specialized nature of storing binary large objects (BLOBs) in relational tables. Your understanding of table design would not be complete without including both vertical and horizontal partitioning, which we review before the chapter ends with an overview of change tracking methods.

Reviewing table design

In this section, we review information that is relevant when designing tables. First, we look at system data types, emphasizing the data design decisions surrounding their use. Next, we briefly discuss primary and foreign key concepts. Then, we cover constraints and their impact on table design. The section ends with user-defined data types and computed columns.

NOTE

Indexing is not covered in this chapter, although table design is not complete without considering it. For guidance on indexing, read Chapter 9 and Chapter 10.

Generic data types

Selecting the appropriate data type when designing relational databases is a crucial activity. Even though you can change the data types of columns, it is an expensive operation at best; at worst, it could lead to a loss of data. A poorly chosen data type can result in suboptimal performance or might allow for unexpected values to be stored in the column. The intent of this section is not to provide exhaustive coverage of each system data type available in SQL Server 2017. Instead, the focus will be on providing the information and guidance necessary to make solid table design decisions.

Inside OUT

When should I use a numeric data type instead of an alphanumeric data type?

You can store any numeric value, such as an amount or an identifier consisting only of digits, in an alphanumeric column or in a numeric data type column. Generally, you would choose a numeric data type if you use the values in some type of calculation or when magnitude matters. For example, on a monetary value, you might need to calculate a discount. Another example for which numeric data types are used is in quantities because you might need to adjust the quantity by adding or subtracting additional units. On the other hand, a US Zip code is best stored as an alphanumeric value because leading zeroes must be preserved. The same can be true in an employee ID number.

In addition to considering whether you need to use the value in calculations, there are also differences in how values are sorted. In a numeric column sorted in ascending order, the value 12 will come before 100. But in an alphanumeric column, 100 will come before 12. Either one can produce the desired answer based on your use case.

If you decide that using a numeric data type is the right choice for a column, you then will need to decide which numeric data type is the best. This decision is a balancing act between precision and storage size required. There is, however, one golden rule: if you are storing financial information, such as monetary values or interest rate percentages, you should always use the decimal type (which is the same as numeric in SQL Server) because it has a fixed precision. This means that there will never be an approximate value stored, as could be the case with the `float` and `real` data types.

Alphanumeric types

Alphanumeric types in SQL Server are commonly discussed in terms of fixed versus variable length, and with Unicode versus without Unicode support. The `char` data type is a fixed length type and `varchar` is variable length. The `nchar` and `nvarchar` data types are fixed and variable length, respectively, and support Unicode.

NOTE

You might need Unicode support more often than you think. Increasingly, users expect to store emojis and other Unicode character data in columns. In addition, increasing internationalization of applications is also best supported by using Unicode string data types.

With string data, collation becomes an important consideration. Among other things, collation determines how the high order bits in each character's byte are interpreted. Collation supports internationalization by allowing different character representations for characters whose integer values is greater than 127. This is determined using the code page, which is one element of the collation. Collation also determines how data is compared and sorted, such as whether casing and accented letters are considered different.

➤ **For complete details about collation and Unicode support, refer to Microsoft Docs at** *https://docs.microsoft.com/sql/relational-databases/collations/ collation-and-unicode-support.*

NOTE

Did you know that a `char` or `varchar` column can also store double-byte character sets (DBCS)? This is an important distinction, because it means that `char(8)` might not be able to store eight characters if the characters require two bytes. However, in the case of `nchar` and `nvarchar`, the size you specify is always the number of characters that you can store.

Finally, no discussion of alphanumeric types would be complete without taking a look at `(N)VARCHAR(MAX)`. By specifying MAX instead of a value between 1 and 8,000 characters (for VARCHAR) or 1 and 4,000 characters (for NVARCHAR), the maximum bytes stored increases to 2 GB. This data, however, is not stored in the table's storage structure. Large-value data is stored out-of-row, though for each such column, 24 bytes of overhead is stored in the row.

Numeric types

When considering numeric types in computer systems, it is important to distinguish between exact and approximate numeric types. Approximate types store values using scientific notation. The number of bits in the mantissa is limited to 24 or 53. Due the nature of the scientific notation and the limited number of bits, these types cannot accurately store all numbers in the supported range. On the other hand, exact types store numbers without a loss of precision, but this comes at a loss of range.

SQL Server provides `real` and `float` as approximate data types, though their implementation is closely related. The `real` data type is lower precision than the `float` data type. It is possible to specify the number of bits for the mantissa when defining `float`, but SQL Server will always use either 24 bits or 53 bits—any other value you specify is rounded up to either 24 or 53. The `real` data type is the same as specifying `float(24)`, or in effect any number of mantissa bits between 1 and 24.

NOTE

The sample script for this chapter includes a case that illustrates important caveats when converting from approximate floating-point numbers to exact types.

Exact numeric types include `tinyint`, `smallint`, `int`, and `bigint`, which are all whole numbers of varying byte sizes and therefore range. SQL Server does not support unsigned integers.

There are exact numeric types that support decimal-point numbers. Foremost among those is the `decimal` data type. In SQL Server, another name for `decimal` is `numeric`. The `decimal` data type supports a precision of up to 38 digits. The number of digits determines the storage size. In addition, you can specify the scale, which determines the number of digits to the right of the decimal point.

Another category of exact numeric types that support decimal point numbers are `money` and `smallmoney`. These data types can store monetary data with a precision of up to four digits to the right of the decimal point, so the precision is to the ten-thousandth. Choosing between `decimal` and `money` or `smallmoney` is primarily determined by your need for range and number of digits to the right of the decimal point. For monetary values, and if your calculations will return the desired result when using only four significant digits to the right of the decimal point, `smallmoney` and `money` are good choices because they are more efficient as it relates to storage space. For high precision and scale, `decimal` is the right choice.

Date and time types

Date and time data types available in SQL Server 2017 include the venerable `datetime` and `smalldatetime` types. Although these are not technically deprecated, we strongly caution against using them for new development due to issues surrounding precision, available date range, and lack of control over the storage size. Additionally, these data types are not aligned with the SQL standard, lowering portability of the data between platforms. Their immediate replacement is `datetime2`, which in no case consumes more than eight bytes of storage space (the same as `datetime`), but addresses precision, increases the date range, and can store dates in less than eight bytes in return for lower precision.

NOTE

All date and time data types discussed here are available in all currently supported versions of SQL Server. They are by no means new data types, but, unfortunately, are too frequently left unused for fear of backward-compatibility problems.

This does not mean, however, that all date or time values should be stored in `datetime2`. There are three additional data types that you should consider for storing date or time values:

- **date.** The `date` data type stores only a date and supports the same date range as `datetime2`. It stores the date in only three bytes, thereby being much more efficient than `datetime` (fixed at eight bytes) and `datetime2` (minimally six bytes). If you need to store only a date without time or time zone information, this is your best choice. An example of such a case is a date of birth. A date of birth is commonly stored to calculate someone's age, and that is not generally dependent on the time zone or on the time. One of the authors was born at 11 PM Central European Summer Time. If he moved to southeast Asia, he would not celebrate his birthday a day later, even though the date in Southeast Asia was the next day. (We appreciate that some applications, such as one used in a neonatal facility, might need to store a more precise "time of birth," but in most cases, the aging logic above holds up.)

- **datetimeoffset.** The `datetimeoffset` data type provides the same precision and range as `datetime2` but includes an offset value in hours and minutes used to indicate the difference from UTC. Even though a discussion of time zones and the impact of Daylight Saving Time (DST), also known as summer time, is beyond the scope of this book, we will note that this data type neither tracks or understands actual time zones nor DST. It would be up to the application to track the time zone where the value originated to allow the application or recent versions of SQL Server (see the note that follows) to perform correct date arithmetic.

  ### NOTE

  Prior to SQL Server 2016, SQL Server did not have any understanding of time zones or DST. SQL Server 2016 and Microsoft Azure SQL Database introduced the AT TIME ZONE function, which you can use to convert between time zones and apply or revert DST offset. The rules SQL Server applies are based on the Windows functionality for time zones and DST. These rules are explained and illustrated with examples at *https://docs. microsoft.com/sql/t-sql/queries/at-time-zone-transact-sql*.

- **time.** The `time` data type stores only a time-of-day value consisting of hours, minutes, seconds, and fractional seconds, with a precision up to 100 nanoseconds. The exact fractional second precision and storage size is user defined by optionally specifying a precision between 0 and 7. The `time` data type is a good choice when storing only a time-of-day value that is not time-zone sensitive, such as for a reminder. A reminder set for 11 AM might need to be activated at 11 AM regardless of time zone and date.

CHAPTER 8

NOTE

The `time` data type is still limited to storing no more than 23 hours, 59 minutes, 59 seconds, and 0.9999999 fractions of a second. This can make this data type unsuitable for storing elapsed time if there is a possibility that elapsed time might be 24 hours or more.

Inside OUT

How can I correctly retrieve the current system date and time?

In addition to continued use of the `datetime` data type, we also observe the common use of the lower-precision functions CURRENT_TIMESTAMP, GETDATE(), and GETUTCDATE(). Although these functions continue to work, they return values of the `datetime` type.

There are replacement functions available in SYSDATETIME(), SYSDATETIMEOFFSET(), and SYSUTCDATETIME(). Despite that their names don't make it immediately clear, the SYSDATETIME() and SYSUTCDATETIME() functions return the improved `datetime2(7)` type. SYSDATETIMEOFFSET() returns a value of type `datetimeoffset(7)`. SYSDATETIME() and SYSUTCDATETIME() are functionally equivalent to GETDATE() and GETUTCDATE(), respectively. SYSDATETIMEOFFSET() did not have a functional equivalent and is thus the only option if you need to include the time zone offset on the server.

Even if you are unable to change the schema of your database to change all `datetime` columns to `datetime2` (or `datetimeoffset`), you might benefit in the long term from adopting the improved functions now. Even though the range of valid dates for `datetime` is much smaller on the lower end than for `datetime2` and `datetimeoffset`, the upper end is the same (December 31, 9999). Discarding the future possibility of time-travel to before the year 1753, none of the improved functions will return a `datetime2` or `datetimeoffset` value that cannot be cast to `datetime`.

➤ For detailed technical comparisons between the available date and time data types, consult Microsoft Docs at *https://docs.microsoft.com/sql/t-sql/functions/date-and-time-data-types-and-functions-transact-sql*.

Binary types

Some data cannot be efficiently represented as an alphanumeric string. For example, data that has been encrypted by the application should be stored as a binary value. The same might also apply to storing contents of binary file formats, such as PDF files.

SQL Server provides the `binary` data type to store fixed-length binary values, and `varbinary` to store variable-length binary values. (The `image` data type is deprecated, and you should no longer use it.) For both data types, you specify the number of bytes that will be stored, up to 8,000. If you need to store more than 8,000 bytes, you can specify `varbinary(max)`. This will allow up to 2 GB to be stored, although those bytes are not stored in the data row.

NOTE

When storing binary values that are on average larger than 1 MB, you should review whether using FILESTREAM is not a better choice. FILESTREAM is discussed in the section "Understanding FILESTREAM" later in the chapter.

You can store the data for `varchar(max)` and `varbinary(max)` columns in a separate filegroup without needing to resort to FILESTREAM. In the CREATE TABLE statement, use the TEXTIMAGE_ON clause to specify the name of the filegroup where large object (LOB) data should be stored.

Specialized data types

In addition to the data types that are designed to store traditional numeric, alphanumeric, and date and time values, SQL Server provides more specialized data types. These data types are more specific to a purpose or use case than the generic data types.

Some specialized data types have SQL Common Language Runtime (CLR) functions that make working with them significantly easier. For example, the `hierarchyid` data type has a `ToString()` function that converts the stored binary value into a human-readable format. Such SQL CLR function names are case-sensitive, regardless of the case sensitivity of the instance or database.

Spatial data types

The spatial data types provide a way to work with planar (flat) or ellipsoidal (round-earth) coordinates. The `geometry` data type is for a flat coordinate system, whereas the `geography` data type is for round-earth coordinates. In addition, both data types also support elevation, or Z, values. Both data types are CLR types available in every database, regardless of whether the SQL CLR feature is turned on.

SQL Server provides several methods to work with the values of these data types, including finding intersections, calculating surface area and distance, and many more. SQL Server supports methods defined by the Open Geospatial Consortium (OGC) as well as extended methods designed by Microsoft. The methods defined by the OGC are identified by their ST prefix.

Generally, you create a geometry or geography value by using the static `STGeomFromText` method. You can use this method to define points, lines, and polygons (closed shapes). The code example that follows creates two geometric points, one with coordinates (0, 0) and the second with coordinates (10, 10), and then the distance between both points is calculated and output:

```
-- Define the variables
DECLARE @point1 GEOMETRY, @point2 GEOMETRY, @distance FLOAT;
-- Initialize the geometric points
SET @point1 = geometry::STGeomFromText('POINT( 0  0)', 0);
SET @point2 = geometry::STGeomFromText('POINT(10 10)', 0);
-- Calculate the distance
SET @distance = @point1.STDistance(@point2);
SELECT @distance;
```

The result in the output is approximately 14.14 (see Figure 8-1; note that no units are defined here). The second argument in the STGeomFromText method is the spatial reference ID (SRID), which is relevant only for the geography data type. Still, it is a required parameter for the function and you should specify 0 for geometry data.

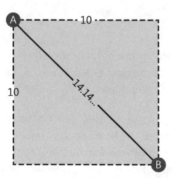

Figure 8-1 The geometry defined in the sample script.

Using spatial data types in a database is valuable when you use the Database Engine to perform spatial queries. You have probably experienced the results of spatial queries in many applications; for example, when searching for nearby pizza restaurants on Bing Maps. Application code could certainly also perform those spatial queries; however, that would require the database to return all pizza restaurants along with their coordinates. By performing the spatial query in the database, the data size that is returned to the application is significantly reduced. SQL Server supports indexing spatial data such that spatial queries can perform optimally.

➤ **For a complete reference on the** geometry **and** geography **data types, the methods they support, and spatial reference identifiers, refer to Microsoft Docs at** *https://docs.microsoft.com/sql/t-sql/spatial-geometry/spatial-types-geometry-transact-sql* **and** *https://docs.microsoft.com/sql/t-sql/spatial-geography/spatial-types-geography.*

NOTE

For an example of the geography data type, refer to the WideWorldImporters sample database. The `Application.StateProvinces` table includes a Border column of type `geography`. To visually see the `geography` data type at work, run a select statement on the table using SQL Server Management Studio. In addition to the row results, SQL Server Management Studio will display a Spatial results tab on which a map will be drawn showing the US states.

The XML data type

A relational database is generally used to store highly structured data, by which we mean data that has a known schema. And even though schemas can change, at any given time every row in a table will have the same columns. Yet, for some scenarios, this strict schema is not appropriate. It might be necessary to accommodate storing data where different rows have different attributes. Sometimes, you can meet this requirement by adding additional nullable sparse columns. Column sets are a feature by which you can manage a group of sparse columns as XML data.

> ➤ You can read more about sparse columns in the section "Sparse columns" later in the chapter.

Other times, this becomes onerous as a substantial number of columns can introduce additional challenges in working with the table. There, the `xml` data type can alleviate the column sprawl. Additionally, if data is frequently used in XML format, it might be more efficient to store the data in that format in the database.

Although XML data could be stored in `(N)VARCHAR` columns, using the specialized data type allows SQL Server to provide functionality for validating, querying, indexing, and modifying the XML data.

SQL Server 2016 introduced support for JSON, though it is not a data type. JSON support includes parsing, querying, and modifying JSON stored in `varchar` columns.

> ➤ For complete information on handling JSON-formatted data in SQL Server 2016 and later, refer to *https://docs.microsoft.com/sql/relational-databases/json/json-data-sql-server*.

Rowversion

This data type generates a database-wide unique binary value upon each modification of row data. This binary value increments with each insert or update statement that affects the row, even if no other row data is actually modified.

CHAPTER 8

NOTE

The rowversion data type was previously known as timestamp. rowversion is the recommended name to use; timestamp is deprecated. Unfortunately, the name timestamp is the same as the SQL ISO standard timestamp, but it does not work according to the ISO standard. Contrary to what the timestamp name might indicate, rowversion data does not map to a moment in time.

A rowversion column in a table is an excellent way to implement *optimistic concurrency*. In optimistic concurrency, a client reads data with the intent of updating it. However, unlike with *pessimistic concurrency*, a lock is not maintained. Instead, in the same transaction as the update statement, the client will verify that the rowversion was not changed by another process. If it hasn't, the update proceeds. But if the rowversion no longer matches what the client originally read, the update will fail. The client application then can retrieve the current values and present the user with a notification and suitable options, depending on the application needs. Many object-relational mappers (ORMs), including Entity Framework, support using a rowversion column type to implement optimistic concurrency.

Inside OUT

Can I implement optimistic concurrency without rowversion?

There are other ways to implement optimistic concurrency. A client application could track the value of each individual column in the row to be updated and verify that only the columns that will be updated by its own update statement have not been modified. Specifically, client A reads a row of data and intends to change only the Name column. Client B reads the same row of data and updates the Address column. When client A attempts to update the Name, it would find that the Name column's value is unchanged and will proceed with the update.

This approach is suitable in some scenarios, but it has some drawbacks. First, each client needs to maintain additional state. In a web application, the amount of state to maintain can grow very large and consume a lot of memory. In a web farm scenario, maintaining such state might require shared state configuration because the web client might not communicate with the same web server on the POST that it did on the GET. But, perhaps more important, the data row can be inconsistent after the second update. If each client updates a column in the same row, the row's data might not reflect a valid business scenario. Certainly, the row's values would not reflect what each client believes it would be.

When designing tables with `rowversion`, keep the following restrictions in mind:

- A table can have only a single `rowversion` column.

- You cannot specify a value for the `rowversion` column in insert or update statements. However, unlike with identity or computed columns, you must specify the columns in insert statements for tables with a `rowversion` column. We should note that not specifying a column list is not recommended anyway.

- Although the Database Engine will not generate duplicate `rowversion` values within a database, `rowversion` values are not unique across databases or across instances.

- Duplicate `rowversion` values can exist in a single database if a new table is created by using the SELECT INTO syntax. The new table's `rowversion` values will be the same as those of the source table. This behavior might be desired, for example, when modifying a table's schema by creating a new table and copying all the data into it. In other instances, this behavior might not be desired. In those cases, do not include the `rowversion` column in the SELECT INTO statement. Instead, alter the new table and add a `rowversion` column. This behavior and workaround are illustrated in a sample script file in the accompanying downloads for this book, which are available at *https://aka.ms/SQLServ2017Admin/downloads*.

The uniqueidentifier data type

The `uniqueidentifier` data type stores a 16-byte value known as a globally unique identifier (GUID). SQL Server can generate GUIDs using one of two functions: NEWID() and NEWSEQUENTIALID(). NEWSEQUENTIALID() generates a GUID that is greater than a previously generated GUID by this function *since the last restart of the server*. You can use NEWSEQUENTIALID() only as a default value for columns, for which it is suitable to use as a clustered primary key. Unlike NEWID(), which generates random values, the increasing nature of the GUIDs generated by NEWSEQUENTIALID() means that data and index pages will fill completely.

> ### NOTE
> Although we are not aware of a use for a SQL Server system without a network interface card (NIC), GUIDs generated on such a system might not be globally unique. A GUID is generated by incorporating MAC address values. On a system without a NIC, the generation algorithm will use random values, instead. The chance of collision is extremely low, though.

➤ The `uniqueidentifier` data type plays an important role in some replication techniques. For more information, see Chapter 12.

CHAPTER 8

The hierarchyid data type

The hierarchyid data type provides a way for an application to store and query hierarchical data in a tree structure. A tree structure means that a row will have one parent and zero or more children. There is a single root element denoted by a single forward slash (/). hierarchyid values are stored as a binary format but are commonly represented in their string format. Each element at the same level in the hierarchy (referred to as siblings) has a unique numeric value (which might include a decimal point). In the string representation of a hierarchyid value, each level is separated by a forward slash. The string representation always begins with a slash (to denote the root element) and ends with a slash.

For example, as illustrated in Figure 8-2, a hierarchyid whose string representation is /1/10/ is a descendant of the /1/ element, which itself is a descendant of the implicit root element /. It must be noted, however, that SQL Server does not enforce the existence of a row with the ancestor element. This means that it is possible to create an element /3/1/ without its ancestor /3/ being a value in a row. Implicitly, it is a child of /3/, even if no row with hierarchyid value /3/ exists. Similarly, the row with hierarchyid element /1/ can be deleted if another row has hierarchyid value /1/10/. If you don't want this, the application or database will need to include logic to enforce the existence of an ancestor when inserting and to prevent the deletion of an ancestor.

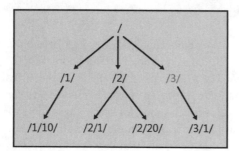

Figure 8-2 hierarchyid values—the value /3/ is in gray to indicate it is implicit.

Perhaps surprisingly, SQL Server does not enforce uniqueness of the hierarchyid values unless you define a unique index or constraint on the hierarchyid column. It is, therefore, possible that the element /3/1/ is defined twice. This is likely not the desired situation, so we recommend that you ensure uniqueness of the hierarchyid values.

Using the hierarchyid data type is an appropriate choice if the tree is most commonly queried to find consecutive children. That is because the hierarchyid stores rows depth-first if it is indexed. You can create a breadth-first index by adding a computed column to the table, which uses the GetLevel() method on the hierarchyid column, and then creating an index on the computed column followed by the `hierarchyid` column. However, you cannot use a computed column in a clustered index, so this solution will still be less efficient compared to creating a clustered index on the `hierarchyid` value alone.

> ➤ For a complete overview of the `hierarchyid` data type, refer to *https://docs.microsoft. com/sql/relational-databases/hierarchical-data-sql-server*.

The sql_variant data type

The `sql_variant` data type allows a single column to store data of diverse types. You can also use the type as a parameter or a variable. In addition to storing the actual value, each `sql_variant` instance also stores metadata about the value, which includes the system data of the value, its maximum size, scale and precision, and collation. Using `sql_variant` can be indicative of a poor database design, and you should use it judiciously. Client libraries that do not know how to handle that data might convert it to NVARCHAR(4000).

Keys and relationships

Proper database design calls for a process called *normalization*. Normalization is not covered in this book; however, suffice it to say that it leads to breaking logical entities into multiple related tables. Without intending to wax poetically, keys are like the nervous system of a relational database; they establish the relationships between the tables. A relational database system provides *primary* and *foreign keys*. In a single table, the primary key values must be unique because those values can be used as foreign key values in the related table. The foreign key values could also be unique in the related table, in which case the established relationship is a one-to-one relationship. This is referenced in the section "Vertical partitioning" later in the chapter.

> ### NOTE
> This chapter does not include any coverage of indexes, though a primary key is always associated with an index. Frequently, foreign keys are also indexed as their values are often used to query the table. For information on indexing, see Chapter 9 and Chapter 10.

A table can have exactly one primary key. The primary key can consist of multiple columns, in which case it's referred to as a *compound primary key*. However, in no case can a nullable column be (part of) the primary key. If additional columns' values should be unique, you can apply a unique index or constraint. (See the next section for coverage on constraints.)

NOTE

In most cases, SQL Server does not require that tables have a primary key. Some features, such as using FILESTREAM or certain types of replication might require that tables have a primary key. In general, though, you should default to designing tables with primary keys unless there is an overriding reason to not do so.

Foreign keys are intended to establish *referential integrity*. Referential integrity enforces that the values found in the foreign key column(s) exist in the primary key column(s). By default, foreign keys in SQL Server have referential integrity enforced. It is possible to establish a foreign key without referential integrity enforced, or alter the foreign key to turn referential integrity off and on. This functionality is useful during import operations or certain types of database maintenance. Foreign keys should have referential integrity turned on to protect the integrity of your data.

NOTE

If a foreign key is a composite key in which one or more columns allow null, a row with a null value in just one of the foreign key columns will pass the integrity check, even if the other columns contain values that do not exist in the parent table. To provide referential integrity, we recommend not allowing null values in any column of a composite foreign key.

One table can have multiple foreign keys. In addition to referencing a primary key, a foreign key can also reference the columns in a nonfiltered unique index.

When defining a foreign key, you can specify *cascading*. Cascading can occur when a parent row's primary key value is updated, or when the parent row is deleted. Cascading specifically means that the same operation will be run on the child row(s) as was run on the parent. Thus, if the primary key value were updated, the foreign key values would be updated. If the parent row is deleted, the foreign key values will be deleted. Alternatively, on updates or deletes in the parent table, no action can be taken (the default, which would cause the update or delete statement to fail if referential integrity is enforced), the foreign-key value can be set to null (effectively creating an orphaned row), or the foreign-key value can be set to its default constraint's specification (effectively mapping the child row to another parent).

Constraints

Constraints define rules to which your data must adhere, and those rules are enforced by the Database Engine. This makes constraints a very powerful mechanism for guaranteeing data integrity. In the previous section, we covered two types of constraints: primary keys and foreign keys. In this section, we provide details on *unique*, *check*, and *default* constraints.

A unique constraint enforces unique values in one column or selected columns. Unlike a primary key, the unique constraint allows the column(s) to be nullable.

A check constraint enforces rules that can be expressed by using a Boolean expression. For example, in the `Sales.Invoices` table in the sample WideWorldImporters database, there is a check constraint defined that requires the `ReturnedDeliveryData` column to either be null or contain valid JSON. Check constraints can reference more than one column. A frequently encountered requirement is that when one column contains a particular value, another column cannot be null.

Using constraints with compound conditions also provides an opportunity to provide check constraints in the face of changing requirements. If a new business rule requires that a nullable column must now contain a value, but no suitable default can be provided for the existing rows, you could consider creating a check constraint that verifies whether an incrementing ID column or date column is larger than the value it held when the rule took effect. For example, consider the table `Sales.Invoices`, which has a nullable column `Comments`. If effective February 1, 2018, every new and modified invoice must have a value in the `Comments` column, the table could be altered using the following script:

```
ALTER TABLE Sales.Invoices WITH CHECK
    ADD CONSTRAINT CH_Comments CHECK (LastEditedWhen < '2018-02-01'
    OR Comments IS NOT NULL);
```

A problem that you cannot solve by using a constraint is when a column must contain unique values, if a value is provided. In other words, the column should allow multiple rows with null, but otherwise should be unique. The solution then is to use a *filtered unique index*.

The third and final constraint type is the *default constraint*. A default constraint specifies the value that will be used as the default value when an INSERT statement does not specify a value for the column.

Sequences

A sequence is a database object that generates a sequence of numeric values. How the sequence is generated is determined by its start value, increment value, and minimum and maximum values. A sequence can be ascending, which is the case when the increment value is positive. When the increment value is negative, the sequence is descending. A sequence object has some similarities to a column with an identity specification, but there are important distinctions:

- You can define a sequence to cycle, meaning that when the numbers in the sequence are exhausted, the next use will return a previously generated number. Which number will be returned when the sequence cycles is determined by the increment: if it is an ascending sequence, the minimum value is returned; if it is a descending sequence, the maximum value is returned.

- A sequence is not bound to any table. You can use numbers generated by the sequence in any table in the database, or outside of a table.

- Sequence numbers can be generated without inserting a new row in a table.

- Uniqueness is not enforced. If unique values are desired, a unique index should be placed on the column where the generated numbers are stored.

- Values generated from a sequence can be updated.

Sequences are used when the application wants to have a numeric sequence generated at any time; for example, before inserting one or more rows. Consider the common case of a parent–child relationship. Even though most developer tools expect to work with identity columns, knowing the value of a new parent row's primary key value and using it as the foreign key value in the child rows can have benefits for the application. A sequence is also useful when a single incrementing range is desired across multiple tables. More creative uses of a sequence include using a sequence with a small range—five, for example—to automatically and randomly place new rows in one of five buckets.

To create a sequence, use the CREATE SEQUENCE command. When creating the sequence, you specify the integer data type; the start, increment, minimum and maximum values; and whether the numbers should cycle when the minimum or maximum value is reached. However, all of these are optional. If no data type is specified, the type will be `bigint`. If no increment is specified, it will be 1. If no minimum or maximum value is specified, the minimum and maximum value of the underlying data type will be used. By default, a sequence does not cycle. The sample script that follows creates a sequence called MySequence of type `int`. The values start at 1001 and increment by 1 until 1003 is reached, after which 1001 will be generated again. The script demonstrates the cycling of the values using the WHILE loop.

```
-- Define the sequence
CREATE SEQUENCE dbo.MySequence AS int
    START WITH 1001
    INCREMENT BY 1
    MINVALUE 1001
    MAXVALUE 1003
    CYCLE;
-- Declare a loop counter
DECLARE @i int = 1;
-- Execute 4 times
WHILE (@i <= 4)
BEGIN
    -- Retrieve the next value from the sequence
    SELECT NEXT VALUE FOR dbo.MySequence AS NextValue;
    -- Increment the loop counter
    SET @i = @i + 1;
END
```

The output of the script will be 1001, 1002, 1003, and 1001. The sequence is used by calling NEXT VALUE FOR. You can use NEXT VALUE FOR as a default constraint or as a function parameter. There are, however, quite a few places where NEXT VALUE FOR cannot be used.

➤ For a listing of limitations, refer to Microsoft Docs at *https://docs.microsoft.com/sql/t-sql/ functions/next-value-for-transact-sql#limitations-and-restrictions*.

NOTE

Sequences are cached by default. You can turn off caching by specifying the NO CACHE clause in the CREATE SEQUENCE statement. You can control the size of the cache by using the CACHE clause and specifying an integer constant.

CAUTION

Using NEXT VALUE FOR multiples times for the same sequence in the same INSERT or UPDATE statement will result in only one value per row being used. For example, in the following Transact-SQL (T-SQL) snippet, the first and the second column of the new row will have the same value:

```
INSERT INTO dbo.SomeTable VALUES (NEXT VALUE FOR MySequence,
    NEXT VALUE FOR MySequence, 'More data...');
```

This is likely not the desired scenario. The solution is to use two separate sequences, though there would not be a guarantee that they would return different numbers even if their start values are different. If you must guarantee that the values are different, you should place a CHECK CONSTRAINT on the table. However, we recommend evaluating the need for having two columns in the same table with autogenerated numeric values.

NEXT VALUE FOR generates and returns a single value at a time. If multiple values should be generated at once, the application can use the `sp_sequence_get_range` stored procedure. This procedure generates as many numbers from the sequence as specified and returns metadata about the generated numbers. The actual values that have been generated are not returned. The sample script that follows uses the `MySequence` sequence to generate five numbers. The metadata is captured in variables and later output. You'll note that the data type of most output parameters is `sql_variant`. The underlying type of those parameters is the data type of the sequence.

```
-- Declare variables to hold the metadata
DECLARE @FirstVal sql_variant, @LastVal sql_variant,
    @Increment sql_variant, @CycleCount int,
    @MinVal sql_variant, @MaxVal sql_variant;
-- Generate 5 numbers and capture all metadata
EXEC sp_sequence_get_range 'MySequence'
    , @range_size = 5
    , @range_first_value = @FirstVal OUTPUT
    , @range_last_value = @LastVal OUTPUT
```

```
    , @range_cycle_count = @CycleCount OUTPUT
    , @sequence_increment = @Increment OUTPUT
    , @sequence_min_value = @MinVal OUTPUT
    , @sequence_max_value = @MaxVal OUTPUT;
-- Output the values of the output parameters
SELECT @FirstVal AS FirstVal, @LastVal AS LastVal
    , @CycleCount AS CycleCount, @Increment AS Increment
    , @MinVal AS MinVal, @MaxVal AS MaxVal;
```

The output of this sample script will vary with each run; however, every three cycles, it will repeat.

NOTE

Although the only required output parameter is @range_first_value, if the application actually intends to use any value but the first, the application should consume all the metadata that is returned as part of the optional output parameters. Without it, the application cannot reliably infer the values that were generated. It is up to the application to calculate the actual numbers that were generated by using the first value, last value, increment, minimum and maximum value, and cycle count output parameters.

TROUBLESHOOTING

You might receive error 11732 when using sequences.

This error indicates that the maximum value of the sequence has been reached and the sequence does not cycle. If this error occurs when using the sp_sequence_get_range stored procedure, no values are issued. That is, the sequence is not affected at all.

User-defined data types and user-defined types

SQL Server supports creating new data types. Two variations exist: user-defined data types (UDTs), which alias existing data types, and user-defined types, which are .NET Framework types. UDTs have no specific requirements because they are merely a new name for an existing system data type, optionally augmented with length or precision, nullability, a default value, or a validation rule. For example, if you want to ensure that a customer name was always defined as an nvarchar column with a max length of 100 characters, you might use the CREATE TYPE statement, as shown here:

```
CREATE TYPE CustomerNameType FROM NVARCHAR(100);
GO
```

After creating this UDT, in any place where you would ordinarily specify NVARCHAR(100), you can use CustomerNameType, instead. This can be in a table's column definition, as the return type of a scalar function, or as a parameter to a stored procedure. The following abbreviated

CREATE TABLE statement, which is based on the WideWorldImporters sample `Customers` table, illustrates how `CustomerNameType` replaces NVARCHAR(100):

```
CREATE TABLE [Sales].[Customers] (
    [CustomerID] INT NOT NULL,
    [CustomerName] CustomerNameType,
    ...
```

Though deprecated functionality, you can further extend the `CustomerNameType` UDT by providing a default value and enforcing validation using a specific rule. The T-SQL snippet that follows first defines a default with value `'NA'` and a rule that requires that the length is at least three characters or equals `'NA'`. It then binds the default and the rule to the `CustomerTypeName` UDT:

```
-- Create a database-wide default
CREATE DEFAULT CustomerNameDefault
AS 'NA';
GO
-- Create a database-wide validation rule
CREATE RULE CustomerNameRule
AS
-- Allow the value 'NA' (the default)
@value = 'NA' OR
-- Or require at least 3 characters
LEN(@value) >= 3;
GO
-- Bind the default and the rule to the CustomerNameType UDT
EXEC sp_bindefault 'CustomerNameDefault', 'CustomerNameType';
EXEC sp_bindrule 'CustomerNameRule', 'CustomerNameType';
```

> **NOTE**
>
> Notice the use of the GO statement between the CREATE statements. This is because each of these CREATE statements must be run in a separate batch.

After running these statements, most uses of the `CustomerNameType` will enforce the validation rule. The notable exception is when the data type is used in a variable declaration.

You develop user-defined types in a .NET language such as C#, and you must compile them into a .NET assembly. This .NET assembly is then registered in the database where the UDT will be used. A database can use these types only if SQL CLR is turned on.

We should warn against the liberal use of either variant of custom data types. They can make a database schema significantly more difficult to understand and troubleshoot. Alias types, in particular, add little value, because they do not create new behavior. SQL CLR types allow SQL Server to expose new behavior, but they come with a significant security risk.

CHAPTER 8

> **NOTE**
>
> User-defined types have a use for memory-optimized tables, which we discuss in the next section.

Sparse columns

As we just saw, a potential workaround for saving storage space for tables with many columns that allow null and have many null values is using sparse columns. When using sparse columns, less storage space for storing null values is traded for increased overhead to retrieve non-null values. Microsoft suggests that a space savings of at least 20 percent should be achieved before the overhead is worth it.

> ➤ The Microsoft Docs at *https://docs.microsoft.com/sql/relational-databases/tables/use-sparse-columns* define the space savings by data type when using sparse columns.

> **NOTE**
>
> Not all data types can be defined as sparse columns. Specifically, you cannot define geography and geometry, image, text and ntext, timestamp, and user-defined data types as sparse columns.

Sparse columns are defined in CREATE or ALTER TABLE statements by using the SPARSE keyword. The sample script that follows creates a table, OrderDetails, with two sparse columns, ReturnedDate and ReturnedReason. Sparse columns are useful here because we might expect most products not to be returned, in addition to retrieving only the ReturnedDate and ReturnedReason columns occasionally.

```
CREATE TABLE OrderDetails (
    OrderId int NOT NULL,
    OrderDetailId int NOT NULL,
    ProductId int NOT NULL,
    Quantity int NOT NULL,
    ReturnedDate date SPARSE NULL,
    ReturnedReason varchar(50) SPARSE NULL);
```

> **NOTE**
>
> For brevity, the CREATE TABLE script in the preceding example does not define primary keys or foreign keys, or indeed columns that you might typically expect in an order details table.

Computed columns

Mostly, columns store data that is original. Derived data—that is, data that is the result of a calculation—is not ordinarily stored. Instead, the application derives it every time it's needed. In some circumstances, storing derived data in the database can be beneficial. SQL Server supports storing derived data using computed columns and indexed views (indexed views are beyond the scope of this chapter). Computed columns are defined in a table as the result of an expression of other columns in the table, function calls, and perhaps constants.

And although derived data can be saved in the database, by default a computed column is not persisted. Any way you use a computed column is a trade-off. When using either type of computed column, you have decided that there is some benefit of having the database be aware of the derived data, which will require putting some business logic that computes the data in the database. You might find that more beneficial because the database could be the central source of the computation instead of having to spread it out across multiple systems. When you use persisted computed columns, you are trading storage space for compute efficiency.

If the expression that computes the computed column's value is deterministic, the computed column can also be indexed. An expression is deterministic if that expression will always return the same result for the same inputs. An example of a nondeterministic expression is one that uses the SYSDATETIME() function.

> **For a complete discussion of indexing computed columns, refer to Microsoft Docs at** *https://docs.microsoft.com/sql/relational-databases/indexes/ indexes-on-computed-columns*.

Using the WideWorldImporters sample database, you will find two computed columns in the Sales.Invoices table. One of those columns is ConfirmedDeliveryTime. It is derived by examining the contents of the JSON value stored in the ReturnedDeliveryData column and converting it to a datetime2 value. The datetime2 value is not persisted in this case. What this means is that each time the ConfirmedDeliveryTime is queried, the expression is evaluated. If the column was persisted, the expression would be evaluated only when the row is created or updated.

When you are defining a computed column, instead of specifying a data type, you specify an expression following the AS clause. Using the Sales.OrderLines table in the same sample database, you can create a computed column to calculate the order line's extended price. The following sample SQL statement illustrates how:

```
ALTER TABLE Sales.OrderLines
    ADD ExtendedPrice AS (Quantity * UnitPrice) PERSISTED;
```

This statement creates a new column in the table called ExtendedPrice. This column's value is computed by using the expression Quantity * UnitPrice. The column is saved because we expect to be querying this value frequently. The type of the computed column is determined by SQL Server based on the result of the expression. In this case, the data type is set to decimal(29,2). If the determined data type is not suitable for your needs, you can apply a cast to a data type that is more appropriate.

Special table types

As data storage needs have become more specialized, SQL Server has gained extended functionality to support these scenarios in the form of special table types. These table types support scenarios that would otherwise have required significant effort on behalf of the DBA to implement. Thus, although the table types discussed in this section support requirements that can be implemented without them, using these tables makes it possible for you to offload some of the work to the Database Engine. This section discusses temporal tables, memory-optimized tables, external tables, and graph tables. We discuss another special table type, FileTable, in the next section.

System-versioned temporal tables

System-versioned temporal tables, or "temporal tables" for short, are designed to keep not only current values of rows, but also historic values. When a table is designed to be a temporal table, it has two explicitly defined columns of type `datetime2` that are used to indicate the validity period of the row. In addition to the current table, there is a companion history table with the same schema. SQL Server can create the history table at the time the current table is created, but you will need to specify the history table's name. Alternatively, you might use an existing table as the history table, in which case the Database Engine will validate that the schema matches.

NOTE

The row's start and end validity columns are managed by SQL Server. The values in those columns are in the UTC time zone. Neither validity period column will ever be NULL.

SQL Server manages the movement of data from the current table to the history table. The following list indicates what happens with each Data Manipulation Language (DML) operation:

- **INSERT and BULK INSERT.**   A new row is added to the current table. The row's validity start time is set to the transaction's start time. The validity end time is set to the `datetime2` type's maximum value: December 31, 9999 at a fractional second, or whole second when using `datetime2(0)`, before midnight. There is no change in the history table.

- **UPDATE.**   A new row is added to the history table with the old values. The validity end time is set to the transaction's start time. In the current table, the row is updated with the new values and the validity start time is updated to the transaction's start time. Should the same row be updated multiple times in the same transaction, multiple history rows with the same validity start and end time will be inserted.

- **DELETE.**   A new row is added to the history table containing the values from the current table. The validity end period is set to the transaction's start time. The row is removed from the current table.

NOTE

A merge statement needs no special consideration: the merge will still run insert, update, and delete statements as needed. Those statements will add and update rows, as just described.

Querying a temporal table is no different from querying another table if your query only needs to return current data. This makes it possible to modify an existing database and alter tables into temporal tables without requiring application modifications. When designing queries that need to return historical data or even a mix of current and historical data, you use the FOR SYSTEM_TIME clause in the FROM clause of the SELECT statement. There are five subclauses used with FOR SYSTEM_TIME that help you define the time frame for which you want to retrieve rows. The list that follows describes these subclauses as well as provides a sample SQL statement of each one that you can run against the WideWorldImporters sample database to see the effects of the subclause.

NOTE

The IsCurrent column in the output indicates whether the row that is retrieved is the current row or a history row. This is accomplished by simply checking whether the ValidTo column contains the maximum datetime2 value. Due to the nature of the WideWorldImporters sample data, you might need to scroll through several hundred rows before encountering a value of 0 for IsCurrent, which indicates that it is a history row.

- **ALL.**   The result set is essentially the union between the current and the history tables. Multiple rows can be returned for the same primary key in the current table. This will be the case for any row that has one or more history entries, as shown here:

```
SELECT PersonID, FullName,
    CASE WHEN ValidTo = '9999-12-31 23:59:59.9999999' THEN 1
        ELSE 0 END AS IsCurrent
FROM Application.People FOR SYSTEM_TIME ALL
ORDER BY ValidFrom;
```

- **AS OF.**   The AS OF clause returns rows that were valid at the single point in time in the UTC time zone. Rows that had been deleted from the current table or didn't exist yet will not be included:

```
SELECT PersonID, FullName,
    CASE WHEN ValidTo = '9999-12-31 23:59:59.9999999' THEN 1
        ELSE 0 END AS IsCurrent
FROM Application.People FOR SYSTEM_TIME AS OF '2016-03-13'
ORDER BY ValidFrom;
```

- **FROM ... TO.** This subclause returns all rows that were active between the specified lower bound and upper bound. In other words, if the row's validity start time is before the upper bound *or* its validity end time is after the lower bound, the row will be included in the result set. Rows that became active exactly on the upper bound are not included. Rows that closed exactly on the lower bound are not included. This clause might return multiple rows for the same primary key value:

```
SELECT PersonID, FullName,
    CASE WHEN ValidTo = '9999-12-31 23:59:59.9999999' THEN 1
        ELSE 0 END AS IsCurrent
FROM Application.People FOR SYSTEM_TIME FROM '2016-03-13' TO '2016-04-23'
ORDER BY ValidFrom;
```

- **BETWEEN ... AND.** This is like FROM ... TO, but rows that opened exactly on the upper bound are included, as well:

```
SELECT PersonID, FullName,
    CASE WHEN ValidTo = '9999-12-31 23:59:59.9999999' THEN 1
        ELSE 0 END AS IsCurrent
FROM Application.People FOR SYSTEM_TIME BETWEEN '2016-03-13' AND '2016-04-23'
ORDER BY ValidFrom;
```

- **CONTAINED IN (,).** This subclause returns rows that were active only between the lower and the upper bound. If a row was valid earlier than the lower bound or valid past the upper bound, it is not included. A row that was opened exactly on the lower bound or closed exactly on the upper bound will be included. If the upper bound is earlier than the maximum value for `datetime2`, only history rows will be included:

```
DECLARE @now DATETIME2 = SYSUTCDATETIME();
SELECT PersonID, FullName,
    CASE WHEN ValidTo = '9999-12-31 23:59:59.9999999' THEN 1
        ELSE 0 END AS IsCurrent
FROM Application.People FOR SYSTEM_TIME CONTAINED IN ('2016-03-13', @now)
ORDER BY ValidFrom;
```

NOTE

In the sample statement for the CONTAINED IN subclause, the variable @now is declared and initialized with the current UTC time. This is necessary because the FOR SYSTEM_TIME clause does not support functions as arguments.

Inside OUT

How can I design temporal tables to use the least amount of space?

New for SQL Server 2017, you can use the new HISTORY_RETENTION_PERIOD
option with the SYSTEM_VERSIONING option when defining or altering system-
versioned temporal tables. By default, the HISTORY_RETENTION_PERIOD is
INFINITE, meaning that SQL Server will not automatically purge history data. By
defining a finite period, such as 6 MONTHS, SQL Server will automatically purge history records with a valid end time older than the finite period. Two conditions must
hold true: first, the temporal history retention flag must be turned on for the database (which it is by default), and second, the history table must have a clustered or
Columnstore index.

In addition to using automatic retention, which controls the growth of the history
table, you can also consider vertically partitioning the temporal table. Vertical partitioning is discussed in more detail in the section "Vertical partitioning" later in this
chapter. By splitting the table vertically into two tables, and only making one table
system versioned, you can achieve significant space savings because history will
be kept only for the columns in the system-versioned table. This does come at the
expense of potentially frequent JOINs between both tables. This approach is also not
suitable if you are system-versioning tables for compliance requirements for which
row data must be available in exactly the form it was at any given point.

In addition to reducing the history kept by setting a retention period and using
vertical partitioning to avoid keeping history for columns that do not require it, you
might also consider Stretch Database, horizontal partitioning, or a custom cleanup
script to manage the history data. These options are described in detail at
*https://docs.microsoft.com/sql/relational-databases/tables/manage-retention-of-historical-data-
in-system-versioned-temporal-tables*.

NOTE

Temporal tables might provide a solution that also can be addressed by change tracking
or change data capture. Later sections in this chapter cover change tracking and change
data capture and provide a comparison of the three features.

Memory-optimized tables

A traditional database table's data is loaded in memory as needed to efficiently run queries. The
operations of loading data from durable storage to memory and removing the data from memory again is handled by the Database Engine. Many factors play a role in when data is loaded or

released from memory. Memory-optimized tables avoid this by ensuring that the data is always available in memory. This data is durable by default by using the transaction log and saving to the drive. A "schema only" option is available, which does not save data between service restarts and certain other operations.

The benefits of keeping all data from specific tables in memory is blazing-fast performance, which often can be improved by another order of magnitude by applying a Columnstore index to the memory-optimized table. (Columnstore indexes are covered in Chapter 9 and Chapter 10.) This of course requires that the server has sufficient memory to hold the memory-optimized tables' data in memory while still leaving enough room for other operations.

➤ This chapter discusses only the setup and configuration of memory-optimized tables along with caveats. You can find complete discussion of the purpose and the use of memory-optimized tables in Chapter 10.

Memory-optimized tables are available in all editions of SQL Server and in Azure SQL Database's Premium Tier.

NOTE

Over time, many limitations of memory-optimized tables that were present in earlier versions of SQL Server have been eliminated.

Database preparation for memory-optimized tables

First, you must prepare the database. There are two database requirements: the database compatibility level must be at least 130 and the snapshot isolation level must be supported. For SQL Server, you need to create a memory-optimized filegroup. There is no such requirement for Azure SQL Database; or, more accurately, the filegroup is intrinsically present.

Microsoft provides a T-SQL script to ensure that these settings are correct and that a memory-optimized filegroup is created. You can even run the script in Azure SQL Database to ensure that the database supports memory-optimized tables. Rather than reprinting this script here, we refer you to the GitHub content.

➤ See the GitHub user content page at *https://raw.githubusercontent.com/Microsoft/sql-server-samples/master/samples/features/in-memory/t-sql-scripts/enable-in-memory-oltp.sql*.

The script first checks to ensure that the instance or database supports memory-optimized tables. If you're running on SQL Server, the script will create a memory-optimized filegroup and container if none already exist. The script also checks and sets the database compatibility level.

After these actions are complete, you are ready to create one or more memory-optimized tables. The WITH (MEMORY_OPTIMIZED = ON) is the key clause that will create a memory-optimized table. Memory-optimized tables support indexing, but you must create and delete them using an ALTER TABLE ... ADD/DROP INDEX statement instead of a CREATE/DROP INDEX statement.

Natively compiled stored procedures and user-defined functions

You can access memory-optimized tables via standard T-SQL statements and stored procedures. However, you can achieve significant additional performance gains if you use natively compiled stored procedures. These stored procedures are compiled to machine code the first time they are run rather than evaluated every time they run.

NOTE

Natively compiled stored procedures can access only memory-optimized tables. Traditional interpreted stored procedures and ad hoc queries can reference both disk-based tables and memory-optimized tables, even in the same statement (for example, to join a memory-optimized table with a disk-table).

To create a natively compiled stored procedure, use the WITH NATIVE_COMPILATION clause of the CREATE PROCEDURE statement. In addition, the BEGIN ATOMIC statement is required instead of BEGIN TRANSACTION for natively compiled procedures and functions. This statement either begins a new transaction or creates a savepoint in an existing transaction on the session. The BEGIN ATOMIC statement has two options:

- **TRANSACTION_ISOLATION.** You must set this value to one of the three supported isolation levels: snapshot, repeatable read, or serializable.

- **LANGUAGE.** This is a name value from the sys.syslanguages system compatibility view. For example, for United States English, it is us_english, and for Dutch it is Nederlands.

The BEGIN ATOMIC statement is also where delayed durability can be specified (DELAYED_DURABILITY = ON). Delayed durability means that the Database Engine will report to the client that the transaction committed before the log record has been committed to a drive. This creates a risk of data loss should the service or server shut down before the asynchronous log write is completed. You should take the same care to use delayed durability with BEGIN ATOMIC as with BEGIN TRANSACTION. Further, to use delayed durability, it must also be allowed at the database level. Schema-only memory-optimized tables already do not use transaction logging, so when modifying data in those tables, there is no benefit in specifying delayed durability.

NOTE

Several T-SQL statements and constructs are not supported combined with memory-optimized tables and natively compiled stored procedures. A full list of these unsupported constructs is available in Microsoft Docs at *https://docs.microsoft.com/sql/relational-databases/in-memory-oltp/ transact-sql-constructs-not-supported-by-in-memory-oltp*.

Caveats to memory-optimized tables

To put it plainly, you should probably not convert all of your tables to memory-optimized tables. There are several caveats that must be considered before adopting memory-optimized tables and when deciding which tables to turn into memory-optimized tables. We discuss these caveats in this section.

Memory-optimized tables support only three transaction isolation levels: snapshot, repeatable read, and serializable. If your application has a need for other isolation levels, you will not be able to implement memory-optimized tables.

CAUTION

Changing the database's read commit snapshot property will cause schema-only memory-optimized tables to be truncated. Although database designers are aware that schema-only memory-optimized tables are not saved and might need to load initial data at service start, they might not know to load data after a database property change.

Due to all table data being kept in memory, you would naturally expect additional memory requirements. However, when planning for memory size, you should consider that the memory requirement of a memory-optimized table can be more than twice that of the size of the data in the table. This is because of processing overhead requirements.

➤ To review specific guidance on planning for memory size, refer to Microsoft Docs at *https://docs.microsoft.com/sql/relational-databases/in-memory-oltp/ estimate-memory-requirements-for-memory-optimized-tables*.

CAUTION

If you do not carefully plan and monitor them, the memory demands of memory-optimized tables can cause out-of-memory (OOM) conditions on the server. This can lead to lost data and server instability. You can read about how to deal with OOM conditions at *https://docs.microsoft.com/sql/relational-databases/in-memory-oltp/ resolve-out-of-memory-issues*.

When persisted memory-optimized tables are used, upon service start, the Database Engine will load all data from the drive to memory. The service is not available while this operation takes place. With large tables, this can lead to significantly longer service start times. Even though you might carefully plan your service or server restarts for a maintenance window, an unplanned failover on a failover cluster instance (FCI) can take significantly longer. This might be detrimental to meeting your Service-Level Agreement (SLA), which might have been the entire reason to configure an FCI in the first place. If the performance of memory-optimized tables is needed in combination with a high-availability configuration, you might consider Always On availability groups, instead. Because the Database Engine service is running on the secondary, there is no delay caused by having to read the data from a drive.

One way to reduce database startup time due to memory-optimized tables is to ensure that checkpoints are taken frequently. That's because checkpoints cause the updated rows in the memory-optimized table to be committed to the data file. Any data that is not committed to the data file must be read from the transaction log. However, for large tables, this benefit is likely small.

Another contributor to delays, though after service start, is when natively compiled stored procedures are run for the first time; this can take about as long as running a traditional stored procedure. This is because the compiled version of the stored procedure is not saved. Any time a natively compiled stored procedure is run subsequently, the compiled version will be faster.

Memory-optimized tables use an optimistic concurrency model. Instead of locks, latches are used. This means that a client application might experience unexpected conflicts. You should design the application to handle those.

Not unlike when faster drive storage is used for SQL Server, when adopting memory-optimized tables, you might find that the CPU usage is much higher. This is because much less time is spent waiting for I/O operations to complete. The first consideration on this point is that this is exactly the reason why you implemented memory-optimized tables: the CPU utilization is higher because data is being processed faster! Another consideration could be that you might inadvertently reduce the number of concurrent requests that can be served, especially if one instance runs multiple databases. If this is a concern, you can consider using a Resource Governor to manage the relative CPU usage for each database.

PolyBase external tables

PolyBase external tables bring SQL Server into the NoSQL era. An external table is a reference to one of two types of nonrelational data stores. (A third type is a reference to a table in another Azure SQL Database to configure elastic query, but that scenario is beyond the scope for this chapter.) Specifically, an external table can reference a Hadoop hive or an Azure Storage blob. The data in the hive or Storage blob must be of a known format; for example, a text-delimited file.

After the external table is defined, you can query it by using T-SQL alongside the relational data stored in the SQL Server database. You also can import data in the relational tables.

To define an external table referencing a Hadoop hive or Azure Storage blob, three steps are required. First, an external data source is defined, which determines the type and location of the external data. Next, an external file format is set. This determines the format of the external data. SQL Server recognizes delimited text, RCFile, and ORC formats. The third and final step is to define the actual external table.

➤ **For details on creating and working with PolyBase external tables, refer to Microsoft Docs at** *https://docs.microsoft.com/sql/t-sql/statements/create-external-table-transact-sql.*

NOTE

PolyBase is not currently available on SQL Server on Linux.

Graph tables

New to SQL Server 2017, graph functionality provides schema extensions to store directed graph data—that is, nodes and edges—in the relational database. Fitting graph data in a relational database is challenging, and this new feature attempts to resolve these challenges. The graph features in SQL Server 2017 solve common issues but are not a complete replacement for dedicated graph databases that support advanced scenarios.

NOTE

Graph features are also generally available in Azure SQL Database as of September 2017.

Graph data is often associated with networks, such as social networks. More generally, graphs are data structures that consist of *nodes* and *edges*. The nodes represent entities, and the edges represent the connections between those entities. We are using the term "entities" here in a more generic fashion than what you commonly think of as entities in a relational model. Nodes are also referred to as *vertices*, and edges as *relationships*.

Some use cases lend themselves particularly well to be stored in a graph model. Examples of such use cases include the following:

- **Interconnected data.**   A commonly used example of interconnected data is that of social networks. Social network data expresses relationships among people, organizations, posts, pictures, events, and more. In such a data model, each entity can be connected to any other entity, creating lots of many-to-many relationships. In a relational database, this requires the creation of a join table for each many-to-many relationship.

Querying such relationships requires two or more INNER JOIN clauses, which can quickly create lengthy SELECT statements. Such statements can be difficult to digest and are potentially error prone. Graph databases support flexible definitions of relationships.

- **Hierarchical data.**   SQL Server provides a specialized data type, `hierarchyid` (discussed earlier) that supports modeling simple tree hierarchies. One limitation of this data type is its inability to support multiple parents. A node in a graph is not limited like that, and a single node can have many parents in addition to many children.

- **Many-to-many relationships that can be extended at any time during the data life cycle.**   Relational databases have strict requirements for the definition of tables and relationships. For a data model that can evolve quickly to require new relationships, this strict schema requirement can get in the way of meeting evolving requirements.

You can effectively implement these use cases by employing a graph database, but it is important to note that SQL Server 2017's graph features do not (yet) provide a solution that is on-par with dedicated graph databases. We discuss some of the limitations of the current implementation in the section "Current graph table shortcomings" later in the chapter.

Defining graph tables

In SQL Server 2017 and Azure SQL Database, you can store graph data in two new types of table: *node* and *edge* tables. These table types are still stored internally as relational structures, but the Database Engine has additional capabilities to manage and query the data that is stored within them. The T-SQL CREATE TABLE syntax has been extended with two new clauses: AS NODE and AS EDGE. The following T-SQL script creates a Person node table and a Relationship edge table, and you can run the script in any existing or new database; there are no specific requirements of the database:

```
CREATE TABLE dbo.People (
    PersonId INT NOT NULL PRIMARY KEY CLUSTERED,
    FirstName NVARCHAR(50) NOT NULL,
    LastName NVARCHAR(50) NOT NULL
) AS NODE;
CREATE TABLE Relationships (
    RelationshipType NVARCHAR(50) NOT NULL
) AS EDGE;
```

In the sample script, both the node and the edge table contain user-defined columns. Edge tables are not required to have user-defined columns, but node tables must have at least one. In the case of edge tables, which model relationships, simply modeling the relationship without additional attributes can be desirable. In the case of node tables, which model entities, there is no value in a node without properties. Designing a node table is comparable to designing a relational table; you would still consider normalization and other concepts.

In addition to user-defined columns, both table types also have one or more implicit columns. Node tables have one implicit (also called pseudo) column, $node_id, which uniquely identifies the node in the database. This pseudo-column is backed by two actual columns:

- **graph_id_<hex_string_1>.**   This is a BIGINT column, which stores the internally generated graph ID for the row. This column is internal and cannot be explicitly queried.

- **$node_id_<hex_string_2>.**   This column can be queried and returns a computed NVARCHAR value that includes the internally generated BIGINT value and schema information. You should avoid explicitly querying this column. Instead, you should query the $node_id implicit pseudo column.

In addition to optional user-defined columns, edge tables have three implicit columns:

- **$edge_id_<hex_string_3>.**   This is a system-managed value, comparable to the $node_id column in a node table.

- **$from_id_<hex_string_4>.**   This references a node ID from any node table in the graph. This is the source node in the directed graph.

- **$to_id_<hex_string_5>.**   This references a node ID from any node table in the graph, whether it is the same or a different table than the $from_id$ node's table. This is the target node in the directed graph.

Inside OUT

When should I choose graph tables over relational tables?

First, it's important to understand that there is nothing inherent to a graph database that makes it possible for you to solve a problem that you cannot also solve using a relational database. The relational database concept has been around for nearly five decades, and relational database management systems are as popular as ever.

The use cases described earlier and queries described momentarily are examples of data models and operations that might be better addressed by a graph database. This is because the Database Engine has specific optimizations to address some of the particular types of queries that are often run against such models.

In addition, a graph table can still contain foreign keys referring to relational tables, and a relational table can contain a foreign key referring to a graph table.

Working with graph data

DML statements generally work the same in graph tables as they do in relational tables. Some operations are not supported, though. An edge table does not support updating either of the node values. Thus, to update a relationship, the existing edge row must be deleted and a new one inserted. User-defined columns of edge tables do support update operations.

When querying graph data, you can write your own table joins to join nodes to edges to nodes, though this approach offers none of the benefits of graph tables. Instead, using the new MATCH subclause in the WHERE clause, you can use a new style of expression, referred to as *ASCII art*, to indicate how nodes and edges should be traversed. You might be surprised to find that the node and edge tables are joined using old-style join syntax first. The MATCH subclause then performs the actual equi-joins necessary to traverse the graph.

> ### NOTE
> Although it is possible to combine the old-style join syntax with JOIN clauses, for long-term maintainability of the query, it might be better for you to stick with a single join style, or to create a correlated subquery using the old-style join syntax and graph MATCH clause.

The brief example that follows is intended to provide an introduction only. It builds on the creation of the People and Relationship tables shown in the previous example. First, a few rows of sample data are inserted. Then, the sample data is queried by using the MATCH subclause:

```
-- Insert a few sample people
-- $node_id is implicit and skipped
INSERT INTO People VALUES
    (1, 'Karina', 'Jakobsen'),
    (2, 'David', 'Hamilton'),
    (3, 'James', 'Hamilton');
-- Insert a few sample relationships
-- The first sub-select retrieves the $node_id of the from_node
-- The second sub-select retrieves the $node_id of the to node
INSERT INTO Relationships VALUES
    ((SELECT $node_id FROM People WHERE PersonId = 1),
     (SELECT $node_id FROM People WHERE PersonId = 2),
     'spouse'),
    ((SELECT $node_id FROM People WHERE PersonId = 2),
     (SELECT $node_id FROM People WHERE PersonId = 3),
     'father');
-- Simple graph query
SELECT P1.FirstName + ' is the ' + R.RelationshipType +
    ' of ' + P2.FirstName + '.'
FROM People P1, People P2, Relationships R
WHERE MATCH(P1-(R)->P2);
```

The ASCII art syntax used in the MATCH subclause means that a node in the `People` table should be related to another node in the `People` table using the `Relations` edge. As with self-referencing many-to-many relationships, the `People` table needs to be present in the FROM clause twice to allow the second `People` node to be different from the first. Otherwise, the query would retrieve only edges in which people are related to themselves (there is no such relationship in our sample).

The true power of the MATCH subclause is evident when traversing edges between three or more nodes. One such example would be finding restaurants your friends have liked in the city where your friends live and where you intend to travel.

> ➤ For a more comprehensive sample graph database, refer to Microsoft Docs at *https://docs.microsoft.com/sql/relational-databases/graphs/sql-graph-sample*.

Current graph table shortcomings

This first release of SQL Server with support for graph models is missing several features that dedicated graph databases usually have. This doesn't mean that the current graph support isn't useful, but if your short-term needs for graph support require these features, SQL Server might not yet be the right solution for you. The following list contains the most notable missing graph features and a brief description of their significance for graph processing. Hopefully, this will provide the information you need to make an informed decision about using SQL Server for graph data.

- **No graph analytic functions.**   Graph processing commonly involves finding answers to common questions, such as, "What is the shortest path between two nodes?" There are specific algorithms that are used to find answers to these questions. However, SQL Server does not implement any graph analytic functions.

- **Need to explicitly define edges as tables.**   Graphs model pairwise relations between entities (the nodes). Flexibility can be key in maximizing the benefits of graph models. Even though the nodes are often well understood, including their properties, new relationships can be modeled as new needs arise or additional possibilities emerge. The need to make schema modifications to support new types of edges reduces flexibility. Some of this can be addressed by defining one or few edge tables and storing the edge properties as XML or JSON. This approach, too, has drawbacks in terms of performance and ease of writing queries against the data.

- **No transitive closures.**   The current MATCH subclause syntax does not support querying recursively. A transitive closure is when node A is connected to node B, which is in turn connected to node C, and we want to traverse the graph from node A to node C, but we don't know that node B is involved at all; or, indeed, that there might even be a node B1 involved. Currently, MATCH can traverse multiple edges but the query needs to be defined knowing which edges and how many edges are involved. As an alternative, you could write a recursive common table expression (CTE) or a T-SQL loop. Dedicated graph databases can traverse graphs without being directed as to which edges and how many edges to use.

- **No polymorphism.**   Polymorphism is the ability to find a node of any type connected to a specified starting node. In SQL Server, a workaround for graph models with few node and edge types is to query all known node and edge types and combine the result sets by using a UNION clause. For large graph models, this solution becomes impractical.

Storing BLOBs

Storing LOBs, and more specifically BLOBs, in the relational database has been known to cause debate. Prior to SQL Server offering the FILESTREAM feature as a specialized way for the Database Engine to manage BLOBs using the file system, database designers had two suboptimal choices:

- Store the BLOB, such as an image, video, or document file, in a VARBINARY column. Downsides of this approach include rapid growth of the data file, frequent page splits, and pollution of the buffer pool. Benefits include transactional integrity and integrated backup and recovery of the BLOB data.

- Have the application store the BLOB in the file system and use an NVARCHAR column to store the file system path to the file. Downsides of this approach include requiring the application to manage data integrity (e.g., avoiding orphaned or missing files) and lack of integrated security (i.e., the security mechanism to secure the BLOBs is an entirely different model than that for protecting the database). There are some benefits, though, primarily around performance and ease of programming for the client to work with the BLOBs (i.e., using traditional file I/O APIs provided by the OS).

The FILESTREAM feature is designed to provide a way to have the best of both alternatives. FILESTREAM is not a data type as much as it is an extension to VARBINARY(max). This section discusses FILESTREAM and FileTable. FileTable builds on FILESTREAM, so we first cover FILESTREAM and then FileTable.

NOTE
This book does not cover the programming models for accessing FILESTREAM data from client applications. There are many online resources available that discuss the nuances of designing applications for FILESTREAM.

CHAPTER 8

Understanding FILESTREAM

To take advantage of FILESTREAM, there are three requirements. First, the instance must be configured to allow at least one of several levels of FILESTREAM. Second, your database will need to have at least one FILESTREAM filegroup. Third, any table containing a FILESTREAM column requires a unique, non-null `rowguid`. A FILESTREAM filegroup refers to a location on an NT File System (NTFS) or Resilient File System (ReFS) volume that is under the control of the Database Engine. This location will be used by the Database Engine to store the binary data and log files for the binary data.

When a FILESTREAM filegroup is available in the database, FILESTREAM can be used as a modifier on VARBINARY(MAX) columns. When creating a table with a FILESTREAM column, you can specify on which filegroup the FILESTREAM data will be stored. When multiple FILESTREAM files are added to a single filegroup, the files will be used in round-robin fashion, as long as they don't exceed their maximum size.

In general, FILESTREAM's performance benefits kick in when the average BLOB size is 1 MB or larger. For smaller BLOB sizes, storing the BLOBs in the database file using a VARBINARY(MAX) column is better for performance. However, you might determine that the ease of programming against file I/O APIs in the client application is an overriding factor and decide to use FILESTREAM even with smaller BLOBs.

Additionally, if any of your BLOBs exceed 2 GB in size, you will need to use FILESTREAM; `varbinary(max)` supports a maximum BLOB size of 2 GB. Another reason for choosing FILESTREAM is the ability to integrate the BLOBs with SQL Server semantic search. To be clear, VARBINARY(MAX) columns can also be integrated with semantic search, but BLOBs stored in traditional file systems files cannot.

➤ More information about Semantic Search is available online at *https://docs.microsoft.com/ sql/relational-databases/search/semantic-search-sql-server*.

Inside OUT

How can I move data from a VARBINARY(MAX) *column to* FILESTREAM*?*

Unfortunately, moving from VARBINARY(MAX) columns to FILESTREAM is not as easy as modifying the column to add the FILESTREAM modifier. Attempting to modify the column in that way will result in an error. Instead, you should use the following three-step process, after creating a FILESTREAM file group:

1. Create a new VARBINARY(MAX) FILESTREAM column in the table or in another table if you want to use vertical partitioning.

2. Copy the data from the existing VARBINARY(MAX) column to the new FILESTREAM column. The amount of database activity that will be caused by this operation can be significant, depending on the number of rows and the size of the BLOBs.

3. Drop the VARBINARY(MAX) column. Optionally, you can then rename the FILESTREAM column to the name of the dropped column. Until you have (optionally) deployed a modified application that uses the I/O APIs with FILESTREAM, the existing T-SQL statements will continue to work on the FILESTREAM column.

In addition to potentially causing significant database activity, you also need to ensure that sufficient storage space is available to hold both copies of the data. Perhaps you are using the opportunity to move the BLOBs to different storage hardware, in which case this might be less of a concern.

Even though FILESTREAM BLOBs are stored in the file system, they are managed by the Database Engine. That includes transactional consistency and point-in-time restores. Thus, when a BLOB is deleted, the file on the drive backing that BLOB is not immediately deleted. Similarly, when a BLOB is updated, an entirely new file is written and the previous version is kept on the drive. When the deleted file or previous file version is no longer needed, the Database Engine will eventually delete the file using a garbage collection process. You are already aware of the importance of taking transaction log backups with databases in the full recovery model. That way, the transaction log can be truncated and stop growing. When using FILESTREAM, this mantra applies double: the number of files will keep growing until they are deleted by the garbage collector.

CAUTION
You should never modify the FILESTREAM folder's (a "data container") contents manually. Doing so can lead to FILESTREAM data corruption.

FileTable

FileTable makes it possible to access BLOBs managed by the Database Engine using traditional file share semantics. Applications that can read and write from a file share can access the BLOBs managed by the SQL Server engine. Although clients can use file I/O APIs to work with FILESTREAM, obtaining a handle to the BLOB requires using specific client libraries and application modifications. There might be applications that cannot be modified to work with FILESTREAM but for which having the BLOBs managed by the relational engine would have significant advantages. To that end, FileTable, which is a special table type, was developed.

CHAPTER 8

NOTE

FileTable is not currently available on SQL Server on Linux.

A FileTable has a fixed schema. This means that you can neither add user-defined columns nor can you remove columns. The only control provided is the ability to define indexes on some FileTable columns. The fixed schema has a FILESTREAM column that stores the actual file data in addition to many metadata columns and the non-null unique `rowguid` column required of any table containing FILESTREAM data. FileTable can organize data hierarchically, meaning folders and subfolders are supported concepts.

➤ **For a detailed discussion of the FileTable schema, refer to Microsoft Docs at** *https://docs.microsoft.com/sql/relational-databases/blob/filetable-schema*.

Table partitioning

Table partitioning occurs when you design a table that stores data from a single logical entity in physically separate structures. In other words, rather than storing all of the entity's data in a single physical data structure, it is split into multiple physical data structures. They continue to be treated by the user as a single unit. Table partitioning has multiple purposes, most of which relate to performance, either when querying or when loading data. We discuss this later in detail. We first distinguish between horizontal and vertical partitioning, as illustrated in Figure 8-3, and then discuss each separately with its common use cases and recommendations.

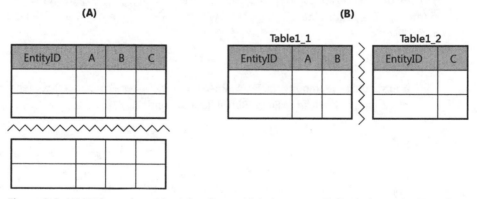

Figure 8-3 (A) Horizontal partitioning splits a table's data rows. (B) Vertical partitioning splits a table's columns.

As Figure 8-3 illustrates, horizontal and vertical partitioning are distinctly different. Horizontal partitioning splits the data rows, and each partition has the same schema. Vertical partitioning splits the entity's columns across multiple tables. The diagram shows a table partitioned in only two partitions. However, you can partition tables into many partitions. You can also mix horizontal and vertical partitioning.

NOTE

In SQL Server, "partitioning" usually refers to horizontal partitioning only. In this book, we discuss both horizontal and vertical partitioning, and, as such, we always explicitly define which partitioning type is being discussed.

Horizontally partitioned tables and indexes

In a large-scale database, in which a single table can grow to hundreds of gigabytes and more, some operations become more difficult. For example, adding new rows can take an excessive amount of time and might also cause SELECT queries against the table to fail due to lock escalation. Similar concerns exist with respect to removing data and index maintenance.

Horizontal partitioning can address these concerns, but it is also important to understand that it is not a silver bullet that will make all performance problems in large tables disappear. On the contrary, when applied incorrectly, horizontal partitioning can have a negative effect on your database workload. This section builds on the brief discussion of partitioning found in Chapter 3.

NOTE

Support for horizontal partitioning was limited to the Enterprise edition of SQL Server until the release of SQL Server 2016 Service Pack 1. Since then, all editions support horizontal table and index partitioning.

About horizontal partitioning

When partitioning a table, the rows of the table are not stored in the same physical place. When designing partitions, you decide on a partition key, which is the column that will be used to assign a row to exactly one partition. From a logical viewpoint, however, all rows belong to the same table. A query without a WHERE clause returns all rows, regardless of which partition they are stored in. This means that the Database Engine must do more work to retrieve rows from different partitions. Your goal when partitioning for query performance should be to write queries that eliminate partitions. You can accomplish this by including the partition key in the WHERE clause.

CHAPTER 8

Additional benefits of horizontal partitioning include the ability to set specific filegroups to read-only. By mapping partitions containing older data to read-only filegroups, you can be assured that this data is unchangeable without affecting your ability to insert new rows. In addition, you could exclude the read-only filegroups from regular backups. Finally, during a restore, filegroups containing the most recent data could be restored first, allowing new transactions to be recorded faster than if the entire database would need to be restored.

NOTE

Restoring selected files or filegroups while keeping the database available is called an _online restore_, which is still supported only in the Enterprise edition.

In addition to horizontal table partitioning, SQL Server also supports _index partitioning_. A partitioned index is said to be aligned with the table if they are partitioned in the same number of partitions using the same column and boundary values. When a partitioned index is aligned, you can direct index maintenance operations to a specific partition. This can significantly speed up the maintenance operation compared to rebuilding the index for the entire table. On the other hand, if the entire index needs to be rebuilt, SQL Server will attempt to do so in a parallel fashion. Rebuilding multiple indexes simultaneously will create memory pressure. Because of this concern, we recommend that you do not use partitioning on a server with less than 16 GB of RAM.

NOTE

Most commonly, achieving an aligned index is done by using the same partition function and scheme as the table. However, it is not strictly necessary to create an aligned partitioned index. When modifying the partition function for the table, you would need to remember to modify the function for the index simultaneously. Therefore, we recommend that you use one partition function for both database objects.

You might benefit from creating a partitioned index without partitioning the table. You can still use this nonaligned index to improve query efficiency if only one or a few of the index partitions need to be used. In this case, you will also use the index' partition key in the WHERE clause to gain the performance benefit of eliminating partitions.

Defining partitions and partitioning a table

We now demonstrate how to create a partitioned table. Three database objects are involved in defining partitions and partitioning a table:

- A partition function, which defines the number of partitions and the boundary values

- A partition scheme, which defines on which filegroup each partition is placed

- The partitioned table

NOTE

For brevity, the following script does not show the creation of the database with the file-groups and files necessary to support the partition scheme. The sample script included with the book downloads does include the CREATE DATABASE statement.

```
-- Create a partition function for February 1, 2017 through January 1, 2018
CREATE PARTITION FUNCTION MonthPartitioningFx (datetime2)
    -- Store the boundary values in the right partition
    AS RANGE RIGHT
    -- Each month is defined by its first day (the boundary value)
    FOR VALUES ('20170201', '20170301', '20170401',
        '20170501', '20170601', '20170701', '20170801',
        '20170901', '20171001', '20171101', '20171201', '20180101');
-- Create a partition scheme using the partition function
-- Place each trimester on its own partition
-- The most recent of the 13 months goes in the latest partition
CREATE PARTITION SCHEME MonthPartitioningScheme
    AS PARTITION MonthPartitioningFx
    TO (FILEGROUP2, FILEGROUP2, FILEGROUP2, FILEGROUP2,
        FILEGROUP3, FILEGROUP3, FILEGROUP3, FILEGROUP3,
        FILEGROUP4, FILEGROUP4, FILEGROUP4, FILEGROUP4, FILEGROUP4);
```

If you visualize the table data as being sorted by the partition key in ascending order, the left partition is the partition that is on top. When defining a partition function, you indicate whether the boundary value—in our example, the first day of each month—will be stored in the partition on the left (which is the default), or the partition on the right (as specified in the sample).

Figure 8-4 shows the relationship between the partition function and the partition scheme. The partition function created 13 partitions using 12 boundary values. The partition scheme directed these 13 partitions to three filegroups by specifying each filegroup four times, and the last filegroup five times because it will hold the last partition.

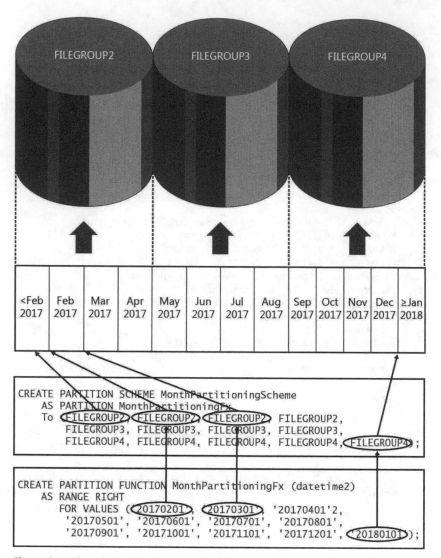

Figure 8-4 The relationship between the partition function and the partition scheme, and the filegroups on which the partitions will be stored.

Partition design guidelines

When designing partitions, keep the following guidelines in mind, though also keep in mind that your mileage may vary:

- The number of parallel operations that can be run depends on the number of processor cores in the system. Using more partitions than processor cores will limit the number of partitions that will be processed in parallel. So, even though SQL Server now supports up to 15,000 partitions, on a system with 12 processor cores, at most 12 partitions will be processed in parallel.

- Choose the partition key based on the column's values growing. This could be a date value or an incrementing identity column. The goal is to always have new rows added to the right-most partition.

- The selected partition key should be immutable, meaning that there should be no business reason for this key value to change. A narrow data type is preferable over a wide data type.

- To achieve most benefits of partitioning, you will need to put each partition into its own filegroup. This is not a requirement, and some or all partitions can share a single filegroup. For example, the next section discusses a sliding window partition strategy, in which partitioning is beneficial even if all are on the same filegroup.

- Consider the storage that is backing the filegroups. Your storage system might not provide higher performance if all filegroups have been placed on the same physical drives.

- Tables that are good candidates for partitioning are tables with many—as in millions or billions—rows for which data is mostly added as opposed to updated, and against which queries are frequently run that would return data from one or a few partitions.

Implementing a sliding window partition strategy

Horizontal partitioning is often applied to relational data warehouses. A common data warehouse operation is loading a significant amount of data to a fact table while simultaneously purging old data. The sliding window partition strategy is particularly well suited for tables for which data is regularly added and removed. For example, data in a data warehouse fact table can be purged after 13 months. Perhaps each time data is loaded into the data warehouse, rows older than 13 months are removed while new rows are added. This is a sliding window in so much as the fact table always contains the most recent 13 months of data.

To set up a sliding window, you'll need a partition function and scheme as well as the fact table. You should also set up a stored procedure that modifies the partition function to accommodate the new boundary values. You will also need a staging table with the same columns and clustered index as the partitioned table.

NOTE

For the next example, we make the assumption that data is loaded in the data warehouse only once every month. This is not particularly realistic, but the example still works when data is loaded more frequently, even in real time. It's only the first load operation for a new month that will need to modify the partition function.

Figure 8-5 illustrates what happens on March 1, 2018, when data is loaded for the month of February 2018. The fact table is partitioned into 13 partitions, one for each month. An automated process takes care of modifying the partition function to accommodate the new date range by splitting the last partition in two. Then, the oldest month's data is switched out to a staging table and the new data is switched in from a staging table. Finally, the left-most partition, which is now empty, is merged.

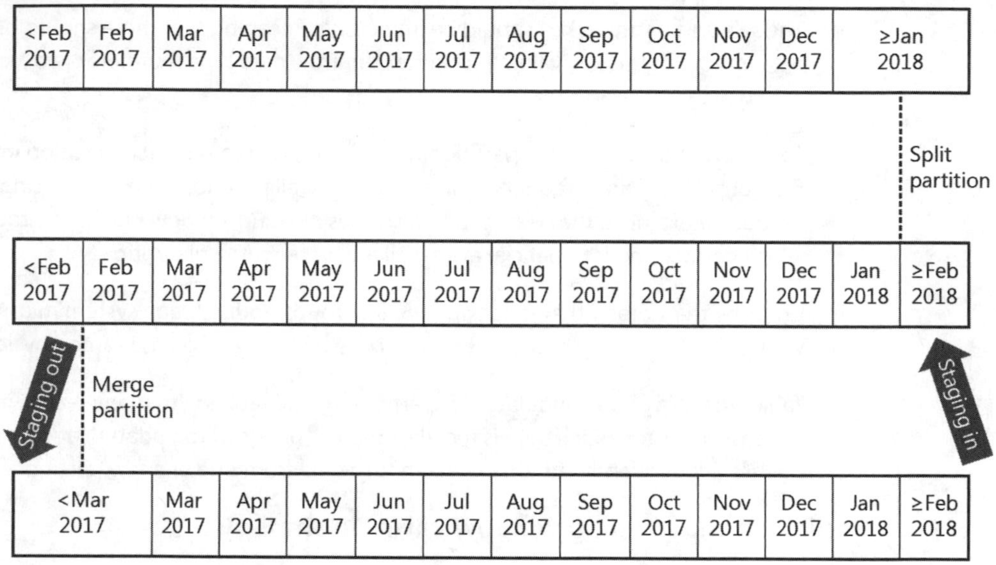

Figure 8-5 An overview of the sliding window partition strategy.

NOTE

Implementing a sliding window partition strategy is not without pitfalls. To fully automate it, job auditing is required to ensure that the process that modifies the partition function operates successfully. Additional complexity is introduced if the switched out, old data is to be archived rather than purged.

You can optimize switching the old partition out and the new partition in by using a memory-optimized table as the staging table.

NOTE

Now that you have read in detail about horizontal partitioning, we encourage you to refer to the earlier section about temporal tables and consider that temporal tables are a specialized case of horizontal partitioning. In addition, you can partition the history table, as described in Microsoft Docs at *https://docs.microsoft.com/sql/relational-databases/tables/manage-retention-of-historical-data-in-system-versioned-temporal-tables#using-table-partitioning-approach*.

Vertical partitioning

An entity that is vertically partitioned into multiple tables can usually be identified by the fact that the tables share the same primary key. A one-to-one relationship exists between the tables, which you can enforce by using a foreign key constraint.

Unlike horizontal partitioning, SQL Server does not have extensive support for vertical partitioning. As the database designer, you will need to create the necessary schema to vertically partition tables yourself.

Vertical partitioning makes sense when a single table would ordinarily contain a large number of columns, some of which might contain large values that are infrequently queried. You can improve performance by storing the infrequently accessed columns in another table. Another problem that you can solve by vertical partitioning is when you run into a maximum row size limit or maximum column count limit. We would encourage you to first review your database design to ensure that one logical entity really needs such wide columns or that many attributes. If that's the case, splitting the entity into two or more tables can be a workaround.

NOTE

Instead of vertical partitioning for infrequently accessed columns, you might also consider using sparse columns, which are described earlier in this chapter.

Be careful not to abuse vertical partitioning as a strategy. Every time data from two tables is needed in a single result set, a join operation will be required. These joins could be expensive operations or are at least more expensive than reading data from a single page, and might nullify other performance benefits if you run them frequently.

There is a special case for using vertical partitioning, and it relates to FileTable. FileTables, as described previously in this chapter, have a fixed schema. You might, however, need to store additional metadata about the files. Because you are unable to extend the schema, you will need to create a new table which uses the same primary key as the FileTable. Using insert and delete triggers, you can guarantee data integrity by ensuring that for every row in the FileTable, there is a matching row in your extended metadata table.

Capturing modifications to data

SQL Server supports several methods for capturing row data that has been modified. Temporal tables have been discussed earlier in this chapter. In this section, we discuss *change tracking* and *change data capture*. Although these features allow applications to detect when data has changed, they operate very differently and serve different purposes. This section first discusses change tracking, then change data capture, and then finally provides recommendations on their use.

NOTE

We should immediately state that neither feature tracks Data Definition Language (DDL) or Data Control Language (DCL) changes. Only DML changes to user tables are tracked, and it does not include the login that made the change. This limitation affects these features' usefulness as an auditing mechanism. When used in combination with auditing, change data capture can provide additional value. For more information about auditing in SQL Server, refer to Chapter 7. For more information about auditing in Azure SQL Database, refer to Chapter 5.

Using change tracking

Change tracking does not actually track the data that has changed, but merely that a row has changed. You use it mostly for synchronizing copies of data with occasionally offline clients or for Extract, Transform, and Load (ETL) operations. For example, an application that facilitates offline editing of data will need to perform a two-way synchronization when reconnected. One approach to implementing this requirement is to copy (a subset of) the data to the client. When the client goes offline, the application reads and updates data using the offline copy. When the client reestablishes connectivity to the server, changes can be merged efficiently. The application is responsible for detecting and managing conflicting changes.

Configuring change tracking is a two-step process: first, change tracking must be turned on for the database. Then, change tracking must be turned on for the table(s) that you want to track. Before performing these steps, we recommend setting up snapshot isolation for the database. Snapshot isolation is not required for proper operation of change tracking, but it is very helpful for accurately querying the changes. Because data can change as you are querying it, using the snapshot isolation level and an explicit transaction, you will see consistent results until you commit the transaction. This is described in the detail in the article "Working with change tracking" referenced at *https://docs.microsoft.com/sql/relational-databases/track-changes/work-with-change-tracking-sql-server*.

The sample script that follows turns on snapshot isolation on the WideWorldImporters sample database. Then, change tracking on the WideWorldImporters sample database and on two tables, `Sales.Orders` and `Sales.OrderLines`, is turned on. Only on the `Sales.Orders` table is column tracking activated. Next, change tracking is turned off for `Sales.OrderLines`. Finally, the `sys.change_tracking_tables` catalog view is queried to retrieve a list of tables with change tracking turned on.

```
USE master;
GO
-- Enable snapshot isolation for the database
ALTER DATABASE WideWorldImporters
    SET ALLOW_SNAPSHOT_ISOLATION ON;
```

```
-- Enable change tracking for the database
ALTER DATABASE WideWorldImporters
    SET CHANGE_TRACKING = ON
    (CHANGE_RETENTION = 5 DAYS, AUTO_CLEANUP = ON);
USE WideWorldImporters;
GO
-- Enable change tracking for Orders
ALTER TABLE Sales.Orders
    ENABLE CHANGE_TRACKING
    -- and track which columns changed
    WITH (TRACK_COLUMNS_UPDATED = ON);
-- Enable change tracking for OrderLines
ALTER TABLE Sales.OrderLines
    ENABLE CHANGE_TRACKING;
-- Disable change tracking for OrderLines
ALTER TABLE Sales.OrderLines
    DISABLE CHANGE_TRACKING;
-- Query the current state of change tracking in the database
SELECT *
FROM sys.change_tracking_tables;
```

➤ **For an end-to-end example of how an application can use change tracking to accomplish two-way data synchronization with an occasionally offline data store, see** *https://docs.microsoft.com/sql/relational-databases/track-changes/work-with-change-tracking-sql-server*.

A major benefit of change tracking compared to implementing a custom solution is that change tracking does not make any schema changes to the user tables that are tracked. In addition, change tracking is available in all editions of SQL Server and in Azure SQL Database. Auto-cleanup ensures that the database does not grow unchecked.

NOTE

We recommend turning on autocleanup and setting a retention period sufficiently long to ensure that data synchronization has taken place. Applications can check whether they have waited too long to synchronize; that is, applications can find out whether cleanup has already removed tracking information since the application last synchronized.

Although change tracking can track which rows, and optionally columns, have changed, it is not able to indicate what the old values were or how often the row has been changed. If your use case does not require this, change tracking provides a light-weight option for tracking. If your use case does require one or both, change data capture might offer a solution.

We discuss change data capture in the next section. The functions for querying changes is the same between change tracking and change data capture. They are also covered in the next section.

Using change data capture

Change data capture varies in some important ways from change tracking. Foremost, change data capture actually captures the historical values of the data. This requires a significantly higher amount of storage than change tracking. Unlike change tracking, change data capture uses an asynchronous process for writing the change data. This means that the client does not need to wait for the change data to be committed before the database returns the result of the DML operation.

> **NOTE**
>
> Change data capture is not available in Azure SQL Database. Starting with SQL Server 2016 Service Pack 1, change data capture is available in the Standard edition.

> **NOTE**
>
> Change data capture and memory-optimized tables are mutually exclusive. A database cannot have both at the same time.

Change data capture stores the captured changes in internal tables. You can query that data by using the CHANGETABLE function. To request the data, the client specifies the table for which history is requested along with a version number of the last time the client synchronized. The following script turns on change data capture on a fictitious database using the sys.sp_cdc_enable_db stored procedure. Then, the script turns on change data capture for the dbo.Orders table. The script assumes that a database role cdc_reader has been created.

```
USE WideWorldImporters;
GO
EXEC sys.sp_cdc_enable_db;
EXEC sys.sp_cdc_enable_table
    @source_schema = 'dbo',
    @source_name = 'Orders',
    @role_name = 'cdc_reader';
```

Additional settings for change data capture include specifying which columns to capture, on which filegroup to store the change table, and more. These are discussed in the Microsoft Docs at *https://docs.microsoft.com/sql/relational-databases/track-changes/enable-and-disable-change-data-capture-sql-server*.

The following list includes a few important considerations when designing applications that take advantage of change tracking and change data capture:

- An application should identify itself by using a source ID when synchronizing data. By providing a source ID, the client can avoid obtaining the same data again. A client specifies its own source ID by using the WITH CHANGE_TRACKING_CONTEXT clause at the start of statements.

- An application should perform the request for changed data in a snapshot isolation–level transaction. This will avoid another application updating data between the check for updated data and sending data updates. The snapshot isolation level needs to be turned on at the database level, which was demonstrated in the previous section.

Comparing change tracking, change data capture, and temporal tables

In this section, we present a comparison between three features that have common use cases. Table 8-1 should prove helpful when you're deciding which change tracking feature is appropriate for your needs.

Table 8-1 A comparison of features and uses of change tracking, change data capture, and temporal tables

	Change tracking	Change data capture	Temporal tables
Requires schema modification	No	No	Yes
Available in Azure SQL Database	Yes	No	Yes
Edition support	Any	Enterprise only	Any
Provides historical data	No	Yes	Yes
History end-user queryable	No	Yes	Yes
Tracks DML type	Yes	Yes	No
Has autocleanup	Yes	Yes	Yes
Change indicator	LSN	LSN	datetime2

Performance tuning SQL Server

In this chapter, we review the database concepts and objects most commonly associated with performance tuning the performance of objects within the Microsoft SQL Server database. We begin with a fundamental exploration of database isolation and its practical effects on queries. We then review the concepts of delayed durability and delayed durability transactions. Then, we explore *execution plans*, including ways to use them with the Query Store feature. We discuss execution plans in detail, what to look for when performance tuning, and how to control when they go parallel.

Entire books have been written on some of the sections in this chapter—we obviously can't go into that degree of detail here in a single chapter, but we do provide a deep enough discussion to jumpstart and accelerate your learning toward SQL Server performance tuning, including features added in SQL Server 2016 and 2017.

Understanding isolation levels and concurrency

It is important to have a fundamental understanding of *isolation levels*. These aren't just arcane keywords you study only when it is certification test time; they can have a profound effect on application performance, stability, and data integrity.

Understanding the differing impact of isolation levels on locking and blocking, and therefore on concurrency, is the key to understanding when you should use an isolation level different from the default of READ COMMITTED. Table 9-1 presents all of the isolation levels available in SQL Server.

Table 9-1 Isolation levels

Transaction isolation level	Allows dirty reads	Allows nonrepeatable reads	Allows phantom rows	Update conflicts possible
READ UNCOMMITTED	X	X	X	
READ COMMITTED		X	X	
REPEATABLE READ			X	
SERIALIZABLE				
READ COMMITTED SNAPSHOT (RCSI)		X	X	
SNAPSHOT				X

Inside OUT

What about READPAST?

READPAST is a table hint, not an isolation level, and you cannot set it at the session level. We discuss more about how and where you can set isolation levels later in this chapter.

But, READPAST can be useful in very specific circumstances, limited to when there are SQL Server tables used as "stack" or "queue," with "first in, first out" architecture. READPAST does not place row-level locks on a table, and instead of being blocked by rows that are locked, it skips them. User transactions can fetch the "first" row in the stack that isn't already being accessed.

In this way, a multithreaded process that is regularly looping through a table can read rows, afford to skip the rows currently being written to, and read them on the "next pass." Outside of these limited scenarios, READPAST is not appropriate because it will likely return incomplete data.

When you are choosing an isolation level for a transaction in an application, you should consider primarily the transactional safety and business requirements of the transaction in a multiuser environment. The performance of the transaction should be a distant second priority when choosing an isolation level. Locking is not bad, it is the way that every transaction in SQL Server cooperates with others when dealing with disk-based tables. READ COMMITTED is generally a safe isolation level because it allows updates to block reads. In the default READ COMMITTED isolation level, reads cannot read uncommitted data and must wait for a transaction to commit or rollback. In this way, READ COMMITTED prevents a SELECT statement from accessing uncommitted data, a problem known as a *dirty read*. This is especially important during multistep transactions, in which parent and child records in a foreign key relationship must be created in the same transaction. In that scenario, reads should not access either table until both tables are updated.

READ COMMITTED does not ensure that row data and row count won't change between two SELECT queries in a multistep transaction. For some application scenarios, this might be acceptable or desired, but not for others. To avoid these two problematic scenarios (which we talk more about soon), you need to increase the transaction's isolation.

For scenarios in which transactions must have a higher degree of isolation from other transactions, escalating the isolation level of a transaction is appropriate. For example, if a transaction must process multistep writes and cannot allow other transactions to change data during the transaction, escalating the isolation level of a transaction is appropriate. Here are two examples:

In this example, REPEATABLE READ would block other transactions from changing or deleting rows needed during a multistep transaction. This phenomenon is called *nonrepeatable reads*. A nonrepeatable read returns different or fewer rows of data when attempting to read the same data twice, which is problematic to multistep transactions. Nonrepeatable reads can affect transactions with less isolation than REPEATABLE READ.

However, if the transaction in this example would need to ensure that the same number of rows in a result set is returned throughout a multistep transaction, the SERIALIZABLE isolation is necessary. It is the only isolation level that prevents other transactions from inserting new rows inside of a range of rows, a problem known as *phantom rows*.

The behavior just described is consistent with transactions affecting only a few rows. In these cases, the Database Engine is performing row and page-level locks to provide protection for transaction isolation. It is possible that REPEATABLE READ transactions could access a large number of rows and then escalate to use table locks, and then protect the transaction against phantom rows.

➤ **For more on monitoring database locking and blocking, see Chapter 13.**

CHAPTER 9

Inside OUT

SQL Server doesn't have a time-out? Really?

That's correct, by default there is no time-out for a local request that is being blocked in SQL Server, although applications can report a "SQL time-out" if query run time surpasses their own time-out limitations.

By default, SQL Server will not cancel a request that is being blocked, but you can change this behavior for individual sessions. The value of the global variable @@LOCK_TIMEOUT is −1 by default, indicating that there is no time-out. You can change this for the current session by using the following statement:

```
SET LOCK_TIMEOUT n;
```

Where n is the number of milliseconds before a request is cancelled by SQL Server, returning error 1222, "Lock request time out period exceeded. The statement has been terminated." Take caution in implementing this change to SQL's default lock time-out, and try to fully understand the cause of the blocking first. If you change the lock time-out in code, ensure that any applications creating the sessions are prepared to handle the errors gracefully and retry.

SQL Server does have a configuration setting for a lock time-out for outgoing remote connections called Remote Query Timeout (s), which defaults to 600 seconds. This time-out applies only to connections to remote data providers, not to requests run on the SQL Server instance.

NOTE

You can declare isolation levels for transactions that read and write to both memory-optimized tables and disk-based tables. Memory-optimized tables do not use locks or latches; instead, they use row versioning to achieve the isolation and concurrency. Chapter 8 covers memory-optimized tables, and we discuss their use in high-transaction volume scenarios in Chapter 10.

Understanding how concurrent sessions become blocked

In this section, we review a series of realistic examples of how concurrency works in a multiuser application interacting with SQL Server tables. First, let's discuss how to diagnose whether a request is being blocked or blocking another request.

How to observe blocking

It's easy to find out live whether a request is being blocked. The dynamic management view `sys.dm_db_requests`, when combined with `sys_dm_db_sessions` on the `session_id` column, provides similar data plus much more information than the legacy `sp_who` or `sp_who2` commands, including the `blocked_by` column, as demonstrated here:

```
SELECT * FROM
sys.dm_exec_sessions s
LEFT OUTER JOIN sys.dm_exec_requests r ON r.session_id = s.session_id;
```

Now, let's review some example scenarios to detail exactly why and how requests can block one another in the real world. This is the foundation of concurrency in SQL Server and helps you understand the reason why NOLOCK appears to make queries perform faster. The examples that follow behave identically in SQL Server instances and databases in Microsoft Azure SQL Database

Understanding concurrency: two requests updating the same rows

Consider the following steps involving two writes, with each transaction coming from a different session. The transactions are explicitly declared by using the BEGIN/COMMIT TRAN syntax. In this example, the transactions are not overriding the default isolation level of READ COMMITTED:

1.   A table contains only rows of Type = 0 and Type = 1. Transaction 1 begins and updates all rows from Type = 1 to Type = 2.

2.   Before Transaction 1 commits, Transaction 2 begins and issues a statement to update Type = 2 to Type = 3. Transaction 2 is blocked and will wait for Transaction 1 to commit.

3.   Transaction 1 commits.

4.   Transaction 2 is no longer blocked and processes its update statement. Transaction 2 then commits.

The result: The resulting table will contain records of Type = 3, and the second transaction will have updated records. This is because when Transaction 2 started, it waited, too, for committed data until after Transaction 1 committed.

Understanding concurrency: a write blocks a read

Next, consider the following steps involving a write and a read, with each transaction coming from a different session. In this scenario, an uncommitted write in Transaction 1 blocks a read in Transaction 2. The transactions are explicitly declared using the BEGIN/COMMIT TRAN syntax. In this example, the transactions are not overriding the default isolation level of READ COMMITTED:

1. A table contains only records of Type = 0 and Type = 1. Transaction 1 begins and updates all rows from Type = 1 to Type = 2.

2. Before Transaction 1 commits, Transaction 2 begins and issues a SELECT statement for records of Type = 2. Transaction 2 is blocked and waits for Transaction 1 to commit.

3. Transaction 1 commits.

4. Transaction 2 is no longer blocked, and processes its SELECT statement. Rows are returned. Transaction 2 then commits.

The result: Transaction 2 returns records of Type = 2. This is because when Transaction 2 started, it waited for committed data until after Transaction 1 committed.

Understanding concurrency: a nonrepeatable read

Consider the following steps involving a read and a write, with each Transaction coming from a different session. In this scenario, Transaction 1 suffers a nonrepeatable read, as READ COMMITTED does not offer any protection against phantom rows or nonrepeatable reads. The transactions are explicitly declared using the BEGIN/COMMIT TRAN syntax. In this example, the transactions are not overriding the default isolation level of READ COMMITTED:

1. A table contains only records of Type = 0 and Type = 1. Transaction 1 starts and selects rows where Type = 1. Rows are returned.

2. Before Transaction 1 commits, Transaction 2 starts and issues an Update statement, setting records of Type = 1 to Type = 2. Transaction 2 is not blocked, and process immediately.

3. Transaction 1 again selects rows where Type = 1, and is blocked.

4. Transaction 2 commits.

5. Transaction 1 is immediately unblocked. No rows are returned. (No committed rows exist where Type=1.) Transaction 1 commits.

The result: The resulting table contains records of Type = 2, and the second transaction has updated records. This is because when Transaction 2 started, Transaction 1 had not placed any exclusive locks on the data, allowing for writes to happen. Because it is doing only reads, Transaction 1 would never have placed any exclusive locks on the data. Transaction 1 suffered from a nonrepeatable read: the same SELECT statement returned different data during the same multistep transaction.

Understanding concurrency: preventing a nonrepeatable read

Consider the following steps involving a read and a write, with each transaction coming from a different session. This time, we protect Transaction 1 from dirty reads and nonrepeatable reads by using the REPEATABLE READ isolation level. A read in the REPEATABLE READ isolation level will block a write. The transactions are explicitly declared by using the BEGIN/COMMIT TRAN syntax:

1. A table contains only records of Type = 0 and Type = 1. Transaction 1 starts and selects rows where Type = 1 in the REPEATABLE READ isolation level. Rows are returned.

2. Before Transaction 1 commits, Transaction 2 starts and issues an UPDATE statement, setting records of Type = 1 to Type = 2. Transaction 2 is blocked by Transaction 1.

3. Transaction 1 again selects rows where Type = 1. Rows are returned.

4. Transaction 1 commits.

5. Transaction 2 is immediately unblocked and processes its update. Transaction 2 commits.

The result: The resulting table will contain records of Type = 2. This is because when Transaction 2 started, Transaction 1 had placed read locks on the data it was selecting, blocking writes to happening until it had committed. Transaction 1 returned the same records each time and did not suffer a nonrepeatable read. Transaction 2 processed its updates only when it could place exclusive locks on the rows it needed.

Understanding concurrency: experiencing phantom reads

Consider the following steps involving a read and a write, with each transaction coming from a different session. In this scenario, we describe a phantom read:

1. A table contains only records of Type = 0 and Type = 1. Transaction 1 starts and selects rows where Type = 1 in the REPEATABLE READ isolation level. Rows are returned.

2. Before Transaction 1 commits, Transaction 2 starts and issues an INSERT statement, adding rows of Type = 1. Transaction 2 is not blocked by Transaction 1.

3. Transaction 1 again selects rows where Type = 1. More rows are returned compared to the first time the select was run in Transaction 1.

4. Transaction 1 commits.

5. Transaction 2 commits.

CHAPTER 9

The result: Transaction 1 experienced a phantom read when it returned a different number of records the second time it selected from the table inside the same transaction. Transaction 1 had not placed any locks on the range of data it needed, allowing for writes in another transaction to happen within the same dataset. The phantom read would have occurred to Transaction 1 in any isolation level, except for SERIALIZABLE. Let's look at that next.

Understanding concurrency: preventing phantom reads

Consider the following steps involving a read and a write, with each transaction coming from a different session. In this scenario, we protect Transaction 1 from a phantom read.

1. A table contains only records of Type = 0 and Type = 1. Transaction 1 starts and selects rows where Type = 1 in the SERIALIZABLE isolation level. Rows are returned.

2. Before Transaction 1 commits, Transaction 2 starts and issues an INSERT statement, adding rows of Type = 1. Transaction 2 is blocked by Transaction 1.

3. Transaction 1 again Selects rows where Type = 1. The same number of rows are returned.

4. Transaction 1 commits.

5. Transaction 2 is immediately unblocked and processes its insert. Transaction 2 commits.

The result: Transaction 1 did not suffer from a phantom read the second time it selected form the table, because it had placed a lock on the range of rows it needed. The table now contains additional records for Type = 1, but they were not inserted until after Transaction 1 had committed.

Stating the case against READ UNCOMMITTED (NOLOCK)

Many developers and database administrators consider the NOLOCK table hint and the equivalent READ UNCOMMITTED isolation level nothing more than the turbo button on their 486DX. "We had performance problems, but we've been putting NOLOCK in all our stored procedures to fix it."

The effect of the table hint NOLOCK or the READ UNCOMMITTED isolation level is that no locks are taken inside the database, save for schema locks. (A query using NOLOCK could still be blocked by Data Definition Language [DDL] commands.) The resulting removal of basic integrity of the mechanisms that retrieve data can result in uncommitted data, obviously, but that is not usually enough to scare away developers. There are more good reasons to avoid the READ UNCOMMITTED isolation level, however.

The case against using the READ UNCOMMITTED isolation level is deeper than the performance and deeper than "data that has yet to be committed." Developers might counter that data is rarely ever rolled back or that the data is for reporting only. In production environments, these are not sufficient grounds to justify the potential problems. The only situations in which READ UNCOMMITTED are an acceptable performance shortcut involve nonproduction systems, estimate-only counts, or estimate-only aggregations.

A query in READ UNCOMMITTED isolation level could return invalid data in the following real-world, provable ways:

- Read uncommitted data (dirty reads)

- Read committed data twice

- Skip committed data

- Return corrupted data

- Or, the query could fail altogether: "Could not continue scan with NOLOCK due to data movement."

One final caveat: in SQL Server you cannot apply NOLOCK to tables when used in modification statements, and it ignores the declaration of READ UNCOMMITTED isolation level in a batch that includes modification statements; for example:

```
INSERT INTO dbo.testnolock1 WITH (NOLOCK)
SELECT * FROM dbo.testnolock2;
```

The preceding code will return the error:

```
Msg 1065, Level 15, State 1, Line 17
The NOLOCK and READUNCOMMITTED lock hints are not allowed for target tables of INSERT,
UPDATE, DELETE or MERGE statements.
```

However, this protection doesn't apply to the *source* of any writes, hence the danger.

This following code *is* allowed and is dangerous because it could write invalid data:

```
INSERT INTO testnolock1
SELECT * FROM testnolock2 WITH (NOLOCK);
```

Changing the isolation level within transactions

In addition to using the SET TRANSACTION ISOLATION LEVEL command, you can use table hints to override previously set behavior. Let's review the two ways by which you can change the isolation level of queries.

Using the transaction isolation level option

The SET TRANSACTION ISOLATION LEVEL command changes the isolation level for the current session, affecting all future transactions until the connection is closed.

But, you can change the isolation level of an explicit transaction after it is created, as long as you are not changing from or to the SNAPSHOT isolation level.

For example, the following code snippet is technically valid:

```
SET TRANSACTION ISOLATION LEVEL READ COMMITTED
BEGIN TRAN
SET TRANSACTION ISOLATION LEVEL SERIALIZABLE
SELECT...
```

However, this snippet is invalid:

```
SET TRANSACTION ISOLATION LEVEL READ COMMITTED
BEGIN TRAN
SET TRANSACTION ISOLATION LEVEL SNAPSHOT
SELECT...
```

Doing so results in the following error:

```
Msg 3951, Level 16, State 1, Line 4
```

```
Transaction failed in database 'databasename' because the statement was run under snap-
shot isolation but the transaction did not start in snapshot isolation. You cannot
change the isolation level of the transaction after the transaction has started.
```

In .NET applications, you should change the isolation level of each transaction when it is created. In Transact-SQL (T-SQL) code and stored procedures, you should change the execution plan of the session before creating an explicit transaction.

Using table hints to change isolation

You also can use isolation level hints to change the isolation level at the individual object level. This is an advanced type of troubleshooting that you shouldn't use commonly, because it increases the complexity of maintenance and muddies architectural decisions with respect to enterprise concurrency.

For example, you might have seen developers use NOLOCK at the end of a table, effectively (and dangerously) dropping access to that table into the READ COMMITTED isolation level:

```
SELECT col1 FROM dbo.Table (NOLOCK)
```

Aside from the unadvisable use of NOLOCK in the preceding example, using a table hint without WITH is deprecated syntax (since SQL Server 2008).

Aside from the cautionary NOLOCK, there are 20-plus other table hints that can have utility, including the ability for a query to use a certain index, to force a seek or scan on an index, or to override the query optimizer's locking strategy. We look at how to use UPDLOCK later in this chapter; for example, to force the use of the SERIALIZABLE isolation level.

All table hints should be considered for temporary and/or highly situational troubleshooting. They could make maintenance of these queries problematic in the future. For example, using the INDEX or FORCESEEK table hints could result in poor query performance or even cause the query to fail if the table's indexes are changed.

> ➤ For detailed information on all possible table hints, see the SQL Server documentation at *https://docs.microsoft.com/sql/t-sql/queries/hints-transact-sql-table*.

Understanding the enterprise solution to concurrency: SNAPSHOT

In the interest of performance, however, application developers too often seek to solve concurrency issues (reduce blocking) by using READ UNCOMMITTED. At first and at scale, the performance gains are too vast to consider other alternatives. But there is a far safer option, without the significant drawbacks and potential for invalid data and errors. Using row versioning with READ_COMMITTED_SNAPSHOT (RCSI) and/or the SNAPSHOT isolation level is the enterprise solution to performance issues related to concurrency.

SNAPSHOT isolation allows queries to read from the same rows that might be locked by other queries by using row versioning. The SQL Server instance's TempDB keeps a copy of committed data, and this data can be served to concurrent requests. In this way, SNAPSHOT allows access only to committed data but without blocking access to data locked by writes. By increasing the utilization and workload of TempDB for disk-based tables, performance is dramatically increased by increasing concurrency without the dangers of accessing uncommitted data.

Although row versioning works silently in the background, you access it at the statement level, not at the transaction or session levels. Each statement will have access to the latest committed row version of the data. In this way, RCSI is still susceptible to nonrepeatable reads and phantom rows. SNAPSHOT isolation uses row versions of affected rows throughout a transaction; thus, it is not susceptible to nonrepeatable reads and phantom rows.

As an example of SNAPSHOT in use internally, all queries run against a secondary readable database in an availability group are run in the SNAPSHOT isolation level, by design. The transaction isolation level and any locking table hints are ignored. This removes any concurrency conflicts between a read-heavy workload on the secondary database and the transactions arriving there from the primary database.

Understanding concurrency: accessing SNAPSHOT data

Consider the following steps involving a read and a write, with each transaction coming from a different session. In this scenario, we see that Transaction 2 has access to previously committed row data, even though those rows are being updated concurrently.

1. A table contains only records of Type = 1. Transaction 1 starts and updates rows where Type = 1 to Type = 2.

2. Before Transaction 1 commits, Transaction 2 sets its session isolation level to SNAPSHOT.

3. Transaction 2 issues a SELECT statement WHERE Type = 1. Transaction 2 is not blocked by Transaction 1. Rows where Type = 1 are returned. Transaction 2 commits.

4. Transaction 1 commits.

5. Transaction 2 again issues a SELECT statement WHERE Type = 1. No rows are returned.

The result: Transaction 2 was not blocked when it attempted to query rows that Transaction 1 was updating. It had access to previously committed data, thanks to row versioning.

Implementing SNAPSHOT isolation

You can implement SNAPSHOT isolation level in a database in two different ways. Turning on SNAPSHOT isolation simply allows for the use of SNAPSHOT isolation and begins the process of row versioning. Alternatively, turning on RCSI changes the default isolation level to READ COMMITTED SNAPSHOT. You can implement both or either. It's important to understand the differences between these two settings, because they are not the same:

- READ COMMITTED SNAPSHOT configures optimistic concurrency for reads by overriding the default isolation level of the database. When turned on, all queries will use RCSI unless overridden.

- SNAPSHOT isolation mode configures optimistic concurrency for reads and writes. You must then specify the SNAPSHOT isolation level for any transaction to use SNAPSHOT isolation level. It is possible to have update conflicts with SNAPSHOT isolation mode that will not occur with READ COMMITTED SNAPSHOT.

The statement to implement SNAPSHOT isolation in the database is simple enough, but is not without consequence. Even if no transactions or statements use the SNAPSHOT isolation level, behind the scenes, TempDB begins storing row version data for disk-based tables. (Memory-optimized tables have row-versioning built in and don't need TempDB.) The Database Engine maintains previous versions for changing data in TempDB regardless of whether that data is currently being accessed by user queries. Here's how to implement SNAPSHOT isolation:

```
ALTER DATABASE databasename SET ALLOW_SNAPSHOT_ISOLATION ON;
```

All transactions will continue to use the default READ COMMITTED isolation level, but you now can specify the use SNAPSHOT isolation at the session level or in table hints, as shown in the following example:

```
SET TRANSACTION ISOLATION LEVEL SNAPSHOT;
```

Alternatively, or in conjunction with ALLOW_SNAPSHOT_ISOLATION, you can turn on RCSI as the new default isolation level in a database. Here's how to turn on RCSI:

```
ALTER DATABASE databasename SET READ_COMMITTED_SNAPSHOT ON;
```

You can set both of the preceding database settings independently of each other. Setting ALLOW_SNAPSHOT_ISOLATION is not required to turn on READ_COMMITTED_SNAPSHOT, and vice versa. Similarly, these settings are not tied to the MEMORY_OPTIMIZED_ELEVATE_TO_SNAPSHOT database setting to promote memory-optimized table access to SNAPSHOT isolation.

➤ We discuss memory-optimized tables in greater detail in Chapter 10.

For either of the previous ALTER DATABASE statements to succeed, no other transactions can be open in the database. It might be necessary to close other connections manually or to put the database in SINGLE_USER mode. Either way, we do not recommend that you perform this change during production activity.

NOTE
Do not change the READ_COMMITTED_SNAPSHOT database option if you have any memory-optimized tables set to DURABILITY = SCHEMA_ONLY. All rows in the table will be lost. You should move the contents of the table to a more durable table before changing READ_COMMITTED_SNAPSHOT to ON or OFF.

Be aware and prepared for the increased utilization in the TempDB, both in the demand and space requirements. To avoid autogrowth events, increase the size of the TempDB data and log files and monitor their size. Although you should try to avoid autogrowth events by growing the TempDB data file(s) yourself, you should also verify that your TempDB file autogrowth settings are appropriate.

➤ For more information on file autogrowth settings, see Chapter 4.

Should the TempDB exhaust all available space on its drive volume, SQL will be unable to row-version records for transactions, and will terminate them with SQL Server error 3958. SQL Server will also issue errors 3967 and 3966 as the oldest row versions are removed from the TempDB to make room for new row versions needed by newer transactions.

NOTE
Prior to SQL Server 2016, READ COMMITTED SNAPSHOT and SNAPSHOT isolation levels were not supported with Columnstore indexes. Beginning with SQL Server 2016, SNAPSHOT isolation and Columnstore indexes are fully compatible.

Understanding updates in SNAPSHOT isolation level

Transactions that read data in SNAPSHOT isolation or RCSI will have access to previously committed data instead of being blocked, when data needed is being changed. This is important to understand and could result in an update statement experiencing a concurrency error. The potential for update conflicts is real and you need to understand it. In the next section, we review ways to mitigate the risk.

For example, consider the following steps, with each transaction coming from a different session. In this example, Transaction 2 fails due to a concurrency conflict or "write-write error":

1.   A table contains many records, each with a unique ID. Transaction 1 begins a transaction in the READ COMMITTED isolation level and performs an update on the row where ID = 1.

2.   Transaction 2 sets its session isolation level to SNAPSHOT and issues a statement to update the row where ID = 1.

3.   Transaction 1 commits first.

4.   Transaction 2 immediately fails with SQL error 3960.

The result: Transaction 1's update to the row where ID = 1 succeeded. Transaction 2 immediately failed with the following error message:

```
Msg 3960, Level 16, State 2, Line 8
```

```
Snapshot isolation transaction aborted due to update conflict. You cannot use snap-
shot isolation to access table 'dbo.AnyTable' directly or indirectly in database
'WideWorldImporters' to update, delete, or insert the row that has been modified or
deleted by another transaction. Retry the transaction or change the isolation level
for the update/delete statement.
```

The transaction for Transaction 2 was rolled back, marked uncommittable. Let's try to understand why this error occurred, what to do, and how to prevent it.

In SQL Server, SNAPSHOT isolation uses locks to create blocking but doesn't block updates from colliding for disk-based tables. It is possible to error when committing an update statement, if another transaction has changed the data needed for an update during a transaction in SNAPSHOT isolation level.

For disk-based tables, the update conflict error will look like the Msg 3960 that we saw a moment ago. For queries on memory-optimized tables, the update conflict error will look like this:

```
Msg 41302, Level 16, State 110, Line 8
```

```
The current transaction attempted to update a record that has been updated since this
transaction started. The transaction was aborted.
```

The preceding error can occur with `ALLOW_SNAPSHOT_ISOLATION` turned on if transactions are run in SNAPSHOT isolation level.

Even though optimistic concurrency of snapshot isolation level (and also memory-optimized tables) increases the potential for update conflicts, you can mitigate these by doing the following:

- When running a transaction in SNAPSHOT isolation level, it is crucial to avoid using any statements that place update locks to disk-based tables inside multistep explicit transactions.

   Similarly, always avoid multistep transactions with writes when working with memory-optimized tables, regardless of isolation level.

- Specifying the UPDLOCK table hint can have utility at preventing update conflict errors for long-running SELECT statements. The UPDLOCK table hints places pessimistic locks on rows needed for the multistep transaction to complete. The use of UPDLOCK on SELECT statements with SNAPSHOT isolation level is not a panacea for update conflicts, and it could in fact create them. Frequent select statements with UPDLOCK could increase the number of update conflicts with updates. Regardless, your application should handle errors and initiate retries when appropriate.

   If two concurrent statements use UPDLOCK, with one updating and one reading the same data, even in implicit transactions, an update conflict failure is possible if not likely.

- Avoid writes altogether while in SNAPSHOT isolation mode. Change the transaction isolation level back to READ COMMITTED before running an UPDATE statement, and then back to SNAPSHOT if desired.

Specifying table granularity hints such as ROWLOCK or TABLOCK can prevent update conflicts, although at the cost of concurrency. The second update transaction must be blocked while the first update transaction is running—essentially bypassing SNAPSHOT isolation for the write. If two concurrent statements are both updating the same data in SNAPSHOT isolation level, an update conflict failure is likely for the statement that started second.

Using memory-optimized tables in SNAPSHOT isolation level

SNAPSHOT isolation is supported for memory-optimized tables, but not with all of the different ways to place a query in SNAPSHOT isolation. There are only ways to ensure that memory-optimized tables use SNAPSHOT isolation:

- Turn on the `MEMORY_OPTIMIZED_ELEVATE_TO_SNAPSHOT` database option. This promotes access to all memory-optimized tables in the database up to SNAPHOT isolation level if the current isolation level is not REPEATABLE READ or SERIALIZABLE. It will promote the isolation level to SNAPSHOT from isolation levels such as READ UNCOMMITTED and READ COMMITTED. This option is off by default, but you should consider it because you otherwise cannot use the READ UNCOMMITTED or SNAPSHOT isolation levels for a session including memory-optimized tables.

- You can specify SNAPSHOT isolation with table hints (see the section "Using table hints to change isolation" earlier in this chapter). Note that only for memory-optimized tables can use this SNAPSHOT table hint, not disk-based tables.

You cannot, for example, include memory-optimized tables in a session that begins with SET TRANSACTION ISOLATION LEVEL SNAPSHOT, even if MEMORY_OPTIMIZED_ELEVATE_TO_SNAPSHOT = ON or you specify the SNAPSHOT table hint.

Inside OUT

Which isolation level does my .NET application use?

Be aware that by default the .NET System.Transaction infrastructure uses the SERIALIZABLE isolation level, the safest but least practical choice. SERIALIZABLE provides the most isolation for transactions, so by default .NET transactions do not suffer from dirty reads, nonrepeatable reads, or phantom rows.

You might find, however, that SERIALIZABLE transactions are being frequently blocked and at the source of blocking, and that reducing the isolation of certain transactions would result in better performance. Evaluate the potential risk of nonrepeatable reads and phantom rows for each new .NET transaction, and reduce the isolation level to REPEATABLE READ or READ COMMITTED only where appropriate, and following guidance throughout this chapter, do not use the READ UNCOMMITTED isolation level in any production code.

For applications with high transactional volume, consider also using SNAPSHOT isolation level to increase concurrency.

You can set the isolation level of any transaction when it is begun by setting the IsolationLevel property of the TransactionScope class. You can also default a new database connection's isolation level upon creation. Remember, however, that you cannot change the isolation level of a transaction after it has begun.

Understanding on-disk versus memory-optimized concurrency

Queries using memory-optimized tables (initially called Project Hekaton prior to the release of SQL 2014) can perform significantly faster than queries based on the same data in disk-based tables. Memory-optimized tables can improve the performance of frequently written-to tables by up to 40 times over disk-based tables.

When in the aforementioned scenarios we use the words "prevents" or "protection," we mean locking, and this applies only to on-disk tables, not memory-optimized tables. When a transaction has rows or a range of rows locked, any other transaction's writes in that range are blocked and wait patiently, queueing up to proceed as soon as the locks are released. Although SQL Server allows requests to wait and be blocked forever, the applications generating the request might easily time out under a minute of waiting.

In the case of memory-optimized tables, locking isn't the mechanism that ensures isolation. Instead, the in-memory engine uses row versioning to provide row content to each transaction. In the in-memory engine, update operations create new rows in the in-memory data structure (actually a heap), that supplant older row versions. Similarly, delete operations create rows in a delta file, marking the row as deleted. Periodically, cleanup is done to merge the in-memory data structure and delta files to reduce the space used in memory, and in the case of tables with durable data, on a drive. If you are familiar with the data warehousing concept of a Slowly Changing Dimension (SCD), this is similar to an SCD Type II.

If two transactions attempt to update the same data at the same time, one transaction will immediately fail due to a concurrency error. Only one transaction can be in the process of updating or deleting the same row at a time. The other will fail with a concurrency conflict (SQL error 41302).

This is the key difference between the behavior of pessimistic and optimistic concurrency. Pessimistic concurrency uses locks to prevent write conflict errors, whereas optimistic concurrency uses row versions with acceptable risk of write conflict errors. On-disk tables offer isolation levels that use pessimistic concurrency to block conflicting transactions, forcing them to wait. Memory-optimized tables offer optimistic concurrency that will cause a conflicting transaction to fail.

In the case of a nonrepeatable read, SQL error 41305 will be raised. In the case of a phantom read, a SQL error 41325 will be raised. Because of these errors, applications that write to memory-optimized tables must include logic that gracefully handles and automatically retries transactions. They should already handle and retry in the case of deadlocks or other fatal database errors.

➤ **For more information on configuring memory-optimized tables, see Chapter 8.**

➤ **We discuss more about indexes for memory-optimized tables in Chapter 10.**

Understanding delayed durability

Delayed durability is a set of transaction features first introduced in SQL Server 2014. It allows for transactions to avoid synchronously committing to a disk; instead, committing only to memory and asynchronously committing to a disk. If this sounds dangerous to you, and opens the possibility to losing records in the event of a server shutdown, you are correct!

However, unless your SQL Server instance's databases are running in a synchronous availability group (and even then, chance exists for the databases to drop into asynchronous under pressure), you already face the likelihood in your database of losing recently written records in the event of a sudden server or drive failure.

So perhaps delayed durability's danger isn't so unfamiliar after all. Databases in Azure SQL Database also support delayed durability transactions, with the same caveat and expectations for data recovery. Some data loss is possible.

> **NOTE**
>
> **Any SQL Server instance service shutdown, whether it be a planned restart or sudden failure, could result in delayed durability transactions being lost. This also applies to the failover of a failover cluster instance (FCI), availability group, or database mirror. Transaction log backups and log shipping will similarly contain only transactions made durable. You must be aware of this potential when implementing delayed durability.**

> **NOTE**
>
> **Distributed (DTC) and cross-database transactions are always durable.**

A delayed durable transaction will be flushed to the disk whenever a threshold of delayed durability transactions builds up, or, whenever any other durable transaction commits in the same database. You also can force a flush of the transaction log with the system stored procedure `sp_flush_log`. Otherwise, the transactions are written to a buffer in-memory and kept away from using I/O resources until a log flush event. SQL Server manages the buffer, but makes no guarantees as to the amount of time a transaction can remain in buffer.

The delayed durability options, implemented either at the database level or at the transaction level, have application in very-high-performance workloads for which the bottleneck to write performance is the transaction log itself. By trading the possibility for new records to be written only to memory and lost in the event of a shutdown, you can gain a significant performance increase, especially with write-heavy workloads.

It's important to note that delayed durability is simply about reducing the I/O bottleneck of committing a massive quantity of writes to the transaction log. This has no effect on isolation (locking, blocking) or access to any data in the database that must be read to perform the write. Otherwise, delayed durability transactions follow the same rules as other transactions.

> **NOTE**
>
> Aside from the basic concept of an in-memory buffer, this topic is not related to memory-optimized tables. The DELAYED_DURABILITY database option is not related to the DURABILITY option when creating optimized tables.

Delayed durability database options

At the database level, you can set the DELAYED_DURABILITY option to DISABLED (default), ALLOWED, or FORCED.

The FORCED option obviously has implications on the entirety of the database, and you should consider it carefully with existing applications and databases. The ALLOWED option permits delayed durability transactions but has no effect on other transactions.

Delayed durability transactions

In the end, delayed durability is a transaction option with simple syntax. This syntax is necessary only when DELAYED_DURABILITY = ALLOWED in the current database.

It is supported for explicit transactions at the time they are committed by using the following sample syntax:

```
BEGIN TRAN
COMMIT TRAN WITH (DELAYED_DURABILITY=ON);
```

In the case of a natively compiled procedure, you can specify DELAYED_DURABILITY in the BEGIN ATOMIC block. Take, for example, this procedure in the WideWorldImporters database:

```
CREATE PROCEDURE [Website].[RecordColdRoomTemperatures_DD]
@SensorReadings Website.SensorDataList READONLY
WITH NATIVE_COMPILATION, SCHEMABINDING, EXECUTE AS OWNER
AS
BEGIN ATOMIC WITH
(
    TRANSACTION ISOLATION LEVEL = SNAPSHOT,
    LANGUAGE = N'English',
    DELAYED_DURABILITY = ON
)
    BEGIN TRY
...
```

Understanding execution plans

Execution plans are a detailed explanation of the query optimizer's plan for processing any statement. Each time you run a statement, including batches with multiple statements, an execution plan is generated.

CHAPTER 9

Execution plans inform the developer of the steps the Database Engine will take to retrieve data, from the tables, through the various transformation steps to sort, join, and filter data, and finally return or affect data. All statements create execution plans, including Data Manipulation Language (DML) and DDL.

Execution plans contain the cost and other metadata of each piece that it takes to process a query—from the data retrieval steps, joins, sorts, and more, and finally the DML or DDL operation itself. This data can be invaluable to developers and database administrators for tuning query performance.

The Procedure Cache, stored in the memory that SQL Server uses, contains query plans for statements that have been run. The Query Store is a powerful built-in repository in each database to track and trend runtime statistics over time.

Execution plans are generated for a query and reused when that exact same query text is called again. (The query text is first and always subjected to simplification, which removes redundancies, including using a code reduction technique called Constant Folding.) Queries will reuse the same plan only if every character of the query statement matches, including capitalization, whitespace, line breaks, and text in comments. There is one exception to this rule of query reuse, and that is when SQL Server parameterizes a query or stored procedure statement.

SQL Server does a smart job at sniffing for parts of a statement that could be parameterized to make a query's cached plan reusable. For example, a query that has a WHERE clause on a LastName field should be able to use the same execution plan whether it is searching for "Smith" or "Green."

Understanding parameterization and "parameter sniffing"

SQL Server parameterization occurs when the query optimizer detects values (such as the search criteria of a WHERE clause statement) that can be parameterized.

With parameterization, it's possible that two potentially helpful or potentially problematic conditions can occur:

- You can reuse a query plan for multiple queries for which the query text is exactly the same, except for parameterized values.

- The same query could use the same execution plan for two different values of a WHERE clause, resulting in vastly different performance.

For example, the following two query statements in the WideWorldImporters database will be parameterized and use the same query plan. (This also means that both queries could be affected by the same Query Store forced plan; more on that later.) The first query returns 13 rows, the second returns 1,055 rows:

```
SELECT ppo.OrderDate, ppo.PurchaseOrderID, pol.PurchaseOrderLineID, ppo.[SupplierID]
  FROM [Purchasing].[PurchaseOrders] AS ppo
  INNER JOIN [Purchasing].[PurchaseOrderLines] AS pol
    ON ppo.PurchaseOrderID = pol.PurchaseOrderID
  INNER JOIN [Purchasing].[Suppliers] AS s  ON s.SupplierID = ppo.SupplierID
  WHERE ppo.SupplierID = 5

SELECT ppo.OrderDate, ppo.PurchaseOrderID, pol.PurchaseOrderLineID, ppo.[SupplierID]
  FROM [Purchasing].[PurchaseOrders] AS ppo
  INNER JOIN [Purchasing].[PurchaseOrderLines] AS pol
    ON ppo.PurchaseOrderID = pol.PurchaseOrderID
  INNER JOIN [Purchasing].[Suppliers] AS s  ON s.SupplierID = ppo.SupplierID
  WHERE ppo.SupplierID = 4
```

In the WideWorldImporters database, we might see the same query plan for both statements results in quick performance for the smaller `rowcount SupplierID` and horrible performance for the larger `rowcount`.

If the larger `rowcount` query (`SupplierID` = 4) is run first and has its query plan cached, there isn't likely to be a problem. Both versions of the query will run well enough. If the smaller `rowcount` query (`SupplierID` = 5) is run first, its version of the plan will be cached. In this case, the plan is different, less efficient for very large row counts, and will be used for all versions of the parameterized statement.

Here are a few advanced troubleshooting avenues to alleviate this scenario:

- You can use the OPTIMIZE FOR query hint to demand that the query analyzer use a cached execution plan that substitutes a provided value for the parameters. You also can use OPTIMIZE FOR UNKNOWN, which instructs the query analyzer to optimize for the most common value, based on statistics of the underlying data object.

- The RECOMPILE query hint or procedure option does not allow the reuse of a cached plan, forcing a fresh query plan to be generated each time the query is run.

- You can use the Plan Guide feature (implemented via stored procedures) to guide the query analyzer to a plan currently in cache. You identify the plan via its `plan_handle`. For information on identifying and analyzing plans in `sys.dm_exec_cached_plans`, see the upcoming section, which contains a `plan_handle`.

- You can use the Query Store feature (implemented with a GUI in SQL Server Management Studio, and via stored procedures behind the scenes) to visually look at plan performance and force a query to use a specific plan currently in cache.

CHAPTER 9

> ➤ For more information, see the section "Using the Query Store feature" later in this chapter.

- You could use the USE PLAN query hint to provide the entire XML query plan for any statement execution. This obviously is the least convenient option, and like other approaches that override the query analyzer, you should consider it an advanced and temporary performance tuning technique.

Understanding the Procedure Cache

New execution plans enter the Procedure Cache only when a new statement is run. If a procedure cache already contains a plan matching a previous run of the current statement, the execution plan is reused, saving valuable time and resources.

This is why complex statements can appear to run faster the second time they are run.

The Procedure Cache is empty when the SQL Server service starts and grows from there. SQL Server manages plans in the cache, removing them as necessary under memory pressure. The size of the Procedure Cache is managed by SQL Server and is inside the memory space configured for the server in the Max Server Memory configuration setting. Plans are removed based on their cost and how recently it has been used. Smaller, older plans and single-user plans are the first to be cleared.

Inside Out

If I run a statement only once, does SQL Server remember its plan?

By default, SQL Server adds an execution plan to the Procedure Cache the first time it is generated. You can view the number and size of cached execution plans with the dynamic management view `sys.dm_exec_cached_plans`. You might find that a large amount of space in the Procedure Cache is dedicated to storing execution plans that have been used only once. These single-use plans can be referred to as *ad hoc* execution plans, from the Latin, meaning "for this situation."

If you find that a SQL Server instance is storing many single-use plans, as many do, selecting the server configuration option Optimize For Ad Hoc Queries will benefit performance. This option does not optimize ad hoc queries; rather, it optimizes SQL Server memory by storing an execution plan in memory only after the same query has been detected twice. Queries might then benefit from the cached plan only upon the third time they are run.

The following query provides the number of single-use versus multiuse query plans, and the space used to store both:

```
SELECT
        PlanUse = CASE WHEN p.usecounts > 1 THEN '>1' ELSE '1' END
,       PlanCount = COUNT(1)
,       SizeInMB = SUM(p.size_in_bytes/1024./1024.)
FROM sys.dm_exec_cached_plans p
GROUP BY CASE WHEN p.usecounts > 1 THEN '>1' ELSE '1' END;
```

Analyzing cached execution plans in aggregate

You can analyze execution plans in aggregate starting with the dynamic management view `sys.dm_exec_cached_plans`, which contains a `plan_handle`.

The `plan_handle` column contains a system-generated `varbinary(64)` string that can be joined to a number of other dynamic management views. As seen in the code example that follows, you can use the `plan_handle` to gather information about aggregate plan usage, plan statement text, and to retrieve the graphical execution plan itself. You might be used to viewing the graphical execution plan only after a statement is run in SQL Server Management Studio, but you can also analyze and retrieve plans by using the following query against a handful of dynamic management views (DMVs). These DMVs return data for all databases in SQL Server instances, and for the current database in Azure SQL Database.

Query cached plan stats

```
SELECT
    UseCount     = p.usecounts
,   PlanSize_KB  = p.size_in_bytes / 1024
,   CPU_ms       = qs.total_worker_time/1000
,   Duration_ms  = qs.total_elapsed_time/1000
,   ObjectType   = p.cacheobjtype + ' (' + p.objtype + ')'
,   DatabaseName = db_name(convert(int, pa.value))
,   txt.ObjectID
,   qs.total_physical_reads
,   qs.total_logical_writes
,   qs.total_logical_reads
,   qs.last_execution_time
,   StatementText =  SUBSTRING (txt.[text], qs.statement_start_offset/2 + 1,
                     CASE WHEN qs.statement_end_offset = -1 THEN LEN
(CONVERT(nvarchar(max), txt.[text]))
                     ELSE qs.statement_end_offset/2 - qs.statement_start_offset/2 + 1 END)
```

```
,  QueryPlan  = qp.query_plan
FROM sys.dm_exec_query_stats AS qs
INNER JOIN sys.dm_exec_cached_plans p ON p.plan_handle = qs.plan_handle
OUTER APPLY sys.dm_exec_plan_attributes (p.plan_handle) AS pa
OUTER APPLY sys.dm_exec_sql_text (p.plan_handle) AS txt
OUTER APPLY sys.dm_exec_query_plan (p.plan_handle) AS qp
WHERE pa.attribute = 'dbid'  --retrieve only the database id from sys.dm_exec_plan_
attributes
ORDER BY qs.total_worker_time + qs.total_elapsed_time DESC;
```

Note that the preceding query orders by a sum of the CPU time and duration, descending, returning the longest running queries first. You can adjust the ORDER BY and WHERE clauses in this query to hunt, for example, for the most CPU-intensive or most busy execution plans. Keep in mind that the Query Store feature, as detailed later in this chapter, will help you visualize the process of identifying the most expensive and longest running queries in cache.

As you can see in the previous query, you can retrieve a wealth of information from these five DMVs, including the statement within a batch that generated the query plan. The query plan appears as blue hyperlink in SQL Server Management Studio's Results To Grid mode, opening the plan as a new .sqlplan file. You can save and store the .sqlplan file for later analysis.

Permissions required to access cached plan metadata

The only permission needed to run the previous query in SQL Server is the server-level VIEW SERVER STATE permissions, which might be appropriate for developers to have access to in a production environment because it does not give them access to any data in user databases.

In Azure SQL Database, because of the differences between the Basic/Standard and Premium tiers, different permissions are needed. In the Basic/Standard tier, you must be the server admin or Azure Active Directory Admin to access objects that would usually require VIEW SERVER STATE. In Premium tier, you can grant VIEW DATABASE STATE in the intended database in Azure SQL Database to a user who needs permission to view the above DMVs.

Clearing the Procedure Cache

You might find that manually clearing the Procedure Cache is useful when performance testing or troubleshooting. Typically, you want to reserve this activity for nonproduction systems. There are a few strategies to clearing out cached plans in SQL Server.

To compare two versions of a query or the performance of a query with different indexes, you could clear the cached plan for the statement to allow for proper comparison. You can manually flush the entire Procedure Cache, or individual plans in cache, with the following database-scoped configuration command. The following command affects only the current database context, as opposed to the entire instance's procedure cache:

```
ALTER DATABASE SCOPED CONFIGURATION CLEAR PROCEDURE_CACHE;
```

CAUTION

Avoid clearing the Procedure Cache in a live production environment during normal business hours. Doing so will cause all new statements to have their execution plans compiled, dramatically increasing processor utilization and potentially dramatically slowing performance.

This command was introduced in SQL Server 2016 and is effectively the same as the command DBCC FREEPROCCACHE within the current database context. It works in both SQL Server and Azure SQL Database. DBCC FREEPROCCACHE is not supported in Azure SQL Database.

You can use DBCC FREEPROCCACHE to clear the procedure cache of the SQL Server instance.

You can also remove a single plan from cache by identifying its `plan_handle` and then providing it as the parameter to the DBCC FREEPROCCACHE function. Perhaps this is a plan you would like to remove for testing or troubleshooting purposes that you have identified with the script in the previous section:

```
DBCC FREEPROCCACHE (0x06000700CA920912307B86
7DB7010000010000000000000000000000000000000000000000000000000000000);
```

You could alternatively flush the cache by object type. This command clears cached execution plans that are the result of ad hoc statements and prepared statements (from applications):

```
DBCC FREESYSTEMCACHE ('SQL Plans');
```

The advantage of this statement is that it does not wipe the cached plans from "Programmability" database objects such as stored procedures, multistatement table-valued functions, scalar user-defined functions, and triggers. The following command clears the cached plans from those type of objects:

```
DBCC FREESYSTEMCACHE ('Object Plans');
```

Note that DBCC FREESYSTEMCACHE is not supported in Azure SQL Database.

You can also use DBCC FREESYSTEMCACHE to clear cached plans association to a specific Resource Governor Pool, as follows:

```
DBCC FREESYSTEMCACHE ('SQL Plans', 'poolname');
```

NOTE

Execution plans are not removed from cache for a database that is OFFLINE. Plan data is cleared from the Procedure Cache for databases dropped or detached from the SQL Server instance.

CHAPTER 9

Retrieving execution plans in SQL Server Management Studio

There are three basic types of graphical execution plans to retrieve for a statement: Estimated, Actual, and Live. Let's review the differences, and how you can view them.

Estimate the execution plan

You can generate the estimated execution plan quickly and view it graphically from within SQL Server Management Studio by choosing the Display Estimated Execution Plan option in the Query menu, or pressing Ctrl+L. An estimated execution plan will return for the highlighted region, or for the entire file if no text is selected.

You can also retrieve an estimated graphical execution plan in T-SQL code by running the following statement:

```
SET SHOWPLAN_XML ON
```

The actual execution plan is returned as an XML string. In SQL Server Management Studio, in Grid mode, the results are displayed as a link. Click the link to open the plan graphically in SQL Server Management Studio. You can save the execution plan as a .sqlplan file by right-clicking in the neutral space of the plan window.

You can also configure the estimated text execution plan in code by running one of the following statements, which return the execution plan in one result set or two, respectively:

```
SET SHOWPLAN_ALL ON
SET SHOWPLAN_TEXT ON
```

> **NOTE**
>
> Be aware that when any of the aforementioned three options are turned on, SQL Server will not run statements, only return estimated execution plans. Remember to turn off the SET SHOWPLAN_ option before you reuse the same session for other queries.

As expected, the estimated execution plan is not guaranteed to match the actual plan used when you run the statement, but it is a very reliable approximation. The query optimizer uses the same information for the estimate as it does for the actual plan when you run it.

One cause for any differences between the estimate and actual execution plans would be any reason for the plan to be recompiled between the estimate and actual plan generation, including if the plan was removed from the Procedure Cache.

To display information for individual steps, hover over a step in the execution plan. You can also click an object, and then open the Properties window by pressing F4 or, in the View menu, clicking Properties Window. You'll notice the estimated execution plan is missing some information that the actual plan returns. The missing fields are self-explanatory; for example, Actual Number Of Rows, Actual Number Of Batches, and Number of Executions.

Displaying the actual execution plan

You can generate the actual execution plan along with the statement's result set from within SQL Server Management Studio by choosing the Include Actual Execution Plan option in the Query menu, or pressing Control+M to turn on the setting. After turning on this setting, when you run a statement, you will see an additional tab along with the execution results.

You'll notice that returning the actual graphical execution plan adds some additional time to the execution. The actual execution plan will return as an additional tab in Management Studio.

You can also configure the actual graphical execution plan in T-SQL code, returning XML that can be viewed graphically in SQL Server Management Studio, by running the following statement:

```
SET STATISTICS XML ON
```

The actual execution plan is returned as an XML string. In SQL Server Management Studio, in Grid mode, the results display as a link.

Remember to turn off the SET STATISTICS option before you reuse the same session, if you don't want to get back the actual plan for every query you run on this connection.

You can save both the estimated and actual execution plans as a .sqlplan file by right-clicking the neutral space of the plan window.

Displaying live query statistics

You can generate and display a "live" version of the execution plan by using SQL Server Management Studio 2016. You can access live statistics on versions of SQL Server starting with SQL Server 2014. You turn on the Live Execution Statistics option in the Query menu of SQL Server Management Studio, as demonstrated in Figure 9-1.

CHAPTER 9

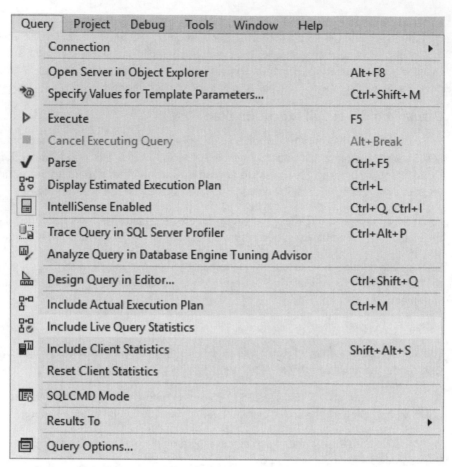

Figure 9-1 The Query menu in SQL Server Management Studio, with the Include Live
Query Statistics option highlighted.

The Live Query Statistics window displays a hybrid version of the Estimated and Actual execution plans while the query is processing. If your query runs too quickly, you'll miss the dotted,
moving lines and the various progress metrics including duration for each step and overall percentage completion. The percentage is based on the Actual rows processed currently incurred
versus a total number of rows processed for that step.

The Live Query Statistics contains more information than the Estimated query plan, such as Actual Number Of Rows and Number Of Executions, but less than the Actual query plan. The Live Query Statistics does not display some data from the Actual Execution Plan, Actual Execution Mode, Number Of Rows Read, Actual Rebinds, and Actual Rebinds.

Notice in Figure 9-2 that returning the execution plan slows down the query, so be aware that the individual and overall execution durations measured will often be longer than when the query is run without the option to display Live Query Statistics.

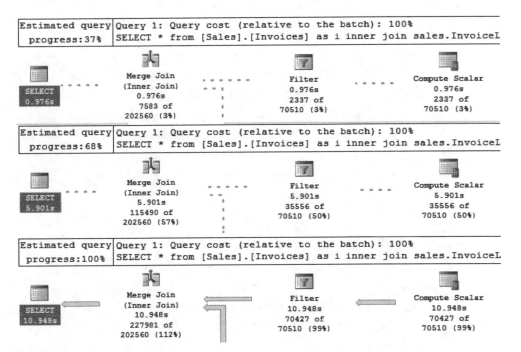

Figure 9-2 Three different screenshots of the Live Query Statistics, moments apart.

You might see that the total rows to be processed does not match total Estimated Number Of Rows for that step; rather, the multiple of that step's Estimated Number Of Rows and a preceding step's Estimated Number Of Rows. In Figure 9-2, the number of rows Estimated is less than the number of rows actually read.

Inside OUT

What's the difference between "Number Of Rows Read" and "Actual Number Of Rows"?

This is an important distinction, and it can tip you off to a significant performance issue.

Both are "Actual" values, but Actual Number Of Rows contains the number of values in the range of rows we expect to retrieve, and Number Of Rows Read contains the number of rows that were actually read. The difference could be significant to performance, and the solution is likely to change the query so that the predicate is narrower and/or better aligned with indexes on the table. Alternatively, you could add indexes to better fit the query predicates and make for more efficient searches.

One of the easiest ways to reproduce this behavior is with a wildcard search, for example in the WideWorldImporters sample database:

```
SELECT i.InvoiceID
FROM [Sales].[Invoices] as i
WHERE i.InvoiceID like '1%'
```

In the XML, in the node for the Index Scan, you will see:

```
<RunTimeInformation>
<RunTimeCountersPerThread Thread="0" ActualRows="11111" ActualRowsRead="70510"
...
```

Defined as "ActualRowsRead" in the XML of the plan, this value is displayed as "Number of Rows Read" in SQL Server Management Studio. Similarly, "ActualRows" is displayed as "Actual Number of Rows."

Permissions necessary to view execution plans

The user must have permissions to actually run the query, even if they are generating only an Estimated execution plan.

Retrieving the Estimated or Actual execution plan requires the SHOWPLAN permission in each database referenced by the query. The Live Query Statistics feature requires SHOWPLAN in each database, plus the VIEW SERVER STATE permission to see live statistics.

It might be appropriate in your environment to grant SHOWPLAN and VIEW SERVER STATE permissions to developers. However, the permission to execute queries against the production database may not be appropriate in your regularly environment. If that is the case, there are alternatives to providing valuable execution plan data to developers without production access:

- Consider providing database developers with saved execution plan (.sqlplan) files for offline analysis.

- Consider also configuring the dynamic data masking feature, which may already be appropriate in your environment for hiding sensitive or personally identifying information for users who are not sysadmins on the server. Do not provide UNMASK permission to developers; assign that only to application users.

➤ For more information on dynamic data masking, see Chapter 7.

Using the Query Store feature

First introduced in SQL Server 2016, the Query Store provides a practical history of execution plan performance. It can be invaluable for the purposes of investigating and troubleshooting sudden negative changes in performance, by allowing the administrator or developer to identify high-cost queries and the quality of their execution plans.

The Query Store is most useful for looking back in time toward the history of statement execution. The Query Store can also assist in identifying and overriding execution plans by using a feature similar to but different from the legacy plan guides feature.

Inside OUT

How should I force a statement to use a certain execution plan?

Your options for forcing a statement to follow a certain execution plan are either the older plan guides stored procedures or the newer Query Store interface (and its underlying stored procedures) to force an execution plan.

Both options are advanced options for temporary or diagnostic use only. Overriding the query optimizer's execution plan choice is an advanced performance tuning technique. It is most often necessitated by query parameter sniffing.

It is possible to create competing plan guides or Query Store forced plans. This is certainly not recommended because it could be extremely confusing. If you create compete plan guides or Query Store forced plans, it's likely you'll see the Query Store forced plan "win."

> In case you are troubleshooting competing plan guides and Query Store forced plans, you can view any existing plan guides and forced query plans with the following DMV queries:
>
> ```
> SELECT * FROM sys.plan_guides
>
> SELECT  *
> FROM    sys.query_store_query AS qsq
> JOIN    sys.query_store_plan AS qsp
>         ON qsp.query_id = qsq.query_id
> WHERE   qsp.is_forced_plan = 1;
> ```
>
> Finally, you could use the USE PLAN query hint to provide the entire XML query plan for any statement execution. This obviously is the least convenient option, and like other approaches that override the query analyzer, should be considered an advanced and temporary performance tuning technique.

Plan guides are used to override an otherwise complicated manual scripting exercise.

You see live Query Store data as it happens from a combination of both memory-optimized and on-disk sources. Query Store minimizes overhead and performance impact by capturing cached plan information to in-memory data structure. The data is "flushed" to disk at an interval defined by Query Store, by default 15 minutes. The Disk Flush Interval setting defines how much Query Store data could be lost in the event of an unexpected system shutdown.

NOTE

Cross-database queries are captured according to the query database context. In the following code example, the query's execution would be captured in the Query Store of the WideWorldImporters database.

```
USE WideWorldImporters;
GO
SELECT * FROM
AdventureWorks.[Purchasing].[PurchaseOrders];
```

The Query Store is a feature that Microsoft delivered to the Azure SQL Database platform *first*, and then to the SQL Server product. In fact, Query Store is at the heart of the Azure SQL Database Advisor feature which provides automatic query tuning. The Query Store feature's overhead is quite manageable, tuned to avoid performance hits, and is already in place on millions of databases in Azure SQL Database.

The VIEW DATABASE STATE permission is all that is needed to view the Query Store data.

Initially configuring the query store

The Query Store feature is identical between the two platforms, except for its default activation. Query Store is turned on automatically on Azure SQL Database, but it is not automatically on for new databases in SQL Server 2017, and it is not a setting that can be inherited by the model database.

You should turn on the Query Store on new production databases in SQL Server 2017 when you anticipate doing any performance tuning. You can turn on Query Store via the database Properties dialog box, in which Query Store is a page on the menu on the left. Or, you can turn it on via T-SQL by using the following command:

```
ALTER DATABASE [DatabaseOne] SET QUERY_STORE = ON;
```

Keep in mind that Query Store begins collecting when you activate it. You will not have any historical data when you first turn on the feature on an existing database, but you will begin to immediately see data for live database activity.

The Query Store Capture Mode default setting of All includes all queries. You might soon realize that this setting does not filter out ad hoc queries, even if you selected the Optimize For Ad Hoc Queries option in the system configuration. Change this setting to Auto because the additional data of one-use plans might not be useful, and can reduce the amount of historical data can be retained.

> **NOTE**
> The Query Store data is stored in the user database. It is backed up and restored along with the database.

The Query Store retains data up to two limits: a Max Size (500 MB by default), and a "Stale Query Threshold" time limit of Days (30 by default). If Query Store reaches its Max Size, it will clean up the oldest data. Because Query Store data is saved on a drive, its historical data is not affected by the commands we looked at earlier in this chapter to clear the Procedure Cache, such as DBCC FREEPROCACHE.

You should keep the Size Based Cleanup Mode set to the default Auto. If not, when the Max Size is reached, Query Store will stop collecting data and enter "Read Only" mode, which does not collect new data. If you find that the Query Store is not storing more historical days of data than your Stale Query Threshold setting in days, increase the Max Size setting.

> **NOTE**
> Starting with SQL Server Management Studio 17.3, you can also see wait stats on existing reports.

Using query store data in your troubleshooting

Query Store has several built-in dashboards, shown in Figure 9-3, to help you examine query performance and overall performance over recent history.

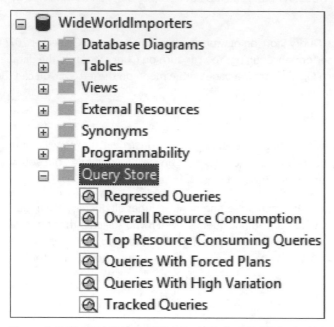

Figure 9-3 The SQL Server Object Explorer list of built-in dashboards available for Query Store in SQL Server Management Studio 2017.

With SQL Server Management Studio 2017, you can view more dashboards in SQL Server 2016 databases than you could in SQL Server Management Studio 2016, including Queries With Forced Plans and Queries With High Variation.

You can also write your own reports against the collection of system DMVs that present Query Store data to administrators and developers by using the VIEW DATABASE STATE permission. You can view the six-view schema of well-documented views and their relationships at *https://docs.microsoft.com/sql/relational-databases/performance/how-query-store-collects-data#views*.

On many of the dashboards, there is a button with a crosshairs symbol, as depicted in Figure 9-4. If a query seems interesting, expensive, or is of high value to the business, you can click this button to view a new screen that tracks the query when it's running as well as various plans identified for that query.

Figure 9-4 The Query Store tool bar at the top of the screen on many of the dashboards, in this example, the tool bar for the Regressed Queries report.

You can also review the various plans for the same statement, compare the plans, and if necessary, force your chosen plan into place. Compare the execution of each plan by CPU Time, Duration, Logical Reads, Logical Writes, Memory Consumption, and Physical Reads.

Most of all, the Query Store can be valuable by informing you when a query started using a new plan. You can see when a plan was generated and the nature of the plan; however, the cause of the plan's creation and replacement is not easily answered, especially when you cannot correlate to a DDL operation. Query plans can become invalidated automatically due to large changes in statistics due to data inserts or deletes, changes made to other statements in the stored procedure, changes to any of the indexes used by the plan, or manual recompilation due to the RECOMPILE option.

Forcing a statement (see Figure 9-5) to use a specific execution plan via the Query Store is not a recommended common activity. You should use this only for specific performance cases, problematic queries demanding unusual plans, workarounds for other unresolvable index or performance scenarios. Note that if the forced plan is invalid, such as an index changing or being dropped, SQL Server will move on without the forced plan without warning or error, though Query Store will still show that the plan is being forced for that statement.

CHAPTER 9

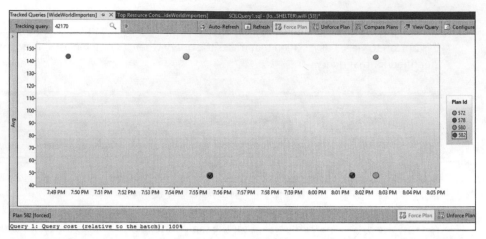

Figure 9-5 The Query Store has recorded the execution results of the query. Note that one plan
has been Forced (using the Force Plan button) for this statement and is displayed with
a check mark.

Understanding automatic plan correction

SQL Server 2017 introduces a new feature called Automatic Plan Tuning, originally developed
for the Azure SQL Database platform. It is capable of detecting and reverting plan regression.

You could use Query Store in 2016 to identify a query that has regressed in performance, and
manually force a past execution plan into use. Now in SQL Server 2017, the database can be
configured to detect plan regression and take this action automatically. The sample syntax for
enabling automatic plan correction is below:

```
ALTER DATABASE [WideWorldImporters] SET AUTOMATIC_TUNING (FORCE_LAST_GOOD_PLAN = ON );
```

Currently, FORCE_LAST_GOOD_PLAN is the only option for automatic plan tuning.

The DMV sys.dm_db_tuning_recommendations captures plan recommendations based
on query performance regression. This doesn't happen immediately – the feature has an algorithm that requires several executions before regression is identified. When a recommendation appears in sys.dm_db_tuning_recommendations, it includes a large amount of diagnostic
data, including a plain-language "reason" explanation for the recommendation to be generated, and a block of JSON data containing diagnostic information. A sample query to parse
this data is available at *https://docs.microsoft.com/sql/relational-databases/automatic-tuning/
automatic-tuning*.

Understanding execution plan operators

After you have a graphical execution plan in front of you, you can begin to understand how the statement is processed.

To display information for individual steps, position your pointer over a step in the execution plan. You can also click an object, and then open the Properties window by pressing F4 or, in the View menu, clicking Properties Window. You'll notice that the information returned estimate and actual values for some metrics, including Number of Rows and Executions. Look for differences here; they can indicate an inefficient execution plan and the source of a poor performing query. Your query might be suffering from a poorly chosen plan because of the impact of parameter sniffing or stale, inaccurate index statistics. (We discussed parameter sniffing earlier in this chapter, and discuss index statistics in Chapter 10.)

However, notice that some values, like Cost information, contain only Estimated values, even when you are viewing the Actual execution plan. This is because the operator costs aren't sourced separately, they are generated the same way for both Estimated and Actual plans, and do not change based on statement execution. Furthermore, cost is not just comprised entirely of duration. You might find that some statements far exceed others in terms of duration, but not in cost.

There are even known plan presentation issues (as recent as SQL Server Management Studio 17.1) that might sometimes result in a sum of Operator Costs that do not add up to 100 percent, specifically in the presence of the concatenation operator.

Interpreting graphical execution plans

In the next list, we review some of the most common things to look for as you review execution plans in SQL Server Management Studio. You can also choose to review execution plans with a well-known third-party tool called Plan Explorer, which is a free download from *https://www.sentryone.com/*.

In this section, it is assumed that you will have access to the Actual execution plan, as not all the information within will exist in the Estimated plan.

Start in the upper left

The upper-left operator will reflect the basic operation that the statement performed. For example, Select, Delete, Update, or Insert for DML statements. This operator might contain warnings or other items that require your immediate attention. These might show up with a small yellow triangle warning icon, with additional detail when you position your pointer on the operator.

Click the upper-left operator, and then press F4 to open the Properties window, or open the Properties window from the View menu in SQL Server Management Studio. In this list are a couple other things to look for. You'll see warnings repeated in here, along with additional aggregate information.

> ### ATTENTION
> Yellow triangles ( ) indicate something that should grab your attention. The alert could tip you off to an implicit conversion—a data type mismatch that could be costly! Investigate any warnings reported before moving on.

Look also for the Optimization Level, which ideally says FULL. If the Optimization Level was TRIVIAL, the plan bypassed the query optimizer altogether because it was too straightforward. The plan contained only a simple Scan or Seek operation the only other operator, perhaps. If not FULL or TRIVIAL, this is something to investigate.

Look next for the presence of a value for Reason For Early Termination, which indicates the query optimizer spent too long on attempting to build the perfect execution plan, and gave up, sometimes literally returning the self-explanatory value, Good Enough Plan Found. If the reason is Time Out, the optimizer tried as many times as it could to find the best plan before deciding, taking the best plan available, which might not be "good enough." If you see this case, consider simplifying the query, especially reducing the use of functions, and by potentially modifying the underlying indexes. Finally, if you see the reason is Memory Limit Exceeded, this is a rare and critical error indicating severe memory pressure on the SQL Server instance.

In the Query Cached Plan Stats script sample shown in the section "Analyzing cached execution plans in aggregate" earlier in this chapter, in which we queried the procedure cache for plan statistics, you can add some code to search only for queries that have a Reason For Early Termination. In the execution plan XML, the Reason For Early Termination will show in a node `StatementOptmEarlyAbortReason`. Before the WHERE clause, add this line:

```
CROSS APPLY sys.dm_exec_text_query_plan(p.plan_handle, qs.statement_start_offset,
qs.statement_end_offset) AS tqp
```

And before the ORDER BY in the script, add this line:

```
and tqp.query_plan LIKE '%StatementOptmEarlyAbortReason%'
```

Next, scroll right, then read from right to left

Graphical execution plans build from sources (rightmost objects), and apply operators to join, sort, and filter data from right to left, eventually arriving at the leftmost operator. In the rightmost objects, you'll see Scans, Seeks, and Lookups of different types. You might find some quick, straightforward insight into how the query is using indexes.

Seek operations are best for when you're looking for a needle or needles in a much larger haystack. They are generally the most efficient operators to see, and can rarely be improved by additional indexes. Keep an eye out for Seeks that are accompanied by Lookups, however. They'll likely appear one on top of the other in the graphical execution plan. Row Lookups indicate that although the optimizer used a seek, it needed a second pass at the table in the form of a Lookup on another object, perhaps the clustered index. Key Lookups (on clustered indexes) and RID Lookups (on heaps) are expensive and inefficient, and likely can be eliminated from the execution plan with the modification to an existing nonclustered index. Lookups are very efficient when looking up a small number of rows, but very inefficient for larger number of rows. In high-cost or high-importance queries, Key Lookups can represent a significant cost, one that is easily resolvable with a nonclustered index.

➤ **For an example, see the section "Designing nonclustered indexes" in Chapter 10.**

Scan operations aren't great unless your query is intentionally performing a query that returns most of the rows out of a table. Scans are in fact that most efficient option for when an index does not provide an ordered dataset, but keep in mind, they do read all rows from the index. Without a nonclustered index with a well-designed key to enable a seek for the query, a scan might be the query optimizer's only option. Scans on nonclustered indexes are often better than scans of clustered indexes, in part due to what is likely a smaller key size. Test and compare the performance of a new or updated nonclustered index, created based on the predicates and outputs of Index Scans and Clustered Index Scans.

> ### NOTE
> Again, very few queries are important enough to deserve their own indexes. Think "big picture" when creating indexes. More than one query should benefit from any nonclustered indexes you create. Avoid redundant or overlapping nonclustered indexes. See Chapter 10 for more information on creating nonclustered indexes, including "missing" indexes.

Other types of scans include the following:

- **Table Scans.** These indicate that the table has no clustered index. We discuss why this is probably not a good idea in Chapter 10.

- **Remote Scans.**   This includes any object that is preceded by "remote," which is the same operation but over a linked server connection. Troubleshoot them the same way, but potentially by making changes to the remote server instead.

- **Constant Scans.**   These appear when the query optimizer deals with scalar values, repeated numbers, and other "constants." These are necessary operators for certain tasks and generally not actionable from a performance standpoint.

- **Columnstore Index Scans.**   These are incredibly efficient operators, and likely will outperform a Clustered Index Scan or Index Seek where millions of rows, for example, must be aggregated. No need to create a nonclustered index to replace this operator.

NOTE

Since SQL Server 2016, Columnstore indexes are a viable option for read-write tables in a transactional system. In previous versions of SQL Server, nonclustered Columnstore indexes did not allow writes to the table, and so couldn't easily be adopted in transactional databases. If you aren't using them already to optimize large row count queries, considering adding them to your toolbelt.

Furthermore, since SQL Server 2016 SP1, Columnstore indexes are even available to all edition licenses of SQL Server, even Express edition, though editions below Enterprise edition have limits to the amount of Columnstore cache in memory. For more information, visit *https://docs.microsoft.com/sql/sql-server/editions-and-components-of-sql-server-2017*.

The weight of the lines connecting operators isn't the full story

SQL Server dynamically changes the thickness of the gray lines to reflect the Actual Number Of Rows. You can get a visual idea of where the bulk of data is coming from by observing the pipes, drawing your attention to the places where performance tuning could have the biggest impact.

The visual weight and the sheer number of rows does not directly translate to cost, however. Look for where the pipe weight changes from light to heavy, or vice versa. Be aware of when thick pipes are joined or sorted.

Operator cost share isn't the full story either

When you run multiple queries, the cost of the query relative to the batch is displayed in the Query Execution Plan header, and within each plan, the batch cost relative to the rest of the operators in the statement is displayed. SQL Server uses a cost-based process to decide which query plan to use. Deciding to address only the highest-cost single operator in the execution plan might be a dead end, but generally you will find the highest cost operators on the rightmost side of the execution plan.

In Figure 9-6, we can see that operator cost might not align with the amount of data. You should investigate performance tuning this execution plan using all of the information provided.

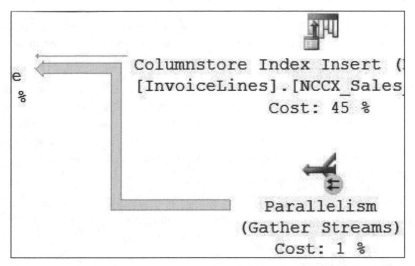

Figure 9-6 In this snippet from an execution plan, much of the cost is associated with the top operator, but more rows are moving on from the bottom operator.

Look for Join operators and understand the different algorithms

As you read from right to left, in a query of any complexity, you'll likely see the paths meet at a join operator. Two tables can be joined, obviously, but different indexes on the table can also meet in a join operator. If you find that a large portion of the cost of an execution plan spent in a Hash Match, Hash Join, Merge Join, or Nested Loop, take a look at what is being joined.

The Hash operators have the most overhead, with a temporary hash table created to bucketize and match rowdata. Merge Joins are the best for ordered data that streams processed data as it receives it. Nested Loops aren't as bad as they sound, but they are essentially the row-by-row comparison of one rowset against another. This can be very efficient for small, indexed datasets.

Each of the following could reduce the cost of a Join operator.

- There may be an opportunity to improve the indexing on the columns being joined, or perhaps, you have a join on a compound key that is incompletely defined. Perhaps you are unintentionally omitting part of the join key in the ON or WHERE clause of the query.

- In the case of a Merge Join, you may see a preceding Sort operator. This could be an opportunity to present the data already sorted according to how the Merge Join requires the data to be sorted. Perhaps changing the ASC/DESC property or the order of index key columns could remove the Sort operator.

- Make sure you that are filtering at the lowest level possible. Perhaps a WHERE clause could exist in a subquery instead of at the top level of the query, or in the definition of a common table expression (CTE) instead of in the lower query.

- Hash Match and Hash Join operators are the most expensive, but are the typically the most efficient for joining two large row sets, especially large unsorted datasets. Reducing the row counts going into the Hash Match or Hash Join could allow the query optimizer to use a less memory-intensive and less costly join operator. You could accomplish this perhaps by adding or modifying nonclustered indexes to eliminate Scan operators in favor of Seek operators.

- Nested Loops are often necessitated by Key Lookups and sometimes quite costly. They too are no longer necessary if a new nonclustered index is added to address the Key Lookup and make an accompanying Index Seek more capable.

Look for Parallel icons

The left-pointing pair of arrows in a yellow circle shown in Figure 9-7 indicate that your query has been run with a parallel-processing execution plan. We talk more about Parallelism later in this chapter, but the important thing here is to be aware that your query has gone parallel.

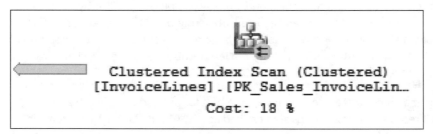

Figure 9-7 the parallel indicator on a Clustered Index Scan operator.

This doesn't mean that multiple sources or pipes are being read in parallel; rather, the work for individual tasks has been broken up behind the scenes. The query optimizer decided it was faster if your workload was split up and run into multiple parallel streams of records.

You might see one of the three different Parallelism operators—the distribute streams, gather streams, and repartition streams operators—each of which appear only for parallel execution plans.

Forcing a parallel execution plan

New to SQL Server 2017 (and also implemented in SQL Server 2016 CU2) is a query hint that can force a statement to compile with a parallel execution plan. This can be valuable in troubleshooting, or to force a behavior in the query optimizer, but is not usually a necessary or recommended option.

Appending the following hint to a query will force a parallel execution plan, which you can see using the Estimate or Actual execution plan output options:

```
OPTION(USE HINT('ENABLE_PARALLEL_PLAN_PREFERENCE'));
```

NOTE

The presence of certain system variables or functions can force a statement to compile to be serial, that is, without any parallelism. This behavior will override the new ENABLE_ PARALLEL_PLAN_PREFERENCE option.

The @@TRANCOUNT system variable will force a serial plan, as will any of the built-in error reporting functions, including ERROR_LINE(), ERROR_MESSAGE(), ERROR_NUMBER(), ERROR_PROCEDURE(), ERROR_SEVERITY(), or ERROR_STATE(). Note that this pertains only to using these objects in a query. Using them in the same batch, such as in a TRY ... CATCH handler, will not affect the execution plans of other queries in the batch.

Understanding parallelism

We mentioned parallelism in execution plans earlier in this chapter. When SQL Server decides to split and stream data needed for requests into multiple threads, it uses more than one processor to get the job done. The number of different parallel threads used for the query is called the degree of parallelism. Because parallelism can never exceed the number of logical processors, naturally the maximum degree of parallelism (MAXDOP) is capped.

The default MAXDOP setting of 0 (allowing all processors to be used in a single statement) allows SQL Server to "go parallel" at will, and, sometimes, to a fault. Although queries may perform fastest in a vacuum going massively parallel, at scale the overuse of parallelism creates a multithreaded bottleneck. Split into too many different parts, queries slow down en masse as CPU utilization rises and SQL Server records increasing values in the CXPACKET wait type.

➤ We talk about CXPACKET here, but for more about wait type statistics, see Chapter 13.

Until SQL Server 2016, MAXDOP was a server-level setting, or a setting enforced at the query level, or a setting enforced to sessions selectively via the Resource Governor, an Enterprise edition feature. Since SQL server 2016, the MAXDOP setting is now available as a database-scoped configuration. You can also use the MAXDOP query hint in any statement to override the database or server level MAXDOP setting.

Another limit to parallelism, called the Cost Threshold for Parallelism (CTFP), enforces a minimum bar for query cost before a query can use a parallel execution plan. The higher the threshold, the fewer queries go parallel. This setting is fairly low by default, but its proper setting in your environment is quite dependent on the workload and processor count. More expensive queries usually benefit from parallelism more than simpler queries, so limiting the use of parallelism to the worst queries in your workload can help. Similarly, setting the CTFP too high could have an opportunity impact, as performance is limited, queries are executed serially, and CPU cores go underutilized. The CTFP is a server-level setting only.

If large queries are already a problem for performance and multiple large queries regularly run simultaneously, raising the CTFP might not solve the problem. In addition to the obvious solutions of query tuning and index changes, including the introduction of Columnstore indexes, use MAXDOP instead to limit very large queries.

When the CXPACKET wait is the predominant wait type experienced over time by your SQL Server, both MAXDOP and CTFP are dials to turn when performance tuning. You can also view the live and last wait types for a request using `sys.dm_exec_requests`. Make these changes in small, measured gestures, and don't overreact to performance problems with a small number of queries. Use the Query Store to benchmark and trend the performance of high-value and high-cost queries as you change configuration settings.

Another flavor of CPU pressure, and in some ways the opposite of the CXPACKET wait type, is the SOS_SCHEDULER_YIELD wait type. The SOS_SCHEDULER_YIELD is an indicator of CPU pressure, indicating that SQL Server had to share time or "yield" to other CPU tasks, which may be normal and expected on busy servers. Whereas CXPACKET is the SQL Server complaining about too many threads in parallel, the SOS_SCHEDULER_YIELD is the acknowledgement that there were more runnable tasks for the available threads. In either case, first take a strategy of reducing CPU-intensive queries and rescheduling or optimizing CPU-intense maintenance operations. This is more economical than simply adding CPU capacity.

Inside OUT

How can I reduce the processor utilization during maintenance operations?

If processor utilization spikes and during maintenance operations such as index maintenance or integrity checks, you can force these to run serially. Although this can increase the duration of maintenance, other queries should be less negatively affected.

You can use the MAXDOP query hint at the end of index maintenance to force index rebuild steps to run serially. Combined with the ONLINE hint, an Enterprise edition feature, your scripted index maintenance might run longer but have a minimal impact of concurrent queries. You can also specify MAXDOP when creating indexes. You cannot specify a MAXDOP for the reorganize step.

```
ALTER INDEX ALL ON WideWorldImporters.Sales.Invoices REBUILD
WITH (MAXDOP = 1, ONLINE = ON);
```

You can also turn on trace flag 2528 to disable parallelism server-wide for DBCC CHECKDB, DBCC CHECKFILEGROUP, and DBCC CHECKTABLE operations. Keep in mind these operations can take hours to complete on large databases, and might run longer if single-threaded.

Understanding and designing indexes

In this chapter, we dive into indexing of all kinds—not just clustered and nonclustered indexes—including practical development techniques for designing indexes. We spend time on memory-optimized tables throughout, including hash indexes for extreme writes, and Columnstore indexes for extreme reads. We review "missing" indexes and index usage, and special types of indexes for niche uses. Finally, we explain statistics, how they are created and updated, and important performance-related options for statistics objects.

Designing clustered indexes

Let's be clear about what the clustered index is and then state the case for why every table in a relational database should have one, with very few exceptions. In this section, we describe the process for choosing the best clustered index key as well as the case against deliberately choosing not to create a clustered index.

Whether you are inheriting and maintaining a database or designing the objects within it, there are important facts to know about clustered indexes. In the case of rowstore and Columnstore tables, the clustered index stores the data rows for all columns in the table, sorted by the clustered index key. Memory-optimized tables don't have a clustered index structure inherent to their design but could have a clustered Columnstore index created for them.

Choosing a proper clustered index key

When designing the clustered index key for a table, keep in mind four marks of a good clustered index key, or in the case of a compound clustered index key, the first column listed. Let's review four key factors that will help you understand what role the clustered index key serves and how best to design one:

- **Increasing sequential value.** A value that increases (such as 1,2,3..., or an increasing point in time, or an increasing alphanumeric) is valuable from a page organization standpoint. This means that the insert pattern of the data as it comes in from the business will match the loading of rows into the table.

A column with the IDENTITY property or populated by a SEQUENCE value matches this perfectly. Use date and time data only if it is highly unlikely to repeat, and then strongly consider using the datetimeoffset data type to avoid repeated data during daylight savings time changes.

Unique.   A clustered index key does not need to be unique, but it really should be. (That said, the clustered key does not need to be the Primary Key of the table, or the only uniqueness enforced in the table.) A unique (or near-unique) clustered index means efficient seeks, and if your application will be searching for individual rows out of this table regularly, you and the business should know what makes those searches unique.

Unique constraints, whether they be nonclustered or clustered, can improve performance on the same data, and create a more efficient structure. If a clustered index is declared without the UNIQUE property, a second key value is added in the background, a four-byte integer uniquifier column. Microsoft SQL Server must have some way to uniquely identify each row.

- **Surrogate.**   The clustered index key shouldn't be visible to end-user applications or reports. In general, when the end users can see data, they will eventually see fit to *change* that data. You do not want clustered index keys to ever change (much less PRIMARY KEY key columns). A system-generated column of sequential values (again, an IDENTITY column is perfect) or one that combines system or application-generated fields such as dates and times, or numbers, is ideal.

  The negative impact of changing the clustering key includes the possibility that the first two aforementioned guidelines would be broken. If the clustered key is also a Primary Key, updating the key's values could also require cascading updates to enforce referential integrity. It is much easier for everyone involved if only columns with business value are exposed to end users and, therefore, could be changed by end users. In normalized database design, we would call these "natural keys" as opposed to "surrogate keys."

- **Narrow data type.**   This is not listed last as an indication that it is least important; quite to the contrary, the decision of data type for your clustered index key can have a large impact on table size, the cost of index maintenance, and the efficiency of queries at scale. The clustered index key value is also stored with every nonclustered index key value, meaning that an unnecessarily wide clustered index key will also cause unnecessarily wide nonclustered indexes on the table. This can have a very large impact on storage on drives and in memory at scale.

  The narrow data type guidance should also steer you away from using the uniqueidentifier field, which is 16 bytes per row, or four times the size of an integer column per row, and twice as large as a bigint. It also steers away from using wide strings, such as names, addresses, or URLs.

Inside OUT

Why are uniqueidentifiers *an overall bad choice for the clustered index key, even for the "oil rig problem"?*

There is a common design challenge to store rows from multiple (perhaps disconnected) data sources in the same table; for example, oil rigs, medical devices, or a supervisory control and data acquisition (SCADA) system. Each source of the data must create unique values for itself, but those values must then be combined into a single table. The uniqueidentifier data type and newid() function appear to be an option because they will generate values uniquely across multiple servers.

This is not a good design for scale, however, because uniqueidentifiers are random, meaning that inserts will perfectly fragment a table with each new row. This will cause page splits (an expensive I/O operation) as the rows naturally merge into the rest with each insert in the "middle" rather than at the end, inserting sequentially. (you can mitigate this, though not completely, by altering the fill factor of each index that uses the uniqueidentier as a key. However, this is also not desirable, because it will further increase the space to store the same data.)

Even the newsequentialid() function, to create sequential uniqueidentifiers, has fatal flaws. After a server restart, the sequence starts again with, meaning that eventually, you will be back to writing new rows in the middle of existing rows, causing page splits again.

Consider instead a solution using multiple integers, one that autoincrements and one that identifies the data source, if you are considering the uniqueidentifier field. Even two four-byte integers are half the size of a uniqueidentifier, and they compress better.

This design problem usually involves these devices merging their data periodically—not continuously. In the case of continuous connected application integration into a single table, consider using the SEQUENCE feature of SQL Server, introduced in SQL Server 2012, instead of a uniqueidentifier. Using the SEQUENCE object will allow for multiple database connections write rows using a unique, autoincrementing, ascending, procedurally generated integer.

It is ironic that a number of Microsoft-developed platforms use `uniqueidentifiers` heavily, and sometimes to very public failures, for example, the Windows 7 RC download page. (Read Paul Randal's blog, "Why did the Windows 7 RC download failure happen?" *https://www.sqlskills.com/blogs/paul/why-did-the-windows-7-rc-download-failure-happen/*) But systems like Microsoft SharePoint and even SQL Server's own merge replication needed to be developed for utility and versatility across unlimited client environments and a wide array of user expertise. When designing your own systems, take advantage of your knowledge of the business environment to design better clustered index keys that escape the inefficiencies of the `uniqueidentifier` data type.

The clustered index is an important decision in the structure of a new table. For the vast majority of tables designed for relational database systems, however, the decision is fairly easy. An `IDENTITY` column with an integer or `bigint` data type is the ideal key for a clustered index because it satisfies the aforementioned four recommended qualities of an ideal clustered index. A procedurally generated timestamp or other incrementing time-related value, combined with a unique, autoincrementing number also provides for a common albeit less-narrow clustered index key design.

When a table is created with a Primary Key constraint and no other mention of a clustered index, the Primary Key's columns become the clustered index's key. This is typically safe, but a table with a compound Primary Key or a Primary Key that does not begin with a sequential column, could result in a suboptimal clustered index. It is important to note that the Primary Key does not need to be the clustered index key. It is possible to create nonunique clustered indexes or to have multiple unique columns or column combinations in a table.

When combining multiple columns into the clustered index key of an index, keep in mind that the column order of an index, clustered or nonclustered, does matter. If you decide to use multiple columns to create a clustered index key, the first column should still align as closely to the other three rules, even if it alone is not unique.

In `sys.indexes`, the clustered index is always identified as `index_id = 1`. If the table is a heap, there will instead be a row with `index_id = 0`. This row represents the heap data.

NOTE

You can also create a clustered index as a clustered Columnstore index, which is optimal in certain situations. More on that later in this chapter.

The case against intentionally designing heaps

Without a clustered index, a rowstore table is known colloquially as a *heap*. The Database Engine uses a structure known as row identifier (RID), which is set up to uniquely identify every row for internal purposes. The structure of the heap has no order when it is logically stored.

Scans are the only method of access to read from a heap structure. It is not possible to perform a seek against a heap; however, it is possible to perform a seek against a nonclustered index that has been added to a heap. In this way, a nonclustered index can provide an ordered copy for some of the table data in a separate structure.

Of the edge cases for designing a table purposely without a clustered index, a case can be made for the situation in which you would only ever insert into a table. Without any order to the data, you might reap some benefits from rapid, massive data inserts into a heap. Other types of writes to the table (deletes and updates) will likely require table scans to complete and likely be far less efficient than the same writes against a table with a clustered index.

Deletes and updates will also probably leave wasted space within the heap's structure, which cannot be reclaimed even with an Index Rebuild operation. To reclaim wasted space inside of a heap, you must ironically create a clustered index on the table and drop the clustered index.

The perceived advantage of heaps for workloads exclusively involving inserts can be easily out-weighed by the significant disadvantages whenever accessing that data—when query perfor-mance would necessitate the creation of a clustered and/or nonclustered index. Table scans and RID lookups are likely to dominate the cost of any execution plan accessing the heap. Without a clustered index, queries reading from a table large enough to gain significant advantage from its inserts would perform poorly.

With Microsoft's expansion into modern unstructured data platforms such as SQL Server inte-gration with Hadoop, or Microsoft Azure Data Lake, other architectures are likely to be more appropriate when rapid, massive data inserts are required. This is especially true for when you will be continuously collecting massive amounts of data and then only ever analyzing the data in aggregate. It's likely that these alternatives, integrated with the Database Engine starting with SQL Server 2016 or a focus of new Azure development, would be a superior alternative.

Further, adding a clustered index to optimize the eventual retrieval of data from a heap is non-trivial. Behind the scenes, the Database Engine must write the entire contents of the heap into the new clustered index structure. If any nonclustered indexes exist on the heap, they also will be re-created, using the clustered key instead of the RID. This will likely result in a large amount of transaction log activity and TempDB space consumed.

CHAPTER 10

Designing nonclustered indexes

Although each table should have a clustered index that assumes the organization of the data in the table, nonclustered indexes provide additional copies of the data in vertically-filtered sets, sorted by nonprimary columns.

You should approach the design of nonclustered indexes in response to application query usage, and then verify over time that you are benefitting from indexes (you can read more about index usage statistics later in this chapter.)

Let's review the properties of good nonclustered indexes:

- Broad enough serve multiple queries, not just designed to suit one

- Well-ordered keys that eliminate unnecessary sorting in high-value queries

- Well-stocked INCLUDE sections prevent Lookups in high-value queries

- Proven beneficial usage over time in the sys.dm_db_index_usage_stats dynamic management view (DMV)

- Unique when possible (keep in mind a table can have multiple uniqueness criteria)

- Key order matters, so the most selective (most distinct) columns should be listed first

- The index key list doesn't overlap other nonclustered indexes

This is the purpose of a nonclustered index; to provide more than one picture of the data in a table. Nonclustered indexes are copies of a rowstore table that take up space on a disk and in memory (when cached). You must back up and maintain them. They are kept transaction-ally consistent with the data in the table, serving a limited, reordered set of the data in a table. Because the nonclustered index reflects the same data per columns that the clustered index has, it also has a degree of overhead in SQL Server. All writes to the table data must also be written to the nonclustered index (in the case of updates, when any indexed column is modified), to keep it up to date.

The positive benefit they can have on SELECT queries, however, is potentially very significant. Keep in mind also that some write queries might appear to perform faster because accessing the data that is being changed can be optimized, as well, just as accessing the data in a SELECT query. It is not a rule that your applications' writes will slow, though adding many nonclustered indexes will certain add up to poor write performance.

You should not create nonclustered indexes haphazardly or clumsily; you should plan, modify, and combine them with one another when appropriate, and review them regularly to make sure they are still useful. Nonclustered indexes represent a significant source of potential performance tuning, however, that every developer and database administration should be aware of, especially in transactional databases. Remember always to create indexes when looking at the "big picture"—rarely does a single query rise to the importance level of justifying its own indexes.

Understanding nonclustered index design

Let's talk about what we meant a moment ago when we said, "you should not create indexes haphazardly or clumsily." When should you create a nonclustered index, and how should you design them? How many should you add to a table?

Even though adding nonclustered indexes on Foreign Key columns can be beneficial if those referencing columns will frequently be used in queries, it's rare that a useful nonclustered index will be properly designed with a single column in mind. This is because outside of joins on foreign keys, it is rare that queries will be designed to seek and return a single column from a table.

Choosing a proper nonclustered index key

Earlier, we mentioned that nonclustered index keys shouldn't overlap with other indexes in the same table. When creating indexes, perhaps one that perfectly suits a very important query, you must always compare the index to existing indexes. The order of the key of the index matters. In Transact-SQL (T-SQL), this looks like this:

```
CREATE INDEX IDX_NC_InvoiceLines_InvoiceID_StockItemID
ON [Sales].[InvoiceLines] (InvoiceID, StockItemID);
```

In this index, `InvoiceID` and `InvoiceLineID` are defined as the key. Via Object Explorer in Management Studio, you can view the index properties to see the same information. This nonclustered index represents a copy of the data of the `InvoiceLines` table, sorted by the column `InvoiceID` first, and then the `StockItemID`.

To emphasize that the order of key columns in a nonclustered index matters, the two indexes that follow are completely different structures, and will best serve different queries. It's not likely that a single query would have much use for both, though SQL Server can still choose to use an nonclustered index with less than optimal key order than to scan a clustered index:

```
CREATE INDEX IDX_NC_InvoiceLines_InvoiceID_StockItemID
ON [Sales].[InvoiceLines] (InvoiceID, StockItemID);
CREATE INDEX IDX_NC_InvoiceLines_StockItemID_InvoiceID
ON [Sales].[InvoiceLines] (StockItemID, InvoiceID);
```

The columns with the most distinct values are more selective and will best serve queries if they are listed before less-selective columns in the index order. Note, though, that the order of columns in the INCLUDE portion of a nonclustered index (more on that later) does not matter.

Remember also from the previous section on clustered indexes that the clustered index key is already inside the key of the nonclustered index. There might be scenarios when the Missing Indexes feature (more on this later) suggests adding a clustered key column to your nonclustered index. It does not change the size of a nonclustered index to do this—the clustered key is already in nonclustered index. The only caveat is that the order of the nonclustered index keys still determines the sort order of the index. So, having the clustered index key column(s) in your nonclustered index key won't change the index's size, but could change the sort order of the keys, creating what is essentially a different index when compared to an index that doesn't include the clustered index key column(s).

Implied in this T-SQL is the sort order of each column which by default is ascending. If queries frequently call for data to be sorted by a column in descending order, you could provide that key value like this:

```
CREATE INDEX IDX_NC_InvoiceLines_InvoiceID_StockItemID
ON [Sales].[InvoiceLines] (InvoiceID DESC, StockItemID);
```

Creating the key's sort order incorrectly might not matter to some queries. Nested Loops do not require data to be sorted, so different sort orders in the keys of a nonclustered index might not make a significant impact to the execution plan. A Merge Join requires sorted data, however, so changing the sort order of the keys of an index, especially the first key, could simplify an execution plan by eliminating unnecessary sort operators. This is among the strategies of index tuning to consider. Remember to review the query plan performance data that the Query Store collects, to observe the impact of index changes on multiple queries.

Understanding redundant indexes

Because index key order matters, we need to be aware of what is and what isn't an overlapping index. Consider the following two nonclustered indexes on the same table:

```
CREATE INDEX IDX_NC_InvoiceLines_InvoiceID_StockItemID_UnitPrice_Quantity
ON [Sales].[InvoiceLines] (InvoiceID, StockItemID, UnitPrice, Quantity);

CREATE INDEX IDX_NC_InvoiceLines_InvoiceID_StockItemID
ON [Sales].[InvoiceLines] (InvoiceID, StockItemID);
```

Both indexes lead with `InvoiceID` and `StockItemID`. The first index includes additional data. The second index is completely overlapped. Queries can still use the second index, but because the leading key columns match the other index, the other index will provide very similar performance gains with less to maintain. The space it requires, the space in memory it consumes when used, and the effort it takes to keep the index up-to-date and maintained could all be considered redundant. The index `IDX_NC_InvoiceLines_InvoiceID_StockItemID` isn't needed and should be dropped, and queries that used it will use `IDX_NC_InvoiceLines_InvoiceID_StockItemID_UnitPrice_Quantity`.

Consider then the following two indexes:

```
CREATE INDEX IDX_NC_InvoiceLines_InvoiceID_StockItemID_UnitPrice_Quantity
ON [Sales].[InvoiceLines] (InvoiceID, StockItemID, UnitPrice, Quantity);

CREATE INDEX IDX_NC_InvoiceLines _StockItemID_InvoiceID
ON [Sales].[InvoiceLines] (StockItemID, InvoiceID);
```

Note that the second index's keys are in a different order. This is physically and logically a different structure than the first index.

Does that mean both of these indexes are needed? Probably. Some queries might perform best using keys in the second index's order. The query optimizer can still use an index with columns in a suboptimal order; for example, to scan the smaller structure rather than the entire table. The query optimizer might instead find that an Index Seek and a Key Lookup on a different index is faster than using an index with the columns in the wrong order.

The Query Store can be an invaluable tool to discover queries that have regressed because of changes to indexes that have been dropped, reordered, or resorted.

Understanding the INCLUDE list of an index

In the B-tree structure of a rowstore nonclustered index, key columns are stored through the two major sections of the index object: the branch levels and the leaf levels. The branch levels are where the logic of seeks happen, starting at a narrow "top" where key data is stored so that it can be traversed by SQL Server using binary decisions. A seek moves "down" the tree via binary decisions. The leaf levels are where the seek ends and data is retrieved. Adding a column to the INCLUDE list of a rowstore nonclustered index adds that data only to the leaf level.

Inside OUT

How can I see the properties and storage for each level of the index's B-tree?

You can view the page_count, record_count, space_used statistics, and more for each level of a B-tree by using the DETAILED mode of the sys.dm_db_index_physical_stats dynamic management function. Only the leaf level (index_level = 0) is visible in other modes. The mode parameter is the fifth parameter passed in, as demonstrated in the following code:

```
USE WideWorldImporters;
GO
SELECT *
FROM sys.dm_db_index_physical_stats
(db_id(), object_id('Sales.Invoices'), null , null, 'DETAILED');
```

Table 10-1 shows the results.

Table 10-1 Results of `sys.dm_db_index_physical_stats` to show index levels

index_id	index_level	page_count	record_count
1	0	11,357	70,510
1	1	41	11,357
1	2	1	41
2	0	164	70,510
2	1	1	164
3	0	152	70,510
3	1	1	152
4	0	237	70,510
4	1	1	237
5	0	122	70,510
5	1	1	122
6	0	164	70,510
6	1	1	164
7	0	152	70,510
7	1	1	152
8	0	136	70,510
8	1	1	136
9	0	142	70,510
9	1	1	142
10	0	434	70,510
10	1	2	434
10	2	1	2

Notice that the leaf level of each index has the same number of rows, but has a different number of pages (because each index has different columns). Note that the branch levels (where `index_level` > 0) of each index's B-tree contain less data. Indexes with more columns and on larger tables will require more levels. Adding a column to the INCLUDE list of a rowstore nonclustered index only adds that data to the leaf level.

The INCLUDE statement of an index allows for data to be retrievable in the leaf level only, but not stored in the branch level. This reduced the overall size and complexity of the index. Consider the following query and execution plan (Figure 10-1) from the WideWorldImporters database:

```
SELECT CustomerID, AccountsPersonID
FROM [Sales].[Invoices]
WHERE CustomerID = 832;
```

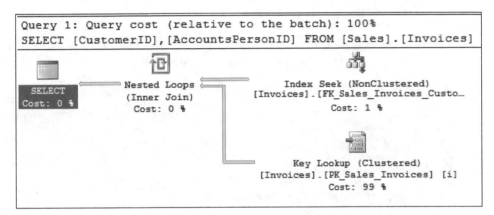

Figure 10-1 This execution plan shows an Index Seek and a Key Lookup on the same table; the Key Lookup represents 99% of the cost of the query.

Assuming that this is a high-priority query, important enough to be considered when modifying indexes in the database, we should consider a change to the nonclustered index being used here. Let's take a look at the properties of the Index Seek in Figure 10-2.

Object
[WideWorldImporters].[Sales].[Invoices].
[FK_Sales_Invoices_CustomerID] [i]
Output List
[WideWorldImporters].[Sales].[Invoices].InvoiceID,
[WideWorldImporters].[Sales].[Invoices].CustomerID
Seek Predicates
Seek Keys[1]: Prefix: [WideWorldImporters].[Sales].
[Invoices].CustomerID = Scalar Operator((832))

Figure 10-2 The properties of the Index Seek in the previous example script. Note that CustomerID is in the Seek Predicate and also in the Output List, but that AccountsPersonID is not listed in the Output List.

Note that `CustomerID` is in the Seek Predicate and also in the Output List, but that `AccountsPersonID` is not listed in the Output List. Our query is searching for and returning `CustomerID` (it appears in both the SELECT and WHERE clauses), but our query also returns `AccountsPersonID`, which is not contained in the index `FK_Sales_Invoices_CustomerID`. Here is the code of the nonclustered index `FK_Sales_Invoices_CustomerID`, named because it is for `CustomerID`, a foreign key reference:

```
CREATE NONCLUSTERED INDEX [FK_Sales_Invoices_CustomerID] ON [Sales].[Invoices]
(    [CustomerID] ASC )
ON [USERDATA];
```

To remove the Key Lookup, let's add an included column to the nonclustered index, so that the query can retrieve all the data it needs from a single object:

```
DROP INDEX IF EXISTS [FK_Sales_Invoices_CustomerID] ON [Sales].[Invoices];
GO
CREATE NONCLUSTERED INDEX [FK_Sales_Invoices_CustomerID] ON [Sales].[Invoices]
(    [CustomerID] ASC )
INCLUDE ( [AccountsPersonID] )
ON [USERDATA];
GO
```

Let's run our sample query again (see also Figure 10-3):

```
SELECT CustomerID, AccountsPersonID
FROM [Sales].[Invoices]
WHERE CustomerID = 832;
```

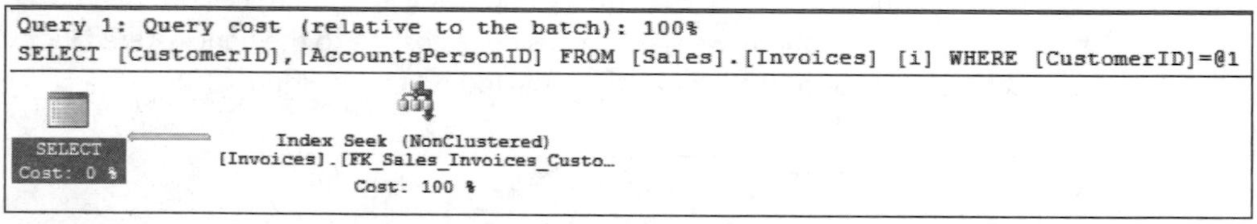

Figure 10-3 The execution plan now shows only an Index Seek; the Key Lookup that appeared in Figure 10-2 has been eliminated from the execution plan.

The Key Lookup has been eliminated. The query was able to retrieve both `CustomerID` and `AccountsPersonID` from the same index and required no second pass through the table for the column `AccountsPersonID`. The estimated subtree cost, in the properties of the SELECT operator, is now 0.0034015, compared to 0.355919 when the Key Lookup was present. Although this query was a small example for demonstration purposes, eliminating the Key Lookup represents a significant improvement to query performance without changing the query.

Just as you do not want to add too many nonclustered indexes, you also do not want to add too many columns unnecessarily to the INCLUDE list of nonclustered indexes. Columns in the INCLUDE list, as we saw in the previous code example, still require storage space. For small, infrequent queries, the key lookup operator is probably not alone worth the cost of storing additional columns in the INCLUDE list of an index.

In summary, you should craft nonclustered indexes to serve many queries smartly, you should always try to avoid creating overlapping or redundant indexes, and you should regularly review to verify that indexes are still being used as applications or report queries change. Keep this guidance in mind as we move into the next section!

Creating "missing" nonclustered indexes

The concept of combining many similar indexes into one super-index is core to the utility of using SQL Server's built-in Missing Indexes feature. First introduced in SQL 2005, the Missing Indexes feature revolutionized the ability to see the "big picture" when crafting nonclustered indexes. The missing indexes feature is passive, on by default on any database since SQL Server 2005, as well as in Azure SQL Database.

The Missing Indexes feature collects information from actual query usage. SQL Server passively records when it would have been better to have a nonclustered index; for example, to replace a Scan for a Seek or to eliminate a Lookup. The Missing Indexes feature then aggregates these requests together, counts how many times they have happened, calculates the cost of the statement operations that could be improved, and estimates the percentage of that cost that would be eliminated (this percentage is labeled the "impact"). Think of the Missing Indexes feature as a wish list of nonclustered indexes.

You can look at missing indexes any time, with no performance overhead to the server, by querying a set of DMVs dedicated to this feature. You can find the following query, which concatenates together the CREATE INDEX statement for you, according to a simple, self-explanatory naming convention. As you can see from the use of system views, this query is intended to be run in a single database:

```
SELECT
  mid.[statement]
, create_index_statement = 'CREATE NONCLUSTERED INDEX IDX_NC_'
--The new Translate syntax is supported for SQL 2017+
    + TRANSLATE(ISNULL(replace(mid.equality_columns, ' ' ,''),''), , '],[' ,' _ ')
    + TRANSLATE(ISNULL(replace(mid.inequality_columns, ' ' ,''),''), '],[' ,' _ ')
    + ' ON ' + [statement]
    + ' (' + ISNULL (mid.equality_columns,'')
    + CASE WHEN mid.equality_columns IS NOT NULL
      AND mid.inequality_columns IS NOT NULL THEN ',' ELSE ''
      END
```

```
      + ISNULL (mid.inequality_columns, '')  + ')'
      + ISNULL (' INCLUDE (' + mid.included_columns + ')',
       '')   COLLATE SQL_Latin1_General_CP1_CI_AS
, unique_compiles, migs.user_seeks, migs.user_scans
, last_user_seek, migs.avg_total_user_cost
, avg_user_impact, mid.equality_columns
,  mid.inequality_columns, mid.included_columns
FROM sys.dm_db_missing_index_groups mig
INNER JOIN sys.dm_db_missing_index_group_stats migs
ON migs.group_handle = mig.index_group_handle
INNER JOIN sys.dm_db_missing_index_details mid
ON mig.index_handle = mid.index_handle
INNER JOIN sys.tables t
ON t.object_id = mid.object_id
INNER JOIN sys.schemas s
ON s.schema_id = t.schema_id
WHERE mid.database_id = db_id()
-- count of query compilations that needed this proposed index
--AND             migs.unique_compiles > 10
-- count of query seeks that needed this proposed index
--AND             migs.user_seeks > 10
-- average percentage of cost that could be alleviated with this proposed index
--AND             migs.avg_user_impact > 75
-- Sort by indexes that will have the most impact to the costliest queries
ORDER BY avg_user_impact * avg_total_user_cost desc;
```

This script is available in the "missing indexes.sql" script in the accompanying downloads for this book, which is available at *https://aka.ms/SQLServ2017Admin/downloads*.

At the bottom of this query are a series of filters that you can use to find only the most-used, highest-value index suggestions. If you have hundreds or thousands of rows returned by this query, consider spending an afternoon crafting together indexes to improve the performance of the actual user activity that generated this data.

This wish list, however, will likely include many overlapping (but not duplicate) suggestions. Each with a very high percentage of impacting high-cost queries. Some indexes returned by the missing indexes queries might not be worth creating because they have a very low impact, or have been part of only one query compilation. For example, you might see these three index suggestions:

```
  CREATE NONCLUSTERED INDEX IDX_NC_Gamelog_Team1 ON dbo.gamelog
(Team1)
INCLUDE (GameYear, GameWeek, Team1Score, Team2Score);

  CREATE NONCLUSTERED INDEX IDX_NC_Gamelog_Team1_GameWeek_GameYear ON dbo.gamelog
(Team1, GameWeek, GameYear)
INCLUDE (Team1Score);

  CREATE NONCLUSTERED INDEX IDX_NC_Gamelog_Team1_GameWeek_GameYear_Team2 ON dbo.gamelog
(Team1, GameWeek, GameYear, Team2)
INCLUDE (GameWeek);
```

You should not create all three of these indexes. Instead, you should combine them into a single index that matches the order of the needed key columns and covers all the included columns, as well. Here is the properly combined index suggestion:

```
CREATE NONCLUSTERED INDEX IDX_NC_Gamelog_Team1_GameWeek_GameYear_Team2 ON dbo.gamelog
(Team1, GameWeek, GameYear, Team2)
INCLUDE (Team1Score, Team2Score);
```

This last index is a good combination of the previous suggestions. It will deliver maximum positive benefit to the most queries, and it minimizes the negative impact to writes, storage, and maintenance. Note that the Key columns list overlaps and is in the correct order for each of the previous index suggestions, and that the INCLUDE columns list also covers all the columns needed in the index suggestions. If a column is in the key of the index, it does not need to exist in the INCLUDE of the index.

However, don't create this index yet. You should still review existing indexes on the table before creating any missing indexes. Perhaps you can combine a new missing index and an existing index, in the Key column list or the INCLUDE column list, further increasing the value of a single index.

Finally, after combining missing index suggestions with one another and with existing indexes, you are ready to create the index and see it in action. Remember always to create indexes when looking at the "big picture": remember, rarely does a single query rise to the importance level of justifying its own indexes. For example, in SQL Server Management Studio, you will sometimes see green text suggesting a missing index for this query, as illustrated in Figure 10-4 (note that in this figure the text is gray).

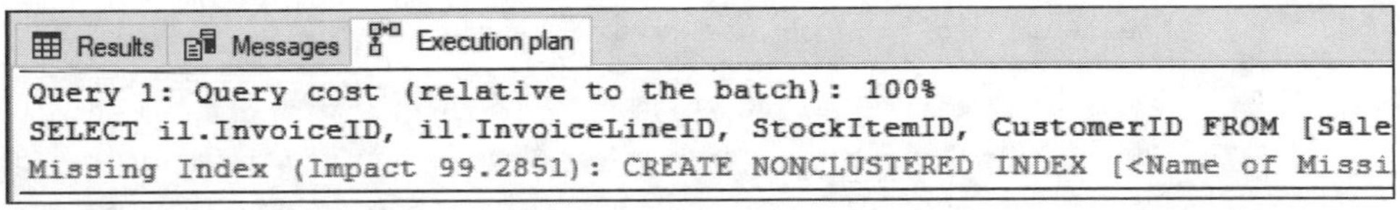

Figure 10-4 In the execution plan tab, in the header of each execution plan, text starting with "Missing Index" will alert you to the possible impact. Do not create this index on the spot!

That's valuable, but do not create that index on the spot! Always refer to the complete set of index suggestions and other existing indexes on the table, combining overlapping indexes when possible. Consider the green missing index alert in SQL Server Management Studio as only a flag that indicates you should spend time investigating new missing indexes.

So, to recap, when creating nonclustered indexes for performance tuning, you should do the following:

1. Use the Missing Indexes DMVs to identify new "big picture" nonclustered indexes:

    a. Don't create indexes that will likely only help out a single query—few queries are important enough to deserve their own indexes.

    b. Consider nonclustered Columnstore indexes instead for very large rowcount tables with very large rowcount queries. (You can read more on Columnstore indexes later in this chapter.)

2. Combine Missing Index suggestions, being aware of key order and INCLUDE lists.

3. Compare new index suggestions with existing indexes; perhaps you can combine them.

4. Remember to review index usage statistics, as well, to verify whether indexes are helping you. (See the next section for more on the index usage statistics DMV.)

Inside OUT

Does the Missing Indexes feature suggest only nonclustered index?

Yes, only nonclustered indexes.

The missing indexes feature can't help you with proper clustered index design—that's up to you, the informed database designer. It can provide some insight into usage after a time, but that would mean running a typical production workload against a heap, and suffering the performance issues likely to arise.

Here's another limitation to the missing indexes feature: it is not aware of clustered or nonclustered Columnstore indexes, which are incredibly powerful structures to add for massive row count queries on large tables. The Missing Indexes feature cannot suggest Columnstore indexes, and it will even suggest an index to replace a well-behaving Columnstore index. Be aware of all indexes in your table, including Columnstore indexes, when considering new indexes.

Therefore, when you have created a Columnstore index on a table, you will need to ignore index suggestions that look like the same workloads that are currently benefitting from the Columnstore. For a query that requires a scan on many rows in the table, the query optimizer is unlikely to pick a nonclustered index over a nonclustered Columnstore index. The Columnstore index will vastly outperform a nonclustered index for massive row count queries, though the missing index feature might still count this as a new nonclustered index suggestion.

Understanding when Missing Index suggestions are removed

Missing Index suggestions are cleared out for any change to the tables; for example, if you add or remove columns, or if you add or remove indexes. Missing Index suggestions are also cleared out when the SQL Server service is started, and cannot be manually cleared easily. (You can take the database offline and back online, which would clear out the Missing Index suggestions, but this seems like overkill.)

Logically, make sure the missing index data that you have collected is also based on a significant sample actual production user activity over time spanning at least one business cycle. Missing index suggestions based on development activity might not be a useful representation of intended application activity, though suggestions based on end-user testing or training could be.

Understanding and proving index usage statistics

You've added indexes to your database, and they are used over time, but meanwhile the query patterns of applications and reports change. Columns are added to the database, new tables are added, and although you add new indexes to suit new functionality, how does a database administrator ensure that existing indexes are still worth keeping?

SQL Server tracks this information for you automatically with yet another valuable DMV: `sys.dm_db_index_usage_stats`. Following is a script that measures index usage within a database, combining `sys.dm_db_index_usage_stats` with other system views and DMVs to return valuable information. Note that the ORDER BY clause will place indexes with the fewest read operations (seeks, scans, lookups) and the most write operations (updates) at the top of the list.

```
SELECT   TableName      = sc.name + '.' + o.name
    ,  IndexName        = i.name
    ,  s.user_seeks
    ,  s.user_scans
    ,  s.user_lookups
    ,  s.user_updates
    ,  ps.row_count
    ,  SizeMb           = (ps.in_row_reserved_page_count*8.)/1024.
    ,  s.last_user_lookup
    ,  s.last_user_scan
    ,  s.last_user_seek
    ,  s.last_user_update
FROM sys.dm_db_index_usage_stats AS s
 INNER JOIN sys.indexes AS i

ON i.object_id = s.object_id AND i.index_id = s.index_id
 INNER JOIN sys.objects AS o
```

```
ON o.object_id=i.object_id
  INNER JOIN sys.schemas AS sc

ON sc.schema_id = o.schema_id
  INNER JOIN sys.partitions AS pr

ON pr.object_id = i.object_id AND pr.index_id = i.index_id
  INNER JOIN sys.dm_db_partition_stats AS ps

ON ps.object_id = i.object_id AND ps.partition_id = pr.partition_id
WHERE    o.is_ms_shipped = 0
ORDER BY user_seeks + user_scans + user_lookups  asc,  s.user_updates desc;
```

This script is available in the "index usage.sql" script in the accompanying downloads for this book, which is available at *https://aka.ms/SQLServ2017Admin/downloads*.

Any indexes that rise to the top of the preceding query should be considered for removal or redesign, given the following caveat:

Before justifying dropping any indexes, you should ensure that you have collected data from the index usage stats DMV that spans at least one business cycle. The index usage stats DMV is cleared when the SQL Server service is restarted. You cannot manually clear it. If your applications have week-end and month-end reporting, you might have indexes present and tuned specifically for those critical performance periods. Like many DMVs that are cleared when the SQL Server service restarts, consider a strategy of capturing data and storing it periodically in persistent tables.

Logically, verify that the index usage data that you have collected is also based on actual production user activity. Index usage data based on testing or development activity would not be a useful representation of intended application activity.

Again, the Query Store can be an invaluable tool to monitor for query regression after indexing changes.

➤ **Chapter 9 discusses the Query Store feature.**

Like many server-level DMVs, the index usage stats data requires the VIEW SERVER STATE permission in SQL Server. In Azure SQL Database Premium tier, the VIEW DATABASE STATE permission is required, but only the server admin or Azure Active Directory admin accounts can access this data in standard and basic tiers.

Designing Columnstore indexes

Columnstore indexes were first introduced in SQL Server 2012, making a splash in their ability to far outperform clustered and nonclustered indexes when it comes to massive table reads. They were typically used in the scenario of nightly-refreshed data warehouses, but now they have beneficial applications on transactional systems, including on memory-optimized tables. Columnstore indexes are superior to rowstore data storage for performance in appropriate situations.

Big changes opened up Columnstore indexes further in SQL Server 2016:

- Prior to SQL Server 2016, the presence of a nonclustered Columnstore index made the table read-only. This drawback and others were removed in SQL Server 2016, and now Columnstore indexes are fully-featured and quite useful.

- With SQL Server 2016 SP1, Columnstore indexes are even available below Enterprise edition licenses of SQL Server (though with a limitation on Columnstore memory utilization).

- Prior to SQL Server 2016, using read committed snapshot and snapshot isolation level were not supported with Columnstore indexes. Starting with SQL Server 2016, snapshot isolation and Columnstore indexes are fully compatible.

- You can place a clustered Columnstore index on a memory-optimized table, providing the ability to do analytics on live real-time Online Transaction Processing (OLTP) data.

These key improvements opened Columnstore indexes to be used in transactional systems, when tables with millions of rows are read, resulting in million-row result sets. This is when Columnstore indexes really shine.

For now, Columnstore indexes are the only objects for which SQL Server can use Batch Mode execution. You'll see "Batch" (instead of the default "Row") in the Actual Execution Mode of an execution plan operator when this faster method is in use. Batch Mode processing benefits queries that process millions of rows or more. This isn't a rule, however, as Columnstore indexes can use both Batch Mode and Row Mode execution for a variety of operators.

> ➤ **For more information on which operators can use Batch Mode execution, go to** *https://docs. microsoft.com/sql/relational-databases/indexes/columnstore-indexes-query-performance*.

Columnstore indexes are not a B-tree; instead, they contain highly compressed data (on disk and in memory), stored in a different architecture from the traditional clustered and nonclustered indexes. You can create "clustered" or "nonclustered" Columnstore indexes, though this terminology is used more to indicate what the Columnstore index is replacing, not what it resembles behind the scenes.

You can also create nonclustered rowstore indexes on tables with a clustered Columnstore index, which is potentially useful to enforce uniqueness. Columnstore indexes cannot be unique, and so cannot replace the table's unique constraint or Primary Key.

You can combine nonclustered and nonclustered Columnstore indexes on the same table, but you can have only one Columnstore index on a table, including clustered and nonclustered

Columnstore indexes. You can even create nonclustered rowstore and nonclustered Columnstore indexes on the same columns. Perhaps you create both because you want to filter on the column value in one set of queries, and aggregate in another. Or, perhaps you create both only temporarily, for comparison.

One significant difference when you choose Columnstore index keys is that the order doesn't matter. You can add columns in any order to satisfy many different queries, greatly increasing the versatility of the Columnstore index in your table. This is because the order of the data is not important to how Columnstore indexes work.

Demonstrating the power of Columnstore indexes

To demonstrate the power of this fully operational Columnstore index, let's review an example scenario in which more than 14 million rows are added to the `WideWorldImporters.Sales.InvoiceLines` table. About half of the rows in the table now contain `InvoiceID = 3932`. This script is available in the "power of columnstore.sql" file in the accompanying downloads for this book, which is available at *https://aka.ms/SQLServ2017Admin/downloads*.

We dropped the existing WideWorldImporters-provided nonclustered Columnstore index and added a new nonclustered index we've created here, which performs an Index Scan on it to return the data. Remember that `InvoiceID = 3932` is roughly half the table, so this isn't a "needle in a haystack" situation; this isn't a seek. If the query can use a seek operator, the nonclustered rowstore index would likely be better. When the query must scan, Columnstore is king.

We'll use the following script as a test:

```
CREATE INDEX IDX_NC_InvoiceLines_InvoiceID_StockItemID_Quantity
ON [Sales].[InvoiceLines] (InvoiceID, StockItemID, Quantity);
GO
SELECT il.StockItemID, AvgQuantity = AVG(il.quantity)
FROM [Sales].[InvoiceLines] as il
WHERE il.InvoiceID = 3932
GROUP BY il.StockItemID;
```

The query returns 227 rows in 538 ms using the Index Scan operator on `IDX_NC_InvoiceLines_InvoiceID_StockItemID_Quantity`, the only operator in the execution plan. The total subtree cost of the plan is 18.9083. Next, we add a Columnstore index with the same key. In fact, the syntax is identical, save for the COLUMNSTORE keyword.

```
CREATE COLUMNSTORE INDEX IDX_CS_InvoiceLines_InvoiceID_StockItemID_quantity
ON [Sales].[InvoiceLines] (InvoiceID, StockItemID, Quantity);
```

The query returns 227 rows in 46 ms using the Columnstore Index Scan operator on `IDX_CS_InvoiceLines_InvoiceID_StockItemID_quantity`, the only operator in the execution plan. The total subtree cost of the plan is 2.56539.

Using compression delay on Columnstore indexes

We haven't done a deep dive into the internals of Columnstore indexes, but we'll touch on it here to discuss a potentially significant configuration option. The COMPRESSION_DELAY option for both nonclustered and clustered Columnstore indexes has to do with how long it takes changed data to be written from the delta store to the highly compressed Columnstore.

The delta store is an ephemeral location where changed data is stored in a clustered B-tree rowstore format. When certain thresholds are reached, specifically 1,048,576 rows, or when a Columnstore index is rebuilt, a group of delta store data is "closed" and then compressed into the Columnstore.

The COMPRESSION_DELAY option does not affect the 1,048,576 number, but rather how long it takes SQL Server to move the data into Columnstore. By setting the COMPRESSION_DELAY option to 10 minutes, data will remain in delta store for an extra 10 minutes before SQL Server compresses it.

The advantage of COMPRESSION_DELAY is noticeable for some write workloads, but not all. If the table is only ever inserted into, COMPRESSION_DELAY doesn't really help. But if a block of recent data is updated and deleted for a period before finally settling in after a time, implementing COMPRESSION_DELAY can speed up the write transactions to the data and reduce the maintenance and storage footprint of the Columnstore index.

Changing the COMPRESSION_DELAY setting of the index, unlike many other index settings, does not require a rebuild of the index, and you can change it at any time; for example:

```
USE WideWorldImporters;
go
ALTER INDEX [IDX_cs_Sales_InvoiceLines]
    ON [Sales].[InvoiceLines]
    SET (COMPRESSION_DELAY = 10 MINUTES);
```

> ### NOTE
> Prior to SQL Server 2016, using read committed snapshot and snapshot isolation levels were not supported with Columnstore indexes. Starting with SQL Server 2016, snapshot isolation and Columnstore indexes are fully compatible.

Understanding indexing in memory-optimized tables

Memory-optimized tables, first introduced in SQL Server 2014 and then greatly enhanced in SQL Server 2016, throw most of the rules of locks and concurrency out the window. They provide for table performance less bound (or in the case of nondurable data, unbound) by I/O constraints. Memory-optimized tables don't use the locking mechanics of pessimistic concurrency, as is discussed in Chapter 9.

CHAPTER 10

Memory-optimized tables have two types of indexes: hash and nonclustered. You must choose one of them to be the structure behind the Primary Key of the table if both data and schema are to be durable. If you do not include Primary Key constraints when a table is created with DURABILITY = SCHEMA_AND_DATA, you will receive an error and the table will not be created.

You can choose to have only the schema of the table be durable, but not the data. This has utility in certain scenarios as a staging table to receive data that will be moved to a durable disk-based or memory-optimized table. You should be aware of the potential for data loss. If only the schema of the memory-optimized table is durable, you do not need to declare a Primary Key. However, in the CREATE TABLE statement, you must still define at least one index or a Primary Key for a table by using DURABILITY = SCHEMA_ONLY.

Keep in mind that adding indexes to memory-optimized tables increases the amount of server memory needed. There is otherwise no limit to the size of memory-optimized tables in Enterprise edition; however, in Standard edition you are limited to 32 GB of memory-optimized tables per database.

Although there is no concept of a clustered index in memory-optimized tables, you can add a clustered Columnstore index to a memory-optimized table, dramatically improving your ability to query the data in aggregate. Because Columnstore indexes cannot be unique, they cannot serve as the Primary Key for a memory-optimized table.

Let's go over the basics of using nonclustered hash and traditional B-tree nonclustered indexes on memory-optimized tables.

Understanding hash indexes for memory-optimized tables

Nonclustered hash indexes are an alternative to the typical B-tree internal architecture for index data storage. Hash indexes are best for queries that look for the needle in the haystack, but they are not effective at range lookups or queries that need a different sort order than the hash index. One other limitation of the hash index is that if you don't query all the columns in a hash index, they are generally not as useful as a nonclustered index (see the next section).

Unlike B-tree–based nonclustered indexes, hash indexes also do not perform as well when there are multiple columns in the key of the indexes but not all columns, or even just the first column, are queried. Hash indexes are currently available only for memory-optimized tables, not disk-based tables. You can declare them by using the UNIQUE keyword, but they default to a non-unique key, similar to how B-tree nonclustered indexes are created. Just as with B-tree nonclustered indexes, you can also create more than one nonclustered hash index.

There is an additional unique consideration for creating hash indexes. Estimating the best number for the BUCKET_COUNT parameter can have a significant impact. The number should be as close to as possible to the number of unique key values that are expected. BUCKET_COUNT should be between 1 and 2 times this number. Hash indexes always use the same amount of space for the same-sized bucket count, regardless of the `rowcount` within.

For example, if you expect the table to have 100,000 unique values in it, the ideal BUCKET_ COUNT value would be between 100,000 and 200,000.

Having too many or too few buckets in a hash index can result in poor performance. More buckets will increase the amount of memory needed and the number of those buckets that are empty. Too few buckets will result in queries needing to access more buckets in a chain to access the same information.

Hash indexes work best when the key values are mostly unique. If the ratio of total rows to unique key values is too high (10:1 is a general upper limit), a hash index is not recommended, and will perform poorly. Ideally, a hash index can be declared unique.

You should periodically and proactively compare the number of unique key values to the total number of rows in the table and then maintain the number of buckets in a memory-optimized hash index by using the ALTER TABLE/ALTER INDEX/REBUILD commands; for example:

```
ALTER TABLE [dbo].[Transactions]
ALTER INDEX [IDX_NC_H Transactions_1]
REBUILD WITH (BUCKET_COUNT = 200000)
```

Understanding nonclustered indexes for memory-optimized tables

Nonclustered indexes for memory-optimized tables behave similarly on memory-optimized tables as they do for disk-based tables. They will outperform hash indexes for queries that perform sorting on the key value(s) of the index, or when the index must be scanned. Further, if you don't query all the columns in a hash index, they are generally not as useful as a nonclustered index.

You can declare nonclustered indexes on memory-optimized tables UNIQUE, however, the CREATE INDEX syntax is not supported. You must use the ALTER TABLE/ADD INDEX commands, or include them in the CREATE TABLE script.

Neither hash indexes nor nonclustered indexes can serve queries on memory-optimized tables for which the keys are sorted in the reverse order from how they are defined in the index. These types of queries simply can't be serviced efficiently right now from memory-optimized indexes.

Moving to memory-optimized tables

When you're considering moving a table from disk-based to memory-optimized, you can use the built-in Memory Optimization Advisor in SQL Server Management Studio. To do so, right-click any disk-based table to start the advisor. The advisor alerts you to table features that are not supported; warns you about some Memory Optimization Caveats, but will not make or recommend changes to applications that will need to incorporate error handling; and retries logic to support optimistic concurrency, if they do not already.

➤ **For more information on configuration of memory-optimized tables, see Chapter 8.**

Understanding other types of indexes

There are other types of indexes that you should be aware of, each with specific, limited uses for certain SQL Server features; for example, the Full-Text Search engine, `spatial` data types, and the `xml` data type.

Understanding full-text indexes

If you have optionally chosen to install the Full-Text Search feature of SQL Server, you can take advantage of the full-text service (fdhost.exe) and query vast amounts of data using special full-text syntax, looking for word forms, phrases, thesaurus lookups, word proximity, and more.

Because they have specific uses for particular architectures and applications, we won't spend much time on them in this reference. The Full-Text Engine is quite powerful and has a syntax of its own.

By design, full-text indexes require a unique nonclustered or clustered rowstore index on the table in which they are created, with a single column in the key. We recommend that this index have an integer key for performance reasons, such as an `IDENTITY` column. Full-text indexes are usually placed on `varchar` or `nvarchar` columns, often with large lengths, but you can also place them on `xml` and `varbinary` columns.

It is also an important to understand the two viable options to updating the full-text index. You can configure Change Tracking on the table that hosts the full-text index, which makes it possible for it to propagate changes to the base table into the full-text index, asynchronously keeping the full-text data synchronized with the table, with minimal overhead. Another option is using a column with the `rowversion` data type in the table and then periodically updating the full-text index. Consider both strategies, along with your requirements for frequency of updates to the full-text index. Both are superior to frequent full populations.

Understanding spatial Indexes

A spatial index is a special B-tree index that uses a suite of special code and geometry methods to perform spatial and geometry calculations. Developers can use these data structures for non-Euclidean geometry calculations, distance and area calculations on spheres, and more. Spatial indexes can improve the performance of queries with spatial operations.

You can create these indexes only on columns that use the `spatial` data types `geometry` or `geography`, and you can create different types of indexes on the same spatial column to server different calculations. To create a spatial index, the table must already have a Primary Key.

You create spatial indexes by using bounding boxes or tessellation schemes for `geometry` and `geography` data types. Consult the documentation and the developers' intended use of spatial data when creating these indexes.

Understanding XML indexes

Eponymous XML indexes are created for much the same benefit for which we use nonclustered indexes: You use them to prevent the runtime shredding of XML files each time they are accessed, and to instead provide a persistent row set of the XML data's tags, values, and paths.

Because the `xml` data type is stored as a BLOB and has an upper limit of 2 GB of data per row, XML data can be massive, and XML indexes can be extremely beneficial to reads. Like nonclustered indexes, they also incur an overhead to writes.

Primary XML indexes prevent the on-demand shredding of the data by providing a reference to the tags, values, and paths. On large XML documents, this can be a major performance improvement. Secondary XML indexes enhance the performance of primary XML indexes. Secondary XML indexes are created on either path, value, or property data in the primary XML index and benefit a read workload that heavily uses one of those three methods of querying XML data. Consult the documentation and the developers' intended use of XML data when creating XML indexes.

Understanding index statistics

When we talk about statistics in SQL Server, we do not mean the term generically. Statistics on tables and views are created to describe the distribution of data within indexes and heaps; they are created as needed by the query optimizer.

Statistics are important to the query optimizer to help it make query plan decisions, and they are heavily involved in the concept of cardinality estimation. The SQL Server Cardinality Estimator provides accurate estimations of the number of rows that queries will return, a big part of producing query plans.

Making sure statistics are available and up to date is essential for choosing a well-performing query plan. "Stale" statistics that have evaded updates for too long contain information that is quite different from the current state of the table and will likely cause poor execution plans.

There are a number of options in each database regarding statistics. We reviewed some in Chapter 4 but we present them again here in the context of performance tuning.

Manually creating and updating statistics

You can also create statistics manually during troubleshooting or performance tuning by using the CREATE STATISTICS statement, but, generally, you create statistics as needed.

You can consider manually creating statistics for large tables, and with design principals similar to how nonclustered indexes should be created. The order of the keys in statistics does matter, and you should choose columns that are regularly queried together to provide the most value to queries.

When venturing into creating your own statistics objects, consider using filtered statistics, which can also be helpful if you are trying to carry out advanced performance tuning on queries with a static filter or specific range of data. Like filtered indexes, or even filtered views and queries, you can create statistics with a similar WHERE clause, which are typically needed for the same reasons filtered indexes are: to limit the scope of the objects to ubiquitous data subsets, such as IsActive=1 or IsDeleted=0 or IsCurrent=1. Filtered statistics are never automatically created.

You can manually verify that indexes are being kept up to date by the query optimizer. The STATS_DATE() function accepts an object_id and stats_id, which is functionally the same as the index_id, if the statistics object corresponds to an index. Not all statistics are associated with an index; for example, indexes that are automatically created. There will generally be more stats objects than index objects. The STATS_DATE() function returns a datetime value of the last time the statistics object was updated. This function works in SQL Server and Azure SQL Database.

You can also use a pair of DMVs to return the statistics object properties including the last_updated date. For tables and indexed views, use sys.dm_db_stats_properties, and for partitioned tables, use sys.dm_db_incremental_stats_properties.

Automatically creating and updating statistics

When the database option _CREATE_STATISTICS is turned on, SQL Server can create single-column statistics objects, based on query need. These can make a big difference in performance. You can determine that a statistics object was created by the AUTO_CREATE_STATISTICS = ON behavior because it will have the name prefix _WA. The behavior that creates statistics for indexes (with a matching name) happens automatically, regardless of the AUTO_CREATE_STATISTICS database option.

Statistics are not automatically created for Columnstore indexes, and instead will use statistics objects that exist on the heap or the clustered index of the table. Like any index, a statistics object of the same name is created; however, for Columnstore indexes it is blank, and in place for logistical reasons only.

As you can imagine, statistics must also be kept up to date with the data in the table. SQL Server has an option in each database for AUTO_UPDATE_STATISTICS, which is ON by default and should almost always remain on.

You should only ever turn off both AUTO_CREATE_STATISTICS and AUTO_UPDATE_STATISTICS when requested by highly complex application designs, with variable schema usage, and a separate regular process that creates and maintains statistics, such as SharePoint. On-premises SharePoint installations include a set of stored procedures that periodically run to create and update the statistics objects for the wide, dynamically assigned table structures within. If you have not designed your application to intelligently create and update statistics using a separate process from that of the SQL Server engine, we recommend that you never turn off these options.

Important performance options for statistics

You can also create and update statistics incrementally, by taking advantage of table partitioning. First introduced in SQL Server 2014, statistics that use table partitioning reduce the overhead of statistics creation. You should turn on the database setting for INCREMENTAL to allow statistics to take advantage of partitioning. It has no impact on statistics for tables that are not partitioned.

Finally, you can update statistics asynchronously, and this is as large a performance gain as has ever been introduced to the concept of statistics. When you turn on the AUTO_UPDATE_STATISTICS_ASYNC database option, running a query will continue even when the query optimizer has identified an out-of-date statistics object. The statistics will be updated afterward, instead of forcing a user query to wait.

CHAPTER 10

Inside OUT

Should I turn on Auto Update Statistics and Auto Update Statistics Asynchronously in SQL 2017?

Yes! (Again, unless an application specifically recommends that you do not, such as SharePoint.)

Starting in SQL Server 2016 (and with database compatibility mode 130), the ratio of data modifications to rows in the table that helps identify out-of-date statistics has been aggressively lowered, causing statistics to be automatically updated more frequently. This is especially evident in large tables in which many rows were regularly updated. In SQL Server 2014 and before, this more aggressive behavior was not turned on by default, but could be turned on via Trace Flag 2371, starting with SQL 2008 R2 SP1.

It is more important now than ever to turn on Auto Update Statistics Asynchronously, which can dramatically reduce the overhead involved in automatic statistics maintenance.

Understanding statistics on memory-optimized tables

Statistics are created and updated automatically on memory-optimized tables. Memory-optimized tables require at least one index to be created, (a Primary Key if durability is set to SCHEMA_AND_DATA), and a matching statistics object is created for that index object.

NOTE

If a memory-optimized table was created in SQL 2014 compatibility level, you must manually update the statistics object yourself by using the UPDATE STATISTICS command. Then, if the AUTO_UPDATE_STATISTICS database option is turned on, statistics will update as normal. Statistics for new memory-optimized tables are not automatically updated when the database compatibility level is below 130 (SQL 2016) when the tables were created. It is always recommended to create memory-optimized tables in databases with the highest compatibility level.

➤ For more on memory-optimized tables, see Chapter 8.

➤ For more on updating statistics, see Chapter 13.

Understanding statistics on external tables

You can also create statistics on external tables; that is, tables that do not exist in the SQL Server database but instead are transparent references to data stored in a Hadoop cluster or in Azure Blob Storage.

You can create indexes on external tables, but currently, you cannot update them. Creating the index involved copying the external data into the SQL Server database only temporarily, and then calculating statistics. To update statistics for these datasets, you must drop them and re-create them. Because of the data sizes typically involved with external tables, using the FULLSCAN method to update statistics is not recommended.

➤ **For more on external tables, see Chapter 8.**

Developing, deploying, and managing data recovery

The first and foremost responsibility of a data professional is to ensure that a database can be recovered in the event of a disaster.

NOTE
As discussed in Chapter 2, a disaster is any unplanned event caused by, but not limited to, natural disaster, hardware or software failure, or human error.

You don't design a *backup strategy*. You design a *restore strategy*. You need to allow for potential downtime and loss of data, within acceptable limits. These are defined by the business requirements for getting an environment back up and running after a disaster.

Technical solutions such as high availability (HA) and disaster recovery (DR) are available in Microsoft SQL Server to support these requirements, which are ultimately governed by the organization itself. In other words, business requirements define the approach that you will take in your organization to plan for and survive a disaster. Remember that this is only a small but important part of a larger business continuity plan.

This chapter does not provide any guidance on recovering from a corrupt database. Microsoft recommends restoring from a last known good database backup if you experience corruption. That being said, our objective is that by the end of the next two chapters, you will understand how to achieve close to zero data loss with minimal downtime.

➤ You can read more about data corruption in Chapter 13.

NOTE
This chapter makes a number of references to Chapter 3, particularly transaction log files, virtual log files (VLFs), and Log Sequence Numbers (LSNs). If you have not yet read that chapter, we highly recommend that you do so before reading any further here.

The fundamentals of data recovery

It is incredibly expensive, and almost impossible, to achieve zero data loss with zero downtime. Recovery is a balance between budget, acceptable downtime, and acceptable data loss. Also, emotions run high when systems are down, so it is incumbent on all organizations to define possible outcomes at the outset and how to deal with them.

The governance of these requirements is outlined in a *Service-Level Agreement* (SLA), which explains the *Recovery Point Objective* (RPO) and *Recovery Time Objective* (RTO) from the organization's perspective, as it relates to business continuity. The SLA might also include the consequences and penalties (financial or otherwise) if you do not meet the timelines.

The SLA is a business document, not a technical one, because the RPO and RTO are business requirements. Although you will use technical solutions to satisfy these requirements, it is important to keep in mind that your recovery strategy should be the best fit for the organization's business needs.

> ➤ **For more information about achieving HA, read Chapter 12.**

A typical disaster recovery scenario

Let's paint a picture of a beautiful, sunny Friday afternoon, at 4:57 PM. This scenario spirals out of control pretty fast, so buckle up.

Disaster strikes in your office, just as you are about to head home for the weekend. The electricity goes out for the entire city block, and the uninterruptible power supply (UPS) under your desk fails because in all the confusion, you knocked over a half-finished can of soda onto it, which blew out the battery.

As the smell of burned electronics wafts up to your nostrils, you begin to panic. You haven't rehearsed this scenario, because no one ever thought the UPS would be moved upstairs after the basement was flooded last spring, let alone end up with soda poured over it.

Your transaction log backups run every 15 minutes because that's what the RPO stipulates, and you have a batch script in the Windows Task Scheduler that copies your files remotely, so your logs should have been copied safely off-premises. Well...that is, you're pretty sure the log backups were copied correctly, right?

Except that you get a sinking feeling in the pit of your stomach as you remember a warning you saw among your email this morning, while a colleague was on the phone to you, and your finger had slipped on the mouse and accidentally deleted the notification instead of moving it. Plus, you have that annoying muscle-memory habit of emptying deleted items whenever you see them.

Your smartphone rings. It's the boss, who is away this week at a conference and wants to check the sales figures for a report the board is putting together for an important meeting this evening. Your phone squawks because it has 2% battery remaining. Your laptop has some charge, but not much because you were planning on charging it when you arrived home.

You crack open your laptop to check whether you can somehow undelete your mail. Oh, right, your internet is down.

And then your phone dies while your boss, who coincidentally doesn't care about power failures because the company spent hundreds of dollars on that UPS under your desk, is asking you when the reports will be available again and wants you to just get it done.

You could charge the phone off the laptop and use the tethered cellular connection to log into the DR site. But the signal in this area is weak, so you need to move to the window on the other side of the office. As you stand up, the laptop decides that it's time to install operating system updates because it's now after 5 PM.

After an agonizing few minutes, your phone finally starts. Meanwhile your laptop has cancelled the updates because there's no internet access. You connect to your off-premises datacenter through a Remote Desktop session. It takes three attempts because you had forgotten that RDP to this server works only with the administrator user account.

The SQL Server instance has its own service account, so you need to download and use `psexec` to run SQL Server Management Studio as the service account in interactive mode, after changing a registry entry to allow that user to use interactive login. You check the backup folder, and thankfully the latest log file is from 4:30 PM. Great. That means the 4:45 PM backup didn't copy over. Oh, it's because the drive is full. That must have been what the email warning was about.

After clearing out some files that another colleague had put on the drive temporarily, you need to write the script you've been meaning to write to restore the database because you didn't have time to set up log shipping.

You export the backup directory listing to a text file and begin looking for the latest *full* backup, *differential* backup, and *transaction log* backup files. But now you've seen that the last differential backup doesn't make sense, because the size is all wrong.

You remember that one of your developers had made a full backup of the production database this week on Monday evening, didn't use the COPY_ONLY option, and you don't have access to that file. The latest differential file is useless. You need to start from Sunday's full backup file and then use Monday afternoon's differential backup and all transaction log files since then. That's more than 400 files to restore.

Eventually, with a bit of luck and text manipulation, you begin running the restore script. One particular log file takes a very long time, and in your panicked state you wonder whether it has somehow become stuck. After a minute or two of clicking around, you realize SQL Server had to grow the transaction log of the restored database because it was replaying that annoying index rebuild script that failed on Tuesday morning and needed to roll back.

Finally, at 6:33 PM, your off-premises database is up and running with the latest database backups up to and including the one from 4:30 PM. Just then, the lights come on in the office, because the power failure that affected the downtown area where your office is has been resolved. Now you need to do a full DBCC CHECKDB of the production server as soon as it starts, which always takes forever because the server is five years old and was installed with ECC RAM, which will push you out of the two-hour RTO that you and your boss agreed to, so you stick with the failover plan.

You update the connection settings in the application to point to the off-premises datacenter just as your phone dies once more, but at least the office again has power to charge everything. You send the boss an email to say the reports should be working. The cellular data bill is coming out of your boss's next trip, you tell yourself as you pack up to go home.

As you walk to the bus stop, it occurs to you that the files you cleared out to free up drive space probably included the full database backup from Monday night, and that you might have saved some time by checking them first.

Losing data with the RPO

When disaster strikes, you might lose a single byte in a single row in a single 8-KB data page due to memory or drive corruption. How do you recover from that corruption? What happens if you lose an entire volume or drive, the storage array, or even the entire building?

The RPO should answer the question: "How much data are you prepared to lose?" You need to consider whether your backups are being done correctly, regularly, and copied off-premises securely and in a timely manner. The RPO is usually measured in seconds or minutes. In other words, this is the acceptable amount of time elapsed between the last known good backup, and the moment of the point of failure.

In this hellish scenario that we just laid out, the organization decided that losing 15 minutes of data was acceptable, but ultimately 27 minutes was lost. This is because the drive on the DR server was full, and the most recent backup did not copy over.

To satisfy a 15-minute window, the transaction log backups would need to be taken more frequently, as would the off-premises copy.

If the organization requires "zero data loss," the budget will need to significantly increase to ensure that whatever unplanned event happens, SQL Server's memory and transaction log remains online and that all backups are working and being securely copied off-premises as soon as possible.

Inside OUT

Why is the RPO measured in time, and not drive usage?

Transactions vary in size, but time is constant.

In Chapter 3, we looked at how every transaction is assigned an LSN to keep track of things in the active portion of the transaction log. Each new LSN is greater than the previous one (this is where the word "sequence" in Log Sequence Number comes from).

The RPO refers to the most recent point in time in the transaction log history to which you will restore the database, based on the most recently committed LSN at that specific moment in time, or the latest LSN in the log backup chain, whichever satisfies the organization's RPO.

Losing time with the RTO

Time is money. Every minute that an organization is unable to work has a cost, and lost productivity adds up quickly. The RTO is the amount of time you need to get everything up and running again after a disaster. This might be orchestrating a failover to your disaster recovery site in another building, or a manual failover using log shipping. The RTO is usually measured in hours.

In our disaster scenario, the RTO was two hours. Our intrepid but woefully unprepared and accident-prone DBA barely made it. A number of factors acted against the plan (if it could be called a plan).

For an organization to require zero downtime, the budget is exponentially increased. This is where a combination of HA and DR technologies combine to support the requirements.

Establishing and using a run book

When panic sets in, you need a clear set of instructions to follow, just like our deer-in-the-headlights DBA in our fictional scenario. This set of instructions is called a *run book*.

The run book is a business continuity document. It covers the steps necessary for someone (including yourself) to bring the databases and supporting services back online after a disaster. In an eventuality in which you or your team members become incapacitated, the document should be accessible and understandable to someone who doesn't have intimate knowledge of the environment.

From our example scenario, issues like the Remote Desktop Protocol (RDP) user account not being able to log in to SQL Server Management Studio, getting `psexec` downloaded, knowing to skip an out-of-band differential backup, and so on would not be immediately obvious to many people. Even the most experienced DBA in a panic will struggle with thinking clearly.

The level of detail in a run book is defined by the complexity of the systems that need recovery and the time available to bring them back again. Your organization might be satisfied with a simple Microsoft Excel spreadsheet containing configurations for a few business-critical systems. Or, it might be something more in-depth, updated regularly, and stored in a version control system (which itself should be backed up properly).

The rest of this chapter describes how SQL Server provides backup and restore features to help you come up with a recovery strategy that is most appropriate to your environment, so that when your organization wants to produce business continuity documentation, you have sufficient knowledge to guide an appropriate and *achievable* technical response.

Most important, you need to be able to rehearse a DR plan. The run book won't be perfect, and rehearsing scenarios will help you to produce better documentation so that when disaster strikes, even the most panicked individual will be able to figure things out.

An overview of recovery models

SQL Server supports three recovery models: full, bulk-logged, and simple. These models provide a high level of control over the types of backups available to your databases. Let's take a brief look at each one:

- **Full recovery model.**   Allows a full point-in-time recovery. Full, differential, and transaction log backups can be taken. All transactions are fully logged.

- **Bulk-logged recovery model.**   Reduces the amount of transaction log used for certain bulk operations. Can allow a point-in-time recovery if no bulk-logged operations are in that portion of the transaction log backup. Full, differential, and transaction log backups can be taken.

- **Simple recovery model.**   No transactions are logged. Full and differential backups can be taken.

NOTE

These are called *recovery models*. If you see the term "recovery mode," it is incorrect.

You can change the recovery model of a database in SQL Server Management Studio in Object Explorer, or by using the following Transact-SQL (T-SQL) statement (and choosing the appropriate option in the square brackets):

```
ALTER DATABASE <dbname> SET RECOVERY [ FULL | BULK_LOGGED | SIMPLE ];
```

Before diving into each recovery model in more detail, let's take a look at point-in-time restores, and how those are affected by the log backup chain.

Recovery to a point in time

If configured properly, it is possible to restore a database to the exact moment in time (or more precisely, to the exact LSN) before disaster struck.

The most common form of disaster is human error, like accidentally leaving out a WHERE clause during an UPDATE statement.

No matter the cause, your reactions should be the same: stop all work on the database in question, find out what happened in a nondestructive way, take a tail-log backup if possible or necessary, and recover to the moment before disaster struck.

Inside OUT

What is a tail-log backup?

A tail-log (or tail-of-the-log) backup, is fundamentally the same thing as an ordinary transaction log backup. The difference is in the circumstances in which you would perform this kind of log backup.

In a disaster scenario, the automation for performing transaction log backups might be offline, or your backup drive is not available. Any time you need to manually perform a transaction log backup to ensure that the remaining transactions in the log are safely stored somewhere after a failure occurred, this is a tail-log backup.

Performing a tail-log backup that you can restore properly later is how you achieve zero data loss.

Keep in mind that a highly available database (using availability groups or database mirroring, for example) is not immune to disasters, especially if these disasters are replicated to downstream database instances.

NOTE

SQL Server 2016 introduced System-Versioned Temporal Tables, which keep a history of changes to a table. When implemented appropriately, temporal tables can reduce productivity loss caused by human error because modified or deleted data is stored in a history table for each temporal table.

Inside OUT

How can I tell when the unplanned event took place?

To find out when a disaster occurred that isn't immediately apparent, you can query the active portion of the transaction log if it is available, making use of an undocumented system function that reads from the active VLF(s), as demonstrated here:

```
SELECT * FROM sys.fn_dblog(NULL, NULL);
```

This displays all transactions that have not yet been flushed as a result of a checkpoint operation.

Using a standard WHERE clause, you can trace back to the point immediately before the event took place. For example, if you know that a user deleted a row from a table, you would write a query looking for all delete operations:

```
SELECT * FROM sys.fn_dblog(NULL, NULL)
WHERE Operation LIKE '%delete%';
```

To get this to work, SQL Server should still be running, and the transaction log should still be available (although this technique does work on offline transaction log files using sys.fn_dump_dblog).

To see more from Paul Randal about reading from the transaction log, go to *https://www.sqlskills.com/blogs/paul/using-fn_dblog-fn_dump_dblog-and-restoring-with-stopbeforemark-to-an-lsn.*

Point-in-time recovery requires transaction logs that cover the full span of time from the most recent full backup to the time of the incident.

➤ You can see an example of how to restore to a point in time in the section "Restoring a database to a point in time" later in this chapter.

The log backup chain

A backup chain starts with a full backup, followed by differential and/or transaction log backups that you can combine into a recovery sequence to restore a database to a particular point in time or to the time of the latest backup, whichever is required.

Databases in the full recovery model can be restored to a point in time because transactions are fully logged in that recovery model.

NOTE

You can also restore a database in the bulk-logged recovery model to a point in time, provided that the transaction log backup does not contain bulk-logged operations up to that point in time.

As Figure 11-1 illustrates, a backup chain starts with a full backup, which contains the most recent LSN of the active portion of the transaction log at the time that backup finished. You can then use a combination of the most recent differential backup (which must be based on that same full backup) and any additional transaction log backups to produce a point-in-time recovery. If you do not have a differential backup or the point in time you want to restore to is before the end of the differential backup, you must use transaction log backups. Either option will work as long as the LSNs required in the sequence are contained in each of those backups.

Figure 11-1 The log backup chain.

A new database is in the full recovery model by default because it is derived from the model database, which itself is in the full recovery model by default. However, the database will not behave like it is in the full recovery model until the first time a full backup is taken, which is what initializes the backup chain.

CAUTION

If you decide to change the default recovery model in the model database, any new databases will inherit that setting. We recommend that you leave the model database in full recovery.

Until you run that first full backup on a database in the full or bulk-logged recovery model, the new database is "pseudo-simple," behaving as though it is in the simple recovery model. Active portions of the log are cleared whenever a database checkpoint is issued, and the transaction log remains at a reasonably stable size, unless a long-running transaction causes it to grow.

For less-experienced data professionals, the sudden and seemingly uncontrolled growth of the transaction log, after the first full backup, can take them by surprise.

We recommend that you configure appropriate maintenance plans (including transaction log backups and monitoring) at the time you create a new database.

NOTE

Backup chains can survive database migrations and upgrades, as long as LSNs remain intact. This is what makes certain HA features possible in SQL Server.

Inside OUT

How long can the backup chain be?

Provided that you have an unbroken backup chain for which the LSNs are all intact, you can potentially have many thousands of log backups stretching back over months or even years. You can apply these backups, along with the full backup on which they are based (and assuming the files are intact), to restore the database to a current point in time, even if the database was moved or upgraded during that time.

However, this can be extremely time consuming and will negatively affect the RTO, especially if the backups need to be retrieved from slow storage (including tape). Legend has it that some organizations were forced to closed down as a result of missing the RTO.

It is far better practice to perform regular full backups (and differential database backups if they are useful) along with transaction log backups so that the dependency chain is shorter.

➤ You can read more about designing an appropriate backup schedule in the section "Creating backups" later in this chapter. For more on maintenance plans, read Chapter 14.

Full recovery model

For databases that require point-in-time recovery, which is the case for most business-critical systems, we recommend the full recovery model (and it is the default for all new SQL Server databases).

In this recovery model, after the first full backup takes place (which initializes the backup chain), the virtual log files in the transaction log remain active and are *not cleared* until a transaction log backup writes these log records to a log backup. Only then will the log be truncated (cleared).

Assuming that you implement a process to ensure that these backups are securely copied off-premises as soon as the backups are completed, and that you regularly test these backups, you can easily restore your database in the event of a disaster. Provided the right circumstances are in play, you might even be able to take a tail-log backup to achieve zero data loss, if that data has been committed and made durable.

➤ You can read more about durability, including delayed durability, in Chapter 2.

NOTE

The Database Engine supports mirrored backups since SQL Server 2016. This makes it possible for you to back up a database to two destinations simultaneously, which could be a local drive or network share as well as an off-premises location such as Microsoft Azure Storage. This tiered approach can also reduce the complexity of securely copying backups off-premises.

Bulk-logged recovery model

Under the bulk-logged recovery model, bulk operations are minimally logged, which reduces the size of the transaction log records and subsequent backups. These operations include BULK INSERT, INSERT ... SELECT, SELECT ... INTO, and bcp operations. Certain indexing operations are also minimally logged.

It is usually not possible to restore a database in the bulk-logged recovery model to a point in time, but there is a way to get *mostly*-point-in-time recovery. This allows a more flexible recovery strategy than the simple recovery model (more on this in the next section), without generating large transaction logs for bulk operations.

Suppose that you want to use the bulk-logged recovery model to perform minimally logged operations, without breaking the log backup chain. Your database must be in the full recovery model before the bulk-logged operation is performed. First, you must take a transaction log backup, and then switch to the bulk-logged recovery model. After the bulk-logged operation is complete, you must immediately switch back to the full recovery model, and then back up the log again. This ensures that the backup chain remains unbroken and allows point-in-time recovery to any point before or after the bulk-logged operation.

➤ For more details, read the TechNet article "Operations That Can Be Minimally Logged," which is available at *https://technet.microsoft.com/library/ms191244.aspx*.

Simple recovery model

Databases in the simple recovery model cannot make use of point-in-time recovery. After a transaction in the simple recovery model is committed or rolled back, a checkpoint is implicitly issued, which truncates (clears) the log.

Databases in the simple recovery model can make use of full and differential backups. This recovery model is better suited to development databases, databases that change infrequently, and databases that can be rebuilt from other sources.

CHAPTER 11

Understanding backup devices

SQL Server writes database backups to physical backup devices. These storage media might be virtualized, but for the purposes of this section, they are considered physical. They include disk, tape, and URL.

Backup disk

The most common form of SQL Server backup is stored directly on a local drive or network path, referred to as the *backup disk*. A backup disk contains one or more backup files, and each file contains one or more database backups. A database backup might also be split across multiple files.

Backup sets and media

As noted previously, SQL Server backups are written to media types (devices), namely tape, hard drives (referred to as backup disks, which include solid-state drives and UNC network paths), and URLs (through Azure Blob Storage). Each of these types have specific properties, including format and block size. You must initialize (format) tapes before you can write to them.

> ### CAUTION
> The option to back up SQL Server databases to tape will be removed from a future version of SQL Server. When creating a recovery strategy, use disk and/or URL. You should change any existing recovery strategies that involve tape to use another media type.

Media set

This is an ordered collection of a fixed type and number of devices (see Figure 11-2). For example, if you are using a backup disk, your media set will comprise a fixed number of one or more files on the file system or UNC network path.

With tape backup now deprecated, media sets with multiple devices are less useful. When backing up to a disk, network, or URL, we recommend limiting backup operations to one file at a time. Nevertheless, a backup will always comprise at least one media set.

> ➤ To read more about mirrored backup media sets, go to *https://docs.microsoft.com/sql/relational-databases/backup-restore/mirrored-backup-media-sets-sql-server*.

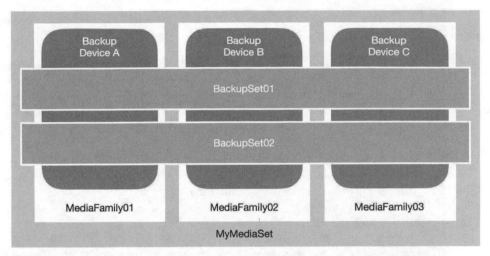

Figure 11-2 A media set, containing three media families spread over three devices.

Media family

In each media set, all backup devices used in that media set make up the media family. The number of devices in that set is the number of media families. If a media set uses three backup devices that are not mirrored, there are three media families in that media set.

Backup set

A successful backup added to a media set is called a backup set. Information about the successful backup is stored here, in the header of a backup set.

You could reuse an existing backup set by adding new backups for a database to the end of that media. This grows the media by appending the backup to the end of it. However, we do not recommend this practice, because the integrity of previous backups relies on the consistency of that media. An errant INIT option in the backup command could even accidentally overwrite existing backups in the backup set.

Inside OUT

What media set, media family, and backup set should I use?

For typical SQL Server instances, we recommend that you back up your databases to strongly named, self-contained files, where only the backup in question is stored in each file. If you are using a third-party solution (free or paid), make sure that they follow a strong naming convention, as well.

In other words, the file name itself should contain the server and instance name, the database name, the type of backup (full, differential, or log), as well as the date and time of the backup. This makes locating, managing, and restoring backups much easier because each file is the backup set, media family, and media set all rolled into one.

For example, a full backup of the WideWorldImporters database on the default instance of a SQL Server called SERVER, taken on February 9th, 2018 at 10:53:44 PM might have the following filename: SERVER_WideWorldImporters_FULL_20180209_225344.BAK.

Physical backup device

This is the actual tape drive, file on a drive, or Azure Blob. You can split a single backup between as many as 64 backup devices of the same type. Splitting across many files can be useful for backing up very large databases (VLDBs), for performance reasons.

Backup to URL

Since SQL Server 2012 (Service Pack 1 with Cumulative Update 2), you can back up your SQL Server database directly to Azure Blob Storage. This is made possible by using a URL as a destination, along with the existing `FILE` and `TAPE` options.

Understanding different types of backups

A SQL Server backup is a process that creates an exact copy of the database, in a transactionally consistent state, at the moment that backup ended.

Regardless of the type of backup, the process will always include the active portion of the transaction log, including relevant LSNs, which ensures full transactional consistency when the backup is restored.

As we discussed earlier in the chapter, you can back up a SQL Server database using three main ways, full, differential, and transaction log, to produce the most efficient recovery strategy. A full database backup is the minimum type required to recover a database. Transaction log backups are incremental backups, based on a full backup, that allow point-in-time restores. Differential backups can reduce the amount of time required to restore a database to a point in time, also based on a full backup.

In Enterprise edition, especially for VLDBs, you can take file-level and filegroup-level backups to allow a more controlled procedure when restoring.

➤ You can read more about the files that make up a SQL Server database in Chapter 3.

Inside OUT

How large is a VLDB?

Opinions differ as to what constitutes a VLDB, based on individual experience and available resources (such as memory and drive space).

For the purposes of this chapter, any database that exceeds 100 GB is considered very large. Although modern solid-state storage arrays do mitigate many of the challenges facing databases of this size, they are not in widespread use as of this writing.

You can read more about solid-state storage, and storage arrays, in Chapter 2.

NOTE

You can use database snapshots to ease administration when testing new functionality to reduce the time required to restore to a particular point in time, but they are at the same risk as regular database files. Snapshots are not guaranteed backups, and you should not use them in place of native SQL Server backups. To learn more about database snapshots, go to *https://docs.microsoft.com/sql/relational-databases/databases/database-snapshots-sql-server*.

Every backup contains a header and a payload. The header describes the backup device, what type of backup it is, backup start and stop information (including LSN information), and information about the database files. The payload is the content of the data and/or transaction log files belonging to that backup. If Transparent Data Encryption (TDE) or Backup Encryption was turned on, the payload is encrypted.

➤ You can read more about TDE in Chapter 7.

Full backups

A full database backup is a transactionally consistent copy of the entire database. This type of backup includes all of the 8-KB data pages in the database file(s) as well as the portion of the transaction log that was active from the start to the end of the backup process.

➤ **You can read more about the active portion of the transaction log in Chapter 3.**

When a full backup runs with the default settings, a reserved data page known as the *differential bitmap* is cleared (see the upcoming section "Differential backups"). Any differential backups that are taken on the database after that will be based off that full backup.

You can perform full backups on databases in all recovery models, and you can compress them. Since SQL Server 2016, you can also compress databases that were encrypted with TDE.

You can perform a full backup to a backup disk target with a minimal amount of T-SQL code. For example, a WideWorldImporters database on a default instance with a machine called SERVER can be backed up by using the following code:

```
BACKUP DATABASE WideWorldImporters
TO DISK = N'C:\SQLData\Backup\SERVER_
WideWorldImporters_FULL_20170918_210912.BAK';
GO
```

Copy-only backup

You can change the default behavior by using the COPY_ONLY option, which does not clear the differential bitmap. Copy-only backups are useful for taking out-of-band backups without affecting the differential backup schedule.

In other words, only differential backups are affected by the COPY_ONLY option. Transaction log backups, and thus the backup chain, are not affected.

Transaction log backups

Transaction log backups are incremental backups of a database. In the full recovery model, all transactions are fully logged. This means that you can bring back a database to the exact state it was when that transaction log was taken, provided that the restore is successful. These backups allow for a recovery at any moment in time in the sequence (the backup chain).

In this type of backup, the active portion of the transaction log is backed up. Transaction log backups apply only to databases in the full and bulk-logged recovery models. Databases in the full recovery model can be restored to a point in time, and databases in the bulk-logged recovery model can be restored to a point in time as long as the transaction log does not contain bulk-logged operations.

Tail-of-the-log backups

As noted previously, tail-of-the-log, or tail-log, backups are functionally no different to a regular transaction log backup. A disaster can occur that does not affect the transaction log itself. For example, the drive or volume for the data file(s) might become unavailable or corrupt, but SQL Server remains online.

After you have disconnected any other users from the database, you can switch it to single-user mode and perform a manual log backup on the active portion of the log. This creates a log backup that can be used at the very end of the backup chain to guarantee zero data loss.

➤ You can read more about tail-log backups at *https://docs.microsoft.com/sql/relational-databases/backup-restore/back-up-the-transaction-log-when-the-database-is-damaged-sql-server*.

Differential backups

Differential backups, which are based on a full database backup, are a convenience feature to reduce the number of transaction log backups (and time) required to restore a database to a point in time.

In many cases, a differential backup is much smaller than a full backup, which allows for a more flexible backup schedule. You can run a full backup less frequently, and have differential backups running more regularly, taking up less space than the full backup would have taken.

Think back to Chapter 3 in which we looked at extents. As a reminder, an extent is a 64-KB segment in the data file, comprising a group of eight physically contiguous 8-KB data pages.

After a full backup completes (i.e., the default full backup without the copy-only option), the differential bitmap is cleared. All subsequent changes in the database, at the extent level, are recorded in the differential bitmap.

When the differential backup runs, it looks at the differential bitmap and backs up only the extents that have been modified since the full backup, along with the active portion of the transaction log.

This is quite different to a transaction log backup, which records every change in the database even if it's to the same tables over and over again.

Thus, a differential backup is not the same thing as an incremental backup. If you want to restore a database using a differential backup, you need only the full backup file plus the most recent differential backup file.

Even though you cannot restore a database to a point in time (or LSN) that occurs within the differential backup itself, it can vastly reduce the number of transaction log files required to effect those same changes.

Differential backups apply to databases in the full, bulk-logged and simple recovery models.

CAUTION

As noted previously, if a full backup is taken out-of-band without the COPY_ONLY option, this will affect subsequent differential backups. In that case, you will be restricted to using transaction log backups exclusively to restore the backup chain. If you want to take a full backup of a database without affecting the differential backup schedule, always use the COPY_ONLY option.

Inside OUT

What do I do if my differential backup is larger than my full backup?

Differential backups will grow larger as the number of changed extents in the database increases. It is feasible that the differential backup can end up being larger than a full backup over time.

This is possible for situations in which every extent is modified in some way (for instance if all the indexes in the database are rebuilt), which makes the differential backup the same size as a full backup. When it adds the active portion of the log, you end up with a differential backup that is larger than a full backup.

SQL Server 2017 provides a new column called `modified_extent_page_count` in the DMV `sys.dm_db_file_space_usage` to let you know how large a differential backup will be. A good rule of thumb is to take a full backup if the differential backup approaches 80% of the size of a full backup.

➤ You can read more about differential backups at *https://docs.microsoft.com/sql/relational-databases/backup-restore/differential-backups-sql-server*.

Fixing a broken backup chain by using differential backups

A backup chain is broken when a database is switched from the full recovery model to the bulk-logged or simple recovery model for any reason (such as shrinking the transaction log file during an emergency situation).

After you switch back to the full recovery model, you can restart the log backup chain without having to perform a full database backup by taking a differential backup. As long as you make use of this or a more recent differential backup in a later recovery, along with the accompanying transaction log backups, the backup chain has been repaired.

➤ You can read more considerations regarding switching between recovery models at *https://msdn.microsoft.com/library/ms178052.aspx*.

File and filegroup backups

With SQL Server Enterprise edition, you can take a more granular approach by backing up individual data files and filegroups, which make use of the full or differential options, as well. Although these options are not available in the SQL Server Management Studio user interface, you can use the official documentation to build appropriate T-SQL queries.

> ## CAUTION
> If a single file in a filegroup is offline (for instance during a restore), the entire filegroup is offline, as well, which affects backups.

Partial backups

Because read-only filegroups do not change, it does not make sense to include them in ongoing backup processes. Primarily used for VLDBs that contain read-only filegroups, partial backups will exclude those read-only filegroups, as required.

Partial backups contain the primary filegroup, any read-write filegroups, and one or more optional read-only filegroups.

> ➤ To read more about partial backups, go to *https://docs.microsoft.com/sql/relational-databases/backup-restore/partial-backups-sql-server*.

File backups

You can use file backups to restore individual files in the event that they become corrupt. This makes restoring easier, because for VLDBs it would take much less time to restore a single file than the entire database, and it interferes with point-in-time restores.

Unfortunately, it does increase the complexity due to increased administration of the additional file backups over and above the full, differential, and transaction log backups. This overhead extends to recovery script maintenance.

> ➤ To read more about file backups, visit *https://docs.microsoft.com/sql/relational-databases/backup-restore/full-file-backups-sql-server*.

Additional backup options

Since SQL Server 2014, it is possible to encrypt database backups using an asymmetric key. This is not the same as the encryption provided for backups with TDE turned on.

As noted in Chapter 3, you can also compress backups, which is recommended in almost all cases, unless the database makes use of page or row compression, or the database is encrypted with TDE.

> ➤ To learn more about security and encryption, read Chapter 7.

CHAPTER 11

Backup encryption

Like any asymmetric encryption process, you will require a cipher (the encryption algorithm) and an asymmetric key or certificate. Supported ciphers are Advanced Encryption Standard (AES; you can use key sizes of 128, 192, and 256 bits), and 3DES (also known as Triple DES). As discussed in depth in Chapter 7, AES is a safer and faster cipher than 3DES. You should back up and store the key or certificate in a secure location.

Memory-optimized tables

Standard backups include memory-optimized tables. During the backup process, a checksum is performed on the data and delta file pairs to check for corruption. Any corruption detected in a memory-optimized filegroup will cause a backup to fail, and you will be required to restore from the last known good backup.

Remember that the storage requirements for a memory-optimized table can be much larger than its usage in memory, which will affect the size of your backups.

> ➤ **To learn more about how to back up memory-optimized files, go to**
> **https://docs.microsoft.com/sql/relational-databases/in-memory-oltp/**
> **backing-up-a-database-with-memory-optimized-tables.**

Other options also exist, including file-snapshot backups for database files that are already stored in Azure (see Chapter 3), or turning on Managed Backups (also covered in Chapter 3). Although these options are convenient, there is no substitute for a native SQL Server backup.

Creating and verifying backups

You should completely automate backups when possible, whether you make use of the built-in Maintenance Plan Wizard in SQL Server Management Studio or a third-party solution (free or paid). Always ensure that backups are successful by observing that the backup files exist and the backup task does not error out. Additionally, you must test those backups by restoring them, which you can also do with an automated process.

> ➤ **You can read more about maintenance plans in Chapter 13.**

SQL Server Agent is an excellent resource for automating backups, and many third-party solutions make use of it too (as does the Maintenance Plan Wizard).

Inside OUT

How frequently should I run backups?

Business requirements and database size will dictate how long your maintenance window is and what needs to be backed up in that window. You might have a critical database small enough that it can be fully backed up daily, and has no need for differential backups. Larger databases might require a weekly schedule, augmented by daily differential backups.

A database in the full recovery model should have transaction log backups occurring as a factor of the RPO. Assuming that your RPO is five minutes, transaction logs should be backed up and securely copied off-premises at a more frequent interval (every minute or 90 seconds, perhaps). This is to accommodate the implicit delay between when a backup ends and when the backup has been copied off-premises. In the case of a disaster, there is a higher chance that the files are copied off-premises with a smaller copy interval. A backup is realistically not considered part of the RPO until it is copied off-premises.

Databases that can be rebuilt using existing processes might not need to be backed up at all.

Creating backups

You can design a backup solution to satisfy a recovery strategy by using all or a combination of the following methods:

- A *full backup* reads the entire database, including the data file(s) and the active portion of the transaction log.

- A *differential backup* reads extents that have changed in the data file(s) since the last full (non-copy-only) backup as well as the active portion of the log.

- A *transaction log backup* reads only the active portion of the log.

- A *partial backup* reads an individual file or filegroup as well as the active portion of the log.

The buffer pool (see Chapter 2) is not used for database backups. The *backup buffer* is a portion of memory outside of the buffer pool, big enough to read pages from the data file and write those page to the backup file. The backup buffer is usually between 16 MB and 32 MB in size. Be aware that memory pressure can reduce the backup and restore buffer sizes, causing backups and restores to take longer.

CAUTION

It is possible to increase the number of backup buffers (using the BUFFERCOUNT option) as well as the transfer size of each block to the backup media (using the MAXTRANSFERSIZE option) to improve throughput, but we recommend this only in certain circumstances. A large number of buffers might cause out-of-memory exceptions. You can read more about this possible issue at *https://blogs.msdn.microsoft.com/sqlserverfaq/2010/05/06/ incorrect-buffercount-data-transfer-option-can-lead-to-oom-condition/*.

Backup checksums

SQL Server can perform optional checksum verifications on database backups. By default, backups do not perform a checksum unless they are compressed.

You can change this behavior either by a trace flag (TF3023), in the SQL Server Management Studio properties of a backup, or in any T-SQL script you create to perform backups. We recommend that you turn on backup checksum where possible.

Without backup checksum turned on, no validation is performed on data pages or log blocks. This means that any logical corruption will also be backed up without showing any of the errors you might see with a DBCC CHECKDB operation. This is to allow for scenarios in which you can back up a corrupt database before attempting to fix the corruption.

➤ **To read more about recovering from corruption, see Chapter 13.**

With backup checksum turned on, a checksum is calculated over the entire backup file. Additionally, the page checksum on every 8-KB data page (for both page verification types of *checksum* or *torn-page detection*), and log block checksum from the active portion of the log, will be validated.

CAUTION

Physical corruption, in which the data cannot be read from the drive, including corruption in memory-optimized filegroups, will cause the backup to fail.

The backup checksum can significantly increase the time for a backup to run, but adds some peace of mind, short of running a recommended DBCC CHECKDB on a restored database. Backup compression can offset this additional overhead.

Verifying backups

After you create a backup, we highly recommend that you immediately verify that the backup was successful. Although rare, corruption is always a possibility. Most of the time it is caused by the storage layer (including as a result of device drivers, network drivers, and filter drivers), but it can also occur in non-ECC RAM or as the result of a bug in SQL Server itself.

NOTE

A filter driver is software that intercepts all drive reads and writes. This class of software includes defragmentation tools and security products like antivirus malware scanners. This is a good opportunity to remind you to exclude SQL Server files (data, log, backups) from antivirus scanners, and also to note that defragmenting solid-state storage is a bad idea because it will dramatically reduce the lifespan of the drive.

There are two ways to verify a backup, and you can probably guess that the best way is to restore it and perform a full consistency check on the restored database by using DBCC CHECKDB.

The other, slightly quicker method, is to use RESTORE VERIFYONLY. If you backed up your database using the checksum option (which is on by default on compressed backups), the restore will verify the backup checksum as well as the data page and log block checksums as it reads through the backup media.

The convenience with RESTORE VERIFYONLY is that you do not need to allocate drive space to restore the data and log files, because the restore will read directly from the backup itself.

However, a DBCC CHECKDB is the only way to know that a database is free of corruption.

Inside OUT

Why should I perform a DBCC CHECKDB *if I have backup checksums turned on?*

Although backup checksums are verified by RESTORE VERIFYONLY, it is possible for corruption to occur after a page was verified as it is being written to the drive or while it is copied off-premises. A successful RESTORE VERIFYONLY is not a clean bill of health for the backup.

You can build an automated process on another server with a lot of cheaper drive space to restore all databases after they have been backed up and perform a DBCC CHECKDB on them. This also gives you an excellent idea of whether you can meet your RTO as databases grow in size.

Restoring a database

To restore a database, you will generally start with a full backup (piecemeal restore is covered in a later section).

If you plan to make use of differential and/or transaction log backups, you must use the NORECOVERY keyword for all but one of the backups.

You restore a database in the simple recovery model by using a full backup to begin, plus the most recent differential backup based on the full backup if one is available.

You can restore a database in the bulk-logged recovery model by using a full backup, along with a most recent differential backup based on that full backup if available. Should you want to restore to a specific point in time for a bulk-logged database, this might be possible if no bulk-logged operations exist in the transaction log backups you use.

You can restore a database in the full recovery model to a point in time using a full backup, plus any transaction log backups that form part of the backup chain. You can use a more recent differential backup (based off that full backup) to bypass a number of those transaction log backups, where appropriate.

CAUTION

Differential and transaction log backups rely on a corresponding full backup. If the full backup is not available, the differential and transaction log backups are useless.

Each transaction log backup is replayed against the restoring database, using the NORECOVERY option, as though those transactions are happening in real time. Each file is restored in sequential order up to the required point in time or until the last transaction log backup is reached, whichever comes first.

NOTE

When restoring a chain of transaction log backups, especially the first one in the sequence after a full or differential backup, it can happen that the LSN of the transaction log backup is earlier than the latest LSN of the full or differential backup that was restored. In most cases, you can ignore the error message that is displayed because the next transaction log file in the restore sequence will usually contain the required LSN.

After the entire chain has been restored (indicated by the WITH RECOVERY option), only then does the recovery kick in (which was covered in some detail in Chapter 3). All transactions that are committed will be rolled forward, and any in-flight transactions will be rolled back.

Some examples of restoring a database are included in the section that follows.

Restoring a database using a full backup

You can perform a database restore through SQL Server Management Studio or by using a T-SQL statement. In this example, only a full backup file is available to restore a database. The full backup comes from a different server, where the path of the original database is different, so the files need to be relocated (moved) on the new server.

To see the progress of the restore, you can set the statistics to display to the output window. The default is to write progress for every 5% complete. No statistics will be output until the files have been created on the file system first.

```
RESTORE DATABASE WideWorldImporters
FROM DISK = N'C:\SQLData\Backup\SERVER_
WideWorldImporters_FULL_20170918_210912.BAK'

WITH

MOVE N'WideWorldImporters' TO N'C:\SQLData\WWI.mdf',

MOVE N'WideWorldImporters_log' TO N'C:\SQLData\WWI.ldf',
STATS = 5,

RECOVERY;

GO
```

The RECOVERY option (the default) at the end brings the database online immediately after the full backup has been restored. This prevents any further backups from being applied. If you want to restore a differential backup after this full backup, you will need to use the NORECOVERY option and bring the database online only after restoring the differential backup (see the next example).

Restoring a database with differential and log backups

Restoring using full, differential, and transaction log backups is more complicated, but you can still perform it through SQL Server Management Studio or by using a series of T-SQL statements.

For this scenario, we recommend creating your own automated scripts. For example, after every transaction log backup, you can use the information in the msdb database to build a script to restore the entire database to that point in time and then save the script in the same folder as the backup file(s).

➤ To see an example by Steve Stedman, go to *http://stevestedman.com/2017/10/building-sql-restore-script-backup-runs/*.

NOTE

When restoring a database using more than one backup type (full, plus differential and/
or transaction log), each RESTORE statement that will be followed by another restore
file must include a WITH NORECOVERY option. This prevents recovery from running until
needed. You can either use the WITH RECOVERY option on the final file to run recovery
and bring the database online or you can add an extra line to the end of the script as in
the following example.

You restore a database by using the RESTORE command. Full and differential restores use the
RESTORE DATABASE option by convention. You can also restore transaction logs by using the
RESTORE DATABASE option, but you might prefer to use RESTORE LOG, instead, for clarity:

```
-- First, restore the full backup
RESTORE DATABASE WideWorldImporters
FROM DISK = N'C:\SQLData\Backup\SERVER_
WideWorldImporters_FULL_20170918_210912.BAK'
WITH
MOVE N'WideWorldImporters' TO N'C:\SQLData\WWI.mdf',
MOVE N'WideWorldImporters_log' TO N'C:\SQLData\WWI.ldf',
STATS = 5,
NORECOVERY;
GO
-- Second, restore the most recent differential backup
RESTORE DATABASE WideWorldImporters
FROM DISK = N'C:\SQLData\Backup\SERVER_
WideWorldImporters_DIFF_20170926_120100.BAK'
WITH STATS = 5,
NORECOVERY;
GO
-- Finally, restore all transaction log backups after the differential
RESTORE LOG WideWorldImporters
FROM DISK = N'C:\SQLData\Backup\SERVER_
WideWorldImporters_LOG_20170926_121500.BAK'
WITH STATS = 5,
NORECOVERY;
GO
RESTORE LOG WideWorldImporters
FROM DISK = N'C:\SQLData\Backup\SERVER_
WideWorldImporters_LOG_20170926_123000.BAK'
WITH STATS = 5,
NORECOVERY;
GO
-- Bring the database online
RESTORE LOG WideWorldImporters WITH RECOVERY;
GO
```

Remember that you can use the WITH RECOVERY option in the final transaction log file restore,
and exclude the final statement in the previous example.

The RECOVERY option instructs SQL Server to run recovery on the database, which might include an upgrade step if the new instance has a newer version of SQL Server on it. When recovery is complete, the database is brought online.

Restoring a database to a point in time

A point-in-time restore requires an LSN or timestamp (meaning a specific date and time value) to let the RESTORE command know when to stop restoring.

You can even restore to a specific mark in the transaction log backup, which you specify at transaction creation time by explicitly naming a transaction, though this is less common.

> ➤ To see more about marking transactions, go to *https://docs.microsoft.com/sql/t-sql/statements/restore-statements-transact-sql*.

CAUTION

The timestamp used for a point-in-time restore comes from the transaction log itself and refers to the local date and time on the SQL Server instance when the transaction started. Remember to take time zones and daylight saving into consideration when restoring a database to a point in time.

A point-in-time restore works only when restoring transaction log backups, not full or differential backups.

The process is the same as in the previous example, except for the final transaction log file, for which the point in time is specified by using the STOPAT or STOPBEFOREMARK options. Let's look at each option:

- **STOPAT.**   A timestamp. You will need to know this value from the time an unexpected event occurred, or from exploring the transaction log.

- **STOPBEFOREMARK** (also **STOPATMARK**).   A log sequence number or transaction name. You will need to know the LSN value from exploring the active portion of the transaction log (see the Inside OUT for `sys.fn_dblog` in the section "Recovery to a point in time" previously in this chapter).

Assuming that you have followed the same sequence as shown in the previous example, the final transaction log restore might look like this:

```
-- Restore point in time using timestamp
RESTORE LOG WideWorldImporters
FROM DISK = N'C:\SQLData\Backup\SERVER_
WideWorldImporters_LOG_20170926_123000.BAK'
WITH STOPAT = 'Sep 26, 2017 12:28 AM',
```

```
STATS = 5,
RECOVERY;
GO
-- Or restore point in time using LSN
-- Assume that this LSN is where the bad thing happened
RESTORE LOG WideWorldImporters
FROM DISK = N'C:\SQLData\Backup\SERVER_
WideWorldImporters_LOG_20170926_123000.BAK'
WITH STOPBEFOREMARK = 'lsn:0x0000029f:00300212:0002',
STATS = 5,
RECOVERY;
GO
```

➤ To read more about database recovery, including syntax and examples, visit *https://docs. microsoft.com/sql/t-sql/statements/restore-statements-transact-sql*.

Restoring a piecemeal database

Partial database backups deal with file and filegroup backups in order to ease the manageability of your VLDB. This is an advanced topic, so this section is a very high-level overview, which does not cover all of the intricacies involved.

Partial recovery is useful for bringing a database online as quickly as possible to allow the organization to continue working. You can then restore any secondary filegroups later, during a planned maintenance window.

Piecemeal restores begin with what is known as the *partial-restore sequence*. In this sequence, the primary filegroup is restored and recovered first. If the database is under the simple recovery model, all read/write filegroups are then restored.

➤ To learn more about the SQL Server recovery process, read Chapter 3.

While this is taking place, the database is offline until restore and recovery is complete. Any unrestored files or filegroups remain offline, but you can bring them online later by restoring them.

Regardless of the database's recovery model, the RESTORE command must include the PARTIAL option when doing a piecemeal restore, but only at the beginning of the sequence. Because transactions might span more than just the recovered filegroups, these transactions can become deferred, meaning that any transactions that needs to roll back cannot do so while a filegroup is offline. The transactions are deferred until the filegroup can be brought online again, and any data involved in that deferred transaction is locked in the meantime.

➤ To read more about deferred transactions, go to *https://docs.microsoft.com/sql/ relational-databases/backup-restore/deferred-transactions-sql-server*.

Restoring a partial database under the simple recovery model

To initialize a partial recovery of a database under the simple recovery model, you must begin with a full database or a partial backup. The restore will bring the primary filegroup online. You can then restore any additional files, if they are valid and transactionally consistent. Finally, if any read-only filegroups were damaged or corrupted and you need to restore them, you will do those last.

Restoring a partial database under the full recovery model

As with the simple recovery model that we just looked at, you must begin with a full database or partial backup (which must include the primary filegroup).

Point-in-time restore is provided under the following conditions:

- The first RESTORE DATABASE command must include the PARTIAL option.

- For a point-in-time restore against read/write filegroups, you need an unbroken log backup chain, and you must specify the time in the restore statement.

  ➤ To see more about piecemeal restores, including code examples, visit *https://docs.microsoft. com/sql/relational-databases/backup-restore/piecemeal-restores-sql-server.*

Limitations

If you skip a FILESTREAM filegroup during partial recovery, you can never again recover it unless the entire database is restored in full.

Defining a recovery strategy

Consider our scenario from the beginning of the chapter, in which anything and everything that could go wrong did go wrong. We will highlight certain issues that could be addressed by an appropriate recovery plan. This recovery plan can then be implemented, step by step, using your run book.

The word "strategy" means that there is a long-term goal. Your recovery strategy will need to adapt to your environmental changes. A run book is a living document; it requires incremental improvements as you test it.

We also discuss recovery strategies around hybrid environments, and briefly discuss Azure SQL Database.

A sample recovery strategy for a DR scenario

Several avoidable problems occurred in the DR scenario at the beginning of the chapter:

- A UPS was in the wrong place, with no redundant backup

- The internet connection did not have a redundant backup

- There was no run book to guide the accident-prone DBA

- The security on the DR server does not follow recommended best practices

- The off-premises backups were failing

Keeping the lights on

First and foremost, the backup power was inappropriate. There was no sufficient way to ensure that electricity would continue to flow after the building lost power, which had a number of knock-on effects including the inability to charge laptops and cellphone batteries. Additionally, the UPS should not have been placed in an area that could be affected by a can of soda falling off a desk.

In your run book, ensure that your backup generators and UPS collection can run all necessary equipment for long enough to keep emergency lights on, laptops charging, network equipment live, and the servers running, so that your DBA can log in to the SQL Server instance long enough to run a tail-log backup if necessary.

It might sound like a small detail, but you should even have a list of diesel suppliers in your run book, especially if your generators need to keep running for several hours.

Clean power is also important. Generators cause power fluctuations, which can damage sensitive electronic equipment. Although a power conditioner should be installed with your generator, you need to make sure that it works correctly.

Redundant internet connection

If your backups are being copied securely off-premises or you have a hybrid environment in which systems are connected across datacenters using Virtual Private Networks (VPNs), make sure that these routes can stay connected if one of the links goes down.

Know where the run book is

The run book itself should be printed out and stored in a secure but easily accessible location (for example, a fireproof safe or lock box). Don't forget to have an electronic copy available, as well, stored with a cloud provider of your choice and kept up to date.

Make sure your off-premises backups are secure and tamper-proof

In our example scenario, our DBA accidentally deleted an email alert indicating that the off-premises storage for backups was almost full. This alert is a good one to have, but it was not acted on appropriately. Also, the cause of the alert was an avoidable situation because the colleague who used up the free space should not have been able to use critical organization resources.

Security of the off-premises location for backups is critical, and no one should have access to that unless they are required to do a recovery.

Check your backups regularly and test them regularly

Our DBA assumed that the backups were taking place every 15 minutes and being copied off-premises immediately afterward. This was not the case, and instead of losing 15 minutes of data, the organization lost as much as 27 minutes' worth.

Automate your backups. Use maintenance plans (see Chapter 13), and make use of established third-party backup tools such as Ola Hallengren's Maintenance Solution (available from *http://ola.hallengren.com*) or MinionWare Backup (available from *http://www.minionware.net*).

Verify that you have a process to check that your backups are taking place. Test that process often. For example, if SQL Server Agent is crashing, none of your notifications might ever fire. Test the backups, as well, by having a machine that restores backups continuously and running DBCC CHECKDB where possible. If you can afford it, have log shipping configured so that all backups are restored as soon as they come into off-premises storage. Ensure that the backup files are being securely copied off-premises as soon as they can.

Run random spot-checks of your backups, as well, by picking a date and time in the backup history and restoring the backup. Aside from testing the databases themselves, this is a good rehearsal for when something goes wrong. Remember to run DBCC CHECKDB on any database you restore.

You might find as databases grow that the SLA becomes out of date and that the RTO is no longer achievable. Running these tests will alert you to this situation long before it becomes a problem and will allow you to tweak how you perform backups in the future.

For example, you might discover that it is much quicker to spin up an Azure virtual machine with SQL Server, and restore the business-critical databases that are stored in Azure Blob Storage, than having to struggle with VPN connections and failed hardware on-premises at another datacenter.

Check the security of your DR site

Your DR site might have outdated security access (physical and virtual). Be sure that you stay up to date, especially when people leave the company. You don't want to be in the position of having to call someone who left your organization two years ago to ask for a firewall password—especially not at 3 AM on a Sunday.

If you must use a remote desktop connection to access a server, protect it by using a VPN. Also, check that you have already downloaded additional tools (like `psexec` in the example) and documented how to use them.

Keep all passwords and keys (symmetric and asymmetric) in a password manager as well as printed and stored in a secure location with the run book where practical. Make sure that all digital certificates are backed up securely.

Automate restore scripts

In the case of an msdb database being inaccessible and you are unable to generate a restore script from a database backup history, make sure that you have a tool that generates a restore script based on files in a folder in your off-premises storage. Many tools exist to do this, including the free dbatools (available from *https://dbatools.io*).

Practice your DR strategy

In concert with your HA strategy, which involves automated and manual failovers (see Chapter 12 for more on this), you should perform regular drills to test your run book. You can also have people in your organization who are unfamiliar with the environment look through the run book. They can provide valuable information with regard to assumptions you might have made.

The cadence is up to your organization, but a full DR scenario should be tested at least once or twice a year. Any changes you need to make to the run book should be made immediately. If the recovery fails, make notes of how it failed and what you did to resolve the failure. All of this information is extremely valuable.

Strategies for a cloud/hybrid environment

Many organizations are making use of a combination of on-premises infrastructure and services in remote locations, including Azure services, third-party datacenters, and other cloud vendors.

Recovering data in a hybrid environment

The strategy for recovering data in a hybrid environment is very similar to an on-premises strategy, except that you must take network connection, latency, and bandwidth into account.

With cloud services, don't keep all of your data in one region. Make use of geo-replication, so that if or when one region becomes unavailable, you still have business continuity.

It can be prudent to make use of virtualization technologies that allow for virtual machine snapshots and file system snapshots to ensure that your virtual servers are backed up regularly. You can augment these with appropriate native SQL Server backups that are tested properly.

When designing a recovery strategy for a hybrid environment, pick a DR site that is central, but geo-replicated.

If you are already making use of Azure Storage for your backups, this reduces the network bandwidth and latency issues if you can restore your organization's databases to Azure virtual machines or databases in Azure SQL Database.

Remember that after failing over to a DR site, you will need to fail back to your on-premises site when it is up and running again.

It's always good to remember that the backup chain can survive migrations and upgrades. Keep your databases in the full recovery model, and take regular full and transaction log backups (and differential backups where appropriate). Make sure these backups are copied securely off-premises on a regular basis to a central location accessible from each node of your hybrid environment. Test your backups and your recovery strategy regularly, and write it down.

You are now prepared to handle almost any disaster recovery scenario.

Recovering a database in Azure SQL Database

Chapter 5 offers an in-depth look at managing Azure SQL Database, including backup and restore; however, there are three options to consider when restoring a point-in-time backup, which plays into your run book:

- **Database replacement.**   You can replace an existing database using a database backup. This requires that you verify the service tier and performance level of the restored database. To replace your existing database, rename the old one and restore the new one to the old name.

- **Database recovery.**   If you need to recover data from a previous point in time, you can restore your database backup with a different database name and then copy the data you need using T-SQL scripts you write yourself.

- **Deleted database.**   If you deleted a database and you are still within the recovery window, you can restore that deleted database to the time just before it was deleted.

The geo-restore feature can restore a full and differential backup to any server in the Azure region from a geo-redundant backup. However, databases on the basic performance tier can take up to 12 hours to geo-restore. This Estimated Recovery Time should be a consideration in your RTO.

➤ **To read more about recovering a database in Azure SQL Database, including associated costs, refer to Chapter 5, or visit** *https://docs.microsoft.com/azure/sql-database/sql-database-recovery-using-backups.*

Implementing high availability and disaster recovery

No server is (intended to be) an island. Application downtime is costly. Loss of data can be fatal to an organization. In this chapter, we detail the Microsoft SQL Server technologies designed to provide high availability and disaster recovery, adding to the discussion of backups in Chapter 11. What's beyond taking backups?

First, we take an overview of the available technologies, including log shipping, replication, failover clustering, and availability groups. Then, we take a detailed look at configuration of failover clusters and availability groups on Windows and Linux. SQL Server 2017 support for Linux extends to availability groups, and we provide an in-depth, step-by-step examination on how to set up your first availability group on Red Hat Linux. Finally, we cover the administration of availability groups, such as monitoring, performance analysis, and alerting.

➤ This chapter deals with SQL Server instances. Disaster recovery technologies provided in Microsoft Azure SQL Database are covered in Chapter 5.

Overview of high availability and disaster recovery technologies in SQL Server

As an enterprise-grade data platform, SQL Server provides features to ensure high availability (HA) and prepare for disaster recovery (DR). You must configure these technologies correctly to provide the desired benefits. This requires some effort and extra investment. The level of effort and investment required in ensuring HA should never exceed the value of the data to the organization.

In other words, not every database on every server must be configured for HA and geo-replicated for DR. Depending on the value of the data and any Service-Level Agreements (SLAs), having backups available off-premises might be sufficient to prepare for disaster. (As always, you should copy your backups off-premises as soon as possible after they are taken, and you should test them regularly.)

For cases in which additional investment is warranted, there are many technologies available. Some are suitable for HA and others for DR, and a few are suitable for both uses. In this first section, we cover the variety of technologies available in SQL Server to build a highly available environment and to prepare for DR.

NOTE

Before covering the different technologies, we should clarify the difference between HA and DR. HA means that your databases remain available, automatically, in the face of hardware or software failures. DR means that your data is not lost after a substantial incident (a "disaster"), though data might be temporarily unavailable until you run your DR plan.

Understanding log shipping

The log shipping feature in SQL Server makes it possible for you to create a copy of a database on a secondary instance by automatically restoring transaction log backups from the database on a primary instance to one or more secondary instances. You need to set up log shipping for each individual database. Therefore, if your application uses multiple databases, you will need to independently configure each database for log shipping.

NOTE

You can perform transaction log backups only if the database uses the full or bulk-logged recovery model. You cannot configure log shipping on a database in the simple recovery model. For more information on this, refer to Chapter 11.

The real role of log shipping isn't to provide HA—unlike other features available to you, there is no way to failover to the secondary copy of the database or redirect user connections. You can configure the log shipping job to set the secondary database to Standby mode, allowing for read-only access. In that case, users concurrently accessing the database will block the next transaction log restore in the chain. You can configure the transaction log restore to kick users out of the secondary database in time for the restore.

All of the logs are stored to the log shipping secondary database and restored WITH NORECOVERY, meaning that the database will remain "In Recovery..." status without any way for you to access them. In the event of a disaster, you can restore the last good transaction log backup from the source, or if no more are available, simply bring the destination database online.

In the most common log shipping use case, it serves simply as a way to stream backups to an off-premises DR SQL Server. You can recover the secondary database, take a new backup of the secondary database, and restore it to the primary after a disaster that claims the primary database. Another common use of log shipping is to provide a "rewind" copy of the database, given that the restoration of the transaction log backups on the secondary instance can be delayed, and provide an uncorrupted backup of the database in the event of a data-related disaster, perhaps caused by an application fault or human error.

You cannot currently configure log shipping with a database in Azure SQL Database as the destination.

Although log shipping is a straightforward and effective way to set up secondary databases, it does have a few shortcomings. First, you can take no other transaction log backups than those used for log shipping. This means that you must find a balance between the replication frequency for DR and the frequency of taking transaction log backups for point-in-time restores, for example, to recover from user error. Second, you can take log-shipped backups quite frequently, even every minute, but you must plan appropriately for the overhead of taking the transaction log backups and having the files copied over the network to the file share.

Overall, log shipping is considered a rudimentary form of DR (indeed, it was first introduced in SQL Server 7.0) that does what it can and does it well, capable of continuously shipping a chain of transaction logs to a remote database for months or even years. Let's take a quick look at configuring log shipping.

Setting up log shipping

Log shipping uses the SQL Server Agent to run scheduled jobs. Be sure that the SQL Server Agent service is scheduled to start automatically.

To begin configuring log shipping, you first create a network share for the folder where the transaction log backups will be stored. This folder and share require specific permissions which depend on a few factors. We recommend using domain proxy accounts for the SQL Server Agent jobs.

Assuming this recommended configuration, the proxy account for the transaction log backup job (which runs on the primary server) must have read and write access to the folder (if the folder is located on the primary server) or the network share (if the folder is not located on the primary server). The proxy account for the backup copy job, which runs on the secondary server, must have read access to the file share.

If you are using SQL Server Management Studio to configure log shipping, it will restore a full backup of the database on the secondary server from the network share, using your credentials. If you are using Transact-SQL (T-SQL) scripts, to create the log shipping you will need to copy and restore this backup manually.

CAUTION

If you let SQL Server create the secondary database(s) during the configuration steps, the data and log files for the secondary database will be placed on the same volume as the data and log file for the destination instance's master database by default. You can use the Restore Options button in the Initialize Secondary Database to change the destination data and log file directories on the secondary server.

On the primary SQL Server instance, log shipping creates a SQL Server Agent job called LSBackup_*dbname* to back up the transaction logs to the network share. You will need to schedule the log shipping log backup job to occur at a schedule that meets your needs for DR, while taking into the account the overhead and duration of taking and restoring the backups.

Log shipping also creates a SQL Server Agent job called LSAlert_*primaryinstancename* that will fail if no backup is detected in the desired window. You should set a failure notification to email an operator if this job fails; otherwise, you should monitor the SQL Server Error Log for the Severity 16 error that it raises.

> ➤ **You can read more about configuring alerts in Chapter 14.**

On the secondary SQL Server instance, log shipping creates three SQL Server Agent jobs: LSCopy_*primaryinstancename* to copy the backup files from the file share to the secondary server, LSRestore_*primaryinstancename* to restore the transaction log backups continually, and LSAlert_*secondaryinstancename* to raise an error if no log backup is detected after a certain time.

When using SQL Server Management Studio, these steps are mostly automated. Otherwise, you will need to manually schedule and turn on these jobs. Following are a couple of recommendations for configuring log shipping optimally:

- You should configure the file share on a server other than the primary database server. That way, the log files need to be copied from the primary server only once. On the other hand, if you configure the file share on the primary server, each secondary will initiate a copy of the backup files. If you have more than one secondary, this will increase the network traffic to your primary server.

- You should monitor the log shipping activity using the report available in SQL Server Management Studio and configure alerts.

Understanding types of replication

Replication provides several approaches to copy schema and data from one database to another. Because this chapter focuses on HA and DR technologies, we discuss replication in this context.

There are three main types of replication: *transactional*, *merge*, and *snapshot*. Each of these types has specific benefits and drawbacks that makes them more or less suitable for HA or DR. Other uses for replication include support for occasionally offline clients, integrating heterogeneous data stores, offloading processing and reporting workloads, and more.

Transactional and merge replication can optionally support two-way replication. These are powerful features, but the databases must be designed to support the fact that updates will take place in more than one place. The application also might need to be aware of such operations.

Peer-to-peer replication supports multimaster replication, and, like merge replication, it can be the core foundation of an application architecture. In addition to scale-out functionality, peer-to-peer replication can provide HA if the application is designed to attempt to connect to another instance in case of failed connection attempts to its preferred instance.

> ### NOTE
> **SQL Server replication is a separately installable Database Engine feature. This means that for any replication method to be available, the instance must be installed or modified with that option selected.**

All types of replication employ a concept of a publisher and one or more subscribers. The *publisher* is the SQL Server instance that holds the original database. A *subscriber* is the SQL Server instance holding a destination database for replication.

In addition, the *distributor* is the component responsible for obtaining data from the publisher and directing it to the subscribers. The distributor is, in effect, the middle man: the publisher and the subscriber do not directly interact. Note that the distributor component can be located on the same SQL Server instance as the publisher, but for performance purposes, it is best to configure a different SQL Server instance to serve as the distributor.

When the publishing instance serves as its own distributor, this is called a *push subscriber model*. This is the only model in which it is possible to replicate to a database in Azure SQL Database. When another instance serves as the distributor, it is called a *pull subscription*.

All types of replication deal with *articles*. An article can be a table, stored procedure, or view, synchronizing both data and most schema changes. With views, the underlying data tables are required to be part of the same replication publication, as well. You can filter articles, and they do not need to include all the columns or rows of a table.

Inside OUT

What are some of the limitations on schema changes in SQL Server replication?

Table schema changes on publication databases can be made only by using T-SQL or SQL Server Management Objects (SMO). SQL Server Management Studio attempts to drop and re-create tables, as opposed to running ALTER TABLE statements.

Dropping replication articles is not allowed, and the schema change will fail when performed within SQL Server Management Studio.

Additionally, some schema changes are not allowed on replication articles. Notably, creating, altering, or dropping indexes explicitly will fail.

➤ To view a list of additional considerations for schema changes and replication, go to Microsoft Docs at *https://docs.microsoft.com/sql/relational-databases/replication/publish/ make-schema-changes-on-publication-databases#considerations-for-schema-changes*.

Snapshot replication

We first cover snapshot replication because it serves a role in the initial distribution of schema and data for transactional and merge replication. Even though there are other ways to get an initial copy of the database to a subscriber, snapshot replication integrates with merge and transactional replication to seed the subscribers.

Snapshot replication is described very well by its name: this replication method takes a snapshot of the database state at a point in time and can then replicate that state to another SQL Server instance. Unlike merge and transactional replication, it's not usually scheduled and repeated to the same subscriber. Data and schema changes are not monitored: if you need additional replication, you take a new snapshot of the entire database and replicate it to all subscribers.

This type of replication can be beneficial if data changes are infrequent, but for those that do occur, they are substantial. Conceptually, it's very similar to taking and restoring a database backup; however, unlike with a backup, you can select individual database objects to include in the snapshot.

A trade-off to consider when using snapshot replication is that there is no continuous overhead for tracking incremental changes, but there is a significant resource requirement when generating and delivering a new snapshot.

When using snapshot replication to create the initial snapshot for transactional or merge replication, you should keep the default synchronization method of concurrent snapshot processing. Otherwise, the creation of the snapshot will place and hold locks on the tables that are selected for replication. Depending on several factors, including the data size and the available resources on the publisher, the snapshot creation can take long enough for update operations to fail due to the locks. With concurrent snapshot processing, locks are not held for the entire snapshot creation operation.

> ➤ For descriptions of the roles played by each component in snapshot replication, refer to Microsoft Docs at *https://docs.microsoft.com/sql/relational-databases/replication/snapshot-replication*.

Merge replication

Merge replication is not commonly used for HA or DR. It is well-suited for two-way synchronization between copies of a database on multiple SQL Server instances. At a high level, merge replication operates by tracking schema and data changes using triggers.

Every table that is published requires a column of type `uniqueidentifier` with the ROWGUIDCOL property set. If no such column exists, one will be created with the name `rowguid`. If such a column exists, its name does not matter.

NOTE
The ROWGUIDCOL property indicates that the column's value will be updated automatically by the Database Engine.

Merge replication can also be the basis of application architecture, used to synchronize changes in articles to and from instances.

> ➤ For more information on merge replication, refer to Microsoft Docs at *https://docs.microsoft.com/sql/relational-databases/replication/merge/merge-replication*.

Transactional replication

Transactional replication is the best suited of the three approaches for DR purposes. It works well with high-volume transactions, provides low latency, and guarantees transactional consistency. Beyond DR, it can even be the foundation of data warehousing projects, moving only needed tables, columns, and rows; however, you might find that custom-developed SQL Server Integration Services packages provide better performance, customizability, and maintainability.

The components of transactional replication are discussed in detail here:

- **Publisher.**   The SQL Server instance that publishes the database for replication.

- **Subscriber.**   The SQL Server instance that receives the replicated data.

CHAPTER 12

- **Distributor.**   The SQL Server instance that distributes the replicated data from the publisher to the subscriber. Think of the distributor as the middle man. This can be the same SQL Server instance as the publisher or subscriber.

- **Article.**   The database object that is replicated. In addition to replicating the schema and data for tables, you can also replicate the running of stored procedures. Articles can have row and column filters to limit the data that is replicated.

- **Distribution database.**   The distribution database is hosted on the distributor. For all types of replication, it stores metadata and history data. For transactional replication, it also contains the transactions that have not yet been moved to the subscriber(s).

- **Log Reader Agent.**   The Log Reader Agent, which runs at the distributor, reads the publication database's transaction log and extracts commands to be replicated. These commands are added to the distribution database, which will hold these commands until all subscribers have received them or until the retention period has been reached.

- **Distribution Agent.**   The Distribution Agent moves transactions from the distribution database to the subscriber(s). Optionally, the Distribution Agent can validate that data between the publisher and the subscriber match. The distribution agent can run on the distributor, which is a push subscription, or at the subscriber, which is a pull subscription.

NOTE

Transactional replication supports updatable subscriptions, peer-to-peer replication, and bidirectional replication. These publication types each have benefits and drawbacks as it relates to handling changes that originated at subscribers. Because a peer-to-peer topology is designed to increase read-scale and move data between instances but is not designed for HA, it is not covered in this chapter.

➤ **For details on the different publication types, refer to Microsoft Docs at**
https://docs.microsoft.com/sql/relational-databases/replication/transactional/
publication-types-for-transactional-replication.

Understanding the capabilities of failover clustering

Failover clustering's purpose is to provide a fully automated HA solution that protects against server failures due to hardware or software. Failover clusters build on the Windows Server Failover Cluster (WSFC) technology to implement this. Conceptually, when the server hardware or software of an active cluster node fails, WSFC detects this and starts the SQL Server Database Engine instance on another node. SQL Server Integration Services and SQL Server Reporting Services are not part of a failover cluster—there are different methods for making those services highly available which are not covered in this book.

NOTE

With SQL Server 2016 (and later) and Windows Server 2016, you can create WSFCs with certificates instead of using Active Directory service accounts, which is known as a Workgroup Cluster. This is based on a Windows Server 2012 R2 concept called Active Directory-Detached Cluster, that still required a domain. You can create a Domain-Independent Availability Group on a Workgroup Cluster, for any mixture of Windows Server nodes that are not joined to the same domain or any domain. For more information, visit *https://docs.microsoft.com/sql/database-engine/availability-groups/windows/domain-independent-availability-groups*.

This is hugely beneficial because the failover is automated, and also because it often just takes mere seconds for the failover of the SQL Server instance from one server to another. And even though clients will experience connection disruption in the event of a failover and the SQL Server experiences a restart, no special configuration on the client is required and reconnection is usually prompt. After a failover, the active instance will have the same DNS name and IP address as before. Clients simply open a new connection using the same connection string and continue operating.

Failover clustering does not require any form of replication or data duplication. Instead, the SQL Server data and logs are stored on shared storage. Each cluster node has access to the shared storage; which node is actively connected to shared storage is determined by WSFC. WSFC ensures that only one node can write to the shared storage at a time. Cluster disks appear only on the server that "owns" them.

NOTE

We refer to any form of storage that all nodes in the cluster can access as shared storage. Versions of SQL Server prior to 2012 required this to be storage that was connected to all cluster nodes using some type of bus topology such as a Fibre Channel Storage-Area Network (SAN) or shared SAS SAN. Since SQL Server 2012, shared storage includes file shares, as well. Since SQL Server 2016 and Windows Server 2016, shared storage can also include Storage Spaces Direct (S2D) and Cluster Shared Volumes (CSV). Although all of these options can make selecting the appropriate one a little more difficult, they bring SQL failover clusters within reach for a much broader set of deployments.

Whichever option you select for storage, make sure that it does not become a single point of failure. The entire path from the cluster nodes to the storage should be redundant. With traditional shared storage, this will likely involve configuring Multipath I/O (MPIO) to avoid a single shared drive from being discovered multiple times by each node. Many storage vendors provide the necessary device-specific module (DSM), a software driver that works with the Windows MPIO feature. For Fibre Channel SANs and iSCSI SANs, you can also use the generic Microsoft DSM if your vendor does not provide one.

> ➤ You can read more about implementing MPIO at *https://technet.microsoft.com/library/ ee619734.aspx.*

Using WSFC poses additional requirements on the hardware and software configuration of each node as well as on shared storage. As to the hardware, WSFC requires that the hardware on each node is the same, including driver versions. The software on each node must also be the same, including operating system (OS) patches. WSFC provides a validation configuration wizard (see Figure 12-1) or the `Test-Cluster` PowerShell cmdlet that will provide detailed analysis and reports about the suitability of the selected servers to become cluster nodes. Microsoft supports only clusters for which the cluster validation tests pass.

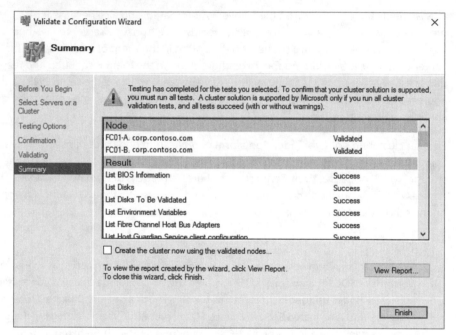

Figure 12-1 The Summary page in the Validate A Configuration Wizard, indicating that the selected cluster nodes were validated.

> ➤ For details on the OS and SQL Server configuration necessary to create a Failover Cluster Instance, see the section "Configuring Failover Cluster Instances" later in the chapter.

Configuring Failover Cluster Instances for DR

SQL Server failover clusters can provide DR options in case a stretch cluster is configured. In a stretch cluster, some of the nodes are located at a distance from one another. The cluster will be configured to work across a Wide-Area Network (WAN) and the outlying nodes will not have access to the same shared storage. This requires that replication is configured from the cluster nodes in the primary site to the cluster nodes in the remote site(s).

➤ For information on multi-subnet clustering with SQL Server, including considerations for the IP address cluster resource, refer to Microsoft Docs at *https://docs.microsoft.com/sql/ sql-server/failover-clusters/windows/sql-server-multi-subnet-clustering-sql-server*. To read more about multi-subnet cluster configuration for availability groups, see the section "Configuring RegisterAllProvidersIP and MultiSubNetFailover correctly" later in the chapter.

NOTE

Instead of configuring a single stretch cluster to provide DR, you should configure two independent clusters, one at each site. To replicate data between sites, set up availability groups.

Understanding the capabilities of availability groups

Availability groups provide both HA and DR capabilities in a single feature. An availability group consists of one or more databases, the *availability databases,* that failover together. Failover can be automatic or manual, and a manual failover can either be planned or forced. Of these three failover methods, only forced failover can cause data loss. The secondary replica(s) can optionally be readable, allowing some read-only access to be offloaded from the primary read-write databases.

As discussed in previous chapters, availability groups are the successor and replacement to the deprecated database mirroring feature. Availability groups provide true disaster recovery and read-only secondary database utility that database mirroring did not. In fact, availability groups have totally encompassed database mirroring—see the subsection "Basic availability groups" later in the chapter.

They also provide a much-improved set of dynamic management views for monitoring and user interface dialog boxes in SQL Server Management Studio (and other tools) compared to database mirroring. Combined with massive performance improvements in SQL Server 2016 and widened architecture possibilities in SQL Server 2017, availability groups offer a formidable and capable feature set of which all DBAs should be aware.

NOTE

Many administrators are familiar with the Microsoft Exchange term "database availability group," and its acronym "DAG." This is not an acronym used to describe SQL Server availability groups; the technologies are very different. To prevent miscommunication, you should not use DAG to describe availability groups or to describe an architecture alternative called Distributed Availability Groups.

Remembering the availability groups feature set

The early code name for the availability groups project internally at Microsoft was *HADRON*. But, this wasn't just a cool name that had contemporary science relevance: you have probably heard of the Large Hadron Collider (LHC) beneath the France–Switzerland border, which first collided beams of high-energy particles in 2010 while HADRON was being developed for its initial release in SQL Server Denali CTP1 in December 2010.

In SQL Server, the acronym HADRON also spells out the three big features of availability groups:

- **HA: High Availability.**   The automatic failover to one or more synchronous secondary replicas, or manual failover to asynchronous secondary replicas.

- **DR: Disaster Recovery.**   The ability to take valid backups directly on secondary replicas, including integrated backup tools that use customizable replica backup priority.

- **ON: ONline.**   The secondary replicas could be read-only, and allow for the offloading of heavy-duty report workloads, utilizing snapshot isolation to prevent blocking of transactions arriving from the primary replica.

Additionally, availability groups include automatic data corruption correction to repair damaged pages with data from other replicas, and database health detection that can initiate failover in response to database status.

> ### NOTE
>
> According to Microsoft Docs (*https://docs.microsoft.com/sql/database-engine/availability-groups/windows/always-on-availability-groups-sql-server*), failovers will not be initiated by a database becoming suspect due to factors such as transaction log corruption, data file loss, or database deletion.

You should keep all the features of availability groups in mind when developing an architecture to meet your environment's requirements for Recovery Point Objective (RPO; or data loss tolerance) Recovery Time Objective (RTO; or how long before the systems are back online after a disaster).

Differentiating availability groups from other HA solutions

Availability groups operate by transmitting segments of transaction log data from a primary replica to one or more secondary nodes.

Like transactional replication, availability groups use the transaction log data itself. Blocks of transaction logs are sent to the replicas, which is a scalable approach.

Superior to database mirroring, availability groups begin to send blocks of log data as soon as the data is ready to be flushed to a drive, not afterward, resulting in transaction log data being sent to the secondary availability replica(s) sooner, tightening the gap between replicas.

Finally, unlike a SQL Server instance running on a Failover Cluster Instance, availability groups require minimally two copies of the data—no shared storage in use here—and minimally two active instances of SQL Server to accomplish HA. Unlike with FCI, both servers can be of use to the enterprise: one as the primary read/write replica, and one as a secondary read-only replica.

Like the behavior of database mirroring, the availability group listener provides redirection to the primary node at all times but additionally can also provide redirection to readable nodes. Applications can use the same connection string and instead provide a new parameter, `ApplicationIntent`, to declare whether the transactions in the connection will be read-write or read-only. You can route read-write connections to the primary replica, and read-only connections to one of the possible secondary replicas, thus splitting the workloads, even across a WAN.

> ➤ **For detailed configuration information, refer to Microsoft Docs at** *https://docs.microsoft.com/sql/database-engine/availability-groups/windows/configure-read-only-access-on-an-availability-replica-sql-server.*

Improving availability groups since SQL Server 2012

Performance improvements introduced to the communications stack of availability groups transaction processing in SQL Server 2016 were significant—up to 10 times faster on the same hardware and network compared to SQL Server 2012 and 2014. One significant performance improvement was the introduction of a multithreaded parallel redo on the secondary replicas, which greatly enhances the throughput in synchronous commit mode. We discuss the possible commit modes and redo queue later in this chapter.

Aside from the obvious issues with expiring support, you should upgrade your SQL Server if you are still running legacy SQL Server 2012 or 2014 availability groups to benefit from these performance gains.

Improvements introduced in SQL Server 2017 include structural expansion to the very foundation of availability groups, including support for replicas to SQL Server on Linux instances and the possibility of cross-platform availability groups using an external cluster manager. Obviously, Linux servers cannot be part of a WSFC, so this means that the architecture of availability groups must be expanded to operate without a WSFC. As a result, clusterless availability groups are now possible in SQL Server 2017. We discuss the several types of cluster setups later in this section.

Improvements to SQL Server Management Studio coinciding with SQL Server 2017 include the ability to configure read-only routing URLs and routing lists per replica in the availability group properties dialog box, a task previously possible only via T-SQL or PowerShell scripts.

Another new feature added to SQL Server 2017 is an option to specify the implementation of a minimum committed replica setting, in availability groups with more than one secondary replica. We review the REQUIRED_SYNCHRONIZED_SECONDARIES_TO_COMMIT setting later in this chapter.

Comparing HA and DR technologies

Table 12-1 compares the four major technologies for HA and DR using a variety of attributes. We do not intend for this table to provide a complete comparison; rather, it gathers the details relevant for HA and DR.

Table 12-1 Comparison of four HA and DR technologies

	Log shipping	Replication	Failover clustering	Basic availability groups	Availability groups
Automatic failover	No	N/A	Yes	Yes*	Yes*
Edition	Web, Standard, Enterprise	Standard, Enterprise[†]	Standard, Enterprise	Standard	Enterprise
Readable secondary	Yes, between log restores	Yes	No	No	Yes
Schema changes required to tables	No	Yes (except snapshot)	No	No	No
Schema changes replicated	Yes	Yes	N/A	Yes	Yes
Primary purpose	DR	Offline sync, DR	HA[‡]	HA/DR	HA/DR

	Log shipping	Replication	Failover clustering	Basic availability groups	Availability groups
Level	Database	Articles	Instance	Databases	Databases
Instance versions	Must match exactly**	Up to two major versions apart	Must match exactly^^^	Must match exactly***	Must match exactly***

*   Configurable.

**   In theory, log shipping to a higher version of SQL Server is possible, in which case there is no path to return to the primary copy after recovering from a disaster.

*** Temporarily, these environments can be different versions while applying cumulative updates in a rolling fashion.

†   All editions, including Azure SQL Database, can be subscribers. Only Standard and Enterprise Edition instances can be publishers.

‡   Unless a multi-subnet failover cluster with replication is configured, in which case it is also suitable for DR.

NOTE

In addition to using these SQL Server technologies, the application itself can also take steps to ensure high availability of its data. The Microsoft Sync Framework, which is beyond the scope of this book, can be helpful for application developers who are working on such applications.

Configuring Failover Cluster Instances

The WSFC is a Windows Server feature (not a role). Each server that will act as a cluster node must have this feature installed. Cluster nodes can join or leave a cluster at any time. However, simply adding a node to a cluster is not all that is required to run the SQL Server instance(s). We first cover (briefly) some key concepts of the WSFC and then move into configuring SQL Server Failover Cluster Instances.

When creating your cluster initially, Windows sets up an Active Directory computer account for the cluster's Virtual Network Name (VNN). By default, this VNN is created in the same Active Directory Organizational Unit (OU) as the cluster node. We recommend creating an OU for each cluster you create because permissions to create additional computer objects are then more easily delegated. Additional computer objects are created for each cluster resource, including each SQL Server instance. The cluster's VNN computer object should be given permission to create new computer objects in the OU. Alternatively, you could pre-stage the computer objects for the new virtual network names in the OU. The IP address associated with any VNN should be a static address instead of a dynamically assigned address.

> **NOTE**
>
> In most configurations, availability groups (covered in the section "Configuring availability groups") have a dependency on a cluster manager. In Windows, this is the WSFC. In Linux, this is an external cluster manager. When using WSFC for availability groups, the same guidance in this section applies.

Operating a WSFC requires an understanding of *quorum*. The quorum of the cluster determines which nodes in the cluster are operating and how many failed nodes the cluster can sustain. Correctly selecting a quorum configuration is important to avoid a *split-brain* scenario, which would occur when two instances of the cluster are running, unaware that each other is running. You can choose from five quorum configurations:

- **Node majority.** This is the recommended configuration choice for clusters that have an odd number of nodes. To determine whether the cluster will function, and if so, which nodes will be active cluster members, a majority of nodes must "vote." The number of failures that can be sustained for the cluster to remain operational is $(n / 2) - 1$, where n is the number of cluster nodes, and the result of the division is rounded up. Thus, in a five-node cluster, you can sustain at most two failed nodes, or two nodes that have lost communication with the other nodes, and so on, because $(5 / 2) - 1 = 3 - 1 = 2$.

- **Node and disk majority.** This is a recommended configuration choice for clusters with an even number of nodes. Each node gets a vote, and the presence of a shared witness disk, designated as the quorum disk, adds a vote to whichever node owns it. In the case of a four-node cluster, two nodes can fail if the shared disk is online or can be brought online on one of the remaining two nodes. If the shared disk cannot be brought online, the number of nodes that can fail is half minus one. In the case of a four-node cluster with the witness disk unavailable, only one node can fail for the cluster to remain available.

- **Node and file share majority.** In this configuration, which is used for clusters with an even number of nodes but without shared drives, the file share adds the extra vote. The witness file share isn't owned by any particular node to increase its vote count, but the nodes that aren't able to reach the file share (due to whatever problem prompted them to no longer be able to communicate with their peers) will not be active.

- **Node and cloud witness.** In this configuration, which is very similar to node and file share majority, the witness is a cloud service; specifically, an Azure storage account. To configure this option, you need to provide the name of the storage account and one of its access keys. Cloud witness is available only in Windows Server 2016 and later.

- **Disk only.** In the legacy disk-only quorum configuration, node count is never considered. Only the shared witness disk's availability to nodes matters. This means that the (single) shared disk becomes a single point of failure: even if all nodes can communicate but the disk is unavailable, the cluster will not be operational. This mode is largely available for legacy purposes, but it can make it possible for you to start the cluster in case of a significant disaster when there is no other way to achieve quorum.

Because of the intricacies of quorum configuration, we recommend that you use node majority (for a cluster with an odd number of nodes) or node and disk majority as the configuration (for a cluster with an even number of nodes) if shared storage is available. If shared storage is not available, configure node and file share majority for a cluster with an even number of nodes. You should not use the disk-only quorum configuration to operate the cluster; its value lies in recovering a severely broken cluster using only a single node.

Inside OUT

Should I use dynamic quorum management for my availability group?

Yes. In Windows Server 2012 R2 and later, dynamic quorum management can remove nodes that drop from a cluster. Dynamic quorum is turned on by default in Windows Server 2012 R2 and 2016.

Consider a five-node cluster. With dynamic quorum, when three nodes are shut down in a planned manner, their votes are removed leaving only two votes remaining, allowing the cluster to maintain quorum and stay functioning because those two votes are available on the two remaining nodes.

But, this can be dangerous in the event of a total site failure. Should a site in a cluster that spans two physical locations be left with no way to achieve Node Majority, no automatic failover would be possible without manually "rigging" the node weights to force a failover. Forcing quorum and manually performing a failover is a temporary measure and will require the reestablishment of proper node weights after DR.

NOTE

In a multi-instance clustered scenario, there is no requirement that every SQL Server instance must be installed on every cluster node. In two-node deployments, it is naturally required to achieve HA. For larger clusters, this is not necessary. For example, on a four-node cluster, each instance can be installed on only three nodes. Three nodes provide HA, even when faced with the failure of a single node. There isn't really an additional benefit in deploying each instance to a fourth node, but there are additional maintenance requirements: you must patch and test each instance on each node. The Inside OUT sidebar "How can I upgrade or patch a failover cluster with a minimal amount of downtime?" explains a process for patching.

CHAPTER 12

Configuring a SQL Server FCI

When configuring SQL Server as a cluster resource, you should configure the cluster resources for a single instance in a single cluster resource group. Cluster resources include the IP address, the SQL Server instance's network name, the shared disks (if any; there aren't any shared disks with CSV and S2D), the SQL Server services, and the FILESTREAM file share. If multiple SQL Server instances are configured on a single cluster, each will need a resource group.

If you would like to have multiple servers running active instances of SQL Server simultaneously, you can install additional instances on each FCI. Each SQL Server instance can be active on only one server at a time, but when using multiple instances, each instance can run independently of another. We recommend always keeping a passive cluster node. Otherwise, in case of a failover, one server will need to run at least one additional instance, increasing the load on the server. If you run each instance on separate hardware, you'll need $n + 1$ cluster nodes, where n is the number of SQL Server instances.

Keep in mind that any cluster configuration of more than two nodes requires SQL Server Enterprise edition. Figure 12-2 illustrates the concept of running two SQL Server instances on a four-node cluster.

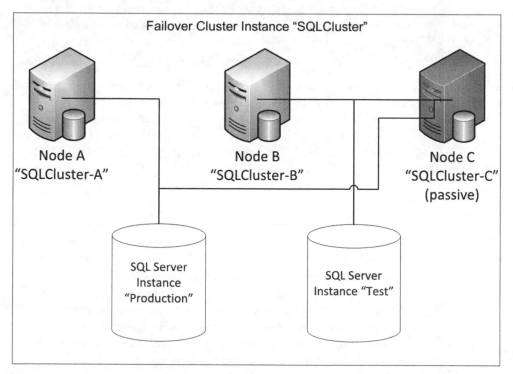

Figure 12-2 A sample three-node, two-instance FCI.

Inside OUT

How should I configure service accounts for SQL Server in a cluster?

With a standalone installation, SQL Server will offer to create virtual service accounts for all services during setup. With a cluster installation, you must specify a domain account for the clustered services: Database Engine, SQL Server Agent, and SQL Server Analysis Services. Shared services, such as SQL Server Reporting Services, can continue to use a virtual service account.

The domain accounts require no special privileges or rights in advance, so use a domain user account for each SQL Server service that will run on the cluster. SQL Server Setup will grant the necessary permissions to each service account, such as access to the data and log folders. The account that is running the installer will need permissions to make these changes.

You can choose to create a group managed service account (gMSA) for each service. It reduces management overhead because the password for these service accounts is managed by Active Directory and regularly changed. In addition, the security configuration is enhanced because there is no one who actually knows the password.

To learn more about configuring gMSAs for SQL Server, refer to the Microsoft blog post at *https://blogs.msdn.microsoft.com/markweberblog/2016/05/25/ group-managed-service-accounts-gmsa-and-sql-server-2016/*.

Just like the hardware and the software must be identical on every cluster node, so should the SQL Server configuration. The best way to guarantee initial exact configuration is to use configuration scripts to first prepare each cluster node, and then complete the cluster installation with another script. The scripts are valuable because they ensure consistent installation of the SQL Server binaries. Additionally, they also serve as DR preparation because they document the configuration of each instance, and you can use them to set up a new cluster in case of a disaster.

You can create these scripts by hand; however, that is a tedious and error-prone process. Instead, we recommend starting SQL Server Setup and initiating the Advanced Cluster Preparation setup. On the Ready To Install step of the installation wizard, the path to the configuration file will be displayed. Open the configuration file and save it somewhere. A network share is ideal because then it can be referenced from all cluster nodes that will run the SQL Server instance.

CHAPTER 12

If you prefer to have a completely automated configuration file, you will need to modify the script as outlined in the example that follows. You start Setup from the command line by using the `/ConfigurationFile=path` parameter and specify the full path to the configuration file:

```
; Add this line
IACCEPTSQLSERVERLICENSETERMS="True"
; Modify the next lines
; Change to True to enable unattended installation to progress
IACCEPTPYTHONLICENSETERMS="True"
; Quiet simple means you'll see the UI auto-progress.
QUIETSIMPLE="True"
; Or, leave QUIETSIMPLE="False" and modify this line for no UI
QUIET="True"
; Delete, or comment out, this line
UIMODE="Normal"
```

To complete the cluster installation, run the Advanced Cluster Completion setup option. There again, you can choose to save the script for later. The cluster completion phase is where you will do the following (in no particular order):

- Select or create the cluster resource group

- Set the virtual network name and IP address for the SQL Server instance—how your clients will connect

- Select the shared storage for the database files

Inside OUT

How can I upgrade or patch a failover cluster with a minimal amount of downtime?

Near-zero downtime is the objective when configuring FCIs. Some events are unexpected, but some regular maintenance tasks such as patching the OS and SQL Server instance are regular activities. You can perform these maintenance tasks with near-zero downtime by using *rolling upgrades.*

To conduct a rolling upgrade, you should have a passive node; that is, a node that under normal circumstances does not run any workload. You upgrade the passive node first and, if necessary, reboot it. This reboot does not cause any downtime because this node is not running a workload. When the reboot is completed and the upgrade is validated, the roles from any active node failover to the passive node.

As we indicated earlier, a brief amount of downtime is incurred while this takes place (on the order of seconds). The newly passive node is then upgraded, and so on, until all nodes in the cluster are at the same software version. Although you can choose to return the original passive node to its passive state when all nodes have finished upgrading, this would incur one more interruption and will likely not provide any benefits other than consistency.

Starting with Windows Server 2012, Cluster-Aware Updating (CAU) automates this process, and you can even schedule it. In addition to rolling upgrades and updates for Windows patches and SQL Server updates, Windows Server 2012 R2 and later also supports rolling upgrades for operating systems. Even though this is not automated, it will be a significant benefit with the frequent updates available for Windows Server 2016.

Configuring availability groups

You can create availability groups within the Availability Groups Wizard in SQL Server Management Studio, via T-SQL, or PowerShell. If this is your first time creating an availability group, we recommend using the Availability Groups Wizard and scripting out the steps and objects it creates with T-SQL to further your understanding.

Creating a copy of a database on a secondary replica SQL Server can be fairly wizard-driven in SQL Server Management Studio, including the ability for SQL Server Management Studio to automate the process of taking a full and transaction log backup of the database, copying the data to a file share, and restoring the database to any secondary replica(s). You can script these tasks at the end of the wizard and deploy them to future availability groups via T-SQL or PowerShell.

As in many places in this book, although we won't provide a step-by-step, click-by-click walk-through, following are pointers and key decisions to make when creating availability groups in Windows. We also provide a more in-depth walk-through of availability groups in SQL Server in Linux later in this chapter.

Inside OUT

What server principal owns an availability group replica?

The server security principal used to create the availability group will own the availability group replica object by default, creating an immediate follow-up action item for administrators after setup. Each replica object has an owner, listed in the dynamic management view (DMV) `sys.availability_replicas`, where the `owner_sid` is a server-level security principal.

It isn't fully documented what the `owner_sid` is used for, but because it could be used as the authority to make changes to availability groups, it should not be an administrator's personal named account. You should either create the availability group (and create future replicas) under the security context of a service account that does not expire, or immediately change the owner of the availability group replica to a service account.

A similar problem occurs when you create an availability group with a login that doesn't have an explicit server principal or SQL Server login, but rather has access via a security group. In that case, an availability group will be created with the built-in public server role as the `owner_id`. In general, ownership or additional permissions should not be granted to the public role, so you should change this.

Changing the owner of the availability group replica to the instance's "sa" login, on instances with mixed mode authentication turned on, is also an acceptable and common practice; for example:

```
ALTER AUTHORIZATION ON AVAILABILITY GROUP::[AG1] to [domain\serviceaccount];
```

Comparing different cluster types and failover

With SQL Server 2017, you can implement availability groups that, like database mirroring, do not require a failover cluster network. One of the biggest sources of complexity and problems (especially during failover) with availability groups based on WSFC was not the SQL Server configuration or behavior, but the configuration or behavior of cluster objects, quorum, and the various forms of witnesses.

Since 2012, it is likely that more availability group failovers have been incomplete or unsuccessful because of misconfigurations of Windows Server, cluster networks, DNS, or cluster quorum settings than because of SQL Server–based misconfigurations

You must turn on the Availability Groups feature in SQL Server Configuration Manager. The Properties page of the SQL Server instance service contains a tab labeled AlwaysOn High Availability (Figure 12-3).

NOTE

As discussed in Chapter 2, the correct term is "Always On," with a space between "Always" and "On." As Figure 12-3 demonstrates, you might still see instances of this name without the space. This is because changes to naming in the product take time to filter through.

You will not be able to access the Availability Group dialog boxes in SQL Server Management Studio until the feature is turned on in Configuration Manager.

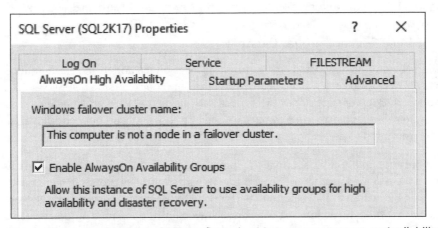

Figure 12-3 In the SQL Server 2017 Configuration Manager, you can turn on Availability Groups even if the Windows Server is not a member of a WSFC.

Unlike in past versions of SQL Server, the instance does not need to reside on a Windows Server that is a member of a WSFC. You can turn on the HA feature and create clusterless availability groups in SQL Server 2017. The only cluster types available when creating an availability group without a Windows Server Failover Cluster are External and None, which are cluster types created for non-Windows cluster managers or clusterless availability groups, respectively.

Let's compare the three cluster type options that are possible with SQL Server 2017 and availability groups. Figure 12-4 shows the New Availability Group dialog box and the Cluster Type list box.

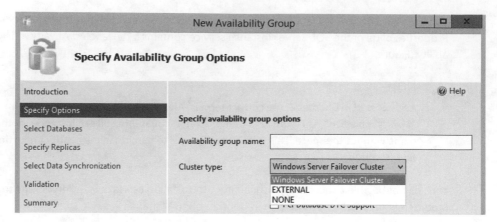

Figure 12-4 The three possible cluster types in the New Availability Group dialog box.

Windows Server Failover Cluster

This is the original supported architecture that relies on the underlying cluster quorum for failover, discussed earlier in this chapter, and the only choice prior to SQL Server 2016. Even though SQL Server creates the objects necessary inside the WSFC and managed settings such as preferred/possible resource ownership, and also runs any user-initiated failovers, the WSFC quorum is used to detect node outage and trigger automatic failover.

Just because failover isn't automatically prompted by SQL, doesn't mean you can't have HA. There are production enterprise environments with availability groups configured for manual failover, but with the failover automated along with other server assets (such web or app servers) so that the automation isn't piecemeal. PowerShell is a common automation tool for this task, and we provide a sample of such a failover script in Chapter 14.

External

New to SQL Server 2017, SQL Server on Linux supports the use of external cluster managers, preferably Pacemaker. Red Hat Enterprise Linux, Ubuntu, and SUSE Linux Enterprise Server are all supported platforms. Availability groups on Linux clusters require at least *two* synchronous replicas to guarantee HA, but at least *three* replicas for automatic recovery, so we recommend that you set up your availability group on at least three nodes.

SQL Server on Linux is not cluster-aware, and availability groups on Linux are not tightly bound to the clustering resource manager as they are on Windows. This means that you cannot control failovers from within SQL Server. To manually perform a failover, for example, you must use the pcs command line to manage the Pacemaker cluster manager.

➤ You can read more about managing availability groups in Linux at
https://docs.microsoft.com/sql/linux/sql-server-linux-availability-group-failover-ha.

➤ To learn more about setting up availability groups in Linux, see the section "Configuring an availability group on Red Hat Linux" later in this chapter.

None

New to SQL Server 2017, the None option (clusterless) provides a subset of features of availability groups, available in Standard and Enterprise editions, the biggest gap currently being the complete lack of automatic failover. Similar to database mirroring, all of the machinery of synchronization and failover is within the SQL Server instances. The None setting also supports SQL Server on Linux replicas.

Although automatic failover is not possible, manual planned and forced failover is still possible as well as the usual availability groups features to which you're accustomed, including both synchronous and asynchronous modes, readable secondary nodes, and secondary replica backups. Availability groups without a WSFC cluster can still provide readable secondary nodes, read-only routing, and load balancing.

CAUTION

The `fn_hadr_backup_is_preferred_replica` function is used to determine whether a replica is the preferred replica for backups. In availability groups with `cluster type = NONE`, it returns an error. This bug might be fixed in an early SQL Server 2017 cumulative update, but for now, it means that you cannot use SQL Server Management Studio Maintenance Plans or other applications to schedule preference-aware backups for clusterless availability groups.

Other possible architectures

Consider also the following alternate architectures, which might be more appropriate for your environment if you are not running Enterprise edition, or if you have geographically separated environment HA requirements.

Basic availability groups   Basic availability groups are a limited version of the real thing and are supported only on SQL Server Standard edition. This feature wholly replaces the deprecated database mirroring feature but with the modern SQL Server Management Studio dialog box options and monitoring tools.

As with database mirroring, the single secondary replica cannot be readable or backed up. Although each basic availability group can support only two replicas, you can create more than one basic availability group per server. Basic availability groups are supported only on SQL Server 2016 and above, and are mostly there to match the features of database mirroring. Instead of basic availability groups, consider clusterless availability groups, unless automatic failover is a requirement.

FCIs + availability groups   SQL Server FCIs can themselves be members of availability groups, though without the possibility for automatic failover of the availability group. The FCI is still capable of automatic failover of the instance, allowing for local HA and hardware availability, but not remote HA.

We do not recommend creating a WSFC that spans a WAN, even if the subnet spans the network. Instead, you should consider availability groups without FCIs, or distributed availability groups if you require local hardware HA.

Distributed availability groups   This allows an availability group to treat another availability group, typically over a WAN, to act as a secondary replica. The two availability groups, each with their own listener, do not need to be in same network or WSFC. This allows for local hardware and geographically remote HA and DR across multisite deployments. With distributed availability groups, you do not need to span a WSFC across the WAN or subnet. There is no risk of accidental failover of the WSFC over the WAN; in fact, there is no automatic failover supported at all between the primary availability group and the secondary availability group.

You can also use distributed availability groups to migrate Windows-based availability groups to Linux-based availability groups, though this is not a permanent, stable, or recommended configuration.

Instead, this feature is better suited to read-only secondary replicas that are globally dispersed, offloading workloads to regional read-only secondary replicas.

This architecture could be especially useful for OS and future SQL Server version upgrades of instances in an availability group because you can have different versions of Windows Server (2012 minimum) and SQL Server (2016 minimum) and perform a fast migration with minimal downtime.

Although each partner availability group in a distributed scenario has its own listener, the distributed availability group as a whole does not. Applications, perhaps with the aid of DNS aliases, will connect to each availability group directly after a failover to take advantage of readable secondary replicas.

The availability group that is not primary can serve only read-only queries, but does have a "primary" replica itself. The "primary" replica in the secondary availability group is charged with replicating transactions to the other secondary replicas in the secondary availability group. Otherwise, distributed availability groups operate in much the same way of a traditional availability group.

Creating WSFC for use with availability groups

We covered WSFCs earlier in this chapter. If you choose to set up an availability group that uses the underlying structure of a WSFC for your availability group, the first big decision is the same for setting up any WSFC. Quorum votes and, specifically, where quorum votes will reside, is key to understanding how the servers will eventually failover.

You should use the Node Majority quorum mode when you have an odd number of voting nodes; use the Node and File Share Majority quorum mode when you have an even number of voting nodes.

Your quorum strategy might also be different based on two factors. First, do you intend to mostly run out of one datacenter, with the other datacenter to be used in disaster operations only? Second, do you intend to have manual failover only, without any automatic failover? If you answered yes to both, having a quorum vote maintaining uptime in the primary node, including placing a file share witness in the primary node datacenter, makes sense. If you answered no to either, you should follow best practices for WSFC quorum alignment, including an odd number of quorum votes, with one of the quorum votes in a third location. This can include an Azure Storage Account Cloud Witness, a relatively inexpensive and very reliable witness feature of Windows Server 2016.

When validating your cluster, don't run validation checks on your storage, and do not select the Add All Eligible Storage check box for the cluster. The storage validation is time consuming and not needed. The WSFC for your availability group won't have any storage, unless you choose to use a shared storage witness as your "odd" vote. Add that separately. You can view the current quorum votes per member roles in the `sys.dm_hadr_cluster_members` DMV.

During the cluster validation and after the WSFC is online, you might see warnings in the Windows Server Failover Cluster Manager that storage is not configured. Because storage is not clustered in availability groups, you can ignore these warnings and, in the future, use the Failover Cluster Manager only to view the overall health state of the cluster or to manage quorum.

Do not initiate failovers from the Failover Cluster Manager unless you are forcing quorum. All failovers for the availability group should be initiated through SQL Server; for example, via SQL Server Management Studio, T-SQL statements, or PowerShell commands.

Inside OUT

What permissions are needed to create the availability group objects?

When creating the WSFC without domain administrator permissions, you might encounter errors when creating a Cluster Name Object (CNO) or the listener objects in Active Directory. The listener object is created by the CNO, so the CNO must have access to read all properties and Create Computer Objects in the cluster's OU. The user creating the cluster must have rights to grant the CNO these permissions, as well, or grant these permissions to the CNO after it is created. The listener object can also be pre-created by a domain administrator instead of giving the CNO these rights.

Understanding the database mirroring endpoint

The endpoint for availability groups is also called the database mirroring endpoint, sharing a type name, functionality, and port with the endpoint created by the deprecated database mirroring feature. The endpoint name `Hadr_endpoint` is given by default to the availability groups endpoint for communication.

By default, the endpoint communicates on TCP port 5022 and does not need to change unless it is already in use by another availability group. You can view information about the endpoint in the system reference tables `sys.database_mirroring_endpoints` (including its current status, role, and encryption settings) and `sys.tcp_endpoints` (including its port number, IP settings, and Listener IP).

If you're creating the availability group database_mirroring endpoint manually, you can use T-SQL, using the CREATE ENDPOINT command, or PowerShell, using the `New-SqlHadrEndpoint` cmdlet.

NOTE

Each availability group endpoint will need a different endpoint URL port number. There is a bug in SQL Server Management Studio prior to 17.2 that did not recognize nonstandard port values and would create the `database_mirroring` endpoint on TCP 5022. Always use the latest version of SQL Server Management Studio.

Configuring the minimum synchronized required nodes

New to SQL Server 2017, the REQUIRED_SYNCHRONIZED_SECONDARIES_TO_COMMIT setting establishes a minimum number of synchronized replicas, which you can set to an integer value between 0 and the number of replicas minus 1.

By default, this setting is 0, which mimics the behavior prior to SQL Server 2017. In that case, a synchronous replica that stops responding does not stop the primary replica from committing transactions. Instead, that problematic synchronous replica's state is set to NOT SYNCHRONIZED until it is reachable again and catches up, at which point its state is set back to SYNCHRONIZED.

When more than zero, this setting creates guarantees that transactions commit to that number of secondary replicas. At least as many secondary replicas as the value of the setting must be SYNCHRONIZED, or transactions on the primary replica will not be allowed to commit!

This guarantees that the primary database replica cannot introduce new data while there are insufficient secondary synchronous replicas, and therefore automatic failover targets. You should carefully consider the impact of transaction rollbacks on client applications and your data-loss tolerance requirements before changing this setting from the default.

Choosing the correct secondary replica availability mode

The most important consideration of choosing between asynchronous-commit availability mode and synchronous-commit availability mode for each secondary replica is the requirement for automatic or manual failover. In this section, we discuss how synchronous-commit availability mode replicas work and how the commit mode affects their behavior and that of the primary replica.

Three overall considerations guide this decision:

- If your HA goals require automatic failover, you must choose synchronous.

- If your databases are geographically separated, even if in the same subnet, you should consider choosing asynchronous-commit availability mode because the performance impact discussed in the section that follows will be significant.

- Asynchronous-commit availability mode will perform faster than synchronous mode, especially over geographically separated datacenters. Performance with only asynchronous-commit availability mode replicas will also be noticeably improved during index maintenance and other bulk data operations.

- If your databases are in the same physical network area, you should consider whether your performance requirements allow for synchronous commit mode.

Choosing synchronous-commit availability mode is not without a performance impact on the primary replica. The performance impact has two causes: the actual delay of the commit due to the time it takes to receive the acknowledgements from the secondary replica(s), and the potential for concurrency issues due to the longer lock periods. The commit delay can be measured by using performance counters (if you want to measure the delay for a specific duration) or by querying wait statistics.

> ➤ Methods for measuring the commit delay are detailed in the Microsoft blog post at *https://blogs.msdn.microsoft.com/saponsqlserver/2013/04/24/ sql-server-2012-alwayson-part-12-performance-aspects-and-performance-monitoring-ii/*.

Understanding the impact of secondary replicas on performance

If you exceed the amount of replica data that your secondary replica hardware can handle, the log redo queue on the secondary replica(s) and the log send queue on the primary replica will begin to fill. These log queues will grow under heavy load and would need to process before the secondary replica could come online. In synchronous commit mode, this delays commits on the primary replica. In asynchronous commit mode, there are still transaction delay repercussions if the secondary replica(s) cannot match the performance of the primary replica.

A redo backlog on a secondary replica will cause the following problematic conditions:

- Delay automatic failover by preventing a failover without data loss, forcing any failover to be a manual failover.

- Delaying database recovery at startup after a crash or reboot.

- The data on the secondary replica will be stale, which might reveal itself in queries against read-only secondary nodes.

- The delay of data being backed up when using the secondary replica for database or log backups.

- Transactions in the primary replica's transaction log will be delayed, truncating only during transaction log backups, due to transactions being unable to be applied to secondary replicas.

For these reasons, to protect the performance of the primary replica, a secondary synchronous replica might switch to asynchronous because of time-outs when communicating with the primary node.

This switch to asynchronous happens automatically and temporarily, and would logically block the possibility for automatic failover. Synchronous replicas are not guaranteed to provide zero data loss in all workloads and are best described as *potential* automatic failover partners.

If a synchronous commit secondary replica does not send confirmation before a time-out period, the primary replica will mark the secondary replica status as DISCONNECTED, essentially removing it from the availability group. The time-out period is 10 seconds by default, but you can change this via the SESSION_TIMEOUT property of the secondary replica. This prevents the primary replica from suffering transaction hardening delays. You can detect when this happens by setting an alert for error 41418. A secondary replica that has become DISCONNECTED will need to be added back to the availability group by an administrator and, depending on how far behind it is, might need to be reseeded.

You should consider switching the availability group's secondary replicas from synchronous to asynchronous if you anticipate a period of heavy, performance-sensitive writes to the system; for example, when performing index maintenance, modifying or moving large tables, or running bulk operations. Afterward, change the replicas back to synchronous. You'll be able to observe their state change from SYNCHRONIZING to SYNCHRONIZED as soon as the secondary replicas have caught up.

Similarly, you could also consider switching your asynchronous secondary replicas to synchronous mode, temporarily, in order to perform a manual failover without data loss, and without having to use the FORCE parameter. After the failover, you can switch the replicas back to the higher-performance asynchronous mode. You'll be able to observe their state change from SYNCHRONIZED to SYNCHRONIZING as soon as the secondary replicas have switched to asynchronous.

Inside OUT

How many potential synchronous automatic failover partners can a replica have?

Prior to SQL Server 2016, only one secondary replica could be a potential automatic failover partner with the primary replica. Starting with SQL Server 2016, you can set up to two synchronous commit secondary replicas as automatic failover partners using the WSFC cluster type, for a total of three (including the current primary) replicas that you can set to automatic failover.

The preferred owner properties of the availability group object in the WSFC determine which of the two secondary replicas is the target of an automatic failover.

SQL Server automatically manages the potential and preferred owners list of availability group resources in the WSFC, and there is no method in SQL Server to control this. If you change these settings in the WSFC, they will be overwritten the next time SQL Server performs a failover, and thus we do not recommend doing so.

You can view the current possible and preferred owners in the Windows Failover Cluster Manager. On the Roles page of the Failover Cluster Manager, double-click the availability group object to open its Properties dialog box. On the General tab, you'll find the Preferred Owners list. Then, back in Failover Cluster Manager, under Other Resources, double-click the availability group object. On the Advanced Policies tab, you'll find the Possible Owners list.

Understanding failovers in availability groups

When an availability group fails over, a secondary replica becomes the new primary, and the primary replica (if available) becomes a secondary replica. The properties of replicas after they become primary or secondary should be reviewed and reconfigured after a failover, especially after an unplanned and/or forced failover. It might not be appropriate given the loss of one or more nodes to support automatic failover, readable secondary nodes, or backup priority settings.

Automatic failover

Automatic failovers provide HA and rely on properly configured listener and WSFC objects for their success. Only a synchronous-commit availability mode replica can be the destination of an automatic failover. You can configure the conditions that prompt an automatic failover on a scale of 1 to 5, where 1 indicates that only a total outage of the SQL Server service on the primary replica would initiate a failover, and 5 indicates any of a number of critical to less-severe SQL Server errors.

The default is 3, which prompts an automatic failure in the case of an outage or unresponsive primary replica, but also for some critical server conditions. These conditions are detailed at *https://docs.microsoft.com/sql/database-engine/availability-groups/windows/flexible-automatic-failover-policy-availability-group#FClevel*.

Automatic failovers will not occur unless they meet the same conditions as a planned failover, which we look at next. Specifically, automatic failovers cannot occur with the possibility of data loss.

Planned failover

A planned failover can occur only if there is possibility for data loss. Specifically, this means the failover occurs without using the FORCE parameter to acknowledge warnings in code or in the SQL Server Management Studio dialog boxes. It is therefore only possible to have a planned failover to a secondary replica in synchronous-commit availability mode, but that doesn't mean that asynchronous is out of the question.

You can move an asynchronous-commit availability mode replica to synchronous, wait for the SYNCHRONIZED state, and then issue a planned failover without data loss. You should not attempt a planned failover from within the Windows Server Failover Cluster Manager. Instead, you should always use SQL Server commands via SQL Server Management Studio, T-SQL, or PowerShell.

➤ **For PowerShell code examples of scripted failover, see Chapter 14.**

Forced failover

You should attempt a forced failover only in response to adverse cluster conditions such as the loss of the primary node. You should not attempt to force failover from within the Windows Server Failover Cluster Manager unless adverse cluster conditions have made it impossible to force failover from SQL Server commands via SQL Server Management Studio, T-SQL, or PowerShell.

After a forced failover, the new primary replica will begin to receive transactions from clients but will not synchronize with other databases until the other databases are resumed. You can accomplish this via SQL Server Management Studio by right-clicking the database and selecting Resume Data Movement, if available. With T-SQL scripting, you use the following command:

```
ALTER DATABASE [AGDB] SET HADR RESUME
```

With PowerShell, use this command for each database in the availability group:

```
Import-Module SQLSERVER
Resume-SqlAvailabilityDatabase -Path `
    SQLSERVER:\Sql\SQLSRV2\SQL17\AvailabilityGroups\AG1\AvailabilityDatabases\AGDB
```

> **NOTE**
>
> You should always use SQL Server commands via the SQL Server Management Studio Availability Group dashboard, T-SQL, or PowerShell to initiate failovers. An exception to this rule is with availability groups for which the `cluster_type` = EXTERNAL. This would be the case for instances on SQL Server on Linux, using a Linux-based cluster manager such as Pacemaker. In this case, you must use the external cluster manager to initiate all failovers.

Seeding options when adding replicas

Copying the data to the secondary replica to begin synchronization is a prerequisite step for adding a database to an availability group. There are a few different ways this can occur, some more automatic than others.

Following are your options when using the Add Database To Availability Group page of the Availability Groups Wizard in SQL Server Management Studio, and an explanation of when you should use each. Each has a different strategy for moving the data across the network to the secondary replica.

Automatic seeding

First introduced in SQL Server 2016, automatic seeding handles the data copy, performing a backup using the endpoint as a virtual backup device. This is a clever way to automate the backup/restore without using network file shares or requiring administrator backup/copy/restore effort. This works seamlessly for most cases, given the following caveats:

- In general, you should use the same data and log file paths for all replicas on the same OS (Windows or Linux), but in SQL Server 2017, this is no longer a requirement for automatic seeding. Keep in mind that the default path to the instance data and log folders includes the named instance names, which could be different from instance to instance; for example, the path on my named instance in Windows

```
F:\Program Files\Microsoft SQL Server\MSSQL14.InstanceA\MSSQL\DATA
```

will not match the path on another server with a different instance name:

```
F:\Program Files\Microsoft SQL Server\MSSQL14.InstanceB\MSSQL\DATA
```

- The only manual intervention required by the administrator is to grant the availability group object permissions to create databases on the secondary replicas. This is slightly different from a typical GRANT statement for permissions:

```
ALTER AVAILABILITY GROUP [AG_WWI] GRANT CREATE ANY DATABASE;
```

- After automatic seeding, the AUTHORIZATION (also known as owner) of the database on the secondary replica might be different from the AUTHORIZATION of the database on the primary. You should check to ensure that they are the same, and alter the database if needed:

```
ALTER AUTHORIZATION ON DATABASE::WideWorldImporters TO [serverprincipal];
```

➤ **For more about database authorization, see Chapter 6.**

- Compression over the network for the automatic seeding backup transfer is turned off by default. You can turn it on to speed the transfer, but with an increase in CPU utilization. We do not recommend that you perform automatic seeding during regular production usage anyway, so turning on compression to speed the transfer might be worthwhile. You cannot currently turn on compression via SQL Server Management Studio dialog boxes; instead, you should turn it on via global trace flag 9567. Keep in mind that turning on automatic seeding compression via the global trace flag will affect all availability groups on the instance.

- The automatic seeding backup can take longer than a normal backup, especially if it is over a WAN network connection or a distributed availability group. During automatic seeding, the source database's transaction log cannot truncate. If automatic seeding takes too long, you can stop it for databases that have yet to complete by using the following code, which changes the replica synchronization preference to MANUAL or Join Only. Use the following T-SQL example on the primary replica:

```
--Stop automatic seeding
ALTER AVAILABILITY GROUP [AG_WWI] --Availability Group name
    MODIFY REPLICA ON 'SQLSERVER-1\SQL2K17' --Replica name
    WITH (SEEDING_MODE = MANUAL); --"Join Only" in SSMS

GO
```

You can view the progress of automatic seeding (on all replicas) in the system DMV `sys.dm_hadr_physical_seeding_stats`, which includes a column that estimates the completion of the automatic seeding, `estimate_time_complete_utc`. Even though data is displayed for `sys.dm_hadr_physical_seeding_stats` on both the primary and secondary replica, an estimate might be available only on the primary node. The `role_desc` field will indicate which end of the automatic seeding the local SQL instance is: source or destination.

You can review the history of automatic seeding activity in the DMV `sys.dm_hadr_automatic_seeding`, on both the primary and the target secondary replica. The `current_state` field will equal 'SEEDING' for in-progress automatic seeding sessions, as shown in the following T-SQL examples:

```
--Monitor automatic seeding
SELECT s.*
FROM sys.dm_hadr_physical_seeding_stats s
ORDER BY start_time_utc desc;

--Automatic seeding History
SELECT TOP 10 ag.name, dc.database_name, s.start_time, s.completion_time,
    s.current_state, s.performed_seeding, s.failure_state_desc, s.error_code,
    s.number_of_attempts
FROM sys.dm_hadr_automatic_seeding s
INNER JOIN sys.availability_databases_cluster dc ON s.ag_db_id = dc.group_database_id
INNER JOIN sys.availability_groups ag ON s.ag_id = ag.group_id
ORDER BY start_time desc;
```

Troubleshooting automatic seeding   Here is a checklist of troubleshooting steps for unsuccessful automatic seeding attempts:

- Check the primary and secondary replica's SQL Server Error Log, which will contain error messages related to the attempted automatic seeding backup and restore events.

- Make sure that the secondary replica's SQL Server service account has permissions to create and have full control over the path where the restore is attempting to place the seeded files. In SQL Server 2016, the database data and log file paths must be the same, and that includes named instance names that could be present in the file path. In SQL Server 2017, you can use different paths, but we do not recommend doing this, because it would increase complexity and could be the source of errors in future reconfigurations or restores.

- Check also that the same features, including FILESTREAM if applicable, are turned on for the secondary instance prior to automatic seeding.

- During a lengthy automatic seeding, turn off transaction log backups on the primary database. Transaction log backups could cause automatic seeding to fail, with the message "The remote copy of database *databasename* has not been rolled forward to a point in time that is encompassed in the local copy of the database log."

If automatic seeding fails, remember to drop the unsuccessfully seeded database on the secondary replica, including the database data and log files in the file path. After you have resolved the errors and want to retry automatic seeding, you can do so by using the following example T-SQL statement. Run this code sample on the primary replica to restart automatic seeding:

```
--Restart automatic seeding after error resolution
ALTER AVAILABILITY GROUP [AG_WWI] --Availability Group name
    MODIFY REPLICA ON 'SQLSERVER-1\SQL2K17' --Replica name
    WITH (SEEDING_MODE = AUTOMATIC); --Automatic Seeding
```

Inside OUT

Can I use automatic seeding to add a database with Transparent Data Encryption (TDE) turned on?

Databases that already have TDE turned on are supported in availability groups, but are problematic with automatic seeding. You cannot have a database with TDE turned on for one replica but not turned on for another replica. If you're setting up a new database, seed it to all secondary replicas first, and then turn on TDE. If adding an existing database with TDE turned on to a new replica, do not use automatic seeding at this time. This might be improved in a future version of SQL Server.

Turning on TDE on a database that is already a member of an availability group is supported in the SQL Server Management Studio wizards starting with SQL Server 2016 with other seeding modes. (This feature was required to place the SQL Server Integration Services database into an availability group.)

Full database and log backup

This option performs a background backup of the database and log, copies them via a network share (Windows or Linux) that you must set up beforehand, and restores the databases. Configuring the network share and its permissions successfully is the trickiest part of this strategy. The SQL Server service account of the primary replica instance must have read and write permissions to the network share. The SQL Server service account of the secondary replica instance(s) must have read permissions to the network share.

Troubleshooting full database and log backup   Make sure that the secondary replica's SQL Server service account has permissions to create and have full control over the path where the restore is attempting to restore the copied backup files. Because you cannot specify REPLACE, the databases and database files should not already exist in place on the secondary replicas. Check also that the same features, including FILESTREAM if applicable, are turned on for the secondary instance prior to adding the database to the secondary replica.

Join Only (Manual Backup/Copy/Restore)

As a fallback to more automated options, when creating an availability group outside of the SQL Server Management Studio dialog boxes, with T-SQL or PowerShell, "Join only" is the default and least complicated option. "Join only" requires the administrator to do the following manually, in this order: take full and log backups of each database (or use recently taken backups), copy them to the secondary replica(s), restore the full backup WITH NORECOVERY, and restore the log backup WITH NORECOVERY. The closer the log chain is to live, the sooner the database will catch up after it is joined to the availability group. After the transaction log backup is restored, the database is ready to be joined to the availability group on that replica, via SQL Server Management Studio or code.

Skip

Using this option, you can complete setup of the rest of the availability group without synchronizing any databases. Choose this if you want to synchronize the replica databases later.

Additional actions after creating an availability group

Availability groups copy databases and database-level configuration, but not server-level configuration, such as logins. As the DBA, your job is to prepare the secondary instances for failover by creating the necessary server-level settings and objects to support normal operations during a failover. We recommend creating these by using a script, which can easily be run on multiple secondaries, including new secondaries which might be added after a disaster affects the primary or secondary server(s). Using scripts will ensure that the server-level configuration is consistently and efficiently applied.

Although database-level settings are moved, including users, user permissions, and database roles, there are server-level objects that the SQL DBA needs to move after creating the availability group during a failover.

Prior to adding a SQL Server instance as a secondary replica of an availability group, you should move the server-level objects from the primary replica to the new secondary replica SQL Server instances.

Consider the following a general checklist for all the server-level objects that should exist on all SQL Server replica instances:

- Server-level security, including logins and server roles, that can be used to access the replicated databases, plus any explicit server-level permissions or role memberships for logins and roles. The `owner_sid` of the database owner should also exist in the new secondary replica instance.

  ➤ **For more on moving SQL Server logins and permissions, see Chapter 6.**

- Server-level certificates, endpoints, Transport Layer Security (TLS) settings, including certificates used by TDE for databases in the availability group, SQL Server Audit configurations.

  ➤ **For more on TDE, TLS, certificates, keys, and SQL Server Audit, see Chapter 7.**

- SQL Agent jobs, operators, alerts, retention policies enforced for backup files, log files, various msdb history, policy-based management (PBM).

  ➤ **For more on SQL Agent jobs, operators, alerts, retention policies, and PBM, see Chapter 14.**

- Server-level configuration options and surface area configuration options.

  ➤ **For more on server-level configuration options, see Chapter 4.**

- Backup devices

  ➤ **For more on backup devices, see Chapter 10.**

- Resource Governor configuration, classifier functions, groups, and pools.

  ➤ **For more on Resource Governor, see Chapter 13.**

- Custom extended events sessions for monitoring.

  ➤ **For more on extended events, see Chapter 13.**

- User-defined messages.

- Server-level triggers including logon triggers.

- Azure Network load balancer backend pools (if applicable).

- Corporate network firewall settings.

After the availability group is set up, review the following checklist:

- Review all settings and document the current configuration. Document the planned settings for each replica in all failover scenarios, which should be synchronous/asynchronous, automatic/manual failover, readable.

- Perform a planned failover to each replica (with replicas in synchronous mode, even if temporarily). Confirm application network connectivity where each replica is primary.

- Confirm that the cluster network `RegisterAllProvidersIP` setting is configured correctly to work with application connection strings (see next section). If turned on, confirm that the listener has IPs in each subnet. Confirm that application connection strings are using the proper value for `MultiSubnetFailover` (see the next section).

- Confirm that application connection strings are using appropriate values for `ApplicationIntent` (see the next section).

- Configure the read-only secondary replica endpoints and routing URLs for all replicas (see the next section).

- Confirm that all SQL Server Agent jobs have been modified if necessary to be aware of the replica status of necessary databases.

- Confirm the new backup strategy for databases in availability groups. If the method for backups is aware of backup priority values, verify that the availability group's Backup Preferences are appropriate.

- ➤ **For more information on configuring SQL Server Agent jobs to be availability group replica–aware, and automating backups to secondary availability group replicas, see Chapter 14.**

Reading secondary database copies

In this section, we provide an overview of how the synchronization of secondary replicas works and then move into using the secondary replicas to offload heavy read-only workloads from the primary replica. This is the *ONline* portion of the original HADRON code name acronym for availability groups, and it can be integral to the architecture of an enterprise transactional system.

One of the biggest advantages of availability groups over the legacy database mirroring feature is the ability to get some value out of the secondary database. Read-only replicas can be part of your enterprise architecture, providing an easy way to offload heavy workloads to another server, including business intelligence (BI); Extract, Transform, and Load (ETL); and integration workloads. Secondary replica databases are not set to read-only using the database settings using the READ_ONLY option; rather, they are written to by the availability group mechanism, and available to be read by transactions.

How synchronizing secondary replicas works

In synchronous commit, transactions must write to the primary server, send to secondary replica(s), commit to secondary replica(s), and then receive an acknowledgement from each secondary replica before it can commit on the primary server.

Log data is written to the drive (also known as being "flushed") to the primary replica log file, and that data is received by the secondary replicas and applied to the secondary replicas' data files. The log data is then written to the drive to the secondary replica(s) log file(s). The amount of data waiting to be flushed on the secondary replica is known as the log redo queue.

In asynchronous commit, transactions must write to the primary server and commit, then transactions are sent to secondary replica(s), commit to secondary replica(s), then the primary replica receives an acknowledgement from each secondary replica.

As a result, asynchronous replicas will never display "SYNCHRONIZED" with the primary replica, but they can be "caught up" to reflect the same state of all row data. You cannot trust an asynchronous replica to be completely caught up with all transactions from the primary, but the replica will rarely be behind by more than a few seconds for most workloads. You can measure the backlog of transactions waiting to be committed to an asynchronous replica by using the `sys.dm_hadr_database_replica_states` DMV.

To avoid blocking transactions that are arriving from the primary replica, secondary replicas use snapshot isolation to return queries using row versioning, stored in the secondary replica's TempDB database. Queries against secondary replicas use the snapshot isolation level, overriding any transaction isolation level settings or table hints.

Readable secondary databases automatically append a 14-byte overhead to each data row to facilitate the row versioning, just as a 14-byte overhead is added to row data on the primary database if snapshot isolation or Read-Committed Snapshot Isolation (RCSI) are used. The TempDB database also is used to store temporary statistics for indexes in secondary replica databases.

➤ For more information about snapshot isolation and RCSI, see Chapter 9.

Using the listener for read-only traffic

The availability groups listener not only forwards traffic to the current primary replica and handles redirection automatically during failover, but the listener can also redirect traffic that identifies itself as read-only to readable secondary replicas. This is especially effective for long-running SELECT statements coming from reports or other BI systems.

Each replica, when primary, provides a list of endpoints to the listener. You can configure this routing list on each listener in advance; however, in certain failover scenarios, your desired routing list might change. Updating the read-only routing lists for each replica should be part of your failover scripting if necessary.

Each replica will also have a read-only routing URL regardless of whether it is currently serving as a secondary replica. You should also set this in advance but use it only when the replica is serving as a readable secondary replica.

The options to maintain the read-only routing URL and Routing List for each replica are available for the first time in the Availability Group Properties (see Figure 12-5) of SQL Server Management Studio as of version 17.3.

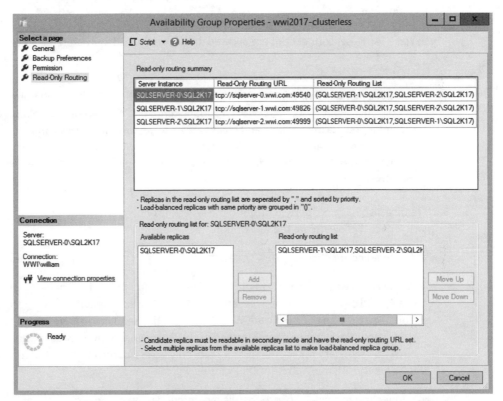

Figure 12-5 The Read-Only Routing page of the Availability Group Properties dialog box in SQL Server Management Studio. You can configure the Read-Only Routing URLs and Routing Lists for each replica. Note that each routing list is wrapped in parenthesis, indicating that the secondary readable replicas will be load balanced.

To be routed to a secondary readable replica by the listener, a connection string must specify the `ApplicationIntent = ReadOnly`. The listener does not otherwise have a way to determine whether the user connection will run only read-only statements.

The read-only routing URL is not used for application connection strings, however. You should use the listener name for connection strings. Each replica has a property indicating what types of connections it can receive when it is a secondary replica. Following are the three options for the `ALLOW_CONNECTIONS` parameter for replicas:

- **No.**   No user connections are allowed to the secondary replica.

- **Read-intent only.**   Only user connections that use the `ApplicationIntent = ReadOnly` parameter in their connection string are allowed, and only read-only statements can be run.

- **Yes.**   Any user connections are allowed, though only read-only statements can be run.

NOTE

Be aware that specifying SECONDARY_ROLE (ALLOW_CONNECTIONS = NO) or SECONDARY_ROLE (ALLOW_CONNECTIONS = READ_ONLY) **makes the databases on a secondary replica inaccessible and blocks access to your normal query connections in SQL Server Management Studio and other applications without changes to their connection strings. This will hide databases on secondary replicas from DMV's and your monitoring tools.**

Each replica also has a property indicating the types of connections it can receive when it is a primary replica. Following are the two options:

- **Allow all connections.**   This is the default.

- **Allow read/write connections.**   Use this when your application connections strings use `ApplicationIntent`. This setting blocks any user connection that specifies `ApplicationIntent = ReadOnly`. This could be useful if you have report connection strings that use instance names instead of the listener name (not recommended). If you have no secondary replicas set up for read-only access, connections to the replica database via the listener with `ReadOnly` intent will fail.

When connecting to availability groups, we recommend that you provide both the `ApplicationIntent` and `MultiSubnetFailover` keywords and appropriate values for each depending on the application. The default value for `ApplicationIntent` is `ReadWrite` if not otherwise provided, which will always be directed to the primary replica of the availability group.

Connections directly to a secondary readable database without using a listener are possible. However, we do not recommend designing connection strings for reporting systems that use a secondary readable SQL Server instance. In future failover scenarios, you would not be able to separate read-write traffic from read-only traffic without reconfiguration. Consider hardcoding a readable secondary replica name only if you're using a connection string that cannot use the `ApplicationIntent` parameter or if using a listener for some reason is not possible.

Configuring RegisterAllProvidersIP and MultiSubNetFailover correctly

In a multi-subnet cluster, you should have the `RegisterAllProvidersIP` setting turned on (1) if your application connection strings will be using the listener using `MultiSubNetFailover = Yes`.

Optimally, you both turn on the `RegisterAllProvidersIP` setting and specify `MultiSubNetFailover = Yes` when in a multi-subnet cluster. The `MultiSubNetFailover` connection string parameter allows both IPs for the listener to be registered at all times and modern connection strings to use a parallel connection attempt to each IP address. The result is a quick connection to the active IP address during normal operation and immediately after failover.

Misconfiguration of the `RegisterAllProvidersIP` and `MultiSubNetFailover` options will be noticeable in the following circumstances:

- If you turn on `RegisterAllProvidersIP` without your connection strings using `MultiSubNetFailover = No` or not specifying `MultiSubNetFailover`, your application could have very high latency connection times because connection strings attempt to connect to both IPs.

- If you turn off `RegisterAllProvidersIP`, `MultiSubNetFailover = Yes` will have no effect, and your applications will not reconnect promptly after availability group failovers. Instead, they will need to wait for DNS to resolve the new primary subnet IP address for the listener. (By default, the TTL is 20 minutes!)

If you are using any non-Microsoft connection strings that do not support `MultiSubNetFailover` or do not have the ability to turn on that connection string parameter, the `RegisterAllProvidersIP` setting in the cluster should be turned off (0), which is the default.

> **NOTE**
> The Object Linking and Embedding Database (OLE DB) connection string in the SQL Server Native Client supports `ApplicationIntent` but does not support the `MultiSubnetFailover` keyword. Use Microsoft Open Database Connectivity (ODBC) instead, which supports both keywords.

CHAPTER 12

You can verify that `RegisterAllProvidersIP` is turned on in your cluster and that the listener has an IP in each subnet by using the following command-line command:

```
nslookup Listener1
```

You should see two IP addresses listed, one per subnet, if `RegisterAllProvidersIP` is turned on.

To change the `RegisterAllProvidersIP` setting in the cluster network, you can use the following PowerShell script:

```
Import-Module FailoverClusters
# Get cluster network name
Get-ClusterResource -Cluster "CLUSTER1"
Get-ClusterResource "AG1_Network" -Cluster "CLUSTER1" | `
    Get-ClusterParameter RegisterAllProvidersIP -Cluster "CLUSTER1"
# 1 to enable, 0 to disable
Get-ClusterResource "AG1_Network" -Cluster "CLUSTER1" | `
    Set-ClusterParameter RegisterAllProvidersIP 1 -Cluster "CLUSTER1"
# All changes will take effect once AG1 is taken offline and brought online again.
Stop-ClusterResource "AG1_Network" -Cluster "CLUSTER1"
Start-ClusterResource "AG1_Network" -Cluster "CLUSTER1"
# Must bring the AAG Back online
Start-ClusterResource "AG1" -Cluster "CLUSTER1"
# Should see the appropriate number of IPs listed now
nslookup Listener1
```

NOTE

The `FailoverPartner` connection keyword used with database mirroring does not apply to availability groups or the listener. If you're upgrading from database mirroring to availability groups, be sure to remove the `FailoverPartner` keyword from connection strings. A connection string will fail if both the `MultiSubetFailover` and `FailoverPartner` keywords are present.

Configuring availability groups load balanced read-only routing

First introduced in SQL Server 2016, you can load-balance connections that use `ApplicationIntent = ReadOnly` across multiple read-only replicas in the availability group. You can implement this easily by changing the read-only routing list to use parenthesis to create load-balanced groups.

For example, the ALTER statement that follows provides a read-only routing list for a three-node availability group that is not load balanced. All read-only queries will be sent to the secondary node SQLSERVER-1, and if it is unavailable, to SQLSERVER-2, and if that is also unavailable, to SQLSERVER-0. This is the behavior prior to SQL Server 2016.

```
ALTER AVAILABILITY GROUP [wwi2017]
MODIFY REPLICA ON 'SQLSERVER-0'
WITH (PRIMARY_ROLE(READ_ONLY_ROUTING_LIST =
('SQLSERVER-1','SQLSERVER-2', SQLSERVER-0')));
```

This ALTER statement provides a read-only routing list that is load balanced. Note the extra set of parentheses.

With the configuration in the following sample, read-only traffic will be routed to a load-balance group of SQLSERVER-1 and SQLSERVER-0, but failing those connections, to SQLSERVER-0:

```
ALTER AVAILABILITY GROUP [wwi2017]
MODIFY REPLICA ON 'SQLSERVER-0'
WITH (PRIMARY_ROLE(READ_ONLY_ROUTING_LIST =
(('SQLSERVER-1','SQLSERVER-2'), SQLSERVER-0')));
```

To add load-balanced replica groups, in SQL Server Management Studio, in the Availability Group Properties dialog box, go to the Read-Only Routing page, and then, in the Availability Replicas window, press the Ctrl key while clicking to select multiple nodes. Then, click Add to add them simultaneously as a load-balanced group.

Although it is possible to add the primary replica itself to its own read-only routing list, this might be a self-defeating strategy of offloading read-only workloads from the primary replica.

Implementing a hybrid availability group topology

You can include new Azure virtual machines (VMs) running SQL Server instances in an availability group alongside on-premises SQL Server instances. Azure VMs in multiple regions can be part of the same availability group, as well. In terms of SQL Server functionality, the availability groups feature operates the same, but there are differences in the network setup. Communication is accomplished via a prerequisite site-to-site VPN with Azure to your on-premises subnet.

The member Azure VMs of the availability group should also be in the same availability set per region. (Note that you cannot move a VM from one availability set to another after they are created in an availability set.)

The Add Replica dialog box in SQL Server Management Studio provides an easy method to add Azure Replicas, and the Add Azure Replicas button appears on the Specify Replicas page of the Add Replica Wizard when the prerequisites have been met.

The Add Azure Replica button does significantly more work than the Add Replica button to the new secondary replica, including creating the Azure VM. You are given an opportunity to select the Azure VM tenant, the image for the VM, and to specify the Domain. The Availability Group Wizard handles creating the VM based off the image, configuring the VM's administrator user, and joining the VM to your domain.

Availability group listeners using Azure VMs use an internal Azure load balancer, one per region. You must create the load balancer before you create the listener, so skip this step in your initial availability group setup and/or wizard. When creating the load balancer, add all Azure SQL Server VMs in that region to the Backend pool. You can then configure the availability group listener configured to use the Load Balancer IP.

> ➤ A step-by-step walk-through of creating an Azure load balancer is available at *https://docs.microsoft.com/azure/virtual-machines/windows/sql/virtual-machines-windows-portal-sql-availability-group-tutorial#create-an-azure-load-balancer*.

Configuring an availability group on Red Hat Linux

In this section, we provide an in-depth summary of how to configure availability groups with SQL Server 2017 on Linux. Red Hat Enterprise Linux (RHEL), Ubuntu, and SUSE Linux Enterprise Server (SLES) are all supported platforms; however, this section focuses specifically on RHEL, using Pacemaker for the cluster manager, for setting up an availability group.

> ➤ To create a read-scale availability group that does not require a cluster manager, go to *https://docs.microsoft.com/sql/linux/sql-server-linux-availability-group-configure-rs*.

In the interest of providing a thorough discussion in this section, we make the assumption that you have fairly limited knowledge of Linux; however, if you feel comfortable with Red Hat, you can probably skim over the notes. Try not to skip them entirely, though, because there might be something you find interesting.

You should run all commands in the sample code in a terminal window by using the `bash` command-line shell (which is the default on most Linux platforms).

NOTE

Many of the commands for installing, configuring, and administering SQL Server on Linux require administrator privileges, just like on Windows. The commands are preceded by the `sudo` keyword, which means "super user do." This is less risky than logging in as the super user (root). The first time you run `sudo`, you will be prompted for the root password.

Installation requirements

As of this writing, SQL Server requires RHEL version 7.3. The minimum system requirements for SQL Server 2017 are as follows:

- CPU: 2 GHz (x64-compatible), with two physical cores

- RAM: 3.25 GB

- Disk: 6 GB (formatted with either ext4 or XFS)

SQL Server 2017 has been tested with 1 TB of RAM.

Setting up an availability group

Linux clusters require at least *two* synchronous replicas to guarantee HA, but at least *three* replicas for automatic recovery. We recommend that you set up your availability group on at least three nodes. Each node can be physical or virtual, but Red Hat requires that VMs use the same hypervisor, to keep the platform-specific fencing agents happy.

Understanding the differences between Windows and Linux clustering

The first thing to note is that SQL Server is not cluster-aware when running on Linux. This is the first key difference from the Windows world, which you can configure to to be clustered or clusterless. Pacemaker is much more limited than Windows Failover Cluster Manager.

Second, because we are not creating a Windows FCI, (nor extending a Windows availability group to a Linux replica), virtual network names do not exist, so you will need to manually add the listener name yourself to DNS, with the virtual IP you create.

Third, you will need to configure a *fencing agent* for your cluster, which ensures that misbehaving nodes in the cluster are returned to a known state (which might include forcing it to shut down and restart).

> ➤ For more information about STONITH, refer to Chapter 2. To read more on how to configure an appropriate fencing agent, visit *https://access.redhat.com/documentation/Red_Hat_Enterprise_Linux/7/html/High_Availability_Add-On_Reference/ch-fencing-HAAR.html*.

To set up an availability group on Linux, you must do the following:

1. Create the availability group (from within SQL Server).

2. Configure the cluster resource manager (Pacemaker).

3. Add the availability group to the cluster.

To reiterate, you must create the availability group *before* the you create the cluster create.

Configuring the server

Each node must have a unique name on the network, which can be no more than 15 characters in length. (This 15-character limit is a legacy requirement dating back to the old NetBIOS service.)

To set the server name, use the following command to edit the host name (remember to do this on all nodes):

```
sudo vi /etc/hostname
```

NOTE

If you're new to Linux, you might find that the vi editor is quite different from text editors you experienced in Windows. You might want to replace it with pico or nano. To save and quit from a vi session, you must type **:wq** and then press Enter. The colon instructs vi that you want to perform a command; the "w" writes (saves) the file; and "q" quits from the session.

If you are making use of a DNS server (which we recommend), you do not need to add entries to each node's hosts file. Otherwise, you will need to add entries for each node that will be in the availability group, including the node on which you edit each hosts file. You can find the hosts file at /etc/hosts.

Setting up the package manager

From a terminal window, run the following command to add the SQL Server repository to the yum package manager:

```
sudo curl -o /etc/yum.repos.d/mssql-server.repo \ https://packages.microsoft.com/config/
rhel/7/mssql-server.repo
```

Note in this example that the trailing space and backslash at the end of the first line is a convention in Bash to indicate that the command spans more than one line.

NOTE

Linux uses package managers to install, manage, update, and delete software—known as packages—using online repositories. Packages are the equivalent of installer files on the Windows platform. Package managers use information from repositories to ensure that packages are compatible with one another, which makes it much easier to keep your system stable and up to date.

Downloading and installing packages

After you have added the repository, run the following two commands to update the package manager and install SQL Server 2017:

```
sudo yum update
```

```
sudo yum install -y mssql-server
```

The SQL Server setup will be quick, which is quite a different experience from Windows. After it is downloaded, the installation will be over in a matter of seconds.

> ➤ **If you want to perform an offline installation for servers that do not have access to the internet, visit** *https://docs.microsoft.com/sql/linux/sql-server-linux-setup#offline.*

SQL Server license agreement and password

Next, run the SQL Server configuration process to set up SQL Server and agree to the software license:

```
sudo /opt/mssql/bin/mssql-conf setup
```

Microsoft recommends a password of at least eight characters; however, there is no harm in picking something much longer.

You can read more about passwords and brute-force attacks in Chapter 7. Now, verify that the SQL Server service is running:

```
systemctl status mssql-server
```

Installing the SQL Server Agent

Next, install the SQL Server Agent. Note that this requires restarting the SQL Server instance:

```
sudo yum install mssql-server-agent
```

```
sudo systemctl restart mssql-server
```

Opening the default port on the firewall

Finally, configure the built-in firewall to allow connections to TCP port 1433. This assumes that you're using the firewall package FirewallD:

```
sudo firewall-cmd --zone=public --add-port=1433/tcp -permanent
```

```
sudo firewall-cmd --reload
```

SQL Server 2017 is now up and running on your RHEL server, and you can connect to it by using SQL Operations Studio or SQL Server Management Studio.

➤ You can read more about installing command-line tools like sqlcmd and bcp at *https://docs. microsoft.com/sql/linux/sql-server-linux-setup-tools.*

Turning on availability groups and optional health session

Now, you need to turn on availability groups on each node. The following two commands configure the instance for availability groups and then restarts SQL Server:

```
sudo /opt/mssql/bin/mssql-conf set hadr.hadrenabled 1

sudo systemctl restart mssql-server
```

Optionally, you can set up an extended events session, which will aid with troubleshooting availability group issues. This is a T-SQL command that you must run from within the SQL Server instance:

```
ALTER EVENT SESSION AvailabilityGroupHealth ON SERVER
WITH (STARTUP_STATE = ON);
```

Creating the database mirroring endpoints

To set up the database mirroring endpoints, you need to create a user on each replica, being sure to use a strong password. Then, you create a certificate to allow the nodes to communicate securely with one another. Finally, you create the database mirroring endpoints on all replicas. The following code shows how to do this:

```
USE master;
GO


-- Create database mirroring endpoint user
CREATE LOGIN dbm_login WITH PASSWORD = '<UseAReallyStrongPassword>';

-- Create user for use by the database certificate later
CREATE USER dbm_user FOR LOGIN dbm_login;
GO


-- Create certificate
IF NOT EXISTS (SELECT * from sys.symmetric_keys
WHERE name = '##MS_DatabaseMasterKey##')

CREATE MASTER KEY ENCRYPTION BY PASSWORD = '<UseAReallyStrongMasterKeyPassword>';
CREATE CERTIFICATE dbm_certificate WITH SUBJECT = 'dbm';
BACKUP CERTIFICATE dbm_certificate
    TO FILE = '/var/opt/mssql/data/dbm_certificate.cer'
    WITH PRIVATE KEY (
        FILE = '/var/opt/mssql/data/dbm_certificate.pvk',
        ENCRYPTION BY PASSWORD = '<UseAReallyStrongPrivateKeyPassword>'
    );
GO
```

Copy the files that are generated to the same location on each availability replica. These are the certificates at `/var/opt/mssql/data/dbm_certificate.cer` and the private key at `/var/opt/mssql/data/dbm_certificate.pvk`.

To create the certificate on the availability replica, after you have copied the files, use the following T-SQL command (remember to use the same MASTER KEY and PRIVATE Key passwords as before):

```
CREATE MASTER KEY ENCRYPTION BY PASSWORD = '<UseAReallyStrongMasterKeyPassword>';
CREATE CERTIFICATE dbm_certificate
    AUTHORIZATION dbm_user
    FROM FILE = '/var/opt/mssql/data/dbm_certificate.cer'
    WITH PRIVATE KEY (
    FILE = '/var/opt/mssql/data/dbm_certificate.pvk',
    DECRYPTION BY PASSWORD = '<UseAReallyStrongPrivateKeyPassword>'
    );
```

Finally, create the actual endpoint, as demonstrated in the code that follows. The TCP port you choose needs to be open on the firewall. You can do this by using the same method for opening TCP port 1433 that we saw earlier.

> **NOTE**
>
> As of this writing, 0.0.0.0 is the only IP address you can use for the availability group listener.

```
CREATE ENDPOINT [Hadr_endpoint]
    AS TCP (LISTENER_IP = (0.0.0.0), LISTENER_PORT = 5022)
    FOR DATA_MIRRORING (
        ROLE = ALL,
        AUTHENTICATION = CERTIFICATE dbm_certificate,
        ENCRYPTION = REQUIRED ALGORITHM AES
        );

ALTER ENDPOINT [Hadr_endpoint] STATE = STARTED;

GRANT CONNECT ON ENDPOINT::[Hadr_endpoint] TO [dbm_login];
```

Create the availability group

Pacemaker is an external cluster resource manager, so you must create the availability group with the cluster type and failover mode set to EXTERNAL.

The code example that follows assumes three synchronous replicas, as we recommended previously. Additionally, the seeding mode is set to automatically create the database on each secondary replica. You can change this if you prefer. Confirm that the names of the servers are correct and that the port is the same one that you chose when creating the listener. You must run this script on the primary replica only.

CHAPTER 12

```
CREATE AVAILABILITY GROUP [LinuxAG1]
    WITH (DB_FAILOVER = ON, CLUSTER_TYPE = EXTERNAL)
    FOR REPLICA ON
        N'server1'
         WITH (
             ENDPOINT_URL = N'tcp://server1:5022',
             AVAILABILITY_MODE = SYNCHRONOUS_COMMIT,
             FAILOVER_MODE = EXTERNAL,
             SEEDING_MODE = AUTOMATIC
             ),
        N'server2'
         WITH (
             ENDPOINT_URL = N'tcp://server2:5022',
             AVAILABILITY_MODE = SYNCHRONOUS_COMMIT,
             FAILOVER_MODE = EXTERNAL,
             SEEDING_MODE = AUTOMATIC
             ),
        N'server3'
         WITH(
             ENDPOINT_URL = N'tcp://server3:5022',
             AVAILABILITY_MODE = SYNCHRONOUS_COMMIT,
             FAILOVER_MODE = EXTERNAL,
             SEEDING_MODE = AUTOMATIC
             );
GO

ALTER AVAILABILITY GROUP [LinuxAG1] GRANT CREATE ANY DATABASE;
GO
```

To join the secondary replicas to your freshly minted availability group, run the following T-SQL on each secondary:

```
ALTER AVAILABILITY GROUP [LinuxAG1] JOIN WITH (CLUSTER_TYPE = EXTERNAL);

ALTER AVAILABILITY GROUP [LinuxAG1] GRANT CREATE ANY DATABASE;
```

Adding a database

This is where things are closer to how Windows works (except, of course, that we haven't set up the cluster yet).

On the primary replica, ensure that the database you want to add to the availability group is in the Full Recovery Model and take a full backup of it.

When the backup is complete, you can add the database to the availability group by using the following T-SQL command:

```
ALTER AVAILABILITY GROUP [LinuxAG1] ADD DATABASE [<dbname>];
```

To check whether the database has been created on the secondary replicas, you can run the statements that follow. Note that the second statement is checking the synchronization status.

```
SELECT * FROM sys.databases WHERE name = '<dbname>';
GO
SELECT
    DB_NAME(database_id) AS 'database',
    synchronization_state_desc
FROM sys.dm_hadr_database_replica_states;
```

Congratulations! You have created an availability group on Linux. The next step is to create the cluster so that your availability group is highly available.

Setting up the cluster

Each node in the cluster must have an appropriate subscription for the HA components in RHEL.

> ➤ **To read more about subscriptions, visit** *http://www.opensourcerers.org/ pacemaker-the-open-source-high-availability-cluster/.*

After you have registered each replica and configured the subscription, you can configure Pacemaker.

Configure the cluster resource manager (Pacemaker)

Pacemaker requires the following ports to be opened on the firewall (you can use the same method as we just described):

- **TCP.** 2224, 3121, and 21064

- **UDP.** 5405

On each node, install Pacemaker from the command line:

```
sudo yum install pacemaker pcs fence-agents-all resource-agents
```

Pacemaker creates a user name called `hacluster` by default, which requires a proper password. Make sure it is the same one for all nodes:

```
sudo passwd hacluster
```

The `pcsd` service is required to allow nodes to rejoin the cluster after a restart. You should run this on all nodes for the cluster:

```
sudo systemctl enable pcsd
sudo systemctl start pcsd
sudo systemctl enable pacemaker
```

Create the cluster

The commands that follow create the cluster. Note that the nodes must have the correct names, and you must use the `hacluster` password you set previously. This is where you get to choose the cluster name (which is not the same as your availability group name, but it can be):

```
sudo pcs cluster auth server1 server2 server3 -u hacluster -p <password>

sudo pcs cluster setup --name <clusterName> server1 server2 server3

sudo pcs cluster start --all
```

And you thought you were done! Run the following command to install the SQL Server resource agent:

```
sudo yum install mssql-server-ha
```

Now that you've installed Pacemaker, you will use the `pcs` command-line tool to manage it. You can run all commands from a single node.

Configuring node-level fencing with STONITH

Organizational requirements will dictate how you configure node fencing in your environment.

> ➤ **For more information about how to set up node fencing, refer to the Red Hat documentation at** *https://docs.microsoft.com/sql/linux/ sql-server-linux-availability-group-cluster-rhel#configure-fencing-stonith*.

Restarting nodes after failure

What you don't want is a node that never restarts after a failure. Turning off this feature relies on a more sensible failure count and associated threshold, which you can do by using the following command on each server:

```
sudo pcs property set start-failure-is-fatal=false
```

Now if a failover occurs, the restarted instance will be demoted to a secondary and automatically rejoins it to the availability group.

Create the Pacemaker login in SQL Server

Now you need to create a SQL Server login for Pacemaker on each server so that it can manage the business of the availability group in the event of a failover. Here's how to do this:

```
USE [master];
GO

CREATE LOGIN [pacemakerLogin] with PASSWORD = N'UseAReallyStrongMasterKeyPassword';
GO
```

```
ALTER SERVER ROLE [sysadmin] ADD MEMBER [pacemakerLogin];

GRANT ALTER, CONTROL, VIEW DEFINITION
ON AVAILABILITY GROUP::LinuxAG1 TO pacemakerLogin;

GRANT VIEW SERVER STATE TO pacemakerLogin;
```

Now, save the credentials on the file system for safety, again on all servers:

```
echo 'pacemakerLogin' >> ~/pacemaker-passwd

echo 'UseAReallyStrongMasterKeyPassword' >> ~/pacemaker-passwd

sudo mv ~/pacemaker-passwd /var/opt/mssql/secrets/passwd

sudo chown root:root /var/opt/mssql/secrets/passwd

sudo chmod 400 /var/opt/mssql/secrets/passwd
```

These passwords will be accessible only by root. You can see the ownership change (**chown**) and access permission (**chmod**) commands in the preceding example.

Creating an availability group resource and virtual IP resource

The following command (which again spans two lines) creates a primary/replica type *availability group resource* (the "master" terminology is unfortunate; it doesn't refer to the master database):

```
sudo pcs resource create ag_cluster ocf:mssql:ag ag_name=LinuxAG1 \
--master meta notify=true
```

In the case of our example with three synchronous replicas, the Pacemaker agent sets REQUIRED_SYNCHRONIZED_SECONDARIES_TO_COMMIT to 1.

> ➤ **You can read more about data protection for availability group configurations specific to SQL Server on Linux at *https://docs.microsoft.com/sql/linux/ sql-server-linux-availability-group-ha*.**

To create the *virtual IP resource*, run the following command on one of the nodes (use a valid IP address here):

```
sudo pcs resource create virtualip ocf:heartbeat:IPaddr2 ip=172.8.0.120
```

Remember that there is no virtual server name equivalent, so ensure that you have DNS configured with the virtual IP resource and virtual server name. Remember to do this in your DR environment, as well.

CHAPTER 12

Create colocation constraint and ordering constraint

As discussed in Chapter 2, WSFC uses votes to decide on how to manage resources in the cluster.

Pacemaker uses a scoring system, which is calculated per resource. You can manipulate the scoring system by using *constraints*.

To make sure that the virtual IP resource runs on the same host as the primary replica, for instance, you can create a constraint with a score of INFINITY. Anything lower than INFINITY is simply taken as a recommendation.

To create a *colocation constraint* to have the virtual IP and primary replica on the same host, run the following command on one node (note that it again spans two lines):

```
sudo pcs constraint colocation add virtualip ag_cluster-master \
INFINITY with-rsc-role=Master
```

A colocation constraint is implicitly ordered. In the previous example, if a failover occurs, the virtual IP will point to a secondary node before the first node is demoted to secondary, and the second node it is promoted to the primary replica.

To resolve this, you can create an *ordering constraint*, which will wait for the promotion before pointing the virtual IP resource to the new node; here's how to do it:

```
sudo pcs constraint order promote ag_cluster-master then start virtualip
```

Administering availability groups

Although the availability groups dashboards provide a base amount of information about overall availability group health, they do not provide much in the way of monitoring the performance, current latency, or throughput of the availability groups cluster.

In this section, we review the insights to be had in monitoring availability groups in three main categories: DMVs, wait types, and extended events. In all three categories, *most* of the data to be had will be on the primary replicas.

> ➤ For more scripts to automate the management of availability groups, including failover, see Chapter 14.

Analyzing DMVs for availability groups

In this section, we review a few scenarios for which using DMVs to retrieve availability group information is useful. You either won't see data or will see incomplete data when viewing HADR DMVs on secondary replicas.

Monitoring availability group health and status

You can view dashboards for individual availability groups within SQL Server Management Studio or by using the script that follows, which uses three different DMVs. Both methods provide a complete snapshot of data only when run on a SQL Server instance that serves as the primary replica for an availability group, but the script will show information for all replicas, for all availability groups in which the instance is the primary replica. This sample is a good foundation script for monitoring.

```
--Monitor Availability Group Health

--On a secondary replica, this query returns a row for every secondary database on the
server instance.

--On the primary replica, this query returns a row for each primary database and an
additional row for the corresponding secondary database. Recommended.

IF NOT EXISTS (
SELECT @@SERVERNAME
    FROM sys.dm_hadr_availability_replica_states  rs
    WHERE rs.is_local = 1
    and rs.role_desc = 'PRIMARY'
)
    SELECT 'Recommend: Run script on Primary, incomplete data on Secondary.';
SELECT
  AG = ag.name
, Instance = ar.replica_server_name + ' ' +
    CASE WHEN is_local = 1 THEN '(local)' ELSE '' END
, DB = db_name(dm.database_id)
, Replica_Role  = CASE
WHEN last_received_time IS NULL THEN 'PRIMARY (Connections: '+ar.primary_role_allow_
connections_desc+')'
ELSE 'SECONDARY (Connections: '+ar.secondary_role_allow_connections_desc+')' END
, dm.synchronization_state_desc
, dm.synchronization_health_desc
, ar.availability_mode_desc
, ar.failover_mode_desc
, Suspended = CASE is_suspended WHEN 1 THEN suspend_reason_desc ELSE 'NO' END
, last_received_time
, last_commit_time
, Redo_queue_size_MB = redo_queue_size/1024.
, dm.secondary_lag_seconds
, ar.backup_priority
, ar.endpoint_url
, ar.read_only_routing_url
FROM sys.dm_hadr_database_replica_states dm
INNER JOIN sys.availability_replicas ar on dm.replica_id = ar.replica_id and dm.group_id
= ar.group_id
INNER JOIN sys.availability_groups ag on ag.group_id = dm.group_id
ORDER BY AG, Instance, DB, Replica_Role;
```

➤ For more information on the data returned in this DMV, read on
to the next code sample and reference *https://docs.microsoft.com/
sql/relational-databases/system-dynamic-management-views/
sys-dm-hadr-database-replica-cluster-states-transact-sql.*

Monitoring for suspect pages and database automatic page repair events

Availability groups, and the database mirroring feature that came before them, used the replicas to automatically repair any corrupted, unreadable data pages on one replica with data
from a replica with a readable copy of the data page. This is different from the behavior of DBCC
CHECKDB and REPAIR_ALLOW_DATA_LOSS, which could result in lost data when repairing
pages.

The automatic page repair is a background process that occurs after the operation that discovered the corrupted page data. Transactions will still fail with an error code 823, 824, or 829.

You should monitor the system table `msdb.dbo.suspect_pages` and the DMV
`sys.dm_hadr_auto_page_repair`, which will contain entries of these events; for example:

```
--Check for suspect pages (hopefully 0 rows returned)
SELECT * FROM msdb.dbo.suspect_pages WHERE (event_type <= 3);
--Check for autorepair events (hopefully 0 rows returned)
SELECT db = db_name(database_id), * FROM sys.dm_hadr_auto_page_repair;
```

Monitoring live availability group performance

Typically, the gap between the primary and an asynchronous replica is mere seconds. You can
measure the backlog of transactions waiting to be committed to an asynchronous replica using
the `sys.dm_hadr_database_replica_states` DMV, which provides a wealth of information of interest to tracking how far behind a secondary replica is:

- **log_send_queue_size.**   Expressed in kilobytes, this is the amount of log data not yet
sent to the secondary replicas.

- **log_send_rate.**   Expressed in kilobytes per second, this is the average of data sent to
secondary replicas. Values only present for primary replicas.

- **redo_queue_size.**   Expressed in kilobytes, this is the amount of log data not yet committed on of the secondary replica. This data must be committed before the secondary
replica can become primary in a failover, a part of RTO.

- **redo_rate.**   Expressed in kilobytes per second, this is the average amount of data committed on of the secondary replica.

- **secondary_lag_seconds.**   Expressed in seconds, this is a more accurate amount of time
the secondary replica is "behind." Does not express how long it would take the secondary
replica to "catch up."

Dividing `log_send_queue_size` (KB) by `log_send_rate` (KB/s) provides a rough estimate for the amount of time it will take to send all data from the primary to secondary replicas. Similarly, dividing `redo_queue_size` (KB) by `redo_rate` (KB/s) provides an estimate for the number of seconds it will take a secondary replica to "catch up" to the primary.

Let's combine what we've learned about the DMVs `sys.dm_hadr_database_replica_states` and `sys.dm_os_performance_counters` to create a script, which you can see in the code sample that follows, which returns a significant amount of availability groups performance data. As usual, you should run this on the primary replica of an availability group.

```
--Monitor Availability Groups performance
--On a secondary replica, this query returns a row for every secondary database
--    on the server instance.
--On the primary replica, this query returns a row for each primary database
--    and an additional row for the corresponding secondary database. Recommended.

IF NOT EXISTS (
SELECT @@SERVERNAME
   FROM sys.dm_hadr_availability_replica_states
   WHERE is_local = 1
   and role_desc = 'PRIMARY'
)
  SELECT 'Recommend: Run This Script on Primary Replica';
DECLARE @BytesFlushed_Start_ms bigint, @BytesFlushed_Start bigint,
@BytesFlushed_End_ms bigint, @BytesFlushed_End bigint;
--Compare counter samples
DECLARE @TransactionDelay TABLE
(    DB sysname not null
,    TransactionDelay_Start_ms decimal(19,2) null
,    TransactionDelay_end_ms decimal(19,2) null
,    TransactionDelay_Start decimal(19,2) null
,    TransactionDelay_end decimal(19,2) null
,    MirroredWriteTranspersec_Start_ms decimal(19,2) null
,    MirroredWriteTranspersec_end_ms decimal(19,2) null
,    MirroredWriteTranspersec_Start decimal(19,2) null
,    MirroredWriteTranspersec_end decimal(19,2) null
,    UNIQUE CLUSTERED (DB)
);
INSERT INTO @TransactionDelay (DB, TransactionDelay_Start_ms, TransactionDelay_Start)
SELECT DB = pc.instance_name
,    TransactionDelay_Start_ms = MAX(ms_ticks)
,    TransactionDelay_Start = MAX(convert(decimal(19,2), pc.cntr_value))
FROM sys.dm_os_sys_info as si
CROSS APPLY sys.dm_os_performance_counters as pc
 WHERE object_name like '%database replica%'
 AND counter_name = 'transaction delay' --cumulative transaction delay in ms
 GROUP BY pc.instance_name;
UPDATE t
SET MirroredWriteTranspersec_Start_ms = t2.MirroredWriteTranspersec_Start_ms
,    MirroredWriteTranspersec_Start = t2.MirroredWriteTranspersec_Start
FROM @TransactionDelay t
```

```
INNER JOIN
(SELECT DB = pc.instance_name
,     MirroredWriteTranspersec_Start_ms = MAX(ms_ticks)
,     MirroredWriteTranspersec_Start = MAX(convert(decimal(19,2), pc.cntr_value))
FROM sys.dm_os_sys_info as si
CROSS APPLY sys.dm_os_performance_counters as pc
 WHERE object_name like '%database replica%'
 AND counter_name = 'mirrored write transactions/sec'
--actually a cumulative transactions count, not per sec
 GROUP BY pc.instance_name
 ) t2 on t.DB = t2.DB;
SELECT @BytesFlushed_Start_ms = MAX(ms_ticks), @BytesFlushed_Start = MAX(cntr_value)
FROM sys.dm_os_sys_info
CROSS APPLY sys.dm_os_performance_counters where counter_name like 'Log Bytes Flushed/
sec%';
WAITFOR DELAY '00:00:05'; --Adjust sample duration between measurements

UPDATE t
SET TransactionDelay_end_ms = t2.TransactionDelay_end_ms
,     TransactionDelay_end = t2.TransactionDelay_end
FROM @TransactionDelay t
INNER JOIN
(SELECT DB = pc.instance_name
,     TransactionDelay_end_ms = MAX(ms_ticks)
,     TransactionDelay_end = MAX(convert(decimal(19,2), pc.cntr_value))
FROM sys.dm_os_sys_info as si
CROSS APPLY sys.dm_os_performance_counters as pc
 WHERE object_name like '%database replica%'
 AND counter_name = 'transaction delay' --cumulative transaction delay in ms
 GROUP BY pc.instance_name
 ) t2 on t.DB = t2.DB;
UPDATE t
SET MirroredWriteTranspersec_end_ms = t2.MirroredWriteTranspersec_end_ms
,     MirroredWriteTranspersec_end = t2.MirroredWriteTranspersec_end
FROM @TransactionDelay t
inner join
(SELECT DB = pc.instance_name
,     MirroredWriteTranspersec_end_ms = MAX(ms_ticks)
,     MirroredWriteTranspersec_end = MAX(convert(decimal(19,2), pc.cntr_value))
FROM sys.dm_os_sys_info as si
CROSS APPLY sys.dm_os_performance_counters as pc
 WHERE object_name like '%database replica%'
 AND counter_name = 'mirrored write transactions/sec'
--actually a cumulative transactions count, not per sec
 GROUP BY pc.instance_name
 ) t2 on t.DB = t2.DB;
SELECT @BytesFlushed_End_ms =  MAX(ms_ticks), @BytesFlushed_End = MAX(cntr_value)
FROM sys.dm_os_sys_info
CROSS APPLY sys.dm_os_performance_counters where counter_name like 'Log Bytes Flushed/
sec%';
DECLARE @LogBytesFushed decimal(19,2)
SET @LogBytesFushed = (@BytesFlushed_End - @BytesFlushed_Start) /
```

```
NULLIF(@BytesFlushed_End_ms - @BytesFlushed_Start_ms,0);
--Current replica metrics
SELECT
    AG = ag.name
,   Instance = ar.replica_server_name + ' ' + case when is_local = 1
    then '(local)' else '' end
,   DB = db_name(dm.database_id)
,   Replica_Role = CASE WHEN last_received_time IS NULL THEN 'PRIMARY
    (Connections: '+ar.primary_role_allow_connections_desc+')' ELSE 'SECONDARY
    (Connections: '+ar.secondary_role_allow_connections_desc+')' END
,   Last_received_time
,   Last_commit_time
,   Redo_queue_size_MB = convert(decimal(19,2),dm.redo_queue_size/1024.)--KB
,   Redo_rate_MB_per_s = convert(decimal(19,2),dm.redo_rate/1024.) --KB/s
,   Redo_Time_Left_s_RTO =
convert(decimal(19,2),dm.redo_queue_size*1./NULLIF(dm.redo_rate*1.,0))
--only part of RTO. NULL value on secondary replica indicates no sampled activity.
,   Log_Send_Queue_RPO =
convert(decimal(19,2),dm.log_send_queue_size*1./NULLIF(@LogBytesFushed ,0))
--Rate. NULL value on secondary replica indicates no sampled activity.
,   Sampled_Transactions_count = (td.MirroredWriteTranspersec_end -
td.MirroredWriteTranspersec_start)
,   Sampled_Transaction_Delay_ms = (td.TransactionDelay_end -
td.TransactionDelay_start)
--Transaction Delay numbers will be 0 if there is no synchronous replica for the DB
,   Avg_Sampled_Transaction_Delay_ms_per_s = convert(decimal(19,2),
(td.TransactionDelay_end - td.TransactionDelay_Start) / ((td.TransactionDelay_end_ms
- td.TransactionDelay_Start_ms)/1000.))
,   Transactions_per_s = convert(decimal(19,2), ((td.MirroredWriteTranspersec_end -
td.MirroredWriteTranspersec_start) / ((td.MirroredWriteTranspersec_End_ms -
td.MirroredWriteTranspersec_Start_ms)/1000.)))
,   dm.secondary_lag_seconds
,   dm.synchronization_state_desc
,   dm.synchronization_health_desc
,   ar.availability_mode_desc
,   ar.failover_mode_desc
,   Suspended = case is_suspended when 1 then suspend_reason_desc else 'NO' end
,   ar.backup_priority --Backup preference priorities for reference
,   ar.modify_date --Replica modified date
,   ar.endpoint_url --EndPoint URL for reference
,   ar.read_only_routing_url --Routing URL for reference
FROM sys.dm_hadr_database_replica_states dm
INNER JOIN sys.availability_replicas ar on dm.replica_id = ar.replica_id and
dm.group_id = ar.group_id
INNER JOIN @TransactionDelay td on td.DB = db_name(dm.database_id)
INNER JOIN sys.availability_groups ag on ag.group_id = dm.group_id
ORDER BY
    AG,
    Instance,
    DB,
    Replica_Role;
GO
```

Analyzing wait types for availability groups

As with all wait types, you should baseline these wait types and take action on increases in this wait type, whether they be sudden or gradual. In this section, we look at some wait types to take note of when administering availability groups.

> ➤ **For more information on wait statistics, such as how to monitor and trend them, see Chapter 13.**

There are 60-plus wait types in SQL Server that are prefixed with HADR_*. Many are background tasks that are expected or will rise when the SQL Server is idle. The following wait types are those of which you should be wary, and when:

- The HADR_SYNC_COMMIT wait type is the transaction delay present when using synchronous mode secondary replicas. It is associated with the wait that primary replicas experience when sending log data to synchronous replicas, and then waiting on the acknowledgement of the synchronous replicas. An increase of HADR_SYNC_COMMIT on the primary replica will be due to performance constraints on the secondary replica. This wait type, and many others, will not be present when running only with asynchronous secondary replicas. This wait type does not include the time spent on the secondary replicas processing the redo log data. The secondary replica might be experiencing WRITELOG.

- The WRITELOG wait type is likely to appear on any SQL Server instance, including availability group primary and secondary replicas, when there is heavy write activity. The WRITELOG wait is time spent flushing the local SQL Server instance log to the drive and is due to physical I/O subsystem performance. The WRITELOG wait occurs on the local instance and would not be affected by secondary replicas.

- A sudden spike in the HADR_SYNCHRONIZING_THROTTLE wait type would indicate that synchronous secondary replicas are trying to get caught up and indicates that transactions are waiting on secondary replicas to commit. You should expect to see this wait when synchronous replicas are still in the SYNCRONIZING state.

- The ASYNC_NETWORK_IO wait is not usually associated with network transport for availability groups; rather, it is with communication via the network stack to remote clients or storage systems. Misconfigured or malfunctioning network cards could explain a sudden spike in this wait, but more than likely is caused by excessive data sent to remote clients, especially long-running report applications.

- The HADR_WORK_QUEUE and WAIT_XTP_OFFLINE_CKPT_NEW_LOG wait types are an indication of worker threads waiting; you do not need to worry about them. The HADR_TIMER_TASK and HADR_CLUSAPI_CALL wait types are also not indicative of a problem, and thus you can ignore them. If it is among the top waits, it generally indicates a lack of activity, not performance problems. The HADR_GROUP_COMMIT wait indicates that log records are waiting for a sufficient quantity to be grouped together, and is also not indicative of any performance issue.

Analyzing extended events for availability groups

SQL Server includes an extended event session called AlwaysOn_health. By default, this session collects Data Definition Language (DDL) events, failover and state changes, and more than 30 SQL Server errors by number. You can view the details of what the session collected by scripting it.

The AlwaysOn_health session is actually used by the dashboard, but it can also be queried in aggregate, and by default keeps up to four 5-MB rolling .xel files in the *Instancepath*\MSSQL\ Log folder.

Look for the log_flush_complete event duration in your extended events sessions; it includes the duration (in milliseconds) which will indicate the amount of time it took for I/O to complete the log flush on any replica.

The ucs_connection_send_msg event signals the communication between replicas. This occurs after the hardening of the block of transaction log data on the secondary replica, and in the case of synchronous replication, occurs before the hardening of the block on the primary replica.

The hadr_log_block_group_commit and hadr_db_commit_mgr_harden events on the primary node are the start and end of the log block replication. The hadr_db_commit_mgr_ harden event follows the acknowledgement from any synchronous secondary replicas and the hardening of the primary transaction log.

You might consider creating an extended events session to watch the timing of synchronization events on your primary and secondary instances. Following is a script to get your started:

> ➤ **For more information on extended events, see Chapter 13.**

> ➤ **For more information on the syntax configuring alerts that follow, see Chapter 14.**

```
--Create extended events session to monitor Availability Group synchronization

--Recommended for diagnostic purposes only

--For monitoring events on Primary Replica

CREATE EVENT SESSION [AG_Synchronization_Events_Primary] ON SERVER
ADD EVENT sqlserver.hadr_log_block_group_commit,
ADD EVENT sqlserver.log_flush_start,
ADD EVENT sqlserver.hadr_log_block_send_complete,
```

CHAPTER 12

```
ADD EVENT sqlserver.log_flush_complete,
ADD EVENT ucs.ucs_connection_send_msg,
ADD EVENT sqlserver.hadr_receive_harden_lsn_message,
ADD EVENT sqlserver.hadr_db_commit_mgr_harden
ADD TARGET package0.event_file
    (SET filename=N'Synchronization_Events_Primary.xel',
    max_file_size=(5),max_rollover_files=(2))
WITH (STARTUP_STATE=ON);
GO

--Recommended for diagnostic purposes only

--For monitoring events on a Secondary Replica

CREATE EVENT SESSION [AG_Synchronization_Events_Secondary] ON SERVER
ADD EVENT sqlserver.hadr_transport_receive_log_block_message,
ADD EVENT sqlserver.log_flush_start,
ADD EVENT sqlserver.log_flush_complete,
ADD EVENT sqlserver.hadr_send_harden_lsn_message,
ADD EVENT ucs.ucs_connection_send_msg
ADD TARGET package0.event_file
    (SET filename=N'Synchronization_Events_Secondary.xel',
    max_file_size=(5),max_rollover_files=(2))
WITH (STARTUP_STATE=ON);
GO
ALTER EVENT SESSION [AG_Synchronization_Events_Secondary] ON SERVER STATE=START
ALTER EVENT SESSION [AG_Synchronization_Events_Primary] ON SERVER STATE=START
```

Alerting for availability groups

Consider placing alerts for a list of errors that are specific to availability groups, which should trigger nontrivial, actionable emails to be sent to your SQL DBA team. If you are not already using SQL Server Agent Alerts for error events to send emails to your SQL DBA team via Database Mail, see Chapter 14. If you are using an external error log monitoring application, be sure to trigger high priority alarms for the following error messages, each of which is significant:

- **35264.** Database movement for a database has been suspended.

- **35265.** Database movement for a database has resumed; informational only.

- **35273, 35274.** Indicate database failure during recovery at failover.

- **35276.** Synchronization of database has stopped and cannot be resumed.

- **41418.** A secondary replica has become disconnected from the primary and will need to be reconnected.

Managing and monitoring SQL Server

Chapter 11 discusses the importance and logistics of database backups, but what else do you need to do on a regular basis to maintain a healthy SQL Server? In this chapter, we lay the foundation for the what and why of Microsoft SQL Server management, including key dynamic management views (DMVs) along the way, and how to set up extended events (the replacement for traces). We review what to look for in the Windows Performance Monitor for SQL Server instances and Database Transaction Unit (DTU) metrics for databases in Microsoft Azure SQL Database. Finally, we review the major changes to the SQL Server servicing model. For example, there are no more service packs: it's cumulative updates from here out.

Detecting database corruption

Aside from database backups, the second most important factor concerning database page integrity is the proper configuration to prevent, and the monitoring to mitigate, database corruption. This isn't a complicated topic and mostly revolves around one setting and one command.

Setting the database's page verify option

For all databases, this setting should be CHECKSUM. The legacy TORN_PAGE option is a sign that this database has been moved over the years, up from a pre–SQL 2005 version, but this setting has never changed. Since SQL 2005, CHECKSUM has the superior and default setting, but it requires an Administrator to manually change after a database is restored up.

If you still have databases with a page verify option that is not CHECKSUM, you should change this setting immediately.

➤ **For more information on database files and filegroups, see Chapter 3.**

NOTE

Changing the page verify option to CHECKSUM **is a quick, unnoticeable change to databases that have no data corruption. However, it is possible that changing a data-base from** NONE **or** TORN_PAGE **to** CHECKSUM **could result in the discovery of database corruption. This could result in databases immediately becoming inaccessible and in the** SUSPECT **state. It is paramount that good backups are taken regularly, and before making the change to** CHECKSUM. **If a database becomes** SUSPECT **after changing the page verify option to** CHECKSUM, **you should restore a copy of the database prior to the change and attempt immediate detection and recovery of the lost data.**

Using DBCC CHECKDB

You should periodically run CHECKDB on all databases. This is a time-consuming but crucial process. You should run DBCC CHECKDB at least as often as your backup retention plan, and consider DBCC CHECKDB nearly as important as regular database backups. It's worth noting that the only reliable solution to database corruption is restoring from a known good backup.

For example, if you keep local backups around for one month, you should ensure that you per-form a successful DBCC CHECKDB no less than once per month. More often as possible is rec-ommended, of course. This ensures that you will at least have a recovery point for uncorrupted, unchanged data, and a starting point for corrupted data fixes. On large databases, DBCC CHECKDB could take hours and block other user queries.

The DBCC CHECKDB command actually covers other more-granular database integrity check tasks, including DBCC CHECKALLOC, DBCC CHECKTABLE, or DBCC CHECKCATALOG, all of which are important, and in only rare cases need to be run separately or to split up the workload.

Running DBCC CHECKDB, with no other parameters or syntax, performs a database integrity test on the current database context. Without specifying a database, however, no other addi-tional options can be provided. There are a number of parameters for CHECKDB detailed at *https://docs.microsoft.com/sql/t-sql/database-console-commands/dbcc-checkdb-transact-sql*.

Here are some parameters worth noting:

- **NOINDEX.**   This can reduce the duration of the integrity check by ignoring nonclustered rowstore and Columnstore indexes.

  Example usage:

  ```
  DBCC CHECKDB (databasename, NOINDEX);
  ```

- **NO_INFOMSGS.**   This suppresses informational status messages and returns only errors.

  Example usage:

  ```
  DBCC CHECKDB (databasename) WITH NO_INFOMSGS;
  ```

- **REPAIR_REBUILD.**   You should run this only as a last resort because although it might have some success, it is unlikely to result in a complete repair. It can also be very time consuming, involving the rebuilding of indexes based on attempted repair data. We suggest that you review the DBCC CHECKDB documentation for a number of caveats.

  Example usage:

  ```
  DBCC CHECKDB (databasename) WITH REPAIR_REBUILD;
  ```

- **REPAIR_ALLOW_DATA_LOSS.**   You should run this only as a last resort to achieve a partial database recovery because it could force a database to resolve errors by simply deallocating pages, potentially creating gaps in rows or columns. You must run this in SINGLE_USER mode, and you should run it in EMERGENCY mode. Review the DBCC CHECKDB documentation for a number of caveats. A complete review of how EMERGENCY mode and REPAIR_ALLOW_DATA_LOSS is detailed in this blog post by Paul Randal: *https://www.sqlskills.com/blogs/paul/ checkdb-from-every-angle-emergency-mode-repair-the-very-very-last-resort/.*

  Example usage: (last resort only, not recommended!)

  ```
  ALTER DATABASE WorldWideImporters SET EMERGENCY, SINGLE_USER;
  DBCC CHECKDB('WideWorldImporters', REPAIR_ALLOW_DATA_LOSS);
  ALTER DATABASE WorldWideImporters SET MULTI_USER;
  ```

- **ESTIMATEONLY.**   This does not provide an estimate of the duration of a CHECKDB (without other parameters), only an amount of space required in TempDB.

  Example usage:

  ```
  DBCC CHECKDB (databasename) WITH ESTIMATEONLY;
  ```

These scripts are all available in the accompanying downloads for this book at *https://aka.ms/SQLServ2017Admin/downloads.*

➤ For more information on automating DBCC CHECKDB, see Chapter 14.

Repairing database data file corruption

Of course, the only real remedy to data corruption after it has happened is by restoring from a backup. The well-documented DBCC CHECKDB REPAIR_ALLOW_DATA_LOSS should be a last resort.

It is possible to repair missing pages in clustered indexes by piecing together missing columns in nonclustered indexes. In reality, this is an academic solution because data corruption rarely happens in such a tidy and convenient way.

Always On availability groups also provide a built-in data corruption detection and automatic repair capability by using uncorrupted data on one replica to replace inaccessible data on another.

➤ **For more information on this feature of availability groups, see Chapter 12.**

Recovering the database transaction log file corruption

In addition to the previous guidance on the importance of backups, you can reconstitute a corrupted or lost database transaction log file (though not recovered) by using the example that follows. A lost transaction log file will likely result in the loss of some recent rows, but in the event of a disaster recovery involving the loss of the .ldf file but an intact .mdf file, this could be a valuable step.

It is possible to rebuild a blank transaction log file in a new file location for a database by using the following command:

```
ALTER DATABASE WorldWideImporters SET EMERGENCY, SINGLE_USER;

ALTER DATABASE WorldWideImporters REBUILD LOG

ON (NAME=WWI_Log, FILENAME='F:\DATA\WideWorldImporters_new.ldf');

ALTER DATABASE WorldWideImporters SET MULTI_USER;
```

These scripts are all available in the accompanying downloads for this book, which are available at *https://aka.ms/SQLServ2017Admin/downloads*.

> ## NOTE
> Rebuilding a blank transaction log file using ALTER DATABASE ... REBUILD LOG is not supported for databases containing a MEMORY_OPTIMIZED_DATA filegroup.

Database corruption in databases in Azure SQL Database

Microsoft takes data integrity in its platform-as-a-service (PaaS) database offering very seriously and provides strong assurances of assistance and recovery for its product. Albeit rare, Azure engineering teams respond 24x7 globally to data corruption reports. The Azure SQL Database engineering team details its response promises at *https://azure.microsoft.com/blog/data-integrity-in-azure-sql-database/*.

Maintaining indexes and statistics

Maintaining index fragmentation is about proper organization of rowstore data within the file that SQL Server maintains, minimizing the number of pages that must be read when queries read or write those data pages. Reducing fragmentation in database objects is vastly different from reducing fragmentation at the drive level and has little in common with the Disk Defragmenter application of Windows. Although this doesn't translate to page locations on magnetic disks (and on Storage-Area Networks, this has even less relevance), it does translate to the activity of I/O systems when retrieving data.

The causes of index fragmentation are, to be put plainly, writes. Our data would stay nice and tidy if applications would stop writing to it! There will inevitably be a significant effect that updates and deletes have on clustered and nonclustered index fragmentation, plus the effect that inserts could have on fragmentation because of clustered index design.

> ### NOTE
> A heap, or a table without a clustered index, doesn't suffer from fragmentation (how can pages be out of order?); rather, it suffers from wasted space within the heap structure. This is due to the use of Forwarding Pointers, a straightforward mechanism for keeping data associated but is realistically far worse for performance than fragmentation. Deletes and updates leave wasted space in a heap that cannot be reclaimed even with an Index Rebuild operation. To reclaim wasted space within a heap, you must, ironically, create a clustered index on the table, and then drop the clustered index.

The information in this section is largely unchanged and applies to SQL Server instances, databases in Azure SQL Database, and even Azure SQL Data Warehouse. (All tables in Azure SQL Data Warehouse have a Columnstore clustered index by default.)

Changing the Fill Factor property when beneficial

Each rowstore index on disk-based objects has a numeric property called Fill Factor that specifies the percentage of space to be filled with rowstore data in each leaf-level data page of the index when it is created or rebuilt. The instance-wide default Fill Factor is 0%, which is the same as 100%; that is each leaf-level data page will be completely filled. A Fill Factor of 80 means that 20% of leaf-level data pages will be intentionally left empty. We can adjust this Fill Factor percentage for each index to manage the efficiency of data pages.

A low Fill Factor will help reduce the number page splits, which occur when the Database Engine attempts to add a new row of data or update an existing row with more data to a page that is already full. In this case, the Database Engine will clear out space for the new row by moving a proportion of the old rows to a new page. This can be a time- and resource-consuming operation, with many page splits possible during writes, and will lead to index fragmentation.

However, setting a low Fill Factor will greatly increase the number of pages needed to store the same data and increase the number of reads during query operations. For example, a Fill Factor of 50 will roughly double the space on the drive that it initially takes to store and therefore access the data, when compared to a Fill Factor of 0 or 100.

In most instances, data is read far more often that it is written and inserted, updated, and deleted upon occasion. Indexes will therefore benefit from a high Fill Factor, almost always more than 80, because it is more important to keep the number of reads to a manageable level than minimizing the resources needed to perform a page split. You can deal with the index fragmentation by using the REBUILD or REORGANIZE commands, as discussed in the next section.

If the key value for an index is constantly increasing, such as an autoincrementing IDENTITY column as the first key of a clustered index, the data would always be added to the end of a data page and any gaps would not need to be filled. In the case of a table for which data is always inserted sequentially and never updated, setting a Fill Factor other than the default of 0/100 will have no benefits. (It is still possible.) Even after fine tuning a Fill Factor, you might not find that the benefit of reducing page splits has any noticeable benefit to write performance.

You can set a Fill Factor when an index is first created, or you can change it by using the ALTER INDEX ... REBUILD syntax, as discussed in the next section.

Tracking page splits

If you are intent on fine-tuning the Fill Factor for important tables to maximize the performance/storage space ratio, you can measure page splits in two ways.

You can use the performance counter DMV to measure page splits in aggregate on Windows server, as shown here:

```
SELECT * FROM sys.dm_os_performance_counters WHERE counter_name ='Page Splits/sec'
```

The cntr_value will increment whenever a page split is detected. This is a bit misleading because to calculate the page splits per second, you must sample the incrementing value twice, and divide by the time difference between the samples. When viewing this metric in Performance Monitor, the math is done for you.

Using extended events session to identify page_split events.

You can track `page_split` events alongside statement execution by adding the `page_split` event to sessions such as the Transact-SQL (T-SQL) template in the extended events wizard.

We review extended events and the `sys.dm_os_performance_counters` DMV later in this chapter, including a sample session script to track `page_split` events.

Monitoring index fragmentation

You can find the extent to which an index is fragmented by interrogating the `sys.dm_db_index_physical_stats` dynamic management function (DMF). Be aware that unlike most DMVs, this function can have a significant impact on server performance because it can tax I/O.

To query this DMF, you must be a member of the sysadmin server role, or the db_ddladmin and db_owner database roles. Alternatively, you can grant CONTROL permission to the object, then also the VIEW DATABASE STATE and VIEW SERVER STATE permissions. For more information, refer to *https://docs.microsoft.com/sql/relational-databases/system-dynamic-management-views/sys-dm-db-index-physical-stats-transact-sql#permissions*.

Keep this in mind when scripting this operation for automated index maintenance. We discuss more about automating index maintenance in Chapter 14.

For example, to find the fragmentation level of all indexes on the `Sales.Orders` table in the WideWorldImporters sample database, we could use a query such as the following:

```
SELECT
  DB = db_name(s.database_id)
, [schema_name] = sc.name
, [table_name] = o.name
, index_name = i.name
, s.index_type_desc
, s.partition_number -- if the object is partitioned
, avg_fragmentation_pct = s.avg_fragmentation_in_percent
, s.page_count -- pages in object partition
FROM  sys.indexes AS i
CROSS APPLY sys.dm_db_index_physical_stats (DB_ID(),i.object_id,i.index_id, NULL, NULL)
AS s
INNER JOIN sys.objects AS o ON o.object_id = s.object_id
INNER JOIN sys.schemas AS sc ON o.schema_id = sc.schema_id
WHERE i.is_disabled = 0
AND o.object_id = OBJECT_ID('Sales.Orders');
```

The `sys.dm_db_index_physical_stats` DMF accepts five parameters: `database_id`, `object_id`, `index_id`, `partition_id`, and `mode`. The mode parameters default to LIMITED, the fastest method, but you can set it to `Sampled` and `Detailed`. These additional modes are rarely necessary, but they provide more data and more-precise data. Some columns will be NULL in LIMITED mode. For the purposes of determining fragmentation, the default mode of LIMITED (used when the parameter value of NULL is provided) suffices.

The five parameters of the `sys.dm_db_index_physical_stats` DMF are all nullable. For example, if you run

```
SELECT * FROM sys.dm_db_index_physical_stats(NULL,NULL,NULL,NULL,NULL);
```

you will see fragmentation statistics for all databases, all objects, all indexes, and all partitions.

We recommend that you do not do this; again, because this can have a significant impact on server resources resulting in a noticeable drop in performance. The previous sample scripts are all available in the accompanying downloads for this book, which are available at *https://aka.ms/SQLServ2017Admin/downloads*.

Rebuilding indexes

Performing an INDEX REBUILD operation on a rowstore index (clustered or nonclustered) will physically re-create the index b-tree leaf level. The goal of moving the pages is to make storage more efficient and to match the logical order provided by the index key. A rebuild operation is both destructive to the index object and will block other queries attempting to access the pages. Because the rebuild operation destroys and re-creates the index, it must update the index statistics afterward, eliminating the need to perform a subsequent UPDATE STATISTICS operation as part of regular maintenace.

Long-term table locks are held during the rebuild operation. One of the major advantages of SQL Server Enterprise edition remains the ability to specify the ONLINE keyword, which allows for rebuild operations to be significantly less disruptive to other queries (though not completely), making feasible index maintenance on SQL Servers with round-the-clock activity.

You should use ONLINE with index rebuild operations whenever possible, if time allows. An ONLINE index rebuild might take longer than an offline rebuild, however. There are also scenarios for which an ONLINE rebuild is not possible, including deprecated data types `image`, `text` and `ntext`, or the `xml` data type. Since SQL Server 2012, it is possible to perform ONLINE index rebuilds on the MAX lengths of the data types `varchar`, `nvarchar`, and `varbinary`.

For the syntax to rebuild the `FK_Sales_Orders_CustomerID` nonclustered index on the `Sales.Orders` table with the ONLINE functionality in Enterprise edition, see the following code sample:

```
ALTER INDEX FK_Sales_Orders_CustomerID
ON Sales.Orders
REBUILD WITH (ONLINE=ON);
```

It's important to note that if you perform any kind of index maintenance on the clustered index of a rowstore table, it does not affect the nonclustered indexes. Nonclustered indexes fragmentation will not change if you rebuild the clustered index, and must be maintained, as well. However, dropping and re-creating the clustered index will require the nonclustered indexes to be rebuilt twice: once to change the nonclustered indexes to reference a heap, and again to reference the new clustered index.

Instead of rebuilding an individual index, you can instead rebuild all indexes on a particular table by replacing the name of the index with the keyword ALL. This is usually overkill and inefficient, and individual index operations when needed are preferred. For example, to rebuild all indexes on the `Sales.Orders` table, do the following:

```
ALTER INDEX ALL ON Sales.Orders REBUILD;
```

You can also do this in SQL Server Management Studio. To do so, under the `Sales.Order` table, expand the Indexes folder. Right-click the FK_Sales_Orders_CustomerID index, and then, on the shortcut menu that opens, select Rebuild. Note, though, that you cannot specify options such as `ONLINE` in this dialog box. (Note also that the right-click shortcut options to Rebuild or Reorganize are unavailable for indexes on memory-optimized tables.)

> **NOTE**
>
> For memory-optimized tables, we recommend a manual routine maintenance step using the ALTER TABLE ... ALTER INDEX ... REBUILD syntax. This is not to reduce fragmentation in the in-memory data; rather, it is to examine the number of buckets in a memory-optimized table's hash index(es). For more information on rebuilding hash indexes and bucket counts, see Chapter 10.

> **NOTE**
>
> You can change the data compression option for indexes by using the rebuild operation using the DATA_COMPRESSION option. For more detail on Data Compression, see Chapter 3.

Aside from `ONLINE`, there are other options that you might want to consider for `INDEX REBUILD` operations. Let's take a look at them:

- **SORT_IN_TEMPDB.**   Use this when you want to create or rebuild an index using TempDB for sorting the index data, potentially increasing performance by distributing the I/O activity across multiple drives. This also means that these sorting work tables are written to the TempDB database transaction log instead of the user database transaction log, potentially reducing the log impact on the user database and allowing for the user database transaction log to be backed up during the operation.

- **MAXDOP.** You can use this to mitigate some of the impact of index maintenance by preventing the operation from using parallel processors. This can cause the index maintenance operation to run longer, but to have less impact on performance.

- **WAIT_AT_LOW_PRIORITY.** Introduced in SQL Server 2014, this is the first of a set of parameters that you can use to instruct the ONLINE index maintenance operation to try not to block other operations, and how. This feature is known as Managed Lock Priority, and this syntax is not usable outside of online index operations and partition switching operations. Here is the full syntax:

```
ALTER INDEX FK_Sales_Orders_CustomerID ON Sales.Orders
REBUILD WITH (ONLINE=ON (WAIT_AT_LOW_PRIORITY (MAX_DURATION = 0 MINUTES,
ABORT_AFTER_WAIT = SELF)));
```

  The parameters for MAX_DURATION and ABORT_AFTER_WAIT instruct the statement how to proceed if it begins to be blocked by another operation. The online index operation will wait, allowing other operations to proceed.

  The MAX_DURATION parameter can be 0 (wait indefinitely) or a measure of time in minutes (no other unit of measure is supported)

  The ABORT_AFTER_WAIT parameter provides an action at the end of the MAX_DURATION wait:

    - SELF instructs the statement to terminate its own process, ending the online rebuild step.

    - BLOCKERS instructs the statement to terminate the other process that is being blocked, terminating what is potentially a user transactions. Use with caution.

    - NONE instructs the statement to continue to wait, and when combined with MAX_DURATION = 0, essentially the same behavior as not specifying WAIT_AT_LOW_PRIORITY.

- **RESUMABLE.** Introduced in SQL Server 2017, this makes it possible to pause an index operation and resume it later, even after a server shutdown. Unlike a reorganize operation, a rebuild operation, if stopped or killed, will cause a potentially lengthy rollback, which itself could be disruptive to other transactions. Killing the session of a long-running index rebuild is no quick remedy: the blocking will continue until the rollback is complete. The RESUMEABLE=ON parameter allows for the index operation to be paused and then resumed manually at a later time.

  You can see a list of resumable and paused index operations in a new DMV, sys.index_resumable_operations, where the state_desc field will reflect RUNNING (and pausable) or PAUSED (and resumable).

The following example shows the syntax for resumable online index rebuilds:

```
--In Connection 1
ALTER INDEX FK_Sales_Orders_CustomerID ON Sales.Orders
REBUILD WITH (ONLINE=ON, RESUMABLE=ON);

--Tn Connection 2
--Show that the index rebuild is RUNNING
SELECT object_name = object_name (object_id), *

FROM sys.index_resumable_operations;
GO
--Pause the Index Rebuild
ALTER INDEX FK_Sales_Orders_CustomerID

ON Sales.Orders PAUSE;
--Connection 1 shows messages indicating the session has been disconnected because
of a high priority DDL operation.
GO
--Show that the index rebulild is PAUSED
SELECT object_name = object_name (object_id), *

FROM sys.index_resumable_operations;
GO
--Allow the index rebuild to complete
ALTER INDEX FK_Sales_Orders_CustomerID ON Sales.Orders RESUME;
```

The RESUMABLE syntax also supports a MAX_DURATION syntax, which has a different mention than the MAX_DURATION syntax used in the ABORT_AFTER_WAIT. MAX_DURATION automatically pauses an ONLINE index operation after a specified amount of time; for example, perhaps allowing for the index operation to be resumed during the next night's maintenance window. MAX_DURATION=0 allows for operation to run indefinitely, and is not a required parameter for RESUMABLE=ON. Here's an example:

```
ALTER INDEX FK_Sales_Orders_CustomerID ON Sales.Orders
REBUILD WITH (ONLINE=ON, RESUMABLE=ON, MAX_DURATION = 60 MINUTES);
```

NOTE

It is possible for a RESUMABLE rebuild operation to be blocked by uncommitted transactions and to be unpausable. In this case, the ALTER INDEX ... PAUSE statement would be blocked by the ALTER INDEX ... REBUILD statement. Long-running transactions can be a problem for many reasons, this among them.

Inside OUT

I only want to maintain indexes if they are above a certain percentage of fragmentation, can I do that with SQL Server Management Studio maintenance plans?

You can, with improvements to the SQL Server Management Studio maintenance plans first released with SQL Server Management Studio in 2016. Older versions of maintenance plans probably drew your ire with an "everything" approach to reorganizing or rebuilding indexes in a database.

You will now see options to intelligently limit index maintenance, starting with the radio buttons to select between Fast (LIMITED), Sampled, and Detailed. This corresponds the parameters provided to the structural statistics DMF, `sys.dm_db_index_physical_stats`.

You can configure the REORGANIZE and REBUILD tasks to maintain only indexes filtered by percentage of fragmentation and page count, both from `sys.dm_db_index_physical_stats` and actual index usage (based on `sys.dm_db_index_usage_stats` DMF). This is a significant improvement in the tooling for maintenance plans, which before these improvements were mostly unusable on larger databases.

Reorganizing indexes

Performing an INDEX REORGANIZE operation on an index uses far less system resources and is much less disruptive than performing a full REBUILD while still accomplishing the goal of reducing fragmentation. It physically reorders the leaf-level pages of the index to match the logical order. It also compacts the pages based on the existing fill factor, though it does not allow the fill factor to be changed. This operation is always performed online, so long-term table locks are not held and queries or modifications to the underlying table will not be blocked during the REORGANIZE transaction.

Because the REORGANIZE operation is not destructive, it does not automatically update the statistics for the index afterward, as a rebuild operation does. Thus, you should consider following a REORGANIZE step with an UPDATE STATISTICS step. We review statistics updates in the next section.

The following example presents the syntax to reorganize the FK_Sales_Orders_CustomerID index on the Sales.Orders table:

```
ALTER INDEX FK_Sales_Orders_CustomerID ON Sales.Orders
REORGANIZE;
```

You also can perform this in SQL Server Management Studio. Under the Sales.Order table, expand the Indexes folder, right-click the FK_Sales_Orders_CustomerID index, and then, on the shortcut menu, select Reorganize.

Instead of reorganizing an individual index, you can instead reorganize all indexes on a particular table by replacing the name of the index with the keyword ALL. For example, to reorganize all indexes on the `Sales.Orders` table, use the following command:

```
ALTER INDEX ALL ON Sales.Orders REORGANIZE;
```

To do this in SQL Server Management Studio, expand the Sales.Order table, right-click the Indexes folder, and then select Reorganize All.

None of the options available to REBUILD that we covered in the previous section are available to the REORGANIZE command. The only additional option that is specific to REORGANIZE is the LOB_COMPACTION option, which affects only large object (LOB) data types: `image`, `text`, `ntext`, `varchar(max)`, `nvarchar(max)`, `varbinary(max)`, and `xml`. By default, this option is turned on, but you can turn it off for non-heap tables to potentially skip some activity, though we do not recommend it. For heap tables, LOB data is always compacted.

➤ **We discuss more about automating index maintenance in Chapter 14.**

Updating index statistics

SQL Server uses statistics to describe the distribution and nature of the data in tables. The query optimizer needs the Auto Create setting turned on so that it can create single-column statistics when compiling queries. These statistics help the query optimizer create optimal runtime plans. Auto Update Statistics prompts statistics to be updated automatically when accessed by a T-SQL query when the statistics object is discovered to be past a threshold of rows changed. Without relevant and up-to-date statistics, the query optimizer might not choose the best way to run queries.

An update of index statistics should accompany INDEX REORGANIZE steps, but not INDEX REBUILD steps. Remember that the INDEX REBUILD command also updates the index statistics.

The basic syntax to update the statistics for an individual table is simple:

```
UPDATE STATISTICS [Sales].[Invoices];
```

The only command option to be aware of concerns the depth to which the statistics are scanned before being recalculated. By default, SQL Server samples a statistically significant number of rows in the table. This sampling is done with a parallel process starting with database compatibility level 130. This is fast and adequate for most workloads. You can optionally choose to scan the entire table, or a sample of the table based on a percentage of rows or a fixed number of rows, but we generally do not recommend these options.

You can manually verify that indexes are being kept up to date by the query optimizer when `auto_create_stats` is turned on. The `sys.dm_db_stats_properties` DMF accepts an `object_id` and `stats_id`, which is functionally the same as the `index_id`, if the statistics object corresponds to an index. The `sys.dm_db_stats_properties` DMF returns information such as `modification_counter` of rows changed since the last statistics update, and the `last_updated` date, which is NULL if the statistics object has never been updated since it was created.

Not all statistics are associated with an index; for example, statistics that are automatically created. There will generally be more stats objects than index objects. This function works in SQL Server and Azure SQL Database.

➤ For more on statistics objects and their impact on performance, see Chapter 10.

Inside OUT

Do I need to update statistics regularly even if `auto_create_stats` *is turned on for the database?*

Yes, you should still maintain the health of Update Statistics with regularity. When `auto_update_stats` is on, statistics are updated periodically based on usage. Statistics are considered out of date by the query optimizer when a ratio of data modifications to rows in the table has been reached. The query optimizer will check for and update the out-of-date statistic before running a query plan. Therefore, the `auto_update_stats` option has some small runtime overhead, though the performance benefit of updated statistics usually outweighs this cost. We also highly recommend turning on the `auto_update_stats_async` option because it helps minimize this runtime overhead by updating the statistics after running the query, instead of before.

We recommend that you turn on the `auto_update_stats` and `auto_update_stats_async` options, as discussed in Chapter 4 and Chapter 9 on all user databases, unless the application specifically requests that it be turned off, such as with Microsoft SharePoint.

Updating both column and index statistics for a database regularly, if your maintenance window time allows, will definitely not hurt, and will likely help. By updating statistics regularly, it could reduce the number of statistics updates that happen automatically during transactions in regular business hours.

Reorganizing Columnstore indexes

Columnstore indexes need to be maintained, as well, but use different internal objects to measure the fragmentation of the internal Columnstore structure. Columnstore indexes need only the REORGANIZE operation.

You can review the current structure of the groups of Columnstore by using the DMV `sys.dm_db_column_store_row_group_physical_stats`. This returns one row per row group of the Columnstore structure. The state of a rowgroup, and the current count of rowgroup by their states, provides some insight into the health of the Columnstore index. The vast majority of row group states should be COMPRESSED. Row groups in the OPEN and CLOSED states are part of the delta store and are awaiting compression. These delta store row groups are served up alongside compressed data seamlessly when queries use a Columnstore data.

The number of deleted rows in a rowgroup is also an indication that the index needs maintenance. As the ratio of `deleted_rows` to total rows in a row group that is in the COMPRESSED state increases, the performance of the Columnstore index will be reduced. If the `delete_rows` is larger than or greater than the total rows in a rowgroup, a REORGANIZE step will be beneficial.

Performing a REBUILD operation on a Columnstore is essentially the same as a drop/re-create and is not necessary. A REORGANIZE step for a Columnstore index, just as for a nonclustered index, is an ONLINE operation that has minimal impact to concurrent queries.

You can also use the option to REORGANIZE WITH (COMPRESS_ALL_ROW_GROUPS=ON) to force all delta store row groups to be compressed into a COMPRESSED row group.

Without COMPRESS_ALL_ROW_GROUPS, only COMPRESSED row groups will be compressed and combined. This can be useful when you observe a large number of COMPRESSED row groups with fewer than 100,000 rows. Typically, COMPRESSED row groups should contain up to one million rows each, but SQL might align rows in COMPRESSED row groups that align with how the rows were inserted, especially if they were inserted in bulk operations.

➤ We discuss more about automating index maintenance in Chapter 14.

Maintaining database file sizes

The difference between the size of a SQL Server database data (.mdf) or log (.trn) file to the data within is an important distinction to understand. Note that this section does not apply to Azure SQL Database, only to SQL Server instances.

CHAPTER 13

In SQL Server Management Studio, you can right-click a database, click Reports, and then view the Disk Usage report for a database, which will contain information about how much data is actually in the database's files.

Alternatively, the following query uses the FILEPROPERTY function to reveal how much data there actually is inside a file reservation; we also use the `sys.master_files` DMV, which returns information about the database files:

```
SELECT DB = d.name
, d.recovery_model_desc
, Logical_File_Name = df.name
, Physical_File_Loc = df.physical_name
, df.File_ID
, df.type_desc
, df.state_desc
-- multiple # of pages by 8 to get KB, divide by 1024 to get MB
, FileSizeMB = size*8/1024.0
, SpaceUsedMB = FILEPROPERTY(df.name, 'SpaceUsed')*8/1024.0
, AvailableMB =  size*8/1024.0
  - CAST(FILEPROPERTY(df.name, 'SpaceUsed') AS int)*8/1024.0
, 'Free%' = (((size*8/1024.0 )
  - (CAST(FILEPROPERTY(df.name, 'SpaceUsed') AS int)*8/1024.0 ))
  / (size*8/1024.0 )) * 100.0
FROM sys.master_files df
INNER JOIN sys.databases d
ON d.database_id = df.database_id
WHERE d.database_id = DB_ID();
```

Run this on a database in your environment to see how much data there is within database files. You might find that some data or log files are near full, whereas others have a large amount of space. Why would this be?

Files that have a large amount of free space might have grown that way in the past but have since been emptied out. If a transaction log in FULL recovery model were to have grown for a long time without having a transaction log backup, the .ldf file would have grown unchecked. Later, when a transaction log backup was taken, causing the log to truncate, it would have been nearly empty, but the size of the .ldf file itself wouldn't have changed. It isn't until a SHRINK FILE operation has taken place that the .ldf file would give its unused space back to the operating system. (And we never recommend shrinking a file flippantly or on a schedule.)

You should pregrow your database and log file sizes to a size that is well ahead of the database's growth pattern. You might fret over the best autogrowth rate, but ideally, autogrowth events are avoided altogether by proactive file management.

Files that are nearly full might be growing; for example, data is being inserted, or in the case of log files, transactions are being written to the transaction log file. Files have an autogrowth setting—the rate with which the files grow when they run out of space—and an autogrowth event might be imminent. (You can turn off autogrowth; however, the database will not be able to accept transactions if it is out of space.)

Autogrowth events can be disruptive to user activity, causing all transactions to wait while the database file asks the Windows server for more space and grows. Depending on the performance of the I/O system, this takes seconds, during which activity on the database must wait. Depending on the autogrowth setting and the size of the write transactions, multiple autogrowth events could be suffered sequentially. Growth of database data files will be greatly sped up by instant file initialization (Chapter 4 covers this in detail).

Understanding and finding autogrowth events

You should change autogrowth rates for database data and log files from the default of 1 MB, but, more important, you should maintain enough free space in your data and log files that autogrowth events do not happen. As a proactive DBA, you should monitor the space in database files and grow the files ahead of time, manually and outside of peak business hours.

You can view recent autogrowth events in a database via a report in SQL Server Management Studio or via a T-SQL script (see the code example that follows) that reads from the SQL Server instance's default trace. In SQL Server Management Studio, in Object Explorer, right-click the database name. On the shortcut menu that opens, select Reports, select Standard Reports, and then click Disk Usage. An expandable/collapsible region of the report contains Data/Log Files Autogrow/Autoshrink Events.

To view autogrowth events faster, and for all databases simultaneously, you can query the SQL Server instance's default trace. The default trace files are limited to 20 MB, and there are at most five rollover files, yielding 100 MB of history. The amount of time this includes depends on server activity. The following sample code query uses the `fn_trace_gettable()` function to open the default trace file in its current location:

```
SELECT
  DB = g.DatabaseName
, Logical_File_Name = mf.name
, Physical_File_Loc = mf.physical_name
, mf.type
-- The size in MB (converted from the number of 8KB pages) the file increased.
, EventGrowth_MB = convert(decimal(19,2),g.IntegerData*8/1024.)
, g.StartTime --Time of the autogrowth event
-- Length of time (in seconds) necessary to extend the file.
, EventDuration_s = convert(decimal(19,2),g.Duration/1000./1000.)
, Current_Auto_Growth_Set = CASE
  WHEN mf.is_percent_growth = 1
  THEN CONVERT(char(2), mf.growth) + '%'
  ELSE CONVERT(varchar(30), mf.growth*8./1024.) + 'MB'
END
```

```
, Current_File_Size_MB = CONVERT(decimal(19,2),mf.size*8./1024.)
, d.recovery_model_desc
FROM fn_trace_gettable(
(select substring((SELECT path
FROM sys.traces WHERE is_default =1), 0, charindex('\log_',
(SELECT path FROM sys.traces WHERE is_default =1),0)+4)
+ '.trc'), default) g
INNER JOIN sys.master_files mf
ON mf.database_id = g.DatabaseID
AND g.FileName = mf.name
INNER JOIN sys.databases d
ON d.database_id = g.DatabaseID
ORDER BY StartTime desc;
```

Shrinking database files

We need to be as clear as possible about this: shrinking database files is not something that you should do regularly and casually.

Files grow by their autogrowth increment based on actual usage. Database data and logs under normal circumstances—and in the case of FULL recovery model with regular transaction log backups—grow to the size they need to be. However, you should try to proactively grow database files to avoid autogrowth events.

You should shrink a file only as one-time events to solve one of two problems:

- A drive volume is out of space, and in an emergency break fix scenario, you reclaim unused space from a database data or log file.

- A database transaction log grew to a much larger size than is normally needed because of an adverse condition and should be reduced back to its normal operating size. An adverse condition could be transaction log backups that stopped working for a timespan, or a large uncommitted transaction, or replication or high availability (HA) issues prevented the transaction log from truncating.

For the case of a database data file, there is rarely any good reason to shrink the file, except for the aforementioned issue of the drive volume being out of space. For the rare situation in which a database had a large amount of data deleted from the file, an amount of data that is unlikely ever to exist in the database again, a one-shrink file operation could be appropriate.

For the case in which a transaction log file should be reduced in size, the best way to reclaim the space and re-create the file with optimal virtual log file (VLF) alignment is to take a transaction log backup to truncate the log file as much as possible, shrink the log file to reclaim all unused space, and then immediately grow the log file back to its expected size in increments of no more than 8,000 MB at a time. This allows SQL Server to create the underlying VLF structures in the most efficient way possible.

➤ For more information on VLFs in your database log files, see Chapter 3.

One of the main concerns with shrinking a file is that it indiscriminately returns free pages to the operating system, helping to create fragmentation. Aside from potentially creating autogrowth events in the future, shrinking a file creates the need for further index maintenance to alleviate the fragmentation. In SQL Server Management Studio, in the Shrink File dialog box, there is the Reorganize Files Before Releasing Unused Space option. Or, you can use the DBCC SHRINKFILE command, but this step can be time consuming, can block other user activity, and is not part of any health database maintenance plan.

A following sample script of this process assumes a preceding transaction log backup has been taken to truncate the database transaction log, and that the database log file is mostly empty. It also grows the transaction log file backup to an example size of 9 GB (9,216 MB or 9,437,184 KB):

```
USE [WideWorldImporters];
--TRUNCATEONLY returns all free space to the OS
DBCC SHRINKFILE (N'WWI_Log' , 0, TRUNCATEONLY);
GO
USE [master];
ALTER DATABASE [WideWorldImporters]
MODIFY FILE ( NAME = N'WWI_Log', SIZE = 8192000KB );
ALTER DATABASE [WideWorldImporters]
MODIFY FILE ( NAME = N'WWI_Log', SIZE = 9437184KB );
GO
```

CAUTION

You should never turn on the autoshrink database setting. It will automatically return any free space of more than 25% of the data file or transaction log. You should shrink a database only as a one-time operation to reduce file size after unplanned or unusual file growth. This setting could result in unnecessary fragmentation, overhead, and frequent rapid log autogrowth events. This setting was originally intended for, and might only be appropriate for, tiny local and/or embedded databases.

Monitoring databases by using DMVs

SQL Server provides a suite of internal, read-only DMVs and DMFs. It is important for you as the DBA to have a working knowledge of these objects because they unlock analysis of SQL Server outside of built-in reporting capabilities and third-party tools. In fact, all third-party tools use these dynamic management objects. DMV and DMF queries are discussed in several other places in this book:

- For more on understanding index usage statistics and missing index statistics, see Chapter 10.

- For more information on reviewing, aggregating, and analyzing cached execution plan statistics, including the Query Store feature introduced in SQL Server 2016, see Chapter 9.

- For more information on monitoring availability groups performance, health, and automatic seeding, see Chapter 12.

- For more information on automatic reporting from DMVs and querying performance monitor metrics from inside SQL Server DMVs, see Chapter 14.

- To read about using a DMF to query index fragmentation refer to the section "Monitoring index fragmentation" earlier in this chapter.

These sample scripts are all available in the accompanying downloads for this book, which are available at *https://aka.ms/SQLServ2017Admin/downloads*.

Sessions and requests

Any connection to a SQL Server instance is a session and is reported live in the DMV `sys.dm_exec_sessions`. Any actively running query on a SQL Server instance is a request and is reported live in the DMV `sys.dm_exec_requests`. Together, these two DMVs provide a thorough and far more detailed replacement to the `sp_who` or `sp_who2` system stored procedures with which long-time DBAs might be more familiar. With DMVs, you can do so much more than replace `sp_who`. We reviewed a simple query to look at sessions and requests active in the SQL Server in Chapter 9, but let's take that query to a higher level of complexity.

By adding references to a handful of other DMVs or DMFs, we can turn this query into a wealth of live information, returning complete connection source information, the actual runtime statement currently being run (similar to `DBCC INPUTBUFFER`), the actual plan being run (provided with a blue hyperlink in the SQL Server Management Studio results grid), request duration and cumulative resource consumption, the current and most recent wait types experienced, and more.

Sure, it might not be as easy to type in as "sp_who2," but it provides much more data, which you can easily query and filter. If you are unfamiliar with any of the data being returned, take some time to dive into the result set and explore the information it provides; it will be an excellent hands-on learning resource. You might choose to add more filters to the `WHERE` clause specific to your environment. Let's take a look at the `sp_who` replacement query:

```
SELECT
  when_observed = sysdatetime()
, r.session_id, r.request_id
, session_status = s.[status] -- running, sleeping, dormant, preconnect
, request_status = r.[status] -- running, runnable, suspended, sleeping, background
```

```
, blocked_by = r.blocking_session_id
, database_name = db_name(r.database_id)
, s.login_time, r.start_time
, query_text = CASE
        WHEN r.statement_start_offset = 0
            and r.statement_end_offset= 0 THEN left(est.text, 4000)
        ELSE SUBSTRING (est.[text],     r.statement_start_offset/2 + 1,
        CASE WHEN r.statement_end_offset = -1
            THEN LEN (CONVERT(nvarchar(max), est.[text]))
            ELSE r.statement_end_offset/2 - r.statement_start_offset/2 + 1
        END
  ) END --the actual query text is stored as nvarchar,
                    --so we must divide by 2 for the character offsets
, qp.query_plan
, cacheobjtype = LEFT (p.cacheobjtype + ' (' + p.objtype + ')', 35)
, est.objectid
, s.login_name, s.client_interface_name
, endpoint_name = e.name, protocol = e.protocol_desc
, s.host_name, s.program_name
, cpu_time_s = r.cpu_time, tot_time_s = r.total_elapsed_time
, wait_time_s = r.wait_time, r.wait_type, r.wait_resource, r.last_wait_type
, r.reads, r.writes, r.logical_reads  --accumulated request statistics
FROM sys.dm_exec_sessions as s
LEFT OUTER JOIN sys.dm_exec_requests as r on r.session_id = s.session_id
LEFT OUTER JOIN sys.endpoints as e ON e.endpoint_id = s.endpoint_id
LEFT OUTER JOIN sys.dm_exec_cached_plans as p ON p.plan_handle = r.plan_handle
OUTER APPLY sys.dm_exec_query_plan (r.plan_handle) as qp
OUTER APPLY sys.dm_exec_sql_text (r.sql_handle) as est
LEFT OUTER JOIN sys.dm_exec_query_stats as stat on stat.plan_handle = r.plan_handle
AND r.statement_start_offset = stat.statement_start_offset
AND r.statement_end_offset = stat.statement_end_offset
WHERE 1=1
AND s.session_id >= 50 --retrieve only user spids
AND s.session_id <> @@SPID --ignore myself
ORDER BY r.blocking_session_id desc, s.session_id asc;
```

Understanding wait types and wait statistics

Wait statistics in SQL Server are an important source of information and can be a key resource to increasing SQL Server performance, both at the aggregate level and at the individual query level. This section attempts to do justice and provide insights to this broad and important topic, but entire books, training sessions, and software packages have been developed to address wait type analysis; thus, this section is not exhaustive.

Wait statistics can be queried and provide value to SQL Server instances as well as databases in Azure SQL Database, though there are some waits specific to the Azure SQL Database platform (which we'll review). Like many dynamic management views and functions, membership in the sysadmin server role is not required, only the permission VIEW SERVER STATE, or in the case of Azure SQL Database, VIEW DATABASE STATE.

We saw in the query in the previous section the ability to see the current and most recent wait type for a session. Let's dive into how to observe wait types in the aggregate, accumulated at the server level or at the session level. Waits are accumulated in many different ways in SQL Server but typically occur when a request is in the `runnable` or `suspended` states. The request is not accumulating waits statistics, only durations statistics, when in the `runnable` state. We saw the ability to see the request state in the previous section's sample query.

SQL Server can track and accumulate many different wait types for a single query, many of which are of negligible duration or are benign in nature. There are quite a few waits that can be ignored or that indicate idle activity, as opposed to waits that indicate resource constraints and blocking. There are more than 900 distinct wait types in SQL Server and more than 1,000 in Azure SQL Database, some more documented and generally understood than others. We review some that you should know about later in this section.

To view accumulated waits for a session, which live only until the close or reset of the session, use the DMV `sys.dm_exec_session_wait_stats`. This code sample shows how the DMV returns one row per session, per wait type experienced, for user sessions:

```
SELECT * FROM sys.dm_exec_session_wait_stats AS wt;
```

There is a distinction between the two time measurements in this query and others. `signal_wait_time_ms` indicates the amount of time the thread waited on CPU activity, correlated with time spent in the `runnable` state. `wait_time_ms` indicates the accumulated amount of time for the wait type and includes the signal wait time, and so includes time the request spent in the `runnable` and `suspended` states. Typically, this is the wait measurement that we aggregate.

We can view aggregate wait types at the instance level with the `sys.dm_os_wait_stats` DMV, which is the same as `sys.dm_exec_session_wait_stats` but without the `session_id`, which includes all activity in the SQL Server instance, without any granularity to database, query, timeframe, and so on. This can be useful for getting the "big picture," but it's limited over long spans of time because the `wait_time_ms` counter accumulates, as illustrated here:

```
SELECT TOP (20)
 wait_type, wait_time_s =  wait_time_ms / 1000.
, Pct = 100. * wait_time_ms/sum(wait_time_ms) OVER()
FROM sys.dm_os_wait_stats as wt ORDER BY Pct desc
```

Over months, the `wait_time_ms` numbers will be so large for certain wait types, that trends or changes in wait type accumulations rates will be mathematically difficult to see. For this reason, if you want to use the wait stats to keep a close eye on server performance as it trends and changes over time, you need to capture these accumulated wait statistics in chunks of time, such as one day or one week. This `sys.dm_os_wait_stats` DMV is reset and all accumulated metrics are lost upon restart of the SQL Server service, but you can also clear them manually. Here is a sample script of how you could capture wait statistics at any interval:

```
--Script to setup capturing these statistics over time
CREATE TABLE dbo.sys_dm_os_wait_stats
(     id int NOT NULL IDENTITY(1,1)
,     datecapture datetimeoffset(0) NOT NULL
,     wait_type nvarchar(512) NOT NULL
,     wait_time_s  decimal(19,1) NOT NULL
,     Pct decimal(9,1)  NOT NULL
,     CONSTRAINT PK_sys_dm_os_wait_stats PRIMARY KEY CLUSTERED (id)
);
--This part of the script should be in a SQL Agent job, run regularly
INSERT INTO
dbo.sys_dm_os_wait_stats  (datecapture, wait_type, wait_time_s, Pct)
SELECT TOP (100)
  datecapture = SYSDATETIMEOFFSET()
, wait_type
, wait_time_s = convert(decimal(19,1), round( wait_time_ms / 1000.0,1))
, Pct = wait_time_ms/sum(wait_time_ms) OVER()
FROM sys.dm_os_wait_stats wt
WHERE wait_time_ms > 0
ORDER BY wait_time_s;
GO
--Reset the accumulated statistics in this DMV
DBCC SQLPERF ('sys.dm_os_wait_stats', CLEAR);
```

You can also view statistics for a query currently running in the DMV `sys.dm_os_waiting_tasks`, which contains more data than simply the `wait_type`; it also shows the blocking resource address in the `resource_description` field. A complete breakdown of the information that can be contained in the `resource_description` field is detailed in the documentation at *https://docs.microsoft.com/sql/relational-databases/system-dynamic-management-views/sys-dm-os-waiting-tasks-transact-sql*.

➤ **For more information on monitoring availability groups wait types, see Chapter 12.**

Wait types that you can safely ignore

Following is a starter list of wait types that you can safely ignore when querying the `sys.dm_os_wait_stats` DMV for aggregate wait statistics. You can append the following sample list WHERE clause.

Through your own research into your workload and in future versions of SQL Server as more wait types are added, you can grow this list so that important and actionable wait types rise to the top of your queries. A prevalence of these wait types shouldn't be a concern, they're unlikely to be generated by or negatively affect user requests.

```
WHERE
    wt.wait_type NOT LIKE '%SLEEP%' --can be safely ignored, sleeping
AND wt.wait_type NOT LIKE 'BROKER%' -- internal process
AND wt.wait_type NOT LIKE '%XTP_WAIT%' -- for memory-optimized tables
AND wt.wait_type NOT LIKE '%SQLTRACE%' -- internal process
AND wt.wait_type NOT LIKE 'QDS%' -- asynchronous Query Store data
AND wt.wait_type NOT IN ( -- common benign wait types
 'CHECKPOINT_QUEUE'
,'CLR_AUTO_EVENT','CLR_MANUAL_EVENT' ,'CLR_SEMAPHORE'
,'DBMIRROR_DBM_MUTEX','DBMIRROR_EVENTS_QUEUE','DBMIRRORING_CMD'
,'DIRTY_PAGE_POLL'
,'DISPATCHER_QUEUE_SEMAPHORE'
,'FT_IFTS_SCHEDULER_IDLE_WAIT','FT_IFTSHC_MUTEX'
,'HADR_FILESTREAM_IOMGR_IOCOMPLETION'
,'KSOURCE_WAKEUP'
,'LOGMGR_QUEUE'
,'ONDEMAND_TASK_QUEUE'
,'REQUEST_FOR_DEADLOCK_SEARCH'
,'XE_DISPATCHER_WAIT','XE_TIMER_EVENT'
 --Ignorable HADR waits
, 'HADR_WORK_QUEUE'
,'HADR_TIMER_TASK'
,'HADR_CLUSAPI_CALL'
)
```

Wait types to be aware of

This section shouldn't be the start and end of your understanding or research into wait types, many of which have multiple avenues to explore in your SQL Server instance, or at the very least, names that are misleading to the DBA considering their origin. Here are some, or groups of some, that you should understand.

Different instance workloads will have a different profile of wait types, and just because a wait type is at the top of the list aggregate `sys.dm_os_wait_stats` list doesn't mean that is the main or only performance problem with a SQL Server instance. It is likely that all SQL Server instances, even those finely tuned, will show these wait types near the top of the aggregate waits list. More important waits include the following:

- **ASYNC_NETWORK_IO.** This wait type is associated with the retrieval of data to a client, and the wait while the remote client receives and finally acknowledges the data received. This wait almost certainly has very little to do with network speed, network interfaces, switches, or firewalls. Any client, including your workstation or even SQL Server Management Studio running locally to the server, can incur small amounts of

ASYNC_NETWORK_IO as `resultsets` are retrieved to be processed. Transactional and snapshot replication distribution will incur ASYNC_NETWORK_IO. You will see a large amount of ASYNC_NETWORK_IO generated by reporting applications such as Cognos, Tableau, SQL Server Reporting Services, and Microsoft Office products such as Access and Excel. The next time a rudimentary Access database application tries to load the entire contents of the `Sales.Orders` table, you'll likely see ASYNC_NETWORK_IO.

Reducing ASYNC_NETWORK_IO, like many of the waits we discuss in this chapter, has little to do with hardware purchases or upgrades; rather, it's more to do with poorly designed queries and applications. Try suggesting to the developers or client applications incurring large amounts of ASYNC_NETWORK_IO that they eliminate redundant queries, use server-side filtering as opposed to client-side filtering, use server-side data paging as opposed to client-side data paging, or to use client-side caching.

- **LCK_M_*.**   Lock waits have to do with blocking and concurrency (or lack thereof). (Chapter 9 looks at isolation levels and concurrency.) When a request is writing and another request in READ COMMITTED or higher isolation is trying to read that same row data, one of the 60-plus different LCK_M_* wait types will be the reported wait type of the blocked request. In the aggregate, this doesn't mean you should reduce the isolation level of your transactions. (Whereas READ UNCOMMITTED is not a good solution, RCSI and snapshot isolation are; see Chapter 9 for more details.) Rather, optimize execution plans for efficient access by reducing scans as well as to avoid long-running multistep transactions. Avoid index rebuild operations without the ONLINE option (see earlier in this chapter for more information).

  The `wait_resource` provided in `sys.dm_exec_requests`, or `resource_description` in `sys.dm_os_waiting_tasks`, each provide a map to the exact location of the lock contention inside the database. A complete breakdown of the information that can be contained in the `resource_description` field is detailed in the documentation at *https://docs.microsoft.com/sql/relational-databases/system-dynamic-management-views/sys-dm-os-waiting-tasks-transact-sql*.

- **CXPACKET.**   A common and often-overreacted-to wait type, CXPACKET is parallelism wait. In a vacuum, execution plans that are created with parallelism run faster. But at scale, with many execution plans running in parallel, the server's resources might take longer to process the requests. This wait is measured in part as CXPACKET waits.

  When the CXPACKET wait is the predominant wait type experienced over time by your SQL Server, both Maximum Degree of Parallelism (MAXDOP) and Cost Threshold for Parallelism (CTFP) settings are dials to turn when performance tuning. Make these changes in small, measured gestures, and don't overreact to performance problems with a small number of queries. Use the Query Store to benchmark and trend the performance of high-value and high-cost queries as you change configuration settings.

If large queries are already a problem for performance and multiple large queries regularly run simultaneously, raising the CTFP might not solve the problem. In addition to the obvious solutions of query tuning and index changes, including the creation of Columnstore indexes, use MAXDOP instead to limit parallelization for very large queries.

Until SQL Server 2016, MAXDOP was a server-level setting, or a setting enforced at the query level, or a setting enforced to sessions selectively via Resource Governor (more on this later in this chapter). Since SQL server 2016, the MAXDOP setting is now available as a Database-Scoped Configuration. You can also use the MAXDOP query hint in any statement to override the database or server level MAXDOP setting.

- **SOS_SCHEDULER_YIELD.** Another flavor of CPU pressure, and in some ways the opposite of the CXPACKET wait type, is the SOS_SCHEDULER_YIELD wait type. The SOS_SCHEDULER_YIELD is an indicator of CPU pressure, indicating that SQL Server had to share time or "yield" to other CPU tasks, which can be normal and expected on busy servers. Whereas CXPACKET is the SQL Server complaining about too many threads in parallel, the SOS_SCHEDULER_YIELD is the acknowledgement that there were more runnable tasks for the available threads. In either case, first take a strategy of reducing CPU-intensive queries and rescheduling or optimizing CPU-intense maintenance operations. This is more economical than simply adding CPU capacity.

- **RESOURCE_SEMAPHORE.** This wait type is accumulated when a request is waiting on memory to be allocated before it can start. Although this could be an indication of memory pressure caused by insufficient memory available to the SQL Server instance, it is more likely caused by poor query design and poor indexing, resulting in inefficient execution plans. Aside from throwing money at more system memory, a more economical solution is to tune queries and reduce the footprint of memory-intensive operations.

- **PAGELATCH_*** and **PAGEIOLATCH_*.** These two wait types are presented together not because they are similar in nature—they are not—but because they are often confused. To be clear, PAGELATCH has to do with contention over pages in memory, whereas PAGEIOLATCH has to do with contention over pages in the I/O system (on the drive).

  PAGELATCH_* contention deals with pages in memory, which can rise because of overuse of temporary objects in memory, potentially with rapid access to the same temporary objects. This could also be experienced when reading in data from an index in memory, or reading from a heap in memory. PAGELATCH_EX waits can be related to inserts that are happening rapidly and/or page splits related to inserts.

PAGEIOLATCH_* contention deals with a far more limiting and troubling performance condition: the overuse of reading from the slowest subsystem of all, the physical drives. PAGEIOLATCH_SH deals with reading data from a drive into memory so that the data can be read. Keep in mind that this doesn't necessarily translate to a request's rowcount, especially if index or table scans are required in the execution plan. PAGEIOLATCH_EX and _UP are waits associated with reading data from a drive into memory so that the data can be written to.

A rise in PAGEIOLATCH_ could be due to performance of the storage system, remembering that the performance of drive systems does not always respond linearly to increases in activity. Aside from throwing (a lot of!) money at faster drives, a more economical solution is to modify queries and/or indexes and reduce the footprint of memory-intensive operations, especially operations involving index and table scans.

- **WRITELOG.**   The WRITELOG wait type is likely to appear on any SQL Server instance, including availability group primary and secondary replicas, when there is heavy write activity. The WRITELOG wait is time spent flushing the transaction log to a drive and is due to physical I/O subsystem performance. On systems with heavy writes, this wait type is expected.

- **IO_COMPLETION.**   Associated with synchronous read and write operations that are not related to row data pages, such as reading log blocks or virtual log file (VLF) information from the transaction log, or reading or writing merge join operator results, spools, and buffers to disk. It is difficult to associate this wait type with a single activity or event, but a spike in IO_COMPLETION could be an indication that these same events are now waiting on the I/O system to complete.

- **WAIT_XTP_RECOVERY.**   This wait type can occur when a database with memory-optimized tables is in recovery at startup and is expected.

- **XE_FILE_TARGET_TVF** and **XE_LIVE_TARGET_TVF.**   These waits are associated with writing extended events sessions to their targets. A sudden spike in these waits would indicate that too much is being captured by an extended events session. Usually these aren't a problem, however, because the asynchronous nature of extended events has much less server impact than traces or SQL Profiler did.

You'll find the new XE Profile in the SQL Server Management Studio Object Explorer window, beneath the SQL Server Agent menu. See Figure 13-1 for an example.

CHAPTER 13

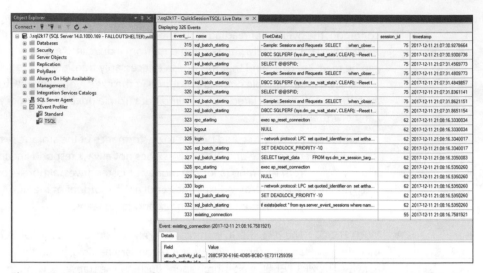

Figure 13-1 The XEvents Profiler T-SQL live events display in SQL Server Management Studio, similar to the deprecated Profiler T-SQL trace template. Note the new XEvent Profiler menu at the bottom of Object Explorer.

- **MEMORYCLERK_XE.**   The MEMORYCLERK_XE wait type could spike if you have allowed extended events session targets to consume too much memory. We discuss extended events in the next section, but you should watch out for the maximum buffer size allowed to the ring_buffer session target, among other in-memory targets.

Reintroducing extended events

Extended events were introduced in SQL Server 2008, though without any sort of official user interface within SQL Server Management Studio. It wasn't until SQL Server 2012 that we got an extended events user interface. Now, with SQL Server Management Studio 17.3 and above, the XEvent Profiler tool is built in to SQL Server Management Studio, which is a real maturation and ease-of-use improvement for administrators and developers. The XEvent Profiler delivers an improved tracing experience that users of the legacy SQL Profiler with SQL Server traces.

Extended events are the future of "live look" at SQL Server activity, replacing deprecated traces. Even though the default extended event sessions are not yet complete replacements for the default system trace (we give an example a bit later), consider extended events for all new activity related to troubleshooting and diagnostic data collection. We understand that the messaging around extended events has been the replacement for traces for nearly a decade. The XEvents UI in SQL Server Management Studio is better than ever, so if you haven't switched to using extended events to do what you used to use traces for, the time is now!

To begin, refer back to Figure 13-1 to see a screenshot of the XEvent Profiler QuickSession functionality new to SQL Server Management Studio. We'll assume that you've not had a lot of experience with creating your own extended events sessions.

Extended events sessions provide a modern, asynchronous, and far more versatile replacement for SQL Server traces, which are, in fact, deprecated. For troubleshooting, debugging, performance tuning, and event gathering, extended events provides a faster and more configurable solution than traces.

Let's become familiar with some of the most basic terminology for extended events:

- **Sessions.**   A set of data collection that can be started and stopped; the new equivalent of a "trace."

- **Events.**   Selected from an event library, events are what you remember "tracing" with SQL Server Profiler. These are predetermined, detectable operations during runtime. Events that you'll want to look for include `sql_statement_completed` and `sql_batch_completed`, for example, for catching an application's running of T-SQL code.

  Examples: `sql_batch_starting`, `sql_statement_completed`, `login`, `error_reported`, `sort_warning`, `table_scan`

- **Actions.**   The headers of the columns of data you'll see in the extended events data describing an event, such as when the event happened, who and what called the event, its duration, the number of writes and reads, CPU time, and so on. So, in this way, actions are additional data captured when an event is recorded. Global Fields is another name for actions, which allow additional information to be captured for any event, whereas event fields are specific to certain actions.

  Examples: `sql_text`, `batch_text`, `timestamp`, `session_id`, `client_hostname`

- **Predicates.**   These are filter conditions created on actions so that you can limit the data you capture. You can filter on any action or field that is returned by an event you have added to the session.

  Examples: `database_id > 4`, `database_name = 'WideWorldImporters`, `is_system=0`

- **Targets.**   This is where the data should be sent. You can always watch detailed and "live" extended events data captured asynchronously in memory for any session. However, a session can also have multiple targets, though only one of each target. We dive into the different targets in the section "Understanding the variety of extended events targets" later in this chapter.

SQL Server installs with three extended events sessions ready to view: two that start by default, `system_health` and `telemetry_xevents`, and another that starts when needed, `AlwaysOn_Health`. These sessions provide a basic coverage for system health, though they are not an exact replacement for the system default trace. Do not stop or delete these sessions, which should start automatically.

NOTE

Should the `system_health`, `telemetry_xevents`, and/or `AlwaysOn_Health` sessions be accidentally dropped from the server, you can find the scripts to re-create them for your instance in this file: *instancepath*\MSSQL\Install\u_tables.sql; for example, F:\Program Files\Microsoft SQL Server\MSSQL14.SQL2K17\MSSQL\Install\u_tables.sql

You'll see the well-documented definitions of the two XEvents sessions toward the bottom of the file. If you'd just like to see the script that created the definitions for the built-in extended events sessions, you can script them via SQL Server Management Studio by right-clicking the session, and then, on the shortcut menu, point to Script Session As, and then click Create To and a destination for the script.

Viewing extended events data

Extended events session can generate simultaneous output to multiple destinations, only one of which closely resembles the .trc files of old. As we said earlier, you can always watch detailed and "live" extended events data captured asynchronously in memory for any session through SQL Server Management Studio by right-clicking a session and then selecting Watch Live Data. You'll see asynchronously delivered detailed data, and you can customize the columns you see, apply filters on the data, and even create groups and on-the-fly aggregations, all by right-clicking in the Live Data window.

The Live Data window, however, isn't a target. The data isn't saved anywhere outside of the SQL Server Management Studio window, and you can't look back at data you missed before launching Watch Live Data. You can create a session without a target, and Watch Live Data is all you'll get, but maybe that's all you'll need for a quick observation.

You can create other targets for a session on the Data Storage page of the New Session dialog box in SQL Server Management Studio. To view data collected by the target, expand the session, right-click the package, and then, on the shortcut menu, click View Target Data, as demonstrated in Figure 13-2.

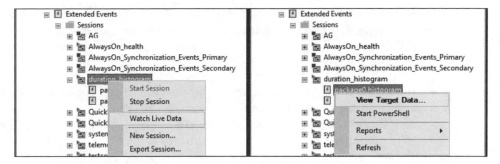

Figure 13-2 A side-by-side look at the difference between Watch Live Data on an extended events session and View Target Data on an extended events session target.

When viewing target data, you can right-click to re-sort, copy the data to clipboard, and export most of the target data to .csv files for analysis in other software.

Unlike Watch Live Data, View Target Data does not refresh automatically, though for some targets, you can configure SQL Server Management Studio to poll the target automatically by right-clicking the View Target Data window and then clicking Refresh Interval.

> **NOTE**
>
> **Currently, there is no built-in way in SQL Server Management Studio to write extended events session data directly to a SQL Server table, but the Watch Live Data interface provides easy point-and-click analysis, grouping, and filtering of live session data. Take some time to explore the other available target types; they can easily and quickly reproduce your analysis of trace data written to SQL Server tables.**

The section that follows presents a breakdown of the possible targets, many of which do some of the serious heavy lifting that you might have done previously by writing or exporting SQL trace data to a table and then performing your own aggregations and queries. Remember that you don't need to pick just one target type to collect data for your session, but that a target can't collect data prior to its creation.

Understanding the variety of extended events targets

Here is a summary of the extended event targets available to be created. Remember you can create more than one target per Session.

- Event File target (.xel), which writes the event data to a physical file on a drive, asynchronously. You can then open and analyze it later, much like deprecated trace files, or merge it with other .xel files to assist analysis (in SQL Server Management Studio, click the File menu, click Open, and then click Merge Extended Events Files).

However, when you view the event file data in SQL Server Management Studio by right-clicking the event file and selecting View Target Data, the data does not refresh live. Data continues to be written to the file behind the scenes while the session is running, so to view the latest data, close the .xel file and open it again.

- Histogram, which counts the number of times an event has occurred and bucketizes an action, storing the data in memory. For example, you could capture a histogram of the `sql_statement_completed` broken down by the number of observed events by client-hostname action, or by the duration field.

  Be sure to provide a number of buckets (or slots, in the T-SQL syntax) that is greater than the number of unique values you expect for the action or field. If you're bucketizing by a numeric value such as duration, be sure to provide a number of buckets larger than the largest duration you could capture over time. If the histogram runs out of buckets for new values for your action or field, it will not capture data for them!

  Note that you can provide any number of histogram buckets, but the histogram target will round the number up to the nearest power of 2. Thus, if you provide a value of 10 buckets, you'll see 16 buckets.

- Pair matching, which is used to match events, such as the start and end of a SQL Server batch execution, and find occasions when an event in a pair occurs without the other, such as `sql_statement_starting` and `sql_statement_completed`. Select a start and an end from the list of actions you've selected.

- `Ring_buffer` provides a fast, in-memory First-In, First-Out (FIFO) asynchronous memory buffer to collect rapidly occurring events. Stored in a memory buffer, the data is never written to a drive, allowing for robust data collection without performance overhead. The customizable dataset is provided in XML format and must be queried. Because this data is in-memory, you should be careful how high you configure the Maximum Buffer Memory size, and never set the size to 0 (unlimited).

- Finally, you can use the Service Broker target to send messages to a target service of a customizable message type.

Although all of the aforementioned targets are high-performing asynchronous targets, there are a pair of synchronous targets: ETW and event counter. Be aware when using synchronous targets that the resource demand of synchronous targets might be more noticeable. Following is a brief description of each asynchronous target:

- **ETW (Event Tracing for Windows).**   This is used to gather SQL Server data for later combination to Windows event log data for troubleshooting and debugging Windows applications.

- **Event counter.**   This simply counts the number of events in an extended events session. You use this to provide data for trending and later aggregate analysis. The resulting dataset has one row per event with a count. This data is stored in memory, so although it's synchronous, you shouldn't expect any noticeable performance impact.

Let's look at querying extended events session data in T-SQL with a couple of practical common examples.

Using extended events to detect deadlocks

We've talked about viewing data in SQL Server Management Studio, so let's review querying extended events data via T-SQL. Let's query one of the default extended events sessions, `system_health`, for deadlocks. Back in the dark ages, before SQL Server 2008, it was not possible to see a deadlock. You had to see it coming—to turn on a trace flag prior to the deadlock.

With the `system_health` extended events session, a recent history (a rolling 4-MB buffer) of event data in the `ring_buffer` target will contain any occurrences of the `xml_deadlock_report` event.

The T-SQL code sample that follows demonstrates the retrieval of the `ring_buffer` target as XML, and the use of XQuery syntax:

```
WITH cteDeadlocks ([Deadlock_XML]) AS (
  --Query RingBufferTarget
  SELECT [Deadlock_XML] = CAST(target_data AS XML)
  FROM sys.dm_xe_sessions AS xs
  INNER JOIN sys.dm_xe_session_targets AS xst
  ON xs.address = xst.event_session_address
  WHERE xs.NAME = 'system_health'
  AND xst.target_name = 'ring_buffer'
 )
SELECT
  Deadlock_XML = x.Graph.query('(event/data/value/deadlock)[1]')  --View as XML for
detail, save this output as .xdl and re-open in SSMS for visual graph
, Deadlock_When = x.Graph.value('(event/data/value/deadlock/process-list/process/@last-
batchstarted)[1]', 'datetime2(3)') --date the last batch in the first process started,
only an approximation of time of deadlock
, DB = DB_Name(x.Graph.value('(event/data/value/deadlock/process-list/process/@cur-
rentdb)[1]', 'int')) --Current database of the first listed process
FROM (
 SELECT Graph.query('.') AS Graph
 FROM cteDeadLocks c
 CROSS APPLY c.[Deadlock_XML].nodes('RingBufferTarget/event[@name="xml_deadlock_
report"]') AS Deadlock_Report(Graph)
) AS x
ORDER BY Deadlock_When desc;
```

This example returns one row per captured `xml_deadlock_report` event and includes an XML document, which in SQL Server Management Studio Grid results will appear to be a blue hyperlink. Click the hyperlink to open the XML document, which will contain the complete detail of all elements of the deadlock. If you'd like to see a Deadlock Graph, save this file as an .xdl file, and then open it in SQL Server Management Studio.

You can download the previous script, CH12_XEvents.sql, and other accompanying sample scripts for this book from *https://aka.ms/SQLServ2017Admin/downloads*.

Using extended events to detect autogrowth events

The SQL Server default trace captures historical database data and log file autogrowth events, but the default extended events sessions shipped with SQL Server do not. The extended events that capture autogrowth events are `database_file_size_change` and `databases_log_file_size_changed`. Both events capture autogrowths and manual file growths run by ALTER DATABASE ... MODIFY FILE statements, and include an event field called `is_automatic` to differentiate. Additionally, you can identify the query statement `sql_text` that prompted the autogrowth event.

Following is a sample T-SQL script to create a startup session that captures autogrowth events to an .xel event file and also a histogram target that counts the number of autogrowth instances per database:

```
CREATE EVENT SESSION [autogrowths] ON SERVER
ADD EVENT sqlserver.database_file_size_change(
    ACTION(package0.collect_system_time,sqlserver.database_id
,sqlserver.database_name,sqlserver.sql_text)),
ADD EVENT sqlserver.databases_log_file_size_changed(
    ACTION(package0.collect_system_time,sqlserver.database_id
,sqlserver.database_name,sqlserver.sql_text))
ADD TARGET package0.event_file(
--.xel file target
SET filename=N'F:\DATA\autogrowths.xel'),
ADD TARGET package0.histogram(
--Histogram target, counting events per database_name
SET filtering_event_name=N'sqlserver.database_file_size_change'
,source=N'database_name',source_type=(0))
--Start session at server startup
WITH (STARTUP_STATE=ON);
GO
--Start the session now
 ALTER EVENT SESSION [autogrowths]
ON SERVER  STATE = START;
```

Using extended events to detect page splits

As we discussed earlier in this chapter, detecting page splits can be useful. You might choose to monitor page_splits when load testing a table design with its intended workload or when finding insert statements that cause the most fragmentation.

The following sample T-SQL script creates a startup session that captures autogrowth events to an .xel event file and also a histogram target that counts the number of page_splits per database:

```
CREATE EVENT SESSION [page_splits] ON SERVER
ADD EVENT sqlserver.page_split(
    ACTION(sqlserver.database_name,sqlserver.sql_text))
ADD TARGET package0.event_file(
SET filename=N'page_splits',max_file_size=(100)),
ADD TARGET package0.histogram(
SET filtering_event_name=N'sqlserver.page_split'
,source=N'database_id',source_type=(0))

--Start session at server startup
WITH (STARTUP_STATE=ON);
GO
--Start the session now
 ALTER EVENT SESSION [page_splits]
ON SERVER  STATE = START;
```

Securing extended events

To access extended events, a developer or analyst needs the ALTER ANY EVERY SESSION permission. This is different from the ALTER TRACE permission needed for traces. This grants that person access to create extended events sessions by using T-SQL commands, but it will not grant access to view server metadata in the New Extended Events Session Wizard in SQL Server Management Studio. For that, the person needs one further commonly granted developer permission, VIEW SERVER STATE. In Azure SQL Database, extended events have the same capability, but for developers to view extended events sessions, you must grant them an ownership-level permission CONTROL DATABASE. However, we do not recommend this for developers or non-administrators in production environments.

There are certain sensitive events that you cannot capture with a trace or extended event session; for example, the T-SQL statement CREATE LOGIN for a SQL-authenticated login.

CHAPTER 13

Capturing Windows performance metrics with DMVs and data collectors

The Performance Monitor (perfmon.exe) application has been used for years by server administrators to visually track and collect performance of server resources, application memory usage, disk response times, and so on. In addition to the live Performance Monitor graph, you can also configure Data Collector Sets to gather the same Performance Monitor metrics over time.

SQL Server has a large number of metrics captured within, as well. Although we have neither the scope nor space to investigate and explain each one in this book, here is a sampling of some performance metrics you might find valuable when reviewing the health and performance of your SQL Server.

These metrics are at the Windows server level or SQL Server instance level, so it is not possible to get granular data for individual databases, workloads, or queries; however, identifying performance with isolated workloads in near-production systems is possible. Like aggregate wait statistics, there is significant value in trending these Performance Monitor metrics on server workloads, monitoring peak behavior metrics, and for immediate troubleshooting and problem diagnosis.

Querying performance metrics by using DMVs

Beyond Performance Monitor, we've already seen in this chapter a DMV that exposes most of the performance metrics within SQL Server, `sys.dm_os_performance_counters`. There are some advantages to this DMV in that you can combine it with other DMVs that report on system resource activity (check out `sys.dm_os_sys_info`, for example), and you can fine-tune the query for ease of monitoring and custom data collecting. However, `sys.dm_os_performance_counters` does not currently have access to metrics outside of the SQL Server instance categories, even the most basic Windows metrics such as "% Processor Time."

This following straightforward code sample uses `sys.dm_os_performance_counters` to return the instance's current target server memory, total server memory, and page life expectancy:

```
SELECT InstanceName = @@SERVERNAME
, Target_Server_Mem_GB = max(CASE counter_name
WHEN 'Target Server Memory (KB)' THEN convert(decimal(19,3), cntr_value/1024./1024.)
END)
, Total_Server_Mem_GB = max(CASE counter_name
WHEN  'Total Server Memory (KB)' THEN convert(decimal(19,3), cntr_value/1024./1024.)
END)
, PLE_s = MAX(CASE counter_name WHEN 'Page life expectancy'  THEN cntr_value END)
FROM sys.dm_os_performance_counters;;
```

NOTE

In servers with multiple SQL Server instances, `sys.dm_os_performance_counters` displays only metrics for the instance on which it is run. You cannot access performance metrics for other instances on the same server via this DMV.

Some queries against `sys.dm_os_performance_counters` are not as straightforward. As an example, although Performance Monitor returns Buffer Cache Hit Ratio as a single value, querying this same memory metric via the DMV requires creating the ratio from two metrics. This code sample divides two metrics to provide the Buffer Cache Hit Ratio:

```
SELECT Buffer_Cache_Hit_Ratio = 100 *
(SELECT cntr_value = convert(decimal (9,1), cntr_value)
FROM sys.dm_os_performance_counters as pc
WHERE pc.COUNTER_NAME = 'Buffer cache hit ratio'
AND pc.OBJECT_NAME like '%:Buffer Manager%')
/
(SELECT cntr_value = convert(decimal (9,1), cntr_value)
FROM sys.dm_os_performance_counters as pc
WHERE pc.COUNTER_NAME = 'Buffer cache hit ratio base'
AND pc.OBJECT_NAME like '%:Buffer Manager%');
```

Finally, some counters returned by `sys.dm_os_performance_counts` are continually incrementing integers. Let's return to our example of finding page splits. The `counter_name` "Page Splits/sec" is misleading when accessed via the DMV, but it is in fact an incrementing number. To calculate the rate of page splits per second, we need two samples. This strategy is appropriate only for single-value counters for the entire server or instance. For counters that return one value per database, you would need a temp table in order to calculate the rate for each database between the two samples.

```
DECLARE @page_splits_Start_ms bigint, @page_splits_Start bigint
, @page_splits_End_ms bigint, @page_splits_End bigint
SELECT @page_splits_Start_ms = ms_ticks
, @page_splits_Start = cntr_value
FROM sys.dm_os_sys_info
CROSS APPLY sys.dm_os_performance_counters
WHERE counter_name ='Page Splits/sec'
AND object_name LIKE '%SQL%Access Methods%'

WAITFOR DELAY '00:00:10' --Adjust sample duration between measurements, 10s sample

SELECT @page_splits_End_ms =  MAX(ms_ticks), @page_splits_End = MAX(cntr_value)
FROM sys.dm_os_sys_info
CROSS APPLY sys.dm_os_performance_counters
WHERE counter_name ='Page Splits/sec'
AND object_name LIKE '%SQL%Access Methods%'
SELECT Page_Splits_per_s = (@page_splits_End - @page_splits_Start)*1.
/ NULLIF(@page_splits_End_ms - @page_splits_Start_ms,0)*1.;
```

However, you can gain access to some Windows metrics via the DMV `sys.dm_os_ring_buffers`, including metrics on CPU utilization and memory. This internal DMV returns thousands of XML documents, generated every second, loaded with information on SQL exceptions, memory, schedulers, connectivity, and more.

In the code sample that follows, we pull the SQL Server instance's current CPU utilization percentage and the current server idle CPU percentage. The remaining CPU percentage can be chalked up to other applications or services running on the Windows server, including other SQL Server instances.

```
SELECT
 [Time] =  DATEADD(ms, -1 * (si.cpu_ticks
 / (si.cpu_ticks/si.ms_ticks) - x.[timestamp])
, SYSDATETIMEOFFSET ())
, CPU_SQL_pct = bufferxml.value('(./Record/SchedulerMonitorEvent
/SystemHealth/ProcessUtilization)[1]', 'int')
, CPU_Idle_pct = bufferxml.value('(./Record/SchedulerMonitorEvent
/SystemHealth/SystemIdle)[1]', 'int')
FROM (SELECT timestamp, CONVERT(xml, record) AS bufferxml
       FROM sys.dm_os_ring_buffers
       WHERE ring_buffer_type = N'RING_BUFFER_SCHEDULER_MONITOR') AS x
CROSS APPLY sys.dm_os_sys_info AS si
ORDER BY [Time] desc;
```

The built-in SQL Server `ring_buffer` data collector isn't Performance Monitor and doesn't resemble it at all, though it does provide data at certain events. In the case of CPU utilization in the `Scheduler_Monitor` ring buffer, we get fresh data once per second. Other data streams aren't as constant. In the case of SQL Server memory utilization, for example, we can get snapshots of key memory metrics only when one of four memory events are initiated: high or low physical memory, low virtual memory, or a steady event that indicates that the previous memory pressure event has been relieved. The frequency of these memory events is inconsistent and might not happen for weeks at a time, but could still be valuable for troubleshooting memory conditions on the SQL Server. Let's look at the code:

```
SELECT
  [Time] =  DATEADD(ms, -1 * (si.cpu_ticks
/ (si.cpu_ticks/si.ms_ticks) - x.[timestamp])
, SYSDATETIMEOFFSET ())
, MemoryEvent = bufferxml.value('(./Record/ResourceMonitor
/Notification)[1]', 'varchar(64)')
, Target_Server_Mem_GB = CONVERT (decimal(19,3),
bufferxml.value('(./Record/MemoryNode/TargetMemory)[1]'
, 'bigint')/1024./1024.)
, Physical_Server_Mem_GB = CONVERT (decimal(19,3),
bufferxml.value('(./Record/MemoryRecord/TotalPhysicalMemory)[1]'
, 'bigint')/1024./1024.)
, Committed_Mem_GB = CONVERT (decimal(19,3),
bufferxml.value('(./Record/MemoryNode/CommittedMemory)[1]'
, 'bigint')/1024./1024.)
```

```
, Shared_Mem_GB = CONVERT (decimal(19,3),
bufferxml.value('(./Record/MemoryNode/SharedMemory)[1]'
, 'bigint')/1024./1024.)
, MemoryUtilization = bufferxml.value('(./Record/MemoryRecord
/MemoryUtilization)[1]', 'bigint')
, Available_Server_Mem_GB = CONVERT (decimal(19,3), bufferxml.value('(./Record/MemoryRe-
cord/AvailablePhysicalMemory)[1]'
, 'bigint')/1024./1024.)
FROM (SELECT timestamp, CONVERT(xml, record) AS bufferxml
FROM sys.dm_os_ring_buffers
WHERE ring_buffer_type = N'RING_BUFFER_RESOURCE_MONITOR') AS x
CROSS APPLY sys.dm_os_sys_info AS si
ORDER BY [Time] desc;
```

Inside OUT

The ring buffer is capturing all of this data to memory constantly. Doesn't that incur some server overhead?

There is some background overhead for `ring_buffer` data collection. That can't be denied. SQL Server instances always have this diagnostic activity present, constantly and by design, so the `ring_buffer` won't be at fault for sudden or even gradual performance degradation.

Only appropriate on resource-limited servers and/or instances with extremely high-frequency transaction activity, it's possible that you could turn off the `ring_buffer` by using trace flags. This can result in a small performance gain, but you should test and measure it against the loss of diagnostic data on which your own administrative queries or third-party products rely. For more information on using trace flags to turn off ring buffer data collection, visit *https://support.microsoft.com/help/920093/ tuning-options-for-sql-server-when-running-in-high-performance-workloa* [sic].

Querying performance metrics by using Performance Monitor

To get a complete and graphical picture of server resource utilization, using a server resource tool is necessary. Performance Monitor is more than just a pretty graph, it is a suite of data collection tools that can persist outside of your user profile.

You can configure the live Performance Monitor graph, available in the Monitoring Tools folder, to show a live picture of server performance. To do so, right-click the (mostly empty) grid to access properties, add counters, clear the graph, and so on. In the Properties dialog box, under General, you can configure the sample rate and duration of the graph. You can display up to 1,000 sample points on the graph live. This can be 1,000 one-second sample points for a total of

16 minutes and 40 seconds, or more time if you continue to decrease the sample frequency. For example, you can display 5,000 five-second sample points for more than 83 minutes of duration in the graph.

To view data collected by Data Collectors, stop the data collector and restart it. In the Reports folder, in the User Defined folder, you'll see a new report that contains the graph that the Data Collector created. Figure 13-3 shows that more than 15 days of data performance was collected in the Data Collector, which we're viewing in the Memory folder, selecting the most recent report that was generated when we stopped the Memory Data Collector Set.

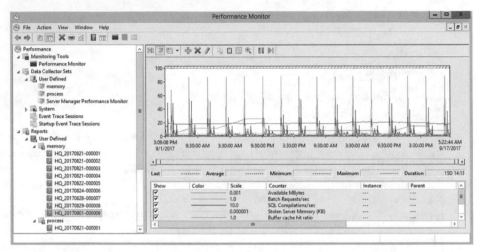

Figure 13-3 The Windows Performance Monitor Application. Instead of showing live data from the Monitoring Tools-Performance Monitor screen, we're showing 15 days' worth of data recorded by a User Defined Data Collector Set, which generated a User Defined Report.

Monitoring key performance metrics

Here are some Performance Monitor metrics to take a look at when gauging the health and performance of your SQL Server. Although we don't have the space in this book to provide a deep dive into each metric, its causes, and indicators, you should take time to investigate and research metrics that appear out of line with the guidelines provided here.

We don't provide many hard numbers in this section; for example, "Metrix X should always be lower than Y." You should trend, measure metrics at peak activity, and investigate how metrics respond to server, query, or configuration changes. What might be normal for an instance with a read-heavy workload might be problematic for an instance with a high-volume write workload, and vice versa.

We do explain how to find the metric in both Performance Monitor's Add Counters menu and the DMV `sys.dm_os_performance_counters`, when available.

Average Disk seconds per Read or Write

Performance Monitor: PhysicalDisk:Avg. Disk sec/Read and PhysicalDisk:Avg. Disk sec/Write

DMV: Not Available

View this metric on each volume. The "_Total" metric doesn't have any value here, you should look at individual volumes in which SQL Server files are present. This metric has the clearest guidance of any with respect to what is acceptable or not for a server. Try to measure this value during your busiest workload and also during backups. You want to see the average disk seconds per read and write operation (considering that a single query could have thousands or millions of operations) below 20 ms, or .02 seconds. Below 10 ms is optimal and very achievable with modern storage systems. (This is the rare case for which we actually have hard and fast numbers specified by Microsoft to rely on.) Seeing this value spike to very high values (such as .1 second or 100 ms) isn't a major cause for concern, but if you see these metrics sustaining an average higher than .02 seconds during peak activity, this is a fairly clear indication that the physical I/O subsystem is being stressed beyond its capacity to keep up. Low, healthy measurements for this number don't provide any insight into the quality of or efficiency of queries and execution plans, only the response from the disk subsystem. The Avg. Disk sec/Transfer counter is simply a combination of both read and write activity, unrelated to Avg. Disk Transfers/sec. (Confusing, we know!)

Page Life Expectancy (PLE)

Performance Monitor: MSSQL$Instance:Buffer Manager/Page Life Expectancy (s)

DMV: MSSQL$Instance:Buffer Manager/Page life expectancy

PLE is a measure of time that indicates the age of data in memory. In general, you want pages of data in memory to grow to a ripe old age—it means that there is ample memory available to SQL Server to store data to serve reads without going back to a drive. A dated metric of 300 seconds might only be appropriate for servers with less than 64 GB of memory. With more and more memory available to a SQL instance, the older the average data page should be as data remains cached longer, so 300 seconds could be appropriate for a server with 4 GB of memory, but far too low for a server with 64 GB of memory. PLE is one of the most direct indicators of memory pressure, though it doesn't provide a complete picture of memory utilization in SQL Server.

Buffer Cache Hit Ratio (BCHR)

Performance Monitor: MSSQL$Instance:Buffer Manager/Buffer Cache Hit Ratio

DMV: MSSQL$Instance:Buffer Manager/Buffer cache hit ratio divided by MSSQL$Instance:Buffer Manager/Buffer cache hit ratio base

A value from 0 to 100, where 100 means that recent traffic has been served entirely out of buffer cache, and 0 means data has been served from a drive. This is not a complete picture of memory pressure, and good high values (>90%) shouldn't be a definitive indication that there is no memory pressure. Low values do indicate a clear indicator that memory is not sufficient for the current workload, but this can also be misleading. Backups and index maintenance can cause BCHR to drop precipitously, to values near zero. Although this metric should be a part of your puzzle, values greater than 80% are desirable.

Page Reads

Performance Monitor: MSSQL$Instance:Buffer Manager/Page reads/sec

DMV: MSSQL$Instance:Buffer Manager/Page reads/sec

The title is a bit misleading—these aren't page reads out of the buffer; rather, they are out of physical pages on the drive, which is slower than data pages coming out of memory. You should make the effort to lower this number by optimizing queries and indexing, efficiency of cache storage, and, of course, as a last resort, increasing the amount of server memory. Although every workload is different, a value less than 90 is a broad guideline. High numbers indicate inefficient query and index design in read-write workloads, or memory constraints in read-heavy workloads.

Memory Pages

Performance Monitor: Memory:Pages/sec

DMV: Not available

Similar to Buffer Manager\Page Reads/sec, this is a way to measure data coming from a drive as opposed to coming out of memory. It is a measure of pages pulled from a drive into memory, which will be high after SQL Server startup. Although every workload is different, a value less than 50 is a broad guideline. Sustained high or climbing levels during typical production usage indicate inefficient query and index design in read-write workloads, or memory constraints in read-heavy workloads. Spikes during database backup and restore operations, bulk copies, and data extracts are expected.

Batch Requests

Performance Monitor: MSSQL$Instance:SQL Statistics\Batch Requests/sec

DMV: MSSQL$Instance:SQL Statistics\Batch Requests/sec

A measure of aggregate SQL Server user activity. Higher sustained numbers are good; they mean your SQL instance is sustaining more traffic. Should this number trend downward during peak business hours, your SQL Server instance is being outstripped by increasing user activity.

Page Faults

Performance Monitor: Memory\Page Faults/sec

DMV: Not Available

A memory page fault occurs when an application seeks a data page in memory, only to find it isn't there because of memory churn. A soft page fault indicates the page was moved or otherwise unavailable; a hard page fault indicates the data page was not in memory and must be retrieved from the drive. The Page Faults/sec metric captures both. Page faults are a symptom, the cause being memory churn, so you might see an accompanying drop in the Page Life Expectancy. Spikes in Page Faults, or an upward trend, indicate the amount of server memory was insufficient to serve requests from all applications, not just SQL Server.

Available Memory

Performance Monitor: Memory\Available Bytes or Memory\Available KBytes or Memory\ Available MBytes

DMV: Available in sys.dm_os_ring_buffers WHERE ring_buffer_type = RING_BUFFER_RESOURCE_ MONITOR (see previous section)

Available Memory is server memory currently unallocated to an application. Server memory above and beyond what the SQL Server instance(s) total MAX_SERVER_MEMORY setting, minus memory in use by other SQL Server features and services or other applications, are available. This will roughly match what shows as available memory in the Windows Task Manager.

Total Server Memory

Performance Monitor: MSSQL$Instance:Memory Manager\Total Server Memory (KB)

DMV: MSSQL$Instance:Memory Manager\Total Server Memory (KB)

This is the actual amount of memory that SQL Server is using. It is often contrasted with the next metric (Target Server Memory). This number might be far larger than what Windows Task Manager shows allocated to the SQL Server Windows NT – 64 Bit background application, which shows only a portion of the memory that sqlserver.exe controls. The Total Server Memory metric is correct.

Target Server Memory

Performance Monitor: MSSQL$Instance:Memory Manager\Target Server Memory (KB)

DMV: MSSQL$Instance:Memory Manager\Target Server Memory (KB)

This is amount of memory to which SQL Server *wants* to have access and is currently working toward consuming. If the difference between Target Server Memory and Total Server Memory is larger than the value for Available Memory, SQL Server wants more memory than the Windows Server can currently acquire. SQL Server will eventually consume all memory available to it under the MAX_SERVER_MEMORY setting, but it might take time.

Protecting important workloads by using Resource Governor

Resource Governor is an Enterprise edition–only feature that you can use to identify connections and limit the resources they can consume.

You can identify connections from virtually any connection property, including the login name, hostname, application name, and so on. After you've identified them, you can limit properties at the individual session level or in a pool of resources. You can override the MAXDOP setting for these sessions; or lower their priority; or cap the CPU, memory, or drive I/O that individual sessions can consume.

For example, you can limit all read-heavy queries coming from a SQL Server Reporting Services server, or long-running reports coming from a third-party reporting application, or dashboard/search queries that use a different application name or login. Then, you can limit these queries as a set, capping them to 25% of the process, disk I/O, or SQL Server memory. SQL Server will enforce these limitations and potentially slow down the identified queries, but meanwhile, the important read-write workloads continue to operate with the remaining 75% of the server's resources.

Be aware that using Resource Governor to limit long-running SELECT statements, for example, does not alleviate concurrency issues caused by locking. See Chapter 9 for strategies to overcome concurrency issues, and keep in mind that using the NOLOCK table hint or the READ UNCOMMITTED isolation level is a risky, clumsy strategy to solving concurrency issues in your applications.

When turned on, Resource Governor is transparent to connecting applications. No code changes are required of the queries to implement Resource Governor.

In Enterprise edition, by default, sessions are split between group = 1 named "system," for system queries internal to the Database Engine, and group = 2 named "default," for all user other user queries. In Standard edition of SQL Server, Resource Governor is not provided, and the only value for group_id is 1. You can find the current groups in the DMV sys. resource_governor_workload_groups.

Configuring the Resource Governor classifier function

Before turning on Resource Governor, you must create a classifier function in the master database that operates at the creation of every new session.

You can write the classifier function however you like, but keep in mind that it will be run for each new connection, and so it should be as efficient and simple as possible. Do not query other user resources such as tables in a user database, because this can cause a noticeable delay in connection creation.

The classifier function must return a Sysname datatype value, which contains the name of the Group to which a new connection is to be assigned. A Group is simply a container of sessions. If no Group name is assigned, the connection is placed in the default group. Remember, it is the default group that you want to protect; it contains "all other" sessions including high business-value connections that perform application-critical functions, writes, and so on.

The sample code that follows defines a classifier function that returns GovGroupReports for all queries coming from two known-fictional reporting servers. You can see in the comments other sample connection identifying functions, with many more options possible.

```
CREATE FUNCTION dbo.fnCLASSIFIER() RETURNS sysname
WITH SCHEMABINDING AS
BEGIN
    -- Note that any request that does not get classified goes into the 'default' group.
 DECLARE @grp_name sysname
IF (
--Use built-in functions for connection string properties
     HOST_NAME() IN ('reportserver1','reportserver2')
 --OR APP_NAME() IN ('some application')
 --AND SUSER_SNAME() IN ('whateveruser')
)
  BEGIN
   SET @grp_name = 'GovGroupReports';
  END
RETURN @grp_name
END;
```

After creating the function, you must register it (which can have any name) as the classifier function for this instance's Resource Governor feature. The feature is not active yet; you still have the following setup to do before turning it on:

```
-- Register the classifier function with Resource Governor
ALTER RESOURCE GOVERNOR WITH (CLASSIFIER_FUNCTION= dbo.fnCLASSIFIER);
```

Configuring Resource Governor pools and groups

Configuring pools (for many sessions to share) and groups (for individual sessions) is the next step. You should take an iterative, gradual approach to configuring the Governor, and avoid making large changes or large initial limitations to the affected groups.

If you have a Developer edition preproduction environment to test the impact of Resource Governor on workloads with realistic production scale, you should consider testing.

The sample code that follows can be an instructional template to creating an initial Pool and Group. If you seek to divide your sessions up further, multiple groups can belong to the same pool, and multiple pools can be limited differently. Commented-out examples of other common uses for Resource Governor are included.

In this example, we create a pool that limits all covered sessions to 50% of the instance's memory, and a group that limits any single query to 30% of the instance's memory, and forces the sessions into MAXDOP = 1, overriding any server, database, or query-level setting:

```
CREATE RESOURCE POOL GovPoolMAXDOP1;
CREATE WORKLOAD GROUP GovGroupReports;
GO
ALTER RESOURCE POOL GovPoolMAXDOP1
WITH (-- MIN_CPU_PERCENT = value
    --,MAX_CPU_PERCENT = value
    --,MIN_MEMORY_PERCENT = value
    MAX_MEMORY_PERCENT = 50
);
GO
ALTER WORKLOAD GROUP GovGroupReports
WITH (
    --IMPORTANCE = { LOW | MEDIUM | HIGH }
    --,REQUEST_MAX_CPU_TIME_SEC = value
    --,REQUEST_MEMORY_GRANT_TIMEOUT_SEC = value
    --,GROUP_MAX_REQUESTS = value
    REQUEST_MAX_MEMORY_GRANT_PERCENT = 30
  , MAX_DOP = 1
)
USING GovPoolMAXDOP1;
```

➤ **For complete documentation of the possible ways to limit groups and pools, go to** *https:// docs.microsoft.com/sql/t-sql/statements/alter-workload-group-transact-sql* **and** *https:// docs.microsoft.com/sql/t-sql/statements/alter-resource-pool-transact-sql*

After you have configured the classifier function, groups, and pools, you can turn on Resource Governor by using the query that follows, placing its functionality into memory. New sessions will begin being sorted by the classifier function and new sessions will appear in their groups. You should also issue the reconfigure command to apply changes made:

```
-- Start or Reconfigure Resource Governor
ALTER RESOURCE GOVERNOR RECONFIGURE;
```

Or, you can turn it off:

```
--Disable Resource Governor
ALTER RESOURCE GOVERNOR DISABLE;
```

After you turn it off, existing sessions will continue to operate under the rules of Resource Governor, but new queries will not be sorted into groups.

After you configure it and turn it on, you can query the status of Resource Governor and the name of the classifier function by using the following sample script:

```
SELECT rgc.is_enabled, o.name

FROM sys.resource_governor_configuration AS rgc
INNER JOIN master.sys.objects AS o
ON rgc.classifier_function_id = o.object_id
    INNER JOIN master.sys.schemas AS s
        ON o.schema_id = s.schema_id;
```

Monitoring pools and groups

The `Group_ID` columns in both `sys.dm_exec_requests` and `sys.dm_exec_sessions` define to which Resource Governor Group the request or session is a part. Groups are members of pools. You can query the groups and pools via the DMVs `sys.resource_governor_workload_groups` and `sys.resource_governor_resource_pools`. Use the following sample query to observe the number of sessions that have been sorted into groups, noting that `group_id` = 1 is the internal group, `group_id` = 2 is the default group, and other groups defined by you, the administrator:

```
SELECT
  rgg.group_id, rgp.pool_id
, Pool_Name = rgp.name, Group_Name = rgg.name
, session_count= ISNULL(count(s.session_id) ,0)
FROM sys.dm_resource_governor_workload_groups AS rgg
LEFT OUTER JOIN sys.dm_resource_governor_resource_pools AS rgp
ON rgg.pool_id = rgp.pool_id
LEFT OUTER JOIN sys.dm_exec_sessions AS s
ON s.group_id = rgg.group_id
GROUP BY rgg.group_id, rgp.pool_id, rgg.name, rgp.name
ORDER BY rgg.name, rgp.name;
```

> ➤ You can reference a (dated) Resource Governor troubleshooting guide for a list of error numbers and their meanings that might be raised by Resource Governor at *https://technet.microsoft.com/library/cc627395%28v=sql.105%29.aspx.*

Understanding the new servicing model

Database administrators and CIOs alike will need to adjust their normal comfort levels with new SQL Server editions. No longer can IT leadership say, "Wait until the first service pack," before moving because there are no more service packs!

Updated servicing model

Microsoft has adopted a new model for its product life cycles. In the past, this servicing model included Service Packs (SPs), Cumulative Updates (CUs), and General Distribution Releases (GDRs). Beginning with SQL Server 2017, the following changes are in effect:

- SPs will no longer be released.

- CUs will be released every month for the first twelve months of general release, and then quarterly for the remaining four years of the five-year duration of the Mainstream Support period.

- CUs might now include localized content and will be delivered on a standardized schedule: as of this writing, this is the week of the third Tuesday of the month.

- Unlike in the past, GDR patches (which contain security-only fixes) will not have their own path for updates between CUs.

Microsoft has maintained in recent years that there is no need to wait for an SP, because the General Availability (GA) release has been extensively tested by both internal Microsoft QA and external preview customers. In fact, Microsoft insists that the Community Technology Preview (CTP) and Release Candidate (RC) versions of SQL Server 2016 and 2017, the steps before Release to Market (RTM), were thoroughly tested in production with selected customers. For those dealing with clients or leadership who are stubborn or reactionary, a possible alternative under the new model could be to target an arbitrary Cumulative Update, such as CU2.

Product support life cycle

In you're planning for long-term use of a particular version of SQL Server, you should keep in mind the following life cycle:

- 0 to 5 Years: Mainstream Support Period

  Security and functional issues are addressed through CUs. Security issues only might also be addressed through GDRs.

- 6 to 10 Years: Extended Support

  Only critical functional issues will be addressed. Security issues might still be addressed through GDRs

- 11 to 16 Years: Premium Assurance

  The Extended Support level can be lengthened with optional payments.

Automating SQL Server administration

This chapter reviews the common forms of automating Microsoft SQL Server instance administration, which includes an exploration of the automation tools of choice for SQL Server administration: SQL Server Agent; basic "care and feeding" maintenance, including Maintenance Plans built in to SQL Server Management Studio; strategies for administering multiple SQL Servers, including Master/Target Agent servers (MSX/TSX); event forwarding and Policy-Based Management (PBM); and, finally, an introduction to PowerShell with realistic sample code. This chapter varies little for SQL Server instances on Windows or Linux except in the case of PowerShell, for which you must run these commands from a Windows server. Where there are exceptions for Linux, we point them out.

Little in this chapter applies to Microsoft Azure SQL Database because the Azure SQL platform automates many of the activities in this chapter, including performance tuning and backups. No initial configuration is needed. If you need more control, many of these features are being released through a new Azure feature, Managed Instances. As the Azure SQL Database platform as a service (PaaS) offering has matured, it has become a powerful cloud-based and complementary platform to SQL Server, neither fully replacing nor overlapping with the feature set or purpose of on-premises SQL Server instances.

Components of SQL Server automated administration

Database Mail makes it possible for SQL Server to send emails to notify DBAs of the outcome of SQL Server Agent Jobs, server performance and error alerts, or custom notifications with Transact-SQL (T-SQL) calls to the `sp_send_dbmail` stored procedure. The SQL Server Agent is the automation engine available in all editions of SQL Server except for Express. Let's review these two key features. Both features are fully supported on Linux as well as Windows.

Database Mail

Database Mail uses Simple Mail Transfer Protocol (SMTP) to send email. By design, this process is run outside of SQL Server using a separate executable DatabaseMail.exe, which is started asynchronously using Service Broker. Email is handled asynchronously and outside of the SQL Server process using Service Broker technology. This isolates both the process and any potential performance impact to the SQL Server instance.

Setting up Database Mail

To begin receiving automated emails, you need to configure Database Mail and then configure SQL Server Agent to use the database mail profile you create. First, in SQL Server Management Studio, use the Database Mail Configuration Wizard, which you can find in the Management folder. You'll need to set up a profile and then an associated account.

The wizard will turn on the Database Mail feature in the Surface Area facet of the SQL Server instance. You need to do this only once. Database Mail is among a select few Surface Area facets that you should turn on for most SQL Server instances.

➤ **For more information on Surface Area facets in each SQL instance, see Chapter 4.**

A Database Mail Profile can be public or private. In the case of private, only specific associated server principals are given access (users or roles in databases). A public profile allows any principal that is a member of the built-in database role DatabaseMailUsersRole in the msdb database.

Ideally, all database mail profiles are private, and only those credentials that will be used to send emails will be given access. In a multitenant environment, or an environment that allows access to external developers or vendors, this is crucial, but even in internal environments this could provide protection against malicious use to send emails.

You can configure a Database Mail Profile to use almost any SMTP configuration, including nonstandard ports and Secure Sockets Layer (SSL). You also can configure it with Windows Authentication (common for SMTP servers in the same domain), basic authentication (common for web authentication), or no authentication (common for anonymous relay in the local network, usually with an IP allow list).

You can configure Database Mail to use any SMTP server that it can reach, including web-based SMTP servers. You can even use Hotmail or other web-based email account if you're configuring for testing purposes or have no other viable internal SMTP options. An internal SMTP server with Windows authentication using a service account is preferred. For Azure infrastructure as a service (IaaS) environments without an internal SMTP presence, SendGrid is a common and supported SMTP solution.

➤ **For more information, visit *https://docs.microsoft.com/azure/sendgrid-dotnet-how-to-send-email*.**

After configuring your account's SMTP settings (you'll need to test them later), the Database Mail account has a number of options that you can adjust:

- **Account Retry Attempts.**   Defaults to 1, which you should probably leave as is to avoid excessive retries that could lock out an account or trigger spam detection.

- **Account Retry Delay (seconds).**   Defaults to 60. Again, you should leave this for the same reasons as for Account Retry Attempts.

- **Maximum File Size (Bytes).**   Defaults to roughly 1 MB. You should change this only if necessary.

- **Prohibited Attachment File Extensions.**   Specifies which file extensions cannot be sent, commonly set if third-party or multitenant development occurs on the SQL instance. This is a comma-delimited list that by default is "exe,dll,vbs,js."

- **Database Mail Executable Minimum Lifetime (seconds).**   Defaults to 10 minutes, which is a counter that starts after an email message is sent. If no other messages are sent in that time frame, the Database Mail executable stops. If stopped, the Database Mail process is started again any time a new email is sent. You'll see messages indicating "Database Mail process is started" and "Database Mail process is shutting down" in the Database Mail Log when this happens.

- **Logging Level.**   Defaults to Extended, which includes basic start/stop and error messages that should be kept in the Database Mail log. Change to Verbose if you are troubleshooting Database Mail and need more information, or Normal to suppress informational messages and see errors only.

After you've set up a Database Mail profile and account, you can send a test email via SQL Server Management Studio. Right-click Database Mail, and then, on the shortcut menu that opens, click Send Test E-Mail. Or, you can send a plain-and-simple test email via T-SQL by using the following code:

```
exec msdb.dbo.sp_send_dbmail
@recipients ='yournamehere@domain.com',
@subject ='test';
```

This code does not specify a @profile parameter, so the command will use the default profile for the current user, the default private if it exists, or the default public profile.

This is all that is necessary for developers and applications to send emails using Database Mail. To allow SQL Server Agent to send emails based on job outcomes and alerts, you will need to create an *Operator* in SQL Server Agent, and then configure SQL Server Agent's Alert System to use a Database Mail profile. We look at SQL Server Agent and its initial configuration in depth later in this chapter.

Maintaining email history in the msdb database   Finally, the email messages sent by Database Mail are queued in a table in the msdb database named dbo.sysmail_mailitems. As you might suspect, data in the msdb tables for Database Mail will grow, potentially to an unmanageable size. This can cause queries to the msdb's Database Mail tables to run for a long time. There is no automated process in place to maintain a retention policy for these tables, though there is a stored procedure to delete older messages as well as a lengthy reference article in place to guide you through creating a set of archive tables and a SQL Server Agent job to maintain data over time. You can find both of these at *https://docs.microsoft.com/sql/ relational-databases/database-mail/create-a-sql-server-agent-job-to-archive-database-mail-messages-and-event-logs*.

Troubleshooting Database Mail

We've already mentioned the Database Mail log, now let's go over the other diagnostics available for Database Mail.

Reading email logging in the msdb database   If the SMTP Server or the database mail process becomes unavailable, the messages are queued in a table in the msdb database named dbo.sysmail_mailitems.

The msdb database contains metadata tables for the Database Mail feature, including msdb.dbo.sysmail_allitems, which tracks all outbound email activity. Look for items for which the sent_status doesn't equal sent for signs of messages that weren't successfully sent; for example:

```
--Find recent unsent emails
SELECT m.send_request_date, m.recipients, m.copy_recipients, m.blind_copy_recipients
, m.[subject], m.send_request_user, m.sent_status
FROM msdb.dbo.sysmail_allitems m
WHERE
-- Only show recent day(s)
m.send_request_date > dateadd(day, -3, sysdatetime())
-- Possible values are sent (successful), unsent (in process), retrying (failed but
retrying), failed (no longer retrying)

AND m.sent_status<>'sent' ORDER BY m.send_request_date DESC;
```

There is also a view provided in the msdb, dbo.sysmail_unsentitems, that filters on (sent_status = 'unsent' OR sent_status = 'retrying'). There are four possible values for sent_status in sysmail_allitems: sent, unsent, retrying, and failed.

NOTE

You cannot use the previous query to troubleshoot failed SQL Server Reporting Services report subscription emails. SQL Server Reporting Services uses an entirely different process, SMTP configuration, and authentication to send report subscriptions via email. Instead, look for SQL Server Reporting Services log messages in the log files in the following subfolder:

%programfiles%\Microsoft SQL Server Reporting Services\SSRS\LogFiles\

Allow anonymous relay for anonymous authentication   If you're using anonymous authentication internally with Microsoft Exchange, verify that the internal SMTP anonymous relay has a dedicated Receive connector that allows for anonymous relay. By design, a Receive connector just for anonymous relay should allow only a small list of internal hosts, your SQL Server(s) among them.

Authentication with the SMTP server is likely the problem if you observe errors in the Database Mail log after attempting to send email, such as

Cannot send mails to mail server. (Mailbox unavailable. The server response was: 5.7.1 Unable to relay...

or:

Cannot send mails to mail server. (Mailbox unavailable. The server response was: 5.7.1 Service unavailable...

Enabling service broker on the msdb database   After restoring the msdb database or setting up database mail for the first time, the Service Broker feature might not be turned on for the msdb database. You can check the `is_broker_enabled` field in the system catalog view `sys.databases`; if it is 0, this is the case, and you must remedy this. You will receive the following self-explanatory error message:

```
Msg 14650, Level 16, State 1, Procedure msdb.dbo.sp_send_dbmail, Line 73 [Batch Start
Line 18] Service Broker message delivery is not enabled in this database. Use the ALTER
DATABASE statement to enable Service Broker message delivery.
```

To turn on Service Broker on the msdb database, you must stop the SQL Server Agent service and close any connections active to the msdb database prior to running the following code:

```
ALTER DATABASE msdb SET ENABLE_BROKER;
```

SQL Server Agent

The SQL Server Agent is the native automation platform for internal task automation, mainte-nance, log and file retention, even backups. SQL Server Agent is similar to the Windows Task Scheduler, but it has a number of advantages for automating SQL Server tasks, including inte-gration with SQL Server security, authentication, logging, and native T-SQL programming. SQL Server Agent can accomplish many of the same tasks as Windows Task Scheduler, including running cmdexec and PowerShell commands. Metadata, configuration, and history data for the SQL Server Agent are kept in the msdb database.

Configuring SQL Server Agent jobs

A job contains a series of steps. Each job step is of a type that allows for different actions to take place. A job can be automatically started based on a number of conditions, including pre-defined schedule or schedules; in response to an alert; as a result of running the `sp_start_job` stored procedure in the msdb database; when SQL Server Agent starts; or even when the host computer is idle.

You can script jobs in their entirety through SQL Server Management Studio, providing a script-level recoverability, migration to other servers, and source control possibility for SQL Server Agent jobs. Jobs are backed up and restored via the msdb database, or scripted for backup and migration.

As you can see in the Job Properties dialog box, job steps do not necessarily need to run lin-early. You can set a job to default to start at any job step, and additionally, when starting a job, you can manually change the start step for the job. Each job step reports back whether it suc-ceeded or failed, and you can configure it to move to another step or fail based on the job step outcome. These step completion actions are defined on the Advanced page of the Job Step Properties dialog box. However, for ease of management in the future, we recommend that you create job steps that run as linearly as possible.

You can assign jobs to categories; in fact, many system-generated jobs (such as replication) are assigned to categories. You can create your own categories in SQL Server Management Stu-dio by right-clicking the Jobs folder under SQL Server Agent, and then, on the shortcut menu, clicking Manage Categories. This should aid your efforts to report on, maintain, redeploy, and migrate jobs in the future.

Understanding job step security

Although creating SQL Server Agent jobs themselves is easy to do through SQL Server Man-agement Studio, a critical step that many developers and administrators skip is the use of Credentials and Proxies in SQL Server Agent job steps. Using a proxy to run a job step instead of the SQL Server Agent service account or another named user is the most secure way to run

jobs. Proxies make it possible for administrators to set job steps to run under a specific credential, rather than giving the SQL Server Agent service account access to everything that each
job needs.

Proxies are used for all job step types but one. It is not possible to run a T-SQL script job step
using a proxy. A T-SQL step will run in the security context of the owner of the job if the owner
is not a sysadmin. If the owner of the job is a member of the sysadmin server role, the job will
run as the SQL Server Agent service account.

For all other job step types, there is a proxy. On the Job Step Properties page, you can select the
job step to "Run as" a proxy. SQL Server Agent checks for access to the subsystem each time the
job step is run to verify that the security has not changed.

You can associate each proxy with one or more subsystems, though to make best use of them,
you should consider not creating one proxy for all subsystems; instead, you should create many
proxies for different job step security requirements and subsystems.

Without a proxy specified, jobs must be owned by a member of the sysadmin role to run job
steps other than the T-SQL step type. These job steps will then run as the SQL Server Agent service account. This isn't ideal, for two reasons:

- The SQL Server Agent service account should not have local administrator privileges on
  the server. This reduces the risk to the operating system (OS) from potential misuse for
  SQL Server Agent jobs. Service accounts are discussed in Chapter 4 and Chapter 6.

- Remember also that the SQL Server Agent service account must be a member of the sysadmin server role, so it might have far too many privileges inside SQL Server than necessary to safely run SQL Agent jobs.

Further, the owner of the job must also have permissions to use any proxy subsystem that the
job's steps use. It is also important because job steps often need to access other servers, and
proxies give you the ability to assign pinpoint rights to the other resources. You will not be able
to create or modify a job step for a subsystem if the job owner is not listed as a principal who
has access to the proxy. Sysadmins automatically have access to all proxies.

Proxies map to credentials on the SQL Server, you'll find a subfolder for credentials in the Security folder on the Server level in Object Explorer in SQL Server Management Studio. Each proxy
is linked to a credential in SQL Server. The credential stores the account's user name and password, which means that if it changes, the proxy and SQL Server Agent job steps that depend
on it will not be able to authenticate and will fail. Therefore, you should use service accounts,
not individual's named accounts, in credentials that will be used by proxies. Credential account
passwords shouldn't be widely known, and the accounts shouldn't be used interactively regularly by administrators, so that they cannot accidentally become locked out.

You can create a credential for a local Windows account or a domain account. You also can create credentials for accounts on Enterprise Key Management (EKM) modules, including the Azure Key Vault service. The Windows account of the credential must have "Log on as a batch job" permission on the server. As a local administrator, you can grant this permission in the Local Security Policy dialog box.

Securing permissions to interact with jobs

Your login must be a member of the sysadmin server role or one of the SQL Server Agent database roles in the msdb database to set up a SQL Server Agent job in SQL Server Management Studio.

The SQLAgentOperatorRole, SQLAgentReaderRole, and SQLAgentUserRole each have permission to create jobs, start jobs, view job history, view, and edit properties of jobs, though mostly only for jobs they own. For granular details on the limitations and overlapping of each role, visit *https://docs.microsoft.com/sql/ssms/agent/sql-server-agent-fixed-database-roles*.

The SQLAgentUserRole is the least privileged of the three roles, but the other two roles are members of the SQLAgentUserRole. Typically, membership to these roles is limited to service accounts and third-party developers. Do not grant permissions directly to the SQLAgentUserRole database role, including the ability to use proxies. Instead, grant permission on proxies to individuals or service accounts.

Scheduling and monitoring jobs

A job is run based on one or more schedules assigned to it. You give schedules a name upon creation and can assign them to multiple jobs, which can be especially useful for uncommon or esoteric job schedules, or to centralized management of jobs that should run simultaneously. To view and select schedules from other jobs, in the Job Properties dialog box, on the Schedules tab, click the Pick button. You will see only the job schedules to which you have access.

There are four schedule types:

- Start automatically when SQL Server Agent starts

- Start whenever the CPUs become idle

- Recurring

- One time (for running a schedule manually, often during testing)

Jobs run asynchronously when they are started by SQL Server Agent or manually. A dialog box with a spinning progress icon appears, but you can close this, and the job will continue to run until completion. You can monitor the progress of jobs in SQL Server Management Studio by viewing the Job Activity Monitor, or you can observe the job's current request in `sys.dm_exec_requests`.

You can also use T-SQL to query the status of jobs with the undocumented stored procedure `master.dbo.xp_sqlagent_enum_jobs`, which you can join to `msdb.dbo.sysjobs`, as shown here:

```
--jobs still running
declare @xp_sqlagent_enum_jobs table (
id int not null IDENTITY(1,1) PRIMARY KEY,
Job_ID uniqueidentifier not null,
Last_Run_Date int not null,
Last_Run_Time int not null,
Next_Run_Date int not null,
Next_Run_Time int not null,
Next_Run_Schedule_ID int not null,
Requested_To_Run int not null,
Request_Source int not null,
Request_Source_ID varchar(100)  null,
Running int not null,
Current_Step int not null,
Current_Retry_Attempt int not null,
[State] int not null);

INSERT INTO @xp_sqlagent_enum_jobs
EXEC master.dbo.xp_sqlagent_enum_jobs 1,'';

SELECT j.name
, state_desc = CASE ej.state
WHEN 0 THEN 'not idle or suspended'
WHEN 1 THEN 'Executing'
WHEN 2 THEN 'Waiting for thread'
WHEN 3 THEN 'Between retries'
WHEN 4 THEN 'Idle'
WHEN 5 THEN 'Suspended'
WHEN 7 THEN 'Performing completion actions'

END
, *
 FROM  msdb.dbo.sysjobs j
 LEFT OUTER JOIN @xp_sqlagent_enum_jobs ej
 ON j.job_id = ej.Job_ID
ORDER BY j.name;
```

You can download this script, CH14_xp_sqlagent_enum_jobs_query.sql, and other accompanying scripts for this book from *https://aka.ms/SQLServ2017Admin/downloads*.

Configuring and viewing job history

Every time a job is run, a record is maintained in system views in the msdb database in the `msdb.dbo.sysjobhistory` table. To review the job's history, in SQL Server Management Studio, right-click it, and then, on the shortcut menu, select Job History. History is stored for each job. You can expand a given job to view the output for each step, including any errors.

With jobs that run frequently (for example, transaction log backup jobs), a large amount of job history will be created and stored in the msdb. It is initially defaulted to two very low and likely unrealistic row caps: 1,000 rows of history for all jobs, and 100 rows of history at most for one job. If a job were to run once per hour, it would lose visibility into history after just four days—a likely unrealistic window for troubleshooting and diagnostic information.

In SQL Server Management Studio, in Object Explorer, right-click SQL Server Agent, and then click Properties. Click the History page. As Figure 14-1 demonstrates, this page is not intuitive and can be confusing. The first option, Limit Size Of Job History Log, is a rolling job history retention setting. You might find it a good start to simply add a 0 to each value, increasing the maximum log history size in rows from the default of 1,000 to 10,000 or more, and also increase the maximum job history per job in rows from the default of 100 to 1,000 or more. These settings would store just more than 41 days of history for a job that runs hourly if this were the only job on the server. You might find these numbers also insufficient on a SQL Server instance with many frequently running jobs, and you should increase until you have a comfortable retention of job run history.

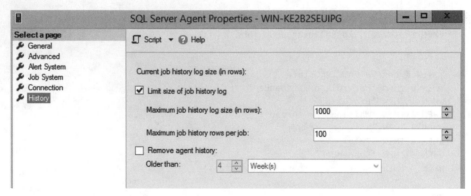

Figure 14-1 The two options to retain SQL Agent job history on the History page of the SQL Server Agent Properties dialog box. The top check box configures a rolling cap on row history; the bottom check box is a one-time manual pruning.

NOTE

SQL Server Agent job history (and Maintenance Plan history logs) are not affected by trace flag 3226, which suppresses successful backup messages in the SQL Server error log and Windows Application event log, such as "BACKUP DATABASE successfully processed."

The job history log can be useful, but there are two limitations of which you should be aware:

- The message text in this Job History viewer is truncated after 1,024 characters. If you need to view the full results of the output, you need to query the `msdb.dbo.sysjobhistory` table. The message window in that table is considerably larger at 8,000 characters.

- The history of SQL Server Integration Services package execution in the SQL Server Agent job history is extremely limited, reduced to details around the fact that the package started, completed, and/or errored, without detail. More verbose detail will appear in the thorough history available in the SSISDB. To access and view that history, in SQL Server Management Studio, use the Integration Services Catalogs menu and then go to the project and packages that failed.

NOTE

Using the Project Deployment model for your SQL Server Integration Services packages provides superior built-in logging and trending when running a package. Since SQL Server 2012, the msdb database isn't the ideal place to deploy your SQL Server Integration Services packages. The Project Deployment model and the SSISDB database, both originally released in SQL Server 2012, combined with further integration with SQL Server Agent, make for a far superior option for SQL Server Integration Services development than the old Package Deployment model. You can still deploy legacy Package Deployment model packages to the msdb, but we do not recommend this for new development.

You can also configure additional logging for each job step in order to capture the full step output and, more commonly, the error text. The following options are available on the Advanced page of the Job Step Properties dialog box:

- The output history to an output text file option, and additionally to append history to that log file. Be careful of keeping the Append Output To Existing File option turned on long term—the output file can grow to a significant size in a short amount of time.

- The Log To Table option, which writes to the `sysjobstepslogs` table in the msdb database. That table has an `nvarchar(max)` data type for the Log field, allowing for more output data to be captured per step if needed. Be careful of this option, as well—the table can grow to a significant size in a short amount of time. You should schedule the stored procedure `sp_delete_jobsteplog` to remove old records from the table over time.

- Finally, there is the Include Step Output In History option, which adds a row to the job history log to include the output of the job step. This should contain valuable information, and, unlike the other two options, job history is automatically maintained over time by SQL Server Agent.

Administering SQL Server Agent operators

Operators are aliases in SQL Server Agent, listing contact information email. (The Net Send and Pager Email Contact options are deprecated, and Net Send no longer appears in SQL Server Management Studio.)

Operators usually should not be pointed at individuals (even though you can create a semi-colon-delimited list of email address), but instead to a distribution group (even if that group initially contains only one person). In most situations, you will create an operator to notify SQL Server first responders in your environment. You should maintain your environment's list of DBA personnel in distribution lists; for example, not inside the Operator lists of each SQL Server instance.

To set up an operator, in SQL Server Management Studio, in Object Explorer, expand the SQL Server Agent folder, right-click Operator, and then, on the shortcut menu, click New Operator.

NOTE

Do you have a big team and an on-call rotation? Set up a scheduled process in a SQL Server Agent job that updates an "on call rotation" operator's email address to resource(s) currently "on call." Use the `sp_update_operator` stored procedure to update the email address for an operator on a schedule.

Alerts

Alerts are created to set conditions and, when met, prompt email notifications or the kickoff of SQL Server Agent jobs in response. Alerts are versatile and can look for SQL Server events in the error log, or performance conditions that you would view in the Performance Monitor application or even by Windows Management Instrumentation (WMI) queries.

As recommended in Chapter 4, you should set up alerts for high-severity SQL Server errors. However, do not overcommit your personal inbox with alerts, and do not set an inbox rule to Mark As Read and file away emails from SQL Server. By careful selection of emails, you can assure yourself and your team that emails from SQL Server will be actionable concerns that rarely arrive.

With a large number of SQL instances under your purview, email alerts for even severe issues can become too numerous. We then recommend a way to gather and queue actionable errors in a system that provides for aggregation, dashboarding, and team assignment. There are a number of third-party "log collection" software applications that perform the task of log aggregation and centralized alerting.

You might also configure the Delay Between Responses in each alert, to prevent an unchecked flooding of emails arriving from a repeating error. Consider a delay of up to five minutes between responses, as your environment deems appropriate.

You can specify only a single error message or severity per alert, so we recommend scripting the mass creation of a standard batch of alerts, to be created consistently on all your SQL Server instances. See the script CH14_add_standard_error_alerts.sql for an example that includes the alerts we examine in just a moment. You can download this script and others from *https://aka.ms/SQLServ2017Admin/downloads*.

Next, we review the three types of Alerts that you can set up: SQL Server event, performance conditions, and WMI event alerts.

SQL Server event   You should set up alerts on actual error messages that are important enough for you to receive emails. SQL Server generates a lot of informational-only events, such as successful backup messages, for which you would not want to receive messages.

You can set up alerts based on the actual error number (samples follow shortly) or any error of a certain severity (1 to 25). You can optionally filter the alert to a single database, or for a specific message text.

It's a good idea to set up alerts for severity 16 through 19 and 21 through 25, because these tend to be actionable errors. Severities 21 and above are severe and unrecoverable errors.

The most common Severity 20 errors are nuisance authentication-related and transient (e.g., the user tried, experienced an error, tried again, and succeeded). An alert for Severity 20 might send out a large number of unactionable alerts to the SQL Server DBA team. You will still see Severity 20 issues in the SQL Server Error Log and should make note of them as they appear, especially if they appear in large numbers, given that this can be a sign of greater authentication or domain issues, or malicious intrusion attempts. The goal of alerts is to send out actionable errors or performance conditions worth investigating.

> **NOTE**
> Every SQL Server error message includes a severity, but that doesn't mean you want to be alerted to them. For example, basic syntax errors that you might make while writing queries in SQL Server Management Studio will surface as Severity 15 errors, which aren't worth alerting.

You might also want to configure alerts to send out error messages for these SQL Server error numbers that are not already covered in the severities 16 through 19 and 21 through 25. These following errors are rare, but immediately actionable:

- **825** (Severity 10).   A dreaded "read-retry" error, after the read of a file succeeded after failing *x* number of times. This is often a harbinger of potential database integrity failure that should prompt immediate action.

- **854, 855, 856** (Severity 10).   This is an uncorrectable hardware memory corruption detected via the operating system's memory diagnostics that indicates a potentially immediate stability thread to the system due to memory.

- **3624** (Severity 20).   This is an internal SQL Server error called an "assertion failure" that is typically a software bug, though it could indicate internal data corruption. This is often-times addressed via a SQL Server service pack or patch.

Performance conditions   You can set up performance condition alerts for any performance counter in the SQLServer category, the same set of alerts you would see in the Windows Performance Monitor application with the prefix "SQLServer" or "MSSQL$*instancename*".

For example, if you want to receive an email when the SQL Server's Page Life Expectancy (PLE) drops below a certain value, you would select PLE in the same way that you would find it in Performance Monitor. Choose the object Buffer Manager, the counter Page Life Expectancy, and the comparison operator Falls Below and comparison value. In the case of PLE, this is measured in seconds.

> **NOTE**
>
> You can also query most performance counters from SQLServer: or MSSQL$*instancename:* objects via the dynamic management view (DMV) sys.dm_os_performance_ counters. There is one caveat: in some cases the calculation is not as straightforward.
>
> For example, consider the Buffer Cache Hit Ratio (BCHR) metric, one piece of the puzzle of looking at memory utilization. Calculating the actual BCHR as it appears in Perfor-mance Monitor requires division of two simultaneous counter values:

```
SELECT [BufferCacheHitRatio] = (bchr * 1.0 / bchrb) * 100.0
FROM
(SELECT bchr = cntr_value FROM
sys.dm_os_performance_counters
WHERE counter_name = 'Buffer cache hit ratio'
AND object_name = 'MSSQL$sql2017:Buffer Manager') AS r
CROSS APPLY
(SELECT bchrb= cntr_value FROM
sys.dm_os_performance_counters
WHERE counter_name = 'Buffer cache hit ratio base'
and object_name = 'MSSQL$sql2017:Buffer Manager') AS rb;
```

> **NOTE**
>
> SQL Server samples the data periodically, so there might be a few seconds' delay between when you receive the alert and when the threshold was reached.

WMI event alert conditions   The third option for SQL Server Agent alerts allows for custom WMI queries to be run. WMI queries can gather and prompt alerts on a variety of Data Definition Language (DDL) events in SQL Server, and WMI queries follow the basic syntax of T-SQL SQL Server queries. The FROM of the WMI query will be a WMI object, not an object in a SQL Server database. You can reference the WMI provider classes and properties at *https://docs.microsoft.com/sql/relational-databases/wmi-provider-server-events/wmi-provider-for-server-events-classes-and-properties*.

This type of alert is not as straightforward. In general, you might find better results, more flexibility, and less complexity by using extended events, SQL Server Agent jobs, SQL Server Audit, and/or third-party monitoring tools than by using WMI alert queries.

Setting up an email recipient for a WMI event alert does not send over any useful or actionable information in the email aside from the alert's name. This does little more than let you know that a WMI event occurred (observed asynchronously, so there might be some delay).

To view the information regarding the event—for example, the T-SQL command associated with the event—you must turn on Token Replacement in the SQL Server Agent Properties dialog box. On the Alert System page, at the bottom, select the Token Replacement check box. This allows for the tokenization (replacement at runtime) of WMI commands in a T-SQL job step. For more on the tokens that you can use in a T-SQL job step, reference *https://docs.microsoft.com/sql/ssms/agent/use-tokens-in-job-steps*.

We have prepared a sample WMI event alert to capture the CREATE DATABASE DDL event. For a simple but lengthy working example of the creation of a sample table, SQL Server Agent job, and alert, see the script CH14_WMI_Alert_data_capture.sql, which you can download along with others for this book from *https://aka.ms/SQLServ2017Admin/downloads*.

SQL Server Agent job considerations when using availability groups

If you are running SQL Server Agent jobs in an availability group environment, you will still need to configure your maintenance plans on each SQL Server instance, some of which will cover databases not included in availability groups and the system databases master and msdb, for example. You should ensure that your maintenance plans, regardless of platform, are consistently updated on all replicas and also are aware of their local replica role, so that maintenance plans do not need to be turned on, turned off, or reconfigured when a failover occurs.

Your SQL Server Agent jobs must exist on all replicas of the availability group and be aware of whether the script is running on the primary replica for a database. You will need multiple versions of any custom maintenance task in order to separate scripts for databases in each availability group and one more for databases not in an availability group (including any system databases that you intend to maintain with custom scripts).

To avoid having SQL Server Agent jobs error when their local replica is not the primary replica for a database, you can add a T-SQL step to the start of the job to detect and raise a failure. The goal of the first step is to prevent subsequent job steps from running and failing against secondary replica databases, which will not be not writeable. Name the first step "Am I Primary?" or something similar, and then add the following script:

```
--add as step 1 on every AAG-aware job
IF NOT EXISTS (
SELECT @@SERVERNAME, *
    FROM sys.dm_hadr_availability_replica_states  rs
    inner join sys.availability_databases_cluster dc
    on rs.group_id = dc.group_id
    WHERE is_local = 1
    and role_desc = 'PRIMARY'
--Any databases in the same Availability Group
    and dc.database_name in (N'databasename1', N'databasename2'))
  BEGIN
     print 'local SQL instance is not primary, skipping';
     throw 50000, 'Do not continue', 1;
  END;
```

This code causes Step 1 to fail when it is not run on a primary replica for the specified database(s). In the Advanced settings of the "Am I Primary?" job step, the On Success Action should be Go To The Next Step, as usual, but the On Failure Action should be Quit The Job Reporting Success, which would not register as a job failure. Instead of a green check mark or a red "X" next to the job, SQL Server Job History displays a yellow Triangle. This prevents subsequent job steps from running and failing against secondary replica databases, which will not be writeable.

This script is available in the CH14_Am_I_Primary.sql script in the accompanying downloads for this book, which are available at *https://aka.ms/SQLServ2017Admin/downloads*.

NOTE

You should not consider the previous script for Maintenance Plans jobs. Any change to the Maintenance Plan will re-create the job and overwrite the new "Am I Primary?" task you added. Instead, take advantage of the availability group–aware backup priority settings in the Back Up Database Task. We look at this in more detail in the next section.

➤ For more about availability groups, see Chapter 12.

Maintaining SQL Server

In this section, we review what you should be doing as a day-to-day database administrator of a SQL Server instance, how to accomplish these tasks, and the built-in tools that SQL Server provides. You can accomplish within SQL Server all of the major maintenance objectives that we cover without the use of third-party tools, or even well-respected free options. SQL Server editions above Express edition (because Express has no Agent) ship fully featured and ready for you to configure to perform basic maintenance.

For the most part, the tasks in this section are built in to Azure SQL Database. In some cases, the maintenance tasks are completely automated, especially in the case of disaster recovery, or partially automated, in the case of index maintenance. We'll be focusing on SQL Server instances in this section because the fast evolution of Azure SQL Database reduces the hands-on maintenance required by DBAs on the PaaS platform.

➤ **For more information on Azure SQL databases and Managed Instances, see Chapter 5.**

Basic "care and feeding" of SQL Server

You can carry out the regular proactive maintenance of a SQL Server instance by applying one or more of the following strategies:

- SQL Server Maintenance Plans, including the option to use a Maintenance Plan Wizard

- Custom scripting using DMVs and T-SQL or PowerShell commands

- Third-party tools

Each has advantages and disadvantages, and each makes different compromises between ease of setup and customizability.

You can run these strategies via SQL Server Agent jobs, except for some third-party software packages that would utilize an external scheduling apparatus. You can configure each to provide customized activity logging, retention, and the ability to view history in different ways.

Regardless of the strategy or strategies adopted, with built-in or third-party tools, you should accomplish the following as a bare minimum on a regular schedule, in no particular order:

1. Backup system and user databases.
   a. Full backups for all databases.
   b. Transaction log backups for database not in SIMPLE recovery mode.
   c. To save space, differential backups between less frequent full backups.

2. Retention policy for database backups, if backups are stored locally, by deleting backups after a business-approved amount of time. In the case of tape backups for which retention isn't necessary, a rotation policy, instead.

3. Retention policy for maintenance plan log files, backup and restore history records in msdb, old database mail row entries.

   a. SQL Server Error Log files are already maintained by SQL Server to a configurable number of log files. (The default is 6 which should be likely be increased.)

   b. SQL Server Agent job history is also maintained automatically by settings in the SQL Server Agent properties.

   c. Backup history is kept in the msdb database and should be pruned over time.

4. Reduce fragmentation in SQL Server indexes.

   a. There are different strategies to reduce fragmentation in clustered and nonclustered indexes.

   b. Columnstore indexes also require maintenance via REORGANIZE steps, as well, and fragmentation is measured differently.

5. Update statistics.

   a. This should accompany INDEX REORGANIZE steps, but not INDEX REBUILD steps. Remember that the INDEX REBUILD command also updates the index statistics.

6. Check database integrity via DBCC CHECKDB.

7. Using off-premises facilities for any backups stored physically local to the SQL Server.

   a. Storage-Area Network (SAN) replication or another file-level backup system can accomplish this, as can integration with Azure Storage for easy cloud-based backup.

   b. Remember that your Data Loss Tolerance isn't defined by how often you take backups, but by how often those backups get off-premises!

What will vary is how often these tasks need to run on each database and even what type of backups you need. This section of the chapter walks you through creating T-SQL scripts in SQL Server Agent, using the Maintenance Plan designer and the Maintenance Plan Wizard.

Even though we won't make any recommendations regarding third-party tools, we should note that many third-party tools do not provide an end-to-end solution for item 7 in the previous list, which typically involves coordination with the storage administrators and/or cloud hosting such as Azure Storage. SQL Server Managed Backup to Azure is a full-featured SQL Server backup solution (though not free, it is relatively cheap). It is the Microsoft-recommended backup solution for SQL Server instances running on Azure virtual machines (VMs).

If you want to maintain direct control of item 7, backing up off-premises, you can use BACKUP ... TO URL statements to write backups directly to Azure Storage, often to complement local backup storage. (Scripting that yourself is free of course, but Azure Storage is not). To meet your Recovery Time Objective (RTO) goals, or in the event of external network failure, you should always maintain local backups within your network for a time.

> ➤ **For more details about backups, schedules, T-SQL command parameters, and backup strategy, refer to Chapter 11.**

Using SQL Server Maintenance Plans

SQL Server Maintenance Plans are a free, low-cost, low-complexity, visually built option to implementing SQL Server maintenance and disaster recovery. The drag-and-drop tasks built in to Maintenance Plans' design surface have some distinct shortcomings that we'll review; although they're much more capable starting in SQL Server 2016, especially for index maintenance, which can now be aware of fragmentation levels, different maintenance strategies, and more. You will see differences when creating Maintenance Plans in SQL Server Management Studio from version to version of SQL Server.

NOTE

As of this writing, Maintenance Plans are not supported for SQL Server on Linux.

The Maintenance Plan Wizard is a step-by-step tour through most of the steps necessary for SQL Server. The Maintenance Plan Wizard guides you through an easy process of creating a Maintenance Plan with most of the basics, which you'll then be able to review with the Maintenance Plan design surface in SQL Server Management Studio. To begin with a fresh slate, click New Maintenance Plan. This prepopulates objects for you in the design surface, with which we recommend you become familiar. If you have any experience with SQL Server Integration Services, the design surface interface will feel very familiar. Behind the scenes, Maintenance Plans actually create and store SQL Server Integration Services packages internally.

The tasks in a Maintenance Plan and the choices in the Maintenance Plan Wizard translate directly to the options you're already familiar with in SQL Server Agent jobs or the options for backups and index maintenance T-SQL commands. For example, the Run As option on the first screen of the wizard or in the Subplan properties of the design surface, provides a list of proxies just as a SQL Server Agent job step does. Instead of using the SQL Server Agent service account, ideally you should choose a proxy that has access to the SQL Server Integration Services Package Execution subsystem.

Also on the first page of the Maintenance Plan Wizard, you have the option to run each task with separate schedules or with a single schedule for the entire plan. We recommend that you choose the Separate Schedules For Each Task option here, or if you're designing the maintenance plan in the design surface, break activities into multiple subplans, each with its own schedules. This is because some tasks such as index maintenance or database integrity checks can take a long time to run, and you do not want your backups in serial with those, and then delayed and inconsistently occurring. To work the maintenance plan into your nonbusiness hours or after-hours windows, you will want more scheduling flexibility than a single start time for all tasks to run serially.

On the Select Maintenance Tasks page of the Maintenance Plan Wizard, there is a list of all of the base built-in maintenance tasks. In the graphical design surface, you have one additional tool to run custom T-SQL scripts titled Execute T-SQL Statement Task. You can use this to run your custom maintenance scripting or other administrative scripts. We review that later in this section.

> **NOTE**
>
> The Maintenance Plan Wizard can create only one copy of each available task. To create two different tasks of the types we'll be looking at in a moment—for example, one for system databases and one for user databases—you will need to use the Maintenance Plan design surface in SQL Server Management Studio.

The following subsections present the available tasks that you can select from, along with descriptions of what they do.

Check Database Integrity task

The Check Database Integrity task runs DBCC CHECKDB to check for database corruption, a necessary task that you should run periodically. You should run DBCC CHECKDB at least as often as your backup retention plan. For example, if you keep local backups around for one month, you should make sure that you perform a successful DBCC CHECKDB no less than once per month. More often, if possible, is recommended. On large databases, this task could take hours and can block other user queries.

> ➤ For more about data corruption and checking database integrity, see Chapter 13.

The options available in the Maintenance Plan task, match the common parameters you would use in the DBCC CHECKDB command. The Physical Only check box uses the PHYSICAL_ONLY parameter of DBCC CHECKDB, which limits the potential disruptive impact of the DBCC CHECKDB and is less comprehensive as a result. However, using PHYSICAL_ONLY takes significantly less time to complete while still detecting the signs of common storage hardware failure.

NOTE

A common practice when using the PHYSICAL_ONLY option of DBCC CHECKDB or the Check Database Integrity Maintenance Plan task is to maintain a system in which production databases are restored on a matching nonproduction system, and running a time-consuming full integrity check (without the PHYSICAL_ONLY parameter) to catch any corruption issues.

Shrink Database task

There is no sound reason to ever perform a Shrink Database task on a schedule. A Shrink Database step removes free space from a file and returns it to the OS, causing the file to experience an autogrowth event the next time data it is written to it. Do not ever include the Shrink Database task in the Maintenance Plan.

Reorganize Index task

A reorganize task runs an ALTER INDEX ... REORGANIZE statement, which reduces index fragmentation but does not update statistics. On large databases, this could take hours, but will have less overhead, much less query disruption, and finish faster than a Rebuild Index.

Because Reorganize Index is an online operation, it will not take long-term table locks and might block other user queries for only a very short period of time. Online index operations will consume server resources and generate large amounts of logged transactions.

CHAPTER 14

Inside OUT

I want to maintain indexes only if they are above a certain percentage of fragmentation, can I do that with Maintenance Plans?

You can, with improvements to the SQL Server Maintenance Plans first released with SQL Server 2016. Older versions of maintenance plans probably drew your ire with an "everything" approach to reorganizing or rebuilding indexes in a database.

You will now see options to intelligently limit index maintenance, starting with the options to select between Fast (LIMITED), Sampled, and Detailed. This corresponds the parameters provided to the structural statistics dynamic management function (DMF), sys.dm_db_index_physical_stats.

You can configure the Reorganize and Rebuild tasks to maintain only indexes filtered by percentage of fragmentation and page count, both from `sys.dm_db_index_physical_stats`, and/or actual index usage (based on the `sys.dm_db_index_usage_stats` DMF). This is a significant improvement in the tooling for Maintenance Plans, which before these improvements were mostly unusable on larger databases. The fragmentation threshold is 15% by default in the Reorganize task, 30% in the Rebuild task, as illustrated in Figure 14-2.

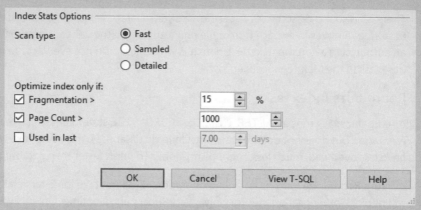

Figure 14-2   The options to maintain indexes available in the Maintenance Plan Index Reorganize and Index Rebuild tasks.

Other options added to the Reorganize and Rebuild tasks match the options for the `ALTER INDEX ... REORGANIZE`, and `REBUILD` T-SQL commands, which we covered in detail in Chapter 13.

Rebuild Index task

More thorough than a Reorganize step at removing index fragmentation, this task runs a `ALTER INDEX ... REBUILD` statement and does update statistics. The options available in the Rebuild Index dialog box correspond to the options for the `ALTER INDEX ... REBUILD` syntax.

NOTE

Maintenance Plans currently do not support `RESUMABLE` index rebuilds, which might be a necessity for you on very large tables. For more information on `ALTER INDEX ... REORGANIZE` and `REBUILD`, see Chapter 13.

You can perform a Rebuild step as an online operation, and then it is not likely to block other user queries. Not all indexes and data types can have an online rebuild performed, so the

Maintenance Plan dialog box for the Rebuild Index task will ask you what you want to happen. The ONLINE option for Index Rebuilds is an Enterprise edition-only feature.

Rebuilding indexes without the ONLINE option has the potential to block other user queries, and will consume server resources. On large databases, this could take hours to finish, and even more without the ONLINE option.

NOTE

Memory-optimized table indexes do not accumulate fragmentation on-disk and do not need regular maintenance for fragmentation. However, you should routinely monitor the number of distinct values in hash index keys, and with the ALTER TABLE ... ALTER INDEX ... REBUILD syntax, adjust the number of buckets in a hash index over time.

Memory-optimized tables are ignored by Maintenance Plans in SQL Server Management Studio.

Update Statistics task

The Update Statistics task runs an UPDATE STATISTICS statement, rebuilding index statistics objects, which we reviewed in Chapter 10. Do not follow an Index Rebuild task with an Update Statistics task for the same objects, this is redundant work. Updating statistics is an online operation, so it will not block other user queries, but it will consume server resources. This task should finish faster than either a REORGANIZE or REBUILD step.

Inside OUT

Is an Update Statistics task necessary in a Maintenance Plan if auto_create_stats *is turned on for the database?*

Yes, you should still maintain the health of Update Statistics with regularity, even if not in a Maintenance Plan. When auto_update_stats is turned on, statistics are updated periodically based on usage. Statistics are considered out of date by the query optimizer when a ratio of data modifications to rows in the table has been reached. The query optimizer checks for and updates the out-of-date statistic before running a query plan. Therefore, auto_update_stats has some small runtime overhead, though the performance benefit of updated statistics usually outweighs this cost. We also recommend turning on auto_update_stats_async option, which helps minimize this runtime overhead by updating the statistics after the query is run, instead of before.

We recommend that you turn on the auto_update_stats and auto_update_ stats_async options, as discussed in Chapters 4 and 10, on all user databases, unless the application specifically requests that it be turned off, such as is the case with Microsoft SharePoint.

You can also manually identify the date on which any statistics object was last updated by using the sys.dm_db_stats_properties DMF. In your databases, you might see that there are statistics that are quite old. This means that they might not have been accessed in a way that prompts the auto_update_stats update and have not had an INDEX REBUILD, which would also update the statistics.

Updating both column and index statistics for a database regularly, if your mainte- nance window time allows, will definitely not hurt, and will certainly help. By updat- ing statistics regularly, you can reduce the number of statistics updates that happen automatically during transactions in regular business hours.

History Cleanup task

This task deletes older rows in msdb tables that contain database backup and restore history, prunes the SQL Server Agent log file, and also removes older Maintenance Plan log records. These are accomplished by running three stored procedures in the msdb database: dbo.sp_ delete_backuphistory, dbo.sp_purge_jobhistory, and dbo.sp_maintplan_ delete_log, respectively. You should run this task to prevent excessively old data from being retained, according to your environmental data retention requirements. This will save space and prevent large table sizes from degrading the performance of maintenance tasks. This step should finish quickly and would not disrupt user queries. This step does not delete backup files or Maintenance Plan log files; that is the job of the Maintenance Cleanup task.

Maintenance Cleanup task

The Maintenance Cleanup task deletes files from folders and is commonly used to delete old database backup files, using the system stored procedure master.dbo.xp_delete_file. You also can use it to clean up the .txt files that Maintenance Plans write their history to in the SQL Server instance's Log folder. You can configure the task to look for and delete any extension and by folder directory, and then specify that subdirectories be included. The date filter uses the Date Modified file attribute (not the Date Created attribute). Combined with the option to cre- ate a subdirectory for each database, this means that you can create and remove backups files in folder structure for each database.

Note that in the case of Maintenance Plans, by default logs are kept in a table, msdb.dbo. sysmaintplan_log, as well as in text files in the SQL Server instance default Log folder.

Deleting one does not delete the other. You should maintain a retention policy on both sources of Maintenance Plan run history.

The Maintenance Cleanup task deletes files only from folders, and thus isn't an option to enforce a retention policy for backups to URL in Azure Storage. And currently, Maintenance Plans in SQL Server Management Studio are not supported at all on SQL for Linux, although this capability might be added in the near future.

Inside OUT

How do I delete old backups in Azure Blob storage?

The stored procedure sp_delete_backup specifically exists to clean up file-snap-shot based backups, which are continuous chains of backup starting from a single FULL backup.

To clean up old backups taken to Blob storage using the BACKUP ... TO URL syntax, you shouldn't try to delete the base blob of the backup, using Microsoft Azure Storage Explorer or the Azure Storage viewer in SQL Server Management Studio, for example. Aside from the files, there are pointers to the file-snapshots in a file-snap-shot backup set that must be deleted, as well.

Note also that SQL Server Managed Backup to Azure has its own retention plan, which is currently limited to a maximum of 30 days.

Execute SQL Server Agent Job task

Using this task, you can orchestrate the asynchronous start of another SQL Server Agent job during the Maintenance Plan, perhaps to start another middle-of-the-night process as soon as possible after maintenance is complete.

Back Up Database (Full, Diff, Transaction Log) task

The most obvious and common of all Maintenance Plan tasks, with this task, you can take a backup of any kind of the specified databases. The options in the Maintenance Plan dialog box for the backup are similar to the SQL Server Management Studio Database Backup dialog box, plus some minor extra options, including an option to ignore replica priority in an availability group database.

NOTE

The standard extensions for backup files are .bak (FULL), .dif (DIFFERENTIAL), and .trn (LOG), but these are just conventions. You can provide any file extension (or none at all) for your backup types, but you should try to be consistent across your entire SQL Server environment with backup file extensions.

The Back Up Database task affords you multiple strategies for backups, including backing up to disk or to Azure Storage via URL as well as to legacy tape backup support.

Backing up to URL writes files directly to Azure Storage natively, without the need to install any software or network connections. This was a fairly limited feature prior to SQL Server 2016 but now can be accomplished via a shared access signature credential for secure access to Azure Blob storage. A step-by-step walkthrough is available at *https://docs.microsoft.com/sql/relational-databases/tutorial-use-azure-blob-storage-service-with-sql-server-2016*.

You can configure disk backups to append multiple database backups multiple times to the same file or files, or create a backup file and a subdirectory for each database per backup. For backups to disk, we recommend that each database have a subdirectory in the folder location you select, to separate the backup files of databases with potentially different retention plans or recovery strategies. The Maintenance Plan backup will automatically create subdirectories for new databases, and when performing backups, append a time stamp and a unique string to backup names in the following format: *databasename*_backup_*yyyy_mm_dd_hhmmss_unique-number.bak|dif|trn*.

We recommend that you select the options for Verify Backup Integrity, CHECKSUM, and Compress Backup for all database types, for all databases. This is supported even for backups to URL. Keep in mind that the Verify Backup step performs a RESTORE VERIFYONLY statement to examine the backup file and verify that it was valid, complete, and should be restorable. "Should be" is key because the only way to truly test whether the backup was valid is to test a restore. The RESTORE VERIFYONLY does not actually restore the database backup, but could give you an early heads-up on a potential drive or backup issue, and is always recommended when time permits. The verify step could significantly increase the duration of the backup, scaling with the size of the database backup, but is time well worth spending in your regular maintenance window.

Execute T-SQL Statement task (not available in the wizard)

This task can run T-SQL statements against any SQL Server connection, with a configurable time-out. A simple text box accepts T-SQL statements, and because of its simplicity, we recommend that instead of pasting lengthy commands, you instead reference a stored procedure. This would be easier to maintain and potentially keep in source control by developing the stored procedure in other tools.

Maintenance Plan report options

By default, Maintenance Plans create a report in two places to record the history for each time a subplan runs. Logs are kept in a table, `msdb.dbo.sysmaintplan_log`, as well as in .txt files in the SQL Server instance default Log folder. You can also choose the Email Report option in the Maintenance Plan Wizard, which adds a Notify Operator Task.

Covering databases with the Maintenance Plan

After you select the maintenance tasks that you want the wizard to configure, you'll be able to select the databases you want to run the tasks against. The options are: all databases, system databases, all user databases, or you can specify a list of databases. You also have the option to ignore databases for which the status is not online, which we also recommend.

To isolate the configuration, maintenance, and logging from one another, it is a common to create two Maintenance Plans: one for system databases (master, model, and msdb) and one for all user databases. The system plan just handles system database backups, the user plan handles everything else. This ensures that if there are any issues with ongoing changes to the User Maintenance Plan, the crucial system database backups are unaffected.

Inside OUT

Will a SQL Server Maintenance Plan automatically detect a new database created on my SQL Server?

Yes, a Maintenance Plan can accomplish this if you configure it correctly, which could be invaluable to you when applications are configured to procedurally create new databases, such as SharePoint.

You should try to configure Maintenance Plan tasks to use either the All Databases or All User Databases (assuming that you have another task that covers system databases). When you select either of these, new databases are automatically included in the maintenance plan. This makes your job as an administrator easier. If you choose a specific fixed list of databases using the These Databases option and list, new databases will be ignored, and you will need to remember to add the databases to the Maintenance Plan.

If you have databases that are no longer in use that you no longer want to cover with Maintenance Plans, consider taking the database offline, and then using the option in many Maintenance Plan tasks to ignore databases where the status is not online.

There is one caveat regarding transaction log backups tasks using either of the two All options for databases. After you create a new database in FULL recovery mode, the backup task that takes transaction log backups in the Maintenance Plan will attempt to take a transaction log backup and will fail. This is because a database must first have a FULL backup taken before a transaction log backup will succeed. When you create a new database, take a manual full backup, or your Maintenance Plan will chirp errors at you until a full backup is taken on that database. Other database's transaction log backups will continue to run as usual, even if one or more databases fail.

Building Maintenance Plans by using the design surface in SQL Server Management Studio

Due to the nature of wizards, there are some inherent issues with configuring a robust maintenance solution that covers all the needs of your databases. The Maintenance Plan design surface in SQL Server Management Studio gives you the ability to set up your task run order and precedence constraints as well as to maintain multiple subplan schedules within a maintenance plan.

The maintenance plan designer has three main sections: the subplans list, the design surface, and the Maintenance Plan tasks toolbox. When you open a maintenance plan, the first two will be obvious, but the toolbox might not be docked. To display the toolbox and pin it to the side of SQL Server Management Studio, press Ctrl+Alt+X, or, on the View menu, click Toolbox. Figure 14-3 displays a sample Maintenance Plan.

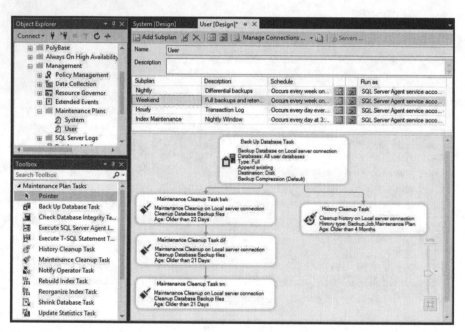

Figure 14-3 A sample maintenance plan for User database has been created, with multiple subplans, each running on a different schedule.

When you save the maintenance plan, each of the subplans in the maintenance plan will become a SQL Server Agent job with a naming convention *maintenance plan name.subplan name*.

NOTE

When you save a Maintenance Plan, the job(s) it creates might be owned by your personal login to the SQL Server. Be aware that if your account becomes disabled or locked out, and this will prevent the SQL Server Agent job from running.

At the top of the Maintenance Plan window is where the subplans are listed; initially, there will be just one plan called Subplan_1. You should break down the tasks that will be accomplished in the subplan by the schedules they will follow, and name them accordingly. You can add subplans and manage their schedules in the Maintenance Plan window. Note that you should not make changes to the SQL Server Agent jobs after they've been created—the next time you edit the Maintenance Plan, your changes might be overwritten.

The large gray area beneath the subplan list is the design surface for Maintenance Plans, a graphical, drag-and-drop interface. To add tasks to a subplan, simply drag a task from the toolbox to the design surface. To serialize the running of multiple tasks, click one, and then click the green arrow beneath the box, dragging it to the task that should follow. You can create a long string of sequential activities or a wide set of parallel-running activities, similar to designing SQL Server Integration Services packages. In fact, Maintenance Plans *are* SQL Server Integration Services packages.

NOTE

When in the Database Maintenance Plan Designer task, there is a View T-SQL button that shows you the exact T-SQL that will be run to perform the maintenance tasks. You can use this to learn the commands for maintenance tasks so that you can make your own customized plans, which we talk about in the next section.

When not to use SQL Server Maintenance Plans

Personal preference, of course, is a fine enough factor to not use built-in Maintenance Plans. You can write your own, as long as your library of scripts or third-party tools accomplish the necessary maintenance tasks with consistency, configurability, and good logging for review.

For SQL Server instances with manageable maintenance windows, SQL Server Maintenance Plans will meet your needs if the schedules are set up appropriately. You can create a variety of Maintenance Plans to cover databases with various levels of importance or availability based on business requirements (with the caveat of not being able to detect new databases [see the previous Inside OUT box]). For very large databases or databases with 24x7 availability requirements, more granularity for maintenance operations will likely be necessary.

Not every business has the luxury of having all night and/or all weekend to perform maintenance outside of business hours. When you become familiar with the T-SQL commands and their various options, you can be creative to overcome tight scheduling, crowded maintenance windows, very large databases, or other Maintenance Plan complications.

After reviewing the capabilities of the Backup Up task and Rebuild Index task, you should consider Maintenance Plans more full-featured and capable of handling the bulk of maintenance, even on larger databases with tight schedules. Ultimately, the success of Maintenance Plans or custom scripts will be dependent on your understanding of the various options available for the seven core maintenance tasks listed earlier in this chapter.

Backups on secondary replicas in availability groups

One of the many useful features in Always On availability groups is the ability to utilize read-only secondary replicas for remote backups. Performing backups on a secondary replica, including a geographically separated replica, introduces complexity but has a big advantage. Backups do not take locks and will never block a user query, but they will incur significant CPU, memory, and I/O overhead. Backups can slow database response, so on servers with large databases and/or busy 24x7 utilization, it might be necessary to find alternative strategies to backups. Taking database backups on secondary replicas is one of the alternatives and moves the resource expense of backups off the primary replica.

Understanding backup priority values

In SQL Server Management Studio, in the Availability Group Properties dialog box, review the Backup Preferences page. It's important to understand the priority values and how they interact with various backup tasks.

The default option is to Prefer Secondary, which specifies that backups occur on the secondary replica first or, if it is not available, on the primary replica. You then can provide priority values (0 to 100, where 100 is highest) to decide which of multiple secondary replicas should be the preferred backup location. The values apply to both full and transaction log backups.

Other self-explanatory options include Primary, Secondary Only, or Any Replica, which uses the priority values to decide which replica is preferred for the backups. When failing over to another replica, you will need to review and script the changes to the backup priority. Your planned failover scripts should include the reassignment of backup priority values.

It's also important to note that this Backup Preferences page affects only backup systems or scripts that are aware of the backup preferences. For example, in SQL Server Management Studio, in Object Explorer, right-click a database, and then, on the shortcut menu, click Tasks, and then Backup. The dialog box that opens takes a backup of a database but does not include any availability groups–aware settings. On the other hand, the Back Up Database task in SQL Server Maintenance Plans is aware of availability group backup priority value settings.

You are limited to taking copy-only FULL backups and transaction log backups on readable secondary replica databases. When including databases in an availability group, the Maintenance Plan Back Up Database task will warn you if you are attempting to configure a FULL backup without copy-only check or differential backup, or if you select the "For availability databases, ignore replica priority for backup and backup on primary settings" check box. If this is misconfigured, it is possible to create a Maintenance Plan that will run but not take backups of databases in an availability group.

> ➤ For more information on using replica backup priorities, visit *https://docs.microsoft.com/ sql/database-engine/availability-groups/windows/active-secondaries-backup-on- secondary-replicas-always-on-availability-groups* and *https://docs.microsoft.com/sql/ database-engine/availability-groups/windows/configure-backup-on-availability- replicas-sql-server*.

Use replica backup priority in your backups schedules

If you attempt to configure a full backup without copy-only or a differential backup, you will see the warning in the Back Up Database task "This backup type is not supported on a secondary replica and this task will fail if the task runs on a secondary replica." If you select the Ignore Replica Priority check box, the warning will read "Note: Ignoring the backup priority and availability group settings may result in simultaneous parallel backups if the maintenance plan is cloned on all replicas."

Maintenance Plans should run on a schedule on all availability group replicas. The priority values for backups can cause a backup not to be taken on a primary or nonpreferred secondary replica, but the Maintenance Plan backup task will start and complete as usual. The Maintenance Plans will use the backup priority values and do not need to be configured when different replicas in the availability group become primary.

You can still take a manual backup of any type of the databases and bypass the availability group backup preferences, and, in fact, your backup strategy might include intentionally taking FULL backups in more than one node of a geographically dispersed availability group.

If you are not using SQL Server Maintenance Plans or scripting to take backups, be aware that not all third-party backup solutions are aware of availability group backup preferences or even availability groups in general. Maintenance Plans in SQL Server Management Studio are aware of the backup preferences, as can be your custom scripting via the function `master.sys.fn_ hadr_backup_is_preferred_replica`. It returns a 0 or 1, based on whether the current SQL Server instance is operating as the preferred backup.

Inside OUT

How do I prevent a broken recovery chain when taking backups on secondary replicas?

Taking backups of the same database on multiple servers could lead to some parts of a backup recovery chain being stored on different servers. The solution to this is rather obvious: You should always ensure that backups are copied off-premises, from one datacenter or secured site to another, which is likely where your availability group replicas are.

Just as you would copy your backups of a standalone SQL Server instance to another location, you must copy your backups of availability group databases off-premises, ideally to each other. You can accomplish this with two strategies.

Copy the backups taken on the secondary node to the primary regularly, and make sure you maintain a chain of transaction log backups together with their root full and/or differential backups, regardless of where the backups were taken. You should keep a complete chain intact in multiple locations.

Strategies for administering multiple SQL Servers

There are some options for creating orchestration in SQL Server, to allow for a multiplication and standardization of SQL Server DBA effort across multiple servers. The potential to set up SQL Server Agent jobs that are run simultaneously on multiple servers is powerful, especially for custom-developed scripts to gather and report information back to a central SQL Server.

If you live in an environment with more than a few SQL Server instances, you should be aware of the Registered Servers and Central Management Server features of SQL Server Management Studio that we reviewed in Chapter 1.

Master and Target servers for SQL Agent jobs

The Master and Target servers (known as the MSX/TSX) feature is built in to SQL Server Agent to aid DBAs who want to manage identical jobs across multiple SQL Server instances. This feature has been in the product since SQL Server 7.0, but many DBAs are unaware of the convenience that it can deliver. The feature shows its age—some of the critical configuration settings are registry keys—but there is no doubt that the feature is useful and works seamlessly with technologies it could not have foreseen, including availability groups (more on that later).

You can designate one SQL Server as a Master server (MSX) and set up multiserver jobs on that server, and configure each instance to have its SQL Server Agent jobs remotely managed into a Target server (TSX). The MSX cannot be a TSX of itself, so using a separate production server to orchestrate multiserver administration of SQL Server Agent jobs is necessary. The MSX server should be a production environment server that does not host performance-sensitive production workloads.

Other considerations for the MSX server include the following:

- Of the servers you have available, choose the most recent version of SQL Server for the MSX server. You can communicate with up to two previous versions for TSX servers.

- Each TSX can have only one MSX.

- Before changing the name of a TSX, first defect it from the MSX and then reenlist it.

- Do not use a built-in account for the SQL Server Agent service account on all servers; instead, use a domain service account, as recommended earlier in this chapter.

Creating MSX and TSX Servers by using SQL Server Management Studio

In SQL Server Management Studio, in Object Explorer, right-click SQL Server Agent, point to Multi Server Administration, and then click Make This A Master, as illustrated in Figure 14-4.

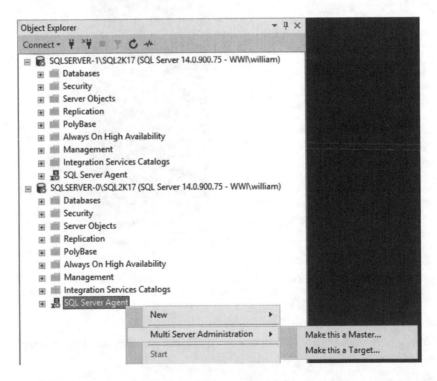

Figure 14-4 The often-overlooked Multi Server Administration options available in SQL Server Management Studio Object Explorer.

The Master Server Wizard launches and first sets up a special operator just for running multi-server jobs, called MSXOperator. You can specify only one operator to run multiserver jobs, so think carefully about who should be notified about these jobs. Specify the email address. As always with operators, it's best not use an individual's email addresses, but to use an email distribution group, instead.

Next, the wizard presents locally registered and central-management registered servers so that you can select them as targets for the MSX. Select the target servers from the list or, at the bottom, click Add Connection and add servers not registered in your list.

> ➤ **For more information about locally registered servers and Central Management Servers, see Chapter 1.**

When you are finished with the wizard, the labels in Object Explorer will be different for both Master and Target SQL Server Agents, as shown in Figure 14-5. SQLSERVER-0\SQL2K17 has been configured as the MSX, and SQLSERVER-1\SQL2K17 has been configured as a TSX.

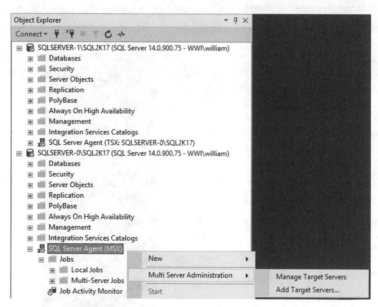

Figure 14-5 With Multi Server Administration configured, the SQL Server Agent in SQL Server Management Studio Object Explorer is labeled, denoting which server is an MSX and which server is a TSX.

Similarly, on the MSX, under SQL Server Agent in Object Explorer, you will see two new subfolders under Jobs: Local Jobs and Multi-Server Jobs.

By default, SSL encryption is used between the servers, but you can change that through a registry setting. See *https://docs.microsoft.com/sql/ssms/agent/*

set-encryption-options-on-target-servers for the exact entries. You should not need to change this, because encrypted communication between the servers is recommended. An SSL certificate will need to be installed on the server before using it through the wizard.

Though we do not recommend it, you can turn off the encryption of Master-Target servers by changing the registry set to not use encryption. The registry key `HKEY_LOCAL_MACHINE\SOFTWARE\Microsoft\Microsoft SQL Server\isntance\SQLServerAgent\MSxEncryptChannelOptions` is by default 2, which means all communication is encrypted. Changing this to 0 on all servers removes encryption.

➤ For more information, visit *https://docs.microsoft.com/sql/ssms/agent/ set-encryption-options-on-target-server*.

Managing multiserver (MSX/TSX) administration

To manage SQL Server Agent jobs in a multiserver environment, set up the job in the same way you would for any other job on the MSX server. Then, navigate to the Targets page on the job, which outside of a multiserver environment has no use. From there, select Target Multiple Servers and then select the servers on which the job should run. In the background, code is run to send the jobs to the TSX servers.

Any jobs with steps that use proxies will need the proxy accounts to have access to the TSX, and a proxy by that same name on the TSX. Otherwise, the job will not find a proxy on the TSX. However, by default, matching proxy names from MSX to TSX isn't allowed, because of the potential for malicious action. This must be turned on via the registry on the TSX.

➤ For more information reference *https://docs.microsoft.com/sql/ssms/agent/ troubleshoot-multiserver-jobs-that-use-proxies*.

On Target servers, jobs will appear in the SQL Server Agent, in the Jobs folder, but you can't edit them.

Sometimes, the synchronizing of job definitions to the TSX will not be queued up and not post to a server. In this case, issue the following the command, but be aware that this cancels any running jobs on the TSX:

```
EXEC msdb.dbo.sp_resync_targetserver '<Target Server Name>';
```

Most other issues with multiserver jobs are solved by defecting the TSX and then adding it again.

Managing multiserver administration in availability groups

The MSX/TSX feature works with availability groups and can be quite useful for ensuring that jobs stay synchronized across servers. The MSX/TSX data is stored in system tables in the msdb database, which cannot be part of an availability group.

CHAPTER 14

You should not have the MSX on a SQL Server instance in the availability group, this would limit your ability to failover and use SQL Server Agent Multi Server Administration. You would lose your ability to orchestrate jobs across the Target servers if one of the nodes in your availability group was unreachable, compromising your failover state. Instead, consider other high availability solutions for the server that functions at the master.

Note that using MSX/TSX for availability group SQL Server Agents doesn't change the need to set up the "Am I Primary?" logic in step 1 of any job that should run only on a SQL Server instance that currently hosts the primary replica.

➤ **For a code sample, refer to the section "SQL Agent Job considerations when using availability groups" earlier in this chapter.**

SQL Server Agent event forwarding

Event forwarding refers to having one central Windows server to receive the SQL Server events of many. The server that is the destination of many servers' event forwarding might handle a heavy workload, especially network traffic. The destination server should be a production-environment server that does not host performance-sensitive production workloads. You can refer to this server as the alerts management server.

Event forwarding allows for the Windows Event Viewer to be a single pane view of events on many instances of SQL Server. Further, it allows for alerts on the alerts management server to prompt a response to the originating server, via SQL Server Agent alerts. Forwarded errors arrive in the Windows Application Event log, not the SQL Server Error Log, and because of this, the SQL Server Agent service account needs to be a local Windows administrator.

Typically, this setup is the same server as your Multi Server Administration (MSX/TSX) server; in fact, the features work together. If your MSX server and alerts management server are on separate SQL Server instances, you will lose the ability to run jobs when events happen.

Setting up event forwarding

You configure event forwarding in the SQL Server Agent Properties dialog box. In SQL Server Management Studio, open the SQL Server Agent Properties dialog box, and then go to the Advanced page. In the SQL Server Event Forwarding section, select the Forward Events To A Different Server check box. In the text box, type the name of the alerts management server. Be aware that the alerts management server that receives forwarded events must be the SQL Server default instance of a server.

You can also choose whether to send all events or only unhandled alerts that have not been handled by local alerts on each SQL Server instance. You can then specify a minimum error severity to be forwarded. We recommend that you select errors of Severity 16 and above, keeping in mind the caveat of nuisance Severity 20 errors.

> ➤ For information about alerts and error severity, see the section "Components of SQL Server automated administration" earlier in this chapter.

Policy-Based Management

Policy-Based Management (PBM) is a powerful tool for enforcing rules for configuration settings, options for databases and servers, security principals, table design, even database object naming conventions. As of this writing, this feature does not yet apply to Azure SQL Database.

PBM is structured around policies. Policies contain a single condition, which is a Boolean expression. The condition expression is evaluated against properties and setting of destination objects, such as the server itself, a database, a table, or an index.

For example, you might set up a condition around the `AdHocRemoteQueries` server-level setting. SQL Server has a large list of facet properties built in to it, such as `AdHocRemove QueriesEnabled` in the Surface Area Configuration facet. (As we covered in Chapter 4, the Surface Area Configuration facet contains a number of security-sensitive features, many of which—but not all—we recommend that you turn off unless needed.) To check that this Surface Area Configuration option is always turned off, create an expression that checks whether `AdHocRemoveQueriesEnabled` can be evaluated to `Enabled = False`.

Policies can contain only one condition, but you can configure many different expressions, any one of which could initiate the expression. You could, for example create a PBM policy called "Configuration Settings," a PBM condition called "Settings That Should be Disabled," and a list of expressions, each of which evaluates a different Surface Area Configuration option.

In fact, in the View Facets dialog box of SQL Server Management Studio, you can click Export Current State As Policy to ease the implementation of many configuration options into policy. You can apply the resulting settings to the local server as a policy right away, or export them as .xml, which then can be imported as a new policy. To export or import a policy, in SQL Server Management Studio, in Object Explorer, in the Policy Management folder, right-click a policy.

Evaluating policies and gathering compliance data

After you create a policy, you have multiple options for when to evaluate it: on demand (manually); on a schedule; and continuously, which either logs or blocks policy violations.

PBM is built in to SQL Server Management Studio, accessible via the Policy Management sub-folder within the Management folder. SQL Server maintains history of all policy evaluations in a Policy History log, which is available within SQL Server Management Studio. To access it, right-click Policy Management, and then, on the shortcut menu, click View History. In the System Policies subfolder, you'll find 14 prebuilt policies for checking the health of availability groups, and two more for the SQL Server Managed Backup feature, first introduced in SQL Server 2014.

For example, after configuring the sample policy in the previous section (see the code example at the end of this section) with On Demand Evaluation Mode, test it by turning on the `AdHocRemoteQueries` setting in the Surface Area Configuration facet. A message will immediately appear in the SQL Server Error Log stating: "Policy 'Disable AdHocRemote QueriesEnabled' has been violated by target 'SQLSERVER:\SQL*servername**instancename*'", accompanied by a Severity 16 error 34053 message.

The on-demand Evaluate Mode gives the administrator an immediate report of all policy compliance. From the Evaluate Policies window, you can view any number of policies, and should any expressions fail, the policy will display a red "X" beside it. In this example, evaluating the policy with the `AdHocRemoteQueries` facet turned on displays an error message and provides you with the ability to apply the change to bring the servers in line with policy.

In the Target Details pane of the Evaluate Policies window, you can click Details to start an analysis of all expression evaluations in the condition.

The scheduled Evaluate Mode generates only SQL Server Error log activity.

Not all facet expressions allow for the On Change: Prevent Evaluation Mode, but this option makes it possible for you to create a policy that will prevent developers or other administrations from making DDL changes that violate condition expressions. This is accomplished by rolling back the transaction that contains the violating statement. As with all rollbacks, this transaction could contain other statements and could cause a database change deployment to fail in a manner that could complicate your change process. This is a heavy-handed way to enforce policy, especially reversible activity such as naming conventions or table designs. Administrators and database developers should be aware of the potential impact to database deployments. You should limit the use of the On Change: Prevent Evaluation Mode to security-related or stability-related properties, such as the following:

- Server Security: `@CrossDBOwnershipChainingEnabled`

  Enforce that this evaluates to `False`, unless this is part application security design

- Server Security: `@PublicServerRoleIsGrantedPermissions`

  Enforce that this evaluates to `False`, in any circumstance

- Login: `@PasswordPolicyEnforced`

  Enforce that this evaluates to `True` for all logins

- Certificate: `@ExpirationDate`

  Enforce that this date is not within a certain time frame in the future (6 months), in every database (sample code to follow)

- Database: @AutoShrink

  Enforce that this evaluates to False, in all databases

- Database: @AutoClose

  Enforce that this evaluates to False, in all databases

Samples

You can script policies to T-SQL for application to multiple servers, though be wary of applying policies for production systems to development systems, and vice versa. Following are the T-SQL scripts to create the two aforementioned samples. (This script is available in the CH14_PBM_samples.ps1 file in the accompanying downloads for this book, which are available at *https://aka.ms/SQLServ2017Admin/downloads*.)

Ad Hoc Remote Queries Enabled   Use the following T-SQL code to create the sample policy to keep the Surface Area Configuration option AdHocRemoteQueries turned off (it will be evaluated on demand):

```
--Create policy to evaluate status of AdHocRemoteQueries option
--This script is generated by SSMS
Declare @condition_id int
--Create Condition
EXEC msdb.dbo.sp_syspolicy_add_condition
@name=N'AHRQE Disabled'
, @description=N'Keep AdHocRemoteQueries disabled.'
, @facet=N'ISurfaceAreaFacet'
, @expression=N'<Operator>
  <TypeClass>Bool</TypeClass>
  <OpType>EQ</OpType>
  <Count>2</Count>
  <Attribute>
    <TypeClass>Bool</TypeClass>
    <Name>AdHocRemoteQueriesEnabled</Name>
  </Attribute>
  <Function>
    <TypeClass>Bool</TypeClass>
    <FunctionType>False</FunctionType>
    <ReturnType>Bool</ReturnType>
    <Count>0</Count>
  </Function>
</Operator>', @is_name_condition=0, @obj_name=N'', @condition_id=@condition_id OUTPUT
Select @condition_id;
GO
--Create internal object set and target sets to support condition
Declare @object_set_id int;
EXEC msdb.dbo.sp_syspolicy_add_object_set
@object_set_name=N'Disable AdHocRemoteQueriesEnabled_ObjectSet'
, @facet=N'ISurfaceAreaFacet'
```

```
, @object_set_id=@object_set_id OUTPUT
Select @object_set_id;
Declare @target_set_id int;
EXEC msdb.dbo.sp_syspolicy_add_target_set
@object_set_name=N'Disable AdHocRemoteQueriesEnabled_ObjectSet'
, @type_skeleton=N'Server', @type=N'SERVER'
, @enabled=True, @target_set_id=@target_set_id OUTPUT
Select @target_set_id;
GO
--Create Policy
Declare @policy_id int;
EXEC msdb.dbo.sp_syspolicy_add_policy
@name=N'Keep AdHocRemoteQueries Disabled'
, @condition_name=N'AHRQE Disabled', @policy_category=N''
, @description=N'', @help_text=N'', @help_link=N''
, @schedule_uid=N'00000000-0000-0000-0000-000000000000'
, @execution_mode=2, @is_enabled=True
, @policy_id=@policy_id OUTPUT, @root_condition_name=N''
, @object_set=N'Disable AdHocRemoteQueriesEnabled_ObjectSet'
Select @policy_id;
GO
```

The result sets returned by these queries contain only the integer IDs of new policy objects that have been created.

User-generated certification expiration   Check to verify whether any nonsystem certificates have an expiration in the next three months, and fails policy if so. Ignores any certificates with "##" in the name because these are built in to SQL Server and are for internal use only. These certificates that begin with "##" are generated when SQL Server is installed, and cannot be modified. Keep in mind also that certificates used for TDE will continue to work just fine after expiration.

```
--Create policy to evaluate certificate expiration
--This script is generated by SSMS
Declare @condition_id int
--Create Condition
EXEC msdb.dbo.sp_syspolicy_add_condition @name=N'Expiration'
, @description=N'Check to verify that any non-system certificates
have an expiration in the next three months, fails policy if so.
Ignores any certificates with "##" in the name.'
, @facet=N'Certificate', @expression=N'<Operator>
  <TypeClass>Bool</TypeClass>
  <OpType>AND</OpType>
  <Count>2</Count>
  <Operator>
    <TypeClass>Bool</TypeClass>
    <OpType>GT</OpType>
    <Count>2</Count>
    <Attribute>
      <TypeClass>DateTime</TypeClass>
```

```
        <Name>ExpirationDate</Name>
      </Attribute>
      <Function>
        <TypeClass>DateTime</TypeClass>
        <FunctionType>DateAdd</FunctionType>
        <ReturnType>DateTime</ReturnType>
        <Count>3</Count>
        <Constant>
          <TypeClass>String</TypeClass>
          <ObjType>System.String</ObjType>
          <Value>m</Value>
        </Constant>
        <Constant>
          <TypeClass>Numeric</TypeClass>
          <ObjType>System.Double</ObjType>
          <Value>6</Value>
        </Constant>
        <Function>
          <TypeClass>DateTime</TypeClass>
          <FunctionType>GetDate</FunctionType>
          <ReturnType>DateTime</ReturnType>
          <Count>0</Count>
        </Function>
      </Function>
    </Operator>
    <Operator>
      <TypeClass>Bool</TypeClass>
      <OpType>LIKE</OpType>
      <Count>2</Count>
      <Attribute>
        <TypeClass>String</TypeClass>
        <Name>Name</Name>
      </Attribute>
      <Constant>
        <TypeClass>String</TypeClass>
        <ObjType>System.String</ObjType>
        <Value>##%</Value>
      </Constant>
    </Operator>
  </Operator>', @is_name_condition=0, @obj_name=N''
, @condition_id=@condition_id OUTPUT
Select @condition_id;
GO
--Create internal object set and target sets to support condition
Declare @object_set_id int;
EXEC msdb.dbo.sp_syspolicy_add_object_set
@object_set_name=N'Cert Expiration_ObjectSet'
, @facet=N'Certificate', @object_set_id=@object_set_id OUTPUT
Select @object_set_id;
GO
Declare @target_set_id int;
EXEC msdb.dbo.sp_syspolicy_add_target_set
```

```
@object_set_name=N'Cert Expiration_ObjectSet'
, @type_skeleton=N'Server/Database/Certificate'
, @type=N'CERTIFICATE', @enabled=True
, @target_set_id=@target_set_id OUTPUT
Select @target_set_id;
EXEC msdb.dbo.sp_syspolicy_add_target_set_level
@target_set_id=@target_set_id
, @type_skeleton=N'Server/Database/Certificate'
, @level_name=N'Certificate', @condition_name=N''
, @target_set_level_id=0;
EXEC msdb.dbo.sp_syspolicy_add_target_set_level
@target_set_id=@target_set_id, @type_skeleton=N'Server/Database'
, @level_name=N'Database', @condition_name=N''
, @target_set_level_id=0;
GO
--Create Policy
Declare @policy_id int;
EXEC msdb.dbo.sp_syspolicy_add_policy
@name=N'Cert Expiration', @condition_name=N'Expiration'
, @policy_category=N'', @description=N''
, @help_text=N'', @help_link=N''
, @schedule_uid=N'00000000-0000-0000-0000-000000000000'
, @execution_mode=2, @is_enabled=True
, @policy_id=@policy_id OUTPUT, @root_condition_name=N''
, @object_set=N'Cert Expiration_ObjectSet'
Select @policy_id;
GO
```

The result sets returned by these queries contain only the integer IDs of new policy objects that have been created.

Using PowerShell to automate SQL Server administration

SQL Server has supported close integration with Windows PowerShell for a decade. PowerShell is a robust scripting shell language with which you can script many administrative tasks. PowerShell was first released in 2006, has integrated with SQL Server since 2008, and was made an open-source, cross-platform language in 2016.

The goal of this section is not to list every possible interaction of PowerShell with SQL Server, Azure, or availability groups, but to provide instructional, realistic samples that will help you to learn the PowerShell language and add it to your DBA tool box.

We reviewed a number of useful PowerShell scripts for Azure SQL Database interaction in Chapter 5. All the scripts in this section are available in the accompanying downloads for this book, which are available at *https://aka.ms/SQLServ2017Admin/downloads*.

IT professionals of all walks of life are learning PowerShell to ease their administrative tasks on various technologies, not just Windows Server and SQL Server, but Active Directory, Machine

Learning, Azure, Microsoft Office 365, SharePoint, Exchange, even Office products like Microsoft Excel. There is very little in the Microsoft stack for which PowerShell cannot help. Developers have created third-party downloadable modules, available for download in the PowerShell Gallery (*http://powershellgallery.com*), to further enhance PowerShell's ability to interact even with non-Microsoft platforms such as Amazon Web Services, Slack, Internet of Things (IoT) devices, Linux, and more.

If you'd like to adopt more PowerShell for administration in your database, you'll need more than the samples in this chapter, though we selected these because we feel them to be good learning examples. Consider adding the *https://dbatools.io/* open-source suite of PowerShell cmdlets to your repertoire, which is available to download from the PowerShell Gallery. Though we won't be looking at any of its highly regarded cmdlets here, this suite has furthered the development of helpful PowerShell cmdlets for automating high availability, security migrations, backups, and more.

There are even scenarios for which PowerShell fills feature gaps in configuration panels and UI, necessitating some basic literacy for PowerShell on the part of the modern system administrator, DBA, or developer. PowerShell is especially useful when building code to automate the failover of Windows Server Failover Clusters or for interacting with DNS. You also can use PowerShell remoting to manage multiple Windows servers and SQL Server instances from a single command prompt.

PowerShell also supports wrappers to run the Windows Command Prompt statements you've been familiar with as a Windows OS user; for example, ping, ipconfig, telnet, and net start. And, they can start commands just like the Command Prompt could; for example, regedit, notepad, SQLCMD, even shutdown.

Instead of the Windows Command Prompt, you should consider getting in the habit of using the PowerShell console window or Visual Studio Code (the replacement for the original PowerShell scripting environment, PowerShell ISE). You can download and start using Visual Studio Code for free at *https://code.visualstudio.com*. A separate installation of Visual Studio is not required.

You can also start a PowerShell console from within SQL Server Management Studio. Right-click most folders, and then, on the shortcut menu, select Launch PowerShell. You might find the Visual Studio Code environment more conducive to authoring multiline PowerShell scripts, especially if you have any prior familiarity with Visual Studio or Visual Studio Code.

PowerShell basics

Cmdlets for PowerShell follow a pattern of *Verb–Noun*. This helps provide ease and consistency when trying to find cmdlets to run your desired task.

For database administration tasks, we will become familiar with cmdlets and using SQL Server Management Objects (SMO). Starting with the release of SQL Server Management Studio 17.0, PowerShell for SQL Server is installed separately from SQL Server Setup or the SQL Server Management Studio Install, and can be installed from the PowerShell Gallery. We demonstrate in this chapter how to install and check the current version of the SQLSERVER module.

NOTE

The SQLPS PowerShell module has been replaced by the SQLSERVER module as of July 2016. All the functionality from SQLPS is included in the newer SQLServer, plus additional features.

For each cmdlet, there is a built-in way to receive a description of the cmdlet and see all of the parameters along with descriptions and examples (if provided by the author) of the cmdlet. Let's try it on `Invoke-Sqlcmd`, a cmdlet that calls `sqlcmd` and runs a SQL query.

First, run the cmdlet:

```
Update-Help
```

This updates the extensive and helpful local help files for PowerShell and installed modules.

Inside OUT!

The Visual Studio Code shortcuts for running scripts are different from SQL Server Management Studio, and you need to be aware of the following:

- **In SQL Server Management Studio, pressing F5 runs the entire script if no text is highlighted, or just the highlighted text if any is selected. Pressing Ctrl+E has the same behavior by default.**

- **In Visual Studio Code, pressing F5 saves then runs the entire script file, regardless of whether any code is highlighted. Pressing F8 runs only highlighted code.**

To access the help information for any cmdlet, use the `Get-Help` cmdlet. Here are some examples:

```
#Basic Reference
Get-Help Invoke-SqlCmd

#See actual examples of code use
Get-Help Invoke-SqlCmd -Examples

#All cmdlets that match a wildcard search
Get-Help -Name "*Backup*database*"
```

Note that the # character begins a single-line comment in PowerShell code. Alternatively, you can use <# and #> to enclose and declare a multiline comment block.

Installing the PowerShell SQLSERVER module

You must be running at least Windows PowerShell 5.0 to download modules from the Power-Shell Gallery. To determine the version of Windows PowerShell on your system, run the following code in the PowerShell window:

```
$PSVersionTable
```

The PSVersion value contains the current installed version of PowerShell.

Inside OUT

As of this writing, the latest version of PowerShell, PowerShell 5.1, ships in Windows Server 2016, the Windows 10 Creator's Edition, and Windows Management Framework 5.1. Up-to-date Windows 10 and Windows Server 2016 do not need any further installation.

To upgrade your version of Windows PowerShell, you should install the latest version of Windows Management Framework 5, which includes PowerShell. PowerShell 5.0 introduced the ability to download and install modules with cmdlets. *https://msdn. microsoft.com/powershell/wmf/readme5.1/install-configure* provides the current download by OS to upgrade your Windows PowerShell. Note that installing this package will require that you reboot your server or workstation.

To install the latest version of the SQLSERVER module, use the following code on an internet-connected device, running the PowerShell console or Visual Studio Code in administrator mode:

```
Install-Module -Name SQLSERVER -Force -AllowClobber
```

In the preceding script, we used a few handy parameters let's review them:

- **-Name.**   Specify the unique name of the module we want.

- **-Force.**   Avoid having to answer Yes to confirm that you want to download.

- **-AllowClobber.**   Allows this module to overwrite cmdlet aliases already in place. Without AllowClobber, the installation will fail if it finds that the new module contains commands with the same name as existing commands.

To find the current installed versions of the SQLSERVER PowerShell module as well as other SQL modules including SQLPS, use the following:

```
Get-Module -ListAvailable -Name '*sql*' | Select-Object Name, Version, RootModule
```

Offline installation

To install the module on a server or workstation that is not internet-connected or cannot reach the PowerShell Gallery, go to a workstation that can reach the PowerShell Gallery and has at least PowerShell 5.0. Then, use the following command to download the module (be aware that it's 82 MB in size):

```
save-module -Name SQLSERVER -LiteralPath "c:\temp\"
```

Then, copy the entire *C:\Temp*\SqlServer\ folder to the machine that cannot reach the PowerShell Gallery. Copy the folder to a path that is in the list of PSModule paths. The potential paths for modules list is stored in an PSModulePath environment variable, which you can view in Windows System Properties, or mode easily with this PowerShell script:

```
$env:PSModulePath.replace(";","'n")
```

The default folder for the module downloaded from the gallery would likely be "C:\Program Files\WindowsPowerShell\Modules". Verify that this path is available or choose another PSModule folder, and then copy the downloaded SQLSERVER folder there. Then, adding the module is as easy as this:

```
Import-Module SQLSERVER
```

You will now see the SQLSERVER module in the Get-Module list of available modules.

> **NOTE**
> When writing code for readability, we recommend that you use the actual cmdlet names. With PowerShell, there are a large number of shorthand and shortcuts possible, but you should try to write easy-to-read code for the next administrator.

Using PowerShell with SQL Server

PowerShell 5.0 can interact with SQL Server instances all the way back to SQL Server 2000 (with some limitations). No book is a good medium to demonstrate the full capability that PowerShell can bring to your regular DBA tasks, nor should a book try to detail all the possibilities. Nonetheless, here are some selected, representative, but simple examples.

Backup-SqlDatabase

Let's learn about some more basics and syntax of PowerShell via the `Backup-SQLDatabase` cmdlet. With this PowerShell cmdlet, you have access to the same parameters as the T-SQL command BACKUP DATABASE.

Again, use PowerShell's built-in help files to see full syntax and examples, many of which will be familiar to you if you have a good understanding of the BACKUP DATABASE options.

```
Get-Help Backup-SQLDatabase -Examples
```

Following is an example of how to back up all databases on a local SQL Server instance, providing the backup path, including a subfolder with the database's name. The script also adds the current date and time to the name of the backup file:

```
#Backup all databases (except for Tempdb)
#TODO: change value for -ServerInstance parameter
Get-SqlDatabase -ServerInstance 'localhost' | `
    Where-Object { $_.Name -ne 'tempdb' } | `
    ForEach-Object {
        Backup-SqlDatabase -DatabaseObject $_ `
        -BackupAction "Database" '
        -CompressionOption On  '
        -BackupFile "F:\Backup\$($_.Name)\$($_.Name)_$(`
        Get-Date -Format "yyyyMMdd")_$(`
        Get-Date -Format "HHmmss_FFFF").bak" `
        -Script     ' #The -Script generates TSQL, but does not execute
    }
```

Here are a few learning notes about this script:

- Adding the `-Script` parameter to this and many other cmdlets outputs only the T-SQL code, split by GO batch separators; it does not actually perform the operation.

- The back tick, or grave accent (`) symbol (below the tilde on most standard keyboards), is a line extension operator. Adding the ` character to the end of a line gives you the ability to display long commands, such as in the previous example, on multiple lines.

- The pipe character (|) is an important concept in PowerShell to grasp. It passes the output of one cmdlet to the next. In the previous script, the list of databases is passed as an array from `Get-SQLDatabase` to `Where-Object`, which filters the array and passes to `ForEach-Object`, which loops through each value in the array.

This script is available in the CH14_powershell_examples.ps1 file in the accompanying downloads for this book, which are available at *https://aka.ms/SQLServ2017Admin/downloads*.

NOTE

There are numerous ways to accomplish the same task in PowerShell, including many different shortcuts and aliases. It is rarely important to write code that uses the fewest characters. Instead, focus on writing code that is easily approachable and maintainable.

Remove-Item

Let's learn some more about common PowerShell syntax parameters. You can use the `Remove-Item` cmdlet to write your own retention policy to delete old files, including backup files, stored locally. Remember to coordinate the removal of old local backups with your off-premises strategy that keeps backups safely in a different location.

In this script, we use the `Get-ChildItem` cmdlet to `Recurse` through a subfolder, ignore folders, and select only files that are more than `$RetentionDays` old and have a file extension in a list we provide:

```
$path = "F:\Backup\"
$RetentionDays = -1
$BackupFileExtensions = ".bak", ".trn", ".dif"
Get-ChildItem -path $path -Recurse | `
    Where-Object { !$_.PSIsContainer `
                -and $_.CreationTime -lt (get-date).AddDays($RetentionDays) `
                -and ($_.Extension -In $BackupFileExtensions) `
                } | Remove-Item -WhatIf
```

Here are a few learning notes about this script:

- The `Get-ChildItem` cmdlet gathers a list of objects from the provided path, including files and folders. The `-Recurse` parameter of `Get-ChildItem` causes the cmdlet to include subfolders.

- The `$_` syntax is used to accept the data from the object prior to the previous pipe character (`|`). In this example, the objects discovered by `Get-ChildItem` are passed to the `Where-Object`, which filters the objects and passes that data to `Remove-Item`.

- Adding the `-WhatIf` parameter to this and many other cmdlets does not actually perform the operation, but provides a verbose summary of the action, instead. For example, rather than deleting old backup files, this PowerShell script returns something similar to the following sample:

```
What if: Performing the operation "Remove File" on target "F:\Backup\backup_
test_201402010200.bak".
```

This script is available in the CH14_powershell_examples.ps1 file in the accompanying downloads for this book, which are available at *https://aka.ms/SQLServ2017Admin/downloads*.

Invoke-Sqlcmd

The `Invoke-Sqlcmd` cmdlet can run T-SQL commands, including on remote SQL Server instances and Azure SQL databases. `Invoke-Sqlcmd` can replace previous batch file scripts that use `sqlcmd`. Use `Invoke-Sqlcmd` when there doesn't exist a cmdlet to return the same data for which you're already looking. In this script, we connect to a database in Azure SQL Database and run a query to see current sessions:

```
Invoke-Sqlcmd -Database master -ServerInstance .\sql2k17 `
-Query "select * from sys.dm_exec_sessions" | `
Format-Table | Out-File -FilePath "C:\Temp\Sessions.txt" -Append
```

Here are a couple learning notes about this script:

- As you might be familiar with in SQL Server Management Studio and other connection strings, the "`.`" character is a shorthand substitute for "localhost".

- The `Invoke-SqlCmd` cmdlet uses Windows Authentication by default. Notice that we passed no authentication information at all. You can provide the `UserName` and `Password` parameters to the `Invoke-SqlCmd` to connect via SQL Authentication to SQL Server instances and Azure SQL databases.

- The | `Format-Table` cmdlet has a big impact on readability of the script output. Without `Format-Table`, the script returns a long list of column names and row values. The `Format-Table` output does not include all columns by default, but returns a wide line of column headers and row values, like how SQL Server Management Studio returns `resultset` output in Text mode.

- The | `Out-File` cmdlet dumps the output to a text file instead of to the PowerShell console, creating the script if needed. The `-Append` parameter adds the text to the bottom of an existing file.

- The `Out-File` can be handy for archival purposes, but for viewing live rowsets, especially SQL Server command results, instead try using the `Out-GridView` cmdlet, which provides a full-featured grid dialog box with re-sortable and filterable columns, and so on. `Out-GridView` is used instead in the following sample:

  ```
  Invoke-Sqlcmd -Database master -ServerInstance .\sql2k17 `
  -Query "select * from sys.dm_exec_sessions" | `
  Out-GridView
  ```

These scripts are available in the CH14_powershell_examples.ps1 file in the accompanying downloads for this book, which are available at *https://aka.ms/SQLServ2017Admin/downloads*.

CHAPTER 14

Inside OUT

After running a PowerShell command in Visual Studio Code, my cursor moves to the results pane, instead of staying in the script pane. Help!

Unlike SQL Server Management Studio, running a script in PowerShell by default moves the cursor to the PowerShell terminal pane (which is actually not a Results window, but a live terminal window). This means that you need to move your cursor back up to the script pane after each run to continue to edit your PowerShell code.

You can change this behavior in Visual Studio Code. Type **Ctrl+,** (comma) to access the Visual Studio Code User Settings, or start Settings by clicking the File Menu, and then choosing Preferences, and then Settings. On the right side, provide the following code to override the Default Setting:

```
"powershell.integratedConsole.focusConsoleOnExecute": false
```

No restart is necessary. Now the cursor will remain in the scripting pane after running a PowerShell command.

Using PowerShell with availability groups

You can script the creation and administration of availability groups and automate them with PowerShell instead of using SQL Server Management Studio commands or wizards. If you work in an environment in which creating, managing, or failing over availability groups is a repeated process, you should invest time in automating and standardizing these activities with PowerShell.

Following are some samples of code that can help you along the way, starting with the very beginning—a new group of servers has been created for availability groups, and you need to add the Failover Clustering feature to each server. This could be time consuming and click-heavy in a remote desktop session to each server. Instead, consider the following script, in which we deploy the Failover Clustering feature and tools on four servers, quickly:

```
Invoke-Command -script {Install-WindowsFeature -Name "Failover-Clustering" } `
    -ComputerName SQLDEV11, SQLDEV12, SQLDEV14, SQLDEV15
Invoke-Command -script {Install-WindowsFeature -Name "RSAT-Clustering-Mgmt" } `
    -ComputerName SQLDEV11, SQLDEV12, SQLDEV14, SQLDEV15
Invoke-Command -script {Install-WindowsFeature -Name "RSAT-Clustering-PowerShell" } `
    -ComputerName SQLDEV11, SQLDEV12, SQLDEV14, SQLDEV15
```

➤ For more about turning on and configuring availability groups, see Chapter 12.

NOTE

Invoke-Command relies on the same modules being installed on the remote machines. You should verify that the same module and versions are installed on any machines to which you will be issuing commands remotely. You can also install the modules via Invoke-Command, as well:

```
#Local server
    Install-Module -Name SQLSERVER -Force -AllowClobber
    Import-Module -Name SQLSERVER

#Remove Server
Invoke-Command -script {
    Install-Module -Name SQLSERVER -Force -AllowClobber
    Import-Module -Name SQLSERVER
    } -ComputerName "SQLSERVER-1"
```

Let's fast forward to an in-place availability group, with two replicas set to asynchronous synchronization. A planned failover is coming up, and you need to automate the script as much as possible. Start with the sample script that follows, which accomplishes these goals:

- Sets asynchronous replicas to synchronous and waits so that we can perform a planned failover with no data loss.

- Performs availability group failover.

- Sets replicas back to asynchronous.

You can adapt the following sample script for your own purposes and environment:

```
#Must run on the primary node
#TODO: configure initial variable values.

    Write-Output "Begin $(Get-Date)"
#Setup: TODO Configure these
    $PrimaryReplicaName = "SQLSERVER-0"
#Named instance or DEFAULT for the default instance
    $PrimaryReplicaInstanceName = "SQL2K17"        $SecondaryReplicaName1 = "SQLSERVER-1"
#Named instance or DEFAULT for the default instance
    $SecondaryReplicaInstanceName1 = "SQL2K17"
    $AvailabilityGroupName = "WWI2017-AG"

#Inventory and test
    Set-Location "SQLSERVER:\SQL\$($PrimaryReplicaName)\$($PrimaryReplicaInstanceName)\`
AvailabilityGroups\$($AvailabilityGroupName)"
    Get-ChildItem "SQLSERVER:\Sql\$($PrimaryReplicaName)\`
$($PrimaryReplicaInstanceName)\`
AvailabilityGroups\$($AvailabilityGroupName)\AvailabilityReplicas\" `
```

```
        | Test-SqlAvailabilityReplica | Format-Table

        $AGPrimaryObjPath = "SQLSERVER:\Sql\$($PrimaryReplicaName)\`
$($PrimaryReplicaInstanceName)\`
AvailabilityGroups\$($AvailabilityGroupName)\AvailabilityReplicas\`
$($PrimaryReplicaName+$(IF($PrimaryReplicaInstanceName `
-ne "DEFAULT"){$("%5C")+$PrimaryReplicaInstanceName} ))"
        $AGPrimaryObj = Get-Item $AGPrimaryObjPath
        $AGSecondaryObjPath = "SQLSERVER:\Sql\$($PrimaryReplicaName)\`
$($PrimaryReplicaInstanceName)\`
AvailabilityGroups\$($AvailabilityGroupName)\AvailabilityReplicas\`
$($SecondaryReplicaName1+$(IF($SecondaryReplicaInstanceName1 -ne
"DEFAULT"){$("%5C")+$SecondaryReplicaInstanceName1} ))"
        $AGSecondaryObj = Get-Item $AGSecondaryObjPath



#Set replicas to synchronous before planned failover

        Set-SqlAvailabilityReplica `
        -Path $AGPrimaryObjPath `
        -AvailabilityMode SynchronousCommit `
        -FailoverMode "Manual" `
        -ErrorAction Stop
        Set-SqlAvailabilityReplica `
        -Path $AGSecondaryObjPath `
        -AvailabilityMode SynchronousCommit `
        -FailoverMode "Manual" `
        -ErrorAction Stop

#Check for when replicas are synchronized.
Do {
    $AGSecondaryObj.Refresh()
    $CurrentSync = ($AGSecondaryObj | `
                                    Select RollupSynchronizationState | Format-Wide |
Out-String).Trim()
    IF ($CurrentSync -ne "Synchronized") {
        Write-Output "Waiting for Synchronized state before failover, still $($Cur-
rentSync)"
        Start-Sleep -s 2
        }
} Until ($CurrentSync -eq 'Synchronized')

#Perform failover
    Write-Output "Beginning Failover $(Get-Date)"
    Switch-SqlAvailabilityGroup `
        -Path "SQLSERVER:\Sql\$($SecondaryReplicaName1)\`
$($SecondaryReplicaInstanceName1)\`
AvailabilityGroups\$($AvailabilityGroupName)\" `
        -ErrorAction Stop `
        #Only include the next line if it is a forced failover
        #-AllowDataLoss -Force
```

```
    Write-Output "Failover Complete $(Get-Date)"
  Start-Sleep -s 10 #Allow failover to resolve

#Return secondary replica to Asynchronous sync
#Note that the values here of Primary and Secondary1 are flipped,
# because the variables predate the failover.
Invoke-Command -script { `
    param($SecondaryReplicaName1, $SecondaryReplicaInstanceName1, `
$AvailabilityGroupName, $PrimaryReplicaName, $PrimaryReplicaInstanceName)

     Set-SqlAvailabilityReplica `
    -Path "SQLSERVER:\Sql\$(($SecondaryReplicaName1))\`
$(($SecondaryReplicaInstanceName1))\`
AvailabilityGroups\$(($AvailabilityGroupName))\AvailabilityReplicas\`
$(($SecondaryReplicaName1)+$(IF(($SecondaryReplicaInstanceName1) -ne `
"DEFAULT"){$("%5C")+(($SecondaryReplicaInstanceName1))} ))"   `
    -AvailabilityMode asynchronousCommit `
    -ErrorAction Stop
       Set-SqlAvailabilityReplica `
    -Path "SQLSERVER:\Sql\$(($SecondaryReplicaName1))\`
$(($SecondaryReplicaInstanceName1))\`
AvailabilityGroups\$(($AvailabilityGroupName))\AvailabilityReplicas\`
$(($PrimaryReplicaName)+$(IF(($PrimaryReplicaInstanceName) `
-ne "DEFAULT"){$("%5C")+(($PrimaryReplicaInstanceName))} ))"   `
    -AvailabilityMode asynchronousCommit `
    -ErrorAction Stop

    Get-ChildItem "SQLSERVER:\Sql\$($SecondaryReplicaName1)\`
$($SecondaryReplicaInstanceName1)\`
AvailabilityGroups\$($AvailabilityGroupName)\AvailabilityReplicas\" | `
Test-SqlAvailabilityReplica | Format-Table
    } -ComputerName $SecondaryReplicaName1
-Args $SecondaryReplicaName1, $SecondaryReplicaInstanceName1, `
$AvailabilityGroupName, $PrimaryReplicaName, $PrimaryReplicaInstanceName

    Write-Output "End $(Get-Date)"
```

Here are a few learning notes about this script:

- We need to do some character trickery to pass in a named instance in the SMO Path
  for the availability group, providing %5C for the backslash \ in the replica name,
  SQLSERVER-0\SQL2K17. The need here is rare albeit frustrating.

- We see another control structure, Do … Until. In this case, we're waiting until the availability group RollupSynchronizationState has changed from Synchronizing
  to Synchronized, indicating that the synchronization has changed from asynchronous to
  synchronous.

- After it is synchronous, the failover can occur without data loss, without being Forced. In an emergency, in which the primary server SQLSERVER-0 is offline, we could skip the steps where we change the synchronization and proceed straight to the most important cmdlet in the script: Switch-SqlAvailabilityGroup. Except in a Forced failover, for which data loss is possible, we must specify the -AllowDataLoss and -Force parameters.

- You must run this entire script from the primary node, as it is currently written. A hint of how you could rewrite the script to be run from anywhere lies in Invoke-Command, where we connect to the original secondary replica (now the primary replica) and set the synchronization from asynchronous back to synchronous.

- Why SQL2K17, not SQL2017? Old DBA habits die hard from the SQL2K5, SQL2K8, SQL2K8R2 days.

This script is available in the CH14_AAG_failover.ps1 file in the accompanying downloads for this book, which are available at *https://aka.ms/SQLServ2017Admin/downloads*.

Using PowerShell with Azure

Similar to the process for installing the SQLSERVER module from the PowerShell Gallery, there is a Microsoft-provided module for administering Azure Resource Manager infrastructure. (There are legacy cmdlets for Azure Classic deployment objects, but we'll focus on Resource Manager here.)

➤ **For much more about administering Azure SQL Databases, see Chapter 5.**

You'll need to install the AzureRM module using a similar process that we covered earlier:

```
Install-Module AzureRM -AllowClobber
```

With AzureRM commands, there is additional authentication required to verify your access to the Azure tenant, using the credentials with which you log in to azure.com. The following PowerShell cmdlet creates a dialog box that asks you to sign in to Azure and provide a password (see Figure 14-6), which can handle two-factor authentication if turned on (two-factor authentication is always recommended!):

```
Login-AzureRmAccount
```

The dialog box outside of the PowerShell console or Visual Studio Code won't be modal, so look for it in the background if it does not appear right away.

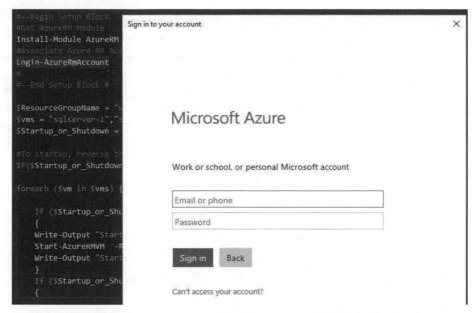

Figure 14-6 The Microsoft Azure sign-in dialog box over Visual Studio Code, after `Login-AzureRmAccount` was run to associate an Azure credential with the current PowerShell session. The same window will later ask for two-factor authentication to your Azure account, if you turn this on.

Using PowerShell with Azure VMs

Many administrators and developers use Azure infrastructure as labs for learning and sandboxes for proofs of concept, often using Azure spending credits that come with MSDN subscriptions. You can create Azure virtual machines (VMs) from the gallery with SQL Server preinstalled and ready to go in minutes. Accidentally leaving the Azure VMs running, however, means that your monthly spending credits will be quickly exhausted. It's even happened to a certain author of this book during the writing process.

A new feature made available in 2017 allows for VMs to automatically be turned off on schedules, or example the time of day, to prevent them from running overnight. Even in production environments, significant cost savings can be had by automatically turning off Azure VMs outside of business hours and then back on again before business hours begin. But what if, as a developer (or book author), you want to spin up and shut down your VMs at will?

The script that follows accomplishes the same task that would take many clicks and minutes through the Azure portal in a browser. Each `Start-AzureRMVM` and `Stop-AzureRMVM` command is synchronous with the VMs startup or shutdown status. Usually this is two to three minutes per VM.

There are also cmdlets available for legacy Azure Classic VMs. These cmdlets are for the newer Azure Resource Manager VMs, first introduced in 2014.

The following script starts or shuts down the five VMs that are created by the SQL Server availability groups template in the Microsoft Azure Portal Gallery. It declares variables including the Azure Resource Group and a list of servers. The list of servers is in the ideal order for the group of servers to be shut down, but when started, we want the two Domain Controllers to come online first, so we add a step to reverse the order of the array. The script also declares a simple-to-understand variable that determines whether the script should be run to shut down or start up the list of VMs.

```
$ResourceGroupName = "w-ag-20170915"
#Order matters!
$vms = "sqlserver-1","sqlserver-0","cluster-fsw"'
,"ad-secondry-dc","ad-primary-dc"
$Startup_or_Shutdown = "startup" # "Shutdown" or "Startup"

#To startup, reverse the order so that DC's come online first.
IF($Startup_or_Shutdown -eq "Startup") {[array]::Reverse($vms)}

#Begin startup/shutdown loop
ForEach ($vm in $vms) {
    If ($Startup_or_Shutdown -eq "Startup")
    {
    Write-Output "Starting VM:($vm.ToString) $(Get-Date -Format G)"
    Start-AzureRMVM  -ResourceGroupName $ResourceGroupName -Name $vm
    Write-Output "Started VM:($vm.ToString) $(Get-Date -Format G)"
    }
    If ($Startup_or_Shutdown -eq "Shutdown")
    {
    Write-Output "Stopping VM:($vm.ToString) $(Get-Date -Format G)"
    Stop-AzureRMVM  -ResourceGroupName $ResourceGroupName -Name $vm -Force
    Write-Output "Stopped VM:($vm.ToString) $(Get-Date -Format G)"
    }
}
```

Here's the sample script output (simplified):

```
Starting VM:(ad-primary-dc.ToString) 9/17/2017 3:28:51 PM
                    True        OK OK
Started VM:(ad-primary-dc.ToString) 9/17/2017 3:31:53 PM
Starting VM:(ad-secondry-dc.ToString) 9/17/2017 3:31:53 PM
                    True        OK OK
Started VM:(ad-secondry-dc.ToString) 9/17/2017 3:34:24 PM
Starting VM:(cluster-fsw.ToString) 9/17/2017 3:34:24 PM
                    True        OK OK
Started VM:(cluster-fsw.ToString) 9/17/2017 3:36:25 PM
Starting VM:(sqlserver-0.ToString) 9/17/2017 3:36:25 PM
                    True        OK OK
```

```
Started VM:(sqlserver-0.ToString) 9/17/2017 3:38:26 PM
Starting VM:(sqlserver-1.ToString) 9/17/2017 3:38:26 PM
                          True         OK OK
Started VM:(sqlserver-1.ToString) 9/17/2017 3:39:56 PM
```

Here are a couple of learning notes from the preceding script:

- PowerShell as a language is not strongly data typed. When we passed in a string, the $ResourceGroupName variable stored a string. When we passed in a list of strings, the $vms variable stored an array. We were then able to treat $vms as an array, and reverse its sort order.

- The ForEach loop runs synchronously. Using PowerShell functions or workflows, the ForEach loop can be set to run its tasks in parallel.

- One common mistake to new PowerShell developers are comparison operators. You cannot use "=" to compare; rather, there is a list of string operators such as "-eq" (equals), "-ne" (not equals), and "-gt" (greater than).

➤ You can learn more about PowerShell comparison operators in the technical reference documentation online at *https://docs.microsoft.com/powershell/module/microsoft. powershell.core/about/about_comparison_operators?view=powershell-5.1.*

This script is available in the CH14_start_or_stop_RM_vms.ps1 file in the accompanying downloads for this book, which are available at *https://aka.ms/SQLServ2017Admin/downloads*.

CHAPTER 14

Index

About the authors

William Assaf

William Assaf, MCSE, is a Microsoft SQL Server consultant and manager and blogs about SQL at *sqltact.com*. William has been a designer, database developer, and admin on application and data warehousing projects for private and public clients. He has helped write the last two generations of Microsoft SQL Server certification exams since 2012 and has been a Regional Mentor for PASS since 2015. William and fellow author Patrick Leblanc worked together on *SQL Server 2012 Step by Step* (Microsoft Press, 2015), having met at and together led the SQL Server User Group and SQLSaturday in Baton Rouge. William and his high school sweetheart enjoy travelling to speak at SQLSaturdays around the south, and hope to see to see you there, too.

Randolph West

Randolph West is a Data Platform MVP from Calgary, Alberta, Canada. He is coorganizer of the Calgary SQL Server User Group and Calgary SQLSaturday. He speaks at various conferences around the world, and acts on stage and screen. Randolph specializes in implementing best practices, performance tuning, disaster recovery, and cloud migrations, through his company Born SQL. You can read his blog at *bornsql.ca*.

Sven Aelterman

Sven Aelterman started with SQL Server when he first deployed version 2000 in a failover cluster scenario. Since then, he has worked as IT manager, principal consultant, and IT director. He currently serves the Trojans (students) of Troy University as a lecturer in information systems in the Sorrell College of Business and as director of IT for the College. In addition, he is cloud software architect for Sorrell Solutions, a business services nonprofit through which Trojans can gain real-world business and IT experience. In a fledgling attempt to give back to the community, he has spoken at many SQLSaturdays and code camps in the southeastern United States since 2005. He spoke about SSIS 2012 at Microsoft TechEd 2011. In 2012, he coauthored a book dedicated to SQL Server FILESTREAM. His involvement with Microsoft Azure resulted in the organization of two Global Azure Bootcamp events at Troy University. Sven blogs about a variety of Microsoft technologies at *svenaelterman.wordpress.com* and tweets and retweets about technology @svenaelterman.

Mindy Curnutt

 Mindy Curnutt, an independent consultant, is 4X Microsoft Data Platform MVP and Idera ACE. She has been actively involved in the SQL Server Community for more than a decade, presenting at various User Group Meetings, SQLPASS Summits, as well as SQLSaturdays across North America. For two years, she was a team lead for the SQLPASS Summit Abstract Review Process and since 2015 has served as one of the three SQLPASS Summit program managers. She was a SME for a couple of the SQL 2012 and 2014 Microsoft SQL Server Certification Exams and helped to author *SQL Server 2014 Step by Step*. Mindy currently serves on the board of directors for the North Texas SQL Server User's Group. She also serves as a mentor to others, helping to educate and promote scalable and sustainable SQL Server architecture and design. She is passionate about Data Security, Accessibility, Usability, Scalability and Performance. You can follow Mindy at her blog, *mindycurnutt.com* and on Twitter where she's known as @sqlgirl.

About the Foreword author

Patrick LeBlanc

 Patrick LeBlanc is a data platform technical solution professional at Microsoft, working directly with customers on the business value of SQL Server. He coauthored *SharePoint 2010 Business Intelligence 24-Hour Trainer* (Wrox, 2011) and *Knight's Microsoft Business Intelligence 24-Hour Trainer* (Wrox, 2010), and founded *www.sqllunch.com*, a website devoted to teaching SQL Server technologies.